The Student's Dictionary of Literary Plains Cree
based on contemporary texts

The Student's Dictionary of Literary Plains Cree
based on contemporary texts

H.C. Wolfart & Freda Ahenakew

Memoir 15

ALGONQUIAN AND IROQUOIAN LINGUISTICS

1998

ALGONQUIAN AND IROQUOIAN LINGUISTICS
John D. Nichols, Editor
Arden C. Ogg, Typography
Norman Schmidt, Cover Design

(c) Algonquian and Iroquoian Linguistics 1998
Fletcher Argue Building
28 Trueman Walk
Winnipeg, Manitoba R3T 2N2

Printed in Canada

The support of the Saskatchewan Indian Languages Institute and the Social Sciences and Humanities Research Council of Canada, without which this work would not have reached publication, is gratefully acknowledged, as is the advice over many years of research of our colleagues in the Cree Language Project at the University of Manitoba and, above all, the unflagging support and encouragement of Arden Ogg.

Canadian Cataloguing in Publication Data

Wolfart, H.C., 1943-

The student's dictionary of literary Plains Cree : based on contemporary texts

(Memoir / Algonquian and Iroquoian linguistics ; 15)

ISBN 0-921064-15-2

1. Cree language – Dictionaries – English. 2. English language – Dictionaries – Cree. I. Ahenakew, Freda, 1932- II. Title. III. Series: Memoir (Algonquian and Iroquoian Linguistics) ; 15.

PM988.W643 1998   497.3   C99-920004-6

Introduction
H.C. Wolfart

This dictionary is intended above all as a key to the growing library of authentic Cree literature. From personal reminiscences to formal speeches,[1] the volumes published over the past two decades all present the text in its original Cree form, accompanied by a translation into English on facing pages. It is the classical language of such texts that is reflected in this work.

Documenting a wealth of spontaneously produced Cree terms that is potentially without limit, a dictionary of the present type has to be carefully circumscribed in aim and plan.[2] As the title proclaims, our work is defined by four principles.

THE STUDENT'S DICTIONARY

The study of a language or literature, one's own or another, is undertaken to best effect if the student can rely on a dictionary providing consistency in orthographic representation, in the grammatical identification of each stem and in the design of the glosses.

With authenticity and reliability as its primary aims, the present dictionary is written for students prepared to be challenged. Even for those who already speak Cree it may take a sustained effort to master the standard orthography, the use of stems instead of fully inflected words and the somewhat technical form of the English glosses. Users without previous exposure to Cree have to face, in addition, the novel structures of a language quite different from English or French.[3]

Unlike the well-worn bilingual dictionaries used by language-and-literature students, the present work, though written in English, is first and foremost a dictionary of Cree. The first part of the book, the CREE DICTIONARY, presents each entry in its full form. The second part, the ENGLISH INDEX, is merely a guide to the first. (Both labels are to be taken quite literally. The second part is, in fact, a selective index to the English glosses; it is not the English-Cree part of a bilingual dictionary.)

The Student's Dictionary, in short, is by no means an elementary dictionary but an initial reference work for the serious student.

LITERARY PLAINS CREE

Before the boundless creativity of language, any dictionary is ultimately reduced to a collection of examples. Never complete and rarely comprehensive – except, perhaps, for a few imperial languages – the best dictionaries are those found to be representative and trustworthy.

For a poorly documented language like Cree, we have to begin with a sampling, representative and reliable, offering breadth and depth alike, of the lexical riches of the language.

The form of Plains Cree here represented is the relatively formal register used by older speakers, usually acknowledged as exemplary, when presenting narrative and mythological texts or paedagogical and religious discourses.

In the elevated style of Cree literature, cognate but distinct stems are used in elaborate patterns of lexical variation. Whether built on initial constituents such as *kakwâtak-* or final elements like *-âhtawî-* (*cf.* the English Index under CLIMB and CRAWL), such stylistic features give depth to a lexicon. (This approach also avoids the complications presented by the competing speech styles of younger speakers, often less comprehensively in command of register than their elders and with a much higher degree of Cree-English bilingualism.)

In terms of geographically defined dialects, this dictionary draws above all on the common Plains Cree spoken across the central prairies of Saskatchewan and Alberta.

While variant forms of individual stems are included as distinct cross-referenced entries, they are not identified as to the various further divisions *within* Plains Cree. (For stems which are most readily documented in the Woods Cree of north-central Saskatchewan but are equally current in Plains Cree, the latter is given without annotation; in the few cases where the non-Plains

Cree usage differs, even though there may be no overt diagnostic of the dialect discrepancy, the dialect code (LR) is added at the end of the entry.)

The literary usage of an otherwise diverse set of speakers has, for many entries, resulted in fairly complex glosses. Where a basic sense can be consistently distinguished from extended or transferred meanings, the latter are separated by a semicolon; a note is added for figurative usage.

CONTEMPORARY

Based on contemporary texts, the entries in this dictionary are designed to represent the current form of the language. Despite their historical and ethnological interest, no comparative evidence is included – whether from other Plains Cree sources, other dialects of Cree or other languages of the Algonquian family and beyond.

Etymological notes are provided only for place-names, which tend to be as problematic as they are important. In other cases we pass over the fact that the secondary stem *nikikomin–* NI, for example, which refers to a variety of blueberries, is derived from a primary stem *nikikw–* NA 'otter' and a noun-forming final *-min-* 'berry of a certain kind'.

Loan words extend from the ancient and deeply entrenched, like *napwênis–* NA 'small frying pan', borrowed from French *la poêle* at a time and place when the vowel corresponded to Cree *-ê-* (rather than *-â-*), to the more recent and obvious *lamilâs–* NI 'syrup' (*cf.* French *la mélasse*) or such English borrowings as *iskôliwi–* VAI 'be in school, go to school' or *cikinis–* NA 'domestic chicken, little chicken', sufficiently integrated to exhibit the Cree diminutive suffix *-is-*. Loan translations often remain opaque, for example *pahkisin–* VAI, which in addition to its common meaning 'fall, fall down' seems to have acquired the calqued meaning 'fall for (him/her)'. Mirrors of cultural change, they test the observant student of the language.

As the English gloss, too, is sometimes obscure or arcane, as in the case of 'reaches', or where the local variety of English diverges from general usage, as in the use of 'sap' for the stringy cambium of poplars or of 'red willow' for red-osier dogwood, further information is given as an elaboration of the gloss (in parentheses) or in the form of a comment [in square brackets].

Variants are cross-referenced mainly when the difference is subtle; in effect, this distinguishes derivational doublets, partial synonyms and the like, which are not flagged, from phonological variants such as stems beginning in either *î-* or *yî-*.

Full words are cited from the texts to illustrate the inflection of monosyllabic stems like *mihkw–* NI or *miht–* NI and the personal prefixes that are obligatory with the dependent stems listed as a set at the head of the dictionary. In the case of vowel-initial dependent stems, the citations further indicate the type of prefixation, either with *k-, n-, w-, m-* (*–aniway–*: *naniway* 'my cheek') or with *kit-, nit-, ot-* (*–awâsimis–*: *nitawâsimis* 'my child'). (Several stems appear not only in a consonant-initial variant, with the personal prefix taking the shape *ki-, ni-, o-, mi-* (*–hkwâkan–*: *ohkwâkan* 'his/her face') but also in a vowel-initial variant with *k-, n-, w-, m-* (*–îhkwâkan–*: *wîhkwâkan* 'his/her face'); as the length of vowels is indeterminate before preaspirated stops in many varieties of Plains Cree, third-person possessor forms constitute the most reliable diagnostic.)

Diminutive and reduplicated stems are labelled if they are grammatically productive. In addition to historical instances (for example, the lexicalised *–skîsikos–* NDI 'spectacles, glasses'), there are many productive cases (notably terms of endearment, for instance *–cânis–* NDA 'daughter, parallel niece', and terms for body parts or intimate possessions, for instance *–cêhis–* NDI 'heart') in which the diminutive status is not reflected in the gloss.

Partly in deference to the diversity of sources from which the stems are drawn, we go beyond other lexicographical traditions in keeping not only homonyms like *askiy–* NI 'land (etc.)' and *askiy–* NI 'moss' distinct, but also polysemous pairs such as *âpacih–* VTA 'use s.o. (etc.)' and *âpacih–* VTA 'be of use to s.o. (etc.)' and, especially, sets differentiated solely by stem-class, for instance *kotawânâpiskw–* NA and NI, *asên–* VTA and VTI, and the many instances of homophonous particles and preverbs such as *ati* IPC and IPV.

Notes and queries of various types may also appear in the comment field [in square brackets] at the end of the entry.

TEXTS

The entries in this dictionary all reflect actual Cree usage as recorded in spoken prose. These original texts, critically edited according to established standards and for the most part already published, vary widely in scale. Some are very brief; taken together, they document the usage of a remarkable range of speakers. In the case of Emma Minde or *kâ-pimwêwêhahk* / Jim Kâ-Nîpitêhtêw, by contrast, we have substantial volumes representing the style of a single speaker.

In subject matter, the texts range from reminiscences of everyday life to formal discussions of ritual observance, from household chores to issues of sacramental affirmation. Trivial or sublime, each of the topics raised is culturally salient. Because of its reliance on authentic texts, the present dictionary is especially rich in terms documenting the lives of women, child-rearing, illness and health and, always, the ceremonial life.

Predictably, a dictionary based on spontaneously produced texts is much less even in coverage than the finely polished dictionaries of the national languages. Even some perfectly ordinary terms will have been omitted simply because they do not happen to occur in the running texts.

The choice of entries, in other words, reflects the topics and verbal resources of the texts that have been excerpted rather than the lexicographical principles adopted by the authors. In the resulting dictionary, the incidental absence of terms for 'schoolbus' or 'cherub' seems amply balanced by the rich texture of terms of long standing, many of them of great cultural weight.

Amongst the asymmetries typical of the lexicon, derivational sets that remain incomplete are most readily apparent. In practice, students learning to speak Cree can normally call on a fluent speaker to fill in specific lacunae – in fact, it is a valuable experience to explore the bounds of lexical productivity. Other students may find it instructive to compare the entries of this dictionary to those found in others, old and new.

Beyond practical answers and, perhaps, a better understanding of Cree literature and Cree culture in general, the present work offers unlimited challenges to all serious students of the Cree language.

---

1 For references see the most recent example: *ana kâ-pimwêwêhahk okakêskihkêmowina / The Counselling Speeches of Jim Kâ-Nîpitêhtêw*, ed. & tr. by Freda Ahenakew & H.C. Wolfart (Publications of the Algonquian Text Society / Collection de la Société d'édition de textes algonquiens, Winnipeg, University of Manitoba Press, 1998).

2 The support of the Saskatchewan Indian Languages Institute and, over many years, of the Social Sciences and Humanities Research Council of Canada is hereby gratefully acknowledged, as is the Killam Research Fellowship the senior author held while shaping the entries and trying to keep track of their play back and forth. Thanks are also due to our colleagues in the Cree Language Project at the University of Manitoba and, especially, to Arden Ogg, who once more assumed a major part in the construction of the English Index.

3 Introductions to the linguistic structure of Cree may be found in *Cree Language Structures: A Cree Approach* (by Freda Ahenakew, Winnipeg, Pemmican Publications, 1987) or *Meet Cree: A Guide to the Cree Language* (by H.C. Wolfart & Janet F. Carroll, 2nd ed., Edmonton, University of Alberta Press, 1982); for more technical discussions see 'Sketch of Cree, an Algonquian language' (by H.C. Wolfart, in *Handbook of North American Indians* [William C. Sturtevant, gen. ed.], vol. 17 [*Languages*], pp. 390-439, Washington, Smithsonian Institution, 1996) and *Plains Cree: A Grammatical Study* (by H.C. Wolfart, American Philosophical Society, Transactions, n.s., vol. 63, pt. 5. Philadelphia, 1973).

CREE DICTIONARY ENTRIES

All noun and verb entries in this dictionary end in a long hyphen, indicating that the form given is a stem.

Only some stems are identical to words; most Cree words consist of stems combined with inflectional endings. In the case of noun stems in post-consonantal -w-, the stem-final -w- does not appear in the singular form of the word.

Dependent noun stems have a long hyphen both at the end and at the beginning: such stems also require a personal prefix.

Entries for dependent stems precede all others. Throughout, long vowels follow their short counterparts; thus: *a, â, c, ê, h, i, î, k, m, n, o, ô, p, s, t, w, y*.

For transitive verb stems belonging to the VTA and VTI types, the primary goal (or object) for which the verb is inflected is indicated by the notations *s.o.* and *s.t.*, to be read 'someone' and 'something', respectively:

> **pânisw–** VTA cut s.o. (e.g., animal) into sheets
> **pânis–** VTI cut s.t. (e.g., meat) into sheets

The secondary goal (or object), which is not specified by inflection, is conventionally indicated by the notation *(it/him)*:

> **nakatamaw–** VTA leave (it/him) behind for s.o., bequeathe (it/him) to s.o.

(*cf.* **nakat–** VTI leave s.t. behind).

For transitive verb stems belonging to the VAI type, the corresponding notation is *(it)* or, less commonly, *(it/him)* or *(her)*, *(him)*, *(them)*:

> **manâcihtâ–** VAI treat (it) with respect
> **mêki–** VAI give (it/him) out as present; give (it/him) away, release (it/him); give (her) in marriage

For a fuller survey of verb types and their syntactic relations see pp. 402-404 in the 'Sketch of Cree, an Algonquian language' (by H.C. Wolfart, in *Handbook of North American Indians* [William C. Sturtevant, gen. ed.], vol. 17 [*Languages*], pp. 390-439, Washington, Smithsonian Institution, 1996).

English Index Entries

This is a *selective* index of the English glosses which correspond to each Cree stem. Thus it is merely a rough guide to the entries in the Cree Dictionary and should not be confused with the English-Cree part of a bilingual dictionary.

In addition, the index entries are abridged; for the full entry, which may include a sample of inflected forms and notes and queries of various types [in square brackets], the user has to refer to the Cree Dictionary.

It often takes several English words or phrases to capture the meaning of a single Cree stem, for instance,

>   **itakiht–** VTI 'count s.t. thus, value s.t. thus, hold s.t. in such esteem; charge so much for s.t.'

In its literal sense, this stem appears under COUNT and VALUE (while no effort has been made also to include stems of this type under headwords like THUS, SO, SUCH); in its extended and transferred senses, it is indexed under ESTEEM and CHARGE. A single Cree stem may thus give rise to several entries in the English Index.

Conversely, the entries listed under a single headword are arranged simply in alphabetical order; no attempt has been made to group them semantically (for instance, 'charge so much for s.t.' vs 'be in charge' vs 'charge headlong' under CHARGE, or 'bark at s.o.' vs 'pull the bark off s.o. (e.g., tree)' under BARK) or syntactically (for instance, under DOCTOR, the noun meaning 'doctor, physician' vs the verb for 'treat s.o., doctor s.o., heal s.o., cure s.o.').

Although the headwords themselves may be ambiguous, the individual entries which are listed under them are fully identified by stem, stem-class code and an explicit gloss. The distinction between headword and cited entry emphasises the fact that this is not a dictionary but merely an index.

Abbreviations

Stem-Class Codes

NA	animate noun
NI	inanimate noun
NDA	animate noun, dependent
NDI	inanimate noun, dependent
VAI	verb of type VAI (animate actor, usually intransitive)
VII	verb of type VII (inanimate actor, intransitive)
VTA	verb of type VTA (animate goal, transitive)
VTI	verb of type VTI (inanimate goal, usually transitive)
PR	pronoun
IPC	indeclinable particle
IPV	indeclinable preverb particle
IPN	indeclinable prenoun particle
INM	indeclinable nominal

Other Codes

cf.	compare [cross-reference]; contrast [general note]
dial.	dialect other than common Plains Cree
diminutive	productively formed diminutive
fig.	figuratively; in a transferred sense
lit.	literally
loc., locative	locative form, inflected with locative ending
reduplicated	productively reduplicated
sic	['indeed'] confirmation that the form is correctly printed
?sic	['really?'] caution that the identification of the stem, gloss, stem-class, etc. remains in doubt
an., inan.	animate, inanimate
excl., incl.	exclusive, inclusive
prox., obv.	proximate, obviative
sg., pl.	singular, plural
s.o.	['someone'] primary goal of VTA stems
s.t.	['something'] primary goal of VTI stems
(it/him)	secondary goal of VTA stems
(it), (it/him), (her), (him), (them)	goal of transitive stems of type VAI

Cree Dictionary

–ahkwan– NDI heel [*e.g.*, nahkwanihk 'on my heel']

–aniway– NDI cheek [*e.g.*, naniwâhk 'on my cheek / cheeks']

–askatay– NDI abdominal wall of animal [*i.e., tough meat layered with fat; e.g.*, waskatay '(an animal's) abdominal wall']

–atay– NDI belly; abdomen (e.g., in childbirth) [*e.g.*, natânâhk 'on our (excl.) abdomens']

–awâsimis– NDA child [*e.g.*, kitawâsimisinawak 'your-and-my (incl.) children']

–ayisiyinîm– NDA people, follower [*e.g.*, kitayisiyinîmak 'your (sg.) people (pl.)']

–âniskocâpânis– NDA great-grandchild [*diminutive; e.g.*, nicâniskocâpânis 'my great-grandchild']

–âniskotâpân– NDA great-grandchild [*e.g.*, nitâniskotâpânak 'my great-grandchildren']

–âskikan– NDI chest [*e.g.*, wâskikanihk 'on his/her chest']

–âskikanis– NDI chest [*diminutive; e.g.*, wâskikanisiwâhk 'on their chests']

–âwikan– NDI backbone, spine (e.g., fish) [*e.g.*, wâwikaniwâhk 'on their spines']

–câhkos– NDA female cross-cousin (woman speaking); sister-in-law (woman speaking) [*e.g.*, nicâhkosak 'my female cross-cousins (woman speaking)', nicâhkosipan 'my late sister-in-law (woman speaking)']

–cânis– NDA daughter, parallel niece [*diminutive; e.g.*, nicânis 'my daughter']

–câpân– NDA great-grandchild [*e.g.*, nicâpânak 'my great-grandchildren']

–câsis– NDA loin-cloth; leggings; trousers, pants [*diminutive; e.g.*, nicâsis 'my pants (sg.)']

–cêhis– NDI heart [*diminutive; e.g.,* ocêhis 'his/her heart']
–cêmisis– NDA little dog [*diminutive; e.g.,* nicêmisis 'my little dog']
–cicâskâs– NDI crotch [*diminutive; e.g.,* nicicâskâsihk 'on my crotch']
–cihciy– NDI hand; paw (e.g., bear) [*e.g.,* kicihcîhk 'on your (sg.) hand / hands'; micihciy mêtawê– VAI 'play the hand-game']
–ciwâm– NDA male parallel cousin (man speaking); (*fig.*) brother, friend, male of the same generation (man speaking); brother, brethren [*e.g.,* kiciwâminawak 'your-and-my (incl.) brethren']
–ciwâmis– NDA male parallel cousin (man speaking); (*fig.*) brother, friend, male of the same generation (man speaking); brother, brethren [*diminutive; e.g.,* kiciwâmisinaw 'your-and-my (incl.) brother']
–cônis– NDI mouth [*diminutive; e.g.,* ocônisiwâwa 'their mouths']
–côskwanis– NDI elbow [*diminutive; e.g.,* ocôskwanisa 'his/her elbows']
–êscakâs– NDI hair [*diminutive; e.g.,* mêscakâs 'a hair (sg.)']
–êstakay– NDI hair [*e.g.,* wêstakâwawa 'their hair (pl.)']
–hcikwan– NDI knee [*sic; cf.* –îhcikwan–; *e.g.,* ohcikwanihk 'on his/her knee / knees']
–hkwâkan– NDI face [*sic; cf.* –îhkwâkan–; *e.g.,* ohkwâkan 'his/her face']
–htawakay– NDI ear [*sic; cf.* –îhtawakay–; *e.g.,* ohtawakâhk 'on his/her ear / ears']
–itâmiyaw– NDI innards, guts [*usually plural; e.g.,* otitâmiyawa '(an animal's) innards (pl.)']
–iyaw– NDI body [*e.g.,* kiyaw 'your (sg.) body', wiyawihk [*sic*] 'on his/her body']
–iyihkos– NDA gland [*diminutive; e.g.,* wiyihkosiwâwa 'their gland / glands']
–iyinîm– NDA people, followers [*usually plural; e.g.,* otiyinîma 'his people']

–îc-âyis– NDA fellow youngster; sibling, parallel cousin [*e.g.*, nîc-âyisak 'my siblings-and-parallel-cousins']

–îc-âyisiyiniw– NDA fellow person, fellow human [*sic; cf.* –îcayisoiyiniw–; *e.g.*, kîc-âyisiyinînaw 'your-and-my (incl.) fellow human']

–îcayisiyiniw– NDA fellow person, fellow human [*sic:* -a-; *cf.* –îc-âyisiyiniw–; *e.g.*, kîcayisiyinînaw 'your-and-my (incl.) fellow human']

–îci-kisêyin– NDA fellow old man, co-elder [*e.g.*, nîci-kisêyin 'my fellow old man']

–îci-kisêyiniw– NDA fellow old man, co-elder [*e.g.*, nîci-kisêyiniw 'my fellow old man']

–îci-kiskinohamawâkan– NDA fellow student, school-mate [*e.g.*, nîci-kiskinohamawâkanak 'my school-mates']

–îci-kîhkâw– NDA aged spouse, fellow old person, fellow oldster, companion of one's old age [*e.g.*, wîci-kîhkâwa 'the companion of his/her old age']

–îcisân– NDA sibling [*sic:* -c-; *e.g.*, nîcisânak 'my brothers-and-sisters', wîcisâna 'his/her sibling / siblings']

–îhcawakâs– NDI ear [*sic:* -î-; *cf.* –htawakay–; *diminutive; e.g.*, wîhcawakâsihk 'on his/her ear / ears']

–îhcikwan– NDI knee [*sic:* -î-; *cf.* –hcikwan–; *e.g.*, wîhcikwana 'his/her knees']

–îhkwâkan– NDI face [*sic:* -î-; *cf.* –hkwâkan–; *e.g.*, wîhkwâkanihk 'on his/her face']

–îhkwâkanis– NDI face [*sic:* -î-; *cf.* –hkwâkan–; *diminutive; e.g.*, nîhkwâkanis 'my face']

–îhtawakay– NDI ear [*sic:* -î-; *cf.* –htawakay–; *e.g.*, nîhtawakâhk 'on my ear / ears', wîhtawakaya 'his/her ears']

–îk– NDI house, dwelling, home [*e.g.*, nîkihk 'in my house', wîki 'his/her house']

–îpit– NDI tooth [*e.g.*, nîpit 'my tooth', wîpita 'his/her teeth']

–îpitihkân– NDI false teeth, dentures [*e.g.*, nîpitihkâna 'my dentures', mîpitihkâna 'false teeth, one's false teeth']

–îscâs– NDA male cross-cousin (man speaking); brother-in-law (man speaking) [*diminutive; e.g.,* wîscâsa 'his male cross-cousin']

–îsopiy– NDI gall bladder; gall, bile [*?sic:* NDI, NI; *e.g.,* wîsopiy 'his/her gall bladder, (an animal's) gall bladder']

–îstâw– NDA male cross-cousin (man speaking); brother-in-law (man speaking) [*e.g.,* wîstâwa 'his male cross-cousin']

–îtimos– NDA cross-cousin of the opposite sex [*sic:* -t-; *diminutive; e.g.,* nîtimos 'my cross-cousin (of the opposite sex)']

–îtisân– NDA sibling [*sic:* -t-; *e.g.,* nîtisânak 'my brothers-and-sisters']

–îw– NDA wife [*e.g.,* wîwa 'his wife / wives', wîwiwâwa 'their wife / wives']

–kâwiy– NDA mother, mother's sister; (*fig.*) Our Mother [*e.g.,* nikâwiy 'my mother', kikâwînawak 'your-and-my (incl.) mother-and-her-sister / -sisters (pl.)'; kikâwînaw 'Our (incl.) Mother']

–kâwîs– NDA mother's sister, parallel aunt; step-mother [*e.g.,* nikâwîs 'my mother's sister']

–kêhtê-ayim– NDA old person, parent, grandparent; elder [*e.g.,* okêhtê-ayimiwâwa 'their old person / old people']

–kisêyinîm– NDA old man, husband [*e.g.,* nikisêyinîm 'my old man']

–kîsikâm– NDI day, day of one's life; (*fig.*) [Our Father's] day, Christmas Day [*e.g.,* kikîsikâminaw 'a day of your-and-my (incl.) life'; kôhtâwînaw okîsikâm 'Our (incl.) Father's day, Christmas Day']

–kohtaskway– NDI throat [*e.g.,* nikohtaskwânâna 'our (excl.) throats']

–kosis– NDA son, parallel nephew; (*fig.*) younger man [*e.g.,* okosisa 'his/her son / sons'; *vocative:* nikosis 'oh my son!']

–kwayaw– NDI neck [*e.g.,* okwayâhk 'on his/her neck / necks']

–manâcimâkan– NDA father-in-law (woman speaking) [*e.g.,* nimanâcimâkan 'my father-in-law (woman speaking)']

–mâmâ– NDA mom, mother [*e.g.*, nimâmâ 'my mom'; *vocative:* mâmâ [*sic*] 'oh my mom!']

–mikiy– NDI scab [*?sic:* NDI, NI; *e.g.*, omikiy 'his/her scab']

–mis– NDA older sister, older female parallel cousin [*e.g.*, nimis 'my older sister'; *vocative:* nimisê 'oh my older sister!']

–misisitân– NDI big toe [*e.g.*, nimisisitân 'my big toe']

–mosôm– NDA grandfather, grandfather's brother; (*fig.*) old man, respected elder [*e.g.*, kimosôminaw 'your-and-my (incl.) grandfather'; *vocative:* nimosô 'oh my grandfather!']

–nâpêm– NDA husband [*e.g.*, onâpêmiwâwa 'their husband / husbands']

–nîkânîm– NDI one's future [*e.g.*, ninîkânîmihk 'in my future']

–nîkihikw– NDA parent [*usually plural; e.g.*, ninîkihikonânak 'our (excl.) parents']

–nôtokwêm– NDA old lady, wife [*e.g.*, ninôtokwêm 'my old lady']

–okimâm– NDA boss [*e.g.*, nitôkimâm 'my boss']

–okimâskwêm– NDA female boss, boss's wife [*e.g.*, nitôkimâskwêm 'my boss-lady']

–osk-âyim– NDA young people, children, grandchildren, the young [*e.g.*, otôsk-âyimiwâwa 'their young person / young people']

–oskinîkiskwêm– NDA young woman; hired girl [*e.g.*, otôskinîkiskwêma 'his/her hired girl / hired girls']

–oskinîkîm– NDA young man, follower; (*fig.*) servant [*e.g.*, otôskinîkîma 'his/her young man / young men']

–oskinîkîmis– NDA young man; hired man [*diminutive; e.g.*, nicôskinîkîmis 'my young man']

–ôhcâwîs– NDA father's brother, parallel uncle; step-father [*e.g.*, ôhcâwîsa 'his/her father's brother / father's brothers']

–ôhkom– NDA grandmother, grandmother's sister, "great-aunt"; (*fig.*) old woman; Our Grandmother [*e.g.*, nôhkom 'my grandmother'; kôhkominaw 'Our (incl.) Grandmother']

–ôhtâwiy– NDA   father, father's brother; (*fig.*) Our Father, Heavenly Father [*e.g.*, kôhtâwînawak 'your-and-my (incl.) father-and-his-brother / -brothers (pl.)'; kôhtâwînaw 'Our (incl.) Father']

–ôhtâwîhkâwin– NDA   step-father [*e.g.*, ôhtâwîhkâwina 'his/her step-father']

–ôsisim– NDA   grandchild; (*fig.*) young person [*e.g.*, kôsisiminaw 'your-and-my (incl.) grandchild'; *vocative:* nôsisê 'oh my grandchild!']

–pawâkan– NDA   dream spirit [*e.g.*, opawâkana 'his/her dream spirit / dream spirits']

–pâpâ– NDA   dad, father [*e.g.*, nipâpâwa 'my dad (obv.)']

–pâpâsis– NDA   dad's brother, father's brother, parallel uncle [*e.g.*, nipâpâsis 'my dad's brother']

–pê-wîc-îspîhcisîmâkan– NDA   age-mate from there on down [*e.g.*, nipê-wîc-îspîhcisîmâkanak 'my age-mates from there on down']

–pêpîm– NDA   baby, infant; youngest child [*e.g.*, nipêpîm 'my baby']

–pîway– NDI   body-hair of animal, fur [?*sic*: NDI, NI; *e.g.*, opîwaya '(an animal's) fur (pl.)']

–pîwâs– NDI   little feathers, down [?*sic:* NDI, NI; *diminutive; e.g.*, opîwâsa '(an animal's) down']

–scikwân– NDI   head [*diminutive; e.g.*, oscikwân 'his/her head']

–scikwânis– NDI   head [*diminutive; e.g.*, oscikwânisiyihk 'on his/her (obv.) head']

–sicis– NDI   foot [*diminutive; e.g.*, osicisa 'his/her feet, (an animal's) feet']

–sikos– NDA   father's sister, mother's brother's wife; mother-in-law, father-in-law's brother's wife, "aunt" [*e.g.*, nisikosak 'my mother-in-law-and-my-father-in-law's-brother's-wife (pl.) / -brothers'-wives']

–sis– NDA   mother's brother, father's sister's husband; father-in-law, father-in-law's brother, "uncle" [*e.g.*, nisisak 'my father-in-law-and-his-brother / -brothers (pl.)']

–sit– NDI foot [*e.g.,* osita 'his/her feet, (an animal's) feet', misita 'feet, one's feet']

–sîm– NDA younger sibling, younger parallel cousin [*e.g., vocative:* nisîmitik 'oh my younger siblings!']

–sîmis– NDA younger sibling, younger parallel cousin [*diminutive; e.g.,* nisîmis 'my younger sibling']

–sîsîpimis– NDA one's little ducks [*diminutive; e.g.,* nisîsîpimisak 'my little ducks']

–skan– NDI bone [*e.g.,* oskana 'his/her bones, (an animal's) bones', miskana 'bones, one's bones']

–skanis– NDI bone [*diminutive; e.g.,* oskanis 'his/her bone (sg.), (an animal's) bone (sg.)']

–skât– NDI leg [*e.g.,* niskâtihk 'on my leg / legs', miskâta 'legs, one's legs']

–skiwan– NDI nose [*e.g.,* oskiwaniwâwa 'their noses']

–skîsikos– NDI spectacles, glasses [*e.g.,* niskîsikosa 'my glasses']

–skîsikw– NDI eye [*e.g.,* kiskîsikwa 'your eyes', miskîsikwa 'eyes, one's eyes']

–skocâkâs– NDI little coat, little dress [*diminutive; e.g.,* miskocâkâsa 'little dresses, one's little dresses']

–skotâkay– NDI coat, dress [*e.g.,* oskotâkâwâwa 'their dresses', miskotâkaya 'dresses, one's dresses']

–soy– NDI tail [*e.g.,* osoya 'his/her tails, (an animal's) tails']

–spiconis– NDI front and hind legs (e.g., of a rabbit) [*diminutive; e.g.,* ospiconisiwâwa 'their extremities']

–spikêkan– NDI rib [*e.g.,* ospikêkana 'his/her ribs, (an animal's) ribs']

–spiskwan– NDI back [*e.g.,* ospiskwaniwâhk 'on their backs']

–spiton– NDI arm [*e.g.,* ospitoniwâwa 'their arms']

–stês– NDA older brother, older male parallel cousin [*e.g.,* nistês 'my older brother']

–stikwân– NDI head; head of hair; mind [*e.g.,* ostikwâniwâw 'their head (sg.)']

–stim– NDA cross-niece; daughter-in-law [*e.g.,* ostima 'his/her daughter-in-law / daughters-in-law']

–stimihkâwin– NDA step-cross-niece, step-daughter-in-law; daughter-in-law-in-common-law [*e.g.,* nistimihkâwin 'my daughter-in-common-law']

–tahtahkwan– NDA wing [*e.g.,* otahtahkwana 'his/her wing / wings']

–takisiy– NDI intestines, guts, entrails [*e.g.,* otakisiya 'his/her intestines, (an animal's) intestines', mitakisiya 'intestines, one's intestines']

–tawêmâw– NDA male parallel cousin (woman speaking); female cross-cousin's husband (woman speaking) [*e.g.,* nitawêmâw 'my male parallel cousin (woman speaking)']

–tânis– NDA daughter, parallel niece [*e.g.,* nitânisak 'my daughters']

–tâpiskan– NDI chin [*e.g.,* otâpiskaniyihk 'on his/her (obv.) chin']

–tâs– NDA loin-cloth; leggings; trousers, pants [*e.g.,* nitâs 'my pants (sg.)', otâsihk 'on his/her pants (sg., pl.)', mitâsa 'pants, one's pants (obv.)']

–têh– NDI heart; (*fig.*) heart, soul [*e.g.,* kitêhinawa 'your-and-my (incl.) hearts']

–têm– NDA dog; horse [*e.g.,* otêmiwâwa 'their horse / horses']

–tihkwatim– NDA cross-nephew; son-in-law [*e.g.,* nitihkwatim 'my son-in-law'; *vocative:* nitihkwâ 'oh my nephew!']

–tipiskâm– NDI night, night of one's life [*e.g.,* kitipiskâmiwâw 'a night of your (pl.) life']

–tôcikan– NDI one's doing, one's fault [*e.g.,* otôcikaniwâw 'their fault (sg.)']

–tôhtôsim– NDA female breast; teat (e.g., cow) [*e.g.,* kitôhtôsimak 'your (sg.) breasts', otôhtôsima 'its (an animal's) teat / teats', mitôhtôsima 'breast / breasts, one's breast / breasts (obv.)']

–tôn– NDI mouth [*e.g.,* otônihk 'on his/her mouth']

–tôsimiskwêm– NDA sister's daughter (woman speaking), parallel niece (woman speaking) [*e.g.*, nitôsimiskwêm 'my sister's daughter (woman speaking)']

–tôtêm– NDA kinsman; friend [*e.g.*, kitôtêminawak 'your-and-my (incl.) friends']

–wâhkômâkan– NDA relative [*e.g.*, kiwâhkômâkaninawak 'your-and-my (incl.) relatives']

–wîcêwâkan– NDA companion, partner; spouse [*e.g.*, kiwîcêwâkaniwâwak 'your (pl.) companions']

–wîcêwâkanis– NDA companion [*diminutive; e.g.*, niwîcêwâkanis 'my companion']

–wîkimâkan– NDA spouse, housemate [*e.g.*, niwîkimâkan 'my spouse']

–wîtatoskêmâkan– NDA fellow worker, co-worker [*e.g.*, niwîtatoskêmâkan 'my fellow worker']

acâhkos– NA star, little star

acâwê– VAI buy a little of (it), buy some of (it) [*diminutive*]

acâwêsi– VAI buy a little of (it), buy some of (it) [*diminutive*]

acikâsipakw– NI bearberry leaf [*sic:* ac–; *cf.* cikâsipakw–; *presumably Arctostaphylos uva-ursi*]

acimosis– NA puppy, young dog, little dog [*diminutive*]

aciyaw IPC for a short while

acosis– NI arrow [*sic:* NI]

acoskâcasi– VAI do some work on (it) [*diminutive*]

ah IPC ho! [*exclamatory*]

ah– VTA place s.o. there, put s.o. there, set s.o. down

ahâw IPC now indeed! ready! let's go! [*hortatory*]

ahcâhko-pimâtisiwin– NI spiritual life

ahcâhkw– NA soul

ahcâpiy– NA bow

ahkitisahw– VTA drive s.o. forward [*sic:* a–; *cf.* yahkitisahw–; *e.g.*, nitahkitisahwâw 'I drove it (cow) forward']

ahpihc IPC very much [*?sic:* ahp–, âp–; *cf.* âpihci IPV]

ahpô IPC even, possibly; or

ahpô cî *IPC* or else

ahpô piko *IPC* even if; and yet

ahpônâni *IPC* of course not, not any [*i.e., foregone conclusion that something is not the case*]

ahtay– *NA* pelt, fur

akâmaskîhk *IPC* across the water, overseas

akâmi-sîpîsisihk *IPC* across the creek

akâmi-tipahaskân *IPC* across the border; across the forty-ninth parallel, in the United States

akâmihk *IPC* across water, across the lake

akâminakasiy– *NA* thorn, thorn-bush [*sic:* akâ–; *cf.* akwâminakasiy–, okâminakasiy–]

akâmôtênaw *IPC* across the camp-circle; across the settlement, across town

akâwât– *VTA* desire s.o., lust for s.o.; want s.o. (e.g., rabbit for food)

akâwât– *VTI* desire s.t., wish for s.t.

akâwâtamaw– *VTA* desire (it/him) of s.o.; envy s.o. over (it/him), begrudge (it/him) to s.o.

akihtê– *VII* be counted

akim– *VTA* count s.o.

akiso– *VAI* be counted; be counted in, be a band member

akocikan– *NI* rack for hanging up fish or meat, storage-rack; cupboard, shelf

akocikanis– *NI* little shelf [*diminutive*]

akocikê– *VAI* hang things up, hang up one's laundry

akocin– *VAI* hang, be suspended; hang in a swing, hang in a snare

akocipayi– *VAI* be caught aloft

akociwêpin– *VTA* throw s.o. to hang, throw s.o. to be suspended; throw s.o. over top (e.g., onto willow bushes)

akohcim– *VTA* immerse s.o. in water (e.g., baby)

akohcin– *VAI* hang in the water, be suspended in water

akohp– *NI* blanket

akohpihkaw– VTA   make a blanket for s.o.
akohpis– NI   small blanket [*diminutive*]
akohtin– VII   float on liquid (e.g., grease on soup)
akohtitâ– VAI   put (it) in water, add (it) to water (e.g., boric acid)
akopiso– VAI   put on medicine, tie on a bandage
akosî– VAI   perch aloft, be perched (e.g., on a tree)
akot– VTA   hang s.o. up; place s.o. on a funeral scaffold
akotâ– VAI   hang (it) up; hang up one's snare, set one's snare
akotê– VII   hang, be suspended
akwamo– VAI   be attached (e.g., thread on spool) [*sic:* -wa-]
akwamohtâ– VAI   attach (it), fasten (it) (e.g., safety-pin)
akwanah– VTA   cover s.o.
akwanah– VTI   cover s.t.
akwanahikan– NI   covering; canvas
akwanaho– VAI   cover oneself, be covered (e.g., by a blanket); use (it) as a cover
akwanahon– NI   cover
akwanâhkwên– VTA   cover s.o.'s (e.g., infant's) face; use (it) to cover s.o.'s face
akwanâhkwêyâmo– VAI   flee with one's face covered, flee by covering one's face, cover one's face in flight
akwanân– NA   shawl
akwanâpowêhikâso– VAI   be covered as vessel containing liquid, have a cover, have a lid (e.g., pot)
akwanâpowêhikâsosi– VAI   be covered as a small vessel containing liquid, have a cover, have a lid (e.g., mussel) [*diminutive*]
akwâminakasiy– NA   thorn, thorn-bush [*sic:* akw-; *cf.* akâminakasiy–, okâminakasiy–]
akwâwân– NI   rack for drying meat
akwâwânâhcikos– NI   rail of drying rack
akwâwê– VAI   hang sheets of meat on drying rack

amisko-sâkahikanihk *INM* (*place-name:*) Beaver Lake (Alberta) [*locative; lit.* at the beaver lake]

amiskw– *NA* beaver

amiskwayânêscocinis– *NI* beaver-pelt hat [*diminutive*]

amiskwayânis– *NA* beaver-pelt [*diminutive*]

amiskwâyow– *NI* beaver-tail

ana *PR* that [*demonstrative; e.g.,* ana, aniki (*also* anikik), anihi; anima, anihi]

anâskânihtakw– *NI* floor-covering, linoleum

anâskânis– *NI* covering, mat, rug [*diminutive*]

anâskât– *VTA* spread matting for s.o.; provide s.o. with bedsheets

anâskê– *VAI* have a mat, spread a blanket; use (it) as matting or floor-covering

ani *IPC* then, indeed, surely [*general enclitic; emphatic*]

anikwacâs– *NA* squirrel; gopher

anima *IPC* it is that; the fact that [*factive; also predicative*]

anis îsi *IPC* in that way; that is how it is [*also predicative*]

anita *IPC* at that place, there

anit[a] êtêhkê isi *IPC* in the direction of that place, in that direction

aniyê *IPC* continuing, on and on [*post-verbal enclitic; cf.* ani]

anohc *IPC* now, today [*cf.* anoht]

anohc-kaskâpiskahikan– *NI* today's canned goods

anohcihkê *IPC* recently

anoht *IPC* now, today [*cf.* anohc]

apahkwân– *NI* roof

apahkwâson– *NI* cover, canvas

apahkwât– *VTI* make a roof over s.t.

apahkwâtê– *VII* have a roof, be roofed; be the roof

apahkwê– *VAI* roof (it); make a roof

apasoy– *NI* lodge-pole

api– *VAI* sit, sit down; be situated, be present, stay; be at home, be available

apihkât– *VTA* braid s.o., knit s.o. (e.g., stocking)
apihkât– *VTI* braid s.t., knit s.t.
apihkâtamaw– *VTA* braid (it/him) for s.o.
apihkâtê– *VII* be braided
apihkê– *VAI* braid, knit
apihkêpicikan– *NI* knitting machine
apisâsin– *VII* be small
apiscâpakwanîs– *NI* small flower, flower pattern (e.g., printed on fabric) [*sic:* -wa-; *diminutive*]
apiscâpêkasin– *VII* be thin string, be thin snare-wire [*diminutive*]
apiscis– *VTI* cut s.t. into small pieces
apiscisasi– *VAI* cut (it) into very small pieces [*diminutive*]
apisi-môsos– *NA* deer, red-deer [*sic: stem-final* -s-; *cf.* apisi-môsosw–]
apisi-môsosw– *NA* deer, red-deer [*sic: stem-final* -sw-; *cf.* apisi-môsos–]
apisi-môsw– *NA* small moose [*e.g.,* apisi-môswa (prox. sg., obv.)]
apisihkwês– *NA* (*man's name:*) Smallface
apisiminakâsin– *VII* be small berries throughout [*diminutive*]
apisimôsoso-oskanis– *NI* small deer-bone [*sic; diminutive*]
apisimôsoso-pahkêkinos– *NI* deer-hide [*sic*]
apisimôsoswayân– *NA* deer-hide
apisis *IPC* a little [*cf.* apisîs]
apisîs *IPC* a little [*cf.* apisis]
apisîsi– *VAI* be small
apisîsisi– *VAI* be quite small, be very small [*diminutive*]
apist– *VTI* sit by s.t., live by s.t., live near s.t., live in s.t. (e.g., lodge) [*sic:* -i-; *cf.* apîst–]
apiwinis– *NI* seat, chair
apîst– *VTI* sit by s.t., live by s.t., live near s.t. [*sic:* -î-; *cf.* apist–]
apîwikamikw– *NI* sitting room, living room

apwêsi– VAI sweat, perspire; work up a sweat
apwêsiwin– NI sweating, labouring
asahkê– VAI feed people, give out food
asahkêwikamikw– NI ration house
asahtowikamikw– NI ration house
asahtowin– NI feeding one another; rations
asam– VTA feed s.o., give s.o. to eat; hand out rations to s.o.
asamastimwân– NA green-feed, oats [*sic:* NA *with reference to oats*]
asamastimwê– VAI feed one's horses
asamâwaso– VAI feed one's children, sustain one's children
asamiso– VAI feed oneself
asapâp– NA thread
asapâpâhtikw– NA thread-spool [*sic:* NA]
asastê– VII be piled up
asawâpam– VTA watch for s.o., look out for s.o., lie in wait for s.o.
asawâpi– VAI be on the lookout; look out for game
asâm– NA snowshoe
ascascwâs– NI curds, cottage cheese [*diminutive*]
ascikê– VAI put things away, store things
ascikêwikamikw– NI storage room, storage building
ascocinis– NI little hat, little cap; infant's bonnet [*diminutive*]
asên– VTA reject s.o., turn s.o. back
asên– VTI reject s.t., turn s.t. back, run away from s.t.
asênikâtê– VII be rejected, be turned back
asêsinw– NI beaded top of moccasin, vamp of moccasin
asici IPC also, in addition, along with, together with [*usually enclitic*]
asikan– NA sock, stocking
asikâpawi– VAI stand about as a loose group
asiniy– NA rock, stone [*cf.* asiniy kâ-kîsisot 'quick-lime']

asinîs– NA stone [*diminutive*]
asinîwaciy– NI the Rocky Mountains [*usually singular*]
asiskiy– NI earth, soil, mud; clay; sod
asiskîhkât– VTI mud s.t., plaster s.t.
asiskîhkê– VAI mud a log-house, do the mudding, hold a mudding bee
asiskîwi-kocawânâpiskos– NA mud stove [*sic:* NA; *diminutive*]
asiskîwi-pahkwêsikan– NA mud-pie
asiskîwihkwê– VAI have soil on one's face, have dirt on one's face
asiskîwikamikos– NI mud shack [*diminutive*]
asiwacikan– NI pocket; container
asiwacikanis– NI little pocket [*diminutive*]
asiwacikê– VAI put things inside, enclose things, put things into boxes; have things inside; be pregnant
asiwacipayin– VII get placed inside, get enclosed; rapidly fill an enclosed space (e.g., water flowing into hoofprint)
asiwah– VTA place s.o. (e.g., sugar, fish) inside, enclose s.o.
asiwaso– VAI be inside, be enclosed; live inside, dwell inside
asiwatan– VII be inside, be enclosed
asiwatâ– VAI place (it) inside, enclose (it), put (it) into a bag or container
asiwatê– VII be placed inside, be enclosed
askihkos– NA little pail, little pot [*usually* NA; *both* NA, NI; *diminutive*]
askihkw– NA kettle, pail; pot
askihtakonikâtê– VII be made blue-green
askihtakosi– VAI be blue-green
askihtakwâ– VII be blue-green
askipwâw– NI potato
askiy– NI land, region, area; earth, world; settlement, colony, country; Métis settlement; (*plural:*) fields under cultivation, pieces of farmland, the lands [*e.g.,* nitaskînâhk

'on our (excl.) settlement'; askiya 'pieces of agricultural land']

askiy– NI moss [*sic*]

askîhkân– NI reserve; band

askîwi– VII be the earth, exist as world; be a year

askîwi-pimiy– NI coal oil, petroleum

askîwisk– VTI subject the earth to oneself, populate the earth, make the earth live

askow– VTA follow s.o., follow behind s.o.

askôskaw– VTA follow s.o. in birth sequence

askôto– VAI follow one another, follow behind one another

asotamaw– VTA promise (it) to s.o.

asotamâkê– VAI make a promise

asotamâkêwin– NI promise, vow [*sc. 'agent-centred' noun; e.g.*, otasotamâkêwin 'what he has promised']

asotamâkowin– NI promise, promise made [*sc. 'patient-centred' noun; e.g.*, kitasotamâkowininaw 'what has been promised to us']

asotamâtowin– NI mutual promise, promises made to one another

aspahâkêmo– VAI rely upon (it/him) in speaking, rely upon (it/him) in telling a story; use (it/him) as an excuse

aspapi– VAI sit against (it), sit on (it) (e.g., blanket)

aspapiwin– NI saddle

aspascâkanis– NI apron [*diminutive*]

aspastâkan– NI apron

aspatisin– VII lie leaning upon (it), lie back upon (it), lie propped up

aspatot– VTA accompany one's request of s.o. with a gift

aspin IPC off, away, from a distance, in departing; since then, the last I knew; back then, so long ago; presumably, evidently [*e.g.*, nîso-askiy aspin 'two years ago'; tânitahto-nîpin aspin 'a few summers ago']

aspisimo– VAI lie upon (it), use (it) as one's mattress

aspisimowin– NI mattress

aspisin– *VAI* lie on (it), lie against (it)

aspiskwêsimon– *NI* pillow

aspitonâmo– *VAI* rely on the spoken word; rely on (it) as a formal confirmation of the spoken word

aspiyîhkâso– *VAI* have a surname; have (it) as one's surname

astamaw– *VTA* place (it/him) for s.o.; put (it/him) on s.o.; apply (it/him) to s.o. (e.g., as medicine)

astamâso– *VAI* place (it/him) for oneself; put (it/him) on oneself

astâ– *VAI* place (it) there, put (it) there

astâh– *VTA* frighten s.o.; (*especially in inverse constructions:*) cause s.o. to be wary, worry s.o. [*e.g.*, k-âstâhikoyân 'when it worries me']

astâhtâso– *VAI* be watched, be considered a threat; evoke fear, be fearsome, be awe-inspiring, be awesome

astê– *VII* be placed, be in place; be piled up; be out (e.g., leaves)

astinwân– *NI* sinew

astis– *NA* mitten, glove [*usually plural*]

astotin– *NI* hat, cap

aswah– *VTI* catch s.t. as it drips

aswahikê– *VAI* watch with a weapon for people, be on the lookout with a weapon, lie in wait with a weapon

aswahw– *VTA* watch with a weapon for s.o., be on the lookout with a weapon for s.o.

atamih– *VTA* make s.o. grateful, make s.o. indebted, please s.o.

atamim– *VTA* make s.o. grateful by speech, please s.o. by speech

atamiskaw– *VTA* greet s.o., shake hands with s.o.

atâhk-akohp– *NA* (*man's name*) [*lit.* Star-Blanket]

atâm– *VTA* buy (it/him) from s.o.

atâmêyim– *VTA* blame s.o. in one's thoughts, accuse s.o. in one's thoughts

atâmihk *IPC* beneath, underneath, inside (e.g., clothing) [*sic:* a-; *cf.* itâmihk]
atâmim– *VTA* blame s.o. by speech
atâwâkê– *VAI* sell (it/him), sell things
atâwê– *VAI* buy (it/him)
atâwêstamaw– *VTA* buy (it/him) for s.o.
atâwêstamâso– *VAI* buy (it/him) for oneself
atâwêwikamikw– *NI* store, trading-post
ati *IPC* gradually, progressively [*sic:* IPC]
ati *IPV* progressively, proceed to
ati nîkân *IPC* in the future
atihkamêkw– *NA* whitefish
atihtê– *VII* be ripe, be of ripe colouring
atim– *VTA* catch up to s.o.
atimipayi– *VAI* move the other way, speed away
atimotâpânêyâpiy– *NI* dog harness [*usually plural*]
atimw– *NA* dog; horse
atis– *VTI* dye s.t.
atisikan– *NI* dye, trade-dye
atisikê– *VAI* dye things
atisikêmakan– *VII* be a dying-agent, yield a dye
atisw– *VTA* dye s.o. (e.g., porcupine quills)
atoskah– *VTA* make s.o. work, employ s.o., hire s.o.
atoskahâkan– *NA* employee, hired man
atoskaw– *VTA* work for s.o.
atoskât– *VTI* work at s.t.
atoskê– *VAI* work
atoskêhâkan– *NA* employee
atoskêmo– *VAI* get people to do things, employ people, hire people
atoskêstamaw– *VTA* work for s.o.
atoskêwin– *NI* work; job; contract (e.g., to complete an assignment)

atot– VTA ask s.o. to do something, engage s.o. for something, employ s.o.

awa PR this [*demonstrative*; *e.g.,* awa, ôki (*also* ôkik), ôhi (*also* ôho); ôma, ôhi (*also* ôho)]

awas IPC go away! away with you! [*e.g.,* awas (sg.), awasitik (pl.)]

awas-âyihk IPC on the other side, on the far side

awasi-nîpinohk IPC the summer before last

awasitâkosihk IPC the day before yesterday

awasitê IPC further over there

awasowi-kotawânâpiskw– NI warming-stove, heater [*sic:* NI]

awaswâkan– NI heater [*sic:* NI]

awaswêwê– VAI disappear from view (e.g., sun) [*sic; cf.* awasêwê–]

awaswêwêtot– VTI disappear behind s.t., go behind s.t. [*sic; cf.* awasêwêtot–]

awâsis– NA child

awâsisi-sôniyâs– NA family allowance

awâsisîhkân– NA doll

awâsisîwi– VAI be a child

awâsisîwiwin– NI being a child, childhood

awâska-mâmitonêyihcikan– NI stable mind, steady mind, balanced mind [*?sic:* awâska]

awêkâ IPC or else

awêska IPC behold! look at that! [*often as proclitic with a demonstrative pronoun; e.g.* awêsk âwa (prox. sg.)]

awih– VTA lend (it/him) to s.o.; rent (it/him) out to s.o.

awihiwê– VAI lend (it/him) to people; rent (it/him) out to people

awiyak PR someone, somebody; (*in negative constructions:*) not anyone, not anybody [*indefinite; e.g.,* awiyak (*also* awiyakak) (prox. sg.), awiya (obv.)]

awîna IPC what was that! [*exclamatory; often as proclitic with a demonstrative pronoun; e.g.,* awîn ôma; *not restricted to animate referents*]

awîna PR who [*interrogative; e.g.,* awîna (prox. sg.), awîniwa (obv.)]

awînipan IPC all gone, no longer present [*absentative; not restricted to animate referents*]

ay IPC hey! [*exclamatory*]

ay-api– VAI sit, be seated [*reduplicated*]

ay-atâmaskamik IPC inside the earth, beneath the ground [*reduplicated*]

ay-âhci IPC from one to another [*reduplicated*]

ay-âpihtaw IPC half-and-half [*reduplicated*]

ay-âskawi IPC from time to time, a few at a time [*reduplicated*]

aya IPC ah, well [*hesitatory; cf.* ayahk, ayi, ayihk]

aya PR the one [*weak demonstrative, often enclitic; e.g.,* aya, ayak, aya; ayi, aya]

ayah– VTI cover s.t. with earth; hill s.t. (e.g., potatoes)

ayahciyiniw– NA Blackfoot

ayahikâkan– NI hiller, tool for covering potatoes with earth

ayahikê– VAI cover things with earth, hill things (e.g., potatoes)

ayahk IPC ah, well [*hesitatory; cf.* aya, ayi, ayihk]

ayami– VAI speak [*dial.* (LR)]

ayamih– VTA speak to s.o. [*dial.* (LR)]

ayamihâ– VAI speak, talk; speak about (it), talk about (it) [*dial.* (LR)]

ayamihâ– VAI pray, say prayers; hold a church service, celebrate mass; participate in a religious rite, go to church; follow a religion [*cf.* ayimihâ–; *e.g.,* nitaw-âyamihâ– 'go on a pilgrimage'; nîpâ-ayamihâ– 'celebrate midnight mass']

ayamihâhtah– VTA make s.o. go to church, take s.o. to mass, go to church with s.o.

ayamihâwin– NI prayer, praying, saying prayers; church service; religious rite; religion, religious denomination; the Roman Catholic church [*cf.* ayimihâwin–]

ayamihcikê– VAI read things, read; go to school

ayamihcikêwin– NI reading; (*fig.*) a reading, bible verse
ayamihêmin– NA rosary-bead; rosary [*usually plural*]
ayamihêstamaw– VTA say Christian prayers for s.o.
ayamihêwâtisi– VAI be of religious disposition
ayamihêwi-kîsikâ– VII be Sunday
ayamihêwi-kîsikâw IPC a week, for a week
ayamihêwi-kîsikâw– NI Sunday
ayamihêwi-nikamo– VAI sing hymns
ayamihêwi-saskamon– NA the host; Holy Communion
ayamihêwikamikw– NI church, church building
ayamihêwiskwêw– NA nun
ayamihêwiyiniw– NA priest; minister; missionary
ayamihito– VAI speak to one another [*dial.* (LR)]
ayamihtâ– VAI read (it); read
ayamiwin– NI speech, message [*dial.* (LR)]
ayapinikê– VAI be all over things, be into things
ayapiy– NA net, fishing-net
ayâ– VAI be there, live there; exist
ayâ– VAI have (it)
ayâ– VII be there, exist
ayânis– NI clothes, clothing [*usually plural; diminutive; cf.* ayânisis–]
ayânisis– NI clothes, clothing [*usually plural; diminutive; cf.* ayânis–]
ayâw– VTA have s.o.
ayâwahkahw– VTA bury s.o. in the ground
ayê IPC wow! [*exclamatory, indicating surprise*]
ayêhkwêsis– NA young castrated bull; steer [*diminutive*]
ayêhkwêw– NA castrated bull; ox
ayêskotisahw– VTA tire s.o. out
ayi IPC ah, well [*hesitatory; cf.* aya, ayahk, ayihk]
ayi IPV ah, well [*hesitatory; sic:* IPV]
ayihk IPC ah, well [*hesitatory; cf.* aya, ayahk, ayi]

ayimihâ– *VAI* pray, say prayers; hold a church service, celebrate mass; participate in a religious rite, go to church; follow a religion [*cf.* ayamihâ–]

ayimihâwin– *NI* prayer, praying, saying prayers; church service; religious rite; religion, religious denomination; the Roman Catholic church [*cf.* ayamihâwin–]

ayinânêw *IPC* eight

ayinânêw-kîsikâw *IPC* eight days, for eight days

ayinânêwi-misit *IPC* eight feet, for eight feet (measure)

ayinânêwimitanaw *IPC* eighty

ayinânêwosâp *IPC* eighteen

ayis *IPC* for, because [*causal conjunction; cf.* ayisk]

ayisiyiniw– *NA* person, human being, people

ayisiyinîhkân– *NA* doll, mannikin; cartoon figure

ayisiyinîsis– *NA* young person [*diminutive*]

ayisiyinîwi– *VAI* be a person, be a human being

ayisiyinîwin– *NI* being human, human existence

ayisk *IPC* for, because [*causal conjunction; cf.* ayis]

ayiwâk *IPC* more; (*in numeral phrases:*) plus

ayiwâk ihkin *IPC* ever more so! this cannot be! would anyone believe this! [*i.e., one's worst premonitions have been fulfilled*]

ayiwâkêyiht– *VTI* think more of s.t., regard s.t. more highly

ayiwâkêyim– *VTA* think more of s.o., regard s.o. more highly

ayiwâkipayi– *VAI* have more than enough, have a surplus, have plenty; run to more, be a surplus (e.g., money)

ayiwêpi– *VAI* rest, take a rest; retire, take retirement

ayiwêpihastimwê– *VAI* give one's horses a rest, rest one's horses

ayiwinis– *NI* clothes, clothing; rags (e.g., as used in bitch-light) [*usually plural; diminutive*]

ayiwinisis– *NI* clothes, clothing, laundry [*diminutive*]

ayîki-pîsimw– *NA* the month of April

ayîkis– NA frog [*diminutive*]
ayôskan– NA raspberry
â IPC well [*introductory; cf.* hâ, wâ]
â IPC ah! oh! [*exclamatory; cf.* âw]
âcim– VTA tell s.o., tell things to s.o., tell about s.o.
âcimiso– VAI tell things about oneself, tell a story about oneself; (*fig.*) confess oneself, go to confession
âcimo– VAI tell things, tell a story, give an account
âcimostaw– VTA tell s.o. about (it/him), tell s.o. a story, give s.o. an account
âcimostâto– VAI tell one another about (it/him), tell stories to one another
âcimowin– NI story, account, report
âcimowinis– NI little story [*diminutive*]
âcimôh– VTA make s.o. tell about (it/him), make s.o. tell a story
âcimômakan– VII tell things, provide an account
âh IPC eh? [*tag question*]
âh-âyin– VTI touch s.t. repeatedly, rub across s.t. by hand [*usually reduplicated*]
âh-âyîtaw IPC on both sides [*reduplicated*]
âha IPC yes [*sic; affirmative; cf.* êha, êhâ, âhâ]
âhâ IPC yes [*sic; affirmative; cf.* êha, êhâ, âha]
âhc-âyâ– VAI move one's abode, move from one place to another
âhcanis– NA ring, wedding-ring
âhci IPC still, nevertheless, despite everything [*adversative*]
âhci IPV by change, by replacement [*sic:* IPV]
âhci piko IPC still, nevertheless, despite everything [*adversative*]
âhcîhtâ– VAI make (it) over, make (it) different, change (it)
âhk îtâp IPC as if, pretendingly [*sic:* â-; *cf.* yâhk îtâp]
âhkamêyimo– VAI persist in one's will, persevere
âhkamêyimotot– VTI persist in s.t., persevere in s.t.

âhkami *IPV* persistently, unceasingly, unwaveringly
âhkasîho– *VAI* dress lightly [*sic:* â-; *cf.* yâhkasîho–]
âhki *IPC* pretend, make-believe [*sic:* â-; *cf.* yâhki]
âhkohtêwiso– *VAI* be sharp, be caustic (e.g., soap)
âhkosi– *VAI* be sick, be ill; have contractions, be in labour
âhkosiski– *VAI* be habitually sick, be sickly
âhkosiwin– *NI* illness
âhkosîwikamikw– *NI* hospital
âhkwaci– *VAI* be cold, freeze, be frozen (e.g., fish)
âhkwaci-pimiy– *NI* hard grease, solid grease [*i.e., grease rendered from fat around abdominal organs, more readily congealed than* iyinito-pimiy–]
âhkwacihcikanis– *NI* small refrigerator, small freezer [*diminutive*]
âhkwakihtê– *VII* cost dearly, cost more, be worth a top-up amount
âhkwatihcikan– *NI* refrigerator, freezer
âhkwatihcikâtê– *VII* be frozen (e.g., in a freezer)
âhkwatihtâ– *VAI* let (it) freeze, freeze (it)
âhkwatim– *VTA* let s.o. freeze (e.g., fish), freeze s.o.
âhkwatin– *VII* be frozen, be frozen solid; be freeze-up
âhkwâpahtê– *VII* give off a sharp odour, produce pungent fumes, emit acidic or caustic fumes
âhkwâtisi– *VAI* be stern, be sharp, be of severe disposition
âhkwêhtawastê– *VII* be piled one over top of the other
âhkwêhtawêskaw– *VTA* wear s.o. (e.g., socks) over top of one another, wear several layers of s.o. (e.g., socks)
âhtahpit– *VTI* move and tie s.t., tie s.t. differently; change the bandage on s.t.
âhtin– *VTI* move s.t. over, push s.t. aside
âhtohtê– *VAI* move to a different place, go elsewhere
âhtokê– *VAI* move camp, move one's camp elsewhere
âkamîna *IPC* also, on the other hand; as usual [*sic; cf.* mâka mîna]

âkaw-âyihk *IPC* hidden, out of view, behind an obstacle to vision

âkayâsîmo– *VAI* speak English

âkayâsîmosi– *VAI* speak a little English [*diminutive*]

âkayâsîmowin– *NI* speaking English, the English language

âkô *IPV* covered, shielded

âkô-wiyîpâ– *VII* be covered in dirt

âkwaskikâpawi– *VAI* stand in the way, stand as an obstacle

âkwaskiskaw– *VTA* head s.o. off, get in s.o.'s way

âkwaskitin– *VTA* embrace s.o., hug s.o.

âkwaskitinito– *VAI* embrace one another, hug one another

âkwâ-tipiskâ– *VII* be late in the evening

âkwâc *IPC* well on its way, a long ways, more than halfway

âkwâskam *IPC* really, rather; (*in negative constructions:*) not really, not as much

âkwâtaskinê– *VAI* be quite full (e.g., pail), be more than half full

âmaciwê– *VAI* go uphill, ascend a hill

âmatisôst– *VTI* perceive the spirit of s.t. (e.g., spirit-bundle)

âmow– *NA* bee

ânisîhcicikan– *NI* antidote [*sic:* -cic-; *?cf.* ânisîhtitâ– VAI]

ânisîhtâ– *VAI* alleviate the effect of (it), be an antidote to (it)

âniskê *IPV* successively, one joining the other, surviving

âniskôkwât– *VTI* sew s.t. on as an extension

âniskôscikê– *VAI* build an extension

âniskôstê– *VII* extend, be extended

âpacih– *VTA* use s.o., make use of s.o., find s.o. useful [*e.g.,* misatimwak ê-âpacihacik 'when you (sg.) are using horses'; sîwinikan t-âpacihat 'for you (sg.) to use sugar']

âpacih– *VTA* (*especially in inverse constructions:*) be of use to s.o., be of service to s.o. [*e.g.,* êwako piko kiyê-âpacihikoyahk 'that is the only thing to sustain us (incl.)'; môy ka-kî-âpacihik 'it cannot benefit him']

âpacihcikan– NI tool, appliance, machine; equipment, furnishings, furniture
âpacihcikanis– NI small tool, small appliance [*diminutive*]
âpacihcikâtê– VII be used, be in use
âpacihtamôh– VTA make s.o. use (it/him), give (it/him) to s.o. to use; use (it/him) for s.o., use (it/him) on s.o.
âpacihtâ– VAI use (it), make use of (it)
âpah– VTI loosen s.t., untie s.t.
âpahkawin– VII be level-headed, be sensible, be conscious
âpahw– VTA loosen s.o., uncover s.o., unbundle s.o. (e.g., child)
âpakosîs– NA mouse [*sic:* â-; *cf.* wâpakosîs–]
âpasâpi– VAI look back, glance back
âpatan– VII be used, be useful
âpatisi– VAI be used, be useful
âpihcaw-âyis– NA halfbreed, Métis [*diminutive*]
âpihci IPV completely, throughout [*?sic:* âp-, ahp-; *cf.* ahpihc IPC]
âpihkon– VTI untie s.t.
âpihtaw IPC half, in half, halfway
âpihtaw-tipahikan IPC half-hour, for half an hour
âpihtawanohk IPC at the halfway point
âpihtawikosisân– NA halfbreed, Métis
âpihtawikosisânaskiy– NI halfbreed settlement, Métis settlement
âpihtawikosisânôcênâs– NI little halfbreed town, Métis settlement [*sic:* -t-, -c-; *diminutive*]
âpihtâ-kîsikani-mîciso– VAI eat one's mid-day meal, eat one's lunch
âpihtâ-kîsikâ– VII be mid-day, be noon, be lunchtime
âpihtâ-kîsikâhk IPC in the south, to the south
âpihtâ-tipiskâ– VII be midnight
âpisisim– VTA revive s.o., bring s.o. back to life

âpisisimito– VAI revive one another, bring one another back to life

âpisisin– VAI revive, come back to life

âpistaw-âyihk IPC at the halfway point [*sic:* -st-; *cf.* âpihtaw]

âpocikwânipayin– VII turn upside down

âpocikwânipit– VTA turn s.o. (e.g., sleigh) upside down

âpocikwânîmakan– VII turn upside down, be turned upside down

âpotah– VTI turn s.t. upside down, turn s.t. inside out

âsawi IPV in passing something on, in continuation [?*cf.* âsowi, âsô]

âsawinamaw– VTA pass (it/him) on to s.o. [*sic:* -awi-; *cf.* âsônamaw–]

âsay IPC already; without delay [*also aspectual; cf.* sâsay]

âsay mîna IPC as usual [*cf.* sâsamîna, sâsay mîna]

âsiciwan– VII run down as liquid

âsipayin– VII move down, hang down, be dragged down

âsipit– VTA pull s.o. down

âsiyân– NA loin-cloth, diaper, menstrual napkin

âsiyânihkêpison– NI diaper [*sic:* NI]

âsîmakan– VII go down, move down

âskaw IPC sometimes; once in a while

âskiti– VAI be raw, be uncooked (e.g., flour)

âsokan– NI dock; bridge

âsosim– VTA lay s.o. to lean against something, lean s.o. against something

âsowah– VTI cross s.t. (e.g., river, creek)

âsowahpitê– VII be stretched across, be strung across

âsowakâmêpici– VAI move one's camp across a body of water

âsowi IPV in turn, in succession [*cf.* âsô; ?*cf.* âsawi]

âsowiskâ– VAI cross by boat, go across by boat

âsowohtah– VTA go across with s.o., take s.o. across

âsowohtê– VAI walk across, cross the road

âsô *IPV* in passing something on, in continuation [*cf.* âsowi; *?cf.* âsawi]

âsô-nakî– *VAI* stop in moving across (e.g., the prairies), stop in one's transit

âsôhtatâ– *VAI* lean (it) across something

âsônamaw– *VTA* pass (it/him) across to s.o., pass (it/him) on to s.o.; hand (it/him) down to s.o., bequeathe (it/him) to s.o.

âsônê *IPC* especially, in particular

âsôskamaw– *VTA* infect s.o. with (it)

âstam *IPC* come here! [*hortatory; e.g.,* âstam (sg.), âstamitik (*also* âstamik) (pl.)]

âstamipayi– *VAI* become less, run low (e.g., money)

âstamispî *IPC* at a time closer to the present; more recently [*cf.* âstamispîhk]

âstamispîhk *IPC* at a time closer to the present; more recently [*cf.* âstamispî]

âstamita *IPC* later, more recently

âstawê– *VII* be without fire; be extinct (e.g., fire)

âstawêhikê– *VAI* be a fire-fighter; fight forest-fires

âstawêpayi– *VAI* have one's light go out (e.g., star), have one's fire extinguished (e.g., star)

âstê-ayâ– *VAI* recover from illness, have one's condition improve, be gradually restored

âstê-kimiwan– *VII* cease being rain, let up as rain

âstê-kîsikâ– *VII* cease being stormy weather, let up as severe weather, be better weather

âswastâ– *VAI* place (it) to lean against something, lean (it) against something

âta *IPC* although; on the other hand [*concessive conjunction*]

âtawêyihcikê– *VAI* reject things; be dissatisfied with things

âtawêyiht– *VTI* reject s.t.; be dissatisfied with s.t.

âtawêyim– *VTA* reject s.o.; be dissatisfied with s.o.

âtayôhkan– *NA* spirit being, dream guardian

âtayôhkan– *NI* sacred story [*sic:* NI]

âtayôhkanakiso– *VAI* be held to be a spirit being, be recognised as a dream guardian
âtayôhkaw– *VTA* tell s.o. a sacred story
âtayôhkât– *VTA* tell about s.o. in the form of a sacred story, tell a sacred story of s.o.
âtayôhkât– *VTI* tell about s.t. in the form of a sacred story, tell a sacred story of s.t.
âtayôhkê– *VAI* tell a sacred story
âtayôhkêwin– *NI* sacred story
âtiht *IPC* some
âtot– *VTI* tell about s.t., give an account of s.t.
âtotâkosi– *VAI* be told about, be told of
âtotâkwan– *VII* be told, be told about, be told of
âw *IPC* ah! oh! [*exclamatory; cf.* â]
âwacikê– *VAI* haul things, do one's hauling
âwacimihtê– *VAI* haul firewood
âwacipit– *VTI* haul s.t. by pulling
âwacitâpê– *VAI* haul (it/him) by dragging
âwatamâso– *VAI* haul (it/him) for oneself
âwataskosiwâkan– *NA* hay-wagon
âwatâ– *VAI* haul (it)
âwatôpê– *VAI* haul water, haul one's drinking water
âyiman– *VII* be difficult
âyimanohk *IPC* in a difficult place
âyimêyiht– *VTI* consider s.t. difficult, consider s.t. too difficult
âyimih– *VTA* make things difficult for s.o., give s.o. a difficult time
âyimim– *VTA* make things difficult for s.o. by speech
âyimisi– *VAI* have a difficult time; be of difficult disposition, be wild, be mean
âyimisîwatimw– *NA* wild horse, difficult horse [*sic:* -at-]
âyimî– *VAI* have a difficult time, have a difficult task; have a hard life

âyimôhto– *VAI* discuss one another; gossip about one another

âyimôhtowin– *NI* discussing one another; gossiping about one another, gossip

âyimôm– *VTA* discuss s.o.; gossip about s.o.

âyimômiso– *VAI* discuss oneself; speak unguardedly about oneself, gossip about oneself

âyimôt– *VTI* speak of s.t., discuss s.t.; gossip about s.t.

âyîcimin– *NA* peas [*usually plural*]

âyîtin– *VTI* hold fast onto s.t., hold on tightly to s.t.

cacâstapipayin– *VII* move rapidly

cah *IPC* gosh! [*exclamatory*]

cahcahkayow– *NA* black-bird

cahcakwahcâsin– *VII* be a small piece of level ground [*diminutive*]

cahkatayên– *VTA* prod s.o. at the belly, spur s.o.'s belly

cahkâpêw-âtayôhkan– *NA* (*name*) [*i.e., name of a spirit being*]

cahkâpicin– *VAI* have one's eye punctured (e.g., by branches or thorns)

cahkon– *VTA* carry s.o. small, hold s.o. small [*diminutive*]

cakahki-nôcikwêsîwi– *VAI* be a nice old woman, be a wonderful old woman [*diminutive*]

canawî– *VAI* keep busy in various ways

capahcâsin– *VII* be quite low [*diminutive*]

capasis *IPC* down, down low [*cf.* capasîs]

capasîs *IPC* down, down low [*cf.* capasis]

cascakiskwês– *NA* (*man's name*) [*lit.* Head-Thrown-Back, Head-Held-Back]

cawâsin– *VII* be a little opening [*diminutive*]

câh-cîkâhtaw *IPC* quite close, quite nearby [*reduplicated*]

câh-cîki *IPC* close to one another

câhcahkipêkahw– *VTA* paint dots on s.o.

câhkin– *VTA* touch s.o. small, touch s.o. a little [*diminutive*]

câpakwânis– *NI* snare, rabbit snare [*diminutive*]

câpakwêsi– VAI set small snares, set rabbit snares; do a little snaring [*diminutive*]

câpihcicikan– NA axe-handle; (*man's name*) [*lit.* Handle]

cêhcapiwinis– NI small chair [*diminutive*]

cêskwa IPC wait! soon; (*in negative constructions:*) not yet [*cf.* êskwa, mêskwa]

cêsos– NA (*name:*) Jésus [*sic, as in French; cf.* cîsas–]

cicipahwânis– NI top, spinning top [*?sic:* NI]

cikâsipakw– NI bearberry leaf [*sic:* c-; *cf.* acikâsipakw–; *presumably Arctostaphylos uva-ursi*]

cikêmâ IPC of course, obviously, as might be expected [*weak concessive, confirming what could not reasonably be doubted*; *cf.* cikêmô]

cikêmô IPC of course, obviously, as might be expected [*weak concessive, confirming what could not reasonably be doubted*; *sic:* -ô; *cf.* cikêmâ]

cikin– NA domestic chicken

cikinis– NA domestic chicken, little chicken [*diminutive*]

cimacês– NI fence-post [*diminutive*]

cimacikê– VAI stook sheaves of grain, do one's stooking

cimah– VTA place s.o. (e.g., tree) upright, plant s.o. upright

cimaso– VAI stand upright, stand erect (e.g., tree)

cimatâ– VAI place (it) upright, plant (it) upright

cimatê– VII stand upright, stand erect

cimâsin– VII be short

cistêmâw– NA tobacco

ciyêkwac IPC instead, in lieu

cî IPC is it the case that [*interrogative enclitic*]

cîhcîkin– VTI scratch s.t. (e.g., one's hip)

cîhcîkî– VAI scratch oneself, scratch

cîhcîkos– VTI cut meat off s.t. (e.g., bone)

cîhkêyiht– VTI like s.t., approve of s.t.; eagerly participate in s.t.

cîkah– VTI chop s.t.

cîkahikanis– NI small axe, hatchet [*diminutive*]
cîkahikê– VAI chop things, chop wood, chop posts
cîkahoso– VAI chop oneself, injure oneself with an axe
cîkahw– VTA chop s.o. (e.g., tree)
cîkâhtaw IPC close, nearby, in the area, in the immediate vicinity
cîki IPC close, close by, nearby, near to
cîkiskîsik IPC close to one's eye
cîpatamo– VAI be attached so as to project out
cîpatapi– VAI sit up, sit upright, sit erect
cîposi– VAI be pointed
cîsas– NA (*name:*) Jesus [*sic, as in English; cf.* cêsos–]
cîsâwât– VTI cut s.t. (e.g., fat) into chunks, chop s.t. fine
cîsiskaw– VTA excite s.o., get s.o. excited (by foot or body movement)
cîstahikan– NI spear, harpoon
cîstahw– VTA spear s.o.
cîstâsêpon– NI fork
cîsw– VTA sting s.o., prick s.o.
cowêskihtê– VAI have one's ears ring, have ringing in one's ears, suffer from tinnitus [*usually reduplicated*]
côfîl– NA (*man's name*) [*?cf.* Théophile]
côhkâpisi– VAI open one's eyes a little, have one's eyes open a little [*diminutive*]
côsap– NA (*name:*) Joseph
êcik âni IPC as it turns out, apparently, evidently, indeed
êcika IPC what is this! [*exclamatory, indicating surprise; proclitic, often with a demonstrative pronoun; e.g.,* êcik ôma]
êha IPC yes [*affirmative; the initial vowel is usually nasalised, and the final vowel often ends in a glottal catch, e.g.,* êha?; *cf.* êhâ, âha, âhâ]
êhâ IPC yes [*sic; affirmative; cf.* êha, âha, âhâ]
êhêhê ahêy IPC oh grief! woe betide! [*sic; cf.* hêhêhêêhahê; *exclamatory, indicating grave regret*]

êkamâ *IPC* it is not the case [*predicative*]

êkâ *IPC* not to [*negator in volitional constructions; cf.* êkâya, êkây, êkâwiya]

êkâwiya *IPC* not to; do not! [*also exclamatory; cf.* êkâ, êkây, êkâya]

êkây *IPC* not to; do not! [*also exclamatory; cf.* êkâ, êkâya, êkâwiya]

êkâya *IPC* not to; do not! [*also exclamatory; cf.* êkâ, êkây, êkâwiya]

êkos âni *IPC* thus indeed [*emphatic; also predicative*]

êkos êsa *IPC* thus then

êkos îsi *IPC* thus, just so, in that way; that is how it is [*also predicative*]

êkosi *IPC* thus, in that way; that is all [*also predicative*]

êkospî *IPC* then, at that time [*cf.* êkospîhk]

êkospîhk *IPC* then, at that time [*cf.* êkospî]

êkota *IPC* there, right there, at that place

êkotê *IPC* over there

êkotowahk *IPC* of that kind

êkotowihk *IPC* in that place

êkoyikohk *IPC* that much, up to that point, to that degree, to that extent [*cf.* êkwayikohk]

êkw âni *IPC* it is then

êkwa *IPC* then, now; and

êkwayâc *IPC* only then, not until then; only now, for the first time [*cf.* êkwêyâc, êkwayâk, êkwayôc]

êkwayâk *IPC* only then, not until then; only now, for the first time [*cf.* êkwayâc, êkwêyâc, êkwayôc]

êkwayikohk *IPC* that much, up to that point, to that degree, to that extent [*cf.* êkoyikohk]

êkwayôc *IPC* only then, not until then; only now, for the first time [*sic:* -ô-; *cf.* êkwayâc, êkwêyâc, êkwayâk]

êkwêyâc *IPC* only then, not until then; only now, for the first time [*also in correlative constructions with* pâtimâ; *cf.* êkwayâc, êkwayâk, êkwayôc]

êmihkwânis– NA spoon

êsa IPC reportedly [*i.e., information received from others, in contrast to* êtokwê *and* pakahkam]

êsis– NA little shell (mollusc)

êska IPC beyond belief [*revelatory*]

êskwa IPC wait! soon; (*in negative constructions:*) not yet [*cf.* cêskwa, mêskwa]

êtataw IPC barely, scarcely

êtatawisi– VAI be barely alive, be weak unto death, be about to die

êtikwê IPC presumably, I guess [*sic; cf.* êtokwê; *dubitative, reflecting personal inference, in contrast to* êsa *and* pakahkam]

êtokwê IPC presumably, I guess [*sic; cf.* êtikwê; *dubitative, reflecting personal inference, in contrast to* êsa *and* pakahkam]

êwako PR that one [*resumptive demonstrative; e.g.,* êwako, êkonik, êkoni; êwako, êkoni; êwakoyiw]

êy IPC hey [*introductory, also exclamatory; cf.* hêy]

êyâpic IPC still, in continuity; yet [*i.e., in future, contrary to expectation; cf.* kêyâpic]

êyiwêhk IPC just in case, nevertheless; despite shortcomings [*cf.* kêyiwêhk]

haha IPC ha! [*exclamatory*]

hâ IPC oh! [*exclamatory, indicating reluctant acknowledgement*]

hâ IPC well [*introductory; cf.* â, wâ]

hâm IPC now then [*hortatory, indicating readiness or impatience*]

hâw IPC now, now then [*hortatory, indicating readiness or impatience*]

hêhêhêêhahê IPC oh grief! woe betide! [*sic; cf.* êhêhê ahêy; *exclamatory, indicating grave regret*]

hêy IPC hey [*exclamatory; cf.* êy]

Hudson's-Bay-ayiwinis– NI Hudson's Bay Company clothes, store-bought clothing [*sic: code-switching within compound*]

icahcopiponêsi– VAI be so many years old (e.g., infant) [*diminutive*]

ici *IPC* later, subsequently

icikâtê– *VII* be called thus

ihkêyiht– *VTI* be tired of s.t.; be impatient

ihkin– *VII* happen thus; occur, take place

ihtahtopiponwêwin– *NI* having so many years, the number of one's years, one's age [*sic:* iht-; *cf.* itahtopiponwê–]

ihtako– *VAI* exist; be born (e.g., infant)

ihtakon– *VII* exist

ihtasi– *VAI* be so many, be as many

ihtatan– *VII* exist there [*?sic: stem, gloss*]

ihtâ– *VAI* be there, exist

ihtâwin– *NI* abode, place of residence; community

is-âyâ– *VAI* be thus in health; be unwell, be in poor health; be out of sorts, have something being the matter [*e.g.*, tânis êtik ôm ê-is-âyâyân 'I wonder what is the matter with me']

isi *IPC* thus, this way; there, in the direction of [*enclitic*]

isi *IPN* thus, this way

isi *IPV* thus, this way; there

isi-mawimoscikêwin– *NI* worshipping thus, such a form of worship; rite of such a type

isi-pîkiskwêwin– *NI* speaking thus; such a language

isikwât– *VTI* sew s.t. thus, sew s.t. to such a design

isinaw– *VTA* look thus to s.o., present such an appearance to s.o.

isinâkosi– *VAI* look thus, give such an appearance

isinâkwan– *VII* look thus, give such an appearance

isiniskêyi– *VAI* move one's arm thus or there, point in that direction with one's arm

isistâ– *VAI* hold such a rite, perform a rite thus

isiwêpin– *VTA* move s.o. (e.g., wing) thus

isiyîhkâcikâtê– *VII* be called thus

isiyîhkâso– *VAI* be called thus, have such a name

isiyîhkât– *VTA* call s.o. thus, use such a name for s.o.

isiyîhkât– VTI call s.t. thus, use such a name for s.t.
isiyîhkâtê– VII be called thus, have such a name
isîh– VTA make s.o. thus, prepare s.o. thus
isîhcikât– VTI do things thus for s.t., proceed thus for s.t.
isîhcikê– VAI do things thus, proceed thus, arrange things thus; perform such a rite, perform a rite thus; conduct negotiations thus
isîhcikêwin– NI what is done, activities; culture; ritual
isîhk– VTI bother with s.t.
isîhkaw– VTA bother s.o. thus
isîho– VAI be so dressed
isîhtâ– VAI prepare (it) thus, make (it) thus
isîhtwâwin– NI performing a rite thus; such a rite; way of worship, way of doing things
isko IPC to such an extent, so far [*cf.* iskohk]
isko IPV to such an extent, so far
iskohk IPC to such an extent, so far [*cf.* isko]
iskon– VTI have so much of s.t. left over
iskon– VTI pull s.t. (e.g., dress) up so far
iskonikan– NI reservation, Indian reserve
iskonikowisi– VAI be left over (e.g., to survive) by the powers
iskopitonê– VAI have one's arm reach so far, extend one's arm so far
iskosâwât– VTA leave meat over in filleting s.o. (e.g., fish), leave some flesh on the bones in filleting s.o.
iskosi– VAI extend so far, be so long, be so tall, be of such height
iskotêhkê– VAI make a fire
iskotêw– NI fire, hearth-fire
iskotêwâpoy– NI alcoholic drink, liquor, whisky
iskoyikohk IPC to such an extent, to such a degree
iskôl– NI school [*sic: stem-final* -l-]
iskôliwi– VAI be in school, go to school [*sic*]

iskw-âcimikosi– *VAI* be told about up to such a point

iskwaht– *VTI* leave so much of s.t. (e.g., food) over; have s.t. (e.g., food) left over

iskwahtâ– *VAI* have so much of (it) left over; have (it) left over, have a plentiful supply of (it)

iskwatahikan– *NA* tree-stump [*sic:* NA]

iskwâ– *VII* extend so far, be of such extent

iskwâhito– *VAI* kill one another off

iskwâhtawât– *VTA* climb up so far after s.o.; climb up (e.g., a tree) after s.o.

iskwâhtawî– *VAI* climb up so far; climb up (e.g., a tree)

iskwâhtawîhtah– *VTA* take s.o. climbing up so far; climb up (e.g., a tree) with s.o.

iskwâhtawîpahtâ– *VAI* climb up so far at a run; climb up (e.g., a tree) at a run

iskwâhtêm– *NI* door

iskwânê– *VAI* be left behind after a widespread illness, survive an epidemic [*sic:* -wâ-]

iskwâpêkamon– *VII* reach so far as rope

iskwêsis– *NI* girl, little girl, female infant

iskwêsisâpoy– *NI* beer, bottle of beer

iskwêsisiwi– *VAI* be a little girl

iskwêw– *NA* woman, female, female adult

iskwêw– *NA* (*woman's name*) [*lit.* Woman]

iskwêw-ây– *NA* female, female (of the species)

iskwêwi– *VAI* be a woman, be female

iskwêwisîh– *VTA* dress s.o. as a girl, dress s.o. as a female

iskwêyâc *IPC* to the end, to the last; the last time

ispacinâs– *NI* small hill [*diminutive*]

ispacinâsin– *VII* be a small hill [*diminutive*]

ispahtâ– *VAI* run there or thus

ispakwan– *VII* taste thus

ispastâ– *VAI* place (it) so high, pile (it) so high

ispatinâ– *VII* be a hill

ispatinâw– NI hill

ispayi– VAI move thus, drive there

ispayi– VAI fare thus, have such an experience, be thus affected; be thus afflicted

ispayi– VII take place thus, occur thus; run thus (in a cycle), be there (in a cycle), come around (in a cycle), be that time again; come by, go by, have passed (e.g., days, years) [*sic; cf.* ispayin–; *e.g.,* nânitaw ispayi– 'take place as an unwelcome event']

ispayih– VTA affect s.o. thus, happen thus to s.o.

ispayiho– VAI throw oneself thus or there, move thus or there

ispayin– VII take place thus, occur thus; run thus (in a cycle), be there (in a cycle), come around (in a cycle), be that time again; come by, go by, have passed (e.g., days, years) [*sic; cf.* ispayi–; *e.g.,* pêyak ê-ispayik 'one week']

ispâhkêkocin– VII rise high up, hang high aloft, be suspended high in the air

ispâhkêpayi– VAI reach a high level, be elevated (e.g., blood-sugar)

ispâhkêpit– VTA pull s.o. high up, pull s.o. high into the sky (e.g., snake)

ispâhkwanêyâ– VII be high-heeled (e.g., shoe)

ispâhtêhikan– NA (*man's name*) [*lit.* Pole; *cf.* ispâhtêhikan– NI]

ispâhtêhikan– NI pole supporting tent-flap (e.g., to permit air-flow)

ispici– VAI move thus or there with one's camp, move one's household there

ispihâ– VAI fly thus or there

ispimihk IPC high up, up above; upstairs

ispisi IPV to such an extent, so far

ispisi-wîhkwêhcâhk IPC in such a sweep of the land, to the extent of the sweep of this valley

ispisîh– VTA make s.o. (e.g., cracklings being boiled) come up so high

ispit– VTI   pull s.t. thither or thus; pull a trailer
ispî IPC   at such a time, then; when
ispîhcâ– VII   extend thus, reach so far as land, be of such size as country
ispîhci IPC   for now, in the meantime; (*in comparative constructions:*) by comparison; than
ispîhci wiya IPC   instead of
ispîhcisi– VAI   be so small, be so young
ispîhtaskamikâ– VII   extend so far as land
ispîhtâskosi– VAI   be so thick (as tree-trunk, braid of tobacco or snake)
ispîhtâskwapihkê– VAI   have braids of such thickness
ispîhtêyihtâkwan– VII   be considered worth so much
ispîhtêyimiso– VAI   think so highly of oneself
ispîhtisî– VAI   extend thus; be of such age
it– VTA   say thus to s.o., say thus of s.o.
it– VTI   say thus of s.t., say thus about s.t.
ita IPC   there
itahkamikan– VII   go on thus, work thus
itahkamikisi– VAI   do things thus, behave thus; work thus or there, busy oneself thus or there [*e.g.,* nânitaw itahkamikisi– 'behave reprehensibly, be up to something']
itahtin– VII   be so many
itahtopiponê– VAI   be so many years old [*sic; cf.* itahtopiponwê–]
itahtopiponwê– VAI   be so many years old [*sic; cf.* itahtopiponê–]
itahtw-âskîwinê– VAI   be so many years old
itahtwapi– VAI   sit as so many, be present as so many
itahtwâkin– VTI   bend so many of s.t. (e.g., willows), bend s.t. (e.g., willows) in such numbers
itakâm IPC   on the hither side of a body of water, on the near side of a body of water

itakiht– *VTI* count s.t. thus, value s.t. thus, hold s.t. in such esteem; charge so much for s.t.

itakihtê– *VII* be counted thus, be valued thus, be held in such esteem; be worth so much, cost so much

itakim– *VTA* count s.o. thus, value s.o. thus, hold s.o. in such esteem

itakiso– *VAI* be counted thus, be valued thus; be held in such esteem; be worth so much; have such a function

itakocin– *VAI* hang thus or there, be suspended thus or there; fly thus or there

itakotâ– *VAI* hang (it) thus or there, suspend (it) thus or there

itakotê– *VII* hang thus or there, be suspended thus or there

itamahciho– *VAI* feel thus, be in such health [*e.g.,* nânitaw itamahciho– 'feel unwell']

itamohtâ– *VAI* attach (it) thus or there

itamon– *VII* run thus or there as a path; be thus attached, be mounted thus

itapi– *VAI* sit thus or there, be present thus or there

itapihkât– *VTI* braid s.t. thus, knit s.t. thus

itapihkê– *VAI* braid thus, knit thus

itasinah– *VTI* mark s.t. thus, draw s.t. thus; write s.t. thus; thus write s.t. down

itasiwât– *VTA* decide thus with respect to s.o.; give s.o. such a command; impose such laws on s.o.

itasiwê– *VAI* decide thus for people, make such a plan for people; give such a command, impose such laws

itaskitê– *VII* stand thus (e.g., lodge)

itaskôto– *VAI* follow one another thither or thus, follow behind one another thither or thus

itastâ– *VAI* place (it) thus or there

itastê– *VII* be placed thus or there; be written thus

itatisw– *VTA* dye s.o. (e.g., porcupine quills) thus; dye s.o. in such a colour

itatoskê– *VAI* work thus or there

itawêhikê– VAI wear one's hair thus

itâciho– VAI travel thither or thus; lead one's life thus

itâcihowin– NI travelling thither or thus; leading one's life thus

itâcim– VTA tell s.o. thus, tell s.o. such things, tell thus about s.o.

itâcimo– VAI tell thus, tell a story thus, tell such a story, give such an account

itâcimostaw– VTA tell s.o. thus about (it/him), tell s.o. such a story, give s.o. such an account

itâcimowinihkât– VTI tell thus about s.t., make such a story of s.t., give such an account of s.t.

itâcimômakan– VII tell thus about (it/him), tell such a story, give such an account

itâhkôm– VTA be thus related to s.o., have s.o. as such a relative, use such a kin-term for s.o.

itâkami– VII be a liquid of such a colour

itâmihk IPC beneath, underneath, inside (e.g., clothing); inside (e.g., mouth) [*sic:* i-; *cf.* atâmihk]

itâmo– VAI flee thither or thus, seek such refuge

itâmôh– VTA make s.o. flee thus or there, direct s.o. to seek such refuge

itâp IPC then, later

itâpacih– VTA use s.o. thus, make such use of s.o., thus find s.o. useful [*e.g.,* tânisi mâk ê-wî-itâpacihacik 'what will you (sg.) do with them']

itâpacih– VTA (*especially in inverse constructions:*) be of such use to s.o., be thus of service to s.o. [*e.g.,* namôy nânitaw kik-êtâpacihikon ôma maskihkiy 'this medicine will not help you in any way']

itâpacihtâ– VAI use (it) thus, make such use of (it)

itâpaminâkwan– VII give such an appearance to look at

itâpatakêyimo– VAI use one's mind thus, make such use of one's mental faculties

itâpatan– VII be thus used, be of such use

itâpatisi– VAI be used thus, be of such use

itâpêkin– VTA align s.o. (e.g., porcupine quills) thus (e.g., end-to-end); lead s.o. (e.g., horse) thus or there

itâpi– VAI look thus or there; take aim thus or there

itâpihkêpayi– VAI move thus or there as a rope or snake, swing thus as a rope or snake

itâskonamaw– VTA thus point the pipe for s.o., thus point the pipe at s.o.

itâskonamawât– VTI thus point the pipe at s.t.

itâskonikâkê– VAI point the pipe or pipestem with (it), use (it) to point the pipe or pipestem

itâskonikê– VAI thus point the pipe or pipestem; thus hold a pipe ceremony

itâskonikêwin– NI thus pointing the pipe or pipestem; such a pipe ceremony

itâspinê– VAI be ill thus, suffer from such a disease

itâspinêm– VTA call s.o. thus in anger, angrily call s.o. such a name, thus scold s.o. in anger

itâtayôhkaw– VTA tell s.o. such a sacred story

itâtayôhkât– VTI tell thus about s.t. in the form of a sacred story, tell such a sacred story of s.t.

itâtayôhkâtê– VII be told thus in the form of a sacred story, be told as such a sacred story

itâtisi– VAI act thus, be of such a disposition

itâtot– VTI tell thus about s.t., give such an account of s.t.

itê IPC there, over there; thither

itê isi IPC thither, in that direction

itêh– VTI stir s.t., stir s.t. in

itêhkê isi IPC thither, in that direction

itêhkêskamik IPC thitherward, in thither region

itêhw– VTA stir s.o., stir s.o. in; stir s.o. (flour) in as thickening

itêkin– VTI fold s.t. flat thus, fold s.t. thus as cloth

itêyati– VAI be such in number, be so many

itêyihcikan– NI thinking thus; such thought
itêyiht– VTI think thus of s.t., regard s.t. thus
itêyihtamopayi– VAI suddenly think thus of (it/him)
itêyihtâkwan– VII be thus thought of
itêyim– VTA think thus of s.o., regard s.o. thus [*e.g.*, mistahi itêyim– 'think a lot of s.o.']
itêyimikowisi– VAI be thus thought of by the powers, be thus regarded by the powers
itêyimiso– VAI think thus of oneself, regard oneself thus
itêyimo– VAI think thus of (it/him) for oneself, have (it/him) in mind for oneself
itihkwâmi– VAI sleep thus
itiht– VTI hear s.t. thus
itihtaw– VTA hear s.o. thus
itihtâkosihkâso– VAI pretend to be heard making such a noise, act as if to make such a noise
itihtâkwan– VII be thus heard, sound thus
itikwamikohkê– VAI hold such a lodge, hold such a rite [*sic:* -kw-]
itin– VTI hold s.t. thus
itinikê– VAI do things thus; act thus; experience such things; get into such things [*e.g.*, nânitaw itinikê– 'get into trouble']
itipê– VAI be thus affected with alcoholic drink, be in such shape from alcoholic drink
itis– VTI cut s.t. thus
itisahamaw– VTA send (it/him) to s.o. thus or there
itisahamâto– VAI send (it/him) to one another thus or there
itisahw– VTA send s.o. thus or there
itisin– VAI lie thus or there
itisinamaw– VTA thus hold (it/him) for s.o., thus hand (it/him) over to s.o.
itiskaw– VTA (*especially in inverse constructions:*) have such an effect on s.o., leave s.o. thus affected [*e.g.*, kwayask

kik-êtiskâkoyahk 'for it to have a beneficial effect on us (incl.)']

itiskwêhkê– VAI act thus as a woman; give the impression of being such a woman

itistahikê– VAI sew things on thus

itistahw– VTA sew s.o. (e.g., porcupine quills) on thus

itito– VAI say thus to one another, say thus about one another

itohtah– VTA take s.o. (e.g., pelt) there or thus; go there with s.o., lead s.o. there

itohtatamaw– VTA take (it/him) to s.o.

itohtatâ– VAI take (it) there or thus, go there with (it)

itohtê– VAI go there or thus

itowahk IPC this kind

itowihk IPC in this place

itôt– VTI do s.t. thus; act thus [*cf.* tôt–]

itôtamaw– VTA do (it) thus for s.o., do thus to s.o.

itôtamôh– VTA make s.o. do (it) thus, cause s.o. to act thus

itôtaw– VTA do (it) thus to s.o., treat s.o. thus

itwahw– VTA point one's finger at s.o., point at s.o.

itwê– VAI say thus, call (it) thus; have such a meaning

itwêmakan– VII say thus, have such a meaning

itwêmakisi– VAI say thus, have such a meaning [*sic*]

itwêski– VAI say thus habitually, always say thus

itwêstamaw– VTA say thus for s.o.; speak for s.o.; interpret for s.o.; transmit s.o.'s message, relay s.o.'s message (e.g., by radio)

itwêwêsin– VAI fall with such a sound, make such a sound with one's shoes

itwêwin– NI what is being said, speech; word; language

itwêwit– VTI make such a noise

iyaskohc IPC next in sequence

iyaw IPC well now; ho! [*sic:* iy-; *cf.* y-; *introductory; also exclamatory, indicating surprise*]

iyawis *IPC* fully, entirely; the whole lot, the entire household; (*in negative constructions:*) only partially, not exclusively

iyâyaw *IPC* eagerly, intently; by preference, rather

iyikohk *IPC* so much, to such a degree, to such an extent

iyinico-pimîs– *NI* ordinary grease [*diminutive*]

iyinimin– *NI* blueberry [*usually plural*]

iyinito *IPN* plain, ordinary

iyinito-pimiy– *NI* ordinary grease [*i.e., grease rendered from fat from around muscle tissue (and including bone-marrow), less readily congealed than* âhkwaci-pimiy–]

iyinitohk *IPC* simply; just as [*in correlative constructions with* êkosi 'just so', iyikohk 'so much']

iyinîhkah– *VTA* heal s.o.

iyinîsi– *VAI* be clever, be smart

iyisâc *IPC* half-heartedly, resistingly

iyisâho– *VAI* resist, resist temptation, exercise restraint

iyisâhowin– *NI* resistance, resisting temptation, restraint

iyôskisi– *VAI* be soft [*sic:* iy-; *cf.* y-]

iyôtinw– *NA* (*name:*) Wind [*sic:* iy-; *cf.* y-]

iyôtinw– *NI* high wind, tornado [*sic:* iy-; *cf.* y-]

îh *IPC* lo! look! behold! [*exclamatory*]

îhkatawâw– *NI* slough, marsh

îhkatawâwipêyâw– *NI* wet slough, marsh

îkatê *IPV* to the side, aside [*sic:* î-; *e.g.,* âh-îkatê [*reduplicated*]; *cf.* yî-, wî-]

îkatêhtê– *VAI* walk off to the side [*sic:* î-; *cf.* yî-, wî-]

îkihtawitâpân– *NA* travois [*sic:* î-; *cf.* yî-, wî-]

îkin– *VTA* milk s.o. (e.g., cow) [*sic:* î-; *cf.* yî-]

îkinamaw– *VTA* milk (it/him) for s.o. [*sic:* î-; *e.g.,* ê-âh-îkinamawak [*reduplicated*]; *cf.* yî-]

îkinikê– *VAI* milk, do the milking [*sic:* î-; *cf.* yî-]

îkinikêsi– *VAI* milk, do one's milking [*sic:* î-; *cf.* yî-; *diminutive*]

îkwaskwan– *VII* be cloudy [*sic:* î-; *cf.* yî-]

îpâcihtâ– *VAI* make (it) dirty, soil (it) [*sic:* î-; *cf.* wiyî-, wî-]

îwahikan– *NA* pounded meat [*sic:* î-; *e.g.*, nîwahikana (obv.); *cf.* yî-; *usually plural*]

îwanisîhisowin– *NI* fasting, denying oneself food [*usually but not always restricted to food*]

îwâsên– *VTI* turn s.t. down by hand (e.g., by turning a knob), dim the light, turn s.t. too low

k-ôsâwisicik *INM* oranges [*i.e., plural form of* osâwisi– *VAI; lit.* yellow ones]

k-ôsihkosiwayâniw *INM* (*man's name:*) Ermineskin [*lit.* Has-an-Ermineskin]

kahkiyaw *IPC* every, all

kakayêyih– *VTA* deceive s.o.

kakâmwâtisi– *VAI* be of quiet disposition

kakâmwâtiskwêhkê– *VAI* act quietly as a woman; give the impression of being a quiet woman

kakâyawâciho– *VAI* live an active life; work hard in one's life, lead an industrious life

kakâyawâtisi– *VAI* be active; be hard-working, be of industrious disposition

kakâyawi *IPV* actively; by working hard, industriously

kakâyawisî– *VAI* be active; be hard-working, be industrious

kakêhtawêyiht– *VTI* have good ideas about s.t.; be intelligent beyond one's years; be sensible

kakêpâhkamikisi– *VAI* fool around, get in the way

kakêskihkêmo– *VAI* counsel people, lecture people, preach at people

kakêskim– *VTA* counsel s.o., lecture s.o., preach at s.o.

kakêskimâwaso– *VAI* counsel one's children, lecture one's children

kakêskimâwasowin– *NI* counselling the young

kakêskimiso– *VAI* counsel oneself

kakiyâskiwin– *NI* lie, tall tale

kakwâhyakâpasikê– *VAI* make a great deal of smoke

kakwâhyakêyati– *VAI* be in great numbers, be plentiful, be very numerous

kakwâhyakêyiht– *VTI* despise s.t.

kakwâhyaki *IPV* greatly, extremely, tremendously, to an extraordinary extent [*sic:* -hy-; *cf.* kakwâyaki]

kakwâhyaki-iskwêw– *NA* extraordinary woman, superwoman

kakwâhyakicin– *VAI* be terribly torn (e.g., by porcupine quills)

kakwâhyakih– *VTA* do a terrible thing to s.o., mistreat s.o. greatly

kakwâtakatoskê– *VAI* work dreadfully hard, do punishing work

kakwâtakâciho– *VAI* suffer dreadfully, live through a dreadful time

kakwâtakâhpi– *VAI* laugh dreadfully

kakwâtakâpâkwaho– *VAI* suffer mortification by denying oneself liquid, make oneself suffer thirst

kakwâtakêyiht– *VTI* be tormented, be tormented about s.t.

kakwâtakêyihtamih– *VTA* bring torment upon s.o., bring suffering upon s.o.

kakwâtaki *IPV* dreadfully, insufferably

kakwâtakih– *VTA* make s.o. suffer; be mean to s.o., be abusive to s.o.; (*especially in inverse constructions:*) affect s.o. terribly (e.g., as disease), ravage s.o. (e.g., as disease) [*e.g.,* ka-kakwâtakihât 'for him to be abusive towards her'; kakwâtakihik 'it [illness] took a terrible toll on him']

kakwâtakihiso– *VAI* make oneself suffer; torture oneself, deny oneself food and drink

kakwâtakiho– *VAI* make oneself suffer; torture oneself, experience suffering; deny oneself food and drink

kakwâtakihowin– *NI* making oneself suffer; denying oneself food and drink

kakwâtakihtâ– *VAI* suffer (it), suffer because of (it), have difficulties because of (it); suffer; experience a crisis (e.g., in the course of an illness)

kakwâtakî– *VAI* suffer, experience difficulty, experience torment

kakwâyaki *IPV* greatly, extremely, tremendously, to an extraordinary extent [*sic:* -y-; *cf.* kakwâhyaki]

kakwâyakinikê– *VAI* act with great speed, act abruptly; buck violently (e.g., horse)

kakwâyakiyawêh– *VTA* make s.o. terribly angry

kakwê *IPV* try to, attempt to; circumstances permitting, by divine grace

kakwêcihkêmo– *VAI* ask people, ask a question of people

kakwêcim– *VTA* ask s.o.; make a request of s.o.; ask s.o. about (it/him)

kakwêtawêyiht– *VTI* long for s.t., miss s.t.

kakwêyâho– *VAI* hurry, hurry up

kanak *IPC* for a short while

kanakê *IPC* at least, even if only [*restrictive concessive; e.g.,* pêyak kanakê 'just one']

kanakêkâ *IPC* more especially

kanawâpahkê– *VAI* watch things, watch people, observe people

kanawâpam– *VTA* look at s.o., watch s.o., observe s.o.; look after s.o.

kanawâpokê– *VAI* look after a household, keep house

kanawêyihcikâtê– *VII* be kept, be preserved

kanawêyiht– *VTI* keep s.t., look after s.t., take care of s.t.; store s.t., preserve s.t.; guard s.t. closely

kanawêyihtamaw– *VTA* look after (it/him) for s.o., take care of (it/him) for s.o.

kanawêyihtamâso– *VAI* guard (it/him) closely for oneself, take good care of (it/him) oneself

kanawêyihtamôh– *VTA* make s.o. guard (it/him) closely; ask s.o. to look after (it/him), leave (it/him) to be looked after by s.o., get s.o. to babysit (her/him)

kanawêyihtâkwan– *VII* be kept, be looked after, the taken care of; be stored, be preserved; be closely guarded

kanawêyim– VTA keep s.o., look after s.o., take care of s.o.; guard s.o. closely

kanawêyimiwê– VAI look after people; guard people (e.g., girls) closely

kanâcâciwahtê– VII be boiled clean, be clean by boiling [*sic: -c-*]

kanâci IPV clean

kanâcih– VTA clean s.o.

kanâcihcikê– VAI clean things, do one's cleaning

kanâcihiso– VAI clean oneself

kanâciho– VAI clean oneself, keep oneself clean

kanâcihtâ– VAI clean (it), clean (it) out (e.g., intestine)

kanâcinâkosi– VAI look clean, give a clean appearance

kanâtahcâ– VII be clean ground, be clean land

kanâtan– VII be clean

kanâtanohk IPC in a clean place

kanâtapi– VAI live in a clean house

kanâtâpâwahiso– VAI wash oneself clean with water

kanâtâpâwatâ– VAI wash (it) clean with water

kanâtâpâwê– VII be washed clean with water

kanâtêyim– VTA have respect for s.o.

kanâtisi– VAI be clean

kani IPC oh yes, I just remembered, I had forgotten [*introductory, indicating an interruption; sometimes enclitic; cf.* kanihk]

kanihk IPC oh yes, I just remembered, I had forgotten [*introductory, indicating an interruption; sometimes enclitic; cf.* kani]

kanôsimon– NI protective talisman (usually worn around the neck, wrapped in leather)

kanôsimototaw– VTA have s.o. (e.g., rattle) as protection

kapatâsiwêpiskaw– VTA kick s.o. ashore, kick s.o. out of the water

kapatên– VTA take s.o. ashore, take s.o. out of the water

kapâ– VAI come ashore, come out of the water

kapê-ayi IPC all along, all the time, for the entire period, throughout

kapê-kîsik IPC all day long, throughout the day

kapê-nîpin IPC all summer long, throughout the summer

kapê-tipisk IPC all night long, throughout the night

kapêsi– VAI stay overnight

kapêsimostaw– VTA stay overnight with s.o., stay overnight at s.o.'s place

kapêsîwikamikw– NI inn, hotel

kartôš– NA (*dog's name:*) Bullet

kaskatwân– VTI break s.t. off (e.g., branch)

kaskawanipêstâ– VII be drizzle, be rainy

kaskâciwahtê– VII be boiled until tender

kaskâciwas– VTI boil s.t. until tender

kaskâpahtê– VII be smoked; be smoky, be hazy

kaskâpas– VTI smoke s.t.

kaskâpaso– VAI be smoked (e.g., rabbit)

kaskâpasw– VTA smoke s.o. (e.g., fish, rabbit)

kaskâpiskah– VTI can s.t., preserve s.t.

kaskâpiskahikan– NI can, preserve, canned goods

kaskâpiskahikâtê– VII be canned, be preserved

kaskêyiht– VTI be sad over s.t.; be sad, be lonesome, have a longing

kaski-tipiskâ– VII be the dark of the night

kaskicêwasinâsosi– VAI have black markings (e.g., dog) [*diminutive*]

kaskih– VTA prevail upon s.o., succeed in imposing one's will on s.o.; be able to deal with s.o.; earn s.o. (e.g., money)

kaskihkasw– VTA cook s.o. (e.g., skunk) until tender

kaskiho– VAI be able, be competent

kaskihtamâso– VAI earn (it) for oneself, deserve (it); make money for oneself

kaskihtâ– VAI be able to do (it), be competent at (it), manage (it)

kaskihtâwin– NI ability to do (it), competence

kaskikwâcikâkê– VAI sew things with (it), use (it) to sew things

kaskikwâso– VAI sew, do one's sewing; sew (it)

kaskikwâsopayihcikanis– NI sewing machine [*diminutive*]

kaskikwâsopayihcikâkê– VAI machine-sew with (it), use (it) to machine-sew

kaskikwâsowat– NI sewing-box

kaskikwâsowin– NI doing one's sewing, the art of sewing; sewing needs, sewing-kit

kaskikwâswâkan– NI sewing machine

kaskikwâswâkê– VAI sew with (it), use (it) in sewing

kaskikwât– VTA sew s.o. (e.g., pants)

kaskikwât– VTI sew s.t.

kaskikwâtamaw– VTA sew (it/him) for s.o.

kaskikwâtamâso– VAI sew (it/him) for oneself

kaskikwâtê– VII be sewn

kaskikwâtiso– VAI sew for oneself

kaskim– VTA prevail upon s.o. by speech

kaskipitê– VII be tied up, be wrapped up

kaskitêsi– VAI be black

kaskitêsip– NA black-duck

kaskitêwasinâstê– VII be black trim, be black edging

kaskitêwatisw– VTA dye s.o. (e.g., stocking) black

kaskitêwâpahtê– VII give off black smoke

kaskitêwiyâs– NA Negro, Black person

katawasisi– VAI be beautiful

katawatêyim– VTA consider s.o. beautiful

katawâhk IPC properly, in seemly manner

katâc IPC insistently; (*in negative constructions:*) not necessarily [*e.g.*, êkây katâc cîki! 'it is not necessary to be so close!'; ..., êkâykatâc sîwinikan t-âpacihat '... that you don't have to use sugar']

katikoni– *VAI* sleep over, spend the night

katisk *IPC* just now, a moment ago; recently, a while ago; exactly, just at that moment, at the very moment; (*in negative constructions:*) not merely

katiskaw *IPC* to exact measure, no more than, barely

kawaci– *VAI* be cold, experience cold; suffer chills

kawacipayi– *VAI* get chilled, get cold

kawatihtâ– *VAI* get (it) chilled, get (it) cold

kawatim– *VTA* get s.o. cold, expose s.o. to cold

kawatimiso– *VAI* get oneself cold

kawikah– *VTI* chop s.t. down, cut s.t. down

kawikîhkâ– *VAI* be bent with age, be prostrated by age

kawipah– *VTA* cause s.o. to fall down with alcoholic drink

kawipayiho– *VAI* throw oneself down

kawisimo– *VAI* lie down, go to bed

kawisimonihkê– *VAI* prepare the bed, get ready for bed

kawisin– *VAI* fall down, lie fallen down

kawiwêpin– *VTA* throw s.o. down

kayâcic *IPC* the spare, the surplus [*?sic: record, gloss*]

kayâhtê *IPC* before, previously, formerly; before the appropriate time, prematurely

kayâs *IPC* long ago, in earlier days; previously

kayâs *IPN* long ago, old-time, traditional [*e.g.,* kayâs-*Hudson's-Bay-blanket* [*sic*], *with code-switching within compound*]

kayâs-ây– *NI* old stuff [*e.g.,* kayâs-âya (pl.)]

kayâs-isîhcikêwin– *NI* the old way of doing things, traditional culture

kayâsês *IPC* quite some time ago; a while ago

kayâsi *IPN* long ago, old-time, traditional

kayâsi-nêhiyâwin– *NI* traditional Creeness, traditional Cree identity

kayâsi-pimâcihowin– NI old life, traditional way of life
kayâsi-wâskahikan– NI old house, traditional house
kayâsiyâkan– NA (*man's name:*) Old-Pan
kâ-cawacinâsik INM (*place-name*) [*lit.* where there is a small opening between the hills; *at an unidentified location in the vicinity of Rocky Mountain House (Alberta)*]
kâ-cîposicik INM pears [*i.e., plural form of* cîposi– VAI; *lit.* pointy ones]
kâ-mahîhkani-pimohtêw INM (*man's name*) [*lit.* Walks-like-a-Wolf]
kâ-nîpitêhtêw INM (*man's name*) [*lit.* Walks-Abreast]
kâ-pimwêwêhahk INM (*man's name:*) Jim Kâ-Nîpitêhtêw [*lit.* Goes-Along-Drumming]
kâ-tipahamâtohk INM at Treaty time, during Treaty Days
kâ-wâkisicik INM bananas [*i.e., plural form of* wâkisi– VAI; *lit.* bent ones]
kâcikê– VAI hide things
kâciwêpin– VTI throw s.t. so as to hide it
kâh-kapê-ayi IPC all the time [*reduplicated*]
kâh-kipîhci IPC stopping now and then [*reduplicated*]
kâh-kito– VAI hoot (e.g., owl); be thunder [*reduplicated*]
kâh-kîhtwâm IPC again and again [*reduplicated*]
kâh-kîhtwâm IPV again and again [*sic:* IPV; *reduplicated*]
kâh-kwêkwask IPC back and forth, criss-cross, crosswise [*cf.* kwêh-kwêkwask; *reduplicated*]
kâhcitin– VTA catch s.o., seize s.o., get s.o. (e.g., a spouse); obtain s.o. (e.g., money) [*cf.* kâhtitin–]
kâhcitin– VTI catch s.t., seize s.t., obtain s.t.; get s.t. back [*cf.* kâhtitin–]
kâhkêwakw– NI dried meat, sheet of dried meat
kâhkwêyim– VTA be jealous of s.o.
kâhtap IPC differently; regularly [*?sic: gloss*]
kâhtitin– VTA catch s.o., seize s.o., get s.o. (e.g., a spouse); obtain s.o. (e.g., money) [*cf.* kâhcitin–]

kâhtitin– VTI catch s.t., seize s.t., obtain s.t.; get s.t. back [*cf.* kâhcitin–]

kâkatâc IPC insistently; (*in negative constructions:*) not necessarily [*cf.* katâc; *e.g.*, namôya kâkatâc maskihkiy 'it was not necessarily physical medicine']

kâkeswân IPC as it happens, by coincidence [*cf.* kêswân]

kâkikê IPC always, at all times, forever; for a very long time, forever (metaphorically)

kâkîsimo– VAI pray, plead, chant prayers

kâkîsimotot– VTI chant prayers for s.t.; chant prayers over s.t.

kâkîsimototaw– VTA chant prayers for s.o.; chant prayers over s.o.

kâkîsimowin– NI chanting prayers

kâkîsimwâkê– VAI chant prayers with (it), use (it) to chant prayers

kâkîtisi– VAI ache, experience pain

kâkw– NA porcupine [*e.g.*, kâkwa (prox. sg., obv.)]

kânâta INM (*place-name:*) Canada

kâsisi– VAI be sharp, be scratchy (e.g., wool); be sharply pointed

kâsisin– VII be sharp (e.g., knife)

kâsispô– VAI reach beyond, exceed; survive into another generation

kâsispôhtêmakan– VII go on, reach beyond, exceed; survive into another generation

kâsîhkwâkê– VAI wash one's face with (it), use (it) to wash one's face

kâsîhkwê– VAI wash one's face

kâsîhkwêwiyâkan– NI wash-basin

kâsînamaw– VTA wipe (it) off for s.o.; (*fig.*) forgive s.o.

kâsînamâso– VAI wipe (it) off for oneself; (*fig.*) have one's sins forgiven, obtain forgiveness

kâsînamâto– VAI wipe (it) off for one another; (*fig.*) forgive one another

kâsîyâkanê– VAI wash dishes, do the dishes

kâskah– VTI scrape s.t., scrape s.t. off

kâskâskihkot– VTA scrape s.o. (e.g., touchwood) off [*reduplicated*]

kâso– VAI hide, hide oneself

kâspihkas– VTI heat s.t. until crisp, heat s.t. until brittle; dry s.t. by heat until crisp

kâspis– VTI heat s.t. until crisp, heat s.t. until brittle

kât– VTA hide s.o.

kâwi IPC again; back, in return [*i.e., restoring a former state*]

kâwiy– NA porcupine quill [*usually plural*]

kêcikon– VTI take s.t. off (e.g., glasses, clothing)

kêcikonêwên– VTA take (it/him) out of s.o.'s mouth

kêcikopayi– VAI come off (e.g., soap), come out of container (e.g., soap)

kêcikopit– VTI pull s.t. free, pull s.t. out; take s.t. off by pulling; pull out of s.t.

kêcikwahw– VTA pull s.o. (e.g., thorns) out, remove s.o. by tool

kêcikwâpitêpit– VTA pull a tooth for s.o., pull s.o.'s tooth

kêcikwâstan– VII be blown down by wind

kêhcê-ayiwi– VAI be old [*diminutive*]

kêhcinâ IPC surely, for certain

kêhcinâho– VAI be certain

kêhtê-ay– NA old person, the old; elder [*e.g.,* kêhtê-aya (prox. sg., obv.), kêhtê-ayak (prox. pl.)]

kêhtê-ayisiyiniw– NDA old person

kêhtê-ayiwi– VAI be an old person, get old; be an elder

kêhtêskwêw– NA old woman, old lady

kêhtêwasinahikan– NI pension cheque, old-age pension

kêhtêyâtisi– VAI be old, be advanced in age

kêhtin– VTA treat s.o. with respect, show deference to s.o.

kêkâ-mitâtahtomitanaw IPC ninety

kêkâc IPC almost [*cf.* kêkât]

kêkât *IPC* almost [*cf.* kêkâc]

kêkisêpâ *IPC* early in the morning [*sic; cf.* kîkisêpâ]

kêswân *IPC* by coincidence [*cf.* kîswân, kâkêswân]

kêtahtawê *IPC* at times, sometimes; at one time, all at once, suddenly [*cf.* kîtahtawê]

kêtastotinê– *VAI* take one's hat off

kêtisk *IPC* just barely, to exact measure

kêyâpic *IPC* still, in continuity; yet [*i.e., in future, contrary to expectation; cf.* êyâpic]

kêyiwêhk *IPC* just in case, nevertheless; despite shortcomings [*cf.* êyiwêhk]

kici *IPC* for then, for later [*sic; e.g.,* kici kâ-pipohk 'for the winter']

kicimah– *VTA* be mean to s.o., treat s.o. cruelly [*diminutive*]

kicimâkisi– *VAI* be pitiable, be miserable; be poor [*diminutive*]

kihc-âtâwêwikamikowiyiniw– *NA* store manager, post manager, Hudson's Bay Company factor

kihc-âtâwêwikamikw– *NI* Hudson's Bay Company store

kihc-âyamihêwiyiniw– *NA* bishop

kihc-îskwêwinâkosi– *VAI* look like a great lady

kihc-ôkâwîmâw– *NA* (*name:*) Great Mother, Mother Earth

kihc-ôkimâskwêw– *NA* queen

kihc-ôkimâw– *NA* king; (*fig.*) government; royalty [*e.g.,* kihc-ôkimânâhk 'in the government']

kihc-ônîkânohtêw– *NA* lead-dog

kihc-ôskâpêwis– *NA* main ritual server; (*name:*) Great Servitor, St Peter

kihcêyihcikâtê– *VII* be highly thought of, be respected; be held sacred

kihcêyiht– *VTI* think highly of s.t., hold s.t. in high regard, respect s.t.; hold s.t. sacred [*sic; cf.* kistêyiht–]

kihcêyihtamaw– *VTA* think highly of (it/him) for s.o.

kihcêyihtâkwan– *VII* be highly thought of, be respected; be held sacred

kihcêyim– VTA think highly of s.o., hold s.o. in high regard, respect s.o.; hold s.o. sacred [*sic; cf.* kistêyim–]

kihci IPC great, superb; the best [*sic:* IPC]

kihci IPN great

kihci IPV greatly; formally

kihci-kiskinahamâtowikamikw– NI university; post-secondary education

kihci-kiskinahamâtowin– NI higher education, post-secondary education

kihci-kîkway PR something important, big things

kihci-kîsikw– NI heaven

kihci-masinahikan– NI (*fig.*) important book; bible

kihci-môhkomân– NA American

kihci-môhkomânaskiy– NI America, the USA

kihci-wayawî– VAI go to relieve oneself in a major way, go to defecate

kihci-wîki– VAI live formally; (*fig.*) live in residence

kihci-wîkihto– VAI be formally married, be married in church

kihci-wîkihtowin– NI formal marriage, Holy Matrimony

kihci-wîkihtowin-âhcanis– NA wedding ring

kihci-wîkim– VTA marry s.o. formally, marry s.o. in church

kihcihtwâwi IPN of exalted character; venerable, holy [*e.g.*, kihcihtwâwi-côsap 'Holy Joseph']

kihcikanisi– VAI hold a rite; spend Christmas

kihciniskihk IPC on the right hand, to the right

kihîw– NA eagle [*sic:* -î-]

kihtimêyiht– VTI be tired of s.t.

kihtimi– VAI be lazy; be self-indulgent

kihtimikanê– VAI be lazy, be a lazy-bones

kikamo– VAI be attached, have a fixed place (e.g., star)

kikamohtâ– VAI attach (it), fasten (it) on, put (it) on something

kikamon– VII be attached, be fastened

kikamôh– VTA   attach s.o. (e.g., yarn, ribbon), put s.o. on
kikapi– VAI   sit along with something
kikask IPC   too soon, prematurely
kikaskisinê– VAI   wear shoes
kikastê– VII   be placed along with something
kikâpôhkê– VAI   add (it) to soup, enhance one's soup with (it)
kiki IPC   along with [*sic:* IPC]
kiki IPV   along with
kikin– VTA   add s.o. (e.g., tobacco) in, mix s.o. in
kikin– VTI   put s.t. on something, add s.t. in (e.g., baking-powder)
kikisk– VTI   wear s.t. (e.g., shoe), have s.t. as an intimate possession, carry s.t. in oneself (e.g., blood)
kikiskaw– VTA   wear s.o. (e.g., ring), have s.o. as an intimate possession (e.g., stocking) [*e.g.,* ahcânisa ê-kikiskawât 'when she was wearing a ring']
kikiskaw– VTA   (*especially in inverse constructions:*) affect s.o., befall s.o.; inhere in s.o., engross s.o. [*e.g.,* môy ânima êtokwê omâmitonêyihcikaniwâw ê-kikiskâkocik 'it must be that their mind (sg.) does not dwell in them']
kikiskawâwaso– VAI   carry a child, be with child, be pregnant
kimisâhowin– NI   wiping oneself, wiping one's anus
kimiwan– VII   rain, be rain
kimotamaw– VTA   steal (it/him) from s.o.
kimoti– VAI   steal (him/it); be a thief
kimotôsê– VAI   bear an illegitimate child
kinêpiko-maskotêhk INM   (*place-name:*) Snake Plain (Saskatchewan); *mistawâsis*'s Reserve [*locative; lit.* at the snake plain]
kinêpikw– NA   snake
kinosêw– NA   fish

kinosêwi-sâkahikanihk *INM* (*place-name:*) Jackfish Lake (Saskatchewan) [*locative; lit.* at the fish lake; *centred on Cochin, the region is also referred to by that name*]

kinosi– *VAI* be long (e.g., sock), be tall

kinwâ– *VII* be long, be tall

kinwâpêkan– *VII* be a long garment, be a long piece of paper; be a long saw-blade, be a long saw

kinwâpêkasâkê– *VAI* wear a long skirt; wear a long robe (e.g., as a Roman Catholic priest)

kinwâpêkisi– *VAI* be long as string, be long as fishing-net

kinwês *IPC* for a long time [*cf.* kinwêsk]

kinwêsêskamik *IPC* for a very long time

kinwêsîs *IPC* for quite a long time

kinwêsk *IPC* for a long time [*cf.* kinwês]

kipah– *VTI* close s.t., shut s.t.

kipahotowikamikw– *NI* jail, prison

kipihtêpayi– *VAI* go deaf, be deafened

kipipayin– *VII* be blocked

kipokwât– *VTI* sew s.t. closed, sew s.t. shut; close s.t. up by sewing

kipokwâtâ– *VAI* sew (it) closed, sew (it) shut, close (it) up by sewing

kiposakahikâtê– *VII* be nailed shut

kipwacâpahpit– *VTA* blindfold s.o.

kipwahpit– *VTI* pull s.t. closed, tie s.t. shut

kipwaskinê– *VII* be filled to the lid, be full to the brim

kisâcî– *VAI* stay behind, stay around, stay nearby

kisâkamicêwâpôs– *NI* warm water [*diminutive*]

kisâkamis– *VTI* heat s.t. as liquid

kisâkamisikê– *VAI* heat a liquid; boil water for tea, make tea

kisâkamitêhkwê– *VAI* drink a hot liquid, have a hot drink

kisâkamitêwâpoy– *NI* hot water

kisâpiskisw– *VTA* heat s.o. as rock (e.g., in sweat-lodge)

kisâstaw *IPC* roughly like, resembling

kisâstê– *VII* be hot weather
kisât– *VTI* stay with s.t., hold fast to s.t.; stay, stay back
kiscikânis– *NA* grain, seed [*sic:* NA; *usually plural; diminutive*]
kiscikânis– *NI* garden [*sic:* NI; *diminutive*]
kiscikêsi– *VAI* plant seeds; have a small garden [*diminutive*]
kisê-manitow– *NA* God the kind, the compassionate God; (*name:*) Merciful God
kisê-manitowi-pîkiskwêwin– *NI* God's word
kisê-nâpêw-asiniy– *NA* (*name*) [*lit.* Kind-Man-Rock]
kisêpêkihtakinikê– *VAI* wash a wooden floor, wash floor-boards
kisêpêkin– *VTA* wash s.o.
kisêpêkin– *VTI* wash s.t. [*cf.* kisîpêkin–]
kisêpêkinikan– *NI* soap [*sic:* NI; *cf.* kisîpêkinikan– NA]
kisêpêkinikê– *VAI* wash things, do the laundry
kisêpêkinikêwin– *NI* laundry, doing the laundry
kisêpêkiniso– *VAI* wash oneself
kisêwâtisi– *VAI* be kind, be of compassionate disposition; (*fig.*) be full of grace
kisêwâtisiwin– *NI* kindness, compassion; (*fig.*) grace
kisêyiniw– *NA* old man
kisêyinîsis– *NA* little old man, wizened old man [*diminutive*]
kisêyinîw-âcimowin– *NI* old man's story, report of the old men
kisêyinîw-ôhpikihâkan– *NA* old man's pupil, ward of the old men
kisêyinîwi *IPN* of an old man, befitting an old man
kisêyinîwi– *VAI* be an old man
kisêyinîwi-pîkiskwêwin– *NI* old man's word, word of the old men
kisik *IPC* at the same time, simultaneously, coincidentally
kisin– *VII* be cold weather, be very cold weather
kisip-âyihk *IPC* at the end, at the edge

kisipakim– VTA count s.o. (e.g., sun) as the end of the month
kisipanohk IPC at the end (in space or time), at the edge
kisipi-kîsikâ– VII be the end of the day
kisipipayi– VII come to an end, reach the end, run out [*sic; cf.* kisipipayin–]
kisipipayin– VII come to an end, reach the end, run out [*sic; cf.* kisipipayi–]
kisipîmakan– VII come to an end, reach the end; have an end
kisis– VTI warm s.t. up, heat s.t. up
kisiskâ IPV quickly, fast
kisiso– VAI be warm, be hot; run a fever, be febrile
kisitê– VII be warmed up, be heated up, be hot; be a hot compress
kisiwâh– VTA anger s.o., make s.o. angry
kisiwâk IPC nearby
kisiwâsi– VAI be angry
kisiwipayi– VAI get angry, fly into rage
kisiwiyo– VAI complain, be angry at one's work
kisîhto– VAI anger one another by speech
kisîkitot– VTA speak to s.o. in anger [*sic:* -î-]
kisîkotê– VII move fast through the sky (e.g., cloud)
kisîm– VTA anger s.o. by speech
kisîpayi– VAI drive fast
kisîpêkin– VTI wash s.t. [*cf.* kisêpêkin–]
kisîpêkinihtakwâkê– VAI wash one's floor-boards with (it), use (it) to wash one's floor-boards
kisîpêkinihtakwê– VAI wash one's floor-boards
kisîpêkinikan– NA soap [*sic:* NA; *cf.* kisêpêkinikan– NI]
kisîpêkinikâtê– VII be washed
kisîpêkinikê– VAI wash things, do the laundry
kisîpêkinikêwikamikw– NI coin laundry, laundromat
kisîpêkinikêwin– NI laundry, doing the laundry

kisîpêkistikwânâkê– *VAI* wash one's head with (it), use (it) to wash one's hair

kisîpêkistikwânê– *VAI* wash one's head, wash one's hair

kisîstaw– *VTA* be angry with s.o., stay angry with s.o.

kisîwê– *VAI* speak angrily; speak loudly

kisîwê– *VII* be loud, speak loudly (e.g., audio-recorder)

kisîwêhkahtaw– *VTA* speak angrily to s.o.; speak loudly to s.o., scold s.o. loudly

kisîwên– *VTI* turn s.t. (e.g., radio) loud by hand

kisîwi *IPV* loudly, angrily, in anger

kiskêyiht– *VTI* know s.t.; have knowledge

kiskêyihtamâ– *VAI* have spiritual knowledge

kiskêyihtamôhikowisi– *VAI* be granted knowledge by the powers

kiskêyihtâkwan– *VII* be known

kiskêyim– *VTA* know s.o.

kiskinahamaw– *VTA* teach (it) to s.o.; teach s.o. [*sic; cf.* kiskinohamaw–]

kiskinahamawâkan– *NA* student

kiskinahamâkê– *VAI* teach (it) to people; teach things; teach, be a teacher

kiskinahamâkêwin– *NI* teaching, education

kiskinahamâkosi– *VAI* be taught; be a student, attend school

kiskinahamâso– *VAI* teach oneself; be taught; be a student, attend school

kiskinahamâtowikamikw– *NI* school-house; school

kiskinahamâtowin– *NI* teaching, education; education system, school board

kiskinahamâwaso– *VAI* teach one's children

kiskinawâcihcikâcêsi– *VII* be marked, be indicated; be decorated (e.g., brooch, barrette) [*diminutive*]

kiskinawâcihowinis– *NI* decorated brooch, decorated barrette [*diminutive*]

kiskinawâpam– *VTA* learn by watching s.o., learn by s.o.'s example [*sic; cf.* kiskinowâpam–]

kiskinawâpi– *VAI* learn by observation, learn by example; learn merely by watching

kiskinawêhikê– *VAI* utter prophesies, prophesy

kiskinohamaw– *VTA* teach (it) to s.o.; teach s.o. [*sic; cf.* kiskinahamaw–]

kiskinohamawâkan– *NA* student

kiskinohamâkê– *VAI* teach (it) to people; teach things; teach, be a teacher

kiskinohamâkosi– *VAI* be taught; be a student, attend school

kiskinohamâkosiwin– *NI* being a student, going to school; schoolwork, homework

kiskinohamâso– *VAI* teach oneself; be taught; be a student, attend school

kiskinohamâsowin– *NI* schooling, education [*sc. 'patient-centred' noun; e.g.,* okiskinohamâsowin 'his schooling']

kiskinohamâto– *VAI* teach one another

kiskinohamâtowikamikw– *NI* school-house; school

kiskinohamâtowin– *NI* teaching, education; education system, school board

kiskinohtah– *VTA* show (it/him) to s.o.; show s.o. the way, direct s.o.

kiskinowâcihcikâtê– *VII* be marked, be indicated; be decorated

kiskinowâpaht– *VTI* learn by watching s.t., learn by the example of s.t.; learn merely by watching s.t.

kiskinowâpahtih– *VTA* teach s.o. by example

kiskinowâpahtihiwê– *VAI* teach people by example

kiskinowâpam– *VTA* learn by watching s.o., learn by s.o.'s example [*sic; cf.* kiskinawâpam–]

kiskinowâpiwin– *NI* learning by observation, learning by example; learning merely by watching

kiskinowâsoht– VTI learn merely by listening to s.t.

kiskisi– VAI remember; remember (it/him)

kiskisoh– VTA make s.o. remember, remind s.o., put s.o. in mind [*sic:* -o-]

kiskisohto– VAI remind one another [*sic:* -o-; *cf.* kiskisôhto–]

kiskisom– VTA remind s.o. [*sic:* -o-; *cf.* kiskisôm–]

kiskisomito– VAI remind one another [*sic:* -o-; *cf.* kiskisômito–]

kiskisopayi– VAI suddenly remember, remember in a flash; suddenly think of (it), have (it) come to mind

kiskisototaw– VTA remember s.o.; remember (it) about s.o.

kiskisôhto– VAI remind one another [*sic:* -ô-; *cf.* kiskisohto–]

kiskisôm– VTA remind s.o. [*sic:* -ô-; *cf.* kiskisom–]

kiskisômito– VAI remind one another [*sic:* -ô-; *cf.* kiskisomito–]

kiskiwêh– VTI utter s.t. as a prophesy; utter prophesies

kiskiwêhikê– VAI utter prophesies; make predictions, forecast things

kiskiwêhikêmakan– VII provide prophesies; make predictions, forecast things

kiskiwêhikêwin– NI prophesy; prediction, forecast

kiskiwêhw– VTA utter prophesies to s.o., utter prophesies about s.o.

kispaki IPV thickly

kispakikwât– VTI sew s.t. thickly

kispakiwêsâkay– NI thick coat, thick jacket [*cf.* kispakasâkay–]

kistêyiht– VTI think highly of s.t., hold s.t. in high regard [*sic; cf.* kihcêyiht–]

kistêyim– VTA think highly of s.o., hold s.o. in high regard [*sic; cf.* kihcêyim–]

kistikân– NA grain, seed; sheaf of grain; oats

kistikân– NI garden, field, farm, arable land

kistikânikamikw– NI granary

kistikê– *VAI* seed things, plant things, do one's seeding, do one's planting; farm the land

kistikêwi-pimâcihowin– *NI* agricultural way of life, farm economy

kitahamaw– *VTA* advise s.o. against (it/him), warn s.o. about (it/him)

kitamw– *VTA* eat all of s.o. (e.g., bear)

kitâ– *VAI* eat (it) up, eat (it) completely, eat all of (it); drink all of (it); finish drinking a bottle of (it); drink an entire bottle

kitânawê– *VAI* eat all of (it)

kitâpahkê– *VAI* watch things, observe people

kitâpaht– *VTI* look at s.t.

kitâpam– *VTA* look at s.o. (e.g., sun), watch s.o.; look at s.o. with respect, regard s.o. with respect; (*fig.*) watch over s.o.

kitâpamikowisi– *VAI* be looked upon by the powers

kitâpayihtamaw– *VTA* eat all of (it/him) on s.o., eat s.o.'s entire supply

kitâsôm– *VTA* warn s.o. about (it/him)

kitêyiht– *VTI* look after s.t., be responsible for s.t.

kitêyihtamaw– *VTA* look after (it/him) for s.o., be responsible (for it/him) to s.o.

kitimah– *VTA* be mean to s.o., treat s.o. cruelly; bring misery upon s.o.

kitimahiso– *VAI* be mean to oneself, treat oneself cruelly; hurt oneself

kitimaho– *VAI* be mean to oneself, treat oneself cruelly; bring misery upon oneself

kitimâk-ôhpikih– *VTA* raise s.o. in poverty; raise s.o. as an orphan

kitimâkan– *VII* be pitiable, be miserable

kitimâkêyihtamâso– *VAI* think of (it/him) with compassion for one's own sake

kitimâkêyihto– *VAI* feel pity towards one another, think of one another with compassion; take pity upon one another, be kind to one another, love one another

kitimâkêyihtowin– *NI* feeling pity towards one another, thinking of one another with compassion; taking pity upon one another, being kind to one another, loving one another

kitimâkêyim– *VTA* feel pity towards s.o., think of s.o. with compassion; take pity upon s.o., be kind to s.o., love s.o.

kitimâkêyimo– *VAI* feel pitiable, feel miserable; feel poor

kitimâkihtaw– *VTA* listen to s.o. with pity, listen to s.o. with compassion

kitimâkinaw– *VTA* look with pity upon s.o., look with compassion upon s.o., feel sorry for s.o.; take pity upon s.o., lovingly tend s.o.; regard s.o. with respect

kitimâkinâkosi– *VAI* look pitiable, look miserable; look poor

kitimâkinâso– *VAI* pity oneself, feel sorry for oneself

kitimâkisi– *VAI* be pitiable, be miserable; be poor

kitimâkisiwin– *NI* misery; poverty

kitin– *VTA* hold s.o. back

kitiskin– *VTA* inadvertently drop s.o., let s.o. fall by awkwardness

kito– *VAI* utter a sound, call, sing (e.g., bird); make noises (e.g., animal), hoot; be a thunderclap [*cf.* kâh-kito–]

kitohcikê– *VAI* play a musical instrument; play one's stereo-player

kitohcikêmakan– *VII* blare out music (e.g., as stereo-player)

kitot– *VTA* address s.o., speak to s.o.; lecture s.o.

kitot– *VTI* address s.t., speak to s.t. (e.g., spirit-bundle)

kitowêyêkinikê– *VAI* make a noise with paper, rustle one's paper

kiya *PR* you (sg.)

kiyakasê– *VAI* have itchy skin, suffer from eczema

kiyawâw *PR* you (pl.)

kiyâm *IPC* oh well, never mind, so much for this; anyway, rather; let it be, let there be no further delay; please
kiyânaw *PR* you-and-I (incl.), you-and-we (incl.), we (incl.)
kiyâskiski– *VAI* habitually tell lies, be a liar
kiyikaw *IPC* in addition, additionally
kiyipa *IPC* quickly, soon
kiyipi *IPV* quickly, fast
kiyipikin– *VII* grow quickly
kiyokaw– *VTA* visit s.o.
kiyokâto– *VAI* visit one another
kiyokê– *VAI* visit people, pay a visit, go visiting
kiyôtê– *VAI* visit afar, travel to visit
kî *IPV* able to
kî *IPV* to completion, completely; in the past [*in positive constructions only: perfective aspect marker*]
kîh– *VTA* get away from s.o., escape from s.o.'s snare
kîhcêkosî– *VAI* climb high up, climb to a high place
kîhcêkosîw-ôhpî– *VAI* jump to a high place
kîhcêkosîwi *IPV* high up, towards a high place
kîhkâm– *VTA* scold s.o.
kîhkânâkwan– *VII* be clearly visible
kîhkâtah– *VTI* make the sound of (it/him) ring out clearly
kîhkâtahamaw– *VTA* make the sound of (it/him) ring out clearly to s.o.
kîhkâtêyihtâkwan– *VII* be held in high esteem, be prominent
kîhkâtêyim– *VTA* hold s.o. in high esteem
kîhkihto– *VAI* resist one another, quarrel
kîhkîhk *IPC* nevertheless
kîhtwâm *IPC* again, once more, the next [*e.g.*, kîhtwâm ê-kîsikâk 'the next day'; kîhtwâm ê-wâpahk 'the next morning, the next day']
kîkawên– *VTI* mix s.t. in, sprinkle s.t. over [*sic:* -ê-]

kîkawin– VTA   mix s.o. (e.g., tobacco) together by hand [*sic:* -i-]

kîkisêp IPC   early in the morning [*sic; cf.* kîkisêpâ]

kîkisêpâ IPC   early in the morning [*cf.* kêkisêpâ, kîkisêp]

kîkisêpâyâ– VII   be early in the morning

kîkw-ây– NA   which one; what kind [*e.g.,* kîkw-âyak (prox. pl.)]

kîkway PR   something, thing; things; (*in negative constructions:*) not anything, nothing, not any [*indefinite; e.g.,* kîkway; *usually both singular and plural may be expressed by* kîkway]

kîkwâpoy IPC   what kind of liquid [*?sic:* IPC, NI]

kîkwâs PR   something, thing; things; (*in negative constructions:*) not anything, nothing, not any [*indefinite; e.g.,* kîkwâs; *diminutive*]

kîkwây PR   what [*interrogative; e.g.,* kîkwây(i), kîkwâya; *usually both singular and plural may be expressed by* kîkwây]

kîkwây piko IPC   the only thing is [*predicative*]

kîmôc IPC   secretly, in secret, stealthily, privately, in private

kîmôci IPV   secretly, in secret, stealthily, privately, in private

kîmôcih– VTA   be stealthily unfaithful to s.o. (e.g., spouse), cheat on s.o. (e.g., spouse)

kîmôtâpi– VAI   look stealthily, look secretly

kînikatahamaw– VTA   chop (it/him) to a point for s.o.

kînikatahikê– VAI   chop things to a point, sharpen posts

kînikâ– VII   be sharp; be well-defined (e.g., hoofprint)

kînwâhkwêh– VTA   (*especially in inverse constructions:*) leave s.o. baffled, confound s.o. [*?sic: stem; e.g.,* nikînwâhkwêhikon 'it had me stumped']

kîpipayi– VAI   fall over

kîs-ôhpiki– VAI   complete one's growing up, reach adulthood, be grown up

kîsahpit– VTI   complete tying s.t. up, complete tying s.t. in

kîsakim– VTA   finish counting s.o.; finish giving orders to s.o., complete one's charge to s.o.

kîsapihkât– VTI braid s.t. to completion, complete the knitting of s.t.

kîsapwê– VII be warm weather [*sic:* -a-; *cf.* kîsopwê–]

kîsasiwât– VTI reach a decision about s.t.; complete making a law about s.t.

kîsâc IPC beforehand, in advance, in preparation

kîsâpiskiso– VAI be completely heated as rock (e.g., in sweat-lodge), be fully heated as rock

kîsêyiht– VTI make up one's mind about s.t., decide on s.t., complete one's plan for s.t.; be decisive

kîsi IPV completely, to completion

kîsi-tipiskâ– VII be completely night

kîsih– VTA complete s.o. (e.g., stocking), finish preparing s.o. [*sic:* -ih-; *cf.* kîsîh–]

kîsikanisi– VAI spend one's day, live through the day

kîsikâ– VII be day, be daylight [*e.g.,* kîhtwâm ê-kîsikâk 'the next day']

kîsikâw– NI day, daylight, day sky

kîsikâw-pîsimw– NA sun [*i.e., as opposed to moon; cf.* kîsikâwi-pîsimw–]

kîsikâwi-pîsimw– NA sun [*i.e., as opposed to moon; cf.* kîsikâw-pîsimw–]

kîsikohk IPC in the sky; (*fig.*) in heaven

kîsikw– NI sky

kîsin– VTA finish s.o. (e.g., raw hide)

kîsin– VTI finish s.t. (e.g., dressed hide)

kîsinamâso– VAI complete (it/him) for oneself, finish (it/him) for oneself

kîsis– VTI cook s.t. to completion

kîsisikâtê– VII be cooked done

kîsisikê– VAI burn things; burn stubble, burn the fields

kîsiso– VAI be cooked to completion; burn oneself, get burnt; get burnt by an acidic or caustic agent

kîsisw– VTA cook s.o. (e.g., bread) to completion

kîsitê– VII be cooked to completion; be burnt; burn down, be burnt down (e.g., building); be burnt (e.g., stubble, fields)

kîsitêpo– VAI cook; cook a feast, cook ritual food

kîsitêw– NI food, ritual food

kîsîh– VTA complete s.o. (e.g., rattle) [sic: -îh-; cf. kîsih–]

kîsîhcikê– VAI complete doing things; bring a ritual to its conclusion; conclude the formal signing of a treaty

kîsîhtamaw– VTA complete (it/him) for s.o.

kîsîhtâ– VAI finish (it), complete (it)

kîskaht– VTI cut s.t. with one's teeth, bite s.t. off

kîskanakwêwayân– NI waistcoat, short-sleeved vest

kîskasâkay– NI skirt

kîskasâkê– VAI wear a skirt

kîskatah– VTI chop s.t. through

kîskatahikâso– VAI be chopped through by tool (e.g., tree)

kîskatahikâtê– VII be chopped through by tool (e.g., branch)

kîskicihcêpit– VTA tear s.o.'s hand off

kîskicin– VAI be cut (e.g., by branches or thorns), be torn

kîskin– VTI cut s.t. off (e.g., panelling) by hand

kîskipayi– VAI break off, be cut through, break apart

kîskipocikan– NI saw, long saw (e.g., with two handles)

kîskipocikê– VAI cut things with a saw, cut cordwood

kîskipotâ– VAI cut (it) with a saw (e.g., cordwood), saw (it) through

kîskis– VTI cut s.t. through

kîskisamaw– VTA cut (it/him) off for s.o.; cut tobacco as an offering to s.o., present tobacco to s.o.

kîskosîmakan– VII whistle, emit a whistling sound

kîskwê– VAI be mentally disturbed, be mad, be crazy

kîskwêpê– VAI be crazy with alcoholic drink, be drunk

kîskwêpêski– VAI be habitually crazy with alcoholic drink, be habitually drunk

kîskwêskaw– VTA (*especially in inverse constructions:*) make s.o. crazy, leave s.o. disoriented [*e.g.,* kâ-kîskwêskâkot 'that which makes him crazy']

kîskwêtonâmo– VAI say all manner of things, chatter on

kîsohpihkê– VAI melt snow into water [*?sic:* -hp-, -p-]

kîsopwê– VII be warm weather [*sic:* -o-; *cf.* kîsapwê–]

kîsowaho– VAI dress warmly, be warmly dressed

kîsowâ– VII be warm, provide warmth

kîsowâspiso– VAI be warmly swaddled

kîsowât– VTI complete one's words, complete one's prayers

kîsowâtamaw– VTA complete one's words for s.o., complete one's prayers for s.o.

kîsowihkaso– VAI warm oneself by a burning fire

kîsôn– VTA keep s.o. warm, warm s.o. by hand

kîsôsi– VAI keep warm, stay warm; be warm (e.g., pants)

kîsôsim– VTA place s.o. to lie warmly, tuck s.o. into bed

kîspin IPC if [*conditional conjunction*]

kîspin êkâ ohci IPC if it were not for [*irreal conditional, usually with noun phrase or simple conjunct*]

kîspinat– VTA earn enough to buy s.o. (e.g., horse)

kîspinat– VTI earn enough to buy s.t.; earn s.t. as reward; earn one's reward

kîspinatamaw– VTA earn one's reward in s.o., earn s.o. (e.g., grandchild) as one's reward

kîspo– VAI have one's fill, be full with food

kîspôh– VTA feed s.o. until full, get s.o. (e.g., horse) fully fed

kîsta PR you (sg.), too; you (sg.), by contrast; you yourself

kîstanaw PR you-and-I (incl.), too; you-and-we (incl.) by contrast; we ourselves

kîstawâw PR you (pl.), too; you (pl.) by contrast; you yourselves

kîswân IPC by coincidence [*cf.* kêswân, kâkêswân]

kîtahtawê IPC at times, sometimes; at one time, all at once, suddenly [*cf.* kêtahtawê]

kîwâc-âwâsis– NA orphan
kîwâtisi– VAI be orphaned, be an orphan
kîwê IPV back, towards home
kîwê– VAI go home, return home
kîwêhtah– VTA take s.o. home, carry s.o. home, go home with s.o.
kîwêhtatamâkê– VAI take (it/him) home for people
kîwêhtatâ– VAI take (it) home, carry (it) home, go home with (it)
kîwêmakan– VII return home, come back
kîwêpayi– VAI drive home, drive back, ride home, ride back
kîwêtâpê– VAI drag (it) home
kîwêtinohk IPC north, in the north
kîwêtisahw– VTA drive s.o. back, drive s.o. home
kîwêtot– VTI return home to s.t.
kîwêtotaw– VTA return home to s.o.
kocawâkanis– NI match, match-stick [*diminutive*]
kocihtâ– VAI try (it), try to do (it)
kocî– VAI try (it); try, have a try
kohcipayihtâ– VAI swallow (it)
kohtân– VTA immerse s.o. (e.g., a piece of ice) in liquid, dunk s.o. into liquid
konit-âcimowinis– NI mere story, simple story, just a little story [*diminutive*]
konita IPC in vain, without reason, without purpose, for nothing; without further ado; anywhere, at random, in a random place [*cf.* pikonita]
konita-kîkway PR something or other, random things
kosa IPC indeed [*usually as proclitic with a demonstrative pronoun; e.g.,* kos âwa; kos ôma]
kosâpaht– VTI hold a shaking-lodge, hold the shaking-lodge ceremony
kosikwan– VII be heavy
koskoh– VTA startle s.o., surprise s.o.

koskom– VTA awaken s.o. by speech; surprise s.o. by speech
koskon– VTA awaken s.o. by hand, wake s.o. up; startle s.o.
koskopayi– VAI wake up
koskwêyiht– VTI be surprised about s.t., marvel at s.t.; be surprised
koskwêyihtâkwan– VII be surprising, be amazing
koskwêyim– VTA be surprised about s.o.; find s.o. surprising
kospî– VAI move away from the water, move off into the bush
kost– VTA fear s.o.
kost– VTI fear s.t.
kostâci– VAI be afraid, have fear
kostâtikwan– VII be fearsome, be awe-inspiring
kotak PR other, another [*e.g.*, kotakak (prox. pl.), kotaka (an. obv., inan. pl.); kotakihk (loc.)]
kotawân– NI campfire, open fire
kotawânâpiskw– NA stove, cook-stove [*sic:* NA]
kotawânâpiskw– NI stove, cook-stove [*sic:* NI]
kotawê– VAI make a campfire, make a cooking fire
kotâwiciwan– VII sink into the ground, run into the ground (e.g., water)
kotâwipayi– VAI rapidly sink into the ground (e.g., into bog or quicksand)
kotêyiht– VTI try s.t. in one's mind, think strenuously about s.t., test s.t.; challenge s.t.
kotêyihto– VAI test one another, try one another's determination, challenge one another
kotêyim– VTA try s.o., test s.o., put s.o.'s mind to the test; challenge s.o.
kotiskâwê– VAI race, be in a race
kotiskâwêwatimw– NA race-horse [*sic:* -at-]
kotist– VTI taste s.t., try the taste of s.t.
kôhkôs– NA pig, domestic pig
kôhkôsi-wiyinw– NA bacon, strip of bacon [*sic:* NA]

kôn– NA snow [e.g., kôna (prox. sg., obv.)]

kôniwâpoy– NI snow water

kôtatê IPC at a loss; due to limitations beyond one's control; it cannot be helped [*also predicative; cf.* kwêtatêyitiskwêyi– VAI, kwîtawêyihcikâtê– VII]

kôtawêyiht– VTI be at a loss for s.t., miss s.t.

kôtawêyim– VTA be aware of s.o.'s absence, feel the loss of s.o., miss s.o.

kwatakatot– VTA meanly order s.o. around, harass s.o.

kwatakiho– VAI suffer [*sic:* -h-]

kwatakim– VTA speak meanly to s.o., nag s.o.

kwatapisim– VTA tip s.o. over, turn s.o. over (e.g., car in an accident)

kwatapiwêpin– VTA throw s.o. over, flip s.o. upside down

kwayakopayin– VII fall out

kwayask IPC properly, by rights

kwayaski IPV properly, by rights

kwayâc IPC ready, prepared in advance

kwayâc-âstâ– VAI place (it) in readiness (e.g., drinking water) [*sic; cf.* kwayâtastâ–]

kwayâci IPV ready, prepared in advance

kwayâci-niton– VTI look for s.t. to hold in readiness

kwayâci-sikwatahikâtê– VII be pounded in readiness, be pre-pounded

kwayâcihtâ– VAI get (it) ready, prepare (it) in advance [*sic; cf.* kwayâtisîhtâ–]

kwayâtah– VTA place s.o. (e.g., rock) in readiness, prepare s.o. (e.g., rock) in advance

kwayâtastamaw– VTA put (it/him) aside in readiness for s.o.

kwayâtastamâso– VAI put (it/him) aside in readiness for oneself

kwayâtastâ– VAI place (it) in readiness, put (it) aside in advance [*cf.* kwayâc-âstâ–]

kwayâtisîhtâ– VAI get (it) ready, prepare (it) in advance [*sic; cf.* kwayâcihtâ–]

kwâhci *IPV* far off

kwâhkotê– *VII* catch fire, be ablaze

kwâhkotênikê– *VAI* start a fire, set things aflame

kwâkopîwi-sâkahikanihk *INM* (*place-name:*) Green Lake (Saskatchewan) [*locative; lit.* at the green-surfaced lake; *sic:* kwâ-; *cf.* akwâkopiy– NI 'green surface algae']

kwâpah– *VTI* dip s.t. out (e.g., water)

kwâpikê– *VAI* dip out water, draw water, haul water, obtain one's drinking water

kwâsih– *VTA* steal s.o., run away with s.o. (e.g., of the opposite sex)

kwâskwê *IPV* upward

kwâskwêkotê– *VII* jump up

kwâskwêpicikan– *NI* fishing-rod

kwâskwêpicikanis– *NI* fishing-rod [*diminutive*]

kwâskwêpicikê– *VAI* fish with a rod

kwêh-kwêkwask *IPC* back and forth [*cf.* kâh-kwêkwask; *reduplicated*]

kwêsk-âyâ– *VAI* turn around to the opposite side, be turned around (e.g., a pivot)

kwêsk-âyihk *IPC* on the opposite side

kwêskahcâhk *IPC* on the opposite side of a rise in the land

kwêskâskon– *VTA* turn s.o. (e.g., pipe) to the opposite side

kwêski *IPV* turned around, turned to the opposite side

kwêskin– *VTA* change s.o. around, turn s.o. around to the opposite side; (*fig.*) convert s.o. to Christianity

kwêskinâkwan– *VII* look changed around, look turned around to the opposite side

kwêskinisk *IPC* the other hand, changing one's hand

kwêskî– *VAI* turn around

kwêskîmo– *VAI* change one's form

kwêtatêyitiskwêyi– *VAI* be at a loss as to where to turn one's head; be at a loss for a response [*cf.* kôtatê IPC, kwîtawêyihcikâtê– VII]

kwîtawêyihcikâtê– VII be missed, be in short supply [*cf.* kôtatê IPC, kwêtatêyitiskwêyi– VAI]

kwîtâpacihtâ– VAI be short of (it) to use, lack tools

lamilâs– NI syrup [*sic: stem-final* -s-]

ma cî IPC is it not the case [*predicative; cf.* nama cî, namôya cî]

ma kîkway PR nothing; not at all; there is none [*also predicative*]

ma-môhcw-âtayôhkêwin– NI stupid sacred story, crazy sacred story [*reduplicated*]

mac-âyiwi– VAI be bad, be evil

mac-îtêyiht– VTI suspect s.t. bad; suspect evil

macan– VII be bad, be evil

macawâsis– NA (*man's name*) [*lit.* Bad-Child]

maci IPV bad, evil

maci-kikiskaw– VTA (*especially in inverse constructions:*) inhere in s.o. as a bad thing, engross s.o. as an evil [*e.g.,* ma kîkway kôhci-pê-maci-kikiskâkon 'there used to be no evil in you (sg.)']

maci-kîkway PR something bad, evil things

maci-kîsikâ– VII be a bad storm, be a severe storm

maci-manitow– NA (*name:*) devil

maci-manitowi-mihkw– NI (*fig.*) devilish blood, the devil's blood [*e.g.,* maci-manitowi-mihko (sg.)]

maci-manitowi-môtêyâpiskw– NI (*fig.*) the devil's bottle

maci-maskihkiy– NI evil medicine

maci-nôcihtâ– VAI pursue evil things, engage in bad medicine

maci-pawâmi– VAI have an evil dream spirit

maci-pisiskiw– NA evil animal, monster

macikwanâs– NI weed [*sic:* -wa-]

macipakw– NI herb; leaves, lettuce

macipayi– VII go badly

macostêh– VTI throw s.t. into the fire

macôhow– NA (*man's name*) [*lit.* Bad-Owl]

macôhôsis– NA (*man's name:*) young *macôhow*, *macôhow*'s son; (*plural:*) *macôhow*'s family, members of *macôhow*'s family [*diminutive*]

mahîhkani-wât– NI wolf-hole [*e.g.,* mahîhkani-wâti (sg.)]

mahîhkanis– NA (*man's name*) [*lit.* Little-Wolf]

mahkahkw– NI barrel, tub

mahkêsîs– NA (*man's name*) [*lit.* Fox]

mahkihtawakê– VAI have a big ear [*usually reduplicated:* mâh-mahkihtawakê– 'have big ears']

mahkipakâ– VII be big leaves, be the time of fully grown leaves

mahti IPC let's see, please [*hortatory, often jussive*]

mamacikastâkê– VAI show off with (it), use (it) to show off

mamacikastê– VAI show off

mamanê– VAI get ready, be busy [*dial.* (LR)]

mamâhpinêmakan– VII moan, emit a moaning sound

mamâhtawêyihtâkwan– VII be thought strange, be thought supernatural

mamâhtâwisi– VAI have supernatural power

mamâyî– VAI be poor at (it), do (it) poorly

mamihcih– VTA (*especially in inverse constructions:*) make s.o. proud, fill s.o. with pride [*e.g.,* ê-mamihcihikoyân 'it made me proud']

mamihcim– VTA boast about s.o.

mamihcimo– VAI be boastful

mamihcisi– VAI be proud

mamihtisihkâso– VAI act proudly, hold back, hesitate with one's response

mamisî– VAI rely on (it/him); place reliance

mamisîtot– VTI rely on s.t.

mamisîtotaw– VTA rely on s.o.

mamisîtowi– VAI place reliance [*?sic: stem*]

mamisîwât– VTA rely on s.o. for (it/him)

mamistêyimo– *VAI* be proud of oneself, be boastful [*sic:* -st-]
manah– *VTI* skim s.t. off (e.g., grease, cream)
manahikan– *NI* cream
manâ *IPC* in avoiding, in sparing, being careful not to [*sic:* IPC]
manâ *IPV* in avoiding, in sparing, being careful not to
manâ-koskon– *VTA* avoid waking s.o. up, be careful not to wake s.o. up
manâ-pîkon– *VTI* avoid breaking s.t.
manâcih– *VTA* be protective about s.o., be careful about s.o., spare s.o.; avoid hurting s.o.; treat s.o. with respect
manâcihito– *VAI* be protective about one another, be careful about one another; avoid hurting one another
manâcihtâ– *VAI* treat (it) with respect
manâcim– *VTA* speak to s.o. with respect, speak of s.o. with respect
manâhkwatatahw– *VTA* peel s.o. hardened off (e.g., spruce-gum)
manâho– *VAI* collect (it); take (it) as trophy; take a trophy
manâpâwê– *VII* be washed down as water, come running down
manâskocihtâ– *VAI* be left in want by having (it) torn by branches or thorns
manâtâstim– *VTA* be careful in making s.o. wave, avoid making s.o. weave about; spare s.o. in driving a wagon, be considerate of s.o.
manêsi– *VAI* run short, be in want; have run out of (it), lack (it)
mani *IPV* with the intent of, with the purpose of
manicôs– *NA* insect, bug
manin– *VTI* take s.t. down, remove s.t. (e.g., snare)
manipit– *VTA* pull s.o. free (e.g., thorn, porcupine quills), pull s.o. in (e.g., net), pull s.o. out, obtain s.o. by pulling
manipit– *VTI* pull s.t. free, pull s.t. out (e.g., flower), obtain s.t. by pulling

manipîhtwâh– VTA provide tobacco for s.o.

manis– VTI cut s.t.

manisw– VTA cut s.o.; perform surgery on s.o.

manitow– NA spirit; (*name:*) God

manitowakim– VTA endow s.o. (e.g., tobacco) with supernatural power; attribute spirit power to s.o.

manitowi– VAI be a spirit; have spirit power

manitowi-kîsikâw– NI Christmas Day

manitowi-masinahikan– NI God's book, bible

manitowi-sâkahikanihk INM (*place-name:*) Manito Lake (Saskatchewan) [*locative; lit.* at the spirit's lake]

manitowih– VTA grant s.o. supernatural power

mariy– NA (*name:*) Marie, the Virgin Mary [*sic, as in French* Marie]

masinah– VTI mark s.t., draw s.t.; write s.t.; write s.t. down, record s.t. in writing; sign s.t. (e.g., treaty)

masinahamâso– VAI draw (it) for oneself, write (it) for oneself; write oneself

masinahikan– NI letter, mail; book; written document, will; (*fig.*) bible

masinahikanêkinowatis– NI paper bag [*sic:* -t-; *cf.* masinahikanêkinowacis–; *diminutive*]

masinahikanêkinw– NI paper; wallpaper

masinahikâso– VAI be drawn, be pictured, be depicted; be written on

masinahikâtê– VII be pictured, be depicted; have marks, have writing; be written

masinahikê– VAI write things; write, be literate; go into debt, have debts

masinahikêh– VTA hire s.o., employ s.o.

masinahikêstamaw– VTA write things for s.o., write things down for s.o.

masinahikêwin– NI writing; letter, character

masinâso– VAI be marked, be striped

masinihtatâ– VAI trace (it), use (it) as pattern

masinipayi– VAI be depicted as moving (e.g., on film)
masinipayihtâ– VAI depict (it) (e.g., on film)
masinipayiwin– NI picture, photograph
masinisin– VAI be drawn, be represented, be shaped (e.g., star, sun)
masinistah– VTI embroider s.t. (e.g., shape, design)
masinistahikê– VAI embroider things, do embroidery
maskahcih– VTA seize (it/him) from s.o.
maskahto– VAI seize (it/him) from one another; rob one another
maskam– VTA seize (it/him) from s.o.; rob s.o.
maskatêpo– VAI roast (it) on a spit
maskawâ– VII be hard (e.g., fat); be strong, be sturdy
maskawâtisi– VAI be strong, be of sturdy disposition
maskawi-nâpêw– NA (*man's name*) [*lit.* Strong-Man, Hard-Man]
maskawisî– VAI be strong, be vigorous
maskawisîwin– NI strength
maskawîskaw– VTA (*especially in inverse constructions:*) make s.o. strong in body, have an invigorating effect on s.o. [*sic:* -î-; *e.g.,* ta-maskawîskâkoyahk 'for it to make us (incl.) strong']
maskêko-*litea* INM labrador tea [*sic: code-switching within compound*]
maskêko-sâkahikanihk INM (*place-name:*) Muskeg Lake (Saskatchewan); *opitihkwahâkêw*'s Reserve [*locative; lit.* at the muskeg lake]
maskêkowiyiniw– NA Muskeg Lake person, member of *opitihkwahâkêw*'s band
maskêkw– NI swamp, bog, muskeg
maskêkwâpoy– NI labrador tea
maskihkiwâpoy– NI tea [*sic:* -i-; *cf.* maskihkîwâpoy–]
maskihkiy– NI herb, plant; seneca-root; medicinal root; medicine; chemicals
maskihkîwâpoy– NI tea [*sic:* -î-; *cf.* maskihkiwâpoy–]

maskihkîwâpôhkatiso– *VAI* prepare an herbal infusion for oneself; make a medicinal drink for oneself

maskihkîwâpôhkê– *VAI* prepare an herbal infusion; make tea

maskihkîwin– *NI* medicinal preparation, medicine

maskihkîwiskwêw– *NA* nurse

maskihkîwiwacis– *NI* medicine chest

maskihkîwiyiniw– *NA* doctor, physician

maskimocis– *NI* small bag [*diminutive*]

maskimot– *NI* bag

maskimotêkinw– *NI* sack, sacking, sack-cloth; flour-bag, cloth from flour-bag

maskisin– *NI* moccasin, shoe

maskisinêkinw– *NI* shoe-leather

maskisinihkê– *VAI* make moccasins

maskisinihkêhkâso– *VAI* pretend to make moccasins

maskisinis– *NI* shoe, little shoe [*diminutive*]

masko-nôcokwêsiw– *NA* (*woman's name*) [*lit.* Bear-Old-Woman, Old-Lady-Bear]

masko-tâpakwân– *NI* bear-trap; bear-snare

masko-wiyâs– *NI* bear-meat

maskosiy– *NI* grass, hay; (*plural:*) reeds; pieces of sod

maskosîhkê– *VAI* make hay

maskosîs– *NI* grass, hay; blade of grass [*diminutive*]

maskw– *NA* bear [*e.g.,* maskwa (prox.sg., obv.)]

maskwacîsihk *INM* (*place-name:*) Hobbema (Alberta) [*locative; lit.* at the bear's hill, at the bear hills; *includes the four reserves surrounding Hobbema*]

maskwamiy– *NA* ice, hail [*sic:* -a-; *cf.* miskwamiy–]

maskwayân– *NA* bearskin

mastaw *IPC* newly, recently

matâwisi– *VAI* move into the open, come out onto the open prairie

matâwisipit– VTI pull s.t. into the open, pull s.t. out onto the open prairie
matotisah– VTA make s.o. hold a sweat-lodge
matotisahtâ– VAI take (it) into the sweat-lodge
matotisân– NI sweat-lodge
matotisi– VAI hold a sweat-lodge
matwân cî IPC I wonder [*polar dubitative*]
matwê IPV audibly, visibly; perceptibly; in full view, in plain sight
matwêhikâtê– VII be a knock; be a drum-beat
matwêhw– VTA sound a beat upon s.o. (e.g., drum), drum on s.o.
matwêwê– VII be heard as a gunshot, be the report of a gun
matwêwêhtâ– VAI detonate (it); shoot off one's gun
mawimo– VAI cry out; cry out in prayer, wail
mawimohkê– VAI howl (e.g., dog)
mawimoscikê– VAI cry out in prayer, wail; worship with (it)
mawimoscikêwin– NI crying out in prayer, wailing; form of worship, rite
mawimost– VTI cry out in prayer to s.t., wail before s.t.
mawimostaw– VTA cry out in prayer to s.o., wail before s.o., implore s.o.; worship s.o.
mawinêhw– VTA challenge s.o. to a contest
mawiso– VAI pick berries, gather berries
mawîhkât– VTA cry out over s.o., lament s.o.
mawîhkât– VTI cry out over s.t., lament s.t.
mawîhkâtamaw– VTA cry out over (it/him) in prayer to s.o., wail over (it/him) before s.o.
mayaw IPC as soon as [*temporal conjunction*]
maywês IPC previously, before [*cf.* maywêsk, mwayê, mwayês, pamwayês, pâmwayês]
maywêsk IPC previously, before [*cf.* maywês, mwayê, mwayês, pamwayês, pâmwayês]

mâc-âtoskê– VAI   begin to work, begin one's work [*sic; cf.* mâcatoskê–, mâtatoskê–]

mâcatoskê– VAI   begin to work, begin one's work [*sic:* -ca-; *cf.* mâtatoskê–, mâc-âtoskê–]

mâci IPV   begin to; initially

mâcihtâ– VAI   begin doing (it)

mâcika IPC   for instance [*weak concessive*]

mâcikôci IPC   by gosh!

mâcikôtitan IPC   wait and see! lo! [*sic; exclamatory*]

mâcipayin– VII   begin to run (e.g., tape-recorder)

mâcî– VAI   hunt, go hunting

mâcîtotaw– VTA   hunt for s.o.

mâcîwâkê– VAI   hunt with (it/him), use (it/him) to hunt

mâcîwihkomân– NI   hunting knife

mâcîwin– NI   hunting, the hunt

mâcosi– VAI   cry a little [*diminutive*]

mâh-maskâc IPC   strangely, marvellously, amazingly [*sic; cf.* mâmaskâc]

mâh-mawaci IPC   (*in superlative constructions:*) most, the very most, the best [*sic; cf.* mâmawaci; *reduplicated*]

mâh-mêskoc IPC   each in turn [*cf.* mâh-mêskot, mêh-mîskoc; *reduplicated*]

mâh-mêskot IPC   each in turn [*cf.* mâh-mêskoc, mêh-mîskoc; *reduplicated*]

mâhmâkwahcikanêyâpiy– NI   rawhide rope [*sic:* -hm-; *cf.* mâmâkwaht– VTI]

mâka IPC   but [*concessive*]

mâka mîna IPC   also, on the other hand; as usual [*cf.* âkamîna]

mâkoh– VTA   press upon s.o., bear down upon s.o., oppress s.o.; worry s.o., trouble s.o., throw s.o. into crisis

mâkon– VTA   press upon s.o. by hand, press s.o.'s hand; push s.o. down (e.g., button on radio)

mâkon– VTI   press upon s.t. by hand

mâkoskaw– VTA press upon s.o. (by foot or body movement)

mâkw– NA loon [*e.g.*, mâkwa (prox. sg., obv.)]

mâkwêyimo– VAI be worried, be troubled

mâmaskâc IPC strangely, marvellously, amazingly; (*in negative constructions:*) not surprisingly, no wonder [*sic; cf.* mâh-maskâc]

mâmaskâsihtaw– VTA be amazed upon listening to s.o.

mâmaskât– VTA find s.o. strange, find s.o. incomprehensible, marvel at s.o.

mâmaskât– VTI find s.t. strange, find s.t. incomprehensible, marvel at s.t.

mâmaw-âyamihâ– VAI pray as a group, participate in a religious rite as a group, celebrate mass as a group; go on a pilgrimage as a group

mâmaw-ôhtâwîmâw– NA (*name:*) All-Father, Father-of-All

mâmawaci IPC (*in superlative constructions:*) most, the very most [*sic; cf.* mâh-mawaci; *reduplicated*]

mâmawaci-kayâs IPC at the very earliest time

mâmawatoskê– VAI work together as a group, work as a team

mâmawêyati– VAI be together as a group, be together in numbers

mâmawi IPN collectively, jointly, all together [*e.g.*, mâmawi-ayisiyiniwa (obv.) 'the assembled people']

mâmawi IPV collectively, jointly, all together

mâmawi-wîcihitowin– NI all helping together, general cooperation

mâmawihkwâmi– VAI sleep together as a group, share a mattress

mâmawin– VTI put s.t. together, sew s.t. together (e.g., quilted squares)

mâmawo-kayâs IPC at the very earliest time

mâmawokwât– VTI sew s.t. together into one, piece s.t. together in sewing

mâmawopiwin– NI meeting, assembly

mâmawôhk– VTI work together at s.t. as a group; engage in a joint effort

mâmawôhkamâto– VAI work together at (it/him) as a group; do things together, help one another, cooperate

mâmawôpayi– VAI get together as a group, have a gathering

mâmawôpi– VAI sit as a group, get together; hold a meeting

mâmawôpîtot– VTI meet about s.t., hold a meeting about s.t. [*sic:* -î-]

mâmâkwaht– VTI chew s.t. (e.g., sinew); bite down on s.t. (e.g., leather, birchbark)

mâmâkwam– VTA chew s.o. (e.g., spruce-gum, thread)

mâmâsîs IPC sparingly, delicately; quickly, roughly, without care

mâmâwacêyas IPC (*in superlative constructions:*) most, the very most [*enclitic; cf.* mâwacêyas; *reduplicated*]

mâmiskôcikâtê– VII be discussed, be expounded

mâmiskôm– VTA talk about s.o., discuss s.o., refer to s.o.

mâmiskôt– VTI talk about s.t., discuss s.t., expound s.t., refer to s.t.

mâmiskôtamaw– VTA discuss (it/him) for s.o., expound (it/him) for s.o., refer to (it/him) for s.o.

mâmitonêyihcikan– NI mind; troubled mind; thought, worry

mâmitonêyiht– VTI think about s.t.; worry about s.t.

mâmitonêyihtamih– VTA cause s.o. to think about (it/him), cause s.o. to worry about (it/him); worry s.o.

mâmitonêyihtamim– VTA worry s.o. by speech

mâmitonêyihtêstamâso– VAI think about (it/him) for oneself; plan for oneself

mâmitonêyim– VTA think about s.o., have s.o. on one's mind; worry about s.o.

mân[a] âta wiya IPC on the other hand

mâna IPC usually, habitually

mânahtê– VAI get one's pelts

mâninakis IPC continually, on and on, persistently [*often in preterite constructions; cf.* mâninakisk]

mâninakisk IPC continually, on and on, persistently [*often in preterite constructions; cf.* mâninakis]

mânokê– VAI build a lodge, set up a tent [*sic:* -kê-]

mâsihito– VAI wrestle with one another, wrestle, jostle one another

mâskosiwân– NI bulrush, edible reed [*sic:* mâ-; *cf.* mwâ-; *?sic: Typha spp., Scirpus spp.*]

mâskôc IPC perhaps, I suppose, undoubtedly [*cf.* mâskôt]

mâskôt IPC perhaps, I suppose, undoubtedly [*cf.* mâskôc]

mâtah– VTI scrape s.t. (e.g., hide)

mâtahpinê– VAI begin to be ill, fall ill

mâtatoskaw– VTA begin to work for s.o.

mâtatoskê– VAI begin to work, begin one's work [*sic:* -ta-; *cf.* mâc-âtoskê–, mâcatoskê–]

mâtayak IPC ahead of time, beforehand, in advance

mâtâcimo– VAI begin to tell a story

mâtâskonikê– VAI begin to point the pipe or pipestem

mâtinamâto– VAI deal (it/him) out to one another

mâtitâpihtêpiso– VAI begin to wear earrings [*sic:* -t-]

mâto– VAI cry, wail

mâtopahtâ– VAI cry while running

mâtowin– NI crying, wailing

mâwacêyas IPC (*in superlative constructions:*) most, the very most [*enclitic; cf.* mâmawacêyas; *e.g.,* nistam mâwacêyas 'the very first time']

mâwaci IPV (*in superlative constructions:*) the most

mâwaci-sôhkan– VII be strongest, be sturdiest

mâwacih– VTA collect s.o. (e.g., pounded meat), gather s.o. up; save s.o.

mâwacihtâ– VAI collect (it), gather (it) up

mâwacisôniyâwê– VAI gather up money, pile up money

mâwacîhito– VAI collect one another, gather [*sic:* -îh-]

mâwasakon– VTA   gather s.o. up, collect s.o. (e.g., spruce-gum)

mâwasakowêpah– VTI   sweep s.t. together

mâwasakwahpit– VTI   tie s.t. together in a bunch

mâyahkamikan– VII   be a bad deed; be a bad situation

mâyahpinat– VTA   treat s.o. badly, beat s.o. severely

mâyamahciho– VAI   feel poorly, be in ill health [*sic; cf.* mâyimahciho–]

mâyatihkopîway– NI   sheep's fleece; wool

mâyâpaso– VAI   smell foul, give off a bad smell, stink

mâyâtan– VII   be ugly, be bad

mâyêyiht– VTI   consider s.t. a challenge; be willing to tackle a difficult task, venture out

mâyêyim– VTA   consider s.o. a challenge; be willing to tackle s.o.

mâyi IPV   bad, evil

mâyi-kîsikâ– VII   be stormy weather, be foul weather, be a severe storm

mâyi-nawasônikê– VAI   choose badly, make a bad choice

mâyi-tôt– VTI   do s.t. evil; do a bad thing, impose a curse

mâyi-tôtaw– VTA   do evil to s.o., harm s.o., make s.o. sick, put a curse on s.o.

mâyi-wîcêhto– VAI   live in discord with one another

mâyimahciho– VAI   feel poorly, be in ill health [*sic; cf.* mâyamahciho–]

mâyinikê– VAI   act badly, do harmful things; experience bad things, come to harm

mâyinikêhkâto– VAI   act badly towards one another, harm one another

mâyinikêwin– NI   wrong-doing; evil deed

mâyipayi– VAI   fare badly, suffer ill; suffer a death, be bereaved, have a death in the family; be bereaved of (her/him)

mâyiskaw– VTA   go through s.o. to bad effect, affect s.o. negatively, fail to agree with s.o.; (*especially in inverse* *constructions:*) have an adverse effect on s.o., make s.o. ill [*e.g.,* ê-kî-mâyiskâkot 'it used to cause allergic reactions in him']

mêh-mîskoc IPC each in turn [*sic:* -ê-, -î-; *cf.* mâh-mêskoc; *reduplicated*]

mêki– VAI give (it/him) out as present; give (it/him) away, release (it/him); give (her) in marriage

mêkiskwêwê– VAI give a woman in marriage; give (her) in marriage

mêkwâ IPV while, during, in the course of; meanwhile; in the midst of [*cf.* mêkwâc IPC]

mêkwâc IPC while, during, in the course of; in the meantime [*cf.* mêkwâ IPV]

mêkwâskaw– VTA encounter s.o. in the midst of (it), catch s.o. in the act

mêmohci IPC in particular, above all; exactly, precisely

mênikan– NI fence

mênikanâhtikw– NI fence-rail

mênikanihkâkê– VAI build a fence with (it), use (it) to build a fence

mêscacâkanis– NA coyote [*diminutive*]

mêscih– VTA kill s.o. off, annihilate s.o.

mêscihtamaw– VTA destroy (it/him) for s.o., annihilate (it/him) for s.o.

mêscihtatâ– VAI get all of (it) torn, get all of (it) ragged

mêscihtâ– VAI destroy (it), annihilate (it)

mêscinê– VAI die out

mêscipayi– VAI be exhausted (e.g., snow), be gone entirely (e.g., snow)

mêscipayin– VII run out, be exhausted on the way

mêscisk– VTI wear s.t. out

mêscitonêsin– VAI have exhausted one's mouth, wear one's mouth out

mêsciwêpah– VTI throw away all of s.t.

mêskanaw– NI path, trail, road

mêskanâs– NI path, trail [*diminutive*]
mêskoc IPC instead, in return, in exchange [*cf.* mîskoc]
mêskocikâpawi– VAI stand up instead
mêskotayiwinisê– VAI change one's clothes
mêskotâpin– VTI change s.t. (e.g., water in boiling a beaver), exchange s.t.
mêskotin– VTI change s.t., replace s.t.
mêskotôn– VTI change s.t. (e.g., water in boiling a beaver), exchange s.t. [*sic; cf.* mîskotônikê– VAI]
mêskwa IPC not yet [*sic; cf.* nam êskwa; êskwa, cêskwa]
mêstan– NA sap, tree-sap [*also the stringy cambium or bast of poplars and certain other trees*]
mêstasahkê– VAI feed people until the supply is exhausted, exhaust one's supply by feeding people
mêstâskocihcâ– VAI get all of (it) torn by branches or thorns [*diminutive*]
mêstâskocihtâ– VAI get all of (it) torn by branches or thorns
mêstihkahtê– VII burn down completely, be completely burnt down
mêstin– VTA use all of s.o. (e.g., thread)
mêstinikê– VAI use things up, exhaust things, spend all of (it); spend all of one's money on things
mêstohtê– VAI die off, become extinct
mêtawâkâniwi– VII be general playing around
mêtawâkê– VAI play with (it), use (it) to play; play around with (it), fool around with (it)
mêtawê– VAI play; gamble [*e.g.,* micihciy mêtawê– VAI 'play the hand-game']
mêtawêwikamikw– NI play-house
mêtoni IPC intensively, fully, really [*rhetorical distortion; cf.* mitoni]
mêyiwiciskê– VAI have feces stuck to one's anus, have one's anus soiled with feces
micimâskwahw– VTA hold s.o. in place as or by wood
micimin– VTA hold on to s.o.; hold s.o. in place

micimin– VTI hold on to s.t.; hold s.t. in place

miciminamaw– VTA hold on to (it/him) for s.o.

miciminamôh– VTA make s.o. hold on to (it/him)

miciminikâtê– VII be held onto, be stuck

micimoskowahtâ– VAI make (it) hold together with mud, mud (it) with clay

micimoskowahtê– VII be held together with mud, be mudded with clay

micimoskowê– VAI be stuck in mud or bog

micimôh– VTA (*especially in inverse constructions:*) cause s.o. to get stuck [*e.g.,* ê-micimôhikoyân 'it is leaving me stuck']

micimôho– VAI be held fast, be stuck [*sic:* -h-]

mihcêt IPC many, much

mihcêti– VAI be numerous, be plentiful

mihcêtin– VII be numerous, be plentiful

mihcêtôsê– VAI have many children, have numerous offspring

mihcêtwastimwê– VAI have many horses

mihcêtwâw IPC many times

mihcis– NI split wood, small firewood, sticks [*usually plural; diminutive*]

mihkit– VTI scrape s.t. (meat) off the hide

mihkon– VTI make s.t. red, redden s.t.

mihkonikâtê– VII be made red, be reddened

mihkosi– VAI be red

mihkostikwânê– VAI have red hair, be red-haired

mihkotonê– VAI have a red mouth, wear lipstick

mihkotonêho– VAI paint one's mouth red, wear lipstick

mihkotonêhon– NI lipstick

mihkotonêhw– VTA paint s.o.'s mouth red, put lipstick on s.o.

mihkw– NI blood [*e.g.,* mihko (sg.), nimihko (sg.) 'my blood']

mihkwasâkay– NA red-coat, officer of the NWMP

mihkwawê– VAI have a red coat (e.g., animal)

mihkwâ– VII be red

mihkwâkami– VII be a red liquid

mihkwâpêmakos– NI young red willow, little red willow [*i.e., red-osier dogwood; diminutive*]

mihkwâpêmakw– NI red willow, red willow scrapings [*i.e., the stringy cambium or bast of red-osier dogwood, used for smoking*]

mihkwâpêmakw-âya IPC red willow stuff [*i.e., red-osier dogwood; sometimes pluralised as if* NI]

miht– NI firewood, piece of firewood [*e.g.,* mihti (sg.), mihta (pl.)]

mihtât– VTA deplore the loss of s.o., sorely miss s.o., grieve for s.o.

mihtât– VTI deplore the loss of s.t., be sorry about s.t.

mikisimo– VAI bark (e.g., dog)

mikit– VTA bark at s.o.

mikoskâcihtâ– VAI trifle with (it), tamper with (it)

minah– VTA give s.o. to drink (e.g., tea, soup); give s.o. tea to drink; give s.o. an alcoholic drink, induce s.o. to drink an alcoholic drink

minahikosis– NA small spruce, young spruce-tree [*diminutive*]

minahikoskâ– VII be a spruce thicket, be an abundance of spruce

minahikw– NA spruce, spruce-tree; spruce-bough [*e.g.,* minahikwak 'spruce-boughs']

minaho– VAI kill game, make a kill

minahôstamaw– VTA kill an animal for s.o., make a kill for s.o.

minahôstamâso– VAI kill an animal for oneself, succeed in a kill

minihkwâcikan– NI cup

minihkwât– VTA trade s.o. for a drink

minihkwê– *VAI* drink (it); have a drink; drink an alcoholic drink; abuse alcohol

minihkwêsi– *VAI* drink a little of (it) (e.g., tea, soup); have a little drink; drink a small amount of an alcoholic drink [*diminutive*]

minihkwêski– *VAI* habitually abuse alcohol, be an alcoholic

minihkwêwin– *NI* drink; drinking, alcohol abuse

ministikoskwâ– *VII* be an individual cloud [*sic:* -o-; *cf.* ministikwaskwâsin–]

ministikwaskwâsin– *VII* be an individual small cloud, be an isolated small cloud [*sic:* -wa-; *cf.* ministikoskwâ–; *diminutive*]

mis-âyamihâ– *VAI* hold mass, celebrate high mass

mis-âyiwâk *IPC* much more

mis-ôtinikê– *VAI* come away with rich winnings (e.g., in a card-game)

misahcinêh– *VTI* buy s.t. in great numbers, buy a lot of s.t.

misahkamik *IPC* a great many, in great number

misahtâ– *VAI* make (it) big

misakâmê *IPC* all along, all the way, in continuity, throughout

misakâmê *IPV* all along, all the way, in continuity, throughout [*sic:* IPV]

misaskê– *VAI* touch the earth (e.g., as a falling star)

misatimokamikw– *NI* horse-barn

misatimw– *NA* horse [*sic:* -s-; *cf.* mistatimw–]

misatimwayân– *NA* horse-hide

misatimwâyow– *NI* horse-tail; tail-hair of a horse

misawâc *IPC* in any case, whatever might be thought

misâ– *VII* be big

misâskwatômin– *NI* saskatoon berry

miscahîs *IPC* quite greatly, quite a bit

miscahîs-kîkway *PR* quite a few things

miscanikwacâs– *NA* gopher

miscikos– NI   little stick (e.g., in collecting sap); little pole, rod, rail (e.g., on drying rack); branch of a small plant (e.g., labrador tea) [*diminutive*]

miscikwaskisinis– NI   firm shoe, sturdy shoe, oxford [*diminutive*]

misi IPN   big, great

misi IPV   big, greatly

misi-minahikw– NA   large spruce-tree

misi-mîci– VAI   eat much of (it), eat a lot of (it)

misi-pîtos IPC   very different; very strange

misi-yôtin– VII   be a big windstorm

misihêw– NA   chicken, domestic chicken

misikiti– VAI   be big (in height or girth); be pregnant

misipocikê– VAI   run hide over a sharp edge

misipotâ– VAI   run (it) (e.g., hide) over a sharp edge

misisîhtâ– VAI   make (it) big

misiw îta IPC   everywhere

misiw îtê IPC   all over, everywhere

misiwanâcihcikêmakan– VII   ruin things, destroy things

misiwanâcihiso– VAI   ruin oneself, destroy oneself; (*fig.*) commit suicide

misiwanâcihtamaw– VTA   ruin (it/him) for s.o., destroy (it/him) for s.o.

misiwanâcihtâ– VAI   ruin (it), destroy (it)

misiwanâcisi– VAI   be ruined, perish

misiwanâcisîmakan– VII   be ruinous, be destructive [*sic: gloss*]

misiwanâtan– VII   be ruined, perish; be spoiled, spoil (e.g., meat)

misiwanâtisi– VAI   be ruined, perish [*sic:* -t-]

misiwê IPC   all over, the entire place

misiwêminakin– VTI   put beads all over s.t.; cover s.t. with beads

misiwêpayihcikan– NI   pill, medication

misiwêpayihcikanis– NI little pill, medication [*diminutive*]
misiwêskamik IPC all over the land, all over the world
misîht– VTI chew s.t.
misîm– VTA chew s.o. (e.g., spruce-gum)
misk– VTI find s.t.
miskamaw– VTA find (it/him) for s.o.
miskamâso– VAI find (it/him) for oneself; find oneself a spouse
miskaw– VTA find s.o.
miskikâtê– VII be found
miskîsik-maskihkiy– NI eye medicine
miskôskaw– VTA come upon s.o.
miskôt– VTI discuss s.t., refer to s.t. [*sic; dial.* (LR)]
miskwam– VTA find s.o. (e.g., coin) by mouth, find s.o. (e.g., coin) in one's food
miskwamiy– NA ice, hail [*sic:* -i-; *cf.* maskwamiy–]
miskwamîs– NA a little ice (e.g., crushed ice, ice-cubes) [*diminutive*]
miskwamîwâpoy– NI melted ice, melting hailstones
miskwâpam– VTA see s.o., espy s.o. (e.g., star)
miskwêyiht– VTI find s.t., think of s.t., come to think of s.t.
miskwêyihtamipayi– VAI suddenly have (it/him) come to mind
mispon– VII be falling snow, be a snow-fall
mistah-âtoskêwin– NI big task, major task
mistahi IPC greatly, very much so, very many
mistahi IPN great
mistahi IPV greatly, very much so, very many [*sic:* IPV]
mistahi-kîkway PR many things, a great deal of something
mistahi-pîtos IPC very strangely, most strangely, very differently
mistakihtê– VII be counted for much, be worth a lot, be valuable, be expensive
mistasiniy– NA big stone, big rock

mistaskihkw– NA big kettle, communal cooking pot
mistatimo-mêy– NI horse-dung [*e.g.,* mistatimo-mêya (pl.)]
mistatimokamikw– NI horse-barn
mistatimw– NA horse [*sic:* -st-; *cf.* misatimw–]
mistawâsis– NA (*man's name*) [*lit.* Big-Child]
mistihkomân– NI hunting-knife
mistiko-nâpêwi– VAI work as a carpenter, do carpentry
mistiko-nipêwin– NI wooden bed, bedstead
mistiko-wanihikan– NI trap, wooden trap [*dial.* (LR)]
mistikokamikw– NI log-house
mistikowat– NI wooden box, trunk; wood-box, box for wood; wagon-box
mistikôsiw– NA Frenchman, Hudson's Bay Company manager [*sic:* mi-; *cf.* wêmistikôsiw–]
mistikw– NA tree, post [*sic*] [*sic:* NA]
mistikw– NI stick, pole, post, log, wooden rail [*sic:* NI]
mistikwaskihkw– NA drum
mistikwaskisin– NI heeled shoe, oxford
mistikwâhkatotê– VII be as hard as wood, be as solid as wood
mistiyâkan– NI big dish, platter, large bowl
mitâsipici– VAI move camp into the open, move one's camp out onto the open prairie
mitâtaht IPC ten
mitâtaht-kosikwan IPC ten pounds
mitâtaht-kosikwan– NA ten-pound pail [*sic:* NA]
mitâtaht-tipahikan IPC at ten o'clock
mitâtahto-pîwâpiskos IPC ten cents
mitâtahtomitanaw IPC one hundred
mitâtahtomitanaw-maskimot IPC a hundred bags, one hundred bags
mitâtahtwâpisk IPC ten dollars
mitêwiwin– NI mitewin lodge, medicine society
mitiht– VTA track s.o., follow s.o.'s tracks

mitiht– *VTI* track s.t., follow the tracks of s.t.

mitimê– *VAI* track along a trail, follow a trail; (*fig.*) follow a path, be guided in one's life

mitonêyihcikan– *NI* mind

mitoni *IPC* intensively, fully, really [*cf.* mêtoni]

mitoni *IPV* intensively, fully, really [*sic:* IPV]

miy– *VTA* give (it/him) to s.o.

miy-ôtin– *VTA* take s.o. in, accept s.o.

miyawâcikâtê– *VII* be rejoiced over, be cause for rejoicing

miyawâkâc *IPV* with particular care

miyawâkâtinikê– *VAI* take particular care with things, handle ritual objects with particular care

miyawât– *VTI* enjoy s.t., rejoice over s.t.; rejoice, be joyful, have fun

miyawâtamowin– *NI* enjoyment; fun, joyfulness

miyâhcikê– *VAI* smell things, sniff about

miyâhkas– *VTI* cense s.t., smudge s.t. with sweetgrass

miyâhkasamaw– *VTA* cense (it/him) for s.o., smudge (it/him) with sweetgrass for s.o.

miyâhkasikâkê– *VAI* cense with (it), use (it) to cense with, use (it) as incense

miyâhkasikê– *VAI* cense things, smudge things with sweetgrass

miyâhkaso– *VAI* give off a burning smell

miyâhkasw– *VTA* cense s.o. (e.g., pipe), smudge s.o. (e.g., pipe) with sweetgrass

miyâht– *VTI* smell s.t., sniff s.t.

miyâm– *VTA* smell s.o., smell s.o.'s presence

miyâmâc *IPC* assuredly; I do believe so

miyân– *VTI* leave behind fresh tracks, have recently passed by

miyâsk– *VTI* pass around s.t., bypass s.t.

miyikowisi– *VAI* be given (it/him) by the powers

miyiskwê– VAI   have a dry throat; speak with a weak voice [*?sic: stem, gloss*]

miyito– VAI   give (it/him) to one another

miyo IPN   good, well, beautiful, valuable

miyo IPV   good, well, beautiful, valuable

miyo-kakêskihkêmowin– NI   good counselling, good preaching

miyo-kîkway PR   something good, good things

miyo-kîsih– VTA   finish s.o. well; educate s.o. well [*sic:* -ih-]

miyo-kîsikâ– VII   be good weather, be mild weather

miyo-nôcihtâ– VAI   pursue good things; (*in negative constructions:*) pursue evil things, engage in bad medicine

miyo-pimâciho– VAI   make a good life for oneself, live well; lead a proper life

miyo-pimâtisi– VAI   live a good life, live well; lead a proper life

miyo-pîkiskwêwin– NI   good speech; (*fig.*) the good news of the bible

miyo-sôniyâhkê– VAI   make good money; earn good wages

miyo-tôt– VTI   do s.t. good; do a good thing

miyo-tôtamowin– NI   good deed, good works

miyo-tôtaw– VTA   do s.o. good, affect s.o. beneficially, do s.o. a good turn

miyo-wîcêht– VTI   be supportive of s.t.; be cooperative

miyo-wîcêhto– VAI   get along well with one another, live in harmony with one another

miyo-wîki– VAI   live comfortably, have a nice dwelling

miyoht– VTI   like the sound of s.t., consider s.t. to sound nice

miyohtah– VTA   guide s.o. well

miyohtwâ– VAI   be good-natured, be of pleasant character

miyoki– VAI   grow well

miyokihtâ– VAI   be good at growing (it)

miyomahciho– VAI fare well, be in good health or spirit; feel well, feel healthy; feel pleased

miyonaw– VTA like the look of s.o., consider s.o. good-looking

miyonâkohcikê– VAI be seen to be good at things, make things look nice, make things look prosperous

miyonâkwan– VII look good, have a nice appearance, look prosperous

miyoniskêhkât– VTI accomplish s.t. by the work of one's hands

miyopayi– VAI fare well, be in luck

miyopayi– VII work well, run well; work out, come to pass [*sic; cf.* miyopayin–]

miyopayin– VII work well, run well [*sic; cf.* miyopayi–]

miyopit– VTI carry s.t. off well, accomplish s.t.

miyosi– VAI be good, be beautiful

miyosîho– VAI be well dressed, be beautifully dressed

miyosîhtâ– VAI make (it) good, make (it) beautiful

miyoskamin– VII be early spring

miyoskaw– VTA (*especially in inverse constructions:*) go through s.o. to good effect, have a salutary effect on s.o., make s.o. well [*e.g.,* êkâ ê-miyoskâkoyân 'that it did not do me any good']

miyô– VAI be good at (it)

miyw-âyâ– VAI be well, be in good health; have a good life

miywakihtê– VII be considered good; (*in negative constructions:*) be considered bad, be considered evil

miywakiso– VAI be considered good, be well esteemed; fetch a good price (e.g., tree)

miywâpacih– VTA use s.o. well, make good use of s.o., find s.o. useful

miywâpacihtâ– VAI use (it) well, make good use of (it)

miywâpatisi– VAI be of good use, be useful

miywâpisin– VAI like the look of (it)

miywâsin– VII be good, be valuable; (*in negative constructions:*) be bad, be evil

miywêyihcikâtê– VII be liked, be enjoyed

miywêyiht– VTI consider s.t. good, like s.t.; be glad, be pleased

miywêyihtâkwan– VII be joy, be rejoicing

miywêyim– VTA consider s.o. good, like s.o.; be pleased with s.o.

miywêyimo– VAI think well of oneself; be pleased with oneself; think well for oneself, take a fancy

mîci– VAI eat (it)

mîcimâpoy– NI broth, soup

mîcimâpôhkâkê– VAI make soup with (it), use (it) to make soup

mîcimâpôs– NI broth, soup [*diminutive*]

mîcimîhkahkcikêsi– VAI use (it) as bait [*diminutive*]

mîciso– VAI eat, have a meal; feed (e.g., bird); chew the cud (e.g., ruminant)

mîcisosi– VAI eat a little, have a small meal [*diminutive*]

mîcisowikamikw– NI cafe, restaurant

mîcisowin– NI eating, meal; eating-habits; food, foodstuff, food supply

mîcisowinâhtikw– NI dining table, table

mîcisôh– VTA give s.o. to eat, make s.o. eat

mîciswâkê– VAI eat with (it), use (it) to eat

mîciswât– VTI eat from s.t., eat off s.t.

mîciwin– NI food

mîciwinis– NI some food, a little food [*diminutive*]

mîkis– NA bead

mîkisasâkay– NI beaded coat, beaded jacket

mîkisayiwinis– NI beaded clothing

mîkisihkahcikê– VAI bead things, do beadwork

mîkisihkahcikêwin– NI beading, beadwork

mîkisihkaht– VTI bead s.t., stitch beads on s.t.

mîkisihkahtê– VII be beaded
mîkisistah– VTI bead s.t., stitch beads on s.t.
mîkisistahikê– VAI bead things, do beadwork
mîkisistahikêwin– NI doing beadwork
mîkisiwi– VII be beaded
mîkiwâhp– NI lodge, tipi
mîkiwâhpis– NI little lodge [*diminutive*]
mîkwan– NA feather
mîna IPC also, and also, again
mînis– NI berry [*usually plural; e.g.,* kimînisimihk 'on your berries']
mînisîhkês– NI seneca-root
mînom– VTA straighten s.o. out, correct s.o. verbally
mînwâskonamaw– VTA straighten (it/him) as wood for s.o.
mîsah– VTI mend s.t.
mîsîwikamikw– NI outhouse, toilet
mîskoc IPC instead, in return, in exchange [*cf.* mêskoc]
mîskotônikê– VAI exchange things, trade things (e.g., horse, wagon) [*sic; cf.* mêskotôn– VTI]
mîstowân– NI beard [*sic:* -î-; *cf.* -îhi-]
mîstowê– VAI be bearded, wear a beard [*sic:* -î-; *cf.* -îhi-]
mîtâkwêwi– VAI ward (it/him) off [?*sic: stem, gloss*]
mîtos– NA poplar; tree
mohcihk IPC on the bare floor, on the bare ground
mohcihtak IPC on the bare floor, on the floor-boards
mosc-âsam– VTA simply provide food to s.o., supply food to s.o. without recompense
mosc-ôsîh– VTA prepare s.o. (e.g., soap) without instrument; make s.o. (e.g., soap) at home
mosc-ôsîhcikâtê– VII be made by hand, be home-made
mosc-ôsîhtâ– VAI prepare (it) without instrument; make (it) at home
mosci IPC simply, directly, without mediation; merely, without instrument; without recompense [*sic:* IPC]

mosci *IPV* simply, directly, without mediation; merely, without instrument; without recompense

mosci-kisîpêkinikê– *VAI* simply wash things, do one's laundry by hand

mosci-kîskipotâ– *VAI* simply cut (it) with a saw, cut (it) with a hand-saw

mosci-masinah– *VTI* simply write s.t., write s.t. down by hand

mosci-mêki– *VAI* simply give (her) in marriage

mosci-miy– *VTA* merely give (it/him) to s.o.

mosci-nôhâwaso– *VAI* simply breastfeed one's child, breastfeed one's child without further ado (e.g., sterilisation of bottles)

mosci-pâhpih– *VTA* merely laugh at s.o., merely deride s.o.

mosci-wêwêkin– *VTA* merely wrap s.o. up (e.g., an infant without moss)

moscicihcên– *VTI* scoop s.t. up with bare hands

moscikwâso– *VAI* sew by hand

moscikwât– *VTI* sew s.t. by hand

moscitôn *IPC* gratuitously by speech, without adding a gift or offering

mosciwâk *IPC* (*in negative constructions:*) not at all, not under any circumstances [*e.g.*, môy mosciwâk 'not on your life!'; *dial.* (LR)]

moscosos– *NA* calf [*diminutive*]

moscosw– *NA* cow [*diminutive*]

moskâcih– *VTA* bother s.o., trouble s.o., hurt s.o.

mosti-tôhtôsâpoy– *NI* mere milk, mere cow's milk [*i.e., rather than mother's milk; sic:* mosti]

mostohtê– *VAI* simply walk, move along without instrument, be on foot

mostohtêyâciho– *VAI* travel on foot

mostoso-wiyâs– *NI* beef

mostosw– *NA* cattle, cow

mostosw-âya *IPC* of a cow, in matters bovine

mostoswayân– NA   cow-hide

mow– VTA   eat s.o. (e.g., bread)

môcêyâpiskos– NI   little bottle [*diminutive*]

môcikan– VII   be fun

môcikêyihc– VTI   be excited about s.t. small; be a little excited [*diminutive*]

môcikêyiht– VTI   be happy about s.t., be excited about s.t.; be excited

môcikihcâsi– VAI   have some fun with (it); have a little fun [*diminutive*]

môcikihtâ– VAI   have fun with (it); have fun, have a good time [*e.g.,* nipahi-wâpani-môcikihtâ– 'make merry in a big way until dawn']

môcikipê– VAI   have fun with alcoholic drink, make merry with alcoholic drink

môh– VTA   make s.o. cry

môhcowi– VAI   be foolish, be stupid, be silly; be mad, be crazy

môhcw-âyâ– VAI   be foolish, be stupid, be silly; be mad, be crazy

môhcwahkamikisi– VAI   behave foolishly, do crazy things

môhcwêyim– VTA   consider s.o. stupid

môhkiciwanipêyâ– VII   be a spring, be a well

môhkomân– NI   knife

môhkomânis– NI   knife [*diminutive*]

mônah– VTI   dig for s.t.; dig roots

mônahaskwâkan– NI   digger, tool used to dig seneca-root

mônahaskwân– NI   digger, tool used to dig seneca-root

mônahaskwê– VAI   dig seneca-root

mônahikê– VAI   dig for things, dig

mônahipân– NI   source, well

mônâtihkê– VAI   dig around, dig a hole

môniyâhkâso– VAI   be like a White person, act White

môniyâs– NA   non-Indian, White person [*diminutive*]

môniyâs– NA (*man's name:*) Norman Fraser [*lit.* Little-Whiteman]

môniyâskwêw– NA White female, White woman

môniyâw– NA non-Indian, White person

môniyâw-âpacihcikan– NI White apparatus, White household appliance

môniyâw-âya IPC White things, White stuff [*sometimes pluralised as if* NI]

môniyâw-âyamihâwin– NI White religion; non-Catholic denomination [*sic; cf.* môniyâwi-ayamihâwin–]

môniyâw-âyisiyiniw– NA White person

môniyâw-îhtwâwin– NI White ritual, White custom

môniyâw-kiskêyihtamowin– NI White knowledge

môniyâw-kîkway PR something White, White things [*sic; cf.* môniyâwi-kîkway–]

môniyâw-ôhpiki– VAI grow up like a White person

môniyâwi-ayamahâwin– NI White religion; non-Catholic denomination [*sic; cf.* môniyâw-âyamihâwin–]

môniyâwi-cistêmâw– NA White tobacco, trade tobacco

môniyâwi-itwê– VAI say the White word, say the English word

môniyâwi-kîkway PR something White, White things [*sic; cf.* môniyâw-kîkway–]

môniyâwi-mêskanaw– NI White path, White road

môniyâwi-mîcisowikamikw– NI White restaurant

môniyâwi-wîhowin– NI White name, English name

môs-ôkimâw– NA game warden [*dial.* (LR)]

môsahkin– VTA gather s.o. up

môsahkin– VTI gather s.t. up

môsâpêwi– VAI be a bachelor, be unmarried, be single

môsih– VTA sense s.o., feel s.o. approaching, perceive s.o.'s presence

môsihtâ– VAI sense (it), feel (it) approaching, perceive (it)

môsiskwêw– NA single woman, widow

môsiskwêwi– VAI be a single woman, be a widow

môskipayi– VAI break out in a rash, erupt in sores (e.g., with thrush)

môsko-miywêyiht– VTI cry with joy about s.t.; be moved to tears of joy

môskom– VTA make s.o. cry by tears or speech

môskomo– VAI talk oneself into crying, cry while talking

môskwêyiht– VTI cry about s.t.

môso-pahkêkin– NI finished moose-hide

môso-wiyâs– NI moose-meat

môsopîway– NI moose-hair

môsosiniy– NI shell, bullet [*sic:* -o-; *cf.* môswasiniy–]

môsw– NA moose [*e.g.,* môswa (prox. sg., obv.)]

môswasiniy– NI shell, bullet [*sic:* -wa-; *cf.* môsosiniy–]

môswêkinw– NI moose-hide

môtêyâpiskw– NI bottle

môy êkâ êtokwê IPC without any doubt, of necessity [*usually with independent indicative*]

môy kakêtihk IPC a great many

môy misikiti– VAI be not big, be small

môy nânitaw IPC it is alright, there is nothing wrong with that [*predicative*]

môya IPC not [*cf.* namôya]

môyêyiht– VTI sense s.t.; suspect s.t.; realise s.t.

môyêyim– VTA sense s.o., suspect s.o.

mwayê IPV before [*sic:* IPV; *temporal conjunction; cf.* maywês, maywêsk, mwayês, pamwayês, pâmwayês; *dial.* (LR)]

mwayês IPC previously, before [*either as temporal conjunction or adverbially; cf.* maywês, maywêsk, mwayê, pamwayês, pâmwayês]

mwâc IPC no, not [*cf.* namwâc; *emphatic negator in independent and non-volitional conjunct constructions*]

mwâsi IPC (*in negative constructions:*) hardly ever, hardly any

mwâskosiwân– NI bulrush, edible reed [sic: mwâ–; cf. mâ–; ?sic: Typha spp., Scirpus spp.]

mwêhci IPC exactly; like

mwêsiskaw– VTA have chosen exactly the wrong time or place for s.o., just miss s.o.

mwêstas IPC later, subsequently

mwêstâcim– VTA bother s.o. by speech, wear s.o. out by speech

mwêstâcîhk– VTI bother s.t.; hang around a place

mwêstâcîhkaw– VTA bother s.o., annoy s.o., make a nuisance of oneself to s.o., be troublesome for s.o.

mwêstât– VTA be tired of s.o., be fed up with s.o.

mwêstâtahkamikisi– VAI be troublesome, behave annoyingly

mwêstâtwêwêm– VTA speak about s.o. as troublesome, complain about s.o. being a nuisance

mwêstâtwêwit– VTI make troublesome noise, make a nuisance of oneself by being noisy

nac IPC hm [exclamatory, indicating deliberation]

nah IPC nonsense! no such thing! [exclamatory, indicating deprecation]

nahah– VTA put s.o. away, store s.o. (e.g., duck)

nahapi– VAI sit down in one's place, be properly seated

nahascikê– VAI put things away, store things

nahastâ– VAI put (it) in its place, put (it) away; store (it)

nahâpi– VAI have one's eyes focussed, have acute vision

nahâwaso– VAI have one's child in the proper place, carry one's child with one

nahêyiht– VTI be satisfied with s.t.; have peace of mind

nahêyihtamih– VTA cause s.o. to be satisfied with (it/him); grant s.o. peace of mind

nahiht– VTI hear s.t. sharply; have acute hearing

nahin– VTA bury s.o., hold a funeral for s.o.

nahipayi– VII be convenient, fall into place

nahiyikohk IPC to the proper degree, to the proper extent, just enough, just right, evenly, fittingly, appropriately

nahî– VAI be adept at (it), be good at (it); be competent, be an expert

nahkawêwin– NI speaking Saulteaux, the Saulteaux language

nahkawiyiniw– NA Saulteaux

nakacih– VTA be familiar with s.o.

nakacihtâ– VAI be familiar with doing (it), be practised at (it)

nakacipah– VTA run away from s.o.

nakamo– VAI sing, sing a ritual song [sic; cf. nikamo–]

nakasiwê– VAI leave people behind, die

nakat– VTA leave s.o. behind; leave s.o. alone (e.g., helpless); abandon s.o. (e.g., child); leave s.o. behind in death, die leaving s.o. behind

nakat– VTI leave s.t. behind

nakatahw– VTA leave s.o. behind in departing by boat or airplane

nakatamaw– VTA leave (it/him) behind for s.o., bequeathe (it/him) to s.o.

nakataskê– VAI leave the earth behind, depart the world, die

nakayâh– VTA get s.o. accustomed to something, break s.o. (e.g., horse), tame s.o., train s.o.

nakayâsk– VTI be accustomed to s.t., be comfortable with s.t., be familiar with s.t.

nakayâskaw– VTA be accustomed to s.o., be comfortable with s.o., be familiar with s.o.

nakân– VTA stop s.o.

nakâwâskwêsin– VAI be brought to a stop by hitting a tree

nakê IPC a little off

nakin– VTA stop s.o., make s.o. stop; turn s.o. off (e.g., kitchen-stove)

nakipicikê– VAI stop one's team

nakiskamohtatamaw– VTA take (it/him) to meet s.o., meet s.o. with (it/him); introduce (it/him) to s.o.

nakiskaw– VTA encounter s.o., meet s.o.

nakî– VAI stop, come to a stop

nakwâso– VAI be snared, be stopped by a snare

nakwât– VTA snare s.o.

nam êskwa IPC not yet [*cf.* mêskwa; cêskwa, êskwa]

nama IPC not [*negator in nominal phrases*]

nama cî IPC is it not the case [*predicative; cf.* ma cî, namôya cî]

nama kîkway PR nothing; not at all; there is none [*also predicative*]

nama mayaw IPC not immediately, later; too late

nama wîhkâc IPC never

namahtinihk IPC on the left hand, to the left

namatakon– VII be non-existent, be absent; have disappeared, be no longer in existence

namatê– VAI be non-existent, be absent; have disappeared, be no longer in existence

namêkosis– NA little trout [*diminutive; dial.* (LR)]

namêstikw– NA smoked fish

namôy âhpô IPC not even

namôy âpisis IPC not a little, quite a lot

namôya IPC not; no [*cf.* môya; *negator in independent and non-volitional conjunct constructions*]

namôya cî IPC is it not the case [*predicative; cf.* nama cî, ma cî]

namôya kakêtihk IPC a great many

namôya nânitaw IPC it is alright [*predicative*]

namwâ IPC not; no [*sic; cf.* namwâc; *emphatic negator in independent and non-volitional conjunct constructions*]

namwâc IPC not; no [*cf.* namwâ; *emphatic negator in independent and non-volitional conjunct constructions*]

nanahiht– VTI listen well to s.t.; obey s.t.

nanahihtaw– VTA listen well to s.o.; obey s.o.

nanamaci– VAI shiver with cold

nanayêhtâwipayiwin– NI misfortune, breakdown [*reduplicated*]

nanâcohkokwâcês– NI patchwork quilt [*diminutive*]

nanânis IPC variously, in bits and pieces, here and there

nanânistipit– VTA tear s.o. into bits and pieces; fragment s.o. (e.g., group of people), divide s.o. (e.g., community) against one another

nanânistiwêpahw– VTA shoot s.o. (e.g., rock) into bits and pieces, shatter s.o. (e.g., rock) into pieces

nanâskom– VTA be grateful to s.o., give thanks to s.o.

nanâskomo– VAI be grateful, give thanks

nanâskot– VTI be grateful for s.t., give thanks for s.t.

nanâtawâpi– VAI look around

nanâtawâpôhkân– NI medicinal draught

nanâtawih– VTA treat s.o., doctor s.o.; heal s.o., cure s.o.

nanâtawihitowin– NI doctoring one another; healing one another, curing one another

nanâtawihiwê– VAI treat people, doctor people; heal people, cure people

nanâtawihwâkê– VAI doctor oneself with (it), use (it) to heal oneself, use (it) medicinally

nanâtohk IPC variously, of various kinds

nanâtohk isi IPC in various ways, in various directions

nanâtohkokwâso– VAI sew various things; sew a patchwork blanket

nanâtohkôskân IPC various kinds, all kinds of things

naniwacihito– VAI tease one another, provoke one another

naniwêyatwê– VAI joke, tell a joke

napakaskisin– NI flat moccasin

napakâ– VII be flat

napakihtakohkâso– VAI have the appearance of boards, be made of boards

napakihtakw– *NI* flat lumber, board, floor-board

napakikamikos– *NI* little house made of lumber or boards [*diminutive*]

napakikamikw– *NI* house made of lumber or boards; flat-top shack

napakin– *VTI* flatten s.t. by hand

napakis– *VTI* cut s.t. into flat pieces, cut s.t. (e.g., meat) into chops

napatâkw– *NI* potato [*usually plural*]

napatê *IPC* on one side

napwênis– *NA* small frying-pan [*diminutive*]

naskom– *VTA* respond to s.o. with (it/him), answer s.o.'s prayer with (it/him)

naskomo– *VAI* respond, make a verbal response

naskot– *VTI* respond to s.t.; swear upon s.t. in response

naskwahamaw– *VTA* respond to s.o.; sing in response to s.o.

naskwahamâkê– *VAI* respond; sing in response, sing one's response

naskwên– *VTA* collect s.o. while moving, pick s.o. up on one's way

naskwêwasim– *VTA* speak to s.o. in response, respond to s.o. by speech; answer back to s.o., respond to s.o. (e.g., inappropriately)

naskwêwasimo– *VAI* speak in response, respond by speech

naspâpan *IPC* at daybreak, before sunrise

natahipayiho– *VAI* move upriver, spawn (e.g., fish)

naton– *VTI* look for s.t., seek s.t., search for s.t. [*sic; cf.* niton–]

nawac *IPC* by comparison; more, better, rather

nawac piko *IPC* sort of, kind of, approximately; more or less; even a little

nawac wâhyaw *IPC* quite far

nawac wîpac *IPC* earlier

nawacî– *VAI* roast (it), roast (it) over an open fire; roast one's food

nawakapi– *VAI* sit bent down, sit huddled over

nawakipayiho– *VAI* throw oneself down, duck down

nawakiskwêsimo– *VAI* dance with one's head down

nawasôn– *VTA* choose s.o.

nawasôn– *VTI* choose s.t.

nawasônamaw– *VTA* choose (it/him) for s.o.; make a choice for s.o.

nawasônikê– *VAI* choose, make a choice

nawaswât– *VTA* pursue s.o., chase after s.o.

nawaswât– *VTI* pursue s.t., chase after s.t.

nawaswê– *VAI* give chase, be in pursuit

nawatahikê– *VAI* shoot (it/him) in flight, shoot ducks as they fly

nawatahw– *VTA* shoot s.o. in flight

nayahcikan– *NI* bundle, sacred bundle, spirit-bundle (e.g., in ghost-dance) [*sic; cf.* nayôhcikan–]

nayahcikê– *VAI* carry things on one's back, carry a load; carry a backpack [*sic; cf.* nayôhcikê–]

nayaht– *VTI* carry s.t. on one's back [*sic; cf.* nayôht–]

nayahto– *VAI* carry one another on one's back; ride up on one another (e.g., beads)

nayawaciki– *VAI* grow up to reach various ages, be variously grown up [*usually plural*]

nayawâs *IPC* after a long wait [*?sic: stem, gloss*]

nayêhtâw-âyâ– *VAI* be troubled, have problems (e.g., health problems)

nayêhtâwan– *VII* be difficult, be troublesome

nayêhtâwêyim– *VTA* find s.o. difficult, find s.o. troublesome

nayêhtâwiki– *VAI* have experienced a troubled birth, be born with a birth defect [*?sic: gloss*]

nayêhtâwipayi– *VAI* run into difficulties, experience trouble

nayêhtâwipayin– *VII* there is trouble, there are problems

nayêstaw *IPC* only, exclusively; it is only that [*often predicative*]

nayêwac *IPC* in mid-air

nayôhcikan– *NI* bundle, sacred bundle, spirit-bundle (e.g., in ghost-dance) [*sic; cf.* nayahcikan–]

nayôhcikê– *VAI* carry things on one's back, carry a load; carry a backpack [*sic; cf.* nayahcikê–]

nayôht– *VTI* carry s.t. on one's back [*sic; cf.* nayaht–]

nayôm– *VTA* carry s.o. on one's back

nâ *IPC* not so! [*exclamatory, indicating disagreement*]

nâcakwêsi– *VAI* check one's small snares (e.g., for rabbits) [*diminutive*]

nâcikâpawist– *VTI* seek to shift one's position to s.t. [*sic:* -i-]

nâcikâtê– *VII* be fetched

nâcimihtê– *VAI* fetch firewood, go for firewood

nâcinêhamaw– *VTA* obtain (it/him) from s.o. by payment, seek to buy medicine from s.o.

nâcinêhikê– *VAI* obtain things by payment, seek to buy medicine

nâcipah– *VTA* run to fetch s.o., make a run for s.o.

nâcipahiwê– *VAI* run to fetch things, make a run for things

nâcitâpê– *VAI* go and drag (it) back, fetch (it) by cart [*sic; cf.* nâtitâpê–]

nâciwanihikanê– *VAI* fetch game from traps, check one's traps

nâciyôscikê– *VAI* sneak up to people

nâcowêw– *NA* (man's name:) Pierre Morin [*cf.* onâcowêsis–]

nâh *IPC* fie! [*exclamatory, indicating disapproval or disgust*]

nâh-nêwi– *VAI* be four each

nâh-nêwo *IPC* four each

nâha *PR* that one yonder [*demonstrative, e.g.,* nâha, nêki, nêhi; nêma, nêhi]

nâhnâskon– *VTA* pull s.o. in (on a rope) [*sic:* -hn-; *reduplicated*]

nâkasohtamohkâso– *VAI* pretend to pay attention

nâkatawâpam– VTA pay attention in looking at s.o., observe s.o. [*sic; cf.* nâkatâpam–, nâkatowâpaht– VTI]

nâkatawêyim– VTA watch s.o., keep one's mind trained on s.o.

nâkatâpam– VTA notice s.o. by sight [*sic; cf.* nâkatawâpam–, nâkatowâpaht– VTI]

nâkatêyiht– VTI pay attention to s.o., attend to s.o., look after s.o.

nâkatowâpaht– VTI pay attention in looking at s.t., observe s.t. [*sic; cf.* nâkatawâpam– VTA, nâkatâpam– VTA]

nâkatôhkâtito– VAI take notice of one another, watch over one another, keep a careful eye on one another

nâkatôhkê– VAI take notice, pay attention, be observant; attend to people, watch over people

nânapâcih– VTA fix s.o. up, mend s.o. (e.g., pants)

nânapâcihiso– VAI fix oneself up; doctor oneself

nânapâcihtâ– VAI fix (it) up, mend (it)

nânapêc IPC late, at the last moment, barely in time (e.g., when it should have been done previously); (*in negative constructions:*) too late

nânapwahpiso– VAI have one's forelegs tied together (e.g., horse), be hobbled

nânâmiskwêyi– VAI nod one's head

nânâspicipayi– VAI have a coughing fit

nânitaw IPC simply; (*with numbers:*) roughly, approximately; variously; something, at some undetermined place; (*in negative constructions:*) not anything; something bad, anything bad; somewhere [*usually with pejorative presupposition*]

nânitaw IPV (*in negative constructions:*) not any [*sic:* IPV]

nânitaw isi IPC in some way, in any way; in various ways; in a random direction [*usually with pejorative presupposition*]

nânitaw ispayi– VII take place as an unwelcome event

nânitaw itahkamikisi– VAI behave reprehensibly, be up to something

nânitaw itamahciho– *VAI* feel unwell

nânitaw itêyiht– *VTI* worry about s.t., fret about s.t.; assign blame for s.t.; (*especially in negative constructions:*) not bear a grudge, be forgiving

nânitaw itêyim– *VTA* hold (it) against s.o.; (*especially in negative constructions:*) not bear a grudge against s.o., forgive s.o.

nâpêhkâso– *VAI* be a brave

nâpêsis– *NA* boy, little boy, male infant

nâpêsisiwi– *VAI* be a small boy

nâpêw– *NA* man, male, adult male

nâpêw-âya *IPC* men's things, men's stuff, men's clothing [*sometimes pluralised as if* NI]

nâpêwasikan– *NA* men's socks

nâpêwatoskê– *VAI* work like a man, do man's work

nâpêwi– *VAI* be a man, be male

nâpêwinâkosi– *VAI* look like a man; be of human appearance

nâpêwisîh– *VTA* dress s.o. as a boy, dress s.o. as a male

nâpêwisîho– *VAI* be dressed as a man, dress as a male

nâsipê– *VAI* go towards the water [*dial.* (LR)]

nâsipêpahtâ– *VAI* run towards the water [*dial.* (LR)]

nâsipêskanaw– *NI* path towards the water [*dial.* (LR)]

nâsipêtimihk *IPC* towards the water, by the water's edge [*dial.* (LR)]

nât– *VTA* fetch s.o.

nât– *VTI* fetch s.t.

nâtahapê– *VAI* check one's nets

nâtahisipê– *VAI* fetch ducks (e.g., as a dog)

nâtahw– *VTA* fetch s.o. by boat or airplane; pick s.o. up (e.g., as an airplane)

nâtakâm *IPC* in the north, to the north

nâtakâsin– *VTI* guide s.t. (e.g., boat) to shore

nâtakwê– *VAI* check one's snares

nâtamaw– *VTA* fetch (it/him) for s.o.; take up for s.o.

nâtamawât– *VTI* seek to obtain s.t. for (it/him); take s.t. up for (it/him)

nâtamâso– *VAI* fetch (it/him) for oneself

nâtamâwaso– *VAI* take up for one's children

nâtaskosiwê– *VAI* fetch hay

nâtâhtawât– *VTA* climb up (e.g., a tree) to fetch s.o.

nâtâmost– *VTI* flee to s.t., turn to s.t. for help, seek refuge in s.t.

nâtâmotot– *VTI* flee to s.t., turn to s.t. for help, seek refuge in s.t.

nâtâmototaw– *VTA* flee to s.o., turn to s.o. for help, seek refuge with s.o.

nâtâwatâ– *VAI* fetch (it) by hauling

nâtitâpê– *VAI* go and drag (it) back, fetch (it) by cart [*cf.* nâcitâpê–]

nâtitisahikê– *VAI* send for things, place an order from a catalogue

nâtitisahikêwasinahikan– *NI* mail-order catalogue

nâtitisahw– *VTA* go to fetch s.o. (e.g., horses); send for s.o., order s.o. (e.g., chickens) by catalogue

nâtôpê– *VAI* go to fetch water; go for a drink; go for alcoholic drink

nâtwâh– *VTI* split s.t., chop s.t. apart

nâtwân– *VTI* split s.t. apart, break s.t. off

nâtwâpayi– *VII* split off (e.g., branch), break off

nâtwâpit– *VTI* split s.t. (e.g., branch) off by pulling, break s.t. off

nâtwâwêpah– *VTI* split s.t. (e.g., branch) off and throw it down, break s.t. off and throw it down

nâway *IPC* behind, at the rear; in the past

nêhiyaw– *NA* Cree; Indian

nêhiyaw– *NA* (*woman's name:*) Glecia Bear [*lit.* Cree]

nêhiyaw-âyisiyiniw– *NA* Cree person; Indian person [*sic; cf.* nêhiyawayisiyiniw–]

nêhiyaw-îhtwâwin– NI the Cree way, Cree culture; Indian culture [*sic:* -î-; *cf.* nêhiyawihtwâwin–]
nêhiyaw-îsiyîhkâtê– VII have a Cree name
nêhiyaw-kîkway PR something Cree, Cree things
nêhiyaw-masinîwin– NI Cree design, Cree motif
nêhiyaw-maskihkiy– NI Cree medicine; Indian medicine
nêhiyaw-mihkw– NI Cree blood; Indian blood [*e.g.*, nêhiyaw-mihko (sg.)]
nêhiyaw-nitotamâwin– NI Cree supplication, the Cree way of supplication
nêhiyawasinahikan– NI Cree book; Cree bible [*cf.* nêhiyawi-masinahikan–]
nêhiyawaskamikâ– VII be Cree land, be Cree terrain; be Indian land, be Indian terrain
nêhiyawaskîwin– VII be Cree land, be Cree territory; be Indian land, be Indian territory
nêhiyawastê– VII be written in Cree; be written in syllabics
nêhiyawayisiyiniw– NA Cree person; Indian person [*sic:* -a-; *cf.* nêhiyaw-âyisiyiniw–]
nêhiyawê– VAI speak Cree
nêhiyawêmototaw– VTA speak Cree to s.o. [*sic; cf.* nêhiyawimototaw–]
nêhiyawêwin– NI speaking Cree, the Cree language
nêhiyawi IPN Cree; Indian
nêhiyawi IPV Cree; Indian
nêhiyawi-kiskinohamâtowi-kakêskihkêmowikamikw– NI (*name:*) Saskatchewan Indian Cultural College [*lit.* counselling building for Cree or Indian teaching]
nêhiyawi-masinahikan– NI Cree book; Cree bible [*sic; cf.* nêhiyawasinahikan–]
nêhiyawi-maskihkiy– NI Cree medicine; Indian medicine
nêhiyawi-maskihkîwiskwêw– NA Cree midwife; Indian midwife
nêhiyawi-mêskanaw– NI Cree path, Cree road; Indian path, Indian road

nêhiyawi-nakamo– *VAI* sing hymns in Cree

nêhiyawi-pîkiskwê– *VAI* speak Cree, use Cree words

nêhiyawi-sîwîhtâkan– *NI* Cree salt; Indian salt

nêhiyawi-wîh– *VTA* use s.o.'s Cree name, call s.o. by a Cree name

nêhiyawi-wîhowin– *NI* Cree name; Indian name

nêhiyawi-wîht– *VTI* use the Cree name of s.t., call s.t. by a Cree name

nêhiyawi-wîhtamawâkan– *NI* Cree etymology; Cree teaching

nêhiyawihtwâwin– *NI* the Cree way, Cree culture; Indian culture [*sic:* -i-; *cf.* nêhiyaw-îhtwâwin–]

nêhiyawimototaw– *VTA* speak Cree to s.o. [*sic; cf.* nêhiyawêmototaw–]

nêhiyawisîhcikêwin– *NI* the Cree way, Cree culture; Indian culture [*sic; cf.* nêhiyawîhcikêwin–]

nêhiyawiskwêw– *NA* Cree woman; Indian woman [*sic:* -i-]

nêhiyawiyîhkâso– *VAI* have a Cree name

nêhiyawiyîhkât– *VTA* give s.o. a Cree name

nêhiyawiyîhkât– *VTI* give s.t. a Cree name

nêhiyawiyîhkâtê– *VII* be a Cree name

nêhiyawîhcikêwin– *NI* the Cree way, Cree culture; Indian culture [*sic; cf.* nêhiyawisîhcikêwin–]

nêhiyâsis– *NA* young Cree; young Indian

nêhiyâwi– *VAI* be Cree; be an Indian

nêhiyâwiwin– *NI* being Cree, Cree identity, Creeness

nêhpêmapi– *VAI* be at the ready, sit at the ready

nêmatowahk *IPC* of that kind yonder

nêmitanaw *IPC* forty [*sic; cf.* nêwo]

nêpêwih– *VTA* shame s.o., put s.o. to shame

nêpêwisi– *VAI* be bashful, be shy; be ashamed, be ashamed of oneself

nêpêwisîst– *VTI* be ashamed of s.t.

nêpêwisîstaw– VTA   be bashful before s.o., be shy towards s.o.

nêscâmocakosihk   IPC   at the bow (of a small boat) [*?sic: stem; locative; diminutive; dial.* (LR)]

nêsowan– VII   be weak (e.g., eyes)

nêsowâtisi– VAI   be weak, have a weak constitution

nêsowisi– VAI   be weak, be exhausted, be near death

nêstosi– VAI   be tired

nêstosiwin– NI   being tired

nêstwâso– VAI   be tired by the sun's heat, be exhausted by hot weather

nêta   IPC   over there, over yonder

nêtê   IPC   over there, over yonder; in that direction

nêw-âskiy   IPC   four years, for four years

nêwâw   IPC   four times

nêwi– VAI   be four in number

nêwo   IPC   four

nêwo-kîsikâ– VII   be four days, be the fourth day; be Thursday

nêwo-kîsikâw   IPC   four days, for four days

nêwo-tipiskâ– VII   be four nights, be the fourth night

nêwosâp   IPC   fourteen

nêyâ– VII   be a point of land

nêyâhk   INM   (*place-name*) [*locative; lit.* at the point of land]

nihtâ   IPV   good at, doing much of, competent, practised, experienced

nihtâ-âhkosi– VAI   fall sick easily, be prone to illness

nihtâwâcimo– VAI   be a good storyteller, tell stories expertly

nihtâwêyiht– VTI   be good at thinking of s.t.; be knowledgeable; be innovative

nihtâwiki– VAI   be born

nihtâwikih– VTA   give birth to s.o., be delivered of s.o.

nihtâwikihâwaso– VAI   give birth to one's child, bring forth a child, bring forth a young one (of the species)

nihtâwikihtâ– *VAI* give birth to (it), bring (it) forth
nihtâwikin– *VII* grow forth (e.g., plant), come forth
nihtâwikinâwaso– *VAI* give birth to one's child, bring forth a child, bring forth a young one (of the species)
nihtâwikîst– *VTI* populate s.t. (e.g., the earth) [*sic:* -î-]
nihtâwikwâso– *VAI* be good at sewing, sew expertly, be an experienced seamstress; do fancy sewing
nihtâwikwâsowin– *NI* fancy sewing
nihtâwikwât– *VTI* be good at sewing s.t., sew s.t. expertly
nihtâwiminakinikê– *VAI* be good at sewing on beads
nihtâwisimo– *VAI* be good at dancing, be an expert dancer
nihtâwisîhcikê– *VAI* be good at doing things, make beautiful things [*sic; cf.* nihtâwîhcikê–]
nihtâwitêpo– *VAI* be good at cooking, be an expert cook
nihtâwîhcikê– *VAI* be good at doing things, make beautiful things [*sic; cf.* nihtâwisîhcikê–]
nihtiy– *NI* tea
nikamo– *VAI* sing, sing a ritual song [*cf.* nakamo–]
nikamon– *NI* song, ritual song
nikamosi– *VAI* sing a little song [*diminutive*]
nikikomin– *NI* blueberry (of a certain variety) [*?sic: Vaccinium spp.*]
nikohtât– *VTI* chop s.t. for firewood
nikohtê– *VAI* collect firewood, chop firewood
nikohtêstamâso– *VAI* make firewood for oneself, make one's own firewood
nikohtêwin– *NI* making firewood
nikotwâsik *IPC* six
nikotwâsik-askiy *IPC* six years, for six years
nikotwâsik-tipahamâtowin– *NI* Treaty Number Six, Treaty Six
nikotwâsiko-kîsikâ– *VII* be six days, be the sixth day; be Saturday
nikotwâsikomitanaw *IPC* sixty [*sic; cf.* nikotwâsomitanaw]

nikotwâsomitanaw *IPC* sixty

nikotwâsomitanaw-askiy *IPC* sixty years, for sixty years

nikotwâsosâp *IPC* sixteen

nikotwâw *IPC* either one, anyone

nipah– *VTA* kill s.o.

nipahâhkatoso– *VAI* starve to death, die from starvation; (*fig.*) be terribly hungry

nipahâhkwan– *VII* be terribly strong, be terribly powerful, hurt terribly

nipahâpâkwê– *VAI* die of thirst; (*fig.*) be terribly thirsty

nipahcikê– *VAI* kill things (e.g., game), make a kill

nipahi *IPV* deadly, terribly, greatly [*e.g.,* nipahi-kâh-kinwês 'a very long time'; nipahi-nôhtêsin– 'be absolutely exhausted'; nipahi-wîsakêyiht– 'have terrible pains'; nipahi-wâpani-môcikihtâ– 'make merry in a big way until dawn']

nipahikanê– *VAI* be terribly lazy, be bone-lazy

nipahipahtâ– *VAI* run to excess, collapse from running

nipahisin– *VAI* get killed in a car accident

nipahiso– *VAI* kill oneself, commit suicide

nipahtamaw– *VTA* kill (it/him) for s.o., make a kill for s.o.

nipahtamâso– *VAI* kill (it/him) for oneself, make a kill for oneself

nipahtâ– *VAI* kill (it) (e.g., game), make a kill

nipahtâkê– *VAI* kill people

nipâ– *VAI* sleep, be asleep

nipâkwêsimo– *VAI* attend a sundance, participate in a sundance, dance the sundance

nipâkwêsimowikamikw– *NI* sundance lodge, sundance ceremony

nipâkwêsimowin– *NI* sundance

nipâkwêsimowinihkê– *VAI* hold a sundance

nipâsi– *VAI* sleep a little, take a nap [*diminutive*]

nipâwin– *NI* sleeping, sleep

nipêpayi– VAI fall asleep
nipêwikamikw– NI bedroom
nipêwin– NI bed
nipêwinis– NI bed, little bed [*diminutive*]
nipi– VAI die; be dead
nipiskât– VTA doctor s.o. by insufflation or aspiration
nipiy kâ-pitihkwêk INM (*place-name*) [*lit.* where the water thunders; *most likely in the vicinity of Fort Carlton (Saskatchewan)*]
nipiy– NI water
nipîmakan– VII die; be dead [*cf.* nipômakan–]
nipîs– NI a little water, a small amount of water [*diminutive*]
nipômakan– VII die; be dead [*cf.* nipîmakan–]
nisihkâc IPC slowly, gradually
nisitawêyihcikâtê– VII be recognised
nisitawêyiht– VTI recognise s.t., know s.t.
nisitawêyim– VTA recognise s.o., know s.o.
nisitawin– VTI recognise s.t.
nisitoht– VTI understand s.t.
nisitohtamohtâ– VAI cause (it) to be understood, make (it) understood
nisitohtamôh– VTA make s.o. understand (it/him)
nisitohtamôhkâso– VAI pretend to understand (it/him)
nisitohtaw– VTA understand s.o.
nisitohtâto– VAI understand one another
nisk– NA goose [*e.g.*, niska (prox. sg., obv.)]
nistam IPC first, at first, for the first time, initially, originally
nistamêmâkan– NA the first one, the original one [*sic:* NA]
nisti– VAI be three in number
nistin– VII be three in number
nisto IPC three
nisto-aya IPC three sets [*sic:* -o-]
nisto-kîsikâw IPC three days, for three days

nistomitanaw *IPC* thirty

nistopiponwê– *VAI* be three years old

nistosâp *IPC* thirteen

nistôskwêwê– *VAI* have three wives

nistw-âskiy *IPC* three years, for three years

nistwapihkât– *VTI* braid s.t. in three

nistwâw *IPC* three times

nitaka *IPC* it is a good thing, by a narrow escape [*predicative; usually with the emphatic enclitic* oti; *e.g.,* nitak ôti]

nitaw-âyamihâ– *VAI* (*fig.*) go on a pilgrimage

nitawastimwê– *VAI* look for one's horses, search for one's horses

nitawâc *IPC* despite all, in spite of it all

nitawâpahkê– *VAI* watch things, observe people

nitawâpaht– *VTI* go to see s.t., observe s.t., check s.t. out

nitawâpam– *VTA* go to see s.o., go to visit s.o.

nitawâpaso– *VAI* smell around, sniff about

nitawâpênaw– *VTA* check up on s.o.

nitawâpênikê– *VAI* check up on people, check up on things

nitawâwê– *VAI* go looking for eggs, go to collect eggs

nitawêyihcikâtê– *VII* be wanted, be wished for

nitawêyiht– *VTI* want s.t.

nitawêyihtamaw– *VTA* want (it/him) for s.o., want (it/him) from s.o.

nitawêyim– *VTA* want s.o., want (it/him) of s.o.

nitawi *IPV* go to, go and

nitâhtâm– *VTA* borrow (it/him) from s.o.

nitâmiso– *VAI* look for berries, go berry-picking

nitihkomât– *VTA* pick lice off s.o., louse s.o.

nitoht– *VTI* listen to s.t.

nitohtaw– *VTA* listen to s.o.

nitohtâkowisi– *VAI* be heard by the powers, be listened to by the powers

nitom– VTA call s.o., beckon to s.o., invite s.o.
niton– VTI look for s.t., seek s.t., search for s.t. [*cf.* naton–]
nitonaw– VTA look for s.o., seek s.o. (e.g., tree), search for s.o.
nitonikâtê– VII be looked for, be searched for
nitonikê– VAI take a look, search for things, make a search
nitopahtwâ– VAI search for (it/him)
nitot– VTI look for s.t.; order s.t. (e.g., in a restaurant)
nitotamaw– VTA ask s.o. for (it/him)
nitotamâ– VAI ask for (it/him) (e.g., sugar), make a request for (it), pray for (it); make a request
nitotamâkêstamaw– VTA make a request for s.o., pray on s.o.'s behalf, ask for (it/him) on s.o.'s behalf
nitotamâwin– NI request [*sc. 'agent-centred' noun; e.g.,* kinitotamâwin 'request made by you']
nitôsk– VTI seek s.t.; make a request for s.t. (e.g., medicine)
nitôskamaw– VTA seek (it/him) of s.o., make a request for (it/him) of s.o.
niya PR I
niyanân PR we (excl.)
niyâ IPC go! [*admonitory*]
niyâk IPC in the future
niyânan IPC five
niyânan-kîsikâw IPC five days, for five days
niyânani– VAI be five in number
niyânano-kîsikâ– VII be the fifth day; be Friday
niyânanomitanaw IPC fifty
niyânanosâp IPC fifteen
niyânanwâpisk IPC five dollars
nîhc-âyihk IPC down, downward; below; down the hill
nîhci IPC down, downward
nîhcipayi– VAI come down, move down, fall down
nîhcipayiho– VAI jump down, jump off (e.g., vehicle)

nîhcipicikâtê– *VII* be taken down (e.g., from a shelf), be chosen for purchase (e.g., in self-service store)

nîhcipit– *VTA* pull s.o. down, drag s.o. down

nîhciwêpin– *VTI* throw s.t. down

nîhtakocin– *VAI* descend from high up, fall down (e.g., star)

nîhtakosî– *VAI* get down, get off (e.g., vehicle)

nîhtâhtawî– *VAI* climb down (e.g., a tree)

nîhtâhtawîpahtâ– *VAI* climb down (e.g., a tree) at a run

nîhtin– *VTI* take s.t. down, throw s.t. down, unload s.t.

nîkân *IPC* first, at the head, in front, in the lead; as a first step; in future

nîkânakim– *VTA* count s.o. in first position, hold s.o. (e.g., tobacco) to be the prime element

nîkânapi– *VAI* be at the head, be in the lead, be in charge; hold the office of director

nîkâni– *VAI* be at the head, be in the lead, take precedence (e.g., tobacco); be the prime element [*sic: stem-final* -i-; *cf.* nîkânî–]

nîkâninikâso– *VAI* take precedence, rank first; be the prime element [*sic*]

nîkânist– *VTI* be at the head of s.t., lead s.t. [*sic:* -i-; *cf.* nîkânîst–]

nîkâniwi– *VII* be ahead, be the future; lie in the future [*sic:* -i-]

nîkânî– *VAI* be a leader [*sic; cf.* nîkâni–]

nîkânîh– *VTA* place s.o. (e.g., tobacco) at the head, place s.o. in the lead

nîkânîmakan– *VII* be in the lead, take precedence

nîkânîst– *VTI* be at the head of s.t., lead s.t. [*sic:* -î-; *cf.* nîkânist–]

nîkânîstamaw– *VTA* be in the lead of s.o., be at the head of s.o., be a leader amongst s.o.

nîkânohk *IPC* in the lead position

nîkânohtatâ– *VAI* be in the lead with (it), carry (it) in the lead

nîkânohtê– VAI walk ahead, walk in the lead

nîkânohtêmakan– VII be in the lead, proceed in the lead position

nîmâ– VAI take provisions; take a packed lunch

nîmâh– VTA make s.o. take provisions; add (it) to s.o.'s packed lunch

nîmâsi– VAI take some provisions; take some packed lunch [*diminutive*]

nîmâskwê– VAI carry a weapon; carry a gun

nîmâwin– NI provisions; packed lunch

nîmâwinihkê– VAI arrange provisions; prepare a packed lunch

nîmâwiwat– NI box for provisions; lunch-box

nîmih– VTA make s.o. (e.g., doll) dance

nîmihito– VAI dance with one another, dance; dance a (secular) dance; dance as prairie-chicken; move about in a dancing motion, dance (e.g., northern lights)

nîmihitowikamikw– NI dance lodge, dance ceremony

nîmihitowin– NI dance

nîmihitowinihkê– VAI hold a dance, hold a dance ceremony; give a dance, organise a (secular) dance

nîmihitôh– VTA make s.o. (e.g., dolls) dance with one another

nîmihtâ– VAI make (it) dance (e.g., spirit-bundle in ghost-dance)

nîmin– VTI hold s.t. aloft, offer s.t. up

nîminamaw– VTA hold (it/him) aloft for s.o., offer (it/him) up for s.o.

nîminikê– VAI hold things aloft, offer things up

nîpawi– VAI stand, stand up, stand upright, stand fast

nîpawipayiho– VAI stand up suddenly

nîpawistamaw– VTA stand up for s.o., be a witness (e.g., at wedding) for s.o.

nîpâ IPV in the dark of the night

nîpâ-ayamihâ– *VAI* celebrate midnight mass (e.g., at Christmas)

nîpâ-tipisk *IPC* in the dark of the night, in the middle of the night

nîpâhtâ– *VAI* stay out until late in the night

nîpêpi– *VAI* sit up late at night with (her/him) (e.g., someone near death); hold a wake, take part in a wake

nîpêpîstaw– *VTA* sit up late at night with s.o.; sit at s.o.'s bedside, sit with s.o. near death; sit at a wake for s.o., hold a wake for s.o.

nîpin– *VII* be summer

nîpisiy– *NI* willow, willow bush; willow branch

nîpisîhkopâw– *NI* stand of willows, willow patch

nîpisîhtakw– *NI* willow piece, willow trunk

nîpisîs– *NI* willow branch, willow switch; little willow [*diminutive*]

nîpitêh– *VTA* place s.o. in a row, place s.o. abreast, place s.o. in a line

nîpitêkotâ– *VAI* hang (it) up in a row, hang (it) up in a line

nîpitêpi– *VAI* sit in a row, sit abreast

nîpiy– *NI* leaf; leafy branch

nîsi– *VAI* be two in number, be two together

nîso *IPC* two

nîso *IPV* two, as two, two together [*e.g.,* nîso-mâcî– *VAI* 'hunt together as two']

nîso-askiy *IPC* two years, for two years [*sic:* -o-; *cf.* nîsw-âskiy]

nîso-kîkway *PR* two things

nîso-kîsikâw *IPC* two days, for two days

nîso-sôniyâs *IPC* fifty cents

nîso-tipahikan *IPC* two hours, for two hours

nîso-tipiskâ– *VII* be two nights, be the second night

nîso-tipiskâw *IPC* two nights, for two nights

nîsokâtê– *VAI* have two legs, be two-legged

nîsonito– VAI dance two-and-two with one another, dance in pairs

nîsopîwâpiskw– NI double rail, railway track

nîsosâp IPC twelve

nîsosimo– VAI dance as two; dance a White dance, dance a jig

nîsotâpânâsk IPC two sleighs, two loads

nîsowê– VAI speak as two at once

nîsôcêsis– NA twin [*diminutive*]

nîsôhkamâto– VAI work together at (it/him) as two

nîsôhkiniskê– VAI use two hands, use both hands [*dial.* (LR)]

nîsôskwêwê– VAI have two wives

nîsta PR I, too; I by contrast; I myself

nîstanaw IPC twenty

nîstanaw-askiy IPC twenty years, for twenty years

nîstanaw-tahtwâpisk IPC twenty dollars

nîstanân PR we (excl.), too; we (excl.) by contrast; we (excl.) ourselves

nîsw-âskiy IPC two years, for two years [*sic:* -w-; *cf.* nîso-askiy]

nîsw-âya IPC two pairs, two sets

nîsw-âyamihêwi-kîsikâw IPC two weeks, for two weeks

nîswahpiso– VAI be harnessed as two, be a team of two, be yoked together

nîswahpit– VTI tie s.t. together as two (e.g., bones)

nîswapi– VAI be situated as two, come together as two

nîswayak isi IPC in both directions; in both forms of ritual (e.g., with both incense and sweetgrass)

nîswâpisk IPC two dollars

nîswâw IPC twice

nowâhc IPC more properly [*?sic: stem, gloss*, -hc, -c]

nôcih– VTA pursue s.o., hunt for s.o. (e.g., animal); go after s.o., oppress s.o., beat s.o. up, fight with s.o.

nôcihcikâkê– VAI trap with (it/him) (e.g., dog), use (it/him) to trap

nôcihcikê– VAI trap things, do one's trapping; do one's hunting

nôcihcikêwaskiy– NI trapping territory, trapline

nôcihcikêwin– NI trapping, one's trapping; trapline

nôcihtâ– VAI pursue (it), work at (it); do one's hunting, hunt

nôcikinosêwê– VAI get fish, be engaged in fishing

nôcisipê– VAI hunt ducks, be engaged in duck-hunting

nôcokwêsiw– NA old woman [*diminutive*]

nôh– VTA suckle s.o., nurse s.o., breastfeed s.o.

nôhâwaso– VAI nurse one's child, breastfeed one's child; suckle the young one (of the species), suckle one's calf (as cow)

nôhcimihk IPC in the bush, away from the water

nôhkwât– VTI lick s.t. [*dial.* (LR)]

nôhtaw IPC less; minus; previously; prematurely, incompletely, short of attainment

nôhtê IPV want to, desire to

nôhtêhkatê– VAI be hungry, suffer want of food

nôhtêhkwasîwipayi– VAI suddenly become sleepy

nôhtêpayi– VAI run short, be in want; run short of supplies; run short of (it), have (it) in short supply

nôhtêsin– VAI be played out, lie exhausted

nôhtêyâpâkwê– VAI be thirsty, suffer want of water

nôkohtâ– VAI let (it) appear, show (it)

nôkosi– VAI be visible, become visible; be born

nôkwan– VII be visible, become visible

nômanak IPC a while

nônâcikan– NI bottle, baby-bottle

nônâcikêhâwaso– VAI bottlefeed one's child

nôni– VAI suck at the breast, nurse at the breast; suck at the teats (e.g., calf)

nôtikwêsiw– NA old woman [*sic; cf.* nôcikwêsiw–; *diminutive*]

nôtikwêw– NA old woman [*cf.* nôtokwêw–]

nôtin– VTA fight s.o., fight with s.o.

nôtin– VTI fight s.t., fight with s.t.

nôtinikê– VAI fight people, put up a fight; take part in war (e.g., World War II)

nôtiniskwêwê– VAI beat one's wife

nôtinito– VAI fight with one another

nôtinitowin– NI fighting one another, fighting

nôtokwêsiw– NA old woman [*sic; cf.* nôcokwêsiw–; *diminutive*]

nôtokwêw– NA old woman [*cf.* nôtikwêw–]

nôtokwêwi– VAI be an old woman

ocawâsimisi– VAI have a child; have offspring, have a calf (as cow); have (her/him) as one's child; be the mother of a child; give birth, be delivered; calve (as cow) [*sic:* -c-; *cf.* otawâsimisi–; *diminutive*]

ocâhkosi– VAI have a female cross-cousin or sister-in-law (woman speaking), have (her) as one's female cross-cousin or sister-in-law (woman speaking)

ocâpânâskos– NA cart; small wagon, small sleigh [*diminutive*]

ocêhtowi-kîsikâ– VII be New Year's Day

ocêm– VTA kiss s.o.

ocêpihk– NI root

ocêpihkis– NI little root [*sic:* -is-; *cf.* ocêpihkos–; *diminutive*]

ocêpihkos– NI little root [*sic:* -os-; *cf.* ocêpihkis–; *diminutive*]

ocihci IPV having lived long enough for something

ocihcihkwanapi– VAI kneel [*cf.* ocihkwanapi–]

ocihcihkwanapih– VTA make s.o. kneel

ocihcikiskisi– VAI remember (it) far back; have memories far back

ocihcipayi– VII come to pass, take place

ocihciskâmakan– *VII* come to pass, take place (by foot or body movement)

ocihkwanapi– *VAI* kneel [*cf.* ocihcihkwanapi–]

ocipâson– *NA* knob, button (e.g., on radio)

ocipicikâtê– *VII* be pulled off, be moved (e.g., house, granary)

ocipit– *VTA* pull s.o. along, pull s.o. in; pull s.o. out (e.g., rabbit from snare, fish out of water)

ocipit– *VTI* pull s.t. out (e.g., from the ground), pull s.t. off; extract s.t. (e.g., grease from soup); move s.t. (e.g., house)

ocipitamâso– *VAI* pull (it/him) in for oneself, secure (it/him) for oneself

ocipôhkahtê– *VII* shrink from heat

ocipwâpâwê– *VII* be shrunk from washing in water

ociski– *VAI* have an anus; have (it) as one's anus

ocistêmâ– *VAI* have tobacco; have (it/him) as tobacco

ocîhkwêhikan– *NI* pleated moccasin

ohci *IPC* thence, from there; with, by means of; for that reason; (*in negative constructions:*) in the past [*enclitic; in negative constructions: perfective aspect marker*]

ohci *IPV* thence, from there; with, by means of; for that reason; (*in negative constructions:*) in the past [*in negative constructions: perfective aspect marker; cf.* ôh]

ohcih– *VTA* fight s.o. over (it/him); hold s.o. off

ohcikawan– *VII* leak out, drip out, trickle out; spring a leak (e.g., vessel)

ohcikawi– *VAI* leak out, drip out, trickle out (e.g., sap from tree)

ohcinê– *VAI* be ill on account of (it), suffer for (it); suffer in retribution

ohcipahtâ– *VAI* run from there

ohcipayin– *VII* come from there, result from that

ohcitaw *IPC* expressly, specifically, purposely, necessarily; it is requisite, it is meet indeed [*cf.* ohtitaw]

ohciyaw– *VTA* win from s.o. with (it), win over s.o. with (it)

ohciyâkê– VAI win from people with (it), use (it) to win from people

ohcî– VAI come from there, be from there

ohcîstamaw– VTA provide s.o. with (it/him) thereby or from there

ohpahamaw– VTA set a trap for s.o. (e.g., prairie-chicken)

ohpaho– VAI fly up (e.g., bird); fly off, lift off by airplane

ohpahowi-pîsimw– NA the month of August

ohpahpahtên– VTI raise up the smoke of s.t. [*?sic: stem*]

ohpahtên– VTI raise up the smoke of s.t.

ohpatinâ– VII be a high hill

ohpâskon– VTA raise s.o. (e.g., pipe)

ohpâskon– VTI raise s.t. (e.g., pipestem)

ohpâskwah– VTI raise s.t. (e.g., cloth) on a wooden pole, hold s.t. aloft on a wooden pole [*sic: -wa-*]

ohpiki– VAI grow up, grow

ohpikih– VTA make s.o. grow up, raise s.o.

ohpikihâwaso– VAI make one's children grow up, raise one's children

ohpikihito– VAI make one another grow up, raise one another

ohpikihtamaw– VTA make (it/him) grow for s.o., raise (it/him) for s.o.

ohpikihtamâso– VAI make (it/him) grow for oneself, raise (it/him) for oneself

ohpikihtâ– VAI make (it) grow

ohpikin– VII grow up, grow

ohpikinâwaso– VAI make one's children grow up, raise one's children

ohpimê IPC off, away, to the side; elsewhere, anywhere

ohpimês IPC a little off, a little away, a little to the side [*diminutive*]

ohpin– VTA raise s.o. (e.g., pipe), lift s.o. up

ohpin– VTI raise s.t., create s.t.

ohpipayi– *VAI* spring up, be catapulted up (e.g., in a snare)
ohpipit– *VTA* pull s.o. up
ohpohtât– *VTI* proceed high across s.t. (e.g., sky), rise up upon s.t. (e.g., sun upon sky)
ohpohtê– *VAI* rise up, proceed high in the sky
ohpwên– *VTI* make s.t. fly up, raise s.t. up (e.g., dust)
ohpwêtot– *VTI* lift oneself upon s.t., rise up upon s.t. (e.g., moon upon night sky)
ohtahipê– *VAI* obtain water from there, draw one's drinking water from there
ohtaskat– *VTA* leave s.o. behind thereby or from there, walk out on s.o.
ohtaskat– *VTI* leave s.t. behind thereby or from there
ohtastê– *VII* be placed thereby or from there
ohtatâwâkê– *VAI* sell (it) thus, sell (it) for that amount
ohtâciho– *VAI* make one's living thereby or from there
ohtêpayi– *VII* boil (e.g., water), be at the boil, bubble
ohtêyim– *VTA* be jealous of s.o.
ohtin– *VTI* take s.t. from there, obtain s.t. thereby or from there
ohtinikê– *VAI* take things from there, obtain things thereby or from there
ohtisi– *VAI* earn (it) thereby or from there, earn (it) for that; obtain payment thereby or from there
ohtiskawapi– *VAI* sit facing, sit so as to show one's face
ohtiskawapîstaw– *VTA* sit facing s.o., sit with one's face towards s.o.
ohtitaw *IPC* expressly, specifically, purposely, necessarily; it is requisite, it is meet indeed [*sic; cf.* ohcitaw]
ohtohtê– *VAI* come from there, come walking from there
ohtowâtamaw– *VTA* speak for s.o. therefore or from there
okâwîmâw– *NA* a mother
okâwîmâwaskiy– *NI* (*name:*) Mother Earth [*sic:* -a-; *e.g.,* okâwîmâwaskîhk [*sic*] (loc.)]

okikocêsîs– NA (*man's name*) [*?lit.* Hooked-Nose]
okimâhkân– NA chief, elected chief
okimâhkâniwi– VAI be chief, serve as elected chief
okimâhkâniwin– NI chieftaincy
okimâsis– NA little chief, boss; (*fig.*) nobility [*diminutive*]
okimâw– NA chief, leader, boss; (*fig.*) band council [*e.g.*, okimânâhk 'in the Band Council, amongst the band authorities'].
okiniy– NA rosehip
okinwâpêkikwayaw– NA (*man's name:*) Longneck
okiskinohamâkêw– NA teacher
okiskinohamâkêwiskwêw– NA female teacher; teacher's wife
okiskinowâpiw– NA one who learns merely by watching, mere imitator
okistikânikamiko– VAI have a granary
okistikêwiyiniw– NA farm instructor
okistikêwiyinîwi– VAI be a farmer, be engaged in agriculture
okistikêwiyinîwiwin– NI farming, farm-work, agriculture
okîsikow– NA (*name*) [*lit.* Sky-Spirit]
okwêmêsi– VAI have a namesake; have (her/him) as one's namesake, be named after (her/him)
omasinahikêsîs– NA scribe, clerk
omâcîw– NA hunter
omâmâ– VAI have a mom or mother, have ones' mom living; have (her) as one's mom [*sic: stem-final -â-*]
omâw– NA "bible", manyplies, omasum [*i.e., third stomach of ruminant*]
omihtimi– VAI have firewood; have (it) as one's firewood
omikî– VAI have a scab, have a sore; have (it) as one's scab
ominahowiyiniw– NA hunter; provisioner
omisi– VAI have an older sister; have (her) as one's older sister

omisimâs– NI the oldest sister [*diminutive*]

omisimâw– NA the oldest sister

omostosomisi– VAI have a few cows [*sic:* -t-; *diminutive*]

onakataskêw– NA the dead, the departed

onâcowêsis– NA (*man's name*) [*cf.* nâcowêw– NA; *?cf.* the name sometimes rendered Natuasis]

onâpêmi– VAI have a husband, be married (woman), have a husband living; get married (woman); have (him) as one's husband

onêpêwisiwini– VAI have shame

onihcikiskwapiwinihk INM (*place-name:*) Saddle Lake (Alberta) [*locative*; ?*lit.* at the place of the indistinct dark figure]

onikahp– NI portage [*dial.* (LR)]

onipêwini– VAI have a bed; have (it) as one's bed

onitawahtâw– NA scout, explorer, spy

onîcâniw– NA female of large quadrupeds; cow, cow-moose, female elk

onîkânîw– NA leader

onîkânohtêw– NA leader

onîkihiko– VAI have parents; have (them) as one's parents

onîkihikomâw– NA parents

onôcihcikêw– NA trapper

opacaskahasîs– NA (*bird's name*)

opawâkanêyâspinat– VTA harm s.o. by means of dream spirits

opawâmi– VAI have a dream spirit [*sic; cf.* pawâmi–]

opâpâ– VAI have a dad or father, have one's dad living; have (him) as one's dad [*sic: stem-final* -â-]

opêpîmi– VAI have an infant, have a baby; have (her/him) as one's infant; be the mother of an infant; give birth, be delivered

opitihkwahâkêw– NA (*man's name*) [*lit.* Makes-a-Thudding-Sound-Thereby]

opîma INM (*place-name:*) Hobbema (Alberta) [*sic*]

opîtatowêw– NA Ukrainian

opîwayakohp– NI feather blanket

orêtiyow– NI radio [*e.g.,* nôrêtiyôm 'my radio'; *dial.* (LR)]

os– VTI boil s.t. (e.g., water), keep s.t. at the boil

osâm IPC too much, excessively [*adverbially*]

osâm IPC because; for [*causal conjunction*]

osâm piko IPC mainly, mostly

osâmêyatin– VII be too many, be plentiful [*usually in negative constructions*]

osâpaht– VTI look at s.t. from there

osâpam– VTA look at s.o. from there

osâwâpêkan– VII be yellow (as rope); be yellow rope

osâwi-sôniyâwâpiskw– NA gold, yellow gold

osâwisi– VAI be yellow, be brown

oscikwânis– NA (*woman's name*) [*lit.* Little-Head]

oscoscocasi– VAI cough up a little of s.t.; cough a little [*diminutive*]

osêhcâ– VII be a rise in the land, be a slope, be a gentle hillside

osêhcâw– NI rise in the land, slope, gentle hillside

osikosâhkôm– VTA have s.o. as one's father's sister, call s.o. one's father's sister

osikosi– VAI have a father's sister or mother-in-law; have (her) as one's father's sister or mother-in-law

osikôho– VAI injure oneself, be injured [*sic:* -h-]

osikwânâs– VTI smoke-dry s.t.

osikwânâstê– VII be smoke-dried

osisi– VAI have a mother's brother or father-in-law; have (him) as one's mother's brother or father-in-law

osiskêpayi– VII fall into place, work itself out, be practicable

osîh– VTA prepare s.o. (e.g., game animal, porcupine quills, rattle), make s.o. (e.g., bread)

osîhcikâkê– VAI prepare things with (it/him), use (it/him) to prepare things

osîhcikâte– VII be made, be prepared; be built, be constructed

osîhcikêwin– NI what is made, handiwork, product

osîhikinosêwê– VAI prepare one's fish, process one's fish [*dial.* (LR)]

osîhtamaw– VTA prepare (it/him) for s.o., make (it/him) for s.o.

osîhtamâso– VAI make (it/him) for oneself

osîhtamowinihkê– VAI have a garment made, have clothes made

osîhtâ– VAI prepare (it), make (it); put (it) in service (e.g., hospital), inaugurate (it)

osîkahonê– VAI have a comb; have (it) as one's comb [*sic: stem-final* -ê-; *cf.* osîkahoni–]

osîmihto– VAI be siblings to one another

osîmimâs– NA the youngest sibling [*diminutive*]

osîmimâw– NA the youngest sibling

osîmimâwi– VAI be the youngest sibling

osîmisi– VAI have a younger sibling; have (him/her) as one's younger sibling

osîmisimâw– NA the youngest sibling [*sic; cf.* osîmimâw–]

osk-ây– NA young one (of the species); young person, the young [*e.g.*, osk-âya (prox. sg., obv.), osk-âyak (prox. pl.)]

osk-âyisiyiniw– NA young person [*sic; cf.* oskayisiyiniw–]

osk-âyiwi– VAI be young; be a young person

osk-îskwêw– NA young woman

oskani-pimiy– NI bone-marrow

oskaninê– VAI be ill with arthritis, suffer from arthritis

oskaskosîwinâkwan– VII look green, have the appearance of fresh shoots

oskawâsis– NA young child, infant

oskayisiyiniw– NA young person [*sic:* -a-; *cf.* osk-âyisiyiniw–]

oskâcâskos– NA carrot [*sic:* NA; *diminutive*]

oskâpêwis– NA ritual server, servitor (e.g., in ritual)

oskâtâskw– NI carrot
oski IPN young, fresh, new
oski-kinosêw– NA fresh fish
oski-napatâkw– NI new potato, fresh potato [*usually plural*]
oskiciy– NI pipestem
oskicîwâhtikw– NI wood of pipestem
oskinîki– VAI be a young man
oskinîkiskwêmakisi– VAI be a young woman [*sic*]
oskinîkiskwêsisiwi– VAI be a young girl (about 10-12 years old) [*sic; cf.* oskinîkiskwêwisi–]
oskinîkiskwêw– NA young woman
oskinîkiskwêwi– VAI be a young woman
oskinîkiskwêwisi– VAI be a young girl (about 10-12 years old) [*sic; cf.* oskinîkiskwêsisiwi–; *diminutive*]
oskinîkiw– NA young man
oskinîkiwiyinîs– NI youth, young man (about 12-13 years old)
oskinîkiwiyinîsiwi– VAI be a youth, be a young man (about 12-13 years old) [*sic; cf.* oskinîkîwiyinîsiwi–]
oskinîkîs– NA young boy, youth
oskinîkîwiyinîsiwi– VAI be a youth, be a young man (about 12-13 years old) [*sic; cf.* oskinîkiwiyinîsiwi–]
oskiskwêwê– VAI have a new wife
oskîsikohkâ– VAI wear glasses
oso– VAI boil (e.g., cracklings), be at the boil
osôniyâmi– VAI have money, carry money on oneself
ospwâkan– NA pipe
ostêsimâw– NA the oldest brother
ostêsimâwi– VAI be the oldest brother
ostostot– VTI cough s.t. up, cough s.t. out; cough, have a coughing spell
osw– VTA boil s.o. (e.g., porcupine quills), bring s.o. to the boil, keep s.o. (e.g., cracklings) at the boil

otahw– *VTA* beat s.o. in competition, win over s.o., win from s.o.

otakisîhkân– *NI* sausage

otakohpi– *VAI* have a blanket; use (it) as one's blanket

otakwanaho– *VAI* have a cover; use (it) as one's bed-cover

otamih– *VTA* keep s.o. busy, keep s.o. preoccupied; delay s.o.; *(especially in inverse constructions:)* get in s.o.'s way, be s.o.'s undoing [*e.g.,* kî-otamihikow 'it was in his way']

otamiskay– *NI* hide-scrapings (meat scraped from hide)

otamiyo– *VAI* busy oneself, keep busy, be preoccupied [*sic:* -y-]

otanâskasowini– *VAI* have a bedsheet; use (it) as one's bedsheet

otasahkêw– *NA* dispenser of rations; Indian agent

otaskî– *VAI* have land; have (it) as one's land, have (it) as one's territory [*sic: stem-final* -î-; *?cf.* otaskê–]

otaspiskwêsimoni– *VAI* have a pillow; use (it) as one's pillow

otatâwêw– *NA* store-keeper, store-manager

otatâwêwi– *VAI* be the store-keeper, be the store-manager

otawâsimisi– *VAI* have a child; have offspring, have a calf (as cow); have (her/him) as one's child; be the mother of a child; give birth, be delivered; calve (as cow) [*sic:* -t-; *cf.* ocawâsimisi–; *diminutive*]

otawâsimisimâw– *NA* a child [*sic:* -t-]

otayamihâw– *NA* Christian, adherent of Christianity

otâhk *IPC* behind, at the rear, in the past

otâhkosiw– *NA* sick person

otâkosihk *IPC* the previous evening; yesterday

otâkosin– *VII* be evening

otânihk *IPC* on one's hind part [*?sic:* IPC, NDI; *cf.* otâniyihk 'on his/her (obv.) hind part']

otânisi– *VAI* have a daughter; have (her) as one's daughter

otâpah– *VTA* drive s.o. (e.g., team of horses)

otâpân– *NA* wagon, vehicle

otâpânâskw– NA wagon, vehicle; automobile
otâpâso– VAI drive a vehicle
otâpê– VAI drag (it)
otâskanâhk IPC behind, at the rear; in the past [*locative, presumably based on a stem* otâskanaw– NI; *dial.* (LR)]
otâstawêhikêw– NA fire-fighter
otêhiminâni-cêpihk– NI strawberry root [*sic; cf.* ocêpihk–]
otêhtapîwatimomi– VAI have a horse; have (him) for one's horse [*sic:* -at-]
oti IPC in fact [*enclitic; emphatic*]
otihkomi– VAI have lice
otiht– VTA reach s.o.
otiht– VTI reach s.t.
otihtamâso– VAI reach (it/him) for oneself
otihtapinahisin– VAI move to lie face-down
otihtâwini– VAI have a dwelling, have a place of residence; have (it) as one's dwelling, have (it) as one's place of residence
otihtin– VTA grab s.o., seize s.o.
otihtin– VTI grab s.t., seize s.t.
otin– VTA take s.o., take s.o. in (e.g., orphan); choose s.o.; steal s.o.; (*especially in inverse constructions:*) take hold of s.o., possess s.o. [*e.g.,* ê-kî-otinikocik 'it had taken hold of them']
otin– VTI take s.t.; pick s.t., choose s.t., select s.t. (e.g., moss); steal s.t.; take s.t. over; extract s.t. (e.g., grease from soup), remove s.t. (e.g., glands in butchering beaver), extract s.t.; accept s.t. (e.g., contract); capture s.t., record s.t. on audio-tape
otinamâso– VAI take (it/him) for oneself, get (it/him) for oneself; steal (it/him)
otinaskê– VAI take land, settle the land, homestead
otinikâtê– VII be taken, be obtained; be chosen
otinikê– VAI take things; buy things, do one's shopping, make a purchase; take away winnings (e.g., in a card-game)

otinikêmakan– *VII* take things away; take the fever away

otinikowisi– *VAI* be taken by the powers

otinito– *VAI* take one another; marry each other

otisâpaht– *VTI* have lived long enough to see s.t.

otisîhkân– *NI* turnip

otitwêstamâkêw– *NA* interpreter; advocate

otônihkâ– *VAI* use (it/him) as one's mouthpiece, make (it/him) one's advocate

otôtêmi– *VAI* have a kinsman or friend; have (her/him) as one's kinsman or friend [*sic; cf.* oyotôtêmi–]

owanihikêw– *NA* trapper

owâwi– *VAI* lay eggs

owiyahpit– *VTI* tie s.t. together, tie s.t. into a bundle [*sic; cf.* wiyahpit–]

owiyasiwêwi– *VAI* be a band councillor

owîcêwâkani– *VAI* have a companion or partner; have (her/him) as one's companion or partner [*sic; cf.* wîcêwâkani–]

owîcisânihto– *VAI* have one another as siblings

owîhowini– *VAI* have a name; have (it) as one's name

owîki– *VAI* live there, dwell there, have one's home there [*sic; cf.* wîki–]

owîtisâni– *VAI* have a sibling, have (her/him) as one's sibling [*sic:* o-]

oyaskinah– *VTA* fill s.o. (e.g., pipe) [*sic; cf.* wiyaskinah–]

oyotôtêmi– *VAI* have a kinsman or friend; have (her/him) as one's kinsman or friend; be friendly [*sic; cf.* otôtêmi–]

oyoyo– *VAI* howl (e.g., dog, wolf)

oyôhkomi– *VAI* have a grandmother, have a grandmother living; have (her) as one's grandmother [*sic; cf.* wiyôhkomi–, ôhkomi–]

oyôhtâwî– *VAI* have a father, have a father living; have (him) as one's father

oyôhtâwîmâw– *NA* a father; (*name:*) The Father

oyôsisimi– VAI have a grandchild; have (her/him) as one's grandchild

oyôsisimimâw– NA a grandchild

ôcênâs– NI small town [*diminutive*]

ôcisis– NI small canoe, small boat [*e.g.*, ôcisisa [*sic*] (pl.); *diminutive; dial.* (LR)]

ôh IPV thence, from there; with, by means of; for that reason; (*in negative constructions:*) in the past [*in negative constructions: perfective aspect marker; cf.* ohci]

ôhkomi– VAI have a grandmother, have a grandmother living; have (her) as one's grandmother [*sic; cf.* oyôhkomi–, wiyôhkomi–]

ôhow– NA owl

ôma IPC then; when; it is this; the fact that [*factive; also predicative*]

ômatowahk IPC of this kind

ômatowihk IPC in this place

ômayikohk IPC this much, to this degree, to this extent

ômis îsi IPC in this way; this is how it is [*also predicative*]

ômisi IPC thus, in this way

ôs– NI canoe, boat [*e.g.*, ôsi (sg.), ôsihk (loc.); *cf. also* ê-kî-ôs[a]-ôsîhtamâsocik [*sic*] 'as they used to make canoes for themselves', *i.e., with* ôsa (*pl.*) *in preverb position; cf. dial.* (LR): ôsi (sg.), ôsa (pl.), nitôt [*sic*], otôtiwâw]

ôta IPC here

ôtê IPC over here, hither

ôtênaw– NI camp-circle; settlement, town

ôyâ PR that one no longer here [*absentative, e.g.*, ôyâ (prox. sg.)]

paci IPV wrongly, in error

paci-tôtaw– VTA wrong s.o.

paciyawêh– VTA wrong s.o. by one's utterance, provoke s.o.'s anger

pahkêkino-mîkiwâhp– NI skin-lodge, lodge made from hides

pahkêkinohkê– VAI   prepare one's skins, dress one's hides; make dressed hides, make leather

pahkêkinos– NI   small dressed hide, small piece of leather [*diminutive*]

pahkêkinw– NA   raw hide [*sic:* NA]

pahkêkinw– NI   dressed hide, tanned hide, finished hide, leather; tent-cover [*sic:* NI]

pahkêkinwêsâkay– NI   leather coat, leather jacket

pahkêkinwêskisin– NI   hide moccasin

pahkêkinwêtâs– NA   hide leggings, hide trousers, hide pants

pahkihtin– VII   fall, fall down

pahkikawin– VTI   let s.t. drip

pahkisikê– VAI   drop things, drop a bomb

pahkisim– VTA   let s.o. fall, drop s.o.

pahkisimohk IPC   in the west, to the west

pahkisimon– VII   be sunset, be west [*e.g.*, kâ-pahkisimohk 'in the west']

pahkisin– VAI   fall, fall down; fall for (her/him) [*sic: second gloss*]

pahkon– VTA   skin s.o. (e.g., animal)

pahkonikê– VAI   skin things (e.g., animals), do one's skinning

pahkopê– VAI   walk into the water

pahkopêtisahw– VTA   drive s.o. into the water

pahkwaciwêpah– VTI   break s.t. off, pry s.t. off (e.g., hide-scrapings), knock s.t. off

pahkwatah– VTI   break s.t. off, pry s.t. off (e.g., hide-scrapings), knock s.t. off

pahkwatin– VTI   break s.t. off by hand, pry s.t. off by hand (e.g., caked dirt from laundry)

pahkwêh– VTI   break a part off s.t., pry a part off s.t.

pahkwênamaw– VTA   pay a part of (it/him) to s.o., make partial payment to s.o.; parcel (it/him) out to s.o., give s.o. a share

pahkwêsikan– NA   flour; bannock, bread

pahkwêsikanihkê– VAI   fry bannock, bake bread
pahkwêsikaniwat– NI   flour-bag
pahpakwaciho– VAI   amuse oneself
pahpakwatêyiht– VTI   enjoy s.t., be amused by s.t.
pahpawiwêpin– VTI   shake s.t. out
pakahkam IPC   I think; perhaps [*i.e., expectation, in contrast to* êsa *and* êtokwê]
pakahkihtaw– VTA   hear s.o. clearly
pakamah– VTI   strike s.t., hit s.t.; pound s.t. (e.g., meat); type s.t., type s.t. out
pakamahw– VTA   hit s.o., strike s.o.; pound s.o. (e.g., earring)
pakamâkanis– NI   hammer
pakamisim– VTA   throw s.o. down
pakamisin– VAI   fall down against (it)
pakaski IPV   brightly coloured
pakastawê IPV   into the water
pakastawêh– VTI   place s.t. in water [*sic; cf.* pakistawêh–]
pakastawêhw– VTA   place s.o. in water
pakâhcikanaskihkw– NA   cooking pot
pakâhcikê– VAI   immerse things in water; boil things in water
pakâhtâ– VAI   immerse (it) in water; boil (it) in water
pakâhtê– VII   be immersed in water; be boiled in water
pakân– NA   (*man's name*) [*lit.* Nut]
pakâsim– VTA   immerse s.o. in water; boil s.o. (e.g., rabbit) in water
pakâsimo– VAI   be immersed, swim, have a bath
pakâsimonah– VTA   immerse s.o., bathe s.o.
pakâsimonahâwaso– VAI   immerse one's child, bathe one's child
pakâso– VAI   be immersed in water; be boiled in water
pakicahwânisihk INM   (*place-name:*) Fishing Lake (Alberta) [*locative; lit.* at the little fishing place]

pakiciwêpin– VTI let go of s.t., abandon s.t.

pakicî– VAI let go, give up; release (it/him), let go of (it/him)

pakistawêh– VTI place s.t. in water [*sic; cf.* pakastawêh–]

pakitahwâ– VAI fish by net, set nets

pakitin– VTA set s.o. down, allow s.o., permit s.o.; permit (it) to s.o., give permission to s.o.; let s.o. go, release s.o.; release s.o. (e.g., fish-spawn into lake), stock a lake with s.o. (e.g., fish); drop s.o. off (e.g., as an airplane)

pakitin– VTI let s.t. go, allow s.t., permit s.t.; release s.t.; give s.t. up, abandon s.t. (e.g., teaching, tradition); put s.t. down on earth; put s.t. in (e.g., seed potatoes)

pakitinamaw– VTA allow (it) for s.o., arrange (it) for s.o.; release (it/him) for s.o.

pakitinâso– VAI hold a give-away ceremony

pakitinâsowin– NI give-away ceremony

pakitinikâso– VAI be allowed, have permission; be released

pakitinikâtê– VII be permitted

pakitinikowisi– VAI be permitted by the powers; be put down on earth by the powers

pakitiniso– VAI choose (him/it) for oneself; make one's own choice

pakitiniwê– VAI put people down on earth

pakosêyim– VTA wish for (it/him) of s.o., expect (it/him) of s.o.

pakosêyimo– VAI wish for (it); have an expectation

pakosih– VTA beg from s.o.; be a hanger-on to s.o., go with s.o., be part of s.o.

pakwahcêhonis– NI belt [*diminutive*]

pakwahtêhon– NI belt

pakwanaw IPC by chance, at random

pakwanawahtâ– VAI go on with (it) at random, know nothing about (it), be clueless about (it)

pakwanêh– VTI make a hole in s.t.; drill a hole

pakwât– VTA hate s.o., dislike s.o., disapprove of s.o.

pakwât– VTI hate s.t., dislike s.t., disapprove of s.t.

pakwâtamaw– *VTA* hate (it/him) for s.o., dislike (it/him) for s.o., disapprove of (it/him) for s.o.

pamih– *VTA* tend to s.o., look after s.o.; attend s.o. in childbirth, serve as midwife to s.o.; guide s.o. (e.g., sleigh), drive s.o. (e.g., sleigh)

pamihastimwê– *VAI* drive one's horses

pamihcikê– *VAI* drive one's team

pamihikowin– *NI* being looked after, welfare [*sc. 'patient-centred' noun; e.g.,* kipamihikowin 'the fact that you are looked after']

pamihiso– *VAI* tend to oneself, look after oneself; attend oneself in childbirth, serve as one's own midwife

pamiho– *VAI* look after oneself; be well off

pamihtamaw– *VTA* tend to (it/him) for s.o., look after (it/him) for s.o.

pamihtamâso– *VAI* tend to (it/him) for or by oneself, look after (it/him) for or by oneself

pamihtâ– *VAI* look after (it)

pamin– *VTA* tend to s.o., look after s.o.; attend s.o. in childbirth, serve as midwife to s.o.

pamin– *VTI* tend to s.t., look after s.t.

paminiso– *VAI* tend to oneself, look after oneself

paminiwê– *VAI* tend to people, look after people

pamwayês *IPC* before [*sic:* pa-; *temporal conjunction; cf.* maywês, maywêsk, mwayê, mwayês, pâmwayês]

papakipotâ– *VAI* sharpen (it) to a thin edge

papakiwayân– *NI* shirt

papakiwayânêkinw– *NI* thin cloth, cotton; canvas

papakiwayânikamikw– *NI* tent

papakiwânêkinw– *NI* thin cloth, cotton; canvas [*sic; cf.* papakiwayânêkinw–]

papakwânikamikos– *NI* small tent [*sic; diminutive*]

papakwânikamikwêkin– *NI* canvas [*sic*]

papâ *IPV* around, about, here and there

papâmatoskê– *VAI* go about working, work here and there

papâmaciho– *VAI* travel about; live in various places; run about, be promiscuous
papâmi *IPV* around, about, here and there
papâmicimê– *VAI* go about by boat
papâmihâ– *VAI* fly about
papâmipahtâ– *VAI* run about (e.g., as a child); run around, be promiscuous
papâmipayi– *VAI* ride about, drive about
papâmipici– *VAI* move about, travel around, camp here and there, move around with one's camp
papâmiskâ– *VAI* paddle about, go about in a boat
papâmitâpâso– *VAI* ride about on a wagon; go on a wagon-ride
papâmitisah– *VTI* chase s.t. about; follow s.t. about (e.g., trail)
papâmitisahikêski– *VAI* habitually follow people about
papâmohtah– *VTA* take s.o. about, take s.o. here and there, go about with s.o.
papâmohtatâ– *VAI* take (it) about, take (it) here and there, go about with (it)
papâmohtê– *VAI* walk about, go about, go here and there; run around, be promiscuous
papâsi *IPV* fast, in a hurry
papâsim– *VTA* hurry s.o. by speech
papâsiwih– *VTA* rattle s.o., cause s.o. to be unsettled
papâtinikê– *VAI* hurry hither and thither, chase about
papêskomin– *NI* peppercorn, pepper
pasahkâpi– *VAI* blink, shut and open one's eyes
pasakoskiw– *NA* tree-gum, gum
pasakoskiw-âya *IPC* sticky stuff [*sometimes pluralised as if* NI]
pasakwahw– *VTA* glue s.o. down (e.g., figure cut out in paper)
pasakwâpi– *VAI* close one's eyes, have one's eyes shut
pasakwâpisimowin– *NI* shut-eye dance

pasakwâpisimowinihkê– VAI give a shut-eye dance, hold a shut-eye dance

pasastêhw– VTA whip s.o.

pasân– NA cattail, edible reed [?sic: Scirpus spp., Typha spp.]

pasicân– NI bulrush

pasikô IPV arising (from sitting or crouching) [?sic: pasikô, pasikôwi]

pasikô– VAI arise (from sitting or crouching); be uplifted

pasikô-kwâskohti– VAI jump up from sitting or crouching

pasikôn– VTA raise s.o. (e.g., to a position of leadership)

pasikôn– VTI raise s.t. (e.g., lodge)

pasiposôs– NA reach (long beam running from front to back in the centre of the undercarriage of a wagon)

pasisâwê– VAI burn stubble, burn the fields

pasisêwaci– VAI suffer frostbite

pasitê– VII be burnt, be burnt out (e.g., by forest-fire)

paskaht– VTI bite through s.t.

paskakwaw– VTA break a snare on s.o., break through s.o.'s snare

paskê– VAI branch off, go off to the side; set up a separate household

paskêpayi– VAI branch off, move off to the side; stop off there

paskêtâpâso– VAI branch off with one's wagon, move off to the side with one's vehicle; pull over with a vehicle

paskêwih– VTA part from s.o., leave s.o.; separate from s.o., divorce s.o.

paskêwihito– VAI part from one another, leave one another; separate from one another, divorce

paskiciwêpin– VTA throw s.o. across; throw s.o. (e.g., rabbit) over drying rack

paskin– VTA break s.o. (e.g., thread)

paskin– VTI break s.t. (e.g., snare-wire)

paskipit– VTI break s.t. (e.g., snare-wire)

paskiyaw– *VTA* beat s.o. in a contest

paskopit– *VTA* pluck s.o. (e.g., bird)

paskwasêsipayi– *VII* turn bald (e.g., head) [*sic:* -wa-]

paskwatah– *VTI* clear brush

paskwâwi-mostosw– *NA* bison, buffalo

paskwâwi-sâkahikanihk *INM* (*place-name:*) Meadow Lake (Saskatchewan) [*locative; lit.* at the prairie lake]

paskwâwiyiniw– *NA* prairie person; Plains Cree

paso– *VAI* smell (it)

paspaskiw– *NI* partridge, bush-partridge

paspâpam– *VTA* look out (e.g., through a window or crack) at s.o.

paspâpi– *VAI* look out (e.g., through a hole or crack), peep out

paswêskôyo– *VAI* get sick from eating excessively fatty food [*sic:* -y-]

paswêyâ– *VII* be excessively fatty

patahôhkât– *VTA* overlook s.o., fail to notice s.o., ignore s.o.

patakopit– *VTA* squash s.o. in pulling, flatten s.o. down by pulling

patakwât– *VTA* miss s.o. with one's snare, fail to snare s.o.

patinikê– *VAI* make a mistake, take a wrong step, transgress; (*fig.*) sin

patisk– *VTI* miss s.t. (by foot or body movement)

patitisahamaw– *VTA* drive (it/him) off the path for s.o., send (it/him) awry for s.o., spoil (it/him) for s.o.

patowât– *VTI* misspeak s.t.; commit an error in one's prayers

pawahikê– *VAI* shake things out by tool; thresh, do one's threshing

pawâmi– *VAI* have a dream spirit [*sic; cf.* opawami–]

pawâmiwin– *NI* spirit power; (*fig.*) witchcraft

pawât– *VTA* dream about s.o.

pawât– *VTI* dream about s.t.

pawin– *VTI* shake s.t. out

payipis– VTI cut s.t. out, cut a hole in s.t.

pâh-pahki IPC here and there [*reduplicated*]

pâh-pêyak IPC singly, one at a time; each one, each individually, each; one each [*cf.* pêh-pêyak; *reduplicated*]

pâh-pêyakwan IPC the same for each [*reduplicated*]

pâh-piskihc IPC each separately [*reduplicated*]

pâh-pîtos IPC each differently [*reduplicated*]

pâhkaci IPC actually, firmly

pâhkahâhkwân– NA chicken, domestic chicken [*sic:* -hk-; *cf.* pâhpahâhkwân–]

pâhkohkwêhon– NI towel

pâhkohkwêhonis– NI small towel [*diminutive*]

pâhkopayi– VAI get dry, dry out

pâhkosi– VAI dry off, be dried off; be dry and crisp (e.g., fried bacon)

pâhkw-âyamihâwin– NI Roman Catholic religion; the Roman Catholic church

pâhkw-âyamihêwiyiniw– NA Roman Catholic priest

pâhkwah– VTI dry s.t. by tool

pâhkwahikâkanis– NI small towel, dish-towel [*diminutive*]

pâhpahâhkwân– NA chicken, domestic chicken [*sic:* -hp-; *cf.* pâhkahâhkwân–]

pâhpahâhkwânisis– NA young chicken, chick [*diminutive*]

pâhpi– VAI laugh, smile

pâhpih– VTA laugh at s.o., deride s.o.; joke with s.o.

pâhpihtâ– VAI laugh at (it), deride (it)

pâhpîmakan– VII (*fig.*) laugh (e.g., one's heart)

pâkâhtowê– VAI play ball; play soccer

pâkisitêpayi– VAI have one's foot swell up, have a swollen foot

pâmwayês IPC before [*temporal conjunction; cf.* maywês, maywêsk, mwayê, mwayês, pamwayês]

pânis– VTI cut s.t. (e.g., meat) into sheets

pânisâwê– VAI cut meat into sheets; cut fish into fillets pânisw– VTA cut s.o. (e.g., animal) into sheets

pâpahtâ– VAI run hither, come running

pâpakwâtahw– VTA (*especially in inverse constructions:*) rub s.o. raw, cause s.o. blisters [*e.g.,* ê-kî-pâpakwâtahokot ôm ômaskisin 'her shoe had caused her blisters']

pâpayi– VAI come hither, ride hither

pâpici– VAI move one's camp hither

pâs– VTI dry s.t. by heat (e.g., meat, berries, moss)

pâsikâtê– VII be dried by heat

pâskac IPC on top of that, to top it all off, to cap it all, as the final touch; coincidentally

pâskâpi– VAI have a ruptured eye; have only one eye

pâskêkin– VTA break s.o. made of paper, break the paper of s.o. (e.g., cigarette)

pâskihtên– VTI open s.t. (e.g., window)

pâskin– VTI open s.t. up, take the cover off s.t.; fold s.t. (e.g., book) open

pâskis– VTI shoot at s.t.

pâskisikan– NI gun

pâskisikê– VAI shoot at things, shoot, take a shot

pâskisw– VTA shoot at s.o.

pâskiwêpin– VTI throw s.t. open (e.g., lodge-cover)

pâso– VAI be dry (by heat), be dried

pâstatah– VTI break s.t. (e.g., bone) by tool

pâstâho– VAI breach the natural order, transgress; (*fig.*) sin, be a sinner

pâstâhowi-mihkw– NI blood tainted by a breach of the natural order; (*fig.*) blood tainted by deicide, sinful blood [*e.g.,* pâstâhowi-mihko (sg.)]

pâstâhowin– NI transgression, breach of the natural order; (*fig.*) sin

pâstâhôtot– VTI commit a transgression in s.t., commit sacrilege in s.t.

pâstê– VII be dry (by heat), be dried

pâstipayin– *VII* break, burst (e.g., bottle, head)

pâsw– *VTA* dry s.o. (e.g., rabbit) by heat

pâtimâ *IPC* no earlier, only later [*also in correlative constructions with* êkwêyâc]

pâtos *IPC* only later

pâwanî– *VAI* be lean, be skinny, be scrawny (e.g., rabbit, human)

pê *IPV* thence, from there on down, hither

pêc-âskiy *IPC* in a past year, in past years [*e.g.,* nâway ôma pêc-âskiy 'this past year']

pêcâstamohtê– *VAI* walk hither, come walking [*sic:* -c-; *cf.* pêtâstamohtê–]

pêci *IPC* thence, from there on down, hither

pêci-nâway *IPC* back then, far in the past; from the earliest times

pêcikâtê– *VII* be brought hither

pêcikê– *VAI* bring things hither

pêcikêsi– *VAI* bring a few things hither [*diminutive*]

pêcipit– *VTI* bring s.t. hither by pulling

pêh– *VTA* wait for s.o.

pêh-pêyak *IPC* one after another, one by one [*cf.* pâh-pêyak; *reduplicated*]

pêho– *VAI* wait

pêhonânihk *INM* (*place-name:*) Fort Carlton (Saskatchewan) [*locative; lit.* at the waiting place]

pêht– *VTI* hear s.t.

pêhtamowin– *NI* what one has heard [*sc.* 'agent-centred' *noun; e.g.,* kipêhtamowininâhk 'in what we have heard']

pêhtaw– *VTA* hear s.o.

pêhtâkosi– *VAI* be heard, make oneself heard, make noise

pêhtâkwan– *VII* be heard

pêkopayi– *VAI* awake, wake up

pêpîsis– *NA* baby, infant [*diminutive*]

pêpîwi– *VAI* be a baby, be an infant

pêsiw– *VTA* bring s.o. hither; bring s.o. (e.g., one's child) back (e.g., from the bush) after delivery

pêskis *IPC* besides; at the same time, simultaneously

pêtamaw– *VTA* bring (it/him) hither for s.o.

pêtâ– *VAI* bring (it) hither

pêtâmo– *VAI* flee hither

pêtâstamohtê– *VAI* walk hither, come walking [*cf.* pêcâstamohtê–]

pêtâwah– *VTA* lead s.o. hither as a crowd, pull s.o. hither

pêtâwatâ– *VAI* haul (it) hither

pêtisâpam– *VTA* see s.o. coming

pêtitisahw– *VTA* drive s.o. hither, send s.o. hither

pêtôpê– *VAI* bring an alcoholic drink hither, bring an alcoholic drink home or into the house

pêtwêwêhtamaw– *VTA* come hither audibly bringing (it/him) for s.o.

pêtwêwên– *VTI* come hither audibly, come with audible steps

pêyak *IPC* one, alone, a single one; the only one; a certain one

pêyak-askiy *IPC* one year, for one year

pêyak-ispayiw *IPC* one week, for one week

pêyak-kîsikâw *IPC* one day, for one day, in one day; per day

pêyak-misit *IPC* one foot, for one foot; measuring one foot

pêyak-pîsim *IPC* one month, for one month

pêyak-sôniyâs *IPC* twenty-five cents, a quarter

pêyak-tipahikan *IPC* one hour

pêyak-tipahôpân *IPC* one gallon of alcoholic drink (e.g., wine)

pêyak-tipiskâw *IPC* one night, for one night

pêyako– *VAI* be alone, be the only one; be left alone; go alone (e.g., as a woman, improperly)

pêyako-kosikwan *IPC* one pound; per pound

pêyakoh– *VTA* have s.o. as the only one, be faithful to s.o. (e.g., spouse)
pêyakopêhikan– *NA* card, playing-card
pêyakosâp *IPC* eleven
pêyakoyâkan *IPC* one dish (measure)
pêyakw-ây– *NA* a single one (e.g., stocking); one pair [*e.g.,* pêyakw-âyak (prox. pl.)]
pêyakw-âya *IPC* one team of horses, a single team of horses
pêyakwahpit– *VTA* harness s.o. singly
pêyakwahpitêw *IPC* one team (of two horses)
pêyakwan *IPC* the same
pêyakwan ispî *IPC* at the same time
pêyakwanohk *IPC* in one place, in a single place; in the same place
pêyakwapi– *VAI* stay alone, be alone in the house
pêyakwayak *IPC* in one place, in a certain place; in the same place
pêyakwâciho– *VAI* live alone, travel alone
pêyakwâpisk *IPC* one dollar
pêyakwâw *IPC* once
pêyakwêskihk *IPC* one kettle (measure)
pêyakwêyimiso– *VAI* think solely of oneself
pêyâhtik *IPC* quietly, gently, softly, slowly [*sic:* -i-]
pici– *VAI* move camp, move with one's camp
picikwâs– *NA* apple [*diminutive*]
pihcipo– *VAI* be poisoned [*cf.* piscipo–]
pihcipohtâ– *VAI* poison (it)
pihcipôh– *VTA* poison s.o. [*sic:* -ô-]
pihêsis– *NA* little prairie-chicken [*diminutive*]
pihêw– *NA* prairie-chicken [*cf.* piyêsîs–]
pihêwisimo– *VAI* dance the prairie-chicken dance
pihkin– *VTI* shape s.t., bend s.t., fold s.t.
pihkoh– *VTA* free s.o., release s.o.

pihkoho– *VAI* free oneself, escape; be released; (*fig.*) free oneself (e.g., to meet an obligation or duty); be saved

pihkw– *NI* ash; ashes (as cleaning agent) [*e.g.*, pihko (sg.)]

pihkwâpoy– *NI* lye

pihpihcêw– *NA* robin

pikiw– *NA* spruce-gum, gum

piko *IPC* must, have to [*clause-initial predicative*]

piko *IPC* only [*enclitic*]

piko kîkway *PR* something or other; anything at all

piko kîkwâs *PR* something or other; anything at all [*diminutive*]

pikonita *IPC* in vain, without reason, without purpose, for nothing; without further ado; anywhere, at random, in a random place [*cf.* konita, pikwanita]

pikoyikohk *IPC* to any extent, no matter how much [*cf.* pikw îyikohk]

pikw âni *IPC* anyway

pikw âwiyak *IPC* anyone; everyone

pikw îta *IPC* in any place, no matter where; everywhere

pikw îtê *IPC* to any place, no matter whither; everywhere

pikw îtê isi *IPC* in any direction

pikw îtowahk *IPC* of any kind, no matter what kind; of all kinds

pikw îtowihk *IPC* in any place, no matter where; in all places

pikw îyikohk *IPC* to any extent, no matter how much [*cf.* pikoyikohk]

pimahkamikisi– *VAI* work along, keep busy

pimakocin– *VAI* move along, go by; work, be in working order (e.g., clock, car)

pimakocin– *VII* make a rush in linear fashion, charge headlong

pimakotê– *VII* be in working order, run (e.g., tape-recorder)

pimamon– *VII* run along (e.g., road, rail)

pimastê– *VII* be placed in linear fashion, run along

pimâcih– *VTA* make s.o. live, give life to s.o., sustain s.o.'s life; revive s.o., save s.o.'s life; make a living for s.o.

pimâcihâwaso– *VAI* give life to one's children, make a living for one's children

pimâcihiso– *VAI* make oneself live; make a living for oneself

pimâcihiwêwin– *NI* way of life; way of making a living

pimâciho– *VAI* make a life for oneself; make one's living; live

pimâcihowin– *NI* way of life, livelihood

pimâcihwâkê– *VAI* make one's living with (it), use (it) to make one's living

pimâcisiwin– *NI* life [*cf.* pimâtisiwin–]

pimâhocikêsi– *VAI* float along in a small boat [*diminutive; dial.* (LR)]

pimâhtawî– *VAI* crawl along

pimâsi– *VAI* be blown along by wind

pimâskwamon– *VII* run fastened along as wood, be nailed along (e.g., at regular intervals)

pimâtisi– *VAI* live, be alive, survive

pimâtisiwin– *NI* life [*cf.* pimâcisiwin–]

pimâtisiwinê– *VAI* have life, seek life

pimâtisiwinowi– *VII* have life, provide life

pimâtisîtot– *VTI* live one's life; live one's life by s.t.

pimâwah– *VTA* lead s.o. along as a crowd, pull s.o. along

pimi *IPV* along, in linear progression; while moving in linear progression

pimi-nakî– *VAI* stop in one's progress, stop in one's travelling

pimic-âyihk *IPC* across, athwart, crosswise, sideways

pimicaskêkâs– *NI* (*place-name:*) Leask (Saskatchewan) [*?lit.* little muskeg running across]

pimicikâpawi– *VAI* stand sideways, stand across

pimiciwan– *VII* flow along

pimihâ– *VAI* fly along

pimihâkan– *NI* airplane [*sic:* -h-; *cf.* pimiyâkan–]

pimihtin– *VII* go along (e.g., river, road); run along, flow by (e.g., creek)

piminawaso– *VAI* cook, do one's cooking [*sic; cf.* pininawaso–]

piminawasosi– *VAI* cook a little, do some cooking [*diminutive*]

piminawasowikamikw– *NI* cookhouse, kitchen

piminawat– *VTA* cook for s.o. [*sic; cf.* pininawat–]

pimipayi– *VII* move along; run, run along; be on, work, function (e.g., motor, electricity); exist currently, take place [*sic; cf.* pimipayin–]

pimipayiho– *VAI* move along, migrate (e.g., fish)

pimipayihtâ– *VAI* run (it), operate (it) (e.g., machine); keep (it) up, exercise (it)

pimipayin– *VII* run, run along; go on, work, function [*sic; cf.* pimipayi–]

pimipayîs– *NA* runner (e.g., on sleigh)

pimipici– *VAI* move camp, move along with one's camp

pimisim– *VTA* lay s.o. down, put s.o. to bed

pimisimo– *VAI* dance by, dance along

pimisin– *VAI* lie extended, lie down; lie confined, lie in childbed

pimiskâ– *VAI* swim by, swim along; go by in a boat, move along by one's own power

pimitapi– *VAI* sit crosswise, sit across (e.g., path)

pimitastê– *VII* be placed crosswise; be the bunk of a wagon

pimitâpâso– *VAI* move along in a vehicle

pimitisah– *VTI* follow s.t.; (*fig.*) adhere to a religion

pimitisahikê– *VAI* follow people, tag along, be a follower

pimitisahw– *VTA* follow s.o. along, go behind s.o., drive s.o. along

pimiy– NI fat, oil; crude petroleum [*e.g.,* ê-kî-mâna-pimiy-tihkisamân [*sic*] 'as I used to melt down some grease', *i.e., with* pimiy *in preverb position*]

pimiyâkan– NI airplane [*sic:* -y-; *cf.* pimihâkan–]

pimîhkân– NI pemmican

pimîwi– VII be grease, be greasy

pimocikanis– NA little arrow [*sic:* NA; *diminutive*]

pimocikê– VAI shoot arrows

pimohtah– VTA take s.o. along, go along with s.o., guide s.o. along; carry s.o. along, sustain s.o.

pimohtatâ– VAI take (it) along, carry (it) along, travel with (it)

pimohtât– VTI travel to s.t. (e.g., work-site); live s.t. (e.g., day), live through s.t.; go through s.t. (e.g., as sun through the sky)

pimohtê– VAI go along, walk along

pimohtêho– VAI travel through life, live one's life

pimohtêhon– NI passage through life, travel through life

pimohtêmakan– VII go along, move along; go on, be in effect (e.g., treaty)

pimohtêmakisi– VAI go, go on, be in use, function [*sic*]

pimohtêskanaw– NI walking path

pimohtêstamaw– VTA go along for s.o., represent s.o.

pimohtêwin– NI travel [*sc.* 'agent-centred' *noun; e.g.,* nipimohtêwin 'my travelling']

pimot– VTA shoot an arrow at s.o.

pimowitâ– VAI carry (it) along

pimw– VTA shoot at s.o., loose an arrow at s.o.

pimwasinât– VTA throw (it/him) at s.o., heave (it/him) at s.o.

pimwasinê– VAI throw (it), heave (it)

pinakocin– VAI fall down from aloft

pininawaso– VAI cook, do one's cooking [*sic; cf.* piminawaso–]

pininawat– VTA cook for s.o. [*sic; cf.* piminawat–]

pinkow– NA (*dog's name:*) Bingo

pinkow– NI bingo [*i.e., game of chance*]

pipon– VII be winter

pisc-ôtin– VTI accidentally take s.t., accidentally ingest s.t. (e.g., pill)

pisci IPV by accident, accidentally, erroneously, in error [*sic:* -sc-]

piscipo– VAI be poisoned [*cf.* pihcipo–]

piscipohtâ– VAI poison (it)

piscipowin– NI poison

piscipôskaw– VTA poison s.o.

pisisik IPC always, every time, routinely

pisiskâpam– VTA notice s.o.

pisiskêyiht– VTI pay attention to s.t., take notice of s.t.; bother with s.t.

pisiskêyim– VTA pay attention to s.o., take notice of s.o., tend to s.o.; bother s.o., harass s.o.

pisiskisîs– NA animal; young animal; small animal (e.g., bird, gopher) [*diminutive*]

pisiskiw– NA animal; domestic animal

pisiw– NA lynx

piskihci IPV separately

piskihci-wîki– VAI live separately, dwell separately, have a separate household

piskihcikamikos– NI separate room, private room

piskihcikwât– VTI sew an extension on s.t.

pistah– VTI knock s.t. down inadvertently, hit s.t. accidentally

pistahw– VTA knock s.o. down inadvertently, hit s.o. accidentally

pistin– VTI take s.t. accidentally, take s.t. by mistake

pistiskaw– VTA knock s.o. down inadvertently (by foot or body movement)

pita *IPC* first, first of all; for a while [*cf.* pitamâ]

pitamâ *IPC* first, first of all; for a while [*cf.* pita]

pitanê *IPC* wish that [*with simple conjunct*]

pitihkwê– *VII* thud, make a thudding noise (e.g., the rushing of water, the fall of hooves, the rapid wing movements of a dancing prairie-chicken)

pitikon– *VTI* make small patties of s.t. (e.g., crushed chokecherries)

pitikonikanâpoy– *NI* meatball soup

pitikonikâtê– *VII* be made into small patties (e.g., crushed chokecherries)

pitikwahpit– *VTI* tie s.t. into a bundle

pitikwapi– *VAI* sit huddled together

pitikwêkin– *VTI* roll s.t. up as cloth

piyasêyimo– *VAI* look forward eagerly, wait in anticipation

piyêsiw– *NA* (*name*) [*lit.* Thunderbird]

piyêsîs– *NA* bird; (*man's name*) [*sic:* -y-; *cf.* pihêw–; *diminutive*]

piyis *IPC* finally, at last [*cf.* piyisk]

piyisk *IPC* finally, at last [*cf.* piyis]

pîhc-âyihk *IPC* inside (e.g., fish, house, hat)

pîhcawêsâkânis– *NI* slip, undershirt [*diminutive*]

pîhci *IPV* in between, inside

pîhcikwah– *VTA* take s.o. small indoors, go indoors with s.o. small; bring s.o. small (e.g., infant) home [*diminutive*]

pîhciwêpin– *VTI* throw s.t. inside, throw s.t. into a wagon-box

pîhconês– *NI* blouse

pîhcwâkanis– *NA* cigarette [*diminutive*]

pîhcwâwinis– *NA* cigarette [*diminutive*]

pîhtaw *IPC* in the event, of course

pîhtawêkin– *VTI* line s.t., put a lining into s.t.

pîhtawêkwât– *VTI* sew s.t. in between, sew covers on s.t.

pîhtawêsâkân– *NI* slip, undergarment

pîhtawêwayiwinis– NI underclothes, underwear
pîhtâpâwah– VTA pour liquid into s.o., give s.o. an enema
pîhtêyask IPC at the central circle of poles inside the dance-lodge
pîhtikwah– VTA enter with s.o., take s.o. indoors
pîhtikwatâ– VAI enter with (it), take (it) indoors
pîhtikwê IPV indoors
pîhtikwê– VAI enter, go indoors [*cf.* pîhtokwê–]
pîhtikwê-âwacimihtêwin– NI hauling firewood indoors
pîhtikwêmakan– VII enter, go indoors
pîhtikwêpahtâ– VAI run indoors
pîhtikwêtot– VTI enter s.t. (e.g., sweat-lodge)
pîhtikwêwêpin– VTA throw s.o. indoors
pîhtikwêyâmo– VAI flee indoors
pîhtikwêyâpâwê– VII be washed indoors as water, run indoors
pîhtokwah– VTA enter with s.o., take s.o. indoors
pîhtokwamik IPC indoors [*sic:* -kw-; *also cf.* pîhtokwamihk; *dial.* (LR)]
pîhtokwatamâkê– VAI take (it/him) indoors for people
pîhtokwatâ– VAI take (it) indoors, enter with (it)
pîhtokwê IPV indoors
pîhtokwê– VAI enter, go indoors [*cf.* pîhtikwê–]
pîhtokwêyâmo– VAI flee indoors
pîhton– VTA take the covering layer off s.o. (e.g., tree), peel s.o.
pîhton– VTI take s.t. (e.g., bark) off as the covering layer, peel s.t. off
pîhtopit– VTA pull the covering layer off s.o. (e.g., tree), peel the bark off s.o.
pîhtopit– VTI pull s.t. (e.g., bark) off as the covering layer, peel s.t. off
pîhtosw– VTA cut the covering layer off s.o. (e.g., tree), cut the bark off s.o.

pîhtwâ– VAI smoke, use the pipe; smoke (him) (e.g., pipe); hold a pipe ceremony; be a nicotine addict

pîhtwâh– VTA make s.o. smoke, give s.o. to smoke

pîhtwâkê– VAI smoke with (it/him), use (it/him) in the pipe

pîhtwât– VTI smoke s.t., use s.t. to smoke

pîhtwâwikamikw– NI pipe lodge, pipe ceremony

pîhtwâwin– NI smoking; (*fig.*) cannabis abuse

pîkanowi-sîpiy– NI (*place-name:*) Missouri River

pîkinatah– VTI grind s.t. to powder

pîkinâ– VII be powder, be powdered

pîkinihkoso– VAI be cut into small pieces

pîkinipayi– VAI fall apart into small pieces

pîkinis– VTI cut s.t. into small pieces

pîkinisâwâtamaw– VTA cut (it/him) into small chunks for s.o.

pîkiskât– VTA long for s.o., grieve for s.o.

pîkiskâtisi– VAI be lonesome, grieve

pîkiskwât– VTA speak to s.o., address s.o.

pîkiskwât– VTI speak about s.t., speak about s.t. with concern; speak a prayer over s.t.; address s.t., speak to s.t. (e.g., spirit-bundle)

pîkiskwê– VAI use words, speak; speak a prayer, pray

pîkiskwêh– VTA make s.o. speak, get s.o. to speak; interview s.o.

pîkiskwêmakan– VII speak (e.g., spirit-bundle)

pîkiskwêmohtâ– VAI cause (it) to speak; make an audio-recording

pîkiskwêmôh– VTA cause s.o. to speak with concern

pîkiskwêpayi– VAI speak suddenly, burst into speech

pîkiskwêstamaw– VTA speak for s.o., speak on s.o.'s behalf

pîkiskwêstamâso– VAI speak for oneself, do one's own speaking

pîkiskwêwin– NI word, phrase, expression, voice; what is being said; speech, language

pîkocin– *VAI* be torn (e.g., by branches or thorns)
pîkohtatâ– *VAI* break (it)
pîkohtin– *VII* break in a fall, be broken
pîkokonêwêpayi– *VAI* have cracks erupt in one's mouth, have one's mouth break out in sores (e.g., with thrush)
pîkon– *VTA* break s.o.; break up one's relation with s.o., disrupt s.o.'s life, spoil s.o.'s plans
pîkon– *VTI* break s.t.
pîkonamâso– *VAI* break (it) for oneself, break it oneself
pîkonikâtê– *VII* be torn; be broken down (e.g., institution)
pîkonikê– *VAI* break things; have things break, experience a mechanical breakdown
pîkonikêmakan– *VII* cause things to break down
pîkopayi– *VAI* break down, be broken; be torn (e.g., trousers); (*fig.*) go broke, go bankrupt
pîkopayi– *VII* break down, be broken [*sic; cf.* pîkopayin–]
pîkopayin– *VII* break down, be broken [*sic; cf.* pîkopayi–]
pîkopicikâtê– *VII* be ploughed soil, be cultivated
pîkopicikê– *VAI* plough, do one's ploughing; break soil
pîkopicikêh– *VTA* make s.o. plough, use s.o. (e.g., oxen) in ploughing
pîkopit– *VTI* break s.t. (e.g., soil), plough s.t. (e.g., field)
pîkopitamaw– *VTA* break (it) for s.o., plough (it) for s.o.
pîkwasinahikê– *VAI* be loaded down with debt, be indebted in several places
pîkwatowan– *VII* be rotten (e.g., tooth)
pîkwêyiht– *VTI* be worried about s.t.
pîkwêyihtamih– *VTA* worry s.o., cause s.o. mental anguish
pîkwêyihtamowin– *NI* mental anguish
pîmah– *VTI* twist s.t. (e.g., rags for bitch-light)
pîmikitêwayiwinis– *NI* embroidered clothing
pîmin– *VTI* twist s.t.; turn s.t. on (e.g., equipment); turn s.t. down (e.g., electric appliance)
pîminahkwân– *NI* rope

pîminahkwânis– NI string, rope [*diminutive*]

pîminikan– NA twist-tobacco

pîmiskwêyi– VAI turn one's head sideways, twist one's neck (e.g., owl)

pîsâkwan– VII contain plenty, offer lots of room; be plentiful, be rich [*sic:* -â-]

pîsi-kiscikânis– NI vegetable [*usually plural; diminutive*]

pîsimôhkân– NI clock, watch

pîsimw– NA sun; moon; month

pîswê-maskisin– NI felt-liner, boot-liner

pîtos IPC strangely, differently

pîtos-kîkway PR something strange, strange things

pîtosinâkwan– VII look different; look strange

pîtotêyihtâkosi– VAI be thought strange, be considered odd

pîwaniyôtin– VII be a blizzard

pîwâpiskomêskanaw– NI railway

pîwâpiskw– NI metal, metal object; steel blade; screen of wire-mesh

pîwâpiskwâ– VII be metal

pîwên– VTA scatter s.o. (e.g., sugar), sprinkle s.o. (e.g., sugar) in small grains

pîwêwêpin– VTI scatter s.t., sprinkle in a pinch of s.t.

pîwêyâwahkwâ– VII be powdery

pîwêyiht– VTI think little of s.t., have a low opinion of s.t.

pîwêyim– VTA think little of s.o., have a low opinion of s.o.; be disrespectful of s.o.

pîwêyimo– VAI think little of oneself, have low self-esteem; (*fig.*) be humble

pîwi-kiscikânis– NA garden seed [*usually plural; diminutive*]

pîwi-kiscikânis– NI vegetable garden [*diminutive*]

pîwihtakahikan– NI wood-chips

pohtayiwinisah– VTA put clothes on s.o., make clothes for s.o., fit s.o. out with clothing, clothe s.o.

pohtayiwinisê– VAI put one's clothes on, get dressed [*sic:* -ht-; *cf.* postayiwinisê–]

pohtisk– VTI put s.t. on (e.g., clothing), get dressed in s.t., wear s.t.; be enclosed by s.t. (e.g., mossbag) [*sic:* -ht-; *cf.* postisk–]

posâkan– NA touchwood, tinder fungus [*presumably Fomes fomentarius*]

postamôh– VTA put s.o. on (e.g., reaches under a wagon), attach s.o.

postayiwinisah– VTA put clothes on s.o., make clothes for s.o., fit s.o. out with clothing, clothe s.o.

postayiwinisahiso– VAI put clothes on oneself, make clothes for oneself, clothe oneself

postayiwinisê– VAI put one's clothes on, get dressed [*sic:* -st-; *cf.* pohtayiwinisê–]

postisk– VTI put s.t. on (e.g., clothing), get dressed in s.t., wear s.t.; be enclosed by s.t. (e.g., mossbag) [*sic:* -st-; *cf.* pohtisk–]

postiskaw– VTA put s.o. on, wear s.o. (e.g., pants)

poy IPC boy! [*exclamatory, indicating surprise; also introductory*]

pôhtâskwah– VTI stick s.t. wooden into a hole; clean out one's ear, poke one's ear

pômê– VAI be discouraged, be disappointed; give up

pômêh– VTA discourage s.o., disappoint s.o.; cause s.o. to give up

pôn– VTI build a fire; make a fire with s.t.

pôn-âpihtâ-kîsikâ– VII be afternoon

pôn-âyamihêwi-kîsikâ– VII be Monday

pônasi– VAI add a little wood to one's fire [*diminutive*]

pônatoskê– VAI cease working

pônêyiht– VTI cease thinking of s.t.; overcome a worrying preoccupation

pônêyihtamaw– VTA forgive s.o. for (it); forgive s.o.

pônêyihtamâto– VAI forgive one another

pôni *IPV* cease

pôni-nôhâwaso– *VAI* stop nursing one's child, wean one's child

pôni-pimâtisi– *VAI* cease to live, die; be no longer alive, be dead

pônihk– *VTI* cease of s.t., leave s.t. alone

pônihtâ– *VAI* cease of (it)

pônikâtê– *VII* be a fire being made; be kept burning as a fire

pônipayi– *VII* cease, stop, come to an end

pônisimo– *VAI* cease dancing

pônwêwit– *VTI* cease making noise; keep quiet

pôsapi– *VAI* be aboard (e.g., boat or vehicle), sit aboard, get aboard

pôsâhtawî– *VAI* climb aboard (e.g., boat or vehicle)

pôsi– *VAI* board, be aboard (e.g., boat or vehicle); ride the train

pôsi-kwâskohti– *VAI* jump aboard (e.g., boat or vehicle)

pôsih– *VTA* make s.o. board (e.g., boat or vehicle), give s.o. a ride; put s.o. on a sleigh, give s.o. a ride on a sleigh

pôsihtâ– *VAI* put (it) aboard (e.g., boat or vehicle), load (it) on

pôsihtâso– *VAI* load up, load one's boat or vehicle

pôsiwêpin– *VTI* throw s.t. on board (e.g., boat or vehicle), throw s.t. on a sleigh

pôsiwin– *NA* train

pôskwahikâso– *VAI* have a hole punched, have oneself pierced

pôskwahw– *VTA* punch a hole in s.o. (e.g., in the reaches under a wagon)

pôskwatahw– *VTA* punch a hole in s.o. (e.g., earring), punch a hole in s.o.

pôtât– *VTA* blow at s.o., blow upon s.o.

pôtât– *VTI* blow on s.t.; blow into s.t., blow s.t. up

pôti *IPC* lo and behold! what is this! [*exclamatory, indicating surprise; e.g.,* pôt êsa; *often as proclitic with a demonstrative pronoun; e.g.,* pôt âwa, pôt ôki, pôt ôhi; pôt ôma, pôt ôhi]

pôyo– *VAI* cease, quit

pwât– *NA* Sioux [*e.g.,* pwâtak (prox. pl.)]

pwâtawihtâ– *VAI* be thwarted at (it), fail of (it)

pwêti *IPC* lo and behold! what is this! [*sic; cf.* pôti; *exclamatory, indicating surprise; e.g., as proclitic with a demonstrative pronoun,* pwêt âwa (prox. sg.)]

sakah– *VTI* nail s.t. on, attach s.t. by nails

sakahikan– *NI* nail

sakahpit– *VTA* tie s.o. up (e.g., horses)

sakâ– *VII* be bush, be woodland

sakâpât– *VTI* attach s.t. by sewing, sew s.t. on

sakâpêkin– *VTA* lead s.o. (e.g., horse) by a rope

sakâpêkipah– *VTA* lead s.o. (e.g., horse) along by a rope

sakâs– *NI* piece of bush, bluff of woodland [*diminutive*]

sakâw– *NI* bush, woodland

sakâwi-mîciwin– *NI* food from the bush

sakâwi-pihêw– *NA* wood-cock, wood-partridge, wood-chicken

sakâwi-pimâcihowin– *NI* life in the bush

sakâwi-pisiskiw– *NA* bush animal, wild animal

sakimêskâw– *NI* abundance of mosquitoes

sakimêwayânêkin– *NI* mosquito screen, insect screen

santakilâws– *NA* (*name:*) Santa Claus [*sic*]

sapiko *IPC* actually, as a matter of fact

sasciwih– *VTA* get ahead of s.o.

sasîhciwih– *VTA* make s.o. ashamed, embarrass s.o.

sasîpiht– *VTI* fail to listen to s.t., disobey s.t.

sasîpihtaw– *VTA* fail to listen to s.o., disobey s.o.

sasîwiskwêw– *NA* Sarci woman

saskaci-wâpaht– *VTI* be tired of looking at s.t.

saskacihtaw– VTA be tired of hearing s.o., be fed up with hearing s.o.

saskah– VTI light s.t. (e.g., lamp)

saskahamaw– VTA light (it/him) for s.o.; light the pipe for s.o.

saskahamâso– VAI light (it/him) for oneself (e.g., fire, pipe)

saskahw– VTA light s.o. (e.g., tobacco)

saskamo– VAI take communion; have one's first communion, have had one's first communion

saskamonah– VTA give s.o. communion

saskamonahiso– VAI give oneself communion, place the host into one's mouth [*i.e., instead of having it placed there by the priest*]

saskamowin– NI host (e.g., in communion)

saskatam– VTA be tired of eating s.o. (e.g., fish, duck) [*sic*]

šavâž– NA savage [*e.g., lî šavâža (obv.)*]

sawêyim– VTA be generous towards s.o.; bless s.o.

sawêyimikowisi– VAI be blessed by the powers

sawôhkât– VTA bestow a palpable blessing upon s.o. [*?sic: stem*]

sâkahikan– NI lake

sâkahikanisis– NI small lake [*diminutive*]

sâkakocin– VAI hang so as to project, hang out of the sky (e.g., snake)

sâkamon– VII stick out, be attached so as to project

sâkaskinah– VTA fill s.o.; fill (it) with s.o. (e.g., snow)

sâkaskinahtâ– VAI make (it) full, fill (it) (e.g., audio-tape)

sâkaskinê– VAI crowd in, fill a place

sâkaskinêkâpawi– VAI stand crowded in, stand to fill a place

sâkâstê– VII be daylight

sâkâstênohk IPC in the east

sâkâwanêhtâ– VAI push (it) to emerge from the ground, make (it) come forth

sâkêkamon– *VII* stick out as cloth, project as cloth
sâkêwê– *VAI* appear, come into view
sâkêwêtâpâso– *VAI* come into view with one's wagon, drive into view
sâkêwêtot– *VTI* come out upon s.t., rise (e.g., sun) upon s.t.
sâkih– *VTA* love s.o., be attached to s.o.
sâkihâwaso– *VAI* love one's children
sâkihito– *VAI* love one another
sâkihito-maskihkiy– *NI* love medicine
sâkihitowaskw– *NI* love medicine
sâkihitowin– *NI* mutual love; charity
sâkihtamaw– *VTA* hold on to (it/him) for s.o.; hold (it/him) back from s.o.
sâkihtâ– *VAI* love (it), be attached to (it)
sâkikihtâ– *VAI* make (it) (e.g., earth) bring forth plants
sâkikin– *VII* grow forth, emerge from the ground
sâkiskwêhpit– *VTA* wrap s.o. up to the neck, swaddle s.o. up to the neck [*i.e., so that only the neck remains unwrapped*]
sâkiskwêpayiho– *VAI* suddenly stick one's head out
sâkito– *VAI* make an announcement, make a proclamation
sâkoh– *VTA* overcome s.o., overpower s.o., overwhelm s.o. [*sic:* -o-; *cf.* sâkôh–]
sâkohtê– *VAI* walk into view, move into view
sâkôcih– *VTA* overcome s.o., defeat s.o.
sâkôcim– *VTA* overcome s.o. by speech; convince s.o. by speech, win s.o. over
sâkôh– *VTA* overcome s.o., overpower s.o., overwhelm s.o. [*sic:* -ô-; *cf.* sâkoh–]
sâkôhtâ– *VAI* overcome (it), accomplish (it), lift (it) up
sâmaht– *VTI* taste s.t.
sâmiskaw– *VTA* rub against s.o.
sâpo *IPV* fully, exhaustively, through and through
sâpohci *IPV* through, all the way through [*sic; cf.* sâposci]
sâpohci-kimiwan– *VII* rain through, come raining through

sâpohtawân– NI long-lodge, through-lodge
sâpohtê– VAI walk through (e.g., through a snare)
sâpohtêmakan– VII go through; persist
sâponikan– NI soap [*sic:* NI]
sâpopatâ– VAI get (it) wet throughout; get one's shoes wet
sâpopê– VAI get wet, be drenched, be wet throughout, be sodden
sâpopê– VII get wet, be drenched, be wet throughout, be sodden
sâposci IPV through, all the way through [*sic; cf.* sâpohci]
sâposci-sakah– VTI nail s.t. through, nail through s.t.
sâpostamon– VII run through; be the reaches (under a wagon) [*usually plural*]
sâpotawâ– VII be open through and through
sâpoyowê– VII be blown through by wind
sâsakici IPV backward
sâsakitisin– VAI lie on one's back
sâsamîna IPC as usual [*sic; cf.* sâsay mîna, âsay mîna, âsamîna]
sâsay IPC already; without delay [*also aspectual; cf.* âsay]
sâsay mîna IPC as usual [*cf.* sâsamîna, âsay mîna, âsamîna]
sâsâkihti– VAI be barefoot
sâsâpiskitê– VII be fried, be pan-fried
sâsâpiskitikâtê– VII be fried, be pan-fried
sâskwatôn INM (*place-name:*) Saskatoon (Saskatchewan) [*sic*]
sêhkêpayîs NA car, automobile [*diminutive*]
sêhkwêpitê– VII be pulled to expand; be an elastic band
sêkah– VTI comb s.t. (e.g., hair)
sêkaho– VAI comb one's hair [*sic; cf.* sîkaho–]
sêkahon– NI comb
sêkih– VTA frighten s.o.
sêkim– VTA frighten s.o. by speech
sêkipatwâ– VAI braid one's hair, have braided hair, wear braids

sêkisi– *VAI* be afraid
sêkon– *VTI* place s.t. underneath; place s.t. beneath the coals
sêkopayin– *VII* run beneath, go underneath, get caught underneath
sêkw-âyihk *IPC* underneath
sêkwamon– *VII* be underneath, be attached underneath
sêkwâ *IPC* underneath
sêkwâhtawî– *VAI* crawl underneath (e.g., a tree)
sêkwâpiskin– *VTA* place s.o. beneath the coals, place s.o. (e.g., beaver) in the oven
sêkwâpiskin– *VTI* place s.t. beneath the coals, place s.t. in the oven
sêmâk *IPC* right away, immediately, instantly
sênapân– *NA* ribbon, satin ribbon [*sic; cf.* sênipân–]
sênipân– *NA* ribbon, satin ribbon [*sic; cf.* sênapân–]
sênipânasâkay– *NI* satin dress
sêsâwin– *VTA* stretch s.o. by hand, exercise s.o.'s limbs (in therapy)
sêsâwipayi– *VAI* stretch, become stretched
sêskisi– *VAI* go into the bush; go into the bush to relieve oneself
sêskitâpâso– *VAI* drive into the bush
sêstakw– *NA* yarn, thread
sêwêpin– *VTA* make s.o. (e.g., rattle) ring out
sêwêpitamaw– *VTA* make (it) ring out for s.o.; call s.o. by telephone
sihko– *VAI* spit, spit out
sihkos– *NA* weasel
sikâkw– *NA* skunk
sikohtatâ– *VAI* get (it) torn; go ragged
sikokahw– *VTA* chop s.o. (e.g., beaver) until small
sikon– *VTI* crush s.t. by hand until small
sikopayi– *VII* be crushed, be reduced to small pieces
sikos– *VTI* chop s.t. small

sikosâwât– VTI chop s.t. small (e.g., onion)

sikwah– VTI crush s.t. by tool until small

sikwahcisikê– VAI cultivate, harrow

sikwaht– VTI chew s.t. until small

sikwatah– VTI pound s.t. (by tool with handle) until small

sikwatahikanâpoy– NI minced-meat soup

sikwatahikâtê– VII be pounded, be minced (e.g., meat)

sikwâciwaso– VAI come apart in boiling, be boiled into small pieces; dissolve in boiling

sikwâskocin– VAI be cut by branches or thorns, have one's clothes torn

simacî– VAI stand upright; rear up (e.g., horse)

simâkanis– NA policeman; (*plural:*) the police

simâkanisihkâniwi– VAI be a soldier; take part in war (e.g., World War II)

sinikohtakahikan– NI scrub-brush, floor brush, brush for wood

sinikohtakinikan– NI scrubber, brush; wash-board

sinikon– VTA rub s.o. (e.g., soap)

sipwê IPV departing, leaving, starting off

sipwêcimê– VAI leave by boat, depart by boat

sipwêhâ– VAI fly off, depart flying, fly away

sipwêhotêwi– VAI leave by boat, depart by boat, go out by boat [*dial.* (LR)]

sipwêhtah– VTA take s.o. away, leave with s.o., depart with s.o.

sipwêhtatâ– VAI leave taking (it), depart with (it)

sipwêhtê– VAI leave, depart

sipwêkocin– VII depart in water or air, or by vehicle; fly off, depart flying

sipwêmon– VII leave as path, trail, road; begin as path, trail, road

sipwêpahtâ– VAI run off, drive off

sipwêpayin– VII start off to run (e.g., tape-recorder)

sipwêpici– *VAI* leave with one's camp, depart with one's camp

sipwêpihâ– *VAI* fly off, depart flying [*sic:* -h-; *cf.* sipwêpiyâ–]

sipwêpiyâ– *VAI* fly off, depart flying [*sic:* -y-; *cf.* sipwêpihâ–]

sipwêtâcimopahtâ– *VAI* rapidly crawl away, depart crawling fast

sipwêtâpâso– *VAI* leave with a team of horses, drive off by wagon

sipwêtâpê– *VAI* drive away with (it/him)

sipwêtisah– *VTI* send s.t. off

sipwêtisahw– *VTA* send s.o. off

sipwêwihw– *VTA* make s.o. leave by boat, depart with s.o. by boat [*dial.* (LR)]

sipwêyâciho– *VAI* travel away, depart in travel; depart as a camp

sisikoc *IPC* suddenly

sisikotêyiht– *VTI* find s.t. surprising, find s.t. shocking; be surprised, be shocked

sisocêskiwakinikê– *VAI* plaster things, do the plastering

sisonê *IPC* alongside

sisopâcikâtê– *VII* be spattered, be sprayed

sisopât– *VTA* spread (it) on s.o., apply (it) to s.o.'s chest

sisopât– *VTI* spread (it) on s.t.; lick s.t. off (e.g., sap) [*?sic: second gloss*]

sisopêkah– *VTI* rub (it) flat on s.t. by tool; paint s.t.

sisopêkahw– *VTA* rub (it/him) flat on s.o. by tool; paint s.o.

sisopêkin– *VTA* rub (it/him) flat on s.o. by hand

sisoskiwakin– *VTI* mud s.t. (e.g., log-house), plaster s.t.

sisoskiwakinamâso– *VAI* do the mudding for oneself

sisoskiwakinikâtê– *VII* be mudded

sisoskiwakinikê– *VAI* do the mudding

sisowaskinikê– *VAI* put on mud or plaster; mud one's log-house

siswêwêpin– *VTI* sprinkle s.t. about (e.g., ashes in cleaning) sîhcâskwahonis– NI brassière [*sic:* -hc-; *cf.* sîscâskwahonis–; *diminutive*]

sîhcihtâ– VAI strain (it) (e.g., one's eyes)

sîhcî– VAI strain, be strained

sîhkim– VTA urge s.o. by speech, encourage s.o. by speech; guide s.o. by speech

sîhkiskaw– VTA urge s.o. (by foot or body movement)

sîhkitisahw– VTA urge s.o. along (e.g., horse); lay charges against s.o.

sîhtwahpisoso– VAI be braced, wear a girdle

sîkahasinânâpoy– NI rock-sprinkling water (e.g., in sweat-lodge)

sîkahasinê– VAI pour water on rocks (e.g., in sweat-lodge), sprinkle rocks with water

sîkahâht– VTI spray s.t. (e.g., the land)

sîkahâhtaw– VTA sprinkle s.o. with water; (*fig.*) baptise s.o., accept s.o. into the Catholic church

sîkaho– VAI comb one's hair [*sic; cf.* sêkaho–]

sîkatêhtamaw– VTA spit (it/him) out for s.o.

sîkihtatamaw– VTA pour (it) for s.o.

sîkin– VTA pour s.o. in (e.g., soap)

sîkin– VTI pour s.t.; pour s.t. in (e.g., lye); let it rain

sîkinamaw– VTA pour (it) for s.o. (e.g., tea)

sîkipêstâ– VII pour down as a rain shower

sîkipicikê– VAI pour things out; spill things

sîkiwêpin– VTI pour s.t. out

sîkopit– VTA press s.o. out by pulling; drain the milk from s.o. (e.g., cow)

sîkosâkan– NA cracklings, greaves [*usually plural*]

sîkwanisi– VAI be there in spring, pass the spring, spend the spring

sîkwâ– VII be spring

sîn– VTI wring s.t. out

sînâskwah– VTI wring s.t. out with a wooden tool

sîpah– *VTI* stretch s.t.
sîpahw– *VTA* stretch s.o. (e.g., an animal in processing skins)
sîpaskwât– *VTI* stuff s.t. (e.g., head of an animal) [*dial*. (LR)]
sîpâ *IPC* beneath, underneath
sîpâhtawî– *VAI* crawl underneath (e.g., a tree)
sîpêkaht– *VTI* stretch s.t. with one's teeth
sîpêkiskâwasâkâs– *NI* sweater [*diminutive*]
sîpi *IPV* stretching far back
sîpihkêyiht– *VTI* endure s.t.; persevere in s.t.; persevere
sîpikiskisi– *VAI* remember far back
sîpiy– *NI* river
sîpîsis– *NI* small river, creek [*diminutive*]
sîscâskwahonis– *NI* brassière [*sic:* -sc-; *cf.* sîhcâskwahonis–; *diminutive*]
sîsîkwan– *NA* rattle
sîsîp– *NA* duck
sîsîp-opîway– *NI* duck feathers, duck-down [*sic; cf.* sîsîpipîway–; *usually plural*]
sîsîpakohp– *NI* duck blanket
sîsîpâw– *NI* duck-egg [*?sic: stem*]
sîsîpi-mîcimâpoy– *NI* duck broth, duck soup
sîsîpi-sâkahikan– *NI* (*place-name:*) Duck Lake (Saskatchewan) [*lit.* duck lake]
sîsîpipîway– *NI* duck feathers, duck-down [*sic; cf.* sîsîp-opîway–; *usually plural*]
sîskêpison– *NI* garters
sîtawâ– *VII* be stiff
sîwahcikê– *VAI* eat sweets
sîwihtâkan– *NI* salt
sîwihtâkani-sâkahikan– *NI* salty lake, salt lake
sîwihtâkani-sâkahikanihk *INM* (*place-name:*) Blaine Lake (Saskatchewan) [*locative; lit.* at the salt lake]
sîwinikan– *NA* sugar
sîwinikê– *VAI* sweeten things; sweeten one's tea

sôhkahât *IPV* greatly, vigorously, powerfully [*sic:* IPV]

sôhkan– *VII* be strong, be sturdy; be important; (*fig.*) be powerful, have supernatural power

sôhkatoskê– *VAI* work vigorously, work hard

sôhkâtisi– *VAI* be strong in body, be fit, have a vigorous disposition

sôhkêhtatâ– *VAI* throw (it) vigorously, throw (it) forcefully

sôhkêkocin– *VAI* travel vigorously, travel at great speed

sôhkêpayin– *VII* be strong, work effectively (e.g., medicine)

sôhkêpit– *VTI* stand firmly behind s.t., promote s.t.

sôhkêsimo– *VAI* dance hard, dance vigorously

sôhkêwêpin– *VTI* throw s.t. vigorously, throw s.t. forcefully

sôhki *IPC* strongly, vigorously, powerfully

sôhkisi– *VAI* be strong, be vigorous; be powerful, have supernatural power

sôhkisiwin– *NI* strength, vigour; power, supernatural power; authority

sôkâs– *NA* sugar; candy [*diminutive*]

sôkâw– *NA* sugar

sôkâwâspinê– *VAI* be ill with diabetes, suffer from diabetes, be a diabetic

sôminis– *NA* raisin

sôniyâhkâkê– *VAI* make money with (it), use (it) to earn wages

sôniyâhkât– *VTI* make money at s.t., earn wages at s.t.

sôniyâhkê– *VAI* make money; earn wages; earn (it) as wages

sôniyâhkêsi– *VAI* make some money, earn a little money; earn some wages [*diminutive*]

sôniyâhkêwin– *NI* earning money; wages; income

sôniyâs– *NA* coin; 25-cents coin, quarter; a little money, some money [*diminutive*]

sôniyâw– *NA* gold, silver; money; wages

sôniyâwâpiskw– *NA* gold; copper

sôniyâwi *IPV* with respect to money, in financial matters

sôniyâwi– *VII* be precious metal; be money

sôniyâwikimâw– *NA* Indian agent

sôpaht– *VTI* put s.t. in one's mouth

sôskwakotê– *VII* simply run down, run off (e.g., water)

sôskwâ *IPC* simply, immediately, without further ado; without regard to the consequences; (*in negative constructions:*) not at all [*sic, ending in* -â-; *cf.* sôskwâc, sôskwât]

sôskwâc *IPC* simply, immediately, without further ado; without regard to the consequences; (*in negative constructions:*) not at all [*cf.* sôskwât, sôskwâ]

sôskwât *IPC* simply, immediately, without further ado; without regard to the consequences; (*in negative constructions:*) not at all [*cf.* sôskwâc, sôskwâ]

taciwih– *VTA* get ahead of s.o.

tahcipit– *VTI* undo s.t.

tahk âyiwâk *IPC* increasingly, more and more

tahkam– *VTA* stab s.o.

tahkâ– *VII* be cool, be cold; cool off

tahkâpâwat– *VTA* pour water to cool s.o. (e.g., rock), cool s.o. (e.g., rock) with water (e.g., in sweat-lodge)

tahkâyâ– *VII* be cold weather

tahkêyiht– *VTI* consider s.t. cold; perceive the cold

tahki *IPC* always, all the time

tahkikamâpoy– *NI* cold water

tahkipayi– *VAI* cool down

tahkisi– *VAI* be cooled off, be cool

tahkiskaw– *VTA* kick s.o.

tahkohc *IPC* on top [*cf.* tahkoht]

tahkohcipahkisin– *VAI* fall on top

tahkohcipicikê– *VAI* drive on top of things, drive over things

tahkoht *IPC* on top [*cf.* tahkohc]

tahkohtastâ– *VAI* place (it) on top

tahkon– *VTA* carry s.o., hold s.o.

tahkon– *VTI* carry s.t., hold s.t.

tahkonamôh– *VTA* make s.o. carry (it/him), make s.o. hold (it/him)

tahkonâwaso– *VAI* hold one's child, cuddle one's child

tahkopiso– *VAI* be tied fast

tahkopit– *VTA* tie s.o. fast (e.g., horse), tie s.o. on (e.g., to a sleigh)

tahkopit– *VTI* tie s.t. fast, tie s.t. shut (e.g., swim-bladder), tie s.t. in, tie s.t. up

tahkopitâwaso– *VAI* swaddle one's child; (*fig.*) be delivered of a child

tahkoskê– *VAI* step, take a step, step upon, make a hoofprint

tahkwam– *VTA* hold s.o. fast by mouth, hold s.o. in one's mouth

tahtinikâtê– *VII* be loosened, be taken off

tahto *IPC* so many, as many [*both with and without a noun-phrase*]

tahto-aya *IPC* so many [*sic:* -o-]

tahto-kîkisêpâ *IPC* every morning, early each morning

tahto-kîkway *PR* so many things, as many things, everything

tahto-kîsikâw *IPC* every day, each day, daily

tahto-nîpin *IPC* every summer, each summer

tahto-nîso-kîsikâw *IPC* every second day, every other day

tahto-nîsw-âyamihêwi-kîsikâw *IPC* every second week, fortnightly

tahto-pîsim *IPC* every month, each month, monthly, menstrual

tahtw-âskiy *IPC* so many years, as many years

tahtw-âyamihêwi-kîsikâw *IPC* every Sunday

tahtwayak *IPC* in so many places, in so many ways

tahtwâpisk *IPC* so many dollars [*enclitic with numerals*]

tahtwâw *IPC* so many times, each time

takahk-âcim– *VTA* tell a beautiful story about s.o.
takahk-âtayôhkêwin– *NI* fine sacred story
takahkatâmo– *VAI* sing out beautifully
takahkatimw– *NA* good horse, beautiful horse [*sic:* -at-]
takahkâciwasw– *VTA* boil s.o. (e.g., rabbit) nicely, boil s.o. well
takahkâpâwê– *VII* be nicely washed with water
takahkâpêwi– *VAI* be a handsome man
takahkêyiht– *VTI* think well of s.t., be glad about s.t., like s.t.; be glad, be pleased
takahkêyihtamih– *VTA* please s.o.
takahkêyim– *VTA* think well of s.o., consider s.o. nice, like s.o.
takahkêyimiso– *VAI* think well of oneself, like oneself
takahkêyimo– *VAI* be pleased with oneself
takahki *IPN* nice, good, beautiful
takahki *IPV* nice, good, beautiful [*sic:* IPV]
takahki-kiskinahamawâkanis– *NA* excellent student [*diminutive*]
takahkihtaw– *VTA* like the sound of s.o., consider s.o. to sound nice
takahkihtâkosi– *VAI* sound nice, sound beautiful
takahkihtâkwan– *VII* sound nice, sound beautiful
takahkikihtâ– *VAI* make (it) grow nicely, make (it) a nice garden; have a nice garden
takahkinaw– *VTA* like the look of s.o., consider s.o. good-looking
takahkinâkohtâ– *VAI* make (it) look nice, make (it) look beautiful
takahkipah– *VTA* make s.o. feel good, cause s.o. to be light-headed with an alcoholic drink, get s.o. inebriated
takahkipahtâ– *VAI* run nicely (e.g., horse), run beautifully
takahkipê– *VAI* feel good with drink, be light-headed with alcoholic drink, be inebriated

takahkipicikê– *VAI* drive a nice team, drive beautiful horses
takahkisîh– *VTA* make s.o. (e.g., earring) beautiful
takahkisîho– *VAI* be well dressed, be beautifully dressed
takahkisîhtâ– *VAI* make (it) nice, make (it) beautiful
takahkwêwêhtitâ– *VAI* make (it) sound nice by drumming or tapping; make a nice drumming or tapping sound
takahkwêwêsin– *VAI* fall with nice sounds, make nice sounds with one's shoes
tako *IPV* in addition, additionally, extra; on arrival
tako-kîskwêpê– *VAI* arrive intoxicated with alcoholic drink, arrive inebriated, come home drunk
tako-tipah– *VTI* measure s.t. in addition; pay s.t. extra, pay for s.t. in addition; pay (it) in addition for s.t.
takohtah– *VTA* take s.o. to arrive, lead s.o. to one's destination, arrive with s.o.
takohtatamaw– *VTA* arrive with (it/him) for s.o., carry (it/him) there for s.o.
takohtatâ– *VAI* take (it) to arrive, arrive with (it)
takohtê– *VAI* arrive, arrive walking
takon– *VTA* add (it) to s.o. (e.g., flour), mix (it) into s.o. (e.g., dough); add s.o. to (it), enrich (it) with s.o.
takonikâtê– *VII* be added in by hand
takopahtâ– *VAI* arrive running
takopayi– *VAI* arrive on horseback, arrive driving, arrive by vehicle
takopayi– *VII* arrive, have sufficient reach
takopici– *VAI* arrive with one's camp
takosin– *VAI* arrive
takotisahw– *VTA* drive s.o. to arrive, chase s.o. to arrive
takwah– *VTI* add s.t. by tool; crush s.t. to be added
takwahiminân– *NI* chokecherries
takwahiminê– *VAI* crush chokecherries
takwakotê– *VII* arrive across the sky (e.g., cloud)

takwaskî– *VAI* arrive on the land, move onto the land, join those already on the land [*sic: stem-final -î-; ?cf.* takwaskê–]

takwastâ– *VAI* add something to (it), mix something in with (it)

takwâhtawî– *VAI* arrive in climbing up (e.g., a tree)

takwâkin– *VII* be fall, be autumn

takwâkohk *IPC* last fall

takwâpôyo– *VAI* arrive by railway, arrive by train

takwâwahito– *VAI* bring one another to arrive, arrive as a group

tapahcipayiho– *VAI* swoop down, swoop low

tapasî– *VAI* flee, run away

tapasîh– *VTA* flee from s.o.

tapâtiskwêyi– *VAI* hold one's head low, lower one's head

tasamân– *NI* smudge (smoky fire, often of sage-brush, made to protect cattle against insects) [*sic:* ta-; *cf.* atisamân–]

tasamânihkê– *VAI* make a smudge (smoky fire, often of sage-brush, made to protect cattle against insects) [*sic:* ta-; *cf.* atisamânihkê–]

tasi *IPC* along in time, at the same time; for such a time, for the duration [*sic:* IPC]

tasi *IPV* along in time, at the same time; for such a time, for the duration

tasin– *VTI* pull the trigger on s.t. (e.g., gun), shoot s.t. off (e.g., gun); emit a sharp noise, make a shot-like noise; sound a thunderclap (e.g., as Thunderbird)

tasîhcikâtê– *VII* be talked about, be discussed

tasîhk– *VTI* bother with s.t., trifle with s.t.; be engaged in s.t.

tasîhkaw– *VTA* be busy with s.o., work on s.o. (e.g., fish), trouble oneself with s.o. (e.g., fish)

tasîht– *VTI* talk about s.t., discuss s.t.

tasîhtamaw– *VTA* discuss (it/him) with s.o.

taskamohtê– *VAI* cut across, walk straight towards one's goal

tasôh– *VTA* entrap s.o. (e.g., bird) by putting feed under a movable lid, trap s.o. underneath

taspinê– *VAI* be ill for such a time, be ill for the duration

tastawayas *IPC* in between, in the middle

tastôstôkan– *VII* be bog, be quicksand [*sic*]

taswêkin– *VTI* unfold s.t. as cloth; open s.t. (e.g., book) up flat

taswêkisâwât– *VTI* cut s.t. (e.g., leg of rabbit) into thin sheets

taswêkiwêpin– *VTA* spread s.o. (e.g., wing) flat

tatahkamikisi– *VAI* busy oneself thus or there; have things to do

tatâyawâ– *VII* be crowded

tawâ– *VII* be open, have room

tawâtamaw– *VTA* open (it) up for s.o.; clear the way for s.o.

tawin– *VTI* open s.t. (e.g., house, bottle); turn s.t. on (e.g., stereo, TV)

tawinamaw– *VTA* open (it/him) for s.o.; (*fig.*) open the door to s.o. (e.g., devil)

tâh-tâpwê *IPC* in fact, in truth [*reduplicated*]

tâh-têpi *IPC* at regular intervals [*reduplicated*]

tâhkôcikâtê– *VII* be discussed

tâhkôm– *VTA* discuss s.o., discourse upon s.o.

tâhkôt– *VTI* discuss s.t., discourse upon s.t.

tâna *PR* which one [*interrogative; e.g.,* tâna, tânihi; tânima]

tânêhki *IPC* why

tânimatahto *IPC* how many; so many, several

tânimatahtw-âskîwinê– *VAI* be how many years old; be so many years old

tânimatowâhtik *IPC* what kind of tree [*sometimes pluralised as if* NA]

tânimayikohk *IPC* to which extent; to such an extent [*e.g.,* tânimayikohk ê-itahtopiponêyan 'how old you are']

tânimayikohkêskamik *IPC* to which extent, for how long

tânisi IPC how, in what way
tânispî IPC when, at what time [*cf.* tâyispî]
tânita IPC where
tânitahto IPC how many; so many
tânitahto-kîsikâw IPC how many days; so many days; several days
tânitahto-nîpin IPC how many summers; so many summers, a few summers [*e.g.*, tânitahto-nîpin aspin 'a few summers ago']
tânitahto-pîsim IPC how many months; so many months
tânitahto-tipahikan IPC what hour, what time; so many hours, that time; several hours
tânitahtw-âskiy IPC how many years; so many years
tânitahtw-âya IPC how many kinds; so many kinds
tânitahtwayak IPC in how many places; in so many places
tânitahtwâw IPC how many times; so many times
tânitê IPC where over there, whither
tânitowahk IPC what kind
tânitowihk IPC in what place
tâniyikohk IPC to what extent; to such an extent; so many, plenty
tâpakwamahw– VTA snare s.o., trap s.o. [*dial.* (LR)]
tâpakwân– NI snare
tâpakwânêyâpiy– NI snare-wire
tâpakwânihkê– VAI make a snare
tâpakwâso– VAI get oneself snared, be caught in a snare
tâpakwât– VTA snare s.o.
tâpakwê– VAI set snares
tâpakwêwêpin– VTA lasso s.o.
tâpapîstamaw– VTA sit in s.o.'s place, succeed s.o. in office
tâpâtot– VTI tell s.t. fittingly, tell s.t. correctly, tell s.t. faithfully
tâpihtêpison– NA earring
tâpisah– VTI lace s.t. (e.g., mossbag)

tâpisikopayi– *VAI* get caught in something

tâpisk– *VTI* wear s.t. fitted, wear s.t. around the neck

tâpiskô *IPC* as if; seemingly, apparently [*sic, ending in* -ô-; *cf.* tâpiskôc, tâpiskôt]

tâpiskôc *IPC* as if; seemingly, apparently [*cf.* tâpiskôt, tâpiskô]

tâpiskôt *IPC* as if; seemingly, apparently [*cf.* tâpiskôc, tâpiskô]

tâpitawi *IPC* all the time, at all times

tâpitonêhpicikan– *NI* bridle

tâpowê– *VAI* speak correctly; recite one's prayer correctly

tâpwê *IPC* truly, indeed

tâpwê piko *IPC* straight away, immediately

tâpwê– *VAI* speak true, speak the truth

tâpwêht– *VTI* agree with s.t., believe s.t.

tâpwêhtaw– *VTA* agree with s.o., believe s.o.

tâpwêmakan– *VII* come true; (*fig.*) be fulfilled (e.g., prophecy)

tâpwêwakêyiht– *VTI* hold s.t. to be true, believe in s.t.; regard s.t. positively

tâpwêwakêyim– *VTA* believe in s.o.

tâpwêwin– *NI* true speech, truth

tâsah– *VTI* grind s.t. (e.g., bone needle) to a point by tool

tâsahikâkê– *VAI* grind things with (it), use (it) to grind things

tâsawisâwât– *VTI* cut into the middle of s.t., slice s.t. open (e.g., veal belly cordon-bleu)

tâsipwâw *IPC* in fact, as a matter of fact [*cf.* tâspwâw]

tâskatah– *VTI* split s.t. (e.g., cordwood) by tool

tâskatahimihtê– *VAI* split firewood

tâskipayi– *VAI* split apart (e.g., reaches under a wagon)

tâskipit– *VTI* split s.t. apart

tâskiwêpahw– *VTA* split s.o. (e.g., rock) by arrow, shoot s.o. (e.g., rock) apart

tâspwâw IPC   in fact, as a matter of fact [*sic; cf.* tâsipwâw]
tâtopit– VTI   tear s.t. up into small pieces
tâw-âyihk IPC   in the centre
tâwakisin– VAI   bump into (her/him)
tâwati– VAI   have one's mouth open
tâwatipayi– VAI   suddenly open one's mouth
tâwic IPC   in the middle (e.g., lake)
tâwin– VTA   encounter s.o., come upon s.o., bump into s.o., hit s.o.
tâwin– VTI   encounter s.t. by hand, come upon s.t., bump into s.t.
tâwisk– VTI   encounter s.t. (by foot or body movement), come upon s.t., bump into s.t.
tâwiskaw– VTA   encounter s.o. (by foot or body movement), bump into s.o., come into contact with s.o.
tâyispî IPC   when, at what time [*cf.* tânispî]
têhcipayiho– VAI   jump on (e.g., on a horse)
têhtapi– VAI   be mounted, ride on horseback
têhtapîwitâs– NA   riding breeches
têhtastâ– VAI   place (it) on top
têpakiht– VTI   count s.t. up
têpakohp IPC   seven
têpakohp-askiy IPC   seven years, for seven years
têpakohpomitanaw IPC   seventy
têpakohposâp IPC   seventeen
têpâpam– VTA   see plenty of s.o., see s.o. fully
têpêyimo– VAI   be content, be willing
têpi IPV   fully, sufficiently, enough
têpihkwâmi– VAI   sleep long enough, have enough sleep
têpinêh– VTI   have enough to pay for s.t.
têpinêhamaw– VTA   make full payment for (it/him) to s.o.
têpipayi– VAI   have the full amount, put away enough; have enough, have a sufficiency; have enough of (it)
têpisk– VTI   fit s.t. (e.g., garment)

têpiwi– VAI tape (it), make an audio-recording of (it) [sic]

têpiyâhk IPC merely; barely, the most (if any); the only thing; so long as; (*in negative constructions:*) all but

têpiyâhk êkâ IPC almost

têpwât– VTA call out to s.o., yell at s.o.; publish the marriage banns for s.o.

têpwâtamaw– VTA call out for s.o., be an advocate for s.o.

têpwê– VAI call out, shout, holler, yell

têtipêwêyâmo– VAI flee around in a circle

têyistikwânê– VAI have one's head hurt, have a headache

tihkis– VTI melt s.t. down

tihkiso– VAI melt, thaw out (e.g., snow, ice, tree, hibernating animal)

tihkisw– VTA melt s.o.; render s.o. (e.g., cracklings)

tihtipin– VTI twist s.t. (e.g., rope); roll s.t. up

tihtipiwêpin– VTA twist s.o.

timikoni– VII be deep snow [*sic: stem-final* -i-; *dial.* (LR)]

tipah– VTI measure s.t.; pay s.t., pay for s.t.; pay (it) for s.t.

tipahamaw– VTA pay s.o. for (it/him), repay a debt to s.o.; pay s.o. a pension

tipahamâto– VAI receive one's Treaty payment, be paid Treaty

tipahamâtowi-sôniyâw– NA Treaty money, Treaty payment

tipahamâtowin– NI Treaty

tipahaskân– NI reserve

tipahâkê– VAI measure things with (it/him), measure things against (it/him), use (it/him) as a benchmark; measure things; rely on things

tipahikê– VAI pay for things, make a payment

tipahw– VTA pay (it) for s.o. (e.g., stove)

tipêyihcikâtê– VII be owned, be controlled, be governed

tipêyihcikê– VAI be master over things, be in charge; (*fig.*) be the Lord

tipêyiht– *VTI* own s.t., control s.t., rule s.t., be master over s.t.; have a voice in the affairs of s.t. (e.g., reserve)

tipêyim– *VTA* own s.o., control s.o., rule s.o.; (*fig.*) be the Lord over s.o.; have s.o. in one's clutches (e.g., devil)

tipêyimiso– *VAI* control oneself, govern oneself; be on one's own, be one's own boss

tipiskâ– *VII* be night [*e.g.*, ta-tipiskâk ôma 'this evening, tonight']

tipiskâw– *NI* night, night sky

tipiskâwi-pîsimw– *NA* moon

tipiskisi– *VAI* spend one's night, live through the night

tipiskohk *IPC* last night

tipiskôc *IPC* even, at the same level, parallel; directly overhead

tipiyaw *IPC* personally, in person; really [*cf.* tipiyawê]

tipiyawê *IPC* personally, in person; really [*cf.* tipiyaw]

tipiyawêho– *VAI* live in one's own dwelling, have one's own household

tipôt– *VTI* discuss s.t. with authority

titipahpit– *VTA* roll and tie (it) around s.o., bandage s.o. with (it)

titipahpit– *VTI* roll and tie (it) around s.t.

titipawêhkas– *VTI* curl s.t. (e.g., head) by heat; have a perm

titipihtin– *VII* be rolled up, be twisted

titipikwanah– *VTI* sew s.t. in overcast stitch (e.g., the spiral loops around the vamp of a moccasin)

titipin– *VTI* twine s.t., twist s.t.; roll s.t. up

titipisim– *VTA* roll s.o. (e.g., thread) up

tôcikâtê– *VII* be done thus

tôcikêmakan– *VII* have such an effect; be the cause of (it)

tôhkâpi– *VAI* open one's eyes, have one's eyes open

tôhtôsâpoy– *NI* milk; milk come in (e.g., seen to have come down into the cow's udder at calving time)

tômâ– *VII* be greased, be greasy

tôt– *VTI* do s.t. thus; act thus [*sic:* t-; *cf.* itôt-]
tôtamaw– *VTA* do (it) thus for s.o.; do thus to s.o.
tôtamâso– *VAI* do (it) thus for oneself
tôtamôh– *VTA* make s.o. do (it) thus, make s.o. act thus
tôtaw– *VTA* do (it) thus to s.o., treat s.o. thus
tôtâso– *VAI* do (it) thus to oneself
tôtâto– *VAI* do (it) thus to one another
twêho– *VAI* alight, land (e.g., bird, airplane)
twêhômakan– *VII* alight, land (e.g., airplane)
twêwêkocin– *VAI* audibly break apart (e.g., rock)
wa *IPC* oh! [*exclamatory*]
wacaskw– *NA* muskrat
wacistwan– *NI* nest
wacîhk *INM* (*place-name*) [*locative; lit.* at the hill, at the hills; in the vicinity of Sandy Lake (Saskatchewan)*]
wahwâ *IPC* oh my! [*exclamatory*]
wanahâht– *VTA* lose s.o.'s tracks
wanaskoc *IPC* at the end, at the tip, at the top
wanastâ– *VAI* misplace (it), mislay (it)
wanâh– *VTA* lead s.o. astray, distract s.o.; disrupt s.o.'s life
wanâm– *VTA* distract s.o. by speech
wanâtapi– *VAI* sit so as to expose oneself
wanêyiht– *VTI* forget s.t., be unsure of s.t.; have one's mind blurred, be confused
wani *IPV* indistinctly, blurred
wani-tipiskâ– *VII* be dark night
wani-tipiskin– *VTI* perceive s.t. as darkness; merely see night, perceive merely darkness
wani-tipiskipayin– *VII* get dark (e.g., sky)
wanih– *VTA* lose s.o.; lose s.o. (e.g., to death)
wanihikamaw– *VTA* set traps for s.o. (e.g., animal)
wanihikan– *NI* trap, metal trap
wanihikê– *VAI* trap, set traps

wanihikêskanaw– *NI* trapline
waniho– *VAI* be lost, get lost
wanihtâ– *VAI* lose (it); get relief from (it)
wanikiskisi– *VAI* forget (it/him); be forgetful
wanisim– *VTA* cause s.o. to get lost, lead s.o. astray
wanisimôhâwaso– *VAI* lead one's children astray
wanisin– *VAI* get lost, be lost
wanisinohtah– *VTA* lead s.o. to lose (it/him)
wanisîho– *VAI* be indistinctly dressed, be confusingly dressed, be wrongly dressed
waniskâ– *VAI* arise (from lying or sleep)
waniskâpahtâ– *VAI* jump up (from lying)
wanitonâmo– *VAI* make a mistake in speaking, commit a slip of the tongue
waniyaw *IPC* any, somebody; at random
wanohtê– *VAI* err, make a mistake, take the wrong road
wanwêhkaw– *VTA* leave s.o. baffled by speech or in speech, confuse s.o.
waskawipit– *VTI* move s.t. by pulling, shake s.t. by pulling [*sic*: -i-]
waskawî– *VAI* move, move about, be energetic
waskawîhtâ– *VAI* keep at (it), keep at one's work
waskawîmakan– *VII* move, move about, be shaken by an earthquake
waskawîstamâso– *VAI* work for oneself, be enterprising
waskawîtot– *VTI* carry on with s.t.
waskawîwin– *NI* being active, enterprise
waskic *IPC* on top, on the surface
waskicaskisinis– *NI* overshoe, rubber [*diminutive*]
waskicipit– *VTI* pull s.t. over top
waskipicikan– *NI* pull-on, overshoe, rubber
waskitakotâ– *VAI* hang (it) on top, hang (it) over
waskitasâkay– *NI* overcoat
waskitaskamik *IPC* on the face of the earth

waskitaskisin– *NI* overshoe, rubber
waskway– *NI* birch-tree, birchbark
waskway– *NI* cloud [*?sic: stem; cf.* waskow– NI, waskwâw– NI]
waskwayi-mîtos– *NA* birch-tree
waskwayi-ôs– *NI* birchbark canoe [*e.g.,* waskwayi-ôsa (pl.)]
waskwayiwat– *NI* birchbark basket
watihkwan– *NI* branch
wawânaskêhtamaw– *VTA* create a peaceful life for s.o.
wawânaskêhtâ– *VAI* live a peaceful life [*sic; cf.* wânaskêwin– NI]
wawânêyiht– *VTI* be at a loss for s.t.; worry about s.t.; be worried
wawânêyihtamih– *VTA* cause s.o. to be at a loss; cause s.o. to worry about (it/him); (*especially in inverse constructions:*) place s.o. in a bind [*e.g.,* niwawânêyihtamihik 'she had me in a quandary']
wawêsihcikâtê– *VII* be decorated
wawêsî– *VAI* dress up, get titivated
wawêsîh– *VTA* dress s.o. up, get s.o. titivated
wawêyapi– *VAI* sit in readiness
wawêyî– *VAI* get ready, make preparations
wawêyîh– *VTA* get s.o. ready, get s.o. dressed
wawêyîst– *VTI* prepare s.t., be prepared
wawiyas *IPC* funny, amusing
wawiyasinâkosi– *VAI* look funny, look amusing
wawiyasipayin– *VII* be funny, be amusing
wawiyatâcimowinis– *NI* funny little story [*diminutive*]
wawiyatêyiht– *VTI* find s.t. funny, consider s.t. amusing; be funny about s.t., behave oddly
wawiyatêyim– *VTA* find s.o. funny, consider s.o. amusing; feel joy about s.o.
wawiyatisi– *VAI* be deservedly ridiculed, receive one's just deserts
wayawî *IPV* outside, outdoors

wayawî– VAI go outside, go outdoors; go to relieve oneself; leave school, leave hospital

wayawîhtatâ– VAI have (it) go outdoors; take (it) out, get (it) back (e.g., from photographer)

wayawîkâpawi– VAI stand outside, go outdoors

wayawîpahtâ– VAI run outside, run outdoors

wayawîpakitin– VTA put s.o. (e.g., diaper) down outdoors

wayawîpit– VTI pull s.t. (e.g., fence-post) out of the bush

wayawîsimo– VAI dance outdoors, dance towards the outside

wayawîstamâso– VAI go outdoors for oneself, go to relieve oneself

wayawîtimihk IPC outside, outdoors

wayawîtisahikêmakan– VII drive things out; drive the fever out

wayawîtisahw– VTA send s.o. outdoors; send s.o. off the reserve, banish s.o. from the reserve

wayawîwikamikw– NI outhouse, toilet

wayawîwin– NI going outside, being outdoors; going to relieve oneself, going to the toilet

wayawîyâmohkê– VAI arrange for s.o. to flee outdoors

wayân– NA hide, skin [*sic; not a dependent stem*]

wayêsih– VTA trick s.o., deceive s.o.; take advantage of s.o.

wayêsim– VTA trick s.o. by speech

wâ IPC well [*introductory; cf.* â, hâ]

wâcistak IPC oh my!

wâcistakâc IPC by golly! lo and behold! [*exclamatory, indicating surprise; cf.* wâcistakât]

wâcistakât IPC by golly! lo and behold! [*exclamatory, indicating surprise; cf.* wâcistakâc]

wâh-wahwahwâ IPC oh my god! oh my lord! oh no! [*exclamatory, indicating surprise; reduplicated*]

wâh-wahwâ IPC oh my god! oh my! [*exclamatory, indicating surprise; reduplicated*]

wâh-wâhyaw IPC in far places [*reduplicated*]

wâh-wâsaskotêpayi– *VII* be lightning [*reduplicated*]

wâh-wîhkâc *IPC* at rare intervals, rarely now and again [*reduplicated*]

wâh-wîpac *IPC* quite often, again and again, repeatedly [*reduplicated*]

wâhkêyêyiht– *VTI* be easily swayed; (*fig.*) be too weak

wâhkôhto– *VAI* be related to one another, have one another as relatives; use kin-terms for one another

wâhkôm– *VTA* be related to s.o., have s.o. as one's relative; use a kin-term for s.o.

wâhkwan– *NA* fish-eggs [*?sic:* NA, NDA; *usually plural*]

wâhyaw *IPC* far away

wâhyawês *IPC* a little away; quite far away [*cf.* wâhyawîs]

wâhyawêskamik *IPC* very far away

wâhyawîs *IPC* quite far away [*cf.* wâhyawês]

wâkayôs– *NA* bear

wâkin– *VTI* bend s.t.

wâkisi– *VAI* be bent

wânaskêwin– *NI* being at peace with oneself [*sic; cf.* wawânaskêhtâ– VAI]

wâpahcikâtê– *VII* be seen, be witnessed

wâpahkê– *VAI* watch things, observe people

wâpahki *IPC* tomorrow

wâpaht– *VTI* see s.t., witness s.t.

wâpahtih– *VTA* make s.o. see (it), show (it) to s.o.

wâpakosîs– *NA* mouse [*sic:* wâ-; *cf.* âpakosîs–]

wâpakwaniy– *NI* flower [*sic:* -wa-]

wâpakwanîs– *NI* flower [*sic:* -wa-; *diminutive*]

wâpam– *VTA* see s.o., witness s.o.

wâpamon– *NI* mirror

wâpan– *VII* be dawn, be early morning; be the next day [*cf.* ê-wâpahk 'the next day'; kîhtwâm ê-wâpahk 'the next morning, the next day'; wâpahki 'tomorrow']

wâpanastâ– *VAI* place (it) until dawn, leave (it) until dawn

wâpanatâhkw– NA morning-star, Venus

wâpani IPV until dawn [*e.g.*, wâpani-takohtê– 'arrive at dawn'; wâpani-môcikihtâ– 'make merry until dawn']

wâpanisimo– VAI dance until dawn

wâpanohtêw INM (*man's name*) [*lit.* Walks-til-Dawn, Walks-at-Dawn, Comes-Back-at-Dawn]

wâpanwêwit– VTI make noise until dawn, bark through the night (e.g., dog)

wâpasinîwiskwêw– NA (*woman's name*) [*lit.* White-Rock-Woman]

wâpastimw– NA white horse

wâpatonisk– NA white clay

wâpâstê– VII be light-coloured, be faded in colour

wâpi– VAI see, be sighted, have vision; (*in negative constructions:*) be blind

wâpikwayâs– NA (*man's name*) [*lit.* White-Neck]

wâpisk-ânâskât– VTA provide s.o. with white bedsheets

wâpiskah– VTI whitewash s.t.

wâpiskahikê– VAI do the whitewashing

wâpiskatayêw– NA gopher

wâpiskayiwinis– NI white cloth [*sic:* -a-]

wâpiskâ– VII be white, be unsmoked (e.g., leather)

wâpiskâpâwê– VAI be white from water (e.g., skin), turn white with washing (e.g., pants); turn white under a compress (e.g., skin)

wâpiski-pimiy– NI lard, rendered lard

wâpiski-wiyâs– NA non-Indian, White person

wâpiskihtakâ– VII be white boards, be white floor

wâpiskinikêmakisi– VAI make things white, whiten things (e.g., as soap) [*sic*]

wâpiskipêkahw– VTA paint s.o. white

wâpiskisi– VAI be white

wâpistikwânê– VAI have white hair; have light hair, be blond

wâpiwin– NI eye-sight

wâposo-câpakwêsi– VAI set small snares, set rabbit snares [*diminutive*]

wâposo-mîcimâpoy– NI rabbit broth, rabbit soup

wâposos– NA young rabbit, small rabbit [*diminutive*]

wâposw– NA rabbit

wâposwayân– NA rabbitskin, raw rabbitskin [*sic:* NA]

wâposwayân– NI rabbitskin, dressed rabbitskin [*sic:* NI]

wâposwayânakohp– NI rabbitskin blanket

wâsakâ IPC around a circle, in a full circle

wâsakâhtê– VAI walk around a circle, walk a circuit [*sic; cf.* wâskâhtê–]

wâsakâm IPC around a circle, in a full circle

wâsakâmêsimo– VAI dance the ghost-dance, participate in the ghost-dance

wâsakâmêsimowikamikw– NI ghost-dance lodge; ghost-dance

wâsakâmêsimowin– NI ghost-dance

wâsakâmêyâpôyo– VAI go around a circle by railway, describe a circuit by rail

wâsakân– VTI turn s.t. around a circle; make s.t. go around, turn s.t. (e.g., treadle), crank s.t. [*sic; cf.* wâskân–]

wâsakâpi– VAI sit in a circle

wâsakâtisahoto– VAI chase one another around a circle

wâsakâyâskon– VTA point s.o. (e.g., pipe) around a circle

wâsaskocênikanis– NI candle [*diminutive*]

wâsaskocêpayîs– NI lamp, electric light [*diminutive*]

wâsaskotawêpi– VAI sit with a lamp, have light from a lamp

wâsaskotê– VII be light, be lit; be a lantern

wâsaskotênamaw– VTA light (it) for s.o., provide light to s.o.

wâsaskotênikan– NI light, lamp, lantern

wâsaskotênikâkê– VAI light things with (it), use (it) to have light, use (it) as a lamp

wâsaskotênikê– VAI light things, have light
wâsaskotêpayi– VII be a bolt of lightning, be a lightning-strike
wâsênamân– NI window [*cf.* wâsênamâwin–]
wâsênamâwin– NI window [*cf.* wâsênamân–]
wâsihkopayi– VAI glitter (e.g., wedding-ring)
wâskahikan– NI house
wâskahikanihkê– VAI build a house
wâskahikanis– NI little house; shack, temporary building, trailer; play-house [*diminutive*]
wâskamisî– VAI settle down; be of quiet disposition
wâskâhtê– VAI walk around a circle, walk a circuit [*sic; cf.* wâsakâhtê–]
wâskân– VTI turn s.t. around a circle; make s.t. go around, turn s.t. (e.g., treadle), crank s.t. [*sic; cf.* wâsakân–]
wâskâsk– VTI go around s.t., circle s.t.
wâspison– NI mossbag
wâspisonis– NI mossbag [*diminutive*]
wâspit– VTA wrap s.o. up in a mossbag, lace s.o. up in a mossbag, swaddle s.o.
wâstinikê– VAI signal by hand, wave
wâtihkân– NI hole, cellar
wâtihkât– VTI make a hole for s.t., dig a hole for s.t.
wâtihkê– VAI make a hole, dig a hole
wâwâc IPC especially, even, even more
wâwâskêsiwacîs– NI (*place-name*) [*diminutive; lit.* elk hill, elk hills, red deer hill, red deer hills]
wâwâstinamaw– VTA wave at s.o., signal to s.o. by hand
wâwiyê IPV round, in a ball
wâwiyêkamâ– VII be a round lake
wâwiyêkwât– VTI sew s.t. round (e.g., rug)
wâwiyên– VTI bend s.t. round
wâwiyêyâ– VII be round
wâwîs IPC especially, particularly

wâwîs cî *IPC* especially, all the more so
wâwonî– *VAI* turn back, return [*sic; cf.* wâyonî–]
wâyonî– *VAI* turn back, return [*sic; cf.* wâwonî–]
wêcîpwayâniw– *NA* Chipewayan
wêhcasin– *VII* be easy
wêhci *IPV* easy, in ease
wêhci-pimâtisi– *VAI* live in ease, have an easy life
wêhcih– *VTA* have an easy time with s.o. (e.g., hide)
wêhciskowipayi– *VII* come easily
wêhtakihtê– *VII* be cheap, be inexpensive
wêhtisi– *VAI* have it easy
wêmistikôsiw– *NA* Frenchman; non-Indian, White person
wêmistikôsîmototaw– *VTA* speak French to s.o., address s.o. in French
wêpah– *VTI* sweep s.t. up; throw s.t. by tool, push s.t. by tool; cock s.t. (e.g., gun)
wêpahikan– *NI* broom
wêpahikâkê– *VAI* sweep things with (it), use (it) to sweep, use (it) as a broom
wêpahikê– *VAI* sweep things, do the sweeping
wêpêyim– *VTA* be inclined to throw s.o. (e.g., money) away
wêpin– *VTA* throw s.o. away; empty s.o. (e.g., pail); throw s.o. down or in (e.g., money in a card-game); leave s.o. (e.g., spouse); abandon s.o. (e.g., child)
wêpin– *VTI* throw s.t. away; abandon s.t.
wêpinamaw– *VTA* throw (it/him) on s.o., dump (it/him) on s.o., leave (it/him) with s.o., abandon (it/him) to s.o.
wêpinâson– *NI* draped cloth, flag, cloth offering
wêpinikan– *NA* abandoned child, neglected child
wêpinikâtê– *VII* be thrown away, be abandoned, be discarded; be lost (e.g., blood)
wêpinikê– *VAI* throw things about; throw people about, dance a European dance

wêpinito– *VAI* leave one another, separate from one another, get divorced

wêpinitowin– *NI* leaving one another, separating from one another, divorce

wêtinahk *IPC* quietly

wêwêkahpit– *VTA* wrap and tie (it) around s.o., bandage s.o. with (it)

wêwêkahpit– *VTI* wrap and tie (it) around s.t.

wêwêkapi– *VAI* sit wrapped up, sit bundled up

wêwêkin– *VTA* wrap (it) around s.o., wrap s.o. up

wêwêkin– *VTI* wrap (it) around s.t.; wrap s.t. around

wêwêkiscikwânêhpisonis– *NA* head-scarf [*diminutive*]

wêwêkisin– *VAI* lie wrapped up

wêwêpison– *NI* swing

wêwêpisonihkê– *VAI* make a swing, arrange a swing

wêyôtan– *VII* be an abundance

wêyôtisi– *VAI* be wealthy, be rich

wiy âta wiya *IPC* but of course [*concessive*]

wiya *IPC* by contrast [*enclitic; cf.* wiyê]

wiya *IPC* for, because [*clause-initial causal conjunction; cf.* wiyê]

wiya *PR* he, she

wiyahisow– *NA* blacksmith

wiyahpicikê– *VAI* harness one's horse; harness up

wiyahpit– *VTA* harness s.o. (e.g., horse)

wiyahpit– *VTI* tie s.t. together, tie s.t. into a bundle [*sic; cf.* owiyahpit–]

wiyakâc *IPC* it is regrettable [*predicative*]

wiyakiht– *VTI* set a price for s.t.

wiyakihtamaw– *VTA* set a price on (it/him) for s.o., charge s.o. for (it/him)

wiyakihtâ– *VAI* treat (it) as worthless; (*especially in negative constructions:*) not waste (it); not destroy a valuable possession

wiyakim– VTA set a price on s.o. (e.g., bread); arrange (it) for s.o.; decide on s.o.; give orders to s.o.
wiyasiwât– VTA decide about s.o.; sit in judgment on s.o., hold court over s.o.
wiyasiwât– VTI decide s.t.; make a rule or law about s.t.
wiyasiwâtiso– VAI make a plan for oneself, make one's plan
wiyasiwêhkâniwi– VAI be a band councillor
wiyasiwêwin– NI decision; rule, law; council, band council
wiyaskinah– VTA fill s.o. (e.g., pipe) [*sic; cf.* oyaskinah–]
wiyastamaw– VTA set the table for s.o.
wiyastê– VII be arranged, be structured
wiyatah– VTI pound s.t., hammer s.t. together
wiyatahamâso– VAI pound (it/him) into shape for oneself
wiyatahw– VTA pound s.o. (e.g., earring), mould s.o., shape s.o.
wiyawâw PR they
wiyâ wîpac cî wiya IPC it is a rare and welcome event that [*predicative governing the changed conjunct*]
wiyâhkwât– VTA swear at s.o., speak to s.o. in obscenities
wiyâhkwêwi-âcimo– VAI swear in telling stories; tell obscene stories, tell risqué stories
wiyâht– VTI wear s.t., wear s.t. as underclothing
wiyâhtikosi– VAI be ebullient, have a bubbly personality
wiyâkan– NI dish, bowl, vessel, pot
wiyâkanikamikw– NI pantry, scullery; walk-in closet
wiyâkanis– NI small dish, small bowl [*diminutive*]
wiyâs– NI meat
wiyâsowi– VAI be meaty, have meat still attached (e.g., cracklings)
wiyê IPC by contrast [*enclitic; cf.* wiya]
wiyê IPC for, because [*clause-initial causal conjunction; cf.* wiya]
wiyêyiht– VTI have an idea, think of what to do
wiyikwât– VTI sew s.t. together, sew s.t. up

wiyino– VAI be fat (e.g., animal); be fat, be plump (e.g., little girl)

wiyino– VII be fat [*sic: stem-final -o-,* VII]

wiyinw– NI fat, fat meat, piece of fat [*i.e., unprocessed; usually plural*]

wiyis– VTI cut s.t. out, cut s.t. to a pattern

wiyisamaw– VTA cut a pattern for s.o.

wiyisamâso– VAI cut a pattern for oneself, cut one's own pattern

wiyisw– VTA cut s.o. out (e.g., figure in a picture-book)

wiyîhcikê– VAI conduct negotiations, conclude negotiations

wiyîpâ– VII be soiled, be dirty [*sic:* wiyî-; *cf.* wî-, î-]

wiyôhkomi– VAI have a grandmother, have a grandmother living; have (her) as one's grandmother [*sic; cf.* oyôhkomi–]

wî IPV intend to, be about to

wîc-âyamihâm– VTA pray together with s.o., join s.o. in prayer

wîc-âyâhto– VAI live together; be married to one another

wîc-âyâm– VTA be together with s.o., live together with s.o.; be married to s.o.

wîc-îspîhcisîm– VTA be of the same age as s.o., have s.o. as one's age-mate

wîc-ôhcîm– VTA come from the same time or place as s.o., share the year of birth with s.o.

wîc-ôhpikîm– VTA grow up together with s.o., be raised together with s.o.

wîcêht– VTI go along with s.t., support s.t., cooperate with s.t.

wîcêhto– VAI live with one another, join with one another; get along with one another; breed with one another

wîcêhtowin– NI living with one another; getting along with one another, living in harmony with one another

wîcêw– VTA accompany s.o., get along with s.o., join s.o., live with s.o.

wîcêwâkani– VAI have a companion or partner, have (her/him) as one's companion or partner [*sic; cf.* owîcêwâkani–]

wîcêwâkanihto– VAI find one another as partner or spouse

wîcêwâkanim– VTA have s.o. as partner, be in partnership with s.o.

wîcêwiskwêwê– VAI have one's wife along

wîci-kiskinohamâkosîm– VTA be in school together with s.o., have s.o. as a fellow student

wîci-mêtawêm– VTA play together with s.o., have s.o. as one's playmate

wîci-minihkwêm– VTA drink together with s.o., have s.o. as a drinking companion

wîci-mîcisôm– VTA eat together with s.o., share one's meal with s.o.

wîci-piponisîm– VTA winter together with s.o., have s.o. as one's wintering partner

wîci-pîhtwâm– VTA smoke together with s.o., have s.o. as one's fellow smoker

wîci-pîkiskwêm– VTA speak together with s.o., have s.o. as one's fellow speaker

wîci-tôtamôm– VTA do (it) together with s.o., participate with s.o. in doing (it)

wîcih– VTA help s.o.

wîcihikowisi– VAI be helped by the powers

wîcihiso– VAI help oneself; apply oneself, study for oneself; rely on oneself in childbirth

wîcihito– VAI help one another, cooperate with one another

wîcihiwê– VAI join in, be along, participate, be part of a group

wîcihtâso– VAI help with things

wîcisimôm– VTA dance together with s.o., have s.o. as one's fellow dancer

wîcôhkamaw– VTA help s.o. by doing (it)

wîh– VTA name s.o., mention s.o. by name

wîhcêkaskosiy– NI onion, wild onion
wîhcêkaskosîwi-sâkahikanihk INM *(place-name:)* Onion Lake (Saskatchewan) [*locative; lit.* at the wild onion lake]
wîhcêkimahkasikê– VAI give off a bad smell, produce a foul odour
wîhkasin– VAI taste good
wîhkasin– VII taste good
wîhkaskoyiniw– NA *(name)* [*lit.* Sweetgrass-Old-Man]
wîhkaskw– NI sweetgrass
wîhkâc IPC ever; *(in negative constructions:)* never [*cf.* wîhkât]
wîhkât IPC ever; *(in negative constructions:)* never [*cf.* wîhkâc]
wîhkês– NI ratroot
wîhkihkasikan– NA cake
wîhkimahkaso– VAI smell sweet in burning
wîhkimâkwan– VII smell good, give off a pleasant odour; have an aromatic odour
wîhkipw– VTA like the taste of s.o. (e.g., duck, beaver), have a preference for the taste of s.o.
wîhkist– VTA like the taste of s.o. (e.g., bread, duck)
wîhkist– VTI like the taste of s.t.
wîhkitisi– VAI taste good (e.g., beaver, fish, bannock)
wîhkohkât– VTI hold a feast for s.t. (e.g., medicinal herbs)
wîhkohkê– VAI hold a feast
wîhkohkêh– VTA hold a feast for s.o., hold a feast in s.o.'s honour
wîhkohkêmo– VAI invite people to a feast
wîhkohto– VAI invite one another to a feast
wîhkom– VTA invite s.o. to a feast [*sic:* -o-; *cf.* wîhkôm–]
wîhkô– VAI strain oneself, use all one's force
wîhkôm– VTA invite s.o. to a feast [*sic:* -ô-; *cf.* wîhkom–]
wîhkway– NI craw (e.g., bird); swim-bladder (e.g., fish)
wîhkwâs– NI craw [*i.e., first stomach of fowl; diminutive*]
wîhkwêhcâ– VII go around as land, be curved as land, be the sweep of the valley [*?sic: gloss*]

wîhkwêhtakâw– NI corner made by wooden walls, corner of the floor, corner of the house

wîhkwêskamikâ– VII be the corners of the earth, be the ends of the earth

wîhkwêskaw– VTA go around s.o., head s.o. off

wîhkwêstê– VII be placed around, stand in the shape of a curve

wîhkwêtâpânâskw– NA rounded toboggan, curved sleigh

wîhowin– NI name

wîht– VTI name s.t., mention s.t. by name; tell about s.t., report s.t.; decree s.t.

wîhtamaw– VTA tell s.o. about (it/him)

wîhtamâkowin– NI speech, what is said to s.o. [*sc. 'patient-centred' noun; e.g.,* owîhtamâkowin 'what has been said to him']

wîhtamâkowisi– VAI be told about (it/him) by the powers

wîhtamâto– VAI tell one another about (it/him)

wîhtamâwaso– VAI tell (it/him) to one's children

wîhtaskât– VTA sing about s.o. with words, sing a texted song about s.o.

wîhtaskât– VTI sing about s.t. with words, sing a texted song

wîhtikow– NA cannibal monster; (*name:*) Wihtikow, Windigo

wîkatêhtê– VAI walk off to the side, get away [*sic:* wî-; *cf.* yî-, î-]

wîkatêtâpê– VAI drag (it) off to the side, drag (it) away [*sic:* wî-; *cf.* yî-, î-]

wîkatêwêpin– VTA push s.o. aside, push s.o. away [*sic:* wî-; *cf.* yî-, î-]

wîki– VAI live there, dwell there, have one's home there [*cf.* owîki-]

wîkihtah– VTA take s.o. to be married, arrange for s.o. to be married; join s.o. (e.g., a couple) in marriage

wîkihto– VAI live together; marry one another, be married to one another
wîkihtowin– NI living together; marriage, matrimony; getting married, wedding
wîkim– VTA live with s.o.; be married to s.o.
wîkiwin– NI household; (*fig.*) home
wîmâskaw– VTA pass around s.o., pass s.o. by
wîn– NI bone-marrow [*e.g.,* wîni (sg.)]
wînâstakay– NI "tripe", paunch [*i.e., largest stomach of ruminant*]
wînisakâcihp– NA badger
wîpac IPC soon, early
wîpakwêpayi– VAI have one's neck snapped (e.g., in a snare)
wîpayiwinis– NI dirty clothes, soiled clothing
wîpâcikin– VII grow out of place, grow wild, grow as weeds
wîpâtayiwinis– NI dirty clothes, soiled clothing [*sic:* wî-; *cf.* wiyî-, î-]
wîsahkêcâhkw– NA (*name:*) Wisahketchahk
wîsakahcahw– VTA make s.o. very envious, get s.o.'s goat
wîsakêyiht– VTI have pain in s.t. (e.g., neck)
wîsaki IPV sharply, painfully; sorely
wîsakisin– VAI get hurt in a fall
wîsakitêhê– VAI (*fig.*) experience heart-ache, have a heavy heart
wîsakîmin– NI cranberry
wîsâm– VTA ask s.o. along, take s.o. along; ask s.o. to dance
wîscihkânis– NI hay-pile [*diminutive*]
wîscihkêsi– VAI pile hay into small heaps [*diminutive*]
wîskipôs– NA whiskey-jack
wîskwas– VTI smoke s.t. (e.g., fish, hide)
wîskwastêwinâkwan– VII be brown in appearance
wîskwasw– VTA smoke s.o. (e.g., fish)

wîsta PR he, too; she, too; he by contrast, she by contrast; he himself, she herself

wîstawâw PR they, too; they, by contrast; they themselves

wîstihkê– VAI pile hay into heaps

wîtapiht– VTI sit by s.t.; hatch one's eggs (e.g., bird)

wîtapihtah– VTA set s.o. (e.g., chicken) to brood

wîtapim– VTA sit with s.o., sit beside s.o., be present with s.o.; work together with s.o.

wîtaskîwêm– VTA live together with s.o., have s.o. as one's compatriot; live in the same country with s.o., live in peace with s.o.

wîtatoskêm– VTA work together with s.o., have s.o. as one's fellow worker

wîtimosi– VAI have a cross-cousin of the opposite sex; have (him/her) as one's cross-cousin of the opposite sex [*sic*: -t-]

wîtokwêm– VTA share a dwelling with s.o., live with s.o., have s.o. as one's housemate

wîwi– VAI have a wife, be married (man); have (her) as one's wife; take a wife

yahkatâmo– VAI sing out vigorously

yahkâtihkât– VTI dig out more of a hole or cellar, push out the size of an existing hole or cellar

yahkitisahw– VTA drive s.o. forward [*sic; cf.* ahkitisahw–]

yaw IPC well now; ho! [*sic*: y-; *cf.* iy-; *introductory; also exclamatory, indicating surprise*]

yââw IPC well now; ho! [*sic*: y-; *cf.* iy-; *introductory; also exclamatory, indicating surprise*]

yâhk îtâp IPC as if, pretendingly [*sic; cf.* âhk îtâp]

yâhkasin– VII be light in weight

yâhkâstimon– NI sail

yâhki IPC pretend, make-believe [*sic; cf.* âhki]

yâyâhk IPC really, for sure, to be sure; especially, all the more so

yâyikâskocin– VAI have one's clothes ripped ragged on branches or thorns

yêkawiskâwikamâhk *INM* (*place-name:*) Sandy Lake (Saskatchewan); *atâhk-akohp*'s Reserve [*locative; lit.* at the sandy lake]

yêyâpisin– *VAI* look on with favour; be tempted by looking at (it)

yêyih– *VTA* get s.o. excited by one's action, tempt s.o. by one's action

yîkatêhtê– *VAI* walk off to the side; (*fig.*) walk away [*sic:* yî-; *cf.* î-, wî-]

yîkatên– *VTI* set s.t. aside [*sic:* yî-; *cf.* î-, wî-]

yîkatêpayin– *VII* move off to the side, move sideways (e.g., braided strips of rabbitskin) [*sic:* yî-; *cf.* î-, wî-]

yîkatêstaw– *VTA* go off to the side from s.o., go away from s.o. [*sic:* yî-; *cf.* î-, wî-]

yîkinikan– *NA* milk-cow [*sic:* yî-; *cf.* î-]

yîkinikê– *VAI* milk, do the milking [*sic:* yî-; *cf.* î-]

yîkinikêstamâso– *VAI* do the milking for oneself [*sic:* yî-; *cf.* î-]

yîwahikan– *NA* pounded meat [*sic:* yî-; *cf.* î-]

yîwêpayi– *VAI* be ragged, be in rags

yîwêyâskocin– *VAI* have one's clothes torn ragged on branches or thorns

yôhô *IPC* oh! [*exclamatory*]

yôhtên– *VTI* open s.t.; turn s.t. (e.g., television set) on

yôhtênamaw– *VTA* open (it/him) for s.o.; turn (it/him) (e.g., television set) on for s.o.

yôhtêwêpin– *VTI* throw s.t. open (e.g., lodge-cover)

yôôôh *IPC* oh! [*sic; cf.* yôh; *exclamatory*]

yôskâ– *VII* be soft

yôskipotâ– *VAI* soften (it) by scraping (e.g., hide)

yôskisi– *VAI* be soft [*sic:* y-; *cf.* iy-]

yôtin– *VII* be wind, be a windstorm [*sic:* y-; *cf.* iy-]

yôtinw– *NA* (*name:*) Wind [*sic:* y-; *cf.* iy-]

yôtinw– *NI* wind, high wind, tornado [*sic:* y-; *cf.* iy-]

English Index

ABANDON
nakat– VTA leave s.o. behind; leave s.o. alone (e.g., helpless); abandon s.o. (e.g., child); leave s.o. behind in death, die leaving s.o. behind
pakiciwêpin– VTI let go of s.t., abandon s.t.
pakitin– VTI let s.t. go, allow s.t., permit s.t.; release s.t.; give s.t. up, abandon s.t. (e.g., teaching, tradition); put s.t. down on earth; put s.t. in (e.g., seed potatoes)
wêpin– VTA throw s.o. away; empty s.o. (e.g., pail); throw s.o. down or in (e.g., money in a card-game); leave s.o. (e.g., spouse); abandon s.o. (e.g., child)
wêpin– VTI throw s.t. away; abandon s.t.
wêpinamaw– VTA throw (it/him) on s.o., dump (it/him) on s.o., leave (it/him) with s.o., abandon (it/him) to s.o.

ABANDONED
wêpinikan– NA abandoned child, neglected child
wêpinikâtê– VII be thrown away, be abandoned, be discarded; be lost (e.g., blood)

ABDOMEN
–atay– NDI belly; abdomen (e.g., in childbirth)

ABDOMINAL
–askatay– NDI abdominal wall of animal

ABILITY
kaskihtâwin– NI ability to do (it), competence

ABLAZE
kwâhkotê– VII catch fire, be ablaze

ABLE
kaskih– VTA prevail upon s.o., succeed in imposing one's will on s.o.; be able to deal with s.o.; earn s.o. (e.g., money)
kaskiho– VAI be able, be competent
kaskihtâ– VAI be able to do (it), be competent at (it), manage (it)
kî IPV able to

ABOARD
pôsapi– VAI be aboard (e.g., boat or vehicle), sit aboard, get aboard
pôsâhtawî– VAI climb aboard (e.g., boat or vehicle)
pôsi– VAI board, be aboard (e.g., boat or vehicle); ride the train
pôsi-kwâskohti– VAI jump aboard (e.g., boat or vehicle)
pôsihtâ– VAI put (it) aboard (e.g., boat or vehicle), load (it) on

ABODE
âhc-âyâ– VAI move one's abode, move from one place to another
ihtâwin– NI abode, place of residence; community

ABOVE
ispimihk IPC high up, up above; upstairs
mêmohci IPC in particular, above all; exactly, precisely

ABREAST
nîpitêh– VTA place s.o. in a row, place s.o. abreast, place s.o. in a line
nîpitêpi– VAI sit in a row, sit abreast

ABRUPTLY
kakwâyakinikê– VAI act with great speed, act abruptly; buck violently (e.g., horse)

ABSENCE
kôtawêyim– VTA be aware of s.o.'s absence, feel the loss of s.o., miss s.o.

ABSENT
namatakon– VII be non-existent, be absent; have disappeared, be no longer in existence
namatê– VAI be non-existent, be absent; have disappeared, be no longer in existence

ABUNDANCE
minahikoskâ– VII be a spruce thicket, be an abundance of spruce
sakimêskâw– NI abundance of mosquitoes
wêyôtan– VII be an abundance

ABUSE
minihkwê– VAI drink (it); have a drink; drink an alcoholic drink; abuse alcohol
minihkwêski– VAI habitually abuse alcohol, be an alcoholic

minihkwêwin– *NI* drink; drinking, alcohol abuse

pîhtwâwin– *NI* smoking; *(fig.)* cannabis abuse

ABUSIVE

kakwâtakih– *VTA* make s.o. suffer; be mean to s.o., be abusive to s.o.; *(especially in inverse constructions:)* affect s.o. terribly (e.g., as disease), ravage s.o.

ACCEPT

miy-ôtin– *VTA* take s.o. in, accept s.o.

otin– *VTI* take s.t.; pick s.t., choose s.t., select s.t. (e.g., moss); steal s.t.; take s.t. over; extract s.t. (e.g., grease from soup), remove s.t. (e.g., glands in butchering beaver), extract s.t.; accept s.t. (e.g., contract); capture s.t., record s.t. on audio-tape

sîkahâhtaw– *VTA* sprinkle s.o. with water; *(fig.)* baptise s.o., accept s.o. into the Catholic church

ACCIDENT

nipahisin– *VAI* get killed in a car accident

ACCIDENTALLY

pisc-ôtin– *VTI* accidentally take s.t., accidentally ingest s.t. (e.g., pill)

pisci *IPV* by accident, accidentally, erroneously, in error

pistah– *VTI* knock s.t. down inadvertently, hit s.t. accidentally

pistahw– *VTA* knock s.o. down inadvertently, hit s.o. accidentally

pistin– *VTI* take s.t. accidentally, take s.t. by mistake

ACCOMPANY

aspatot– *VTA* accompany one's request of s.o. with a gift

wîcêw– *VTA* accompany s.o., get along with s.o., join s.o., live with s.o.

ACCOMPLISH

miyoniskêhkât– *VTI* accomplish s.t. by the work of one's hands

miyopit– *VTI* carry s.t. off well, accomplish s.t.

sâkôhtâ– *VAI* overcome (it), accomplish (it), lift (it) up

ACCOUNT

âcimo– *VAI* tell things, tell a story, give an account

âcimostaw– *VTA* tell s.o. about (it/him), tell s.o. a story, give s.o. an account

âcimowin– *NI* story, account, report

âcimômakan– *VII* tell things, provide an account

âtot– *VTI* tell about s.t., give an account of s.t.

itâcimo– *VAI* tell thus, tell a story thus, tell such a story, give such an account

itâcimostaw– *VTA* tell s.o. thus about (it/him), tell s.o. such a story, give s.o. such an account

itâcimowinihkât– *VTI* tell thus about s.t., make such a story of s.t., give such an account of s.t.

itâcimômakan– *VII* tell thus about (it/him), tell such a story, give such an account

itâtot– *VTI* tell thus about s.t., give such an account of s.t.

ACCUSE

atâmêyim– *VTA* blame s.o. in one's thoughts, accuse s.o. in one's thoughts

ACCUSTOMED

nakayâh– *VTA* get s.o. accustomed to something, break s.o. (e.g., horse), tame s.o., train s.o.

nakayâsk– *VTI* be accustomed to s.t., be comfortable with s.t., be familiar with s.t.

nakayâskaw– *VTA* be accustomed to s.o., be comfortable with s.o., be familiar with s.o.

ACHE

kâkîtisi– *VAI* ache, experience pain

ACIDIC

âhkwâpahtê– *VII* give off a sharp odour, produce pungent fumes, emit acidic or caustic fumes

kîsiso– *VAI* be cooked to completion; burn oneself, get burnt; get burnt by an acidic or caustic agent

ACROSS

akâmaskîhk *IPC* across the water, overseas

akâmi-sîpîsisihk *IPC* across the creek

akâmi-tipahaskân *IPC* across the border; across the forty-ninth parallel, in the United States

akâmihk *IPC* across water, across the lake

akâmôtênaw *IPC* across the camp-circle; across the settlement, across town

âh-âyin– *VTI* touch s.t. repeatedly, rub across s.t. by hand

âsowahpitê– *VII* be stretched across, be strung across

âsowakâmêpici– *VAI* move one's camp across a body of water âsowiskâ– *VAI* cross by boat, go across by boat

âsowohtah– *VTA* go across with s.o., take s.o. across

âsowohtê– *VAI* walk across, cross the road

âsô-nakî– *VAI* stop in moving across (e.g., the prairies), stop in one's transit

âsôhtatâ– *VAI* lean (it) across something

âsônamaw– *VTA* pass (it/him) across to s.o., pass (it/him) on to s.o.; hand (it/him) down to s.o., bequeathe (it/him) to s.o.

ohpohtât– *VTI* proceed high across s.t. (e.g., sky), rise up upon s.t. (e.g., sun upon sky)

paskiciwêpin– *VTA* throw s.o. across; throw s.o. (e.g., rabbit) over drying rack

pimic-âyihk *IPC* across, athwart, crosswise, sideways

pimicikâpawi– *VAI* stand sideways, stand across

pimitapi– *VAI* sit crosswise, sit across (e.g., path)

takwakotê– *VII* arrive across the sky (e.g., cloud)

taskamohtê– *VAI* cut across, walk straight towards one's goal

ACT

itâtisi– *VAI* act thus, be of such a disposition

itihtâkosihkâso– *VAI* pretend to be heard making such a noise, act as if to make such a noise

itinikê– *VAI* do things thus; act thus; experience such things; get into such things

itiskwêhkê– *VAI* act thus as a woman; give the impression of being such a woman

itôt– *VTI* do s.t. thus; act thus

itôtamôh– *VTA* make s.o. do (it) thus, cause s.o. to act thus

kakâmwâtiskwêhkê– *VAI* act quietly as a woman; give the impression of being a quiet woman

kakwâyakinikê– *VAI* act with great speed, act abruptly; buck violently (e.g., horse)

mamihtisihkâso– *VAI* act proudly, hold back, hesitate with one's response

mâyinikê– *VAI* act badly, do harmful things; experience bad things, come to harm

mâyinikêhkâto– *VAI* act badly towards one another, harm one another

mêkwâskaw– *VTA* encounter s.o. in the midst of (it), catch s.o. in the act

môniyâhkâso– *VAI* be like a White person, act White

tôt– *VTI* do s.t. thus; act thus

tôtamôh– *VTA* make s.o. do (it) thus, make s.o. act thus

ACTION

yêyih– *VTA* get s.o. excited by one's action, tempt s.o. by one's action

ACTIVE

kakâyawâciho– *VAI* live an active life; work hard in one's life, lead an industrious life

kakâyawâtisi– *VAI* be active; be hardworking, be of industrious disposition

kakâyawi *IPV* actively; by working hard, industriously

kakâyawisî– *VAI* be active; be hardworking, be industrious

waskawîwin– *NI* being active, enterprise

ACTUALLY

pâhkaci *IPC* actually, firmly

sapiko *IPC* actually, as a matter of fact

ACUTE

nahâpi– *VAI* have one's eyes focussed, have acute vision

nahiht– *VTI* hear s.t. sharply; have acute hearing

ADD

akohtitâ– *VAI* put (it) in water, add (it) to water (e.g., boric acid)

kikâpôhkê– *VAI* add (it) to soup, enhance one's soup with (it)

kikin– *VTA* add s.o. (e.g., tobacco) in, mix s.o. in

kikin– *VTI* put s.t. on something, add s.t. in (e.g., baking-powder)

nîmâh– *VTA* make s.o. take provisions; add (it) to s.o.'s packed lunch

pônasi– *VAI* add a little wood to one's fire

takon– *VTA* add (it) to s.o. (e.g., flour), mix (it) into s.o. (e.g., dough); add s.o. to (it), enrich (it) with s.o.

takwah– *VTI* add s.t. by tool; crush s.t. to be added

takwastâ– *VAI* add something to (it), mix something in with (it)

ADDITION
asici *IPC* also, in addition, along with, together with
kiyikaw *IPC* in addition, additionally
tako *IPV* in addition, additionally, extra; on arrival
tako-tipah– *VTI* measure s.t. in addition; pay s.t. extra, pay for s.t. in addition; pay (it) in addition for s.t.

ADDRESS
kitot– *VTA* address s.o., speak to s.o.; lecture s.o.
kitot– *VTI* address s.t., speak to s.t. (e.g., spirit-bundle)
pîkiskwât– *VTA* speak to s.o., address s.o.
pîkiskwât– *VTI* speak about s.t., speak about s.t. with concern; speak a prayer over s.t.; address s.t., speak to s.t. (e.g., spirit-bundle)
wêmistikôsîmototaw– *VTA* speak French to s.o., address s.o. in French

ADEPT
nahî– *VAI* be adept at (it), be good at (it); be competent, be an expert

ADHERE
pimitisah– *VTI* follow s.t.; *(fig.)* adhere to a religion

ADHERENT
otayamihâw– *NA* Christian, adherent of Christianity

ADULT
iskwêw– *NA* woman, female, female adult
nâpêw– *NA* man, male, adult male

ADULTHOOD
kîs-ôhpiki– *VAI* complete one's growing up, reach adulthood, be grown up

ADVANCE
kîsâc *IPC* beforehand, in advance, in preparation
kwayâc *IPC* ready, prepared in advance
kwayâcihtâ– *VAI* get (it) ready, prepare (it) in advance
kwayâtah– *VTA* place s.o. (e.g., rock) in readiness, prepare s.o. (e.g., rock) in advance
kwayâtastâ– *VAI* place (it) in readiness, put (it) aside in advance
mâtayak *IPC* ahead of time, beforehand, in advance

ADVANCED
kêhtêyâtisi– *VAI* be old, be advanced in age

ADVANTAGE
wayêsih– *VTA* trick s.o., deceive s.o.; take advantage of s.o.

ADVERSE
mâyiskaw– *VTA* go through s.o. to bad effect, affect s.o. negatively, fail to agree with s.o.; *(especially in inverse constructions:)* have an adverse effect on s.o., make s.o. ill

ADVISE
kitahamaw– *VTA* advise s.o. against (it/him), warn s.o. about (it/him)

ADVOCATE
otitwêstamâkêw– *NA* interpreter; advocate
otônihkâ– *VAI* use (it/him) as one's mouthpiece, make (it/him) one's advocate
têpwâtamaw– *VTA* call out for s.o., be an advocate for s.o.

AFFECT
ispayih– *VTA* affect s.o. thus, happen thus to s.o.
itiskaw– *VTA* *(especially in inverse constructions:)* have such an effect on s.o., leave s.o. thus affected
kakwâtakih– *VTA* make s.o. suffer; be mean to s.o., be abusive to s.o.; *(especially in inverse constructions:)* affect s.o. terribly (e.g., as disease), ravage s.o.
kikiskaw– *VTA* *(especially in inverse constructions:)* affect s.o., befall s.o.; inhere in s.o., engross s.o.
mâyiskaw– *VTA* go through s.o. to bad effect, affect s.o. negatively, fail to agree with s.o.; *(especially in inverse constructions:)* have an adverse effect on s.o., make s.o. ill
miyo-tôtaw– *VTA* do s.o. good, affect s.o. beneficially, do s.o. a good turn

AFFECTED
ispayi– *VAI* fare thus, have such an experience, be thus affected; be thus afflicted
itipê– *VAI* be thus affected with alcoholic drink, be in such shape from alcoholic drink

AFLAME
kwâhkotênikê– *VAI* start a fire, set things aflame

AFRAID
kostâci– *VAI* be afraid, have fear
sêkisi– *VAI* be afraid

AFTERNOON
pôn-âpihtâ-kîsikâ– *VII* be afternoon

AGAIN
ispayin– *VII* take place thus, occur thus; run thus (in a cycle), be there (in

a cycle), come around (in a cycle), be that time again; come by, go by, have passed (e.g., days, years)
kâh-kîhtwâm *IPC* again and again
kâwi *IPC* again; back, in return
kîhtwâm *IPC* again, once more, the next
mîna *IPC* also, and also, again
wâh-wîhkâc *IPC* at rare intervals, rarely now and again
wâh-wîpac *IPC* quite often, again and again, repeatedly
AGE
–îci-kîhkâw– *NDA* aged spouse, fellow old person, fellow oldster, companion of one's old age
ihtahtopiponwêwin– *NI* having so many years, the number of one's years, one's age
ispîhtisî– *VAI* extend thus; be of such age
kawikîhkâ– *VAI* be bent with age, be prostrated by age
kêhtêyâtisi– *VAI* be old, be advanced in age
nayawaciki– *VAI* grow up to reach various ages, be variously grown up
wîc-îspîhcisîm– *VTA* be of the same age as s.o., have s.o. as one's age-mate
AGE-MATE
–pê-wîc-îspîhcisîmâkan– *NDA* age-mate from there on down
wîc-îspîhcisîm– *VTA* be of the same age as s.o., have s.o. as one's age-mate
AGENT
otasahkêw– *NA* dispenser of rations; Indian agent
sôniyâwikimâw– *NA* Indian agent
AGREE
mâyiskaw– *VTA* go through s.o. to bad effect, affect s.o. negatively, fail to agree with s.o.; *(especially in inverse constructions:)* have an adverse effect on s.o., make s.o. ill
tâpwêht– *VTI* agree with s.t., believe s.t.
tâpwêhtaw– *VTA* agree with s.o., believe s.o.
AGRICULTURE
kistikêwi-pimâcihowin– *NI* agricultural way of life, farm economy
okistikêwiyinîwi– *VAI* be a farmer, be engaged in agriculture
okistikêwiyinîwiwin– *NI* farming, farm-work, agriculture

AHEAD
mâtayak *IPC* ahead of time, beforehand, in advance
nîkâniwi– *VII* be ahead, be the future; lie in the future
nîkânohtê– *VAI* walk ahead, walk in the lead
sasciwih– *VTA* get ahead of s.o.
taciwih– *VTA* get ahead of s.o.
AIM
itâpi– *VAI* look thus or there; take aim thus or there
AIR
ispâhkêkocin– *VII* rise high up, hang high aloft, be suspended high in the air
sipwêkocin– *VII* depart in water or air, or by vehicle; fly off, depart flying
AIRPLANE
nakatahw– *VTA* leave s.o. behind in departing by boat or airplane
nâtahw– *VTA* fetch s.o. by boat or airplane; pick s.o. up (e.g., as an airplane)
ohpaho– *VAI* fly up (e.g., bird); fly off, lift off by airplane
pimihâkan– *NI* airplane
ALCOHOL
iskotêwâpoy– *NI* alcoholic drink, liquor, whisky
itipê– *VAI* be thus affected with alcoholic drink, be in such shape from alcoholic drink
kawipah– *VTA* cause s.o. to fall down with alcoholic drink
kîskwêpê– *VAI* be crazy with alcoholic drink, be drunk
kîskwêpêski– *VAI* be habitually crazy with alcoholic drink, be habitually drunk
minah– *VTA* give s.o. to drink (e.g., tea, soup); give s.o. tea to drink; give s.o. an alcoholic drink, induce s.o. to drink an alcoholic drink
minihkwê– *VAI* drink (it); have a drink; drink an alcoholic drink; abuse alcohol
minihkwêsi– *VAI* drink a little of (it) (e.g., tea, soup); have a little drink; drink a small amount of an alcoholic drink
minihkwêski– *VAI* habitually abuse alcohol, be an alcoholic
minihkwêwin– *NI* drink; drinking, alcohol abuse
môcikipê– *VAI* have fun with alcohol, make merry with alcoholic drink

nâtôpê– VAI go to fetch water; go for a drink; go for alcoholic drink

pêtôpê– VAI bring an alcoholic drink hither, bring an alcoholic drink home or into the house

pêyak-tipahôpân IPC one gallon of alcoholic drink (e.g., wine)

takahkipah– VTA make s.o. feel good, cause s.o. to be light-headed with an alcoholic drink, get s.o. inebriated

takahkipê– VAI feel good with drink, be light-headed with alcoholic drink, be inebriated

tako-kîskwêpê– VAI arrive intoxicated with alcoholic drink, arrive inebriated, come home drunk

ALIGHT

twêho– VAI alight, land (e.g., bird, airplane)

twêhômakan– VII alight, land (e.g., airplane)

ALIGN

itâpêkin– VTA align s.o. (e.g., porcupine quills) thus (e.g., end-to-end); lead s.o. (e.g., horse) thus or there

ALIVE

êtatawisi– VAI be barely alive, be weak unto death, be about to die

pimâtisi– VAI live, be alive, survive

pôni-pimâtisi– VAI cease to live, die; be no longer alive, be dead

ALL

ayapinikê– VAI be all over things, be into things

êkosi IPC thus, in that way; that is all

kahkiyaw IPC every, all

kapê-ayi IPC all along, all the time, for the entire period, throughout

kâh-kapê-ayi IPC all the time

kâkikê IPC always, at all times, forever; for a very long time, forever (metaphorically)

kitamw– VTA eat all of s.o. (e.g., bear)

kitâ– VAI eat (it) up, eat (it) completely, eat all of (it); drink all of (it); finish drinking a bottle of (it); drink an entire bottle

kitânawê– VAI eat all of (it)

kitâpayihtamaw– VTA eat all of (it/him) on s.o., eat s.o.'s entire supply

mâmawi-wîcihitowin– NI all helping together, general cooperation

mêscihtatâ– VAI get all of (it) torn, get all of (it) ragged

mêsciwêpah– VTI throw away all of s.t.

mêstâskocihtâ– VAI get all of (it) torn by branches or thorns

mêstin– VTA use all of s.o. (e.g., thread)

mêstinikê– VAI use things up, exhaust things, spend all of (it); spend all of one's money on things

misakâmê IPC all along, all the way, in continuity, throughout

misiw îtê IPC all over, everywhere

misiwê IPC all over, the entire place

misiwêminakin– VTI put beads all over s.t.; cover s.t. with beads

misiwêskamik IPC all over the land, all over the world

tahki IPC always, all the time

tâpitawi IPC all the time, at all times

ALLEVIATE

ânisîhtâ– VAI alleviate the effect of (it), be an antidote to (it)

ALLOW

pakitin– VTA set s.o. down, allow s.o., permit s.o.; permit (it) to s.o., give permission to s.o.; let s.o. go, release s.o.; release s.o. (e.g., fish-spawn into lake), stock a lake with s.o. (e.g., fish); drop s.o. off (e.g., as an airplane)

pakitin– VTI let s.t. go, allow s.t., permit s.t.; release s.t.; give s.t. up, abandon s.t. (e.g., teaching, tradition); put s.t. down on earth; put s.t. in (e.g., seed potatoes)

pakitinamaw– VTA allow (it) for s.o., arrange (it) for s.o.; release (it/him) for s.o.

pakitinikâso– VAI be allowed, have permission; be released

ALLOWANCE

awâsisi-sôniyâs– NA family allowance

ALMOST

kêkâc IPC almost

têpiyâhk êkâ IPC almost

ALOFT

akocipayi– VAI be caught aloft

akosî– VAI perch aloft, be perched (e.g., on a tree)

ispâhkêkocin– VII rise high up, hang high aloft, be suspended high in the air

nîmin– VTI hold s.t. aloft, offer s.t. up

nîminamaw– VTA hold (it/him) aloft for s.o., offer (it/him) up for s.o.

nîminikê– VAI hold things aloft, offer things up

ohpâskwah– VTI raise s.t. (e.g., cloth) on a wooden pole, hold s.t. aloft on a wooden pole

pinakocin– VAI fall down from aloft

ALONE
nakat– VTA leave s.o. behind; leave s.o. alone (e.g., helpless); abandon s.o. (e.g., child); leave s.o. behind in death, die leaving s.o. behind
pêyak IPC one, alone, a single one; the only one; a certain one
pêyako– VAI be alone, be the only one; be left alone; go alone (e.g., as a woman, improperly)
pêyakwapi– VAI stay alone, be alone in the house
pêyakwâciho– VAI live alone, travel alone

ALONG
kiki IPC along with
kiki IPV along with
pimi IPV along, in linear progression; while moving in linear progression

ALONGSIDE
sisonê IPC alongside

ALREADY
âsay IPC already; without delay
sâsay IPC already; without delay

ALRIGHT
namôya nânitaw IPC it is alright

ALSO
asici IPC also, in addition, along with, together with
mâka mîna IPC also, on the other hand; as usual
mîna IPC also, and also, again

ALTHOUGH
âta IPC although; on the other hand

ALWAYS
itwêski– VAI say thus habitually, always say thus
kâkikê IPC always, at all times, forever; for a very long time, forever (metaphorically)
pisisik IPC always, every time, routinely
tahki IPC always, all the time

AMAZED
mâmaskâsihtaw– VTA be amazed upon listening to s.o.

AMAZING
koskwêyihtâkwan– VII be surprising, be amazing

AMAZINGLY
mâmaskâc IPC strangely, marvellously, amazingly; *(in negative constructions:)* not surprisingly, no wonder

AMERICA
kihci-môhkomânaskiy– NI America, the USA

AMERICAN
kihci-môhkomân– NA American

AMOUNT
âhkwakihtê– VII cost dearly, cost more, be worth a top-up amount
ohtatâwâkê– VAI sell (it) thus, sell (it) for that amount
têpipayi– VAI have the full amount, put away enough; have enough, have a sufficiency; have enough of (it)

AMUSE
pahpakwaciho– VAI amuse oneself

AMUSED
pahpakwatêyiht– VTI enjoy s.t., be amused by s.t.

AMUSING
wawiyas IPC funny, amusing
wawiyasinâkosi– VAI look funny, look amusing
wawiyasipayin– VII be funny, be amusing
wawiyatêyiht– VTI find s.t. funny, consider s.t. amusing; be funny about s.t., behave oddly
wawiyatêyim– VTA find s.o. funny, consider s.o. amusing; feel joy about s.o.

AND
êkwa IPC then, now; and
mîna IPC also, and also, again

ANGER
itâspinêm– VTA call s.o. thus in anger, angrily call s.o. such a name, thus scold s.o. in anger
kisiwâh– VTA anger s.o., make s.o. angry
kisîhto– VAI anger one another by speech
kisîkitot– VTA speak to s.o. in anger
kisîm– VTA anger s.o. by speech
kisîwê– VAI speak angrily; speak loudly
kisîwêhkahtaw– VTA speak angrily to s.o.; speak loudly to s.o., scold s.o. loudly
kisîwi IPV loudly, angrily, in anger
paciyawêh– VTA wrong s.o. by one's utterance, provoke s.o.'s anger

ANGRY
kakwâyakiyawêh– VTA make s.o. terribly angry
kisiwâh– VTA anger s.o., make s.o. angry

kisiwâsi– VAI be angry
kisiwipayi– VAI get angry, fly into rage
kisiwiyo– VAI complain, be angry at one's work
kisîstaw– VTA be angry with s.o., stay angry with s.o.

ANGUISH
pîkwêyihtamih– VTA worry s.o., cause s.o. mental anguish
pîkwêyihtamowin– NI mental anguish

ANIMAL
maci-pisiskiw– NA evil animal, monster
pisiskisîs– NA animal; young animal; small animal (e.g., bird, gopher)
pisiskiw– NA animal; domestic animal
sakâwi-pisiskiw– NA bush animal, wild animal

ANNIHILATE
mêscih– VTA kill s.o. off, annihilate s.o.
mêscihtamaw– VTA destroy (it/him) for s.o., annihilate (it/him) for s.o.
mêscihtâ– VAI destroy (it), annihilate (it)

ANNOUNCEMENT
sâkito– VAI make an announcement, make a proclamation

ANNOY
mwêstacîhkaw– VTA bother s.o., annoy s.o., make a nuisance of oneself to s.o., be troublesome for s.o.

ANNOYINGLY
mwêstâtahkamikisi– VAI be troublesome, behave annoyingly

ANSWER
naskom– VTA respond to s.o. with (it/him), answer s.o.'s prayer with (it/him)
naskwêwasim– VTA speak to s.o. in response, respond to s.o. by speech; answer back to s.o., respond to s.o. (e.g., inappropriately)

ANTICIPATION
piyasêyimo– VAI look forward eagerly, wait in anticipation

ANTIDOTE
ânisîhcicikan– NI antidote
ânisîhtâ– VAI alleviate the effect of (it), be an antidote to (it)

ANUS
kimisâhowin– NI wiping oneself, wiping one's anus
mêyiwiciskê– VAI have feces stuck to one's anus, have one's anus soiled with feces
ociski– VAI have an anus; have (it) as one's anus

ANY
ahpônâni IPC of course not, not any
kîkway PR something, thing; things; *(in negative constructions:)* not anything, nothing, not any
kîkwâs PR something, thing; things; *(in negative constructions:)* not anything, nothing, not any
misawâc IPC in any case, whatever might be thought
mosciwâk IPC *(in negative constructions:)* not at all, not under any circumstances
môy êkâ êtokwê IPC without any doubt, of necessity
mwâsi IPC *(in negative constructions:)* hardly ever, hardly any
nânitaw IPV *(in negative constructions:)* not any
nânitaw isi IPC in some way, in any way; in various ways; in a random direction
pikoyikohk IPC to any extent, no matter how much
pikw îta IPC in any place, no matter where; everywhere
pikw îtê IPC to any place, no matter whither; everywhere
pikw îtê isi IPC in any direction
waniyaw IPC any, somebody; at random

ANYONE
awiyak PR someone, somebody; *(in negative constructions:)* not anyone, not anybody
ayiwâk ihkin IPC ever more so! this cannot be! would anyone believe this!
nikotwâw IPC either one, anyone
pikw âwiyak IPC anyone; everyone

ANYTHING
kîkway PR something, thing; things; *(in negative constructions:)* not anything, nothing, not any
kîkwâs PR something, thing; things; *(in negative constructions:)* not anything, nothing, not any
nânitaw IPC simply; *(with numbers:)* roughly, approximately; variously; something, at some undetermined place; *(in negative constructions:)* not anything; something bad, anything bad; somewhere

piko kîkway *PR* something or other; anything at all
piko kîkwâs *PR* something or other; anything at all

ANYWAY
kiyâm *IPC* oh well, never mind, so much for this; anyway, rather; let it be, let there be no further delay; please
pikw âni *IPC* anyway

ANYWHERE
konita *IPC* in vain, without reason, without purpose, for nothing; without further ado; anywhere, at random, in a random place
ohpimê *IPC* off, away, to the side; elsewhere, anywhere

APPARENTLY
êcik âni *IPC* as it turns out, apparently, evidently, indeed
tâpiskôc *IPC* as if; seemingly, apparently

APPEAR
nôkohtâ– *VAI* let (it) appear, show (it)
sâkêwê– *VAI* appear, come into view

APPLE
picikwâs– *NA* apple

APPLIANCE
âpacihcikan– *NI* tool, appliance, machine; equipment, furnishings, furniture
âpacihcikanis– *NI* small tool, small appliance
môniyâw-âpacihcikan– *NI* White apparatus, White household appliance

APPLY
astamaw– *VTA* place (it/him) for s.o.; put (it/him) on s.o.; apply (it/him) to s.o. (e.g., as medicine)
sisopât– *VTA* spread (it) on s.o., apply (it) to s.o.'s chest
wîcihiso– *VAI* help oneself; apply oneself, study for oneself; rely on oneself in childbirth

APPROACHING
môsih– *VTA* sense s.o., feel s.o. approaching, perceive s.o.'s presence
môsihtâ– *VAI* sense (it), feel (it) approaching, perceive (it)

APPROPRIATE
kayâhtê *IPC* before, previously, formerly; before the appropriate time, prematurely
nahiyikohk *IPC* to the proper degree, to the proper extent, just enough, just right, evenly, fittingly, appropriately

APPROVE
cîhkêyiht– *VTI* like s.t., approve of s.t.; eagerly participate in s.t.

APPROXIMATELY
nawac piko *IPC* sort of, kind of, approximately; more or less; even a little
nânitaw *IPC* simply; *(with numbers:)* roughly, approximately; variously; something, at some undetermined place; *(in negative constructions:)* not anything; something bad, anything bad; somewhere

APRIL
ayîki-pîsimw– *NA* the month of April

APRON
aspascâkanis– *NI* apron
aspastâkan– *NI* apron

ARISE
pasikô– *VAI* arise (from sitting or crouching); be uplifted
waniskâ– *VAI* arise (from lying or sleep)

ARM
–spiton– *NDI* arm
isiniskêyi– *VAI* move one's arm thus or there, point in that direction with one's arm
iskopitonê– *VAI* have one's arm reach so far, extend one's arm so far

AROMATIC
wîhkimâkwan– *VII* smell good, give off a pleasant odour; have an aromatic odour

AROUND
ispayin– *VII* take place thus, occur thus; run thus (in a cycle), be there (in a cycle), come around (in a cycle), be that time again; come by, go by, have passed (e.g., days, years)
kwêsk-âya– *VAI* turn around to the opposite side, be turned around (e.g., a pivot)
kwêski *IPV* turned around, turned to the opposite side
kwêskin– *VTA* change s.o. around, turn s.o. around to the opposite side; *(fig.)* convert s.o. to Christianity
kwêskinâkwan– *VII* look changed around, look turned around to the opposite side
kwêskî– *VAI* turn around
miyâsk– *VTI* pass around s.t., bypass s.t.
nanâtawâpi– *VAI* look around
nitawâpaso– *VAI* smell around, sniff about

papâ *IPV* around, about, here and there

papâmi *IPV* around, about, here and there

papâmipahtâ– *VAI* run about (e.g., as a child); run around, be promiscuous

papâmipici– *VAI* move about, travel around, camp here and there, move around with one's camp

papâmohtê– *VAI* walk about, go about, go here and there; run around, be promiscuous

tâpisk– *VTI* wear s.t. fitted, wear s.t. around the neck

têtipêwêyâmo– *VAI* flee around in a circle

titipahpit– *VTA* roll and tie (it) around s.o., bandage s.o. with (it)

titipahpit– *VTI* roll and tie (it) around s.t.

wâsakâ *IPC* around a circle, in a full circle

wâsakâhtê– *VAI* walk around a circle, walk a circuit

wâsakâm *IPC* around a circle, in a full circle

wâsakâmêyâpôyo– *VAI* go around a circle by railway, describe a circuit by rail

wâsakân– *VTI* turn s.t. around a circle; make s.t. go around, turn s.t. (e.g. treadle), crank s.t.

wâsakâtisahoto– *VAI* chase one another around a circle

wâsakâyâskon– *VTA* point s.o. (e.g., pipe) around a full circle

wâskâhtê– *VAI* walk around a circle, walk a circuit

wâskân– *VTI* turn s.t. around a circle; make s.t. go around, turn s.t. (e.g., treadle), crank s.t.

wâskâsk– *VTI* go around s.t., circle s.t.

wêwêkahpit– *VTA* wrap and tie (it) around s.o., bandage s.o. with (it)

wêwêkahpit– *VTI* wrap and tie (it) around s.t.

wêwêkin– *VTA* wrap (it) around s.o., wrap s.o. up

wêwêkin– *VTI* wrap (it) around s.t.; wrap s.t. around

wîhkwêhcâ– *VII* go around as land, be curved as land, be the sweep of the valley

wîhkwêskaw– *VTA* go around s.o., head s.o. off

wîhkwêstê– *VII* be placed around, stand in the shape of a curve

wîmâskaw– *VTA* pass around s.o., pass s.o. by

ARRANGE

isîhcikê– *VAI* do things thus, proceed thus, arrange things thus; perform such a rite, perform a rite thus; conduct negotiations thus

pakitinamaw– *VTA* allow (it) for s.o., arrange (it) for s.o.; release (it/him) for s.o.

wiyakim– *VTA* set a price on s.o. (e.g., bread); arrange (it) for s.o.; decide on s.o.; give orders to s.o.

wiyastê– *VII* be arranged, be structured

ARRIVE

tako-kîskwêpê– *VAI* arrive intoxicated with alcoholic drink, arrive inebriated, come home drunk

takohtah– *VTA* take s.o. to arrive, lead s.o. to one's destination, arrive with s.o.

takohtatamaw– *VTA* arrive with (it/him) for s.o., carry (it/him) there for s.o.

takohtatâ– *VAI* take (it) to arrive, arrive with (it)

takohtê– *VAI* arrive, arrive walking

takopahtâ– *VAI* arrive running

takopayi– *VAI* arrive on horseback, arrive driving, arrive by vehicle

takopayi– *VII* arrive, have sufficient reach

takopici– *VAI* arrive with one's camp

takosin– *VAI* arrive

takotisahw– *VTA* drive s.o. to arrive, chase s.o. to arrive

takwakotê– *VII* arrive across the sky (e.g., cloud)

takwaskî– *VAI* arrive on the land, move onto the land, join those already on the land

takwâhtawî– *VAI* arrive in climbing up (e.g., a tree)

takwâpôyo– *VAI* arrive by railway, arrive by train

takwâwahito– *VAI* bring one another to arrive, arrive as a group

ARROW

acosis– *NI* arrow

pimocikanis– *NA* little arrow

pimocikê– *VAI* shoot arrows

pimot– *VTA* shoot an arrow at s.o.

pimw– *VTA* shoot at s.o., loose an arrow at s.o.

tâskiwêpahw– *VTA* split s.o. (e.g., rock) by arrow, shoot s.o. (e.g., rock) apart

ARTHRITIS
oskaninê– *VAI* be ill with arthritis, suffer from arthritis

ASCEND
âmaciwê– *VAI* go uphill, ascend a hill

ASH
pihkw– *NI* ash; ashes (as cleaning agent)

ASHAMED
nêpêwisi– *VAI* be bashful, be shy; be ashamed, be ashamed of oneself
nêpêwisîst– *VTI* be ashamed of s.t.
sasîhciwih– *VTA* make s.o. ashamed, embarrass s.o.

ASHORE
kapatâsiwêpiskaw– *VTA* kick s.o. ashore, kick s.o. out of the water
kapatên– *VTA* take s.o. ashore, take s.o. out of the water
kapâ– *VAI* come ashore, come out of the water

ASIDE
âhtin– *VTI* move s.t. over, push s.t. aside
îkatê *IPV* to the side, aside
kwayâtastamaw– *VTA* put (it/him) aside in readiness for s.o.
kwayâtastamâso– *VAI* put (it/him) aside in readiness for oneself
kwayâtastâ– *VAI* place (it) in readiness, put (it) aside in advance
wîkatêwêpin– *VTA* push s.o. aside, push s.o. away
yîkatên– *VTI* set s.t. aside

ASK
atot– *VTA* ask s.o. to do something, engage s.o. for something, employ s.o.
kakwêcihkêmo– *VAI* ask people, ask a question of people
kakwêcim– *VTA* ask s.o.; make a request of s.o.; ask s.o. about (it/him)
nitotamaw– *VTA* ask s.o. for (it/him)
nitotamâ– *VAI* ask for (it/him) (e.g., sugar), make a request for (it), pray for (it); make a request
nitotamâkêstamaw– *VTA* make a request for s.o., pray on s.o.'s behalf, ask for (it/him) on s.o.'s behalf
wîsâm– *VTA* ask s.o. along, take s.o. along; ask s.o. to dance

ASLEEP
nipâ– *VAI* sleep, be asleep
nipêpayi– *VAI* fall asleep

ASPIRATION
nipiskât– *VTA* doctor s.o. by insufflation or aspiration

ASSEMBLY
mâmawopiwin– *NI* meeting, assembly

ASSUREDLY
miyâmâc *IPC* assuredly; I do believe so

ASTRAY
wanâh– *VTA* lead s.o. astray, distract s.o.; disrupt s.o.'s life
wanisim– *VTA* cause s.o. to get lost, lead s.o. astray
wanisimôhâwaso– *VAI* lead one's children astray

ATHWART
pimic-âyihk *IPC* across, athwart, crosswise, sideways

ATTACH
akwamohtâ– *VAI* attach (it), fasten (it) (e.g., safety-pin)
itamohtâ– *VAI* attach (it) thus or there
kikamohtâ– *VAI* attach (it), fasten (it) on, put (it) on something
kikamôh– *VTA* attach s.o. (e.g., yarn, ribbon), put s.o. on
postamôh– *VTA* put s.o. on (e.g., reaches under a wagon), attach s.o.
sakah– *VTI* nail s.t. on, attach s.t. by nails
sakâpât– *VTI* attach s.t. by sewing, sew s.t. on

ATTACHED
akwamo– *VAI* be attached (e.g., thread on spool)
cîpatamo– *VAI* be attached so as to project out
itamon– *VII* run thus or there as a path; be thus attached, be mounted thus
kikamo– *VAI* be attached, have a fixed place (e.g., star)
kikamon– *VII* be attached, be fastened
sâkamon– *VII* stick out, be attached so as to project
sâkih– *VTA* love s.o., be attached to s.o.
sâkihtâ– *VAI* love (it), be attached to (it)
sêkwamon– *VII* be underneath, be attached underneath
wiyâsowi– *VAI* be meaty, have meat still attached (e.g., cracklings)

ATTEMPT
kakwê *IPV* try to, attempt to; circumstances permitting, by divine grace

ATTEND
kiskinohamâkosi– *VAI* be taught; be a student, attend school
kiskinohamâso– *VAI* teach oneself; be taught; be a student, attend school
nâkatêyiht– *VTI* pay attention to s.o., attend to s.o., look after s.o.
nâkatôhkê– *VAI* take notice, pay attention, be observant; attend to people, watch over people
pamih– *VTA* tend to s.o., look after s.o.; attend s.o. in childbirth, serve as midwife to s.o.; guide s.o. (e.g., sleigh), drive s.o. (e.g., sleigh)
pamihiso– *VAI* tend to oneself, look after oneself; attend oneself in childbirth, serve as one's own midwife
pamin– *VTA* tend to s.o., look after s.o.; attend s.o. in childbirth, serve as midwife to s.o.

ATTENTION
nâkasohtamohkâso– *VAI* pretend to pay attention
nâkatawâpam– *VTA* pay attention in looking at s.o., observe s.o.
nâkatêyiht– *VTI* pay attention to s.o., attend to s.o., look after s.o.
nâkatowâpaht– *VTI* pay attention in looking at s.t., observe s.t.
nâkatôhkê– *VAI* take notice, pay attention, be observant; attend to people, watch over people
pisiskêyiht– *VTI* pay attention to s.t., take notice of s.t.; bother with s.t.
pisiskêyim– *VTA* pay attention to s.o., take notice of s.o., tend to s.o.; bother s.o., harass s.o.

ATTRIBUTE
manitowakim– *VTA* endow s.o. (e.g., tobacco) with supernatural power; attribute spirit power to s.o.

AUDIBLY
matwê *IPV* audibly, visibly; perceptibly; in full view, in plain sight
pêtwêwêhtamaw– *VTA* come hither audibly bringing (it/him) for s.o.
pêtwêwên– *VTI* come hither audibly, come with audible steps
twêwêkocin– *VAI* audibly break apart (e.g., rock)

AUDIO-RECORDING
pîkiskwêmohtâ– *VAI* cause (it) to speak; make an audio-recording
têpiwi– *VAI* tape (it), make an audio-recording of (it)

AUDIO-TAPE
otin– *VTI* take s.t.; pick s.t., choose s.t., select s.t. (e.g., moss); steal s.t.; take s.t. over; extract s.t. (e.g., grease from soup), remove s.t. (e.g., glands in butchering beaver), extract s.t.; accept s.t. (e.g., contract); capture s.t., record s.t. on audio-tape

AUGUST
ohpahowi-pîsimw– *NA* the month of August

AUNT
–kâwîs– *NDA* mother's sister, parallel aunt; step-mother
–sikos– *NDA* father's sister, mother's brother's wife; mother-in-law, father-in-law's brother's wife, "aunt"

AUTHORITY
sôhkisiwin– *NI* strength, vigour; power, supernatural power; authority
tipôt– *VTI* discuss s.t. with authority

AUTOMOBILE
otâpânâskw– *NA* wagon, vehicle; automobile
sêhkêpayîs– *NA* car, automobile

AUTUMN
takwâkin– *VII* be fall, be autumn

AVAILABLE
api– *VAI* sit, sit down; be situated, be present, stay; be at home, be available

AVOID
manâ *IPC* in avoiding, in sparing, being careful not to
manâ-koskon– *VTA* avoid waking s.o. up, be careful not to wake s.o. up
manâ-pîkon– *VTI* avoid breaking s.t.
manâcih– *VTA* be protective about s.o., be careful about s.o., spare s.o.; avoid hurting s.o.; treat s.o. with respect
manâcihito– *VAI* be protective about one another, be careful about one another; avoid hurting one another
manâtâstim– *VTA* be careful in making s.o. wave, avoid making s.o. weave about; spare s.o. in driving a wagon, be considerate of s.o.

AWAKE
pêkopayi– *VAI* awake, wake up

AWAKEN
koskom– *VTA* awaken s.o. by speech; surprise s.o. by speech
koskon– *VTA* awaken s.o. by hand, wake s.o. up; startle s.o.

ENGLISH INDEX

AWARE
kôtawêyim– *VTA* be aware of s.o.'s absence, feel the loss of s.o., miss s.o.

AWE-INSPIRING
astâhtâso– *VAI* be watched, be considered a threat; evoke fear, be fearsome, be awe-inspiring, be awesome
kostâtikwan– *VII* be fearsome, be awe-inspiring

AWKWARDNESS
kitiskin– *VTA* inadvertently drop s.o., let s.o. fall by awkwardness

AWRY
patitisahamaw– *VTA* drive (it/him) off the path for s.o., send (it/him) awry for s.o., spoil (it/him) for s.o.

AXE
câpihcicikan– *NA* axe-handle
cîkahikanis– *NI* small axe, hatchet
cîkahoso– *VAI* chop oneself, injure oneself with an axe

BABY
–pêpîm– *NDA* baby, infant; youngest child
opêpîmi– *VAI* have an infant, have a baby; have (her/him) as one's infant; be the mother of an infant; give birth, be delivered
pêpîsis– *NA* baby, infant
pêpîwi– *VAI* be a baby, be an infant

BABY-BOTTLE
nônâcikan– *NI* bottle, baby-bottle

BABYSIT
kanawêyihtamôh– *VTA* make s.o. guard (it/him) closely; ask s.o. to look after (it/him), leave (it/him) to be looked after by s.o., get s.o. to babysit (her/him)

BACHELOR
môsâpêwi– *VAI* be a bachelor, be unmarried, be single

BACK
–spiskwan– *NDI* back
kâwi *IPC* again; back, in return
kîwê *IPV* back, towards home
nayôhcikê– *VAI* carry things on one's back, carry a load; carry a backpack

BACK AND FORTH
kâh-kwêkwask *IPC* back and forth, criss-cross, crosswise

BACKBONE
–âwikan– *NDI* backbone, spine (e.g., fish)

BACKPACK
nayôhcikê– *VAI* carry things on one's back, carry a load; carry a backpack

BACKWARD
sâsakici *IPV* backward

BACON
kôhkôsi-wiyinw– *NA* bacon, strip of bacon

BAD
mac-âyiwi– *VAI* be bad, be evil
mac-îtêyiht– *VTI* suspect s.t. bad; suspect evil
macan– *VII* be bad, be evil
maci *IPV* bad, evil
maci-kikiskaw– *VTA (especially in inverse constructions:)* inhere in s.o. as a bad thing, engross s.o. as an evil
maci-kîkway *PR* something bad, evil things
maci-kîsikâ– *VII* be a bad storm, be a severe storm
maci-nôcihtâ– *VAI* pursue evil things, engage in bad medicine
macipayi– *VII* go badly
mâyahkamikan– *VII* be a bad deed; be a bad situation
mâyahpinat– *VTA* treat s.o. badly, beat s.o. severely
mâyâpaso– *VAI* smell foul, give off a bad smell, stink
mâyâtan– *VII* be ugly, be bad
mâyi *IPV* bad, evil
mâyi-nawasônikê– *VAI* choose badly, make a bad choice
mâyi-tôt– *VTI* do s.t. evil; do a bad thing, impose a curse
mâyinikê– *VAI* act badly, do harmful things; experience bad things, come to harm
mâyinikêhkâto– *VAI* act badly towards one another, harm one another
mâyipayi– *VAI* fare badly, suffer ill; suffer a death, be bereaved, have a death in the family; be bereaved of (her/him)
mâyiskaw– *VTA* go through s.o. to bad effect, affect s.o. negatively, fail to agree with s.o.; *(especially in inverse constructions:)* have an adverse effect on s.o., make s.o. ill
miyo-nôcihtâ– *VAI* pursue good things; *(in negative constructions:)* pursue evil things, engage in bad medicine
miywakihtê– *VII* be considered good; *(in negative constructions:)* be considered bad, be considered evil

miywâsin– *VII* be good, be valuable; *(in negative constructions:)* be bad, be evil

nânitaw *IPC* simply; *(with numbers:)* roughly, approximately; variously; something, at some undetermined place; *(in negative constructions:)* not anything; something bad, anything bad; somewhere

wîhcêkimahkasikê– *VAI* give off a bad smell, produce a foul odour

BADGER
wînisakâcihp– *NA* badger

BAFFLED
kînwâhkwêh– *VTA (especially in inverse constructions:)* leave s.o. baffled, confound s.o.
wanwêhkaw– *VTA* leave s.o. baffled by speech or in speech, confuse s.o.

BAG
asiwatâ– *VAI* place (it) inside, enclose (it), put (it) into a bag or container
masinahikanêkinowatis– *NI* paper bag
maskimocis– *NI* small bag
maskimot– *NI* bag
mitâtahtomitanaw-maskimot *IPC* a hundred bags, one hundred bags

BAIT
mîcimîhkahkcikêsi– *VAI* use (it) as bait

BAKE
pahkwêsikanihkê– *VAI* fry bannock, bake bread

BALD
paskwasêsipayi– *VII* turn bald (e.g., head)

BALL
pâkâhtowê– *VAI* play ball; play soccer
wâwiyê *IPV* round, in a ball

BANANAS
kâ-wâkisicik *INM* bananas

BAND
akiso– *VAI* be counted; be counted in, be a band member
askîhkân– *NI* reserve; band
okimâw– *NA* chief, leader, boss; *(fig.)* band council
owiyasiwêwi– *VAI* be a band councillor
sêhkwêpitê– *VII* be pulled to expand; be an elastic band
wiyasiwêhkâniwi– *VAI* be a band councillor
wiyasiwêwin– *NI* decision; rule, law; council, band council

BANDAGE
akopiso– *VAI* put on medicine, tie on a bandage
âhtahpit– *VTI* move and tie s.t., tie s.t. differently; change the bandage on s.t.
titipahpit– *VTA* roll and tie (it) around s.o., bandage s.o. with (it)
wêwêkahpit– *VTA* wrap and tie (it) around s.o., bandage s.o. with (it)

BANISH
wayawîtisahw– *VTA* send s.o. outdoors; send s.o. off the reserve, banish s.o. from the reserve

BANKRUPT
pîkopayi– *VAI* break down, be broken; be torn (e.g., trousers); *(fig.)* go broke, go bankrupt

BANNOCK
pahkwêsikan– *NA* flour; bannock, bread
pahkwêsikanihkê– *VAI* fry bannock, bake bread

BANNS
têpwât– *VTA* call out to s.o., yell at s.o.; publish the marriage banns for s.o.

BAPTISE
sîkahâhtaw– *VTA* sprinkle s.o. with water; *(fig.)* baptise s.o., accept s.o. into the Catholic church

BARE
mohcihk *IPC* on the bare floor, on the bare ground
mohcihtak *IPC* on the bare floor, on the floor-boards
moscicihcên– *VTI* scoop s.t. up with bare hands

BAREFOOT
sâsâkihti– *VAI* be barefoot

BARELY
êtataw *IPC* barely, scarcely
êtatawisi– *VAI* be barely alive, be weak unto death, be about to die
katiskaw *IPC* to exact measure, no more than, barely
kêtisk *IPC* just barely, to exact measure
nânapêc *IPC* late, at the last moment, barely in time (e.g., when it should have been done previously); *(in negative constructions:)* too late
têpiyâhk *IPC* merely; barely, the most (if any); the only thing; so long as; *(in negative constructions:)* all but

BARK
mikisimo– *VAI* bark (e.g., dog)
mikit– *VTA* bark at s.o.

pîhtopit– *VTA* pull the covering layer off s.o. (e.g., tree), peel the bark off s.o.
pîhtosw– *VTA* cut the covering layer off s.o. (e.g., tree), cut the bark off s.o.
wâpanwêwit– *VTI* make noise until dawn, bark through the night (e.g., dog)
BARREL
mahkahkw– *NI* barrel, tub
BARRETTE
kiskinawâcihowinis– *NI* decorated brooch, decorated barrette
BASHFUL
nêpêwisi– *VAI* be bashful, be shy; be ashamed, be ashamed of oneself
nêpêwisîstaw– *VTA* be bashful before s.o., be shy towards s.o.
BASKET
waskwayiwat– *NI* birchbark basket
BATH
pakâsimo– *VAI* be immersed, swim, have a bath
BATHE
pakâsimonah– *VTA* immerse s.o., bathe s.o.
pakâsimonahâwaso– *VAI* immerse one's child, bathe one's child
BEAD
misiwêminakin– *VTI* put beads all over s.t.; cover s.t. with beads
mîkis– *NA* bead
mîkisihkahcikê– *VAI* bead things, do beadwork
mîkisihkaht– *VTI* bead s.t., stitch beads on s.t.
mîkisistah– *VTI* bead s.t., stitch beads on s.t.
mîkisistahikê– *VAI* bead things, do beadwork
nihtâwiminakinikê– *VAI* be good at sewing on beads
BEADED
asêsinw– *NI* beaded top of moccasin, vamp of moccasin
mîkisasâkay– *NI* beaded coat, beaded jacket
mîkisayiwinis– *NI* beaded clothing
mîkisihkahtê– *VII* be beaded
mîkisiwi– *VII* be beaded
BEADING
mîkisihkahcikêwin– *NI* beading, beadwork
BEADWORK
mîkisihkahcikê– *VAI* bead things, do beadwork

mîkisihkahcikêwin– *NI* beading, beadwork
mîkisistahikê– *VAI* bead things, do beadwork
mîkisistahikêwin– *NI* doing beadwork
BEAR
kimotôsê– *VAI* bear an illegitimate child
maskw– *NA* bear
mâkoh– *VTA* press upon s.o., bear down upon s.o., oppress s.o.; worry s.o., trouble s.o., throw s.o. into crisis
wâkayôs– *NA* bear
BEAR-MEAT
masko-wiyâs– *NI* bear-meat
BEAR-TRAP
masko-tâpakwân– *NI* bear-trap; bear-snare
BEARBERRY
acikâsipakw– *NI* bearberry leaf
BEARD
mîstowân– *NI* beard
mîstowê– *VAI* be bearded, wear a beard
BEARSKIN
maskwayân– *NA* bearskin
BEAT
matwêhw– *VTA* sound a beat upon s.o. (e.g., drum), drum on s.o.
mâyahpinat– *VTA* treat s.o. badly, beat s.o. severely
nôcih– *VTA* pursue s.o., hunt for s.o. (e.g., animal); go after s.o., oppress s.o., beat s.o. up, fight with s.o.
nôtiniskwêwê– *VAI* beat one's wife
otahw– *VTA* beat s.o. in competition, win over s.o., win from s.o.
paskiyaw– *VTA* beat s.o. in a contest
BEAUTIFUL
katawasisi– *VAI* be beautiful
katawatêyim– *VTA* consider s.o. beautiful
miyo *IPN* good, well, beautiful, valuable
miyo *IPV* good, well, beautiful, valuable
miyosi– *VAI* be good, be beautiful
miyosîho– *VAI* be well dressed, be beautifully dressed
miyosîhtâ– *VAI* make (it) good, make (it) beautiful
nihtâwisîhcikê– *VAI* be good at doing things, make beautiful things
nihtâwîhcikê– *VAI* be good at doing things, make beautiful things

takahk-âcim– *VTA* tell a beautiful story about s.o.
takahkatâmo– *VAI* sing out beautifully
takahkatimw– *NA* good horse, beautiful horse
takahki *IPN* nice, good, beautiful
takahki *IPV* nice, good, beautiful
takahkihtâkosi– *VAI* sound nice, sound beautiful
takahkihtâkwan– *VII* sound nice, sound beautiful
takahkinâkohtâ– *VAI* make (it) look nice, make (it) look beautiful
takahkipahtâ– *VAI* run nicely (e.g., horse), run beautifully
takahkipicikê– *VAI* drive a nice team, drive beautiful horses
takahkisîh– *VTA* make s.o. (e.g., earring) beautiful
takahkisîho– *VAI* be well dressed, be beautifully dressed
takahkisîhtâ– *VAI* make (it) nice, make (it) beautiful

BEAVER
amiskw– *NA* beaver

BEAVER LAKE
amisko-sâkahikanihk *INM* (place-name:) Beaver Lake (Alberta)

BEAVER-PELT
amiskwayânêscocinis– *NI* beaver-pelt hat
amiskwayânis– *NA* beaver-pelt

BEAVER-TAIL
amiskwâyow– *NI* beaver-tail

BECAUSE
ayisk *IPC* for, because
osâm *IPC* because; for
wiya *IPC* for, because

BECKON
nitom– *VTA* call s.o., beckon to s.o., invite s.o.

BECOME
âstamipayi– *VAI* become less, run low (e.g., money)
mêstohtê– *VAI* die off, become extinct
nôhtêhkwasîwipayi– *VAI* suddenly become sleepy
nôkosi– *VAI* be visible, become visible; be born
nôkwan– *VII* be visible, become visible
sêsâwipayi– *VAI* stretch, become stretched

BED
kawisimo– *VAI* lie down, go to bed
kawisimonihkê– *VAI* prepare the bed, get ready for bed
kîsôsim– *VTA* place s.o. to lie warmly, tuck s.o. into bed
mistiko-nipêwin– *NI* wooden bed, bedstead
nipêwin– *NI* bed
nipêwinis– *NI* bed, little bed
onipêwini– *VAI* have a bed; have (it) as one's bed
pimisim– *VTA* lay s.o. down, put s.o. to bed

BED-COVER
otakwanaho– *VAI* have a cover; use (it) as one's bed-cover

BEDROOM
nipêwikamikw– *NI* bedroom

BEDSHEET
anâskât– *VTA* spread matting for s.o.; provide s.o. with bedsheets
otanâskasowini– *VAI* have a bedsheet; use (it) as one's bedsheet
wâpisk-ânâskât– *VTA* provide s.o. with white bedsheets

BEE
asiskîhkê– *VAI* mud a log-house, do the mudding, hold a mudding bee
âmow– *NA* bee

BEEF
mostoso-wiyâs– *NI* beef

BEER
iskwêsisâpoy– *NI* beer, bottle of beer

BEFORE
awasi-nîpinohk *IPC* the summer before last
awasitâkosihk *IPC* the day before yesterday
kayâhtê *IPC* before, previously, formerly; before the appropriate time, prematurely
kîsâc *IPC* beforehand, in advance, in preparation
mawimost– *VTI* cry out in prayer to s.t., wail before s.t.
mawimostaw– *VTA* cry out in prayer to s.o., wail before s.o., implore s.o.; worship s.o.
mawîhkâtamaw– *VTA* cry out over (it/him) in prayer to s.o., wail over (it/him) before s.o.
maywêsk *IPC* previously, before
mâtayak *IPC* ahead of time, beforehand, in advance
mwayês *IPC* previously, before

naspâpan *IPC* at daybreak, before sunrise
nêpêwisîstaw– *VTA* be bashful before s.o., be shy towards s.o.

BEG
pakosih– *VTA* beg from s.o.; be a hanger-on to s.o., go with s.o., be part of s.o.

BEGIN
mâci *IPV* begin to; initially
mâcihtâ– *VAI* begin doing (it)
mâcipayin– *VII* begin to run (e.g., tape-recorder)
mâtahpinê– *VAI* begin to be ill, fall ill
mâtatoskaw– *VTA* begin to work for s.o.
mâtatoskê– *VAI* begin to work, begin one's work
mâtâcimo– *VAI* begin to tell a story
mâtâskonikê– *VAI* begin to point the pipe or pipestem
mâtitâpihtêpiso– *VAI* begin to wear earrings
sipwêmon– *VII* leave as path, trail, road; begin as path, trail, road

BEGRUDGE
akâwâtamaw– *VTA* desire (it/him) of s.o.; envy s.o. over (it/him), begrudge (it/him) to s.o.

BEHALF
nitotamâkêstamaw– *VTA* make a request for s.o., pray on s.o.'s behalf, ask for (it/him) on s.o.'s behalf
pîkiskwêstamaw– *VTA* speak for s.o., speak on s.o.'s behalf

BEHAVE
itahkamikisi– *VAI* do things thus, behave thus; work thus or there, busy oneself thus or there
môhcwahkamikisi– *VAI* behave foolishly, do crazy things
mwêstâtahkamikisi– *VAI* be troublesome, behave annoyingly
nânitaw itahkamikisi– *VAI* behave reprehensibly, be up to something
wawiyatêyiht– *VTI* find s.t. funny, consider s.t. amusing; be funny about s.t., behave oddly

BEHIND
askow– *VTA* follow s.o., follow behind s.o.
askôto– *VAI* follow one another, follow behind one another
awaswêwêtot– *VTI* disappear behind s.t., go behind s.t.
âkaw-âyihk *IPC* hidden, out of view, behind an obstacle to vision
iskwânê– *VAI* be left behind after a widespread illness, survive an epidemic
itaskôto– *VAI* follow one another thither or thus, follow behind one another thither or thus
kisâcî– *VAI* stay behind, stay around, stay nearby
miyân– *VTI* leave behind fresh tracks, have recently passed by
nakasiwê– *VAI* leave people behind, die
nakat– *VTA* leave s.o. behind; leave s.o. alone (e.g., helpless); abandon s.o. (e.g., child); leave s.o. behind in death, die leaving s.o. behind
nakat– *VTI* leave s.t. behind
nakatahw– *VTA* leave s.o. behind in departing by boat or airplane
nakatamaw– *VTA* leave (it/him) behind for s.o., bequeathe (it/him) to s.o.
nakataskê– *VAI* leave the earth behind, depart the world, die
nâway *IPC* behind, at the rear; in the past
ohtaskat– *VTA* leave s.o. behind thereby or from there, walk out on s.o.
otâhk *IPC* behind, at the rear, in the past
otâskanâhk *IPC* behind, at the rear; in the past
pimitisahw– *VTA* follow s.o. along, go behind s.o., drive s.o. along
sôhkêpit– *VTI* stand firmly behind s.t., promote s.t.

BEHOLD
awêska *IPC* behold! look at that!
îh *IPC* lo! look! behold!
pôti *IPC* lo and behold! what is this!
pwêti *IPC* lo and behold! what is this!
wâcistakâc *IPC* by golly! lo and behold!

BELIEVE
miyâmâc *IPC* assuredly; I do believe so
tâpwêht– *VTI* agree with s.t., believe s.t.
tâpwêhtaw– *VTA* agree with s.o., believe s.o.
tâpwêwakêyiht– *VTI* hold s.t. to be true, believe in s.t.; regard s.t. positively
tâpwêwakêyim– *VTA* believe in s.o.

BELLY
 -atay- *NDI* belly; abdomen (e.g., in childbirth)
 cahkatayên- *VTA* prod s.o. at the belly, spur s.o.'s belly
BELOW
 nîhc-âyihk *IPC* down, downward; below; down the hill
BELT
 pakwahcêhonis- *NI* belt
 pakwahtêhon- *NI* belt
BENCHMARK
 tipahâkê- *VAI* measure things with (it/him), measure things against (it/him), use (it/him) as a benchmark; measure things; rely on things
BEND
 itahtwâkin- *VTI* bend so many of s.t. (e.g., willows), bend s.t. (e.g., willows) in such numbers
 pihkin- *VTI* shape s.t., bend s.t., fold s.t.
 wâkin- *VTI* bend s.t.
 wâwiyên- *VTI* bend s.t. round
BENEATH
 atâmihk *IPC* beneath, underneath, inside (e.g., clothing)
 ay-atâmaskamik *IPC* inside the earth, beneath the ground
 itâmihk *IPC* beneath, underneath, inside (e.g., clothing); inside (e.g., mouth)
 sêkon- *VTI* place s.t. underneath; place s.t. beneath the coals
 sêkopayin- *VII* run beneath, go underneath, get caught underneath
 sêkwâpiskin- *VTA* place s.o. beneath the coals, place s.o. (e.g., beaver) in the oven
 sêkwâpiskin- *VTI* place s.t. beneath the coals, place s.t. in the oven
 sîpâ *IPC* beneath, underneath
BENT
 kawikîhkâ- *VAI* be bent with age, be prostrated by age
 nawakapi- *VAI* sit bent down, sit huddled over
 wâkisi- *VAI* be bent
BEQUEATHE
 âsônamaw- *VTA* pass (it/him) across to s.o., pass (it/him) on to s.o.; hand (it/him) down to s.o., bequeathe (it/him) to s.o.
 nakatamaw- *VTA* leave (it/him) behind for s.o., bequeathe (it/him) to s.o.

BEREAVED
 mâyipayi- *VAI* fare badly, suffer ill; suffer a death, be bereaved, have a death in the family; be bereaved of (her/him)
BERRIES
 apisiminakâsin- *VII* be small berries throughout
 mawiso- *VAI* pick berries, gather berries
 nitâmiso- *VAI* look for berries, go berry-picking
BERRY
 misâskwatômin- *NI* saskatoon berry
 mînis- *NI* berry
BESIDE
 wîtapim- *VTA* sit with s.o., sit beside s.o., be present with s.o.; work together with s.o.
BESIDES
 pêskis *IPC* besides; at the same time, simultaneously
BEST
 kihci *IPC* great, superb; the best
 mâh-mawaci *IPC* *(in superlative constructions:)* most, the very most, the best
BESTOW
 sawôhkât- *VTA* bestow a palpable blessing upon s.o.
BETTER
 âstê-kîsikâ- *VII* cease being stormy weather, let up as severe weather, be better weather
 nawac *IPC* by comparison; more, better, rather
BETWEEN
 pîhci *IPV* in between, inside
 pîhtawêkwât- *VTI* sew s.t. in between, sew covers on s.t.
 tastawayas *IPC* in between, in the middle
BEYOND
 kakêhtawêyiht- *VTI* have good ideas about s.t.; be intelligent beyond one's years; be sensible
 kâsispô- *VAI* reach beyond, exceed; survive into another generation
 kâsispôhtêmakan- *VII* go on, reach beyond, exceed; survive into another generation
BIBLE
 ayamihcikêwin- *NI* reading; *(fig.)* a reading, bible verse
 kihci-masinahikan- *NI* *(fig.)* important book; bible

manitowi-masinahikan– NI God's book, bible
masinahikan– NI letter, mail; book; written document, will; *(fig.)* bible
nêhiyawasinahikan– NI Cree book; Cree bible
omâw– NA "bible", manyplies, omasum

BIG
–misisitân– NDI big toe
mahkihtawakê– VAI have a big ear
mahkipakâ– VII be big leaves, be the time of fully grown leaves
misahtâ– VAI make (it) big
misâ– VII be big
misi IPV big, greatly
misi-yôtin– VII be a big windstorm
misikiti– VAI be big (in height or girth); be pregnant
misisîhtâ– VAI make (it) big
mistah-âtoskêwin– NI big task, major task
mistasiniy– NA big stone, big rock
mistaskihkw– NA big kettle, communal cooking pot
mistiyâkan– NI big dish, platter, large bowl
môy misikiti– VAI be not big, be small

BILE
–îsopiy– NDI gall bladder; gall, bile

BIND
wawânêyihtamih– VTA cause s.o. to be at a loss; cause s.o. to worry about (it/him); *(especially in inverse constructions:)* place s.o. in a bind

BINGO
pinkow– NI bingo

BIRCH-TREE
waskway– NI birch-tree, birchbark
waskwayi-mîtos– NA birch-tree

BIRCHBARK
waskway– NI birch-tree, birchbark
waskwayi-ôs– NI birchbark canoe
waskwayiwat– NI birchbark basket

BIRD
piyêsîs– NA bird

BIRTH
askôskaw– VTA follow s.o. in birth sequence
nayêhtâwiki– VAI have experienced a troubled birth, be born with a birth defect
nihtâwikih– VTA give birth to s.o., be delivered of s.o.
nihtâwikihâwaso– VAI give birth to one's child, bring forth a child, bring forth a young one (of the species)
nihtâwikihtâ– VAI give birth to (it), bring (it) forth
nihtâwikinâwaso– VAI give birth to one's child, bring forth a child, bring forth a young one (of the species)
ocawâsimisi– VAI have a child; have offspring, have a calf (as cow); have (her/him) as one's child; be the mother of a child; give birth, be delivered; calve (as cow)
opêpîmi– VAI have an infant, have a baby; have (her/him) as one's infant; be the mother of an infant; give birth, be delivered
wîc-ôhcîm– VTA come from the same time or place as s.o., share the year of birth with s.o.

BISHOP
kihc-âyamihêwiyiniw– NA bishop

BISON
paskwâwi-mostosw– NA bison, buffalo

BIT
miscahîs IPC quite greatly, quite a bit

BITE
kîskaht– VTI cut s.t. with one's teeth, bite s.t. off
mâmâkwaht– VTI chew s.t. (e.g., sinew); bite down on s.t. (e.g., leather, birchbark)
paskaht– VTI bite through s.t.

BITS
nanânis IPC variously, in bits and pieces, here and there
nanânistipit– VTA tear s.o. into bits and pieces; fragment s.o. (e.g., group of people), divide s.o. (e.g., community) against one another
nanânistiwêpahw– VTA shoot s.o. (e.g., rock) into bits and pieces, shatter s.o. (e.g., rock) into pieces

BLACK
kaskicêwasinâsosi– VAI have black markings (e.g., dog)
kaskitêsi– VAI be black
kaskitêwasinâstê– VII be black trim, be black edging
kaskitêwatisw– VTA dye s.o. (e.g., stocking) black
kaskitêwâpahtê– VII give off black smoke
kaskitêwiyâs– NA Negro, Black person

BLACK-BIRD
cahcahkayow– NA black-bird

BLACK-DUCK
kaskitêsip– NA black-duck

BLACKFOOT
ayahciyiniw– NA Blackfoot

BLACKSMITH
wiyahisow– NA blacksmith

BLADE
maskosîs– NI grass, hay; blade of grass
pîwâpiskw– NI metal, metal object; steel blade; screen of wire-mesh

BLAINE LAKE
sîwihtâkani-sâkahikanihk INM *(place-name:)* Blaine Lake (Saskatchewan)

BLAME
atâmêyim– VTA blame s.o. in one's thoughts, accuse s.o. in one's thoughts
atâmim– VTA blame s.o. by speech
nânitaw itêyiht– VTI worry about s.t., fret about s.t.; assign blame for s.t.; *(especially in negative constructions:)* not bear a grudge, be forgiving

BLANKET
akohp– NI blanket
akohpihkaw– VTA make a blanket for s.o.
akohpis– NI small blanket
anâskê– VAI have a mat, spread a blanket; use (it) as matting or floor-covering
nanâtohkokwâso– VAI sew various things; sew a patchwork blanket
opîwayakohp– NI feather blanket
otakohpi– VAI have a blanket; use (it) as one's blanket
sîsîpakohp– NI duck blanket
wâposwayânakohp– NI rabbitskin blanket

BLARE
kitohcikêmakan– VII blare out music (e.g., as stereo-player)

BLESS
sawêyim– VTA be generous towards s.o.; bless s.o.
sawêyimikowisi– VAI be blessed by the powers

BLESSING
sawôhkât– VTA bestow a palpable blessing upon s.o.

BLIND
wâpi– VAI see, be sighted, have vision; *(in negative constructions:)* be blind

BLINDFOLD
kipwacâpahpit– VTA blindfold s.o.

BLINK
pasahkâpi– VAI blink, shut and open one's eyes

BLISTERS
pâpakwâtahw– VTA *(especially in inverse constructions:)* rub s.o. raw, cause s.o. blisters

BLIZZARD
pîwaniyôtin– VII be a blizzard

BLOCKED
kipipayin– VII be blocked

BLOND
wâpistikwânê– VAI have white hair; have light hair, be blond

BLOOD
maci-manitowi-mihkw– NI *(fig.)* devilish blood, the devil's blood
mihkw– NI blood
nêhiyaw-mihkw– NI Cree blood; Indian blood
pâstâhowi-mihkw– NI blood tainted by a breach of the natural order; *(fig.)* blood tainted by deicide, sinful blood

BLOUSE
pîhconês– NI blouse

BLOW
pôtât– VTA blow at s.o., blow upon s.o.
pôtât– VTI blow on s.t.; blow into s.t., blow s.t. up

BLOWN
kêcikwâstan– VII be blown down by wind
pimâsi– VAI be blown along by wind
sâpoyowê– VII be blown through by wind

BLUE-GREEN
askihtakonikâtê– VII be made blue-green
askihtakosi– VAI be blue-green
askihtakwâ– VII be blue-green

BLUEBERRY
iyinimin– NI blueberry
nikikomin– NI blueberry (of a certain variety)

BLUFF
sakâs– NI piece of bush, bluff of woodland

BLURRED
wanêyiht– VTI forget s.t., be unsure of s.t.; have one's mind blurred, be confused
wani IPV indistinctly, blurred

BOARD
kiskinohamâtowin– NI teaching, education; education system, school board
napakihtakohkâso– VAI have the appearance of boards, be made of boards
napakihtakw– NI flat lumber, board, floor-board
napakikamikos– NI little house made of lumber or boards
napakikamikw– NI house made of lumber or boards; flat-top shack
pôsi– VAI board, be aboard (e.g., boat or vehicle); ride the train
pôsih– VTA make s.o. board (e.g., boat or vehicle), give s.o. a ride; put s.o. on a sleigh, give s.o. a ride on a sleigh
pôsiwêpin– VTI throw s.t. on board (e.g., boat or vehicle), throw s.t. on a sleigh
wâpiskihtakâ– VII be white boards, be white floor

BOAST
mamihcim– VTA boast about s.o.

BOASTFUL
mamihcimo– VAI be boastful
mamistêyimo– VAI be proud of oneself, be boastful

BOAT
âsowiskâ– VAI cross by boat, go across by boat
nakatahw– VTA leave s.o. behind in departing by boat or airplane
nâtahw– VTA fetch s.o. by boat or airplane; pick s.o. up (e.g., as an airplane)
ôcisis– NI small canoe, small boat
ôs– NI canoe, boat
papâmicimê– VAI go about by boat
papâmiskâ– VAI paddle about, go about in a boat
pimâhocikêsi– VAI float along in a small boat
pimiskâ– VAI swim by, swim along; go by in a boat, move along by one's own power
pôsihtâso– VAI load up, load one's boat or vehicle
sipwêcimê– VAI leave by boat, depart by boat
sipwêhotêwi– VAI leave by boat, depart by boat, go out by boat
sipwêwihw– VTA make s.o. leave by boat, depart with s.o. by boat

BODY
–iyaw– NDI body
maskawîskaw– VTA *(especially in inverse constructions:)* make s.o. strong in body, have an invigorating effect on s.o.
sôhkâtisi– VAI be strong in body, be fit, have a vigorous disposition

BODY-HAIR
–pîway– NDI body-hair of animal, fur

BOG
maskêkw– NI swamp, bog, muskeg
micimoskowê– VAI be stuck in mud or bog
tastôstôkan– VII be bog, be quicksand

BOIL
kanâcâciwahtê– VII be boiled clean, be clean by boiling
kaskâciwahtê– VII be boiled until tender
kaskâciwas– VTI boil s.t. until tender
kisâkamisikê– VAI heat a liquid; boil water for tea, make tea
ohtêpayi– VII boil (e.g., water), be at the boil, bubble
os– VTI boil s.t. (e.g., water), keep s.t. at the boil
oso– VAI boil (e.g., cracklings), be at the boil
osw– VTA boil s.o. (e.g., porcupine quills), bring s.o. to the boil, keep s.o. (e.g., cracklings) at the boil
pakâhcikê– VAI immerse things in water; boil things in water
pakâhtâ– VAI immerse (it) in water; boil (it) in water
pakâhtê– VII be immersed in water; be boiled in water
pakâsim– VTA immerse s.o. in water; boil s.o. (e.g., rabbit) in water
pakâso– VAI be immersed in water; be boiled in water
sikwâciwaso– VAI come apart in boiling, be boiled into small pieces; dissolve in boiling
takahkâciwasw– VTA boil s.o. (e.g., rabbit) nicely, boil s.o. well

BOLT
wâsaskotêpayi– VII be a bolt of lightning, be a lightning-strike

BOMB
pahkisikê– VAI drop things, drop a bomb

BONE
–skan– NDI bone
–skanis– NDI bone

iskosâwât– VTA leave meat over in filleting s.o. (e.g., fish), leave some flesh on the bones in filleting s.o.

BONE-LAZY
nipahikanê– VAI be terribly lazy, be bone-lazy

BONE-MARROW
oskani-pimiy– NI bone-marrow
wîn– NI bone-marrow

BONNET
ascocinis– NI little hat, little cap; infant's bonnet

BOOK
kihci-masinahikan– NI *(fig.)* important book; bible
manitowi-masinahikan– NI God's book, bible
masinahikan– NI letter, mail; book; written document, will; *(fig.)* bible
nêhiyawasinahikan– NI Cree book; Cree bible

BOOT-LINER
pîswê-maskisin– NI felt-liner, boot-liner

BORDER
akâmi-tipahaskân IPC across the border; across the forty-ninth parallel, in the United States

BORN
ihtako– VAI exist; be born (e.g., infant)
nayêhtâwiki– VAI have experienced a troubled birth, be born with a birth defect
nihtâwiki– VAI be born
nôkosi– VAI be visible, become visible; be born

BORROW
nitâhtâm– VTA borrow (it/him) from s.o.

BOSS
–okimâm– NDA boss
–okimâskwêm– NDA female boss, boss's wife
okimâsis– NA little chief, boss; *(fig.)* nobility
okimâw– NA chief, leader, boss; *(fig.)* band council
tipêyimiso– VAI control oneself, govern oneself; be on one's own, be one's own boss

BOTH
âh-âyîtaw IPC on both sides
nîsôhkiniskê– VAI use two hands, use both hands

nîswayak isi IPC in both directions; in both forms of ritual (e.g., with both incense and sweetgrass)

BOTHER
isîhk– VTI bother with s.t.
isîhkaw– VTA bother s.o. thus
moskâcih– VTA bother s.o., trouble s.o., hurt s.o.
mwêstâcim– VTA bother s.o. by speech, wear s.o. out by speech
mwêstâcîhk– VTI bother s.t.; hang around a place
mwêstâcîhkaw– VTA bother s.o., annoy s.o., make a nuisance of oneself to s.o., be troublesome for s.o.
pisiskêyiht– VTI pay attention to s.t., take notice of s.t.; bother with s.t.
pisiskêyim– VTA pay attention to s.o., take notice of s.o., tend to s.o.; bother s.o., harass s.o.
tasîhk– VTI bother with s.t., trifle with s.t.; be engaged in s.t.

BOTTLE
iskwêsisâpoy– NI beer, bottle of beer
kitâ– VAI eat (it) up, eat (it) completely, eat all of (it); drink all of (it); finish drinking a bottle of (it); drink an entire bottle
maci-manitowi-môtêyâpiskw– NI *(fig.)* the devil's bottle
môcêyâpiskos– NI little bottle
môtêyâpiskw– NI bottle
nônâcikan– NI bottle, baby-bottle
nônâcikêhâwaso– VAI bottlefeed one's child

BOVINE
mostosw-âya IPC of a cow, in matters bovine

BOW
ahcâpiy– NA bow
nêscâmocakosihk IPC at the bow (of a small boat)

BOWL
mistiyâkan– NI big dish, platter, large bowl
wiyâkan– NI dish, bowl, vessel, pot
wiyâkanis– NI small dish, small bowl

BOX
asiwacikê– VAI put things inside, enclose things, put things into boxes; have things inside; be pregnant
mistikowat– NI wooden box, trunk; wood-box, box for wood; wagon-box
nîmâwiwat– NI box for provisions; lunch-box

BOY
nâpêsis– *NA* boy, little boy, male infant
nâpêsisiwi– *VAI* be a small boy
nâpêwisîh– *VTA* dress s.o. as a boy, dress s.o. as a male
oskinîkîs– *NA* young boy, youth
poy *IPC* boy!

BRACED
sîhtwahpisoso– *VAI* be braced, wear a girdle

BRAID
apihkât– *VTA* braid s.o., knit s.o. (e.g., stocking)
apihkât– *VTI* braid s.t., knit s.t.
apihkâtamaw– *VTA* braid (it/him) for s.o.
apihkâtê– *VII* be braided
apihkê– *VAI* braid, knit
ispîhtâskwapihkê– *VAI* have braids of such thickness
itapihkât– *VTI* braid s.t. thus, knit s.t. thus
itapihkê– *VAI* braid thus, knit thus
kîsapihkât– *VTI* braid s.t. to completion, complete the knitting of s.t.
nistwapihkât– *VTI* braid s.t. in three
sêkipatwâ– *VAI* braid one's hair, have braided hair, wear braids

BRANCH
miscikos– *NI* little stick (e.g., in collecting sap); little pole, rod, rail (e.g., on drying rack); branch of a small plant (e.g., labrador tea)
nîpisiy– *NI* willow, willow bush; willow branch
nîpisîs– *NI* willow branch, willow switch; little willow
nîpiy– *NI* leaf; leafy branch
paskê– *VAI* branch off, go off to the side; set up a separate household
paskêpayi– *VAI* branch off, move off to the side; stop off there
paskêtâpâso– *VAI* branch off with one's wagon, move off to the side with one's vehicle; pull over with a vehicle
watihkwan– *NI* branch

BRANCHES
manâskocihtâ– *VAI* be left in want by having (it) torn by branches or thorns
mêstâskocihtâ– *VAI* get all of (it) torn by branches or thorns
sikwâskocin– *VAI* be cut by branches or thorns, have one's clothes torn

yâyikâskocin– *VAI* have one's clothes ripped ragged on branches or thorns
yîwêyâskocin– *VAI* have one's clothes torn ragged on branches or thorns

BRASSIERE
sîhcâskwahonis– *NI* brassière

BRAVE
nâpêhkâso– *VAI* be a brave

BREACH
pâstâho– *VAI* breach the natural order, transgress; *(fig.)* sin, be a sinner
pâstâhowi-mihkw– *NI* blood tainted by a breach of the natural order; *(fig.)* blood tainted by deicide, sinful blood
pâstâhowin– *NI* transgression, breach of the natural order; *(fig.)* sin

BREAD
pahkwêsikan– *NA* flour; bannock, bread
pahkwêsikanihkê– *VAI* fry bannock, bake bread

BREAK
kaskatwân– *VTI* break s.t. off (e.g., branch)
kîskipayi– *VAI* break off, be cut through, break apart
manâ-pîkon– *VTI* avoid breaking s.t.
nakayâh– *VTA* get s.o. accustomed to something, break s.o. (e.g., horse), tame s.o., train s.o.
nâtwân– *VTI* split s.t. apart, break s.t. off
nâtwâpayi– *VII* split off (e.g., branch), break off
nâtwâpit– *VTI* split s.t. (e.g., branch) off by pulling, break s.t. off
nâtwâwêpah– *VTI* split s.t. (e.g., branch) off and throw it down, break s.t. off and throw it down
pahkwaciwêpah– *VTI* break s.t. off, pry s.t. off (e.g., hide-scrapings), knock s.t. off
pahkwatah– *VTI* break s.t. off, pry s.t. off (e.g., hide-scrapings), knock s.t. off
pahkwatin– *VTI* break s.t. off by hand, pry s.t. off by hand (e.g., caked dirt from laundry)
pahkwêh– *VTI* break a part off s.t., pry a part off s.t.
paskakwaw– *VTA* break a snare on s.o., break through s.o.'s snare
paskin– *VTA* break s.o. (e.g., thread)
paskin– *VTI* break s.t. (e.g., snare-wire)
paskipit– *VTI* break s.t. (e.g., snare-wire)

pâskêkin– *VTA* break s.o. made of paper, break the paper of s.o. (e.g., cigarette)

pâstatah– *VTI* break s.t. (e.g., bone) by tool

pâstipayin– *VII* break, burst (e.g., bottle, head)

pîkohtatâ– *VAI* break (it)

pîkohtin– *VII* break in a fall, be broken

pîkon– *VTA* break s.o.; break up one's relation with s.o., disrupt s.o.'s life, spoil s.o.'s plans

pîkon– *VTI* break s.t.

pîkonamâso– *VAI* break (it) for oneself, break it oneself

pîkonikê– *VAI* break things; have things break, experience a mechanical breakdown

pîkonikêmakan– *VII* cause things to break down

pîkopayi– *VAI* break down, be broken; be torn (e.g., trousers); *(fig.)* go broke, go bankrupt

pîkopayi– *VII* break down, be broken

pîkopayin– *VII* break down, be broken

pîkopicikê– *VAI* plough, do one's ploughing; break soil

pîkopit– *VTI* break s.t. (e.g., soil), plough s.t. (e.g., field)

pîkopitamaw– *VTA* break (it) for s.o., plough (it) for s.o.

twêwêkocin– *VAI* audibly break apart (e.g., rock)

BREAK OUT

môskipayi– *VAI* break out in a rash, erupt in sores (e.g., with thrush)

pîkokonêwêpayi– *VAI* have cracks erupt in one's mouth, have one's mouth break out in sores (e.g., with thrush)

BREAKDOWN

nanayêhtâwipayiwin– *NI* misfortune, breakdown

pîkonikê– *VAI* break things; have things break, experience a mechanical breakdown

BREAST

–tôhtôsim– *NDA* female breast; teat (e.g., cow)

nôni– *VAI* suck at the breast, nurse at the breast; suck at the teats (e.g., calf)

BREASTFEED

mosci-nôhâwaso– *VAI* simply breastfeed one's child, breastfeed one's child without further ado (e.g., sterilisation of bottles)

nôh– *VTA* suckle s.o., nurse s.o., breastfeed s.o.

nôhâwaso– *VAI* nurse one's child, breastfeed one's child; suckle the young one (of the species), suckle one's calf (as cow)

BREECHES

têhtapîwitâs– *NA* riding breeches

BREED

wîcêhto– *VAI* live with one another, join with one another; get along with one another; breed with one another

BRIDGE

âsokan– *NI* dock; bridge

BRIDLE

tâpitonêhpicikan– *NI* bridle

BRING

pêcikê– *VAI* bring things hither

pêcikêsi– *VAI* bring a few things hither

pêcipit– *VTI* bring s.t. hither by pulling

pêsiw– *VTA* bring s.o. hither; bring s.o. (e.g., one's child) back (e.g., from the bush) after delivery

pêtamaw– *VTA* bring (it/him) hither for s.o.

pêtâ– *VAI* bring (it) hither

pêtôpê– *VAI* bring an alcoholic drink hither, bring an alcoholic drink home or into the house

pêtwêwêhtamaw– *VTA* come hither audibly bringing (it/him) for s.o.

pîhcikwah– *VTA* take s.o. small indoors, go indoors with s.o. small; bring s.o. small (e.g., infant) home

takwâwahito– *VAI* bring one another to arrive, arrive as a group

BRITTLE

kâspihkas– *VTI* heat s.t. until crisp, heat s.t. until brittle; dry s.t. by heat until crisp

kâspis– *VTI* heat s.t. until crisp, heat s.t. until brittle

BROKE

pîkopayi– *VAI* break down, be broken; be torn (e.g., trousers); *(fig.)* go broke, go bankrupt

BROOCH

kiskinawâcihowinis– *NI* decorated brooch, decorated barrette

BROOD

wîtapihtah– *VTA* set s.o. (e.g., chicken) to brood

BROOM
wêpahikan– *NI* broom
wêpahikâkê– *VAI* sweep things with (it), use (it) to sweep, use (it) as a broom
BROTH
mîcimâpoy– *NI* broth, soup
mîcimâpôs– *NI* broth, soup
sîsîpi-mîcimâpoy– *NI* duck broth, duck soup
wâposo-mîcimâpoy– *NI* rabbit broth, rabbit soup
BROTHER
–ciwâm– *NDA* male parallel cousin (man speaking); *(fig.)* brother, friend, male of the same generation (man speaking); brother, brethren
–ciwâmis– *NDA* male parallel cousin (man speaking); *(fig.)* brother, friend, male of the same generation (man speaking); brother, brethren
–mosôm– *NDA* grandfather, grandfather's brother; *(fig.)* old man, respected elder
–ôhcâwîs– *NDA* father's brother, parallel uncle; step-father
–ôhtâwiy– *NDA* father, father's brother; *(fig.)* Our Father, Heavenly Father
–pâpâsis– *NDA* dad's brother, father's brother, parallel uncle
–sikos– *NDA* father's sister, mother's brother's wife; mother-in-law, father-in-law's brother's wife, "aunt"
–sis– *NDA* mother's brother, father's sister's husband; father-in-law, father-in-law's brother, "uncle"
–stês– *NDA* older brother, older male parallel cousin
osisi– *VAI* have a mother's brother or father-in-law; have (him) as one's mother's brother or father-in-law
ostêsimâw– *NA* the oldest brother
ostêsimâwi– *VAI* be the oldest brother
BROTHER-IN-LAW
–îscâs– *NDA* male cross-cousin (man speaking); brother-in-law (man speaking)
–îstâw– *NDA* male cross-cousin (man speaking); brother-in-law (man speaking)
BROUGHT
nakâwâskwêsin– *VAI* be brought to a stop by hitting a tree
pêcikâtê– *VII* be brought hither
BROWN
osâwisi– *VAI* be yellow, be brown

wîskwastêwinâkwan– *VII* be brown in appearance
BRUSH
paskwatah– *VTI* clear brush
sinikohtakahikan– *NI* scrub-brush, floor brush, brush for wood
sinikohtakinikan– *NI* scrubber, brush; wash-board
BUBBLE
ohtêpayi– *VII* boil (e.g., water), be at the boil, bubble
BUBBLY
wiyâhtikosi– *VAI* be ebullient, have a bubbly personality
BUCK
kakwâyakinikê– *VAI* act with great speed, act abruptly; buck violently (e.g., horse)
BUFFALO
paskwâwi-mostosw– *NA* bison, buffalo
BUG
manicôs– *NA* insect, bug
BUILD
âniskôscikê– *VAI* build an extension
mânokê– *VAI* build a lodge, set up a tent
mênikanihkâkê– *VAI* build a fence with (it), use (it) to build a fence
osîhcikâtê– *VII* be made, be prepared; be built, be constructed
pôn– *VTI* build a fire; make a fire with s.t.
wâskahikanihkê– *VAI* build a house
BUILDING
ascikêwikamikw– *NI* storage room, storage building
ayamihêwikamikw– *NI* church, church building
wâskahikanis– *NI* little house; shack, temporary building, trailer; play-house
BULL
ayêhkwêsis– *NA* young castrated bull; steer
ayêhkwêw– *NA* castrated bull; ox
BULLET
môsosiniy– *NI* shell, bullet
BULRUSH
mwâskosiwân– *NI* bulrush, edible reed
pasicân– *NI* bulrush
BUMP INTO
tâwakisin– *VAI* bump into (her/him)
tâwin– *VTA* encounter s.o., come upon s.o., bump into s.o., hit s.o.

tâwin– *VTI* encounter s.t. by hand, come upon s.t., bump into s.t.
tâwisk– *VTI* encounter s.t. (by foot or body movement), come upon s.t., bump into s.t.
tâwiskaw– *VTA* encounter s.o. (by foot or body movement), bump into s.o., come into contact with s.o.

BUNDLE
nayôhcikan– *NI* bundle, sacred bundle, spirit-bundle (e.g., in ghost-dance)
owiyahpit– *VTI* tie s.t. together, tie s.t. into a bundle
pitikwahpit– *VTI* tie s.t. into a bundle
wêwêkapi– *VAI* sit wrapped up, sit bundled up
wiyahpit– *VTI* tie s.t. together, tie s.t. into a bundle

BUNK
pimitastê– *VII* be placed crosswise; be the bunk of a wagon

BURN
kîsisikê– *VAI* burn things; burn stubble, burn the fields
kîsiso– *VAI* be cooked to completion; burn oneself, get burnt; get burnt by an acidic or caustic agent
kîsitê– *VII* be cooked to completion; be burnt; burn down, be burnt down (e.g., building); be burnt (e.g., stubble, fields)
kîsowihkaso– *VAI* warm oneself by a burning fire
mêstihkahtê– *VII* burn down completely, be completely burnt down
miyâhkaso– *VAI* give off a burning smell
pasisâwê– *VAI* burn stubble, burn the fields
pasitê– *VII* be burnt, be burnt out (e.g., by forest-fire)
pônikâtê– *VII* be a fire being made; be kept burning as a fire
wîhkimahkaso– *VAI* smell sweet in burning

BURST
pâstipayin– *VII* break, burst (e.g., bottle, head)
pîkiskwêpayi– *VAI* speak suddenly, burst into speech

BURY
ayâwahkahw– *VTA* bury s.o. in the ground
nahin– *VTA* bury s.o., hold a funeral for s.o.

BUSH
kospî– *VAI* move away from the water, move off into the bush
nîpisiy– *NI* willow, willow bush; willow branch
nôhcimihk *IPC* in the bush, away from the water
sakâ– *VII* be bush, be woodland
sakâs– *NI* piece of bush, bluff of woodland
sakâw– *NI* bush, woodland
sakâwi-mîciwin– *NI* food from the bush
sakâwi-pimâcihowin– *NI* life in the bush
sakâwi-pisiskiw– *NA* bush animal, wild animal
sêskisi– *VAI* go into the bush; go into the bush to relieve oneself
sêskitâpâso– *VAI* drive into the bush
wayawîpit– *VTI* pull s.t. (e.g., fence-post) out of the bush

BUSH-PARTRIDGE
paspaskiw– *NI* partridge, bush-partridge

BUSY
canawî– *VAI* keep busy in various ways
itahkamikisi– *VAI* do things thus, behave thus; work thus or there, busy oneself thus or there
mamanê– *VAI* get ready, be busy
otamih– *VTA* keep s.o. busy, keep s.o. preoccupied; delay s.o.; *(especially in inverse constructions:)* get in s.o.'s way, be s.o.'s undoing
otamiyo– *VAI* busy oneself, keep busy, be preoccupied
pimahkamikisi– *VAI* work along, keep busy
tasîhkaw– *VTA* be busy with s.o., work on s.o. (e.g., fish), trouble oneself with s.o. (e.g., fish)
tatahkamikisi– *VAI* busy oneself thus or there; have things to do

BUT
mâka *IPC* but
wiy âta wiya *IPC* but of course

BUTTON
ocipâson– *NA* knob, button (e.g., on radio)

BUY
acâwê– *VAI* buy a little of (it), buy some of (it)
acâwêsi– *VAI* buy a little of (it), buy some of (it)

atâm– *VTA* buy (it/him) from s.o.
atâwê– *VAI* buy (it/him)
atâwêstamaw– *VTA* buy (it/him) for s.o.
atâwêstamâso– *VAI* buy (it/him) for oneself
kîspinat– *VTA* earn enough to buy s.o. (e.g., horse)
kîspinat– *VTI* earn enough to buy s.t.; earn s.t. as reward; earn one's reward
misahcinêh– *VTI* buy s.t. in great numbers, buy a lot of s.t.
nâcinêhamaw– *VTA* obtain (it/him) from s.o. by payment, seek to buy medicine from s.o.
nâcinêhikê– *VAI* obtain things by payment, seek to buy medicine
otinikê– *VAI* take things; buy things, do one's shopping, make a purchase; take away winnings (e.g., in a card-game)

BYPASS
miyâsk– *VTI* pass around s.t., bypass s.t.

CAFE
mîcisowikamikw– *NI* cafe, restaurant

CAKE
wîhkihkasikan– *NA* cake

CALF
moscosos– *NA* calf
nôhâwaso– *VAI* nurse one's child, breastfeed one's child; suckle the young one (of the species), suckle one's calf (as cow)
ocawâsimisi– *VAI* have a child; have offspring, have a calf (as cow); have (her/him) as one's child; be the mother of a child; give birth, be delivered; calve (as cow)

CALL
isiyîhkât– *VTA* call s.o. thus, use such a name for s.o.
isiyîhkât– *VTI* call s.t. thus, use such a name for s.t.
itâspinêm– *VTA* call s.o. thus in anger, angrily call s.o. such a name, thus scold s.o. in anger
itwê– *VAI* say thus, call (it) thus; have such a meaning
kito– *VAI* utter a sound, call, sing (e.g., bird); make noises (e.g., animal), hoot; be a thunderclap
nêhiyawi-wîh– *VTA* use s.o.'s Cree name, call s.o. by a Cree name
nêhiyawi-wîht– *VTI* use the Cree name of s.t., call s.t. by a Cree name
nitom– *VTA* call s.o., beckon to s.o., invite s.o.
osikosâhkôm– *VTA* have s.o. as one's father's sister, call s.o. one's father's sister
sêwêpitamaw– *VTA* make (it) ring out for s.o.; call s.o. by telephone
têpwât– *VTA* call out to s.o., yell at s.o.; publish the marriage banns for s.o.
têpwâtamaw– *VTA* call out for s.o., be an advocate for s.o.
têpwê– *VAI* call out, shout, holler, yell

CALLED
icikâtê– *VII* be called thus
isiyîhkâcikâtê– *VII* be called thus
isiyîhkâso– *VAI* be called thus, have such a name
isiyîhkâtê– *VII* be called thus, have such a name

CALVE
ocawâsimisi– *VAI* have a child; have offspring, have a calf (as cow); have (her/him) as one's child; be the mother of a child; give birth, be delivered; calve (as cow)

CAMP
âhtokê– *VAI* move camp, move one's camp elsewhere
âsowakâmêpici– *VAI* move one's camp across a body of water
ispici– *VAI* move thus or there with one's camp, move one's household there
mitâsipici– *VAI* move camp into the open, move one's camp out onto the open prairie
papâmipici– *VAI* move about, travel around, camp here and there, move around with one's camp
pâpici– *VAI* move one's camp hither
pici– *VAI* move camp, move with one's camp
pimipici– *VAI* move camp, move along with one's camp
sipwêpici– *VAI* leave with one's camp, depart with one's camp
sipwêyâciho– *VAI* travel away, depart in travel; depart as a camp
takopici– *VAI* arrive with one's camp

CAMP-CIRCLE
akâmôtênaw *IPC* across the camp-circle; across the settlement, across town
ôtênaw– *NI* camp-circle; settlement, town

CAMPFIRE
kotawân– *NI* campfire, open fire
kotawê– *VAI* make a campfire, make a cooking fire

CAN
kaskâpiskah– *VTI* can s.t., preserve s.t.
kaskâpiskahikan– *NI* can, preserve, canned goods

CANADA
kânata *INM* *(place-name:)* Canada

CANDLE
wâsaskocênikanis– *NI* candle

CANDY
sôkâs– *NA* sugar; candy

CANNABIS
pîhtwâwin– *NI* smoking; *(fig.)* cannabis abuse

CANNED
anohc-kaskâpiskahikan– *NI* today's canned goods
kaskâpiskahikan– *NI* can, preserve, canned goods
kaskâpiskahikâtê– *VII* be canned, be preserved

CANNIBAL
wîhtikow– *NA* cannibal monster; *(name:)* Wihtikow, Windigo

CANOE
ôcisis– *NI* small canoe, small boat
ôs– *NI* canoe, boat
waskwayi-ôs– *NI* birchbark canoe

CANVAS
akwanahikan– *NI* covering; canvas
apahkwâson– *NI* cover, canvas
papakiwayânêkinw– *NI* thin cloth, cotton; canvas
papakwânikamikwêkin– *NI* canvas

CAP
ascocinis– *NI* little hat, little cap; infant's bonnet
astotin– *NI* hat, cap

CAPTURE
otin– *VTI* take s.t.; pick s.t., choose s.t., select s.t. (e.g., moss); steal s.t.; take s.t. over; extract s.t. (e.g., grease from soup), remove s.t. (e.g., glands in butchering beaver), extract s.t.; accept s.t. (e.g., contract); capture s.t., record s.t. on audio-tape

CAR
nipahisin– *VAI* get killed in a car accident
sêhkêpayîs– *NA* car, automobile

CARD
pêyakopêhikan– *NA* card, playing-card

CARE
kanawêyiht– *VTI* keep s.t., look after s.t., take care of s.t.; store s.t., preserve s.t.; guard s.t. closely
kanawêyihtamaw– *VTA* look after (it/him) for s.o., take care of (it/him) for s.o.
kanawêyihtamâso– *VAI* guard (it/him) closely for oneself, take good care of (it/him) oneself
kanawêyihtâkwan– *VII* be kept, be looked after, the taken care of; be stored, be preserved; be closely guarded
kanawêyim– *VTA* keep s.o., look after s.o., take care of s.o.; guard s.o. closely
mâmâsîs *IPC* sparingly, delicately; quickly, roughly, without care
miyawâkâc *IPV* with particular care
miyawâkâtinikê– *VAI* take particular care with things, handle ritual objects with particular care

CAREFUL
manâ *IPV* in avoiding, in sparing, being careful not to
manâ-koskon– *VTA* avoid waking s.o. up, be careful not to wake s.o. up
manâcih– *VTA* be protective about s.o., be careful about s.o., spare s.o.; avoid hurting s.o.; treat s.o. with respect
manâcihito– *VAI* be protective about one another, be careful about one another; avoid hurting one another
manâtâstim– *VTA* be careful in making s.o. wave, avoid making s.o. weave about; spare s.o. in driving a wagon, be considerate of s.o.
nâkatôhkâtito– *VAI* take notice of one another, watch over one another, keep a careful eye on one another

CARPENTER
mistiko-nâpêwi– *VAI* work as a carpenter, do carpentry

CARROT
oskâcâskos– *NA* carrot
oskâtâskw– *NI* carrot

CARRY
cahkon– *VTA* carry s.o. small, hold s.o. small
kikisk– *VTI* wear s.t. (e.g., shoe), have s.t. as an intimate possession, carry s.t. in oneself (e.g., blood)
kikiskawâwaso– *VAI* carry a child, be with child, be pregnant

kîwêhtah– *VTA* take s.o. home, carry s.o. home, go home with s.o.
kîwêhtatâ– *VAI* take (it) home, carry (it) home, go home with (it)
nahâwaso– *VAI* have one's child in the proper place, carry one's child with one
nayahto– *VAI* carry one another on one's back; ride up on one another (e.g., beads)
nayôhcikê– *VAI* carry things on one's back, carry a load; carry a backpack
nayôht– *VTI* carry s.t. on one's back
nayôm– *VTA* carry s.o. on one's back
nîkânohtatâ– *VAI* be in the lead with (it), carry (it) in the lead
nîmâskwê– *VAI* carry a weapon; carry a gun
osôniyâmi– *VAI* have money, carry money on oneself
pimohtah– *VTA* take s.o. along, go along with s.o., guide s.o. along; carry s.o. along, sustain s.o.
pimohtatâ– *VAI* take (it) along, carry (it) along, travel with (it)
pimowitâ– *VAI* carry (it) along
tahkon– *VTA* carry s.o., hold s.o.
tahkon– *VTI* carry s.t., hold s.t.
tahkonamôh– *VTA* make s.o. carry (it/him), make s.o. hold (it/him)
takohtatamaw– *VTA* arrive with (it/him) for s.o., carry (it/him) there for s.o.
waskawîtot– *VTI* carry on with s.t.
CART
nâcitâpê– *VAI* go and drag (it) back, fetch (it) by cart
nâtitâpê– *VAI* go and drag (it) back, fetch (it) by cart
ocâpânâskos– *NA* cart; small wagon, small sleigh
CARTOON
ayisiyinîhkân– *NA* doll, mannikin; cartoon figure
CASE
êkamâ *IPC* it is not the case
kêyiwêhk *IPC* just in case, nevertheless; despite shortcomings
misawâc *IPC* in any case, whatever might be thought
nama cî *IPC* is it not the case
CASTRATED
ayêhkwêsis– *NA* young castrated bull; steer
ayêhkwêw– *NA* castrated bull; ox

CATALOGUE
nâtitisahikê– *VAI* send for things, place an order from a catalogue
nâtitisahikêwasinahikan– *NI* mail-order catalogue
nâtitisahw– *VTA* go to fetch s.o. (e.g., horses); send for s.o., order s.o. (e.g., chickens) by catalogue
CATAPULTED
ohpipayi– *VAI* spring up, be catapulted up (e.g., in a snare)
CATCH
aswah– *VTI* catch s.t. as it drips
atim– *VTA* catch up to s.o.
kâhcitin– *VTA* catch s.o., seize s.o., get s.o. (e.g., a spouse); obtain s.o. (e.g., money)
kâhcitin– *VTI* catch s.t., seize s.t., obtain s.t.; get s.t. back
kwâhkotê– *VII* catch fire, be ablaze
mêkwâskaw– *VTA* encounter s.o. in the midst of (it), catch s.o. in the act
CATHOLIC
ayamihâwin– *NI* prayer, praying, saying prayers; church service; religious rite; religion, religious denomination; the Roman Catholic church
pâhkw-âyamihâwin– *NI* Roman Catholic religion; the Roman Catholic church
pâhkw-âyamihêwiyiniw– *NA* Roman Catholic priest
sîkahâhtaw– *VTA* sprinkle s.o. with water; *(fig.)* baptise s.o., accept s.o. into the Catholic church
CATTAIL
pasân– *NA* cattail, edible reed
CATTLE
mostosw– *NA* cattle, cow
CAUGHT
akocipayi– *VAI* be caught aloft
sêkopayin– *VII* run beneath, go underneath, get caught underneath
tâpakwâso– *VAI* get oneself snared, be caught in a snare
tâpisikopayi– *VAI* get caught in something
CAUSE
tôcikêmakan– *VII* have such an effect; be the cause of (it)
CAUSTIC
âhkohtêwiso– *VAI* be sharp, be caustic (e.g., soap)
âhkwâpahtê– *VII* give off a sharp odour, produce pungent fumes, emit acidic or caustic fumes

kîsiso– VAI be cooked to completion; burn oneself, get burnt; get burnt by an acidic or caustic agent

CEASE

âstê-kimiwan– VII cease being rain, let up as rain

âstê-kîsikâ– VII cease being stormy weather, let up as severe weather, be better weather

pônatoskê– VAI cease working

pônêyiht– VTI cease thinking of s.t.; overcome a worrying preoccupation

pôni IPV cease

pôni-pimâtisi– VAI cease to live, die; be no longer alive, be dead

pônihk– VTI cease of s.t., leave s.t. alone

pônihtâ– VAI cease of (it)

pônipayi– VII cease, stop, come to an end

pônisimo– VAI cease dancing

pônwêwit– VTI cease making noise; keep quiet

pôyo– VAI cease, quit

CELEBRATE

ayamihâ– VAI pray, say prayers; hold a church service, celebrate mass; participate in a religious rite, go to church; follow a religion

mâmaw-âyamihâ– VAI pray as a group, participate in a religious rite as a group, celebrate mass as a group; go on a pilgrimage as a group

mis-âyamihâ– VAI hold mass, celebrate high mass

nîpâ-ayamihâ– VAI celebrate midnight mass (e.g., at Christmas)

CELLAR

wâtihkân– NI hole, cellar

yahkâtihkât– VTI dig out more of a hole or cellar, push out the size of an existing hole or cellar

CENSE

miyâhkas– VTI cense s.t., smudge s.t. with sweetgrass

miyâhkasamaw– VTA cense (it/him) for s.o., smudge (it/him) with sweetgrass for s.o.

miyâhkasikâkê– VAI cense with (it), use (it) to cense with, use (it) as incense

miyâhkasikê– VAI cense things, smudge things with sweetgrass

miyâhkasw– VTA cense s.o. (e.g., pipe), smudge s.o. (e.g., pipe) with sweetgrass

CENTRAL

pîhtêyask IPC at the central circle of poles inside the dance-lodge

CENTRE

tâw-âyihk IPC in the centre

CENTS

mitâtahto-pîwâpiskos IPC ten cents

nîso-sôniyâs IPC fifty cents

pêyak-sôniyâs IPC twenty-five cents, a quarter

CEREMONY

itâskonikê– VAI thus point the pipe or pipestem; thus hold a pipe ceremony

itâskonikêwin– NI thus pointing the pipe or pipestem; such a pipe ceremony

kosâpaht– VTI hold a shaking-lodge, hold the shaking-lodge ceremony

nipâkwêsimowikamikw– NI sundance lodge, sundance ceremony

nîmihitowikamikw– NI dance lodge, dance ceremony

nîmihitowinihkê– VAI hold a dance, hold a dance ceremony; give a dance, organise a (secular) dance

pakitinâso– VAI hold a give-away ceremony

pakitinâsowin– NI give-away ceremony

pîhtwâ– VAI smoke, use the pipe; smoke (him) (e.g., pipe); hold a pipe ceremony; be a nicotine addict

pîhtwâwikamikw– NI pipe lodge, pipe ceremony

CERTAIN

kêhcinâ IPC surely, for certain

kêhcinâho– VAI be certain

pêyak IPC one, alone, a single one; the only one; a certain one

pêyakwayak IPC in one place, in a certain place; in the same place

CHAIR

apiwinis– NI seat, chair

cêhcapiwinis– NI small chair

CHALLENGE

kotêyiht– VTI try s.t. in one's mind, think strenuously about s.t., test s.t.; challenge s.t.

kotêyihto– VAI test one another, try one another's determination, challenge one another

kotêyim– VTA try s.o., test s.o., put s.o.'s mind to the test; challenge s.o.

mawinêhw– VTA challenge s.o. to a contest

ENGLISH INDEX   235

mâyêyiht– VTI consider s.t. a challenge; be willing to tackle a difficult task, venture out
mâyêyim– VTA consider s.o. a challenge; be willing to tackle s.o.
CHANCE
pakwanaw IPC by chance, at random
CHANGE
âhci IPV by change, by replacement
âhcîhtâ– VAI make (it) over, make (it) different, change (it)
âhtahpit– VTI move and tie s.t., tie s.t. differently; change the bandage on s.t.
kwêskin– VTA change s.o. around, turn s.o. around to the opposite side; *(fig.)* convert s.o. to Christianity
kwêskinâkwan– VII look changed around, look turned around to the opposite side
kwêskinisk IPC the other hand, changing one's hand
kwêskîmo– VAI change one's form
mêskotayiwinisê– VAI change one's clothes
mêskotâpin– VTI change s.t. (e.g., water in boiling a beaver), exchange s.t.
mêskotin– VTI change s.t., replace s.t.
mêskotôn– VTI change s.t. (e.g., water in boiling a beaver), exchange s.t.
CHANT
kâkîsimo– VAI pray, plead, chant prayers
kâkîsimotot– VTI chant prayers for s.t.; chant prayers over s.t.
kâkîsimototaw– VTA chant prayers for s.o.; chant prayers over s.o.
kâkîsimwâkê– VAI chant prayers with (it), use (it) to chant prayers
CHANTING
kâkîsimowin– NI chanting prayers
CHARACTER
kihcihtwâwi IPN of exalted character; venerable, holy
masinahikêwin– NI writing; letter, character
miyohtwâ– VAI be good-natured, be of pleasant character
CHARGE
itakiht– VTI count s.t. thus, value s.t. thus, hold s.t. in such esteem; charge so much for s.t.
kîsakim– VTA finish counting s.o.; finish giving orders to s.o., complete one's charge to s.o.

nîkânapi– VAI be at the head, be in the lead, be in charge; hold the office of director
pimakocin– VII make a rush in linear fashion, charge headlong
sîhkitisahw– VTA urge s.o. along (e.g., horse); lay charges against s.o.
tipêyihcikê– VAI be master over things, be in charge; *(fig.)* be the Lord
wiyakihtamaw– VTA set a price on (it/him) for s.o., charge s.o. for (it/him)
CHARITY
sâkihitowin– NI mutual love; charity
CHASE
nawaswât– VTA pursue s.o., chase after s.o.
nawaswât– VTI pursue s.t., chase after s.t.
nawaswê– VAI give chase, be in pursuit
papâmitisah– VTI chase s.t. about; follow s.t. about (e.g., trail)
papâtinikê– VAI hurry hither and thither, chase about
takotisahw– VTA drive s.o. to arrive, chase s.o. to arrive
wâsakâtisahoto– VAI chase one another around a circle
CHATTER
kîskwêtonâmo– VAI say all manner of things, chatter on
CHEAP
wêhtakihtê– VII be cheap, be inexpensive
CHEAT
kîmôcih– VTA be stealthily unfaithful to s.o. (e.g., spouse), cheat on s.o. (e.g., spouse)
CHECK
nâcakwêsi– VAI check one's small snares (e.g., for rabbits)
nâciwanihikanê– VAI fetch game from traps, check one's traps
nâtahapê– VAI check one's nets
nâtakwê– VAI check one's snares
nitawâpaht– VTI go to see s.t., observe s.t., check s.t. out
nitawâpênaw– VTA check up on s.o.
nitawâpênikê– VAI check up on people, check up on things
CHEEK
–aniway– NDI cheek
CHEESE
ascascwâs– NI curds, cottage cheese

CHEMICALS
maskihkiy– NI herb, plant; seneca-root; medicinal root; medicine; chemicals

CHEQUE
kêhtêwasinahikan– NI pension cheque, old-age pension

CHEST
–âskikan– NDI chest
–âskikanis– NDI chest
maskihkîwiwacis– NI medicine chest
sisopât– VTA spread (it) on s.o., apply (it) to s.o.'s chest

CHEW
mâmâkwaht– VTI chew s.t. (e.g., sinew); bite down on s.t. (e.g., leather, birchbark)
mâmâkwam– VTA chew s.o. (e.g., spruce-gum, thread)
misîht– VTI chew s.t.
misîm– VTA chew s.o. (e.g., spruce-gum)
mîciso– VAI eat, have a meal; feed (e.g., bird); chew the cud (e.g., ruminant)
sikwaht– VTI chew s.t. until small

CHICKEN
cikin– NA domestic chicken
cikinis– NA domestic chicken, little chicken
misihêw– NA chicken, domestic chicken
pâhpahâhkwân– NA chicken, domestic chicken
pâhpahâhkwânisis– NA young chicken, chick

CHIEF
okimâhkân– NA chief, elected chief
okimâhkâniwi– VAI be chief, serve as elected chief
okimâsis– NA little chief, boss; *(fig.)* nobility
okimâw– NA chief, leader, boss; *(fig.)* band council

CHIEFTAINCY
okimâhkâniwin– NI chieftaincy

CHILD
–awâsimis– NDA child
–osk-âyim– NDA young people, children, grandchildren, the young
–pêpîm– NDA baby, infant; youngest child
asamâwaso– VAI feed one's children, sustain one's children
awâsis– NA child
awâsisîwi– VAI be a child
awâsisîwiwin– NI being a child, childhood
kakêskimâwaso– VAI counsel one's children, lecture one's children
kikiskawâwaso– VAI carry a child, be with child, be pregnant
kimotôsê– VAI bear an illegitimate child
kiskinahamâwaso– VAI teach one's children
mihcêtôsê– VAI have many children, have numerous offspring
mosci-nôhâwaso– VAI simply breastfeed one's child, breastfeed one's child without further ado (e.g., sterilisation of bottles)
nahâwaso– VAI have one's child in the proper place, carry one's child with one
nâtamâwaso– VAI take up for one's children
nihtâwikihâwaso– VAI give birth to one's child, bring forth a child, bring forth a young one (of the species)
nihtâwikinâwaso– VAI give birth to one's child, bring forth a child, bring forth a young one (of the species)
nôhâwaso– VAI nurse one's child, breastfeed one's child; suckle the young one (of the species), suckle one's calf (as cow)
nônâcikêhâwaso– VAI bottlefeed one's child
ocawâsimisi– VAI have a child; have offspring, have a calf (as cow); have (her/him) as one's child; be the mother of a child; give birth, be delivered; calve (as cow)
ohpikihâwaso– VAI make one's children grow up, raise one's children
ohpikinâwaso– VAI make one's children grow up, raise one's children
oskawâsis– NA young child, infant
otawâsimisimâw– NA a child
pakâsimonahâwaso– VAI immerse one's child, bathe one's child
pimâcihâwaso– VAI give life to one's children, make a living for one's children
pôni-nôhâwaso– VAI stop nursing one's child, wean one's child
sâkihâwaso– VAI love one's children
tahkonâwaso– VAI hold one's child, cuddle one's child
tahkopitâwaso– VAI swaddle one's child; *(fig.)* be delivered of a child

wanisimôhâwaso– *VAI* lead one's children astray
wêpinikan– *NA* abandoned child, neglected child
wîhtamâwaso– *VAI* tell (it/him) to one's children

CHILDBED
pimisin– *VAI* lie extended, lie down; lie confined, lie in childbed

CHILDBIRTH
pamih– *VTA* tend to s.o., look after s.o.; attend s.o. in childbirth, serve as midwife to s.o.; guide s.o. (e.g., sleigh), drive s.o. (e.g., sleigh)
pamihiso– *VAI* tend to oneself, look after oneself; attend oneself in childbirth, serve as one's own midwife
pamin– *VTA* tend to s.o., look after s.o.; attend s.o. in childbirth, serve as midwife to s.o.
wîcihiso– *VAI* help oneself; apply oneself, study for oneself; rely on oneself in childbirth

CHILDHOOD
awâsisîwiwin– *NI* being a child, childhood

CHILL
kawaci– *VAI* be cold, experience cold; suffer chills
kawacipayi– *VAI* get chilled, get cold
kawatihtâ– *VAI* get (it) chilled, get (it) cold

CHIN
–tâpiskan– *NDI* chin

CHIPEWAYAN
wêcîpwayâniw– *NA* Chipewayan

CHOKECHERRIES
takwahiminân– *NI* chokecherries
takwahiminê– *VAI* crush chokecherries

CHOOSE
mâyi-nawasônikê– *VAI* choose badly, make a bad choice
nawasôn– *VTA* choose s.o.
nawasôn– *VTI* choose s.t.
nawasônamaw– *VTA* choose (it/him) for s.o.; make a choice for s.o.
nawasônikê– *VAI* choose, make a choice
otin– *VTA* take s.o., take s.o. in (e.g., orphan); choose s.o.; steal s.o.; *(especially in inverse constructions:)* take hold of s.o., possess s.o.
otin– *VTI* take s.t.; pick s.t., choose s.t., select s.t. (e.g., moss); steal s.t.; take s.t. over; extract s.t. (e.g., grease from soup), remove s.t. (e.g., glands in butchering beaver), extract s.t.; accept s.t. (e.g., contract); capture s.t., record s.t. on audio-tape
pakitiniso– *VAI* choose (him/it) for oneself; make one's own choice

CHOP
cîkah– *VTI* chop s.t.
cîkahikê– *VAI* chop things, chop wood, chop posts
cîkahoso– *VAI* chop oneself, injure oneself with an axe
cîkahw– *VTA* chop s.o. (e.g., tree)
cîsâwât– *VTI* cut s.t. (e.g., fat) into chunks, chop s.t. fine
kawikah– *VTI* chop s.t. down, cut s.t. down
kînikatahamaw– *VTA* chop (it/him) to a point for s.o.
kînikatahikê– *VAI* chop things to a point, sharpen posts
kîskatah– *VTI* chop s.t. through
kîskatahikâso– *VAI* be chopped through by tool (e.g., tree)
kîskatahikâtê– *VII* be chopped through by tool (e.g., branch)
napakis– *VTI* cut s.t. into flat pieces, cut s.t. (e.g., meat) into chops
nâtwâh– *VTI* split s.t., chop s.t. apart
nikohtât– *VTI* chop s.t. for firewood
nikohtê– *VAI* collect firewood, chop firewood
sikokahw– *VTA* chop s.o. (e.g., beaver) until small
sikos– *VTI* chop s.t. small
sikosâwât– *VTI* chop s.t. small (e.g., onion)

CHOSEN
mwêsiskaw– *VTA* have chosen exactly the wrong time or place for s.o., just miss s.o.
nîhcipicikâtê– *VII* be taken down (e.g., from a shelf), be chosen for purchase (e.g., in self-service store)
otinikâtê– *VII* be taken, be obtained; be chosen

CHRISTIAN
ayamihêstamaw– *VTA* say Christian prayers for s.o.
kwêskin– *VTA* change s.o. around, turn s.o. around to the opposite side; *(fig.)* convert s.o. to Christianity
otayamihâw– *NA* Christian, adherent of Christianity

CHRISTMAS
–kîsikâm– *NDI* day, day of one's life; *(fig.)* [Our Father's] day, Christmas Day

kihcikanisi– VAI hold a rite; spend Christmas
manitowi-kîsikâw– NI Christmas Day

CHUNK
cîsâwât– VTI cut s.t. (e.g., fat) into chunks, chop s.t. fine
pîkinisâwâtamaw– VTA cut (it/him) into small chunks for s.o.

CHURCH
ayamihâ– VAI pray, say prayers; hold a church service, celebrate mass; participate in a religious rite, go to church; follow a religion
ayamihâhtah– VTA make s.o. go to church, take s.o. to mass, go to church with s.o.
ayamihâwin– NI prayer, praying, saying prayers; church service; religious rite; religion, religious denomination; the Roman Catholic church
ayamihêwikamikw– NI church, church building
kihci-wîkihto– VAI be formally married, be married in church
kihci-wîkim– VTA marry s.o. formally, marry s.o. in church
pâhkw-âyamihâwin– NI Roman Catholic religion; the Roman Catholic church
sîkahâhtaw– VTA sprinkle s.o. with water; *(fig.)* baptise s.o., accept s.o. into the Catholic church

CIGARETTE
pîhcwâkanis– NA cigarette
pîhcwâwinis– NA cigarette

CIRCLE
pîhtêyask IPC at the central circle of poles inside the dance-lodge
têtipêwêyâmo– VAI flee around in a circle
wâsakâ IPC around a circle, in a full circle
wâsakâhtê– VAI walk around a circle, walk a circuit
wâsakâm IPC around a circle, in a full circle
wâsakâmêyâpôyo– VAI go around a circle by railway, describe a circuit by rail
wâsakân– VTI turn s.t. around a circle; make s.t. go around, turn s.t. (e.g. treadle), crank s.t.
wâsakâpi– VAI sit in a circle
wâsakâtisahoto– VAI chase one another around a circle
wâsakâyâskon– VTA point s.o. (e.g., pipe) around a full circle
wâskâhtê– VAI walk around a circle, walk a circuit
wâskân– VTI turn s.t. around a circle; make s.t. go around, turn s.t. (e.g., treadle), crank s.t.
wâskâsk– VTI go around s.t., circle s.t.

CLAY
asiskiy– NI earth, soil, mud; clay; sod
micimoskowahtâ– VAI make (it) hold together with mud, mud (it) with clay
micimoskowahtê– VII be held together with mud, be mudded with clay
wâpatonisk– NA white clay

CLEAN
kanâcâciwahtê– VII be boiled clean, be clean by boiling
kanâci IPV clean
kanâcih– VTA clean s.o.
kanâcihcikê– VAI clean things, do one's cleaning
kanâcihiso– VAI clean oneself
kanâciho– VAI clean oneself, keep oneself clean
kanâcihtâ– VAI clean (it), clean (it) out (e.g., intestine)
kanâcinâkosi– VAI look clean, give a clean appearance
kanâtahcâ– VII be clean ground, be clean land
kanâtan– VII be clean
kanâtanohk IPC in a clean place
kanâtapi– VAI live in a clean house
kanâtâpâwahiso– VAI wash oneself clean with water
kanâtâpâwatâ– VAI wash (it) clean with water
kanâtâpâwê– VII be washed clean with water
kanâtisi– VAI be clean
pôhtâskwah– VTI stick s.t. wooden into a hole; clean out one's ear, poke one's ear

CLEAR
paskwatah– VTI clear brush
tawâtamaw– VTA open (it) up for s.o.; clear the way for s.o.

CLEARLY
kîhkânâkwan– VII be clearly visible
kîhkâtah– VTI make the sound of (it/him) ring out clearly
kîhkâtahamaw– VTA make the sound of (it/him) ring out clearly to s.o.
pakahkihtaw– VTA hear s.o. clearly

ENGLISH INDEX 239

CLERK
omasinahikêsîs– *NA* scribe, clerk
CLEVER
iyinîsi– *VAI* be clever, be smart
CLIMB
iskwâhtawât– *VTA* climb up so far after s.o.; climb up (e.g., a tree) after s.o.
iskwâhtawî– *VAI* climb up so far; climb up (e.g., a tree)
iskwâhtawîhtah– *VTA* take s.o. climbing up so far; climb up (e.g., a tree) with s.o.
iskwâhtawîpahtâ– *VAI* climb up so far at a run; climb up (e.g., a tree) at a run
kîhcêkosî– *VAI* climb high up, climb to a high place
nâtâhtawât– *VTA* climb up (e.g., a tree) to fetch s.o.
nîhtâhtawî– *VAI* climb down (e.g., a tree)
nîhtâhtawîpahtâ– *VAI* climb down (e.g., a tree) at a run
pôsâhtawî– *VAI* climb aboard (e.g., boat or vehicle)
takwâhtawî– *VAI* arrive in climbing up (e.g., a tree)
CLOCK
pîsimôhkân– *NI* clock, watch
CLOSE
câh-cîkâhtaw *IPC* quite close, quite nearby
câh-cîki *IPC* close to one another
cîkâhtaw *IPC* close, nearby, in the area, in the immediate vicinity
cîki *IPC* close, close by, nearby, near to
cîkiskîsik *IPC* close to one's eye
kipah– *VTI* close s.t., shut s.t.
kipokwât– *VTI* sew s.t. closed, sew s.t. shut; close s.t. up by sewing
kipokwâtâ– *VAI* sew (it) closed, sew (it) shut, close (it) up by sewing
kipwahpit– *VTI* pull s.t. closed, tie s.t. shut
pasakwâpi– *VAI* close one's eyes, have one's eyes shut
CLOSER
âstamispîhk *IPC* at a time closer to the present; more recently
CLOSET
wiyâkanikamikw– *NI* pantry, scullery; walk-in closet

CLOTH
itêkin– *VTI* fold s.t. flat thus, fold s.t. thus as cloth
maskimotêkinw– *NI* sack, sacking, sack-cloth; flour-bag, cloth from flour-bag
papakiwayânêkinw– *NI* thin cloth, cotton; canvas
pitikwêkin– *VTI* roll s.t. up as cloth
sâkêkamon– *VII* stick out as cloth, project as cloth
taswêkin– *VTI* unfold s.t. as cloth; open s.t. (e.g., book) up flat
wâpiskayiwinis– *NI* white cloth
wêpinâson– *NI* draped cloth, flag, cloth offering
CLOTHE
pohtayiwinisah– *VTA* put clothes on s.o., make clothes for s.o., fit s.o. out with clothing, clothe s.o.
postayiwinisahiso– *VAI* put clothes on oneself, make clothes for oneself, clothe oneself
CLOTHES
ayânis– *NI* clothes, clothing
ayânisis– *NI* clothes, clothing
ayiwinis– *NI* clothes, clothing; rags (e.g., as used in bitch-light)
ayiwinisis– *NI* clothes, clothing, laundry
***Hudson's-Bay*-ayiwinis–** *NI* Hudson's Bay Company clothes, store-bought clothing
mêskotayiwinisê– *VAI* change one's clothes
mîkisayiwinis– *NI* beaded clothing
nâpêw-âya *IPC* men's things, men's stuff, men's clothing
osîhtamowinihkê– *VAI* have a garment made, have clothes made
pîmikitêwayiwinis– *NI* embroidered clothing
pohtayiwinisah– *VTA* put clothes on s.o., make clothes for s.o., fit s.o. out with clothing, clothe s.o.
pohtayiwinisê– *VAI* put one's clothes on, get dressed
postayiwinisahiso– *VAI* put clothes on oneself, make clothes for oneself, clothe oneself
sikwâskocin– *VAI* be cut by branches or thorns, have one's clothes torn
wîpayiwinis– *NI* dirty clothes, soiled clothing

wîpâtayiwinis– *NI* dirty clothes, soiled clothing
yâyikâskocin– *VAI* have one's clothes ripped ragged on branches or thorns
yîwêyâskocin– *VAI* have one's clothes torn ragged on branches or thorns

CLOUD
îkwaskwan– *VII* be cloudy
ministikoskwâ– *VII* be an individual cloud
ministikwaskwâsin– *VII* be an individual small cloud, be an isolated small cloud
waskway– *NI* cloud

CLUELESS
pakwanawahtâ– *VAI* go on with (it) at random, know nothing about (it), be clueless about (it)

COALS
sêkon– *VTI* place s.t. underneath; place s.t. beneath the coals
sêkwâpiskin– *VTA* place s.o. beneath the coals, place s.o. (e.g., beaver) in the oven
sêkwâpiskin– *VTI* place s.t. beneath the coals, place s.t. in the oven

COAT
–skocâkâs– *NDI* little coat, little dress
–skotâkay– *NDI* coat, dress
kispakiwêsâkay– *NI* thick coat, thick jacket
mihkwawê– *VAI* have a red coat (e.g., animal)
mîkisasâkay– *NI* beaded coat, beaded jacket
pahkêkinwêsâkay– *NI* leather coat, leather jacket

COCK
wêpah– *VTI* sweep s.t. up; throw s.t. by tool, push s.t. by tool; cock s.t. (e.g., gun)

COIN
kisîpêkinikêwikamikw– *NI* coin laundry, laundromat
sôniyâs– *NA* coin; 25-cents coin, quarter; a little money, some money

COINCIDENCE
kâkêswân *IPC* as it happens, by coincidence
kêswân *IPC* by coincidence

COINCIDENTALLY
kisik *IPC* at the same time, simultaneously, coincidentally
pâskac *IPC* on top of that, to top it all off, to cap it all, as the final touch; coincidentally

COLD
âhkwaci– *VAI* be cold, freeze, be frozen (e.g., fish)
kawaci– *VAI* be cold, experience cold; suffer chills
kawacipayi– *VAI* get chilled, get cold
kawatihtâ– *VAI* get (it) chilled, get (it) cold
kawatim– *VTA* get s.o. cold, expose s.o. to cold
kawatimiso– *VAI* get oneself cold
kisin– *VII* be cold weather, be very cold weather
nanamaci– *VAI* shiver with cold
tahkâ– *VII* be cool, be cold; cool off
tahkâyâ– *VII* be cold weather
tahkêyiht– *VTI* consider s.t. cold; perceive the cold
tahkikamâpoy– *NI* cold water

COLLAPSE
nipahipahtâ– *VAI* run to excess, collapse from running

COLLECT
manâho– *VAI* collect (it); take (it) as trophy; take a trophy
mâwacih– *VTA* collect s.o. (e.g., pounded meat), gather s.o. up; save s.o.
mâwacihtâ– *VAI* collect (it), gather (it) up
mâwacîhito– *VAI* collect one another, gather
mâwasakon– *VTA* gather s.o. up, collect s.o. (e.g., spruce-gum)
nikohtê– *VAI* collect firewood, chop firewood
nitawâwê– *VAI* go looking for eggs, go to collect eggs

COLLECTIVELY
mâmawi *IPN* collectively, jointly, all together
mâmawi *IPV* collectively, jointly, all together

COLONY
askiy– *NI* land, region, area; earth, world; settlement, colony, country; Métis settlement; *(plural:)* fields under cultivation, pieces of farmland, the lands

COLOUR
atihtê– *VII* be ripe, be of ripe colouring
itatisw– *VTA* dye s.o. (e.g., porcupine quills) thus; dye s.o. in such a colour
itâkami– *VII* be a liquid of such a colour
pakaski *IPV* brightly coloured

wâpâstê– *VII* be light-coloured, be faded in colour

COMB
osîkahonê– *VAI* have a comb; have (it) as one's comb
sêkah– *VTI* comb s.t. (e.g., hair)
sêkaho– *VAI* comb one's hair
sêkahon– *NI* comb

COME
âstam *IPC* come here!
ohcipayin– *VII* come from there, result from that
ohcî– *VAI* come from there, be from there
ohtohtê– *VAI* come from there, come walking from there
pâpahtâ– *VAI* run hither, come running
pâpayi– *VAI* come hither, ride hither
pêtâstamohtê– *VAI* walk hither, come walking
pêtisâpam– *VTA* see s.o. coming
pêtwêwêhtamaw– *VTA* come hither audibly bringing (it/him) for s.o.
pêtwêwên– *VTI* come hither audibly, come with audible steps
sâkâwanêhtâ– *VAI* push (it) to emerge from the ground, make (it) come forth
sâkêwê– *VAI* appear, come into view
sâkêwêtâpâso– *VAI* come into view with one's wagon, drive into view
sâkêwêtot– *VTI* come out upon s.t., rise (e.g., sun) upon s.t.
tako-kîskwêpê– *VAI* arrive intoxicated with alcoholic drink, arrive inebriated, come home drunk
wîc-ôhcîm– *VTA* come from the same time or place as s.o., share the year of birth with s.o.

COME ASHORE
kapâ– *VAI* come ashore, come out of the water

COME BACK
âpisisin– *VAI* revive, come back to life
kîwêmakan– *VII* return home, come back

COME FORTH
nihtâwikin– *VII* grow forth (e.g., plant), come forth

COME OFF
kêcikopayi– *VAI* come off (e.g., soap), come out of container (e.g., soap)

COME OUT
matâwisi– *VAI* move into the open, come out onto the open prairie

COME UP
ispisîh– *VTA* make s.o. (e.g., cracklings being boiled) come up so high

COME UPON
miskôskaw– *VTA* come upon s.o.
tâwin– *VTA* encounter s.o., come upon s.o., bump into s.o., hit s.o.
tâwin– *VTI* encounter s.t. by hand, come upon s.t., bump into s.t.
tâwisk– *VTI* encounter s.t. (by foot or body movement), come upon s.t., bump into s.t.
tâwiskaw– *VTA* encounter s.o. (by foot or body movement), bump into s.o., come into contact with s.o.

COMFORTABLE
nakayâsk– *VTI* be accustomed to s.t., be comfortable with s.t., be familiar with s.t.
nakayâskaw– *VTA* be accustomed to s.o., be comfortable with s.o., be familiar with s.o.

COMFORTABLY
miyo-wîki– *VAI* live comfortably, have a nice dwelling

COMMAND
itasiwât– *VTA* decide thus with respect to s.o.; give s.o. such a command; impose such laws on s.o.
itasiwê– *VAI* decide thus for people, make such a plan for people; give such a command, impose such laws

COMMUNION
ayamihêwi-saskamon– *NA* the host; Holy Communion
saskamo– *VAI* take communion; have one's first communion, have had one's first communion
saskamonah– *VTA* give s.o. communion
saskamonahiso– *VAI* give oneself communion, place the host into one's mouth

COMMUNITY
ihtâwin– *NI* abode, place of residence; community

COMPANION
–îci-kîhkâw– *NDA* aged spouse, fellow old person, fellow oldster, companion of one's old age
–wîcêwâkan– *NDA* companion, partner; spouse
–wîcêwâkanis– *NDA* companion
owîcêwâkani– *VAI* have a companion or partner; have (her/him) as one's companion or partner

wîci-minihkwêm– VTA drink together with s.o., have s.o. as a drinking companion

COMPARISON

ispîhci IPC for now, in the meantime; *(in comparative constructions:)* by comparison; than

nawac IPC by comparison; more, better, rather

COMPASSION

kisê-manitow– NA God the kind, the compassionate God; *(name:)* Merciful God

kisêwâtisi– VAI be kind, be of compassionate disposition; *(fig.)* be full of grace

kisêwâtisiwin– NI kindness, compassion; *(fig.)* grace

kitimâkêyihtamâso– VAI think of (it/him) with compassion for one's own sake

kitimâkêyihto– VAI feel pity towards one another, think of one another with compassion; take pity upon one another, be kind to one another, love one another

kitimâkêyihtowin– NI feeling pity towards one another, thinking of one another with compassion; taking pity upon one another, being kind to one another, loving one

kitimâkêyim– VTA feel pity towards s.o., think of s.o. with compassion; take pity upon s.o., be kind to s.o., love s.o.

kitimâkihtaw– VTA listen to s.o. with pity, listen to s.o. with compassion

kitimâkinaw– VTA look with pity upon s.o., look with compassion upon s.o., feel sorry for s.o.; take pity upon s.o., lovingly tend s.o.; regard s.o. with respect

COMPATRIOT

wîtaskîwêm– VTA live together with s.o., have s.o. as one's compatriot; live in the same country with s.o., live in peace with s.o.

COMPETENCE

kaskihtâwin– NI ability to do (it), competence

COMPETENT

kaskiho– VAI be able, be competent

kaskihtâ– VAI be able to do (it), be competent at (it), manage (it)

nahî– VAI be adept at (it), be good at (it); be competent, be an expert

nihtâ IPV good at, doing much of, competent, practised, experienced

COMPETITION

otahw– VTA beat s.o. in competition, win over s.o., win from s.o.

COMPLAIN

kisiwiyo– VAI complain, be angry at one's work

mwêstâtwêwêm– VTA speak about s.o. as troublesome, complain about s.o. being a nuisance

COMPLETE

âpihci IPV completely, throughout

kitâ– VAI eat (it) up, eat (it) completely, eat all of (it); drink all of (it); finish drinking a bottle of (it); drink an entire bottle

kî IPV to completion, completely

kîs-ôhpiki– VAI complete one's growing up, reach adulthood, be grown up

kîsahpit– VTI complete tying s.t. up, complete tying s.t. in

kîsakim– VTA finish counting s.o.; finish giving orders to s.o., complete one's charge to s.o.

kîsapihkât– VTI braid s.t. to completion, complete the knitting of s.t.

kîsasiwât– VTI reach a decision about s.t.; complete making a law about s.t.

kîsâpiskiso– VAI be completely heated as rock (e.g., in sweat-lodge), be fully heated as rock

kîsêyiht– VTI make up one's mind about s.t., decide on s.t., complete one's plan for s.t.; be decisive

kîsi IPV completely, to completion

kîsi-tipiskâ– VII be completely night

kîsinamâso– VAI complete (it/him) for oneself, finish (it/him) for oneself

kîsis– VTI cook s.t. to completion

kîsiso– VAI be cooked to completion; burn oneself, get burnt; get burnt by an acidic or caustic agent

kîsisw– VTA cook s.o. (e.g., bread) to completion

kîsitê– VII be cooked to completion; be burnt; burn down, be burnt down (e.g., building); be burnt (e.g., stubble, fields)

kîsîh– VTA complete s.o. (e.g., rattle)

kîsîhcikê– VAI complete doing things; bring a ritual to its conclusion; conclude the formal signing of a treaty

kîsîhtamaw– VTA complete (it/him) for s.o.

kîsîhtâ– VAI finish (it), complete (it)

kîsowât– VTI complete one's words, complete one's prayers
kîsowâtamaw– VTA complete one's words for s.o., complete one's prayers for s.o.
mêstihkahtê– VII burn down completely, be completely burnt down

COMPRESS
kisitê– VII be warmed up, be heated up, be hot; be a hot compress
wâpiskâpâwê– VAI be white from water (e.g., skin), turn white with washing (e.g., pants); turn white under a compress (e.g., skin)

CONCERN
pîkiskwât– VTI speak about s.t., speak about s.t. with concern; speak a prayer over s.t.; address s.t., speak to s.t. (e.g., spirit-bundle)
pîkiskwêmôh– VTA cause s.o. to speak with concern

CONCLUDE
kîsîhcikê– VAI complete doing things; bring a ritual to its conclusion; conclude the formal signing of a treaty
wiyîhcikê– VAI conduct negotiations, conclude negotiations

CONFESS
âcimiso– VAI tell things about oneself, tell a story about oneself; *(fig.)* confess oneself, go to confession

CONFINED
pimisin– VAI lie extended, lie down; lie confined, lie in childbed

CONFIRMATION
aspitonâmo– VAI rely on the spoken word; rely on (it) as a formal confirmation of the spoken word

CONFOUND
kînwâhkwêh– VTA *(especially in inverse constructions:)* leave s.o. baffled, confound s.o.

CONFUSE
wanêyiht– VTI forget s.t., be unsure of s.t.; have one's mind blurred, be confused
wanisîho– VAI be indistinctly dressed, be confusingly dressed, be wrongly dressed
wanwêhkaw– VTA leave s.o. baffled by speech or in speech, confuse s.o.

CONSCIOUS
âpahkawin– VII be level-headed, be sensible, be conscious

CONSIDERATE
manâtâstim– VTA be careful in making s.o. wave, avoid making s.o. weave about; spare s.o. in driving a wagon, be considerate of s.o.

CONTAIN
akwanâpowêhikâso– VAI be covered as vessel containing liquid, have a cover, have a lid (e.g., pot)
akwanâpowêhikâsosi– VAI be covered as a small vessel containing liquid, have a cover, have a lid (e.g., mussel)
pîsâkwan– VII contain plenty, offer lots of room; be plentiful, be rich

CONTAINER
asiwacikan– NI pocket; container
asiwatâ– VAI place (it) inside, enclose (it), put (it) into a bag or container
kêcikopayi– VAI come off (e.g., soap), come out of container (e.g., soap)

CONTENT
têpêyimo– VAI be content, be willing

CONTEST
mawinêhw– VTA challenge s.o. to a contest
paskiyaw– VTA beat s.o. in a contest

CONTINUALLY
mâninakisk IPC continually, on and on, persistently

CONTINUATION
âsawi IPV in passing something on, in continuation
âsô IPV in passing something on, in continuation

CONTINUING
aniyê IPC continuing, on and on

CONTINUITY
kêyâpic IPC still, in continuity; yet
misakâmê IPC all along, all the way, in continuity, throughout

CONTRACT
atoskêwin– NI work; job; contract (e.g., to complete an assignment)

CONTRACTIONS
âhkosi– VAI be sick, be ill; have contractions, be in labour

CONTRAST
wiya IPC by contrast

CONTROL
tipêyihcikâtê– VII be owned, be controlled, be governed
tipêyiht– VTI own s.t., control s.t., rule s.t., be master over s.t.; have a voice in the affairs of s.t. (e.g., reserve)
tipêyim– VTA own s.o., control s.o., rule s.o.; *(fig.)* be the Lord over s.o.; have s.o. in one's clutches (e.g., devil)

tipêyimiso– *VAI* control oneself, govern oneself; be on one's own, be one's own boss

CONVENIENT
nahipayi– *VII* be convenient, fall into place

CONVERT
kwêskin– *VTA* change s.o. around, turn s.o. around to the opposite side; *(fig.)* convert s.o. to Christianity

CONVINCE
sâkôcim– *VTA* overcome s.o. by speech; convince s.o. by speech, win s.o. over

COOK
kaskihkasw– *VTA* cook s.o. (e.g., skunk) until tender
kîsis– *VTI* cook s.t. to completion
kîsisikâtê– *VII* be cooked done
kîsiso– *VAI* be cooked to completion; burn oneself, get burnt; get burnt by an acidic or caustic agent
kîsisw– *VTA* cook s.o. (e.g., bread) to completion
kîsitê– *VII* be cooked to completion; be burnt; burn down, be burnt down (e.g., building); be burnt (e.g., stubble, fields)
kîsitêpo– *VAI* cook; cook a feast, cook ritual food
nihtâwitêpo– *VAI* be good at cooking, be an expert cook
piminawaso– *VAI* cook, do one's cooking
piminawasosi– *VAI* cook a little, do some cooking
piminawat– *VTA* cook for s.o.

COOK-STOVE
kotawânâpiskw– *NA* stove, cook-stove
kotawânâpiskw– *NI* stove, cook-stove

COOKHOUSE
piminawasowikamikw– *NI* cookhouse, kitchen

COOKING
kotawê– *VAI* make a campfire, make a cooking fire
mistaskihkw– *NA* big kettle, communal cooking pot
nihtâwitêpo– *VAI* be good at cooking, be an expert cook
pakâhcikanaskihkw– *NA* cooking pot

COOL
tahkâ– *VII* be cool, be cold; cool off

tahkâpâwat– *VTA* pour water to cool s.o. (e.g., rock), cool s.o. (e.g., rock) with water (e.g., in sweat-lodge)
tahkipayi– *VAI* cool down
tahkisi– *VAI* be cooled off, be cool

COOPERATE
mâmawi-wîcihitowin– *NI* all helping together, general cooperation
mâmawôhkamâto– *VAI* work together at (it/him) as a group; do things together, help one another, cooperate
miyo-wîcêht– *VTI* be supportive of s.t.; be cooperative
wîcêht– *VTI* go along with s.t., support s.t., cooperate with s.t.
wîcihito– *VAI* help one another, cooperate with one another

COPPER
sôniyâwâpiskw– *NA* gold; copper

CORDWOOD
kîskipocikê– *VAI* cut things with a saw, cut cordwood

CORNER
wîhkwêhtakâw– *NI* corner made by wooden walls, corner of the floor, corner of the house
wîhkwêskamikâ– *VII* be the corners of the earth, be the ends of the earth

CORRECT
mînom– *VTA* straighten s.o. out, correct s.o. verbally

CORRECTLY
tâpâtot– *VTI* tell s.t. fittingly, tell s.t. correctly, tell s.t. faithfully
tâpowê– *VAI* speak correctly; recite one's prayer correctly

COST
âhkwakihtê– *VII* cost dearly, cost more, be worth a top-up amount
itakihtê– *VII* be counted thus, be valued thus, be held in such esteem; be worth so much, cost so much

COTTON
papakiwayânêkinw– *NI* thin cloth, cotton; canvas

COUGH
nânâspicipayi– *VAI* have a coughing fit
oscoscocasi– *VAI* cough up a little of s.t.; cough a little
ostostot– *VTI* cough s.t. up, cough s.t. out; cough, have a coughing spell

COUNCIL
okimâw– *NA* chief, leader, boss; *(fig.)* band council

wiyasiwêwin– NI decision; rule, law; council, band council

COUNCILLOR
owiyasiwêwi– VAI be a band councillor
wiyasiwêhkâniwi– VAI be a band councillor

COUNSEL
kakêskihkêmo– VAI counsel people, lecture people, preach at people
kakêskim– VTA counsel s.o., lecture s.o., preach at s.o.
kakêskimâwaso– VAI counsel one's children, lecture one's children
kakêskimiso– VAI counsel oneself

COUNSELLING
kakêskimâwasowin– NI counselling the young
miyo-kakêskihkêmowin– NI good counselling, good preaching

COUNT
akihtê– VII be counted
akim– VTA count s.o.
akiso– VAI be counted; be counted in, be a band member
itakiht– VTI count s.t. thus, value s.t. thus, hold s.t. in such esteem; charge so much for s.t.
itakihtê– VII be counted thus, be valued thus, be held in such esteem; be worth so much, cost so much
itakim– VTA count s.o. thus, value s.o. thus, hold s.o. in such esteem
itakiso– VAI be counted thus, be valued thus; be held in such esteem; be worth so much; have such a function
kisipakim– VTA count s.o. (e.g., sun) as the end of the month
kîsakim– VTA finish counting s.o.; finish giving orders to s.o., complete one's charge to s.o.
mistakihtê– VII be counted for much, be worth a lot, be valuable, be expensive
nîkânakim– VTA count s.o. in first position, hold s.o. (e.g., tobacco) to be the prime element
têpakiht– VTI count s.t. up

COUNTRY
askiy– NI land, region, area; earth, world; settlement, colony, country; Métis settlement; *(plural:)* fields under cultivation, pieces of farmland, the lands
ispîhcâ– VII extend thus, reach so far as land, be of such size as country

wîtaskîwêm– VTA live together with s.o., have s.o. as one's compatriot; live in the same country with s.o., live in peace with s.o.

COURT
wiyasiwât– VTA decide about s.o.; sit in judgment on s.o., hold court over s.o.

COUSIN
–ciwâm– NDA male parallel cousin (man speaking); *(fig.)* brother, friend, male of the same generation (man speaking); brother, brethren
–ciwâmis– NDA male parallel cousin (man speaking); *(fig.)* brother, friend, male of the same generation (man speaking); brother, brethren
–îc-âyis– NDA fellow youngster; sibling, parallel cousin
–mis– NDA older sister, older female parallel cousin
–sîm– NDA younger sibling, younger parallel cousin
–sîmis– NDA younger sibling, younger parallel cousin
–stês– NDA older brother, older male parallel cousin
–tawêmâw– NDA male parallel cousin (woman speaking); female cross-cousin's husband (woman speaking)

COVER
akwanah– VTA cover s.o.
akwanah– VTI cover s.t.
akwanaho– VAI cover oneself, be covered (e.g., by a blanket); use (it) as a cover
akwanahon– NI cover
akwanâhkwên– VTA cover s.o.'s (e.g., infant's) face; use (it) to cover s.o.'s face
akwanâhkwêyâmo– VAI flee with one's face covered, flee by covering one's face, cover one's face in flight
akwanâpowêhikâso– VAI be covered as vessel containing liquid, have a cover, have a lid (e.g., pot)
akwanâpowêhikâsosi– VAI be covered as a small vessel containing liquid, have a cover, have a lid (e.g., mussel)
apahkwâson– NI cover, canvas
ayah– VTI cover s.t. with earth; hill s.t. (e.g., potatoes)
ayahikê– VAI cover things with earth, hill things (e.g., potatoes)
misiwêminakin– VTI put beads all over s.t.; cover s.t. with beads

otakwanaho– *VAI* have a cover; use (it) as one's bed-cover
pâskin– *VTI* open s.t. up, take the cover off s.t.; fold s.t. (e.g., book) open
pîhtawêkwât– *VTI* sew s.t. in between, sew covers on s.t.

COVERED
âkô *IPV* covered, shielded
âkô-wiyîpâ– *VII* be covered in dirt

COVERING
akwanahikan– *NI* covering; canvas
anâskânis– *NI* covering, mat, rug
ayahikâkan– *NI* hiller, tool for covering potatoes with earth
pîhton– *VTA* take the covering layer off s.o. (e.g., tree), peel s.o.
pîhton– *VTI* take s.t. (e.g., bark) off as the covering layer, peel s.t. off
pîhtopit– *VTA* pull the covering layer off s.o. (e.g., tree), peel the bark off s.o.
pîhtopit– *VTI* pull s.t. (e.g., bark) off as the covering layer, peel s.t. off
pîhtosw– *VTA* cut the covering layer off s.o. (e.g., tree), cut the bark off s.o.

COW
moscosw– *NA* cow
mosti-tôhtôsâpoy– *NI* mere milk, mere cow's milk
mostosw– *NA* cattle, cow
mostosw-âya *IPC* of a cow, in matters bovine
omostosomisi– *VAI* have a few cows
onîcâniw– *NA* female of large quadrupeds; cow, cow-moose, female elk

COW-HIDE
mostoswayân– *NA* cow-hide

COW-MOOSE
onîcâniw– *NA* female of large quadrupeds; cow, cow-moose, female elk

COYOTE
mêscacâkanis– *NA* coyote

CRACK
pîkokonêwêpayi– *VAI* have cracks erupt in one's mouth, have one's mouth break out in sores (e.g., with thrush)

CRACKLINGS
sîkosâkan– *NA* cracklings, greaves

CRANBERRY
wîsakîmin– *NI* cranberry

CRANK
wâskân– *VTI* turn s.t. around a circle; make s.t. go around, turn s.t. (e.g., treadle), crank s.t.

CRAW
wîhkway– *NI* craw (e.g., bird); swim-bladder (e.g., fish)
wîhkwâs– *NI* craw

CRAWL
pimâhtawî– *VAI* crawl along
sêkwâhtawî– *VAI* crawl underneath (e.g., a tree)
sipwêtâcimopahtâ– *VAI* rapidly crawl away, depart crawling fast
sîpâhtawî– *VAI* crawl underneath (e.g., a tree)

CRAZY
kîskwê– *VAI* be mentally disturbed, be mad, be crazy
kîskwêpê– *VAI* be crazy with alcoholic drink, be drunk
kîskwêpêski– *VAI* be habitually crazy with alcoholic drink, be habitually drunk
kîskwêskaw– *VTA* (*especially in inverse constructions:*) make s.o. crazy, leave s.o. disoriented
ma-môhcw-âtayôhkêwin– *NI* stupid sacred story, crazy sacred story
môhcowi– *VAI* be foolish, be stupid, be silly; be mad, be crazy
môhcw-âyâ– *VAI* be foolish, be stupid, be silly; be mad, be crazy
môhcwahkamikisi– *VAI* behave foolishly, do crazy things

CREAM
manahikan– *NI* cream

CREATE
ohpin– *VTI* raise s.t., create s.t.
wawânaskêhtamaw– *VTA* create a peaceful life for s.o.

CREE
kayâsi-nêhiyâwin– *NI* traditional Creeness, traditional Cree identity
nêhiyaw– *NA* Cree; Indian
nêhiyaw-îsiyîhkâtê– *VII* have a Cree name
nêhiyaw-kîkway *PR* something Cree, Cree things
nêhiyaw-masinîwin– *NI* Cree design, Cree motif
nêhiyaw-mihkw– *NI* Cree blood; Indian blood
nêhiyaw-nitotamâwin– *NI* Cree supplication, the Cree way of supplication
nêhiyawasinahikan– *NI* Cree book; Cree bible

nêhiyawaskamikâ– VII be Cree land, be Cree terrain; be Indian land, be Indian terrain
nêhiyawaskîwin– VII be Cree land, be Cree territory; be Indian land, be Indian territory
nêhiyawastê– VII be written in Cree; be written in syllabics
nêhiyawayisiyiniw– NA Cree person; Indian person
nêhiyawê– VAI speak Cree
nêhiyawêmototaw– VTA speak Cree to s.o.
nêhiyawêwin– NI speaking Cree, the Cree language
nêhiyawi IPN Cree; Indian
nêhiyawi IPV Cree; Indian
nêhiyawi-maskihkiy– NI Cree medicine; Indian medicine
nêhiyawi-maskihkîwiskwêw– NA Cree midwife; Indian midwife
nêhiyawi-mêskanaw– NI Cree path, Cree road; Indian path, Indian road
nêhiyawi-nakamo– VAI sing hymns in Cree
nêhiyawi-pîkiskwê– VAI speak Cree, use Cree words
nêhiyawi-sîwîhtâkan– NI Cree salt; Indian salt
nêhiyawi-wîh– VTA use s.o.'s Cree name, call s.o. by a Cree name
nêhiyawi-wîhowin– NI Cree name; Indian name
nêhiyawi-wîht– VTI use the Cree name of s.t., call s.t. by a Cree name
nêhiyawi-wîhtamawâkan– NI Cree etymology; Cree teaching
nêhiyawihtwâwin– NI the Cree way, Cree culture; Indian culture
nêhiyawimototaw– VTA speak Cree to s.o.
nêhiyawisîhcikêwin– NI the Cree way, Cree culture; Indian culture
nêhiyawiskwêw– NA Cree woman; Indian woman
nêhiyawiyîhkâso– VAI have a Cree name
nêhiyawiyîhkât– VTA give s.o. a Cree name
nêhiyawiyîhkât– VTI give s.t. a Cree name
nêhiyawiyîhkâtê– VII be a Cree name
nêhiyawîhcikêwin– NI the Cree way, Cree culture; Indian culture
nêhiyâsis– NA young Cree; young Indian

nêhiyâwi– VAI be Cree; be an Indian
nêhiyâwiwin– NI being Cree, Cree identity, Creeness
paskwâwiyiniw– NA prairie person; Plains Cree
CREEK
akâmi-sîpîsisihk IPC across the creek
sîpîsis– NI small river, creek
CRISIS
kakwâtakihtâ– VAI suffer (it), suffer because of (it), have difficulties because of (it); suffer; experience a crisis (e.g., in the course of an illness)
mâkoh– VTA press upon s.o., bear down upon s.o., oppress s.o.; worry s.o., trouble s.o., throw s.o. into crisis
CRISP
kâspihkas– VTI heat s.t. until crisp, heat s.t. until brittle; dry s.t. by heat until crisp
kâspis– VTI heat s.t. until crisp, heat s.t. until brittle
pâhkosi– VAI dry off, be dried off; be dry and crisp (e.g., fried bacon)
CRISS-CROSS
kâh-kwêkwask IPC back and forth, criss-cross, crosswise
CROSS
âsowah– VTI cross s.t. (e.g., river, creek)
âsowiskâ– VAI cross by boat, go across by boat
âsowohtê– VAI walk across, cross the road
CROSS-COUSIN
–câhkos– NDA female cross-cousin (woman speaking); sister-in-law (woman speaking)
–îscâs– NDA male cross-cousin (man speaking); brother-in-law (man speaking)
–îstâw– NDA male cross-cousin (man speaking); brother-in-law (man speaking)
–îtimos– NDA cross-cousin of the opposite sex
–tawêmâw– NDA male parallel cousin (woman speaking); female cross-cousin's husband (woman speaking)
ocâhkosi– VAI have a female cross-cousin or sister-in-law (woman speaking), have (her) as one's female cross-cousin or sister-in-law (woman speaking)
wîtimosi– VAI have a cross-cousin of the opposite sex; have (him/her) as one's cross-cousin of the opposite sex

CROSS-NEPHEW
–tihkwatim– *NDA* cross-nephew; son-in-law

CROSS-NIECE
–stim– *NDA* cross-niece; daughter-in-law

CROSSWISE
kâh-kwêkwask *IPC* back and forth, criss-cross, crosswise

pimic-âyihk *IPC* across, athwart, crosswise, sideways

pimitapi– *VAI* sit crosswise, sit across (e.g., path)

pimitastê– *VII* be placed crosswise; be the bunk of a wagon

CROTCH
–cicâskâs– *NDI* crotch

CROWD
pêtâwah– *VTA* lead s.o. hither as a crowd, pull s.o. hither

pimâwah– *VTA* lead s.o. along as a crowd, pull s.o. along

sâkaskinê– *VAI* crowd in, fill a place

CROWDED
sâkaskinêkâpawi– *VAI* stand crowded in, stand to fill a place

tatâyawâ– *VII* be crowded

CRUDE
pimiy– *NI* fat, oil; crude petroleum

CRUELLY
kicimah– *VTA* be mean to s.o., treat s.o. cruelly

kitimah– *VTA* be mean to s.o., treat s.o. cruelly; bring misery upon s.o.

kitimahiso– *VAI* be mean to oneself, treat oneself cruelly; hurt oneself

kitimaho– *VAI* be mean to oneself, treat oneself cruelly; bring misery upon oneself

CRUSH
sikon– *VTI* crush s.t. by hand until small

sikopayi– *VII* be crushed, be reduced to small pieces

sikwah– *VTI* crush s.t. by tool until small

takwah– *VTI* add s.t. by tool; crush s.t. to be added

takwahiminê– *VAI* crush chokecherries

CRY
mawimo– *VAI* cry out; cry out in prayer, wail

mawimoscikê– *VAI* cry out in prayer, wail; worship with (it)

mawimost– *VTI* cry out in prayer to s.t., wail before s.t.

mawimostaw– *VTA* cry out in prayer to s.o., wail before s.o., implore s.o.; worship s.o.

mawîhkât– *VTA* cry out over s.o., lament s.o.

mawîhkât– *VTI* cry out over s.t., lament s.t.

mawîhkâtamaw– *VTA* cry out over (it/him) in prayer to s.o., wail over (it/him) before s.o.

mâcosi– *VAI* cry a little

mâto– *VAI* cry, wail

mâtopahtâ– *VAI* cry while running

môh– *VTA* make s.o. cry

môsko-miywêyiht– *VTI* cry with joy about s.t.; be moved to tears of joy

môskom– *VTA* make s.o. cry by tears or speech

môskomo– *VAI* talk oneself into crying, cry while talking

môskwêyiht– *VTI* cry about s.t.

CRYING
mawimoscikêwin– *NI* crying out in prayer, wailing; form of worship, rite

mâtowin– *NI* crying, wailing

CUD
mîciso– *VAI* eat, have a meal; feed (e.g., bird); chew the cud (e.g., ruminant)

CUDDLE
tahkonâwaso– *VAI* hold one's child, cuddle one's child

CULTIVATE
askiy– *NI* land, region, area; earth, world; settlement, colony, country; Métis settlement; *(plural:)* fields under cultivation, pieces of farmland, the lands

pîkopicikâtê– *VII* be ploughed soil, be cultivated

sikwahcisikê– *VAI* cultivate, harrow

CULTURE
isîhcikêwin– *NI* what is done, activities; culture; ritual

kayâs-isîhcikêwin– *NI* the old way of doing things, traditional culture

nêhiyawihtwâwin– *NI* the Cree way, Cree culture; Indian culture

nêhiyawisîhcikêwin– *NI* the Cree way, Cree culture; Indian culture

nêhiyawîhcikêwin– *NI* the Cree way, Cree culture; Indian culture

CUP
minihkwâcikan– *NI* cup

CUPBOARD
akocikan– *NI* rack for hanging up fish or meat, storage-rack; cupboard, shelf
CURDS
ascascwâs– *NI* curds, cottage cheese
CURE
nanâtawih– *VTA* treat s.o., doctor s.o.; heal s.o., cure s.o.
nanâtawihiwê– *VAI* treat people, doctor people; heal people, cure people
CURING
nanâtawihitowin– *NI* doctoring one another; healing one another, curing one another
CURL
titipawêhkas– *VTI* curl s.t. (e.g., head) by heat; have a perm
CURSE
mâyi-tôt– *VTI* do s.t. evil; do a bad thing, impose a curse
mâyi-tôtaw– *VTA* do evil to s.o., harm s.o., make s.o. sick, put a curse on s.o.
CURVE
wîhkwêhcâ– *VII* go around as land, be curved as land, be the sweep of the valley
wîhkwêstê– *VII* be placed around, stand in the shape of a curve
wîhkwêtâpânâskw– *NA* rounded toboggan, curved sleigh
CUSTOM
môniyâw-îhtwâwin– *NI* White ritual, White custom
CUT
apiscis– *VTI* cut s.t. into small pieces
apiscisasi– *VAI* cut (it) into very small pieces
cîhcîkos– *VTI* cut meat off s.t. (e.g., bone)
cîsâwât– *VTI* cut s.t. (e.g., fat) into chunks, chop s.t. fine
itis– *VTI* cut s.t. thus
kawikah– *VTI* chop s.t. down, cut s.t. down
kîskaht– *VTI* cut s.t. with one's teeth, bite s.t. off
kîskicin– *VAI* be cut (e.g., by branches or thorns), be torn
kîskin– *VTI* cut s.t. off (e.g., panelling) by hand
kîskipayi– *VAI* break off, be cut through, break apart
kîskipocikê– *VAI* cut things with a saw, cut cordwood
kîskipotâ– *VAI* cut (it) with a saw (e.g., cordwood), saw (it) through
kîskis– *VTI* cut s.t. through
kîskisamaw– *VTA* cut (it/him) off for s.o.; cut tobacco as an offering to s.o., present tobacco to s.o.
manis– *VTI* cut s.t.
manisw– *VTA* cut s.o.; perform surgery on s.o.
mosci-kîskipotâ– *VAI* simply cut (it) with a saw, cut (it) with a hand-saw
napakis– *VTI* cut s.t. into flat pieces, cut s.t. (e.g., meat) into chops
payipis– *VTI* cut s.t. out, cut a hole in s.t.
pânis– *VTI* cut s.t. (e.g., meat) into sheets
pânisâwê– *VAI* cut meat into sheets; cut fish into fillets
pânisw– *VTA* cut s.o. (e.g., animal) into sheets
pîhtosw– *VTA* cut the covering layer off s.o. (e.g., tree), cut the bark off s.o.
pîkinihkoso– *VAI* be cut into small pieces
pîkinis– *VTI* cut s.t. into small pieces
pîkinisâwâtamaw– *VTA* cut (it/him) into small chunks for s.o.
sikwâskocin– *VAI* be cut by branches or thorns, have one's clothes torn
taskamohtê– *VAI* cut across, walk straight towards one's goal
taswêkisâwât– *VTI* cut s.t. (e.g., leg of rabbit) into thin sheets
tâsawisâwât– *VTI* cut into the middle of s.t., slice s.t. open (e.g., veal belly cordon-bleu)
wiyis– *VTI* cut s.t. out, cut s.t. to a pattern
wiyisamaw– *VTA* cut a pattern for s.o.
wiyisamâso– *VAI* cut a pattern for oneself, cut one's own pattern
wiyisw– *VTA* cut s.o. out (e.g., figure in a picture-book)
DAD
–pâpâ– *NDA* dad, father
–pâpâsis– *NDA* dad's brother, father's brother, parallel uncle
opâpâ– *VAI* have a dad or father, have one's dad living; have (him) as one's dad
DAILY
tahto-kîsikâw *IPC* every day, each day, daily
DANCE
nawakiskwêsimo– *VAI* dance with one's head down

nihtâwisimo– VAI be good at dancing, be an expert dancer
nipâkwêsimo– VAI attend a sundance, participate in a sundance, dance the sundance
nîmih– VTA make s.o. (e.g., doll) dance
nîmihito– VAI dance with one another, dance; dance a (secular) dance; dance as prairie-chicken; move about in a dancing motion, dance (e.g., northern lights)
nîmihitowikamikw– NI dance lodge, dance ceremony
nîmihitowin– NI dance
nîmihitowinihkê– VAI hold a dance, hold a dance ceremony; give a dance, organise a (secular) dance
nîmihitôh– VTA make s.o. (e.g., dolls) dance with one another
nîmihtâ– VAI make (it) dance (e.g., spirit-bundle in ghost-dance)
nîsonito– VAI dance two-and-two with one another, dance in pairs
nîsosimo– VAI dance as two; dance a White dance, dance a jig
pasakwâpisimowin– NI shut-eye dance
pasakwâpisimowinihkê– VAI give a shut-eye dance, hold a shut-eye dance
pihêwisimo– VAI dance the prairie-chicken dance
pimisimo– VAI dance by, dance along
pônisimo– VAI cease dancing
sôhkêsimo– VAI dance hard, dance vigorously
wayawîsimo– VAI dance outdoors, dance towards the outside
wâpanisimo– VAI dance until dawn
wâsakâmêsimo– VAI dance the ghost-dance, participate in the ghost-dance
wêpinikê– VAI throw things about; throw people about, dance a European dance
wîcisimôm– VTA dance together with s.o., have s.o. as one's fellow dancer
wîsâm– VTA ask s.o. along, take s.o. along; ask s.o. to dance

DANCE-LODGE
pîhtêyask IPC at the central circle of poles inside the dance-lodge

DANCER
nihtâwisimo– VAI be good at dancing, be an expert dancer
wîcisimôm– VTA dance together with s.o., have s.o. as one's fellow dancer

DARK
kaski-tipiskâ– VII be the dark of the night
nîpâ IPV in the dark of the night
nîpâ-tipisk IPC in the dark of the night, in the middle of the night
wani-tipiskâ– VII be dark night
wani-tipiskin– VTI perceive s.t. as darkness; merely see night, perceive merely darkness
wani-tipiskipayin– VII get dark (e.g., sky)

DAUGHTER
–cânis– NDA daughter, parallel niece
–tânis– NDA daughter, parallel niece
–tôsimiskwêm– NDA sister's daughter (woman speaking), parallel niece (woman speaking)
otânisi– VAI have a daughter; have (her) as one's daughter

DAUGHTER-IN-LAW
–stim– NDA cross-niece; daughter-in-law
–stimihkâwin– NDA step-cross-niece, step-daughter-in-law; daughter-in-law-in-common-law

DAWN
wâpan– VII be dawn, be early morning; be the next day
wâpanastâ– VAI place (it) until dawn, leave (it) until dawn
wâpani IPV until dawn
wâpanisimo– VAI dance until dawn
wâpanwêwit– VTI make noise until dawn, bark through the night (e.g., dog)

DAY
–kîsikâm– NDI day, day of one's life; *(fig.)* [Our Father's] day, Christmas Day
awasitâkosihk IPC the day before yesterday
ayinânêw-kîsikâw IPC eight days, for eight days
kapê-kîsik IPC all day long, throughout the day
kayâs IPC long ago, in earlier days; previously
kâ-tipahamâtohk INM at Treaty time, during Treaty Days
kisipi-kîsikâ– VII be the end of the day
kîsikanisi– VAI spend one's day, live through the day
kîsikâ– VII be day, be daylight
kîsikâw– NI day, daylight, day sky
manitowi-kîsikâw– NI Christmas Day

nêwo-kîsikâ– *VII* be four days, be the fourth day; be Thursday
nêwo-kîsikâw *IPC* four days, for four days
nikotwâsiko-kîsikâ– *VII* be six days, be the sixth day; be Saturday
nisto-kîsikâw *IPC* three days, for three days
niyânan-kîsikâw *IPC* five days, for five days
niyânano-kîsikâ– *VII* be the fifth day; be Friday
nîso-kîsikâw *IPC* two days, for two days
ocêhtowi-kîsikâ– *VII* be New Year's Day
pêyak-kîsikâw *IPC* one day, for one day, in one day; per day
tahto-kîsikâw *IPC* every day, each day, daily
tahto-nîso-kîsikâw *IPC* every second day, every other day
tânitahto-kîsikâw *IPC* how many days; so many days; several days
wâpan– *VII* be dawn, be early morning; be the next day

DAYBREAK
naspâpan *IPC* at daybreak, before sunrise

DAYLIGHT
kîsikâ– *VII* be day, be daylight
kîsikâw– *NI* day, daylight, day sky
sâkâstê– *VII* be daylight

DEAD
nipi– *VAI* die; be dead
nipîmakan– *VII* die; be dead
onakataskêw– *NA* the dead, the departed
pôni-pimâtisi– *VAI* cease to live, die; be no longer alive, be dead

DEADLY
nipahi *IPV* deadly, terribly, greatly

DEAF
kipihtêpayi– *VAI* go deaf, be deafened

DEAL
kaskih– *VTA* prevail upon s.o., succeed in imposing one's will on s.o.; be able to deal with s.o.; earn s.o. (e.g., money)
mâtinamâto– *VAI* deal (it/him) out to one another

DEATH
êtatawisi– *VAI* be barely alive, be weak unto death, be about to die
mâyipayi– *VAI* fare badly, suffer ill; suffer a death, be bereaved, have a death in the family; be bereaved of (her/him)
nakat– *VTA* leave s.o. behind; leave s.o. alone (e.g., helpless); abandon s.o. (e.g., child); leave s.o. behind in death, die leaving s.o. behind
nêsowisi– *VAI* be weak, be exhausted, be near death
nipahâhkatoso– *VAI* starve to death, die from starvation; *(fig.)* be terribly hungry
nîpêpîstaw– *VTA* sit up late at night with s.o.; sit at s.o.'s bedside, sit with s.o. near death; sit at a wake for s.o., hold a wake for s.o.

DEBT
masinahikê– *VAI* write things; write, be literate; go into debt, have debts
pîkwasinahikê– *VAI* be loaded down with debt, be indebted in several places
tipahamaw– *VTA* pay s.o. for (it/him), repay a debt to s.o.; pay s.o. a pension

DECEIVE
kakayêyih– *VTA* deceive s.o.
wayêsih– *VTA* trick s.o., deceive s.o.; take advantage of s.o.

DECIDE
itasiwât– *VTA* decide thus with respect to s.o.; give s.o. such a command; impose such laws on s.o.
itasiwê– *VAI* decide thus for people, make such a plan for people; give such a command, impose such laws
kîsêyiht– *VTI* make up one's mind about s.t., decide on s.t., complete one's plan for s.t.; be decisive
wiyakim– *VTA* set a price on s.o. (e.g., bread); arrange (it) for s.o.; decide on s.o.; give orders to s.o.
wiyasiwât– *VTA* decide about s.o.; sit in judgment on s.o., hold court over s.o.
wiyasiwât– *VTI* decide s.t.; make a rule or law about s.t.

DECISION
kîsasiwât– *VTI* reach a decision about s.t.; complete making a law about s.t.
wiyasiwêwin– *NI* decision; rule, law; council, band council

DECISIVE
kîsêyiht– *VTI* make up one's mind about s.t., decide on s.t., complete one's plan for s.t.; be decisive

DECORATED
kiskinawâcihcikâcêsi– *VII* be marked, be indicated; be decorated (e.g., brooch, barrette)

kiskinawâcihowinis– *NI* decorated brooch, decorated barrette
kiskinowâcihcikâtê– *VII* be marked, be indicated; be decorated
wawêsihcikâtê– *VII* be decorated

DECREE
wîht– *VTI* name s.t., mention s.t. by name; tell about s.t., report s.t.; decree s.t.

DEED
mâyahkamikan– *VII* be a bad deed; be a bad situation
mâyinikêwin– *NI* wrong-doing; evil deed
miyo-tôtamowin– *NI* good deed, good works

DEEP
timikoni– *VII* be deep snow

DEER
apisi-môsos– *NA* deer, red-deer

DEER-BONE
apisimôsoso-oskanis– *NI* small deer-bone

DEER-HIDE
apisimôsoso-pahkêkinos– *NI* deer-hide
apisimôsoswayân– *NA* deer-hide

DEFEAT
sâkôcih– *VTA* overcome s.o., defeat s.o.

DEFECATE
kihci-wayawî– *VAI* go to relieve oneself in a major way, go to defecate

DEFECT
nayêhtâwiki– *VAI* have experienced a troubled birth, be born with a birth defect

DEFERENCE
kêhtin– *VTA* treat s.o. with respect, show deference to s.o.

DEGREE
êkoyikohk *IPC* that much, up to that point, to that degree, to that extent
iskoyikohk *IPC* to such an extent, to such a degree
iyikohk *IPC* so much, to such a degree, to such an extent
nahiyikohk *IPC* to the proper degree, to the proper extent, just enough, just right, evenly, fittingly, appropriately
ômayikohk *IPC* this much, to this degree, to this extent

DEICIDE
pâstâhowi-mihkw– *NI* blood tainted by a breach of the natural order; *(fig.)* blood tainted by deicide, sinful blood

DELAY
âsay *IPC* already; without delay
kiyâm *IPC* oh well, never mind, so much for this; anyway, rather; let it be, let there be no further delay; please
otamih– *VTA* keep s.o. busy, keep s.o. preoccupied; delay s.o.; *(especially in inverse constructions:)* get in s.o.'s way, be s.o.'s undoing
sâsay *IPC* already; without delay

DELICATELY
mâmâsîs *IPC* sparingly, delicately; quickly, roughly, without care

DELIVERED
nihtâwikih– *VTA* give birth to s.o., be delivered of s.o.
ocawâsimisi– *VAI* have a child; have offspring, have a calf (as cow); have (her/him) as one's child; be the mother of a child; give birth, be delivered; calve (as cow)
opêpîmi– *VAI* have an infant, have a baby; have (her/him) as one's infant; be the mother of an infant; give birth, be delivered
tahkopitâwaso– *VAI* swaddle one's child; *(fig.)* be delivered of a child

DELIVERY
pêsiw– *VTA* bring s.o. hither; bring s.o. (e.g., one's child) back (e.g., from the bush) after delivery

DENOMINATION
ayamihâwin– *NI* prayer, praying, saying prayers; church service; religious rite; religion, religious denomination; the Roman Catholic church
môniyâw-âyamihâwin– *NI* White religion; non-Catholic denomination

DENTURES
–îpitihkân– *NDI* false teeth, dentures

DENY ONESELF
îwanisîhisowin– *NI* fasting, denying oneself food
kakwâtakâpâkwaho– *VAI* suffer mortification by denying oneself liquid, make oneself suffer thirst
kakwâtakihiso– *VAI* make oneself suffer; torture oneself, deny oneself food and drink
kakwâtakiho– *VAI* make oneself suffer; torture oneself, experience suffering; deny oneself food and drink
kakwâtakihowin– *NI* making oneself suffer; denying oneself food and drink

DEPART
nakataskê– *VAI* leave the earth behind, depart the world, die

ENGLISH INDEX 253

sipwêcimê– *VAI* leave by boat, depart by boat
sipwêhâ– *VAI* fly off, depart flying, fly away
sipwêhotêwi– *VAI* leave by boat, depart by boat, go out by boat
sipwêhtah– *VTA* take s.o. away, leave with s.o., depart with s.o.
sipwêhtatâ– *VAI* leave taking (it), depart with (it)
sipwêhtê– *VAI* leave, depart
sipwêkocin– *VII* depart in water or air, or by vehicle; fly off, depart flying
sipwêpici– *VAI* leave with one's camp, depart with one's camp
sipwêpihâ– *VAI* fly off, depart flying
sipwêtâcimopahtâ– *VAI* rapidly crawl away, depart crawling fast
sipwêwihw– *VTA* make s.o. leave by boat, depart with s.o. by boat
sipwêyâciho– *VAI* travel away, depart in travel; depart as a camp

DEPARTED
onakataskêw– *NA* the dead, the departed

DEPARTING
aspin *IPC* off, away, from a distance, in departing; since then, the last I knew; back then, so long ago; presumably, evidently
sipwê *IPV* departing, leaving, starting off

DEPICT
masinahikâso– *VAI* be drawn, be pictured, be depicted; be written on
masinahikâtê– *VII* be pictured, be depicted; have marks, have writing; be written
masinipayi– *VAI* be depicted as moving (e.g., on film)
masinipayihtâ– *VAI* depict (it) (e.g., on film)

DEPLORE
mihtât– *VTA* deplore the loss of s.o., sorely miss s.o., grieve for s.o.
mihtât– *VTI* deplore the loss of s.t., be sorry about s.t.

DERIDE
mosci-pâhpih– *VTA* merely laugh at s.o., merely deride s.o.
pâhpih– *VTA* laugh at s.o., deride s.o.; joke with s.o.
pâhpihtâ– *VAI* laugh at (it), deride (it)

DESCEND
nîhtakocin– *VAI* descend from high up, fall down (e.g., star)

DESERVE
kaskihtamâso– *VAI* earn (it) for oneself, deserve (it); make money for oneself

DESERVEDLY
wawiyatisi– *VAI* be deservedly ridiculed, receive one's just deserts

DESIGN
isikwât– *VTI* sew s.t. thus, sew s.t. to such a design
nêhiyaw-masinîwin– *NI* Cree design, Cree motif

DESIRE
akâwât– *VTA* desire s.o., lust for s.o.; want s.o. (e.g., rabbit for food)
akâwât– *VTI* desire s.t., wish for s.t.
akâwâtamaw– *VTA* desire (it/him) of s.o.; envy s.o. over (it/him), begrudge (it/him) to s.o.
nôhtê *IPV* want to, desire to

DESPISE
kakwâhyakêyiht– *VTI* despise s.t.

DESPITE
âhci *IPC* still, nevertheless, despite everything
âhci piko *IPC* still, nevertheless, despite everything
kêyiwêhk *IPC* just in case, nevertheless; despite shortcomings
nitawâc *IPC* despite all, in spite of it all

DESTINATION
takohtah– *VTA* take s.o. to arrive, lead s.o. to one's destination, arrive with s.o.

DESTROY
mêscihtamaw– *VTA* destroy (it/him) for s.o., annihilate (it/him) for s.o.
mêscihtâ– *VAI* destroy (it), annihilate (it)
misiwanâcihcikêmakan– *VII* ruin things, destroy things
misiwanâcihiso– *VAI* ruin oneself, destroy oneself; *(fig.)* commit suicide
misiwanâcihtamaw– *VTA* ruin (it/him) for s.o., destroy (it/him) for s.o.
misiwanâcihtâ– *VAI* ruin (it), destroy (it)
wiyakihtâ– *VAI* treat (it) as worthless; *(especially in negative constructions:)* not waste (it); not destroy a valuable possession

DESTRUCTIVE
misiwanâcisîmakan– *VII* be ruinous, be destructive

DETERMINATION
kotêyihto– VAI test one another, try one another's determination, challenge one another

DETONATE
matwêwêhtâ– VAI detonate (it); shoot off one's gun

DEVIL
maci-manitow– NA *(name:)* devil
maci-manitowi-mihkw– NI *(fig.)* devilish blood, the devil's blood
maci-manitowi-môtêyâpiskw– NI *(fig.)* the devil's bottle

DIABETES
sôkâwâspinê– VAI be ill with diabetes, suffer from diabetes, be a diabetic

DIAPER
âsiyân– NA loin-cloth, diaper, menstrual napkin
âsiyânihkêpison– NI diaper

DIE
êtatawisi– VAI be barely alive, be weak unto death, be about to die
mêscinê– VAI die out
mêstohtê– VAI die off, become extinct
nakasiwê– VAI leave people behind, die
nakat– VTA leave s.o. behind; leave s.o. alone (e.g., helpless); abandon s.o. (e.g., child); leave s.o. behind in death, die leaving s.o. behind
nakataskê– VAI leave the earth behind, depart the world, die
nipahâhkatoso– VAI starve to death, die from starvation; *(fig.)* be terribly hungry
nipahâpâkwê– VAI die of thirst; *(fig.)* be terribly thirsty
nipi– VAI die; be dead
nipîmakan– VII die; be dead
pôni-pimâtisi– VAI cease to live, die; be no longer alive, be dead

DIFFERENT
âhcîhtâ– VAI make (it) over, make (it) different, change (it)
âhtahpit– VTI move and tie s.t., tie s.t. differently; change the bandage on s.t.
âhtohtê– VAI move to a different place, go elsewhere
kâhtap IPC differently; regularly
misi-pîtos IPC very different; very strange
mistahi-pîtos IPC very strangely, most strangely, very differently
pâh-pîtos IPC each differently
pîtos IPC strangely, differently
pîtosinâkwan– VII look different; look strange

DIFFICULT
âyiman– VII be difficult
âyimanohk IPC in a difficult place
âyimêyiht– VTI consider s.t. difficult, consider s.t. too difficult
âyimih– VTA make things difficult for s.o., give s.o. a difficult time
âyimim– VTA make things difficult for s.o. by speech
âyimisi– VAI have a difficult time; be of difficult disposition, be wild, be mean
âyimisîwatimw– NA wild horse, difficult horse
âyimî– VAI have a difficult time, have a difficult task; have a hard life
kakwâtakihtâ– VAI suffer (it), suffer because of (it), have difficulties because of (it); suffer; experience a crisis (e.g., in the course of an illness)
kakwâtakî– VAI suffer, experience difficulty, experience torment
mâyêyiht– VTI consider s.t. a challenge; be willing to tackle a difficult task, venture out
nayêhtâwan– VII be difficult, be troublesome
nayêhtâwêyim– VTA find s.o. difficult, find s.o. troublesome
nayêhtâwipayi– VAI run into difficulties, experience trouble

DIG
mônah– VTI dig for s.t.; dig roots
mônahaskwâkan– NI digger, tool used to dig seneca-root
mônahaskwân– NI digger, tool used to dig seneca-root
mônahaskwê– VAI dig seneca-root
mônahikê– VAI dig for things, dig
mônâtihkê– VAI dig around, dig a hole
wâtihkât– VTI make a hole for s.t., dig a hole for s.t.
wâtihkê– VAI make a hole, dig a hole
yahkâtihkât– VTI dig out more of a hole or cellar, push out the size of an existing hole or cellar

DIGGER
mônahaskwâkan– NI digger, tool used to dig seneca-root
mônahaskwân– NI digger, tool used to dig seneca-root

DIM
îwâsên– VTI turn s.t. down by hand (e.g., by turning a knob), dim the light, turn s.t. too low

DINING
mîcisowinâhtikw– NI dining table, table

DIP
kwâpah– VTI dip s.t. out (e.g., water)
kwâpikê– VAI dip out water, draw water, haul water, obtain one's drinking water

DIRECT
itâmôh– VTA make s.o. flee thus or there, direct s.o. to seek such refuge
kiskinohtah– VTA show (it/him) to s.o.; show s.o. the way, direct s.o.

DIRECTION
anit[a] êtêhkê isi IPC in the direction of that place, in that direction
isi IPC thus, this way; there, in the direction of
isiniskêyi– VAI move one's arm thus or there, point in that direction with one's arm
itê isi IPC thither, in that direction
itêhkê isi IPC thither, in that direction
nanâtohk isi IPC in various ways, in various directions
nânitaw isi IPC in some way, in any way; in various ways; in a random direction
nêtê IPC over there, over yonder; in that direction
nîswayak isi IPC in both directions; in both forms of ritual (e.g., with both incense and sweetgrass)
pikw îtê isi IPC in any direction

DIRECTLY
mosci IPV simply, directly, without mediation; merely, without instrument; without recompense
tipiskôc IPC even, at the same level, parallel; directly overhead

DIRECTOR
nîkânapi– VAI be at the head, be in the lead, be in charge; hold the office of director

DIRTY
asiskîwihkwê– VAI have soil on one's face, have dirt on one's face
âkô-wiyîpâ– VII be covered in dirt
îpâcihtâ– VAI make (it) dirty, soil (it)
wiyîpâ– VII be soiled, be dirty
wîpayiwinis– NI dirty clothes, soiled clothing
wîpâtayiwinis– NI dirty clothes, soiled clothing

DISAPPEAR
awaswêwê– VAI disappear from view (e.g., sun)
awaswêwêtot– VTI disappear behind s.t., go behind s.t.
namatakon– VII be non-existent, be absent; have disappeared, be no longer in existence
namatê– VAI be non-existent, be absent; have disappeared, be no longer in existence

DISAPPOINT
pômê– VAI be discouraged, be disappointed; give up
pômêh– VTA discourage s.o., disappoint s.o.; cause s.o. to give up

DISAPPROVE
pakwât– VTA hate s.o., dislike s.o., disapprove of s.o.
pakwât– VTI hate s.t., dislike s.t., disapprove of s.t.
pakwâtamaw– VTA hate (it/him) for s.o., dislike (it/him) for s.o., disapprove of (it/him) for s.o.

DISCARDED
wêpinikâtê– VII be thrown away, be abandoned, be discarded; be lost (e.g., blood)

DISCORD
mâyi-wîcêhto– VAI live in discord with one another

DISCOURAGE
pômê– VAI be discouraged, be disappointed; give up
pômêh– VTA discourage s.o., disappoint s.o.; cause s.o. to give up

DISCUSS
âyimôhto– VAI discuss one another; gossip about one another
âyimôhtowin– NI discussing one another; gossiping about one another, gossip
âyimôm– VTA discuss s.o.; gossip about s.o.
âyimômiso– VAI discuss oneself; speak unguardedly about oneself, gossip about oneself
âyimôt– VTI speak of s.t., discuss s.t.; gossip about s.t.
mâmiskôcikâtê– VII be discussed, be expounded
mâmiskôm– VTA talk about s.o., discuss s.o., refer to s.o.
mâmiskôt– VTI talk about s.t., discuss s.t., expound s.t., refer to s.t.

mâmiskôtamaw– *VTA* discuss (it/him) for s.o., expound (it/him) for s.o., refer to (it/him) for s.o.
miskôt– *VTI* discuss s.t., refer to s.t.
tasîhcikâtê– *VII* be talked about, be discussed
tasîht– *VTI* talk about s.t., discuss s.t.
tasîhtamaw– *VTA* discuss (it/him) with s.o.
tâhkôcikâtê– *VII* be discussed
tâhkôm– *VTA* discuss s.o., discourse upon s.o.
tâhkôt– *VTI* discuss s.t., discourse upon s.t.
tipôt– *VTI* discuss s.t. with authority

DISEASE
itâspinê– *VAI* be ill thus, suffer from such a disease

DISH
mistiyâkan– *NI* big dish, platter, large bowl
pêyakoyâkan *IPC* one dish (measure)
wiyâkan– *NI* dish, bowl, vessel, pot
wiyâkanis– *NI* small dish, small bowl

DISH-TOWEL
pâhkwahikâkanis– *NI* small towel, dish-towel

DISHES
kâsîyâkanê– *VAI* wash dishes, do the dishes

DISLIKE
pakwât– *VTA* hate s.o., dislike s.o., disapprove of s.o.
pakwât– *VTI* hate s.t., dislike s.t., disapprove of s.t.
pakwâtamaw– *VTA* hate (it/him) for s.o., dislike (it/him) for s.o., disapprove of (it/him) for s.o.

DISOBEY
sasîpiht– *VTI* fail to listen to s.t., disobey s.t.
sasîpihtaw– *VTA* fail to listen to s.o., disobey s.o.

DISORIENTED
kîskwêskaw– *VTA* *(especially in inverse constructions:)* make s.o. crazy, leave s.o. disoriented

DISPOSITION
ayamihêwâtisi– *VAI* be of religious disposition
âhkwâtisi– *VAI* be stern, be sharp, be of severe disposition
âyimisi– *VAI* have a difficult time; be of difficult disposition, be wild, be mean
itâtisi– *VAI* act thus, be of such a disposition
kakâmwâtisi– *VAI* be of quiet disposition
kakâyawâtisi– *VAI* be active; be hard-working, be of industrious disposition
kisêwâtisi– *VAI* be kind, be of compassionate disposition; *(fig.)* be full of grace
maskawâtisi– *VAI* be strong, be of sturdy disposition
sôhkâtisi– *VAI* be strong in body, be fit, have a vigorous disposition
wâskamisî– *VAI* settle down; be of quiet disposition

DISRESPECTFUL
pîwêyim– *VTA* think little of s.o., have a low opinion of s.o.; be disrespectful of s.o.

DISRUPT
pîkon– *VTA* break s.o.; break up one's relation with s.o., disrupt s.o.'s life, spoil s.o.'s plans
wanâh– *VTA* lead s.o. astray, distract s.o.; disrupt s.o.'s life

DISSATISFIED
âtawêyihcikê– *VAI* reject things; be dissatisfied with things
âtawêyiht– *VTI* reject s.t.; be dissatisfied with s.t.
âtawêyim– *VTA* reject s.o.; be dissatisfied with s.o.

DISSOLVE
sikwâciwaso– *VAI* come apart in boiling, be boiled into small pieces; dissolve in boiling

DISTANCE
aspin *IPC* off, away, from a distance, in departing; since then, the last I knew; back then, so long ago; presumably, evidently

DISTRACT
wanâh– *VTA* lead s.o. astray, distract s.o.; disrupt s.o.'s life
wanâm– *VTA* distract s.o. by speech

DISTURBED
kîskwê– *VAI* be mentally disturbed, be mad, be crazy

DIVIDE
nanânistipit– *VTA* tear s.o. into bits and pieces; fragment s.o. (e.g., group of people), divide s.o. (e.g., community) against one another

DIVINE
kakwê *IPV* try to, attempt to; circumstances permitting, by divine grace

DIVORCE
paskêwih– *VTA* part from s.o., leave s.o.; separate from s.o., divorce s.o.
paskêwihito– *VAI* part from one another, leave one another; separate from one another, divorce
wêpinito– *VAI* leave one another, separate from one another, get divorced
wêpinitowin– *NI* leaving one another, separating from one another, divorce

DO
isîhcikât– *VTI* do things thus for s.t., proceed thus for s.t.
isîhcikê– *VAI* do things thus, proceed thus, arrange things thus; perform such a rite, perform a rite thus; conduct negotiations thus
itahkamikisi– *VAI* do things thus, behave thus; work thus or there, busy oneself thus or there
itinikê– *VAI* do things thus; act thus; experience such things; get into such things
itôt– *VTI* do s.t. thus; act thus
itôtamaw– *VTA* do (it) thus for s.o., do thus to s.o.
itôtamôh– *VTA* make s.o. do (it) thus, cause s.o. to act thus
itôtaw– *VTA* do (it) thus to s.o., treat s.o. thus
mâmawôhkamâto– *VAI* work together at (it/him) as a group; do things together, help one another, cooperate
tôt– *VTI* do s.t. thus; act thus
tôtamaw– *VTA* do (it) thus for s.o.; do thus to s.o.
tôtamâso– *VAI* do (it) thus for oneself
tôtamôh– *VTA* make s.o. do (it) thus, make s.o. act thus
tôtaw– *VTA* do (it) thus to s.o., treat s.o. thus
tôtâso– *VAI* do (it) thus to oneself
tôtâto– *VAI* do (it) thus to one another
wîci-tôtamôm– *VTA* do (it) together with s.o., participate with s.o. in doing (it)

DOCK
âsokan– *NI* dock; bridge

DOCTOR
maskihkîwiyiniw– *NA* doctor, physician
nanâtawih– *VTA* treat s.o., doctor s.o.; heal s.o., cure s.o.
nanâtawihitowin– *NI* doctoring one another; healing one another, curing one another
nanâtawihiwê– *VAI* treat people, doctor people; heal people, cure people
nanâtawihwâkê– *VAI* doctor oneself with (it), use (it) to heal oneself, use (it) medicinally
nânapâcihiso– *VAI* fix oneself up; doctor oneself
nipiskât– *VTA* doctor s.o. by insufflation or aspiration

DOCUMENT
masinahikan– *NI* letter, mail; book; written document, will; *(fig.)* bible

DOG
–cêmisis– *NDA* little dog
–têm– *NDA* dog; horse
acimosis– *NA* puppy, young dog, little dog
atimotâpâneyâpiy– *NI* dog harness
atimw– *NA* dog; horse

DOLL
awâsisîhkân– *NA* doll
ayisiyinîhkân– *NA* doll, mannikin; cartoon figure

DOLLAR
mitâtahtwâpisk *IPC* ten dollars
niyânanwâpisk *IPC* five dollars
nîstanaw-tahtwâpisk *IPC* twenty dollars
nîswâpisk *IPC* two dollars
pêyakwâpisk *IPC* one dollar
tahtwâpisk *IPC* so many dollars

DOMESTIC
cikin– *NA* domestic chicken
cikinis– *NA* domestic chicken, little chicken
kôhkôs– *NA* pig, domestic pig
misihêw– *NA* chicken, domestic chicken
pâhpahâhkwân– *NA* chicken, domestic chicken
pisiskiw– *NA* animal; domestic animal

DOOR
iskwâhtêm– *NI* door
tawinamaw– *VTA* open (it/him) for s.o.; *(fig.)* open the door to s.o. (e.g., devil)

DOTS
câhcahkipêkahw– *VTA* paint dots on s.o.

DOUBLE
nîsopîwâpiskw– *NI* double rail, railway track

DOWN
–pîwâs– *NDI* little feathers, down
capasis *IPC* down, down low
nîhc-âyihk *IPC* down, downward; below; down the hill
nîhci *IPC* down, downward

DRAG
âsipayin– *VII* move down, hang down, be dragged down
âwacitâpê– *VAI* haul (it/him) by dragging
kîwêtâpê– *VAI* drag (it) home
nâcitâpê– *VAI* go and drag (it) back, fetch (it) by cart
nâtitâpê– *VAI* go and drag (it) back, fetch (it) by cart
nîhcipit– *VTA* pull s.o. down, drag s.o. down
otâpê– *VAI* drag (it)
wîkatêtâpê– *VAI* drag (it) off to the side, drag (it) away

DRAIN
sîkopit– *VTA* press s.o. out by pulling; drain the milk from s.o. (e.g., cow)

DRAPED
wêpinâson– *NI* draped cloth, flag, cloth offering

DRAUGHT
nanâtawâpôhkân– *NI* medicinal draught

DRAW
itasinah– *VTI* mark s.t. thus, draw s.t. thus; write s.t. thus; thus write s.t. down
kwâpikê– *VAI* dip out water, draw water, haul water, obtain one's drinking water
masinah– *VTI* mark s.t., draw s.t.; write s.t.; write s.t. down, record s.t. in writing; sign s.t. (e.g., treaty)
masinahamâso– *VAI* draw (it) for oneself, write (it) for oneself; write oneself
masinahikâso– *VAI* be drawn, be pictured, be depicted; be written on
masinisin– *VAI* be drawn, be represented, be shaped (e.g., star, sun)
ohtahipê– *VAI* obtain water from there, draw one's drinking water from there

DREADFULLY
kakwâtakatoskê– *VAI* work dreadfully hard, do punishing work
kakwâtakâciho– *VAI* suffer dreadfully, live through a dreadful time
kakwâtakâhpi– *VAI* laugh dreadfully
kakwâtaki *IPV* dreadfully, insufferably

DREAM
–pawâkan– *NDA* dream spirit
âtayôhkan– *NA* spirit being, dream guardian
âtayôhkanakiso– *VAI* be held to be a spirit being, be recognised as a dream guardian
maci-pawâmi– *VAI* have an evil dream spirit
opawâkanêyâspinat– *VTA* harm s.o. by means of dream spirits
opawâmi– *VAI* have a dream spirit
pawâmi– *VAI* have a dream spirit
pawât– *VTA* dream about s.o.
pawât– *VTI* dream about s.t.

DRENCHED
sâpopê– *VAI* get wet, be drenched, be wet throughout, be sodden
sâpopê– *VII* get wet, be drenched, be wet throughout, be sodden

DRESS
–skocâkâs– *NDI* little coat, little dress
–skotâkay– *NDI* coat, dress
âhkasîho– *VAI* dress lightly
isîho– *VAI* be so dressed
iskwêwisîh– *VTA* dress s.o. as a girl, dress s.o. as a female
kîsowaho– *VAI* dress warmly, be warmly dressed
miyosîho– *VAI* be well dressed, be beautifully dressed
nâpêwisîh– *VTA* dress s.o. as a boy, dress s.o. as a male
nâpêwisîho– *VAI* be dressed as a man, dress as a male
pohtayiwinisê– *VAI* put one's clothes on, get dressed
pohtisk– *VTI* put s.t. on (e.g., clothing), get dressed in s.t., wear s.t.; be enclosed by s.t. (e.g., mossbag)
postayiwinisê– *VAI* put one's clothes on, get dressed
postisk– *VTI* put s.t. on (e.g., clothing), get dressed in s.t., wear s.t.; be enclosed by s.t. (e.g., mossbag)
sênipânasâkay– *NI* satin dress
takahkisîho– *VAI* be well dressed, be beautifully dressed
wanisîho– *VAI* be indistinctly dressed, be confusingly dressed, be wrongly dressed
wawêsî– *VAI* dress up, get titivated
wawêsîh– *VTA* dress s.o. up, get s.o. titivated

wawêyîh– *VTA* get s.o. ready, get s.o. dressed
wâposwayân– *NI* rabbitskin, dressed rabbitskin

DRESSED HIDE
pahkêkinohkê– *VAI* prepare one's skins, dress one's hides; make dressed hides, make leather
pahkêkinos– *NI* small dressed hide, small piece of leather
pahkêkinw– *NI* dressed hide, tanned hide, finished hide, leather; tent-cover

DRILL
pakwanêh– *VTI* make a hole in s.t.; drill a hole

DRINK
âwatôpê– *VAI* haul water, haul one's drinking water
iskotêwâpoy– *NI* alcoholic drink, liquor, whisky
itipê– *VAI* be thus affected with alcoholic drink, be in such shape from alcoholic drink
kakwâtakihiso– *VAI* make oneself suffer; torture oneself, deny oneself food and drink
kakwâtakiho– *VAI* make oneself suffer; torture oneself, experience suffering; deny oneself food and drink
kakwâtakihowin– *NI* making oneself suffer; denying oneself food and drink
kawipah– *VTA* cause s.o. to fall down with alcoholic drink
kisâkamitêhkwê– *VAI* drink a hot liquid, have a hot drink
kitâ– *VAI* eat (it) up, eat (it) completely, eat all of (it); drink all of (it); finish drinking a bottle of (it); drink an entire bottle
kîskwêpê– *VAI* be crazy with alcoholic drink, be drunk
kîskwêpêski– *VAI* be habitually crazy with alcoholic drink, be habitually drunk
kwâpikê– *VAI* dip out water, draw water, haul water, obtain one's drinking water
maskihkîwâpôhkatiso– *VAI* prepare an herbal infusion for oneself; make a medicinal drink for oneself
minah– *VTA* give s.o. to drink (e.g., tea, soup); give s.o. tea to drink; give s.o. an alcoholic drink, induce s.o. to drink an alcoholic drink
minihkwât– *VTA* trade s.o. for a drink
minihkwê– *VAI* drink (it); have a drink; drink an alcoholic drink; abuse alcohol
minihkwêsi– *VAI* drink a little of (it) (e.g., tea, soup); have a little drink; drink a small amount of an alcoholic drink
minihkwêwin– *NI* drink; drinking, alcohol abuse
môcikipê– *VAI* have fun with alcohol, make merry with alcoholic drink
nâtôpê– *VAI* go to fetch water; go for a drink; go for alcoholic drink
ohtahipê– *VAI* obtain water from there, draw one's drinking water from there
pêtôpê– *VAI* bring an alcoholic drink hither, bring an alcoholic drink home or into the house
pêyak-tipahôpân *IPC* one gallon of alcoholic drink (e.g., wine)
takahkipah– *VTA* make s.o. feel good, cause s.o. to be light-headed with an alcoholic drink, get s.o. inebriated
takahkipê– *VAI* feel good with drink, be light-headed with alcoholic drink, be inebriated
tako-kîskwêpê– *VAI* arrive intoxicated with alcoholic drink, arrive inebriated, come home drunk
wîci-minihkwêm– *VTA* drink together with s.o., have s.o. as a drinking companion

DRIP
aswah– *VTI* catch s.t. as it drips
ohcikawan– *VII* leak out, drip out, trickle out; spring a leak (e.g., vessel)
ohcikawi– *VAI* leak out, drip out, trickle out (e.g., sap from tree)
pahkikawin– *VTI* let s.t. drip

DRIVE
ispayi– *VAI* move thus, drive there
kisîpayi– *VAI* drive fast
kîwêpayi– *VAI* drive home, drive back, ride home, ride back
kîwêtisahw– *VTA* drive s.o. back, drive s.o. home
manâtâstim– *VTA* be careful in making s.o. wave, avoid making s.o. weave about; spare s.o. in driving a wagon, be considerate of s.o.
otâpah– *VTA* drive s.o. (e.g., team of horses)
otâpâso– *VAI* drive a vehicle
pahkopêtisahw– *VTA* drive s.o. into the water

pamih– *VTA* tend to s.o., look after s.o.; attend s.o. in childbirth, serve as midwife to s.o.; guide s.o. (e.g., sleigh), drive s.o. (e.g., sleigh)
pamihastimwê– *VAI* drive one's horses
pamihcikê– *VAI* drive one's team
papâmipayi– *VAI* ride about, drive about
patitisahamaw– *VTA* drive (it/him) off the path for s.o., send (it/him) awry for s.o., spoil (it/him) for s.o.
pêtitisahw– *VTA* drive s.o. hither, send s.o. hither
pimitisahw– *VTA* follow s.o. along, go behind s.o., drive s.o. along
sâkêwêtâpâso– *VAI* come into view with one's wagon, drive into view
sêskitâpâso– *VAI* drive into the bush
sipwêpahtâ– *VAI* run off, drive off
sipwêtâpâso– *VAI* leave with a team of horses, drive off by wagon
sipwêtâpê– *VAI* drive away with (it/him)
tahkohcipicikê– *VAI* drive on top of things, drive over things
takahkipicikê– *VAI* drive a nice team, drive beautiful horses
takopayi– *VAI* arrive on horseback, arrive driving, arrive by vehicle
takotisahw– *VTA* drive s.o. to arrive, chase s.o. to arrive
wayawîtisahikêmakan– *VII* drive things out; drive the fever out
yahkitisahw– *VTA* drive s.o. forward

DRIZZLE
kaskawanipêstâ– *VII* be drizzle, be rainy

DROP
kitiskin– *VTA* inadvertently drop s.o., let s.o. fall by awkwardness
pahkisikê– *VAI* drop things, drop a bomb
pahkisim– *VTA* let s.o. fall, drop s.o.
pakitin– *VTA* set s.o. down, allow s.o., permit s.o.; permit (it) to s.o., give permission to s.o.; let s.o. go, release s.o.; release s.o. (e.g., fish-spawn into lake), stock a lake with s.o. (e.g., fish); drop s.o. off (e.g., as an airplane)

DRUM
matwêhw– *VTA* sound a beat upon s.o. (e.g., drum), drum on s.o.
mistikwaskihkw– *NA* drum
takahkwêwêhtitâ– *VAI* make (it) sound nice by drumming or tapping; make a nice drumming or tapping sound

DRUM-BEAT
matwêhikâtê– *VII* be a knock; be a drum-beat

DRY
kâhkêwakw– *NI* dried meat, sheet of dried meat
kâspihkas– *VTI* heat s.t. until crisp, heat s.t. until brittle; dry s.t. by heat until crisp
miyiskwê– *VAI* have a dry throat; speak with a weak voice
pâhkopayi– *VAI* get dry, dry out
pâhkosi– *VAI* dry off, be dried off; be dry and crisp (e.g., fried bacon)
pâhkwah– *VTI* dry s.t. by tool
pâs– *VTI* dry s.t. by heat (e.g., meat, berries, moss)
pâsikâtê– *VII* be dried by heat
pâso– *VAI* be dry (by heat), be dried
pâstê– *VII* be dry (by heat), be dried
pâsw– *VTA* dry s.o. (e.g., rabbit) by heat

DRYING
akwâwân– *NI* rack for drying meat
akwâwânâhcikos– *NI* rail of drying rack
akwâwê– *VAI* hang sheets of meat on drying rack
paskiciwêpin– *VTA* throw s.o. across; throw s.o. (e.g., rabbit) over drying rack

DUCK
–sîsîpimis– *NDA* one's little ducks
nawakipayiho– *VAI* throw oneself down, duck down
nawatahikê– *VAI* shoot (it/him) in flight, shoot ducks as they fly
nâtahisipê– *VAI* fetch ducks (e.g., as a dog)
nôcisipê– *VAI* hunt ducks, be engaged in duck-hunting
sîsîp– *NA* duck
sîsîp-opîway– *NI* duck feathers, duck-down
sîsîpakohp– *NI* duck blanket
sîsîpi-mîcimâpoy– *NI* duck broth, duck soup
sîsîpipîway– *NI* duck feathers, duck-down

DUCK-DOWN
sîsîp-opîway– *NI* duck feathers, duck-down

English Index   261

sîsîpipîway– NI duck feathers, duck-down
DUCK-EGG
sîsîpâw– NI duck-egg
DUCK-HUNTING
nôcisipê– VAI hunt ducks, be engaged in duck-hunting
DUCK LAKE
sîsîpi-sâkahikan– NI *(place-name:)* Duck Lake (Saskatchewan)
DUMP
wêpinamaw– VTA throw (it/him) on s.o., dump (it/him) on s.o., leave (it/him) with s.o., abandon (it/him) to s.o.
DUNK
kohtân– VTA immerse s.o. (e.g., a piece of ice) in liquid, dunk s.o. into liquid
DURING
mêkwâ IPV while, during, in the course of; meanwhile; in the midst of
mêkwâc IPC while, during, in the course of; in the meantime
tasi IPC along in time, at the same time; for suck a time, for the duration
taspinê– VAI be ill for such a time, be ill for the duration
DWELL
asiwaso– VAI be inside, be enclosed; live inside, dwell inside
piskihci-wîki– VAI live separately, dwell separately, have a separate household
wîki– VAI live there, dwell there, have one's home there
DWELLING
–îk– NDI house, dwelling, home
miyo-wîki– VAI live comfortably, have a nice dwelling
otihtâwini– VAI have a dwelling, have a place of residence; have (it) as one's dwelling, have (it) as one's place of residence
tipiyawêho– VAI live in one's own dwelling, have one's own household
wîtokwêm– VTA share a dwelling with s.o., live with s.o., have s.o. as one's housemate
DYE
atis– VTI dye s.t.
atisikan– NI dye, trade-dye
atisikê– VAI dye things
atisikêmakan– VII be a dying-agent, yield a dye
atisw– VTA dye s.o. (e.g., porcupine quills)

itatisw– VTA dye s.o. (e.g., porcupine quills) thus; dye s.o. in such a colour
kaskitêwatisw– VTA dye s.o. (e.g., stocking) black
EACH
mâh-mêskoc IPC each in turn
nâh-nêwo IPC four each
pâh-pêyak IPC singly, one at a time; each one, each individually, each; one each
pâh-piskihc IPC each separately
pâh-pîtos IPC each differently
tahto-kîkisêpâ IPC every morning, early each morning
tahto-kîsikâw IPC every day, each day, daily
tahto-nîpin IPC every summer, each summer
tahto-pîsim IPC every month, each month, monthly, menstrual
tahtwâw IPC so many times, each time
EAGERLY
cîhkêyiht– VTI like s.t., approve of s.t.; eagerly participate in s.t.
iyâyaw IPC eagerly, intently; by preference, rather
piyasêyimo– VAI look forward eagerly, wait in anticipation
EAGLE
kihîw– NA eagle
EAR
–htawakay– NDI ear
–îhcawakâs– NDI ear
cowêskihtê– VAI have one's ears ring, have ringing in one's ears, suffer from tinnitus
mahkihtawakê– VAI have a big ear
pôhtâskwah– VTI stick s.t. wooden into a hole; clean out one's ear, poke one's ear
EARLIER
kayâs IPC long ago, in earlier days; previously
nawac wîpac IPC earlier
pâtimâ IPC no earlier, only later
EARLIEST
mâmawaci-kayâs IPC at the very earliest time
mâmawo-kayâs IPC at the very earliest time
pêci-nâway IPC back then, far in the past; from the earliest times
EARLY
kîkisêpâ IPC early in the morning

kîkisêpâyâ– *VII* be early in the morning
miyoskamin– *VII* be early spring
tahto-kîkisêpâ *IPC* every morning, early each morning
wâpan– *VII* be dawn, be early morning; be the next day
wîpac *IPC* soon, early

EARN
kaskih– *VTA* prevail upon s.o., succeed in imposing one's will on s.o.; be able to deal with s.o.; earn s.o. (e.g., money)
kaskihtamâso– *VAI* earn (it) for oneself, deserve (it); make money for oneself
kîspinat– *VTA* earn enough to buy s.o. (e.g., horse)
kîspinat– *VTI* earn enough to buy s.t.; earn s.t. as reward; earn one's reward
kîspinatamaw– *VTA* earn one's reward in s.o., earn s.o. (e.g., grandchild) as one's reward
miyo-sôniyâhkê– *VAI* make good money; earn good wages
ohtisi– *VAI* earn (it) thereby or from there, earn (it) for that; obtain payment thereby or from there
sôniyâhkâkê– *VAI* make money with (it), use (it) to earn wages
sôniyâhkât– *VTI* make money at s.t., earn wages at s.t.
sôniyâhkê– *VAI* make money; earn wages; earn (it) as wages
sôniyâhkêsi– *VAI* make some money, earn a little money; earn some wages
sôniyâhkêwin– *NI* earning money; wages; income

EARRING
mâtitâpihtêpiso– *VAI* begin to wear earrings
tâpihtêpison– *NA* earring

EARTH
asiskiy– *NI* earth, soil, mud; clay; sod
askiy– *NI* land, region, area; earth, world; settlement, colony, country; Métis settlement; *(plural:)* fields under cultivation, pieces of farmland, the lands
askîwi– *VII* be the earth, exist as world; be a year
askîwisk– *VTI* subject the earth to oneself, populate the earth, make the earth live
ay-atâmaskamik *IPC* inside the earth, beneath the ground
ayah– *VTI* cover s.t. with earth; hill s.t. (e.g., potatoes)
ayahikâkan– *NI* hiller, tool for covering potatoes with earth
ayahikê– *VAI* cover things with earth, hill things (e.g., potatoes)
kihc-ôkâwîmâw– *NA (name:)* Great Mother, Mother Earth
misaskê– *VAI* touch the earth (e.g., as a falling star)
nakataskê– *VAI* leave the earth behind, depart the world, die
okâwîmâwaskiy– *NI (name:)* Mother Earth
pakitin– *VTI* let s.t. go, allow s.t., permit s.t.; release s.t.; give s.t. up, abandon s.t. (e.g., teaching, tradition); put s.t. down on earth; put s.t. in (e.g., seed potatoes)
pakitinikowisi– *VAI* be permitted by the powers; be put down on earth by the powers
pakitiniwê– *VAI* put people down on earth
waskitaskamik *IPC* on the face of the earth
wîhkwêskamikâ– *VII* be the corners of the earth, be the ends of the earth

EARTHQUAKE
waskawîmakan– *VII* move, move about, be shaken by an earthquake

EAST
sâkâstênohk *IPC* in the east

EASY
nihtâ-âhkosi– *VAI* fall sick easily, be prone to illness
wâhkêyêyiht– *VTI* be easily swayed; *(fig.)* be too weak
wêhcasin– *VII* be easy
wêhci *IPV* easy, in ease
wêhci-pimâtisi– *VAI* live in ease, have an easy life
wêhcih– *VTA* have an easy time with s.o. (e.g., hide)
wêhciskowipayi– *VII* come easily
wêhtisi– *VAI* have it easy

EAT
asam– *VTA* feed s.o., give s.o. to eat; hand out rations to s.o.
âpihtâ-kîsikani-mîciso– *VAI* eat one's mid-day meal, eat one's lunch
kitamw– *VTA* eat all of s.o. (e.g., bear)
kitâ– *VAI* eat (it) up, eat (it) completely, eat all of (it); drink all of (it); finish drinking a bottle of (it); drink an entire bottle

kitânawê– *VAI* eat all of (it)
kitâpayihtamaw– *VTA* eat all of (it/him) on s.o., eat s.o.'s entire supply
misi-mîci– *VAI* eat much of (it), eat a lot of (it)
mîci– *VAI* eat (it)
mîciso– *VAI* eat, have a meal; feed (e.g., bird); chew the cud (e.g., ruminant)
mîcisosi– *VAI* eat a little, have a small meal
mîcisowin– *NI* eating, meal; eating-habits; food, foodstuff, food supply
mîcisôh– *VTA* give s.o. to eat, make s.o. eat
mîciswâkê– *VAI* eat with (it), use (it) to eat
mîciswât– *VTI* eat from s.t., eat off s.t.
mow– *VTA* eat s.o. (e.g., bread)
paswêskôyo– *VAI* get sick from eating excessively fatty food
saskatam– *VTA* be tired of eating s.o. (e.g., fish, duck)
sîwahcikê– *VAI* eat sweets
wîci-mîcisôm– *VTA* eat together with s.o., share one's meal with s.o.

EATING-HABITS
mîcisowin– *NI* eating, meal; eating-habits; food, foodstuff, food supply

EBULLIENT
wiyâhtikosi– *VAI* be ebullient, have a bubbly personality

ECONOMY
kistikêwi-pimâcihowin– *NI* agricultural way of life, farm economy

ECZEMA
kiyakasê– *VAI* have itchy skin, suffer from eczema

EDGE
kisip-âyihk *IPC* at the end, at the edge
kisipanohk *IPC* at the end (in space or time), at the edge
misipocikê– *VAI* run hide over a sharp edge
misipotâ– *VAI* run (it) (e.g., hide) over a sharp edge
nâsipêtimihk *IPC* towards the water, by the water's edge
papakipotâ– *VAI* sharpen (it) to a thin edge

EDGING
kaskitêwasinâstê– *VII* be black trim, be black edging

EDUCATION
kihci-kiskinahamâtowikamikw– *NI* university; post-secondary education
kihci-kiskinahamâtowin– *NI* higher education, post-secondary education
kiskinahamâkêwin– *NI* teaching, education
kiskinohamâsowin– *NI* schooling, education
kiskinohamâtowin– *NI* teaching, education; education system, school board
miyo-kîsih– *VTA* finish s.o. well; educate s.o. well

EFFECT
ânisîhtâ– *VAI* alleviate the effect of (it), be an antidote to (it)
itiskaw– *VTA* (especially in inverse constructions:) have such an effect on s.o., leave s.o. thus affected
maskawîskaw– *VTA* (especially in inverse constructions:) make s.o. strong in body, have an invigorating effect on s.o.
mâyiskaw– *VTA* go through s.o. to bad effect, affect s.o. negatively, fail to agree with s.o.; (especially in inverse constructions:) have an adverse effect on s.o., make s.o. ill
miyoskaw– *VTA* (especially in inverse constructions:) go through s.o. to good effect, have a salutary effect on s.o., make s.o. well
pimohtêmakan– *VII* go along, move along; go on, be in effect (e.g., treaty)
tôcikêmakan– *VII* have such an effect; be the cause of (it)

EFFECTIVELY
sôhkêpayin– *VII* be strong, work effectively (e.g., medicine)

EFFORT
mâmawôhk– *VTI* work together at s.t. as a group; engage in a joint effort

EGGS
nitawâwê– *VAI* go looking for eggs, go to collect eggs
owâwi– *VAI* lay eggs
wîtapiht– *VTI* sit by s.t.; hatch one's eggs (e.g., bird)

EIGHT
ayinânêw *IPC* eight
ayinânêw-kîsikâw *IPC* eight days, for eight days
ayinânêwi-misit *IPC* eight feet, for eight feet (measure)

EIGHTEEN
ayinânêwosâp *IPC* eighteen

EIGHTY
ayinânêwimitanaw *IPC* eighty

EITHER
nikotwâw *IPC* either one, anyone

ELASTIC
sêhkwêpitê– *VII* be pulled to expand; be an elastic band

ELBOW
–côskwanis– *NDI* elbow

ELDER
–îci-kisêyin– *NDA* fellow old man, co-elder
–îci-kisêyiniw– *NDA* fellow old man, co-elder
–kêhtê-ayim– *NDA* old person, parent, grandparent; elder
–mosôm– *NDA* grandfather, grandfather's brother; *(fig.)* old man, respected elder
kêhtê-ay– *NA* old person, the old; elder
kêhtê-ayiwi– *VAI* be an old person, get old; be an elder

ELECTED
okimâhkân– *NA* chief, elected chief
okimâhkâniwi– *VAI* be chief, serve as elected chief

ELECTRIC
wâsaskocêpayîs– *NI* lamp, electric light

ELEMENT
nîkânakim– *VTA* count s.o. in first position, hold s.o. (e.g., tobacco) to be the prime element
nîkâni– *VAI* be at the head, be in the lead, take precedence (e.g., tobacco); be the prime element
nîkâninikâso– *VAI* take precedence, rank first; be the prime element

ELEVATED
ispâhkêpayi– *VAI* reach a high level, be elevated (e.g., blood-sugar)

ELEVEN
pêyakosâp *IPC* eleven

ELK
onîcâniw– *NA* female of large quadrupeds; cow, cow-moose, female elk

ELSE
ahpô cî *IPC* or else
awêkâ *IPC* or else

ELSEWHERE
âhtohtê– *VAI* move to a different place, go elsewhere
âhtokê– *VAI* move camp, move one's camp elsewhere
ohpimê *IPC* off, away, to the side; elsewhere, anywhere

EMBARRASS
sasîhciwih– *VTA* make s.o. ashamed, embarrass s.o.

EMBRACE
âkwaskitin– *VTA* embrace s.o., hug s.o.
âkwaskitinito– *VAI* embrace one another, hug one another

EMBROIDER
masinistah– *VTI* embroider s.t. (e.g., shape, design)
masinistahikê– *VAI* embroider things, do embroidery
pîmikitêwayiwinis– *NI* embroidered clothing

EMERGE
sâkâwanêhtâ– *VAI* push (it) to emerge from the ground, make (it) come forth
sâkikin– *VII* grow forth, emerge from the ground

EMIT
âhkwâpahtê– *VII* give off a sharp odour, produce pungent fumes, emit acidic or caustic fumes
kîskosîmakan– *VII* whistle, emit a whistling sound
mamâhpinêmakan– *VII* moan, emit a moaning sound
tasin– *VTI* pull the trigger on s.t. (e.g., gun), shoot s.t. off (e.g., gun); emit a sharp noise, make a shot-like noise; sound a thunderclap (e.g., as Thunderbird)

EMPLOY
atoskah– *VTA* make s.o. work, employ s.o., hire s.o.
atoskêmo– *VAI* get people to do things, employ people, hire people
atot– *VTA* ask s.o. to do something, engage s.o. for something, employ s.o.
masinahikêh– *VTA* hire s.o., employ s.o.

EMPLOYEE
atoskahâkan– *NA* employee, hired man
atoskêhâkan– *NA* employee

EMPTY
wêpin– *VTA* throw s.o. away; empty s.o. (e.g., pail); throw s.o. down or in (e.g., money in a card-game); leave s.o. (e.g., spouse); abandon s.o. (e.g., child)

ENCLOSE
asiwacikê– *VAI* put things inside, enclose things, put things into boxes; have things inside; be pregnant
asiwah– *VTA* place s.o. (e.g., sugar, fish) inside, enclose s.o.

asiwatâ– VAI place (it) inside, enclose (it), put (it) into a bag or container

ENCLOSED
asiwacipayin– VII get placed inside, get enclosed; rapidly fill an enclosed space (e.g., water flowing into hoofprint)
asiwaso– VAI be inside, be enclosed; live inside, dwell inside
asiwatan– VII be inside, be enclosed
asiwatê– VII be placed inside, be enclosed
pohtisk– VTI put s.t. on (e.g., clothing), get dressed in s.t., wear s.t.; be enclosed by s.t. (e.g., mossbag)

ENCOUNTER
mêkwâskaw– VTA encounter s.o. in the midst of (it), catch s.o. in the act
nakiskaw– VTA encounter s.o., meet s.o.
tâwin– VTA encounter s.o., come upon s.o., bump into s.o., hit s.o.
tâwin– VTI encounter s.t. by hand, come upon s.t., bump into s.t.
tâwisk– VTI encounter s.t. (by foot or body movement), come upon s.t., bump into s.t.
tâwiskaw– VTA encounter s.o. (by foot or body movement), bump into s.o., come into contact with s.o.

ENCOURAGE
sîhkim– VTA urge s.o. by speech, encourage s.o. by speech; guide s.o. by speech

END
iskwêyâc IPC to the end, to the last; the last time
kisip-âyihk IPC at the end, at the edge
kisipakim– VTA count s.o. (e.g., sun) as the end of the month
kisipanohk IPC at the end (in space or time), at the edge
kisipi-kîsikâ– VII be the end of the day
kisipipayin– VII come to an end, reach the end, run out
kisipîmakan– VII come to an end, reach the end; have an end
pônipayi– VII cease, stop, come to an end
wanaskoc IPC at the end, at the tip, at the top
wîhkwêskamikâ– VII be the corners of the earth, be the ends of the earth

ENDOW
manitowakim– VTA endow s.o. (e.g., tobacco) with supernatural power; attribute spirit power to s.o.

ENDURE
sîpihkêyiht– VTI endure s.t.; persevere in s.t.; persevere

ENEMA
pîhtâpâwah– VTA pour liquid into s.o., give s.o. an enema

ENERGETIC
waskawî– VAI move, move about, be energetic

ENGAGE
atot– VTA ask s.o. to do something, engage s.o. for something, employ s.o.
maci-nôcihtâ– VAI pursue evil things, engage in bad medicine
mâmawôhk– VTI work together at s.t. as a group; engage in a joint effort
miyo-nôcihtâ– VAI pursue good things; *(in negative constructions:)* pursue evil things, engage in bad medicine
nôcikinosêwê– VAI get fish, be engaged in fishing
nôcisipê– VAI hunt ducks, be engaged in duck-hunting
okistikêwiyinîwi– VAI be a farmer, be engaged in agriculture
tasîhk– VTI bother with s.t., trifle with s.t.; be engaged in s.t.

ENGLISH
âkayâsîmo– VAI speak English
âkayâsîmosi– VAI speak a little English
âkayâsîmowin– NI speaking English, the English language
môniyâwi-itwê– VAI say the White word, say the English word
môniyâwi-wîhowin– NI White name, English name

ENGROSS
kikiskaw– VTA *(especially in inverse constructions:)* affect s.o., befall s.o.; inhere in s.o., engross s.o.
maci-kikiskaw– VTA *(especially in inverse constructions:)* inhere in s.o. as a bad thing, engross s.o. as an evil

ENHANCE
kikâpôhkê– VAI add (it) to soup, enhance one's soup with (it)

ENJOY
miyawât– VTI enjoy s.t., rejoice over s.t.; rejoice, be joyful, have fun
miywêyihcikâtê– VII be liked, be enjoyed
pahpakwatêyiht– VTI enjoy s.t., be amused by s.t.

ENJOYMENT
miyawâtamowin– *NI* enjoyment; fun, joyfulness

ENOUGH
ayiwâkipayi– *VAI* have more than enough, have a surplus, have plenty; run to more, be a surplus (e.g., money)
kîspinat– *VTA* earn enough to buy s.o. (e.g., horse)
kîspinat– *VTI* earn enough to buy s.t.; earn s.t. as reward; earn one's reward
nahiyikohk *IPC* to the proper degree, to the proper extent, just enough, just right, evenly, fittingly, appropriately
ocihci *IPV* having lived long enough for something
otisâpaht– *VTI* have lived long enough to see s.t.
têpi *IPV* fully, sufficiently, enough
têpihkwâmi– *VAI* sleep long enough, have enough sleep
têpinêh– *VTI* have enough to pay for s.t.
têpipayi– *VAI* have the full amount, put away enough; have enough, have a sufficiency; have enough of (it)

ENRICH
takon– *VTA* add (it) to s.o. (e.g., flour), mix (it) into s.o. (e.g., dough); add s.o. to (it), enrich (it) with s.o.

ENTER
pîhtikwêmakan– *VII* enter, go indoors
pîhtikwêtot– *VTI* enter s.t. (e.g., sweat-lodge)
pîhtokwah– *VTA* enter with s.o., take s.o. indoors
pîhtokwatâ– *VAI* take (it) indoors, enter with (it)
pîhtokwê– *VAI* enter, go indoors

ENTERPRISE
waskawîstamâso– *VAI* work for oneself, be enterprising
waskawîwin– *NI* being active, enterprise

ENTIRE
iyawis *IPC* fully, entirely; the whole lot, the entire household; *(in negative constructions:)* only partially, not exclusively
kapê-ayi *IPC* all along, all the time, for the entire period, throughout
kitâ– *VAI* eat (it) up, eat (it) completely, eat all of (it); drink all of (it); finish drinking a bottle of (it); drink an entire bottle
kitâpayihtamaw– *VTA* eat all of (it/him) on s.o., eat s.o.'s entire supply
mêscipayi– *VAI* be exhausted (e.g., snow), be gone entirely (e.g., snow)
misiwê *IPC* all over, the entire place

ENTRAILS
–takisiy– *NDI* intestines, guts, entrails

ENTRAP
tasôh– *VTA* entrap s.o. (e.g., bird) by putting feed under a movable lid, trap s.o. underneath

ENVIOUS
wîsakahcahw– *VTA* make s.o. very envious, get s.o.'s goat

ENVY
akâwâtamaw– *VTA* desire (it/him) of s.o.; envy s.o. over (it/him), begrudge (it/him) to s.o.

EPIDEMIC
iskwânê– *VAI* be left behind after a widespread illness, survive an epidemic

EQUIPMENT
âpacihcikan– *NI* tool, appliance, machine; equipment, furnishings, furniture

ERECT
cimaso– *VAI* stand upright, stand erect (e.g., tree)
cimatê– *VII* stand upright, stand erect
cîpatapi– *VAI* sit up, sit upright, sit erect

ERR
wanohtê– *VAI* err, make a mistake, take the wrong road

ERROR
paci *IPV* wrongly, in error
patowât– *VTI* misspeak s.t.; commit an error in one's prayers
pisci *IPV* by accident, accidentally, erroneously, in error

ERUPT
môskipayi– *VAI* break out in a rash, erupt in sores (e.g., with thrush)
pîkokonêwêpayi– *VAI* have cracks erupt in one's mouth, have one's mouth break out in sores (e.g., with thrush)

ESCAPE
kîh– *VTA* get away from s.o., escape from s.o.'s snare
nitaka *IPC* it is a good thing, by a narrow escape
pihkoho– *VAI* free oneself, escape; be released; *(fig.)* free oneself (e.g., to meet an obligation or duty); be saved

ESPECIALLY
âsônê *IPC* especially, in particular
kanakêkâ *IPC* more especially
wâwâc *IPC* especially, even, even more
wâwîs *IPC* especially, particularly
wâwîs cî *IPC* especially, all the more so
yâyâhk *IPC* really, for sure, to be sure; especially, all the more so

ESPY
miskwâpam– *VTA* see s.o., espy s.o. (e.g., star)

ESTEEM
itakiht– *VTI* count s.t. thus, value s.t. thus, hold s.t. in such esteem; charge so much for s.t.
itakihtê– *VII* be counted thus, be valued thus, be held in such esteem; be worth so much, cost so much
itakim– *VTA* count s.o. thus, value s.o. thus, hold s.o. in such esteem
itakiso– *VAI* be counted thus, be valued thus; be held in such esteem; be worth so much; have such a function
kîhkâtêyihtâkwan– *VII* be held in high esteem, be prominent
kîhkâtêyim– *VTA* hold s.o. in high esteem
miywakiso– *VAI* be considered good, be well esteemed; fetch a good price (e.g., tree)

ETYMOLOGY
nêhiyawi-wîhtamawâkan– *NI* Cree etymology; Cree teaching

EVEN
ahpô *IPC* even, possibly; or
ahpô piko *IPC* even if; and yet
kanakê *IPC* at least, even if only
nahiyikohk *IPC* to the proper degree, to the proper extent, just enough, just right, evenly, fittingly, appropriately
namôy âhpô *IPC* not even
nawac piko *IPC* sort of, kind of, approximately; more or less; even a little
tipiskôc *IPC* even, at the same level, parallel; directly overhead
wâwâc *IPC* especially, even, even more

EVENING
âkwâ-tipiskâ– *VII* be late in the evening
otâkosihk *IPC* the previous evening; yesterday
otâkosin– *VII* be evening

EVENT
pîhtaw *IPC* in the event, of course
wiyâ wîpac cî wiya *IPC* it is a rare and welcome event that

EVER
mwâsi *IPC* *(in negative constructions:)* hardly ever, hardly any
wîhkâc *IPC* ever; *(in negative constructions:)* never

EVERY
kahkiyaw *IPC* every, all
pisisik *IPC* always, every time, routinely
tahto-kîkisêpâ *IPC* every morning, early each morning
tahto-kîsikâw *IPC* every day, each day, daily
tahto-nîpin *IPC* every summer, each summer
tahto-nîso-kîsikâw *IPC* every second day, every other day
tahto-nîsw-âyamihêwi-kîsikâw *IPC* every second week, fortnightly
tahto-pîsim *IPC* every month, each month, monthly, menstrual
tahtw-âyamihêwi-kîsikâw *IPC* every Sunday

EVERYONE
pikw âwiyak *IPC* anyone; everyone

EVERYTHING
âhci *IPC* still, nevertheless, despite everything
âhci piko *IPC* still, nevertheless, despite everything
tahto-kîkway *PR* so many things, as many things, everything

EVERYWHERE
misiw îta *IPC* everywhere
misiw îtê *IPC* all over, everywhere
pikw îta *IPC* in any place, no matter where; everywhere
pikw îtê *IPC* to any place, no matter whither; everywhere

EVIDENTLY
aspin *IPC* off, away, from a distance, in departing; since then, the last I knew; back then, so long ago; presumably, evidently
êcik âni *IPC* as it turns out, apparently, evidently, indeed

EVIL
mac-âyiwi– *VAI* be bad, be evil
mac-îtêyiht– *VTI* suspect s.t. bad; suspect evil
macan– *VII* be bad, be evil
maci *IPV* bad, evil

maci-kikiskaw– VTA *(especially in inverse constructions:)* inhere in s.o. as a bad thing, engross s.o. as an evil

maci-kîkway PR something bad, evil things

maci-maskihkiy– NI evil medicine

maci-nôcihtâ– VAI pursue evil things, engage in bad medicine

maci-pawâmi– VAI have an evil dream spirit

maci-pisiskiw– NA evil animal, monster

mâyi IPV bad, evil

mâyi-tôt– VTI do s.t. evil; do a bad thing, impose a curse

mâyi-tôtaw– VTA do evil to s.o., harm s.o., make s.o. sick, put a curse on s.o.

mâyinikêwin– NI wrong-doing; evil deed

miyo-nôcihtâ– VAI pursue good things; *(in negative constructions:)* pursue evil things, engage in bad medicine

miywakihtê– VII be considered good; *(in negative constructions:)* be considered bad, be considered evil

miywâsin– VII be good, be valuable; *(in negative constructions:)* be bad, be evil

EXACT

katisk IPC just now, a moment ago; recently, a while ago; exactly, just at that moment, at the very moment; *(in negative constructions:)* not merely

katiskaw IPC to exact measure, no more than, barely

kêtisk IPC just barely, to exact measure

mêmohci IPC in particular, above all; exactly, precisely

mwêhci IPC exactly; like

mwêsiskaw– VTA have chosen exactly the wrong time or place for s.o., just miss s.o.

EXALTED

kihcihtwâwi IPN of exalted character, venerable, holy

EXAMPLE

kiskinawâpi– VAI learn by observation, learn by example; learn merely by watching

kiskinowâpaht– VTI learn by watching s.t., learn by the example of s.t.; learn merely by watching s.t.

kiskinowâpahtih– VTA teach s.o. by example

kiskinowâpahtihiwê– VAI teach people by example

kiskinowâpam– VTA learn by watching s.o., learn by s.o.'s example

kiskinowâpiwin– NI learning by observation, learning by example; learning merely by watching

EXCEED

kâsispô– VAI reach beyond, exceed; survive into another generation

kâsispôhtêmakan– VII go on, reach beyond, exceed; survive into another generation

EXCELLENT

takahki-kiskinahamawâkanis– NA excellent student

EXCESS

nipahipahtâ– VAI run to excess, collapse from running

osâm IPC too much, excessively

paswêskôyo– VAI get sick from eating excessively fatty food

paswêyâ– VII be excessively fatty

EXCHANGE

mêskoc IPC instead, in return, in exchange

mêskotâpin– VTI change s.t. (e.g., water in boiling a beaver), exchange s.t.

mêskotôn– VTI change s.t. (e.g., water in boiling a beaver), exchange s.t.

mîskoc IPC instead, in return, in exchange

mîskotônikê– VAI exchange things, trade things (e.g., horse, wagon)

EXCITED

cîsiskaw– VTA excite s.o., get s.o. excited (by foot or body movement)

môcikêyihc– VTI be excited about s.t. small; be a little excited

môcikêyiht– VTI be happy about s.t., be excited about s.t.; be excited

yêyih– VTA get s.o. excited by one's action, tempt s.o. by one's action

EXCLUSIVELY

iyawis IPC fully, entirely; the whole lot, the entire household; *(in negative constructions:)* only partially, not exclusively

nayêstaw IPC only, exclusively; it is only that

EXCUSE

aspahâkêmo– VAI rely upon (it/him) in speaking, rely upon (it/him) in telling a story; use (it/him) as an excuse

EXERCISE
pimipayihtâ– *VAI* run (it), operate (it) (e.g., machine); keep (it) up, exercise (it)

sêsâwin– *VTA* stretch s.o. by hand, exercise s.o.'s limbs (in therapy)

EXHAUSTED
mêscipayi– *VAI* be exhausted (e.g., snow), be gone entirely (e.g., snow)

mêscipayin– *VII* run out, be exhausted on the way

mêscitonêsin– *VAI* have exhausted one's mouth, wear one's mouth out

mêstasahkê– *VAI* feed people until the supply is exhausted, exhaust one's supply by feeding people

mêstinikê– *VAI* use things up, exhaust things, spend all of (it); spend all of one's money on things

nêsowisi– *VAI* be weak, be exhausted, be near death

nêstwâso– *VAI* be tired by the sun's heat, be exhausted by hot weather

nôhtêsin– *VAI* be played out, lie exhausted

sâpo *IPV* fully, exhaustively, through and through

EXIST
askîwi– *VII* be the earth, exist as world; be a year

ayâ– *VAI* be there, live there; exist

ayâ– *VII* be there, exist

ihtako– *VAI* exist; be born (e.g., infant)

ihtakon– *VII* exist

ihtatan– *VII* exist there

ihtâ– *VAI* be there, exist

pimipayi– *VII* move along; run, run along; be on, work, function (e.g., motor, electricity); exist currently, take place

EXISTENCE
ayisiyinîwin– *NI* being human, human existence

namatakon– *VII* be non-existent, be absent; have disappeared, be no longer in existence

namatê– *VAI* be non-existent, be absent; have disappeared, be no longer in existence

EXPAND
sêhkwêpitê– *VII* be pulled to expand; be an elastic band

EXPECT
cikêmâ *IPC* of course, obviously, as might be expected

pakosêyim– *VTA* wish for (it/him) of s.o., expect (it/him) of s.o.

pakosêyimo– *VAI* wish for (it); have an expectation

EXPENSIVE
mistakihtê– *VII* be counted for much, be worth a lot, be valuable, be expensive

EXPERT
nahî– *VAI* be adept at (it), be good at (it); be competent, be an expert

nihtâwâcimo– *VAI* be a good storyteller, tell stories expertly

nihtâwikwâso– *VAI* be good at sewing, sew expertly, be an experienced seamstress; do fancy sewing

nihtâwikwât– *VTI* be good at sewing s.t., sew s.t. expertly

nihtâwisimo– *VAI* be good at dancing, be an expert dancer

nihtâwitêpo– *VAI* be good at cooking, be an expert cook

EXPLORER
onitawahtâw– *NA* scout, explorer, spy

EXPOSE
kawatim– *VTA* get s.o. cold, expose s.o. to cold

wanâtapi– *VAI* sit so as to expose oneself

EXPOUND
mâmiskôcikâtê– *VII* be discussed, be expounded

mâmiskôt– *VTI* talk about s.t., discuss s.t., expound s.t., refer to s.t.

mâmiskôtamaw– *VTA* discuss (it/him) for s.o., expound (it/him) for s.o., refer to (it/him) for s.o.

EXPRESSION
pîkiskwêwin– *NI* word, phrase, expression, voice; what is being said; speech, language

EXPRESSLY
ohcitaw *IPC* expressly, specifically, purposely, necessarily; it is requisite, it is meet indeed

EXTEND
âniskôstê– *VII* extend, be extended

iskopitonê– *VAI* have one's arm reach so far, extend one's arm so far

iskosi– *VAI* extend so far, be so long, be so tall, be of such height

iskwâ– *VII* extend so far, be of such extent

ispîhcâ– *VII* extend thus, reach so far as land, be of such size as country

ispîhtaskamikâ– *VII* extend so far as land
ispîhtisî– *VAI* extend thus; be of such age
pimisin– *VAI* lie extended, lie down; lie confined, lie in childbed

EXTENSION
âniskôkwât– *VTI* sew s.t. on as an extension
âniskôscikê– *VAI* build an extension
piskihcikwât– *VTI* sew an extension on s.t.

EXTENT
êkoyikohk *IPC* that much, up to that point, to that degree, to that extent
iskohk *IPC* to such an extent, so far
iskoyikohk *IPC* to such an extent, to such a degree
ispisi *IPV* to such an extent, so far
iyikohk *IPC* so much, to such a degree, to such an extent
kakwâhyaki *IPV* greatly, extremely, tremendously, to an extraordinary extent
nahiyikohk *IPC* to the proper degree, to the proper extent, just enough, just right, evenly, fittingly, appropriately
ômayikohk *IPC* this much, to this degree, to this extent
pikoyikohk *IPC* to any extent, no matter how much
tânimayikohk *IPC* to which extent; to such an extent
tânimayikohkêskamik *IPC* to which extent, for how long
tâniyikohk *IPC* to what extent; to such an extent; so many, plenty

EXTINCT
âstawê– *VII* be without fire; be extinct (e.g., fire)
mêstohtê– *VAI* die off, become extinct

EXTINGUISHED
âstawêpayi– *VAI* have one's light go out (e.g., star), have one's fire extinguished (e.g., star)

EXTRA
tako *IPV* in addition, additionally, extra; on arrival
tako-tipah– *VTI* measure s.t. in addition; pay s.t. extra, pay for s.t. in addition; pay (it) in addition for s.t.

EXTRACT
ocipit– *VTI* pull s.t. out (e.g., from the ground), pull s.t. off; extract s.t. (e.g., grease from soup); move s.t. (e.g., house)

otin– *VTI* take s.t.; pick s.t., choose s.t., select s.t. (e.g., moss); steal s.t.; take s.t. over; extract s.t. (e.g., grease from soup), remove s.t. (e.g., glands in butchering beaver), extract s.t.; accept s.t. (e.g., contract); capture s.t., record s.t. on audio-tape

EXTRAORDINARY
kakwâhyaki *IPV* greatly, extremely, tremendously, to an extraordinary extent
kakwâhyaki-iskwêw– *NA* extraordinary woman, super-woman

EYE
–skîsikw– *NDI* eye
cahkâpicin– *VAI* have one's eye punctured (e.g., by branches or thorns)
cîkiskîsik *IPC* close to one's eye
côhkâpisi– *VAI* open one's eyes a little, have one's eyes open a little
miskîsik-maskihkiy– *NI* eye medicine
nahâpi– *VAI* have one's eyes focussed, have acute vision
pasahkâpi– *VAI* blink, shut and open one's eyes
pasakwâpi– *VAI* close one's eyes, have one's eyes shut
pâskâpi– *VAI* have a ruptured eye; have only one eye
tôhkâpi– *VAI* open one's eyes, have one's eyes open

EYE-SIGHT
wâpiwin– *NI* eye-sight

FACE
–hkwâkan– *NDI* face
akwanâhkwên– *VTA* cover s.o.'s (e.g., infant's) face; use (it) to cover s.o.'s face
akwanâhkwêyâmo– *VAI* flee with one's face covered, flee by covering one's face, cover one's face in flight
asiskîwihkwê– *VAI* have soil on one's face, have dirt on one's face
kâsîhkwâkê– *VAI* wash one's face with (it), use (it) to wash one's face
kâsîhkwê– *VAI* wash one's face
otihtapinahisin– *VAI* move to lie face-down
ohtiskawapi– *VAI* sit facing, sit so as to show one's face
ohtiskawapîstaw– *VTA* sit facing s.o., sit with one's face towards s.o.
waskitaskamik *IPC* on the face of the earth

FACT
anima *IPC* it is that; the fact that

oti *IPC* in fact
ôma *IPC* then; when; it is this; the fact that
sapiko *IPC* actually, as a matter of fact
tâh-tâpwê *IPC* in fact, in truth
tâspwâw *IPC* in fact, as a matter of fact

FACTOR
kihc-âtâwêwikamikowiyiniw– *NA* store manager, post manager, Hudson's Bay Company factor

FACULTIES
itâpatakêyimo– *VAI* use one's mind thus, make such use of one's mental faculties

FADED
wâpâstê– *VII* be light-coloured, be faded in colour

FAIL
pwâtawihtâ– *VAI* be thwarted at (it), fail of (it)

FAITHFUL
pêyakoh– *VTA* have s.o. as the only one, be faithful to s.o. (e.g., spouse)
tâpâtot– *VTI* tell s.t. fittingly, tell s.t. correctly, tell s.t. faithfully

FALL
itwêwêsin– *VAI* fall with such a sound, make such a sound with one's shoes
kawipah– *VTA* cause s.o. to fall down with alcoholic drink
kawisin– *VAI* fall down, lie fallen down
kitiskin– *VTA* inadvertently drop s.o., let s.o. fall by awkwardness
kîpipayi– *VAI* fall over
kwayakopayin– *VII* fall out
mispon– *VII* be falling snow, be a snow-fall
nîhcipayi– *VAI* come down, move down, fall down
nîhtakocin– *VAI* descend from high up, fall down (e.g., star)
pahkihtin– *VII* fall, fall down
pahkisim– *VTA* let s.o. fall, drop s.o.
pahkisin– *VAI* fall, fall down; fall for (her/him)
pakamisin– *VAI* fall down against (it)
pinakocin– *VAI* fall down from aloft
pîkinipayi– *VAI* fall apart into small pieces
pîkohtin– *VII* break in a fall, be broken
tahkohcipahkisin– *VAI* fall on top

takahkwêwêsin– *VAI* fall with nice sounds, make nice sounds with one's shoes
takwâkin– *VII* be fall, be autumn
takwâkohk *IPC* last fall
wîsakisin– *VAI* get hurt in a fall

FALSE
–îpitihkân– *NDI* false teeth, dentures

FAMILIAR
nakacih– *VTA* be familiar with s.o.
nakacihtâ– *VAI* be familiar with doing (it), be practised at (it)
nakayâsk– *VTI* be accustomed to s.t., be comfortable with s.t., be familiar with s.t.
nakayâskaw– *VTA* be accustomed to s.o., be comfortable with s.o., be familiar with s.o.

FAMILY
awâsisi-sôniyâs– *NA* family allowance
mâyipayi– *VAI* fare badly, suffer ill; suffer a death, be bereaved, have a death in the family; be bereaved of (her/him)

FANCY
miywêyimo– *VAI* think well of oneself; be pleased with oneself; think well for oneself, take a fancy
nihtâwikwâso– *VAI* be good at sewing, sew expertly, be an experienced seamstress; do fancy sewing
nihtâwikwâsowin– *NI* fancy sewing

FAR
awas-âyihk *IPC* on the other side, on the far side
iskohk *IPC* to such an extent, so far
iskon– *VTI* pull s.t. (e.g., dress) up so far
iskopitonê– *VAI* have one's arm reach so far, extend one's arm so far
iskosi– *VAI* extend so far, be so long, be so tall, be of such height
iskwâ– *VII* extend so far, be of such extent
iskwâhtawât– *VTA* climb up so far after s.o.; climb up (e.g., a tree) after s.o.
iskwâhtawî– *VAI* climb up so far; climb up (e.g., a tree)
iskwâhtawîhtah– *VTA* take s.o. climbing up so far; climb up (e.g., a tree) with s.o.
iskwâhtawîpahtâ– *VAI* climb up so far at a run; climb up (e.g., a tree) at a run

iskwâpêkamon– *VII* reach so far as rope
ispisi *IPV* to such an extent, so far
ispîhcâ– *VII* extend thus, reach so far as land, be of such size as country
ispîhtaskamikâ– *VII* extend so far as land
kwâhci *IPV* far off
nawac wâhyaw *IPC* quite far
ocihcikiskisi– *VAI* remember (it) far back; have memories far back
pêci-nâway *IPC* back then, far in the past; from the earliest times
sîpi *IPV* stretching far back
sîpikiskisi– *VAI* remember far back
wâh-wâhyaw *IPC* in far places
wâhyaw *IPC* far away
wâhyawês *IPC* a little away; quite far away
wâhyawêskamik *IPC* very far away
wâhyawîs *IPC* quite far away

FARE
ispayi– *VAI* fare thus, have such an experience, be thus affected; be thus afflicted
mâyipayi– *VAI* fare badly, suffer ill; suffer a death, be bereaved, have a death in the family; be bereaved of (her/him)
miyomahciho– *VAI* fare well, be in good health or spirit; feel well, feel healthy; feel pleased
miyopayi– *VAI* fare well, be in luck

FARM
kistikân– *NI* garden, field, farm, arable land
kistikê– *VAI* seed things, plant things, do one's seeding, do one's planting; farm the land
kistikêwi-pimâcihowin– *NI* agricultural way of life, farm economy
okistikêwiyiniw– *NA* farm instructor

FARMER
okistikêwiyinîwi– *VAI* be a farmer, be engaged in agriculture

FARMLAND
askiy– *NI* land, region, area; earth, world; settlement, colony, country; Métis settlement; *(plural:)* fields under cultivation, pieces of farmland, the lands

FAST
âyîtin– *VTI* hold fast onto s.t., hold on tightly to s.t.
kisât– *VTI* stay with s.t., hold fast to s.t.; stay, stay back
kisiskâ *IPV* quickly, fast
kisîkotê– *VII* move fast through the sky (e.g., cloud)
kisîpayi– *VAI* drive fast
kiyipi *IPV* quickly, fast
micimôho– *VAI* be held fast, be stuck
nîpawi– *VAI* stand, stand up, stand upright, stand fast
papâsi *IPV* fast, in a hurry
sipwêtâcimopahtâ– *VAI* rapidly crawl away, depart crawling fast
tahkopiso– *VAI* be tied fast
tahkopit– *VTA* tie s.o. fast (e.g., horse), tie s.o. on (e.g., to a sleigh)
tahkopit– *VTI* tie s.t. fast, tie s.t. shut (e.g., swim-bladder), tie s.t. in, tie s.t. up
tahkwam– *VTA* hold s.o. fast by mouth, hold s.o. in one's mouth

FASTEN
akwamohtâ– *VAI* attach (it), fasten (it) (e.g., safety-pin)
kikamohtâ– *VAI* attach (it), fasten (it) on, put (it) on something
kikamon– *VII* be attached, be fastened
pimâskwamon– *VII* run fastened along as wood, be nailed along (e.g., at regular intervals)

FASTING
îwanisîhisowin– *NI* fasting, denying oneself food

FAT
pimiy– *NI* fat, oil; crude petroleum
wiyino– *VAI* be fat (e.g., animal); be fat, be plump (e.g., little girl)
wiyino– *VII* be fat
wiyinw– *NI* fat, fat meat, piece of fat

FATHER
–ôhcâwîs– *NDA* father's brother, parallel uncle; step-father
–ôhtâwiy– *NDA* father, father's brother; *(fig.)* Our Father, Heavenly Father
–pâpâ– *NDA* dad, father
–pâpâsis– *NDA* dad's brother, father's brother, parallel uncle
–sikos– *NDA* father's sister, mother's brother's wife; mother-in-law, father-in-law's brother's wife, "aunt"
–sis– *NDA* mother's brother, father's sister's husband; father-in-law, father-in-law's brother, "uncle"
mâmaw-ôhtâwîmâw– *NA (name:)* All-Father, Father-of-All

opâpâ– *VAI* have a dad or father, have one's dad living; have (him) as one's dad
osikosâhkôm– *VTA* have s.o. as one's father's sister, call s.o. one's father's sister
osikosi– *VAI* have a father's sister or mother-in-law; have (her) as one's father's sister or mother-in-law
oyôhtâwî– *VAI* have a father, have a father living; have (him) as one's father
oyôhtâwîmâw– *NA* a father; *(name:)* The Father

FATHER-IN-LAW
–manâcimâkan– *NDA* father-in-law (woman speaking)
–sikos– *NDA* father's sister, mother's brother's wife; mother-in-law, father-in-law's brother's wife, "aunt"
–sis– *NDA* mother's brother, father's sister's husband; father-in-law, father-in-law's brother, "uncle"
osisi– *VAI* have a mother's brother or father-in-law; have (him) as one's mother's brother or father-in-law

FATTY
paswêskôyo– *VAI* get sick from eating excessively fatty food
paswêyâ– *VII* be excessively fatty

FAULT
–tôcikan– *NDI* one's doing, one's fault

FAVOUR
yêyâpisin– *VAI* look on with favour; be tempted by looking at (it)

FEAR
kost– *VTA* fear s.o.
kost– *VTI* fear s.t.
kostâci– *VAI* be afraid, have fear

FEARSOME
astâhtâso– *VAI* be watched, be considered a threat; evoke fear, be fearsome, be awe-inspiring, be awesome
kostâtikwan– *VII* be fearsome, be awe-inspiring

FEAST
kîsitêpo– *VAI* cook; cook a feast, cook ritual food
wîhkohkât– *VTI* hold a feast for s.t. (e.g., medicinal herbs)
wîhkohkê– *VAI* hold a feast
wîhkohkêh– *VTA* hold a feast for s.o., hold a feast in s.o.'s honour
wîhkohkêmo– *VAI* invite people to a feast
wîhkohto– *VAI* invite one another to a feast

wîhkom– *VTA* invite s.o. to a feast

FEATHER
–pîwâs– *NDI* little feathers, down
mîkwan– *NA* feather
opîwayakohp– *NI* feather blanket
sîsîp-opîway– *NI* duck feathers, duck-down
sîsîpipîway– *NI* duck feathers, duck-down

FECES
mêyiwiciskê– *VAI* have feces stuck to one's anus, have one's anus soiled with feces

FED UP
mwêstât– *VTA* be tired of s.o., be fed up with s.o.
saskacihtaw– *VTA* be tired of hearing s.o., be fed up with hearing s.o.

FEED
asahkê– *VAI* feed people, give out food
asahtowin– *NI* feeding one another; rations
asam– *VTA* feed s.o., give s.o. to eat; hand out rations to s.o.
asamastimwê– *VAI* feed one's horses
asamâwaso– *VAI* feed one's children, sustain one's children
asamiso– *VAI* feed oneself
kîspôh– *VTA* feed s.o. until full, get s.o. (e.g., horse) fully fed
mêstasahkê– *VAI* feed people until the supply is exhausted, exhaust one's supply by feeding people
mîciso– *VAI* eat, have a meal; feed (e.g., bird); chew the cud (e.g., ruminant)
tasôh– *VTA* entrap s.o. (e.g., bird) by putting feed under a movable lid, trap s.o. underneath

FEEL
itamahciho– *VAI* feel thus, be in such health
kitimâkêyihto– *VAI* feel pity towards one another, think of one another with compassion; take pity upon one another, be kind to one another, love one another
kitimâkêyim– *VTA* feel pity towards s.o., think of s.o. with compassion; take pity upon s.o., be kind to s.o., love s.o.
kitimâkêyimo– *VAI* feel pitiable, feel miserable; feel poor
kitimâkinaw– *VTA* look with pity upon s.o., look with compassion upon s.o., feel sorry for s.o.; take pity upon

s.o., lovingly tend s.o.; regard s.o. with respect
kitimâkinâso– VAI pity oneself, feel sorry for oneself
kôtawêyim– VTA be aware of s.o.'s absence, feel the loss of s.o., miss s.o.
mâyamahciho– VAI feel poorly, be in ill health
miyomahciho– VAI fare well, be in good health or spirit; feel well, feel healthy; feel pleased
môsih– VTA sense s.o., feel s.o. approaching, perceive s.o.'s presence
môsihtâ– VAI sense (it), feel (it) approaching, perceive (it)
nânitaw itamahciho– VAI feel unwell
takahkipah– VTA make s.o. feel good, cause s.o. to be light-headed with an alcoholic drink, get s.o. inebriated
takahkipê– VAI feel good with drink, be light-headed with alcoholic drink, be inebriated
wawiyatêyim– VTA find s.o. funny, consider s.o. amusing; feel joy about s.o.

FEELING
kitimâkêyihtowin– NI feeling pity towards one another, thinking of one another with compassion; taking pity upon one another, being kind to one another, loving one

FEET
ayinânêwi-misit IPC eight feet, for eight feet (measure)

FELLOW
–îc-âyis– NDA fellow youngster; sibling, parallel cousin
–îcayisiyiniw– NDA fellow person, fellow human
–îci-kisêyin– NDA fellow old man, co-elder
–îci-kisêyiniw– NDA fellow old man, co-elder
–îci-kiskinohamawâkan– NDA fellow student, school-mate
–îci-kîhkâw– NDA aged spouse, fellow old person, fellow oldster, companion of one's old age
–wîtatoskêmâkan– NDA fellow worker, co-worker
wîci-kiskinohamâkosîm– VTA be in school together with s.o., have s.o. as a fellow student
wîci-pîhtwâm– VTA smoke together with s.o., have s.o. as one's fellow smoker
wîci-pîkiskwêm– VTA speak together with s.o., have s.o. as one's fellow speaker
wîcisimôm– VTA dance together with s.o., have s.o. as one's fellow dancer
wîtatoskêm– VTA work together with s.o., have s.o. as one's fellow worker

FELT-LINER
pîswê-maskisin– NI felt-liner, boot-liner

FEMALE
–câhkos– NDA female cross-cousin (woman speaking); sister-in-law (woman speaking)
–mis– NDA older sister, older female parallel cousin
–okimâskwêm– NDA female boss, boss's wife
–tawêmâw– NDA male parallel cousin (woman speaking); female cross-cousin's husband (woman speaking)
–tôhtôsim– NDA female breast; teat (e.g., cow)
iskwêsis– NI girl, little girl, female infant
iskwêw– NA woman, female, female adult
iskwêw-ây– NA female, female (of the species)
iskwêwi– VAI be a woman, be female
iskwêwisîh– VTA dress s.o. as a girl, dress s.o. as a female
môniyâskwêw– NA White female, White woman
ocâhkosi– VAI have a female cross-cousin or sister-in-law (woman speaking), have (her) as one's female cross-cousin or sister-in-law (woman speaking)
okiskinohamâkêwiskwêw– NA female teacher; teacher's wife
onîcâniw– NA female of large quadrupeds; cow, cow-moose, female elk

FENCE
mênikan– NI fence
mênikanihkâkê– VAI build a fence with (it), use (it) to build a fence

FENCE-POST
cimacês– NI fence-post

FENCE-RAIL
mênikanâhtikw– NI fence-rail

FETCH
miywakiso– VAI be considered good, be well esteemed; fetch a good price (e.g., tree)
nâcikâtê– VII be fetched

nâcimihtê– *VAI* fetch firewood, go for firewood
nâcipah– *VTA* run to fetch s.o., make a run for s.o.
nâcipahiwê– *VAI* run to fetch things, make a run for things
nâcitâpê– *VAI* go and drag (it) back, fetch (it) by cart
nâciwanihikanê– *VAI* fetch game from traps, check one's traps
nât– *VTA* fetch s.o.
nât– *VTI* fetch s.t.
nâtahisipê– *VAI* fetch ducks (e.g., as a dog)
nâtahw– *VTA* fetch s.o. by boat or airplane; pick s.o. up (e.g., as an airplane)
nâtamaw– *VTA* fetch (it/him) for s.o.; take up for s.o.
nâtamâso– *VAI* fetch (it/him) for oneself
nâtaskosiwê– *VAI* fetch hay
nâtâhtawât– *VTA* climb up (e.g., a tree) to fetch s.o.
nâtâwatâ– *VAI* fetch (it) by hauling
nâtitâpê– *VAI* go and drag (it) back, fetch (it) by cart
nâtitisahw– *VTA* go to fetch s.o. (e.g., horses); send for s.o., order s.o. (e.g., chickens) by catalogue
nâtôpê– *VAI* go to fetch water; go for a drink; go for alcoholic drink

FEVER
kisiso– *VAI* be warm, be hot; run a fever, be febrile
otinikêmakan– *VII* take things away; take the fever away
wayawîtisahikêmakan– *VII* drive things out; drive the fever out

FEW
ay-âskawi *IPC* from time to time, a few at a time
miscahîs-kîkway *PR* quite a few things
omostosomisi– *VAI* have a few cows
pêcikêsi– *VAI* bring a few things hither
tânitahto-nîpin *IPC* how many summers; so many summers, a few summers

FIE
nâh *IPC* fie!

FIELD
askiy– *NI* land, region, area; earth, world; settlement, colony, country; Métis settlement; *(plural:)* fields under cultivation, pieces of farmland, the lands
kistikân– *NI* garden, field, farm, arable land
kîsisikê– *VAI* burn things; burn stubble, burn the fields
pasisâwê– *VAI* burn stubble, burn the fields

FIFTEEN
niyânanosâp *IPC* fifteen

FIFTH
niyânano-kîsikâ– *VII* be the fifth day; be Friday

FIFTY
niyânanomitanaw *IPC* fifty
nîso-sôniyâs *IPC* fifty cents

FIGHT
âstawêhikê– *VAI* be a fire-fighter; fight forest-fires
nôcih– *VTA* pursue s.o., hunt for s.o. (e.g., animal); go after s.o., oppress s.o., beat s.o. up, fight with s.o.
nôtin– *VTA* fight s.o., fight with s.o.
nôtin– *VTI* fight s.t., fight with s.t.
nôtinikê– *VAI* fight people, put up a fight; take part in war (e.g., World War II)
nôtinito– *VAI* fight with one another
ohcih– *VTA* fight s.o. over (it/him); hold s.o. off

FIGHTING
nôtinitowin– *NI* fighting one another, fighting

FIGURE
ayisiyinîhkân– *NA* doll, mannikin; cartoon figure

FILL
asiwacipayin– *VII* get placed inside, get enclosed; rapidly fill an enclosed space (e.g., water flowing into hoofprint)
kipwaskinê– *VII* be filled to the lid, be full to the brim
kîspo– *VAI* have one's fill, be full with food
mamihcih– *VTA* *(especially in inverse constructions:)* make s.o. proud, fill s.o. with pride
sâkaskinah– *VTA* fill s.o.; fill (it) with s.o. (e.g., snow)
sâkaskinahtâ– *VAI* make (it) full, fill (it) (e.g., audio-tape)
sâkaskinê– *VAI* crowd in, fill a place
sâkaskinêkâpawi– *VAI* stand crowded in, stand to fill a place
wiyaskinah– *VTA* fill s.o. (e.g., pipe)

FILLET
iskosâwât– *VTA* leave meat over in filleting s.o. (e.g., fish), leave some flesh on the bones in filleting s.o.
pânisâwê– *VAI* cut meat into sheets; cut fish into fillets

FINALLY
pâskac *IPC* on top of that, to top it all off, to cap it all, as the final touch; coincidentally
piyisk *IPC* finally, at last

FINANCIAL
sôniyâwi *IPV* with respect to money, in financial matters

FIND
misk– *VTI* find s.t.
miskamaw– *VTA* find (it/him) for s.o.
miskamâso– *VAI* find (it/him) for oneself; find oneself a spouse
miskaw– *VTA* find s.o.
miskwam– *VTA* find s.o. (e.g., coin) by mouth, find s.o. (e.g., coin) in one's food
miskwêyiht– *VTI* find s.t., think of s.t., come to think of s.t.
wîcêwâkanihto– *VAI* find one another as partner or spouse

FINE
cîsâwât– *VTI* cut s.t. (e.g., fat) into chunks, chop s.t. fine

FINGER
itwahw– *VTA* point one's finger at s.o., point at s.o.

FINISH
kitâ– *VAI* eat (it) up, eat (it) completely, eat all of (it); drink all of (it); finish drinking a bottle of (it); drink an entire bottle
kîsakim– *VTA* finish counting s.o.; finish giving orders to s.o., complete one's charge to s.o.
kîsih– *VTA* complete s.o. (e.g., stocking), finish preparing s.o.
kîsin– *VTA* finish s.o. (e.g., raw hide)
kîsin– *VTI* finish s.t. (e.g., dressed hide)
kîsinamâso– *VAI* complete (it/him) for oneself, finish (it/him) for oneself
kîsîhtâ– *VAI* finish (it), complete (it)
miyo-kîsih– *VTA* finish s.o. well; educate s.o. well

FINISHED HIDE
môso-pahkêkin– *NI* finished moose-hide
pahkêkinw– *NI* dressed hide, tanned hide, finished hide, leather; tent-cover

FIRE
âstawê– *VII* be without fire; be extinct (e.g., fire)
âstawêpayi– *VAI* have one's light go out (e.g., star), have one's fire extinguished (e.g., star)
iskotêhkê– *VAI* make a fire
iskotêw– *NI* fire, hearth-fire
kîsowihkaso– *VAI* warm oneself by a burning fire
kotawân– *NI* campfire, open fire
kotawê– *VAI* make a campfire, make a cooking fire
kwâhkotê– *VII* catch fire, be ablaze
kwâhkotênikê– *VAI* start a fire, set things aflame
macostêh– *VTI* throw s.t. into the fire
nawacî– *VAI* roast (it), roast (it) over an open fire; roast one's food
pôn– *VTI* build a fire; make a fire with s.t.
pônasi– *VAI* add a little wood to one's fire
pônikâtê– *VII* be a fire being made; be kept burning as a fire

FIRE-FIGHTER
âstawêhikê– *VAI* be a fire-fighter; fight forest-fires
otâstawêhikêw– *NA* fire-fighter

FIREWOOD
âwacimihtê– *VAI* haul firewood
mihcis– *NI* split wood, small firewood, sticks
miht– *NI* firewood, piece of firewood
nâcimihtê– *VAI* fetch firewood, go for firewood
nikohtât– *VTI* chop s.t. for firewood
nikohtê– *VAI* collect firewood, chop firewood
nikohtêstamâso– *VAI* make firewood for oneself, make one's own firewood
nikohtêwin– *NI* making firewood
omihtimi– *VAI* have firewood; have (it) as one's firewood
pîhtikwê-âwacimihtêwin– *NI* hauling firewood indoors
tâskatahimihtê– *VAI* split firewood

FIRMLY
pâhkaci *IPC* actually, firmly
sôhkêpit– *VTI* stand firmly behind s.t., promote s.t.

FIRST
êkwayâc *IPC* only then, not until then; only now, for the first time

nistam *IPC* first, at first, for the first time, initially, originally
nistamêmâkan– *NA* the first one, the original one
nîkân *IPC* first, at the head, in front, in the lead; as a first step; in future
nîkânakim– *VTA* count s.o. in first position, hold s.o. (e.g., tobacco) to be the prime element
nîkâninikâso– *VAI* take precedence, rank first; be the prime element
pita *IPC* first, first of all; for a while
pitamâ *IPC* first, first of all; for a while
saskamo– *VAI* take communion; have one's first communion, have had one's first communion

FISH
akocikan– *NI* rack for hanging up fish or meat, storage-rack; cupboard, shelf
kinosêw– *NA* fish
kwâskwêpicikê– *VAI* fish with a rod
namêstikw– *NA* smoked fish
nôcikinosêwê– *VAI* get fish, be engaged in fishing
osîhikinosêwê– *VAI* prepare one's fish, process one's fish
oski-kinosêw– *NA* fresh fish
pakitahwâ– *VAI* fish by net, set nets
pânisâwê– *VAI* cut meat into sheets; cut fish into fillets

FISH-EGGS
wâhkwan– *NA* fish-eggs

FISHING LAKE
pakicahwânisihk *INM* *(place-name:)* Fishing Lake (Alberta)

FISHING-NET
ayapiy– *NA* net, fishing-net
kinwâpêkisi– *VAI* be long as string, be long as fishing-net

FISHING-ROD
kwâskwêpicikan– *NI* fishing-rod
kwâskwêpicikanis– *NI* fishing-rod

FIT
nânâspicipayi– *VAI* have a coughing fit
pohtayiwinisah– *VTA* put clothes on s.o., make clothes for s.o., fit s.o. out with clothing, clothe s.o.
sôhkâtisi– *VAI* be strong in body, be fit, have a vigorous disposition
têpisk– *VTI* fit s.t. (e.g., garment)

FITTED
tâpisk– *VTI* wear s.t. fitted, wear s.t. around the neck

FITTINGLY
nahiyikohk *IPC* to the proper degree, to the proper extent, just enough, just right, evenly, fittingly, appropriately
tâpâtot– *VTI* tell s.t. fittingly, tell s.t. correctly, tell s.t. faithfully

FIVE
niyânan *IPC* five
niyânan-kîsikâw *IPC* five days, for five days
niyânani– *VAI* be five in number
niyânanwâpisk *IPC* five dollars

FIX
nânapâcih– *VTA* fix s.o. up, mend s.o. (e.g., pants)
nânapâcihiso– *VAI* fix oneself up; doctor oneself
nânapâcihtâ– *VAI* fix (it) up, mend (it)

FIXED
kikamo– *VAI* be attached, have a fixed place (e.g., star)

FLAG
wêpinâson– *NI* draped cloth, flag, cloth offering

FLAT
itêkin– *VTI* fold s.t. flat thus, fold s.t. thus as cloth
napakaskisin– *NI* flat moccasin
napakâ– *VII* be flat
napakihtakw– *NI* flat lumber, board, floor-board
napakis– *VTI* cut s.t. into flat pieces, cut s.t. (e.g., meat) into chops
sisopêkah– *VTI* rub (it) flat on s.t. by tool; paint s.t.
sisopêkahw– *VTA* rub (it/him) flat on s.o. by tool; paint s.o.
sisopêkin– *VTA* rub (it/him) flat on s.o. by hand
taswêkin– *VTI* unfold s.t. as cloth; open s.t. (e.g., book) up flat
taswêkiwêpin– *VTA* spread s.o. (e.g., wing) flat

FLAT-TOP
napakikamikw– *NI* house made of lumber or boards; flat-top shack

FLATTEN
napakin– *VTI* flatten s.t. by hand
patakopit– *VTA* squash s.o. in pulling, flatten s.o. down by pulling

FLEE
akwanâhkwêyâmo– *VAI* flee with one's face covered, flee by covering one's face, cover one's face in flight

itâmo– VAI flee thither or thus, seek such refuge
itâmôh– VTA make s.o. flee thus or there, direct s.o. to seek such refuge
nâtâmost– VTI flee to s.t., turn to s.t. for help, seek refuge in s.t.
nâtâmotot– VTI flee to s.t., turn to s.t. for help, seek refuge in s.t.
nâtâmototaw– VTA flee to s.o., turn to s.o. for help, seek refuge with s.o.
pêtâmo– VAI flee hither
pîhtikwêyâmo– VAI flee indoors
tapasî– VAI flee, run away
tapasîh– VTA flee from s.o.
têtipêwêyâmo– VAI flee around in a circle
wayawîyâmohkê– VAI arrange for s.o. to flee outdoors

FLEECE
mâyatihkopîway– NI sheep's fleece; wool

FLIGHT
akwanâhkwêyâmo– VAI flee with one's face covered, flee by covering one's face, cover one's face in flight
nawatahikê– VAI shoot (it/him) in flight, shoot ducks as they fly
nawatahw– VTA shoot s.o. in flight

FLIP
kwatapiwêpin– VTA throw s.o. over, flip s.o. upside down

FLOAT
akohtin– VII float on liquid (e.g., grease on soup)
pimâhocikêsi– VAI float along in a small boat

FLOOR
kisêpêkihtakinikê– VAI wash a wooden floor, wash floor-boards
mohcihk IPC on the bare floor, on the bare ground
mohcihtak IPC on the bare floor, on the floor-boards
sinikohtakahikan– NI scrub-brush, floor brush, brush for wood
wâpiskihtakâ– VII be white boards, be white floor
wîhkwêhtakâw– NI corner made by wooden walls, corner of the floor, corner of the house

FLOOR-BOARD
kisêpêkihtakinikê– VAI wash a wooden floor, wash floor-boards
kisîpêkinihtakwâkê– VAI wash one's floor-boards with (it), use (it) to wash one's floor-boards
kisîpêkinihtakwê– VAI wash one's floor-boards
mohcihtak IPC on the bare floor, on the floor-boards
napakihtakw– NI flat lumber, board, floor-board

FLOOR-COVERING
anâskânihtakw– NI floor-covering, linoleum
anâskê– VAI have a mat, spread a blanket; use (it) as matting or floor-covering

FLOUR
pahkwêsikan– NA flour; bannock, bread

FLOUR-BAG
maskimotêkinw– NI sack, sacking, sack-cloth; flour-bag, cloth from flour-bag
pahkwêsikaniwat– NI flour-bag

FLOW
pimiciwan– VII flow along
pimihtin– VII go along (e.g., river, road); run along, flow by (e.g., creek)

FLOWER
apiscâpakwanîs– NI small flower, flower pattern (e.g., printed on fabric)
wâpakwaniy– NI flower
wâpakwanîs– NI flower

FLY
ispihâ– VAI fly thus or there
itakocin– VAI hang thus or there, be suspended thus or there; fly thus or there
kisiwipayi– VAI get angry, fly into rage
nawatahikê– VAI shoot (it/him) in flight, shoot ducks as they fly
ohpaho– VAI fly up (e.g., bird); fly off, lift off by airplane
ohpwên– VTI make s.t. fly up, raise s.t. up (e.g., dust)
papâmihâ– VAI fly about
pimihâ– VAI fly along
sipwêhâ– VAI fly off, depart flying, fly away
sipwêkocin– VII depart in water or air, or by vehicle; fly off, depart flying
sipwêpihâ– VAI fly off, depart flying

FOCUSSED
nahâpi– VAI have one's eyes focussed, have acute vision

FOLD
itêkin– VTI fold s.t. flat thus, fold s.t. thus as cloth

pâskin– *VTI* open s.t. up, take the cover off s.t.; fold s.t. (e.g., book) open
pihkin– *VTI* shape s.t., bend s.t., fold s.t.

FOLLOW
askow– *VTA* follow s.o., follow behind s.o.
askôskaw– *VTA* follow s.o. in birth sequence
askôto– *VAI* follow one another, follow behind one another
ayamihâ– *VAI* pray, say prayers; hold a church service, celebrate mass; participate in a religious rite, go to church; follow a religion
itaskôto– *VAI* follow one another thither or thus, follow behind one another thither or thus
mitiht– *VTA* track s.o., follow s.o.'s tracks
mitiht– *VTI* track s.t., follow the tracks of s.t.
mitimê– *VAI* track along a trail, follow a trail; *(fig.)* follow a path, be guided in one's life
papâmitisah– *VTI* chase s.t. about; follow s.t. about (e.g., trail)
papâmitisahikêski– *VAI* habitually follow people about
pimitisah– *VTI* follow s.t.; *(fig.)* adhere to a religion
pimitisahikê– *VAI* follow people, tag along, be a follower
pimitisahw– *VTA* follow s.o. along, go behind s.o., drive s.o. along

FOLLOWER
–ayisiyinîm– *NDA* people, follower
–iyinîm– *NDA* people, followers
–oskinîkîm– *NDA* young man, follower; *(fig.)* servant
pimitisahikê– *VAI* follow people, tag along, be a follower

FOOD
asahkê– *VAI* feed people, give out food
îwanisîhisowin– *NI* fasting, denying oneself food
kakwâtakihiso– *VAI* make oneself suffer; torture oneself, deny oneself food and drink
kakwâtakiho– *VAI* make oneself suffer; torture oneself, experience suffering; deny oneself food and drink
kakwâtakihowin– *NI* making oneself suffer; denying oneself food and drink
kîsitêpo– *VAI* cook; cook a feast, cook ritual food
kîsitêw– *NI* food, ritual food
kîspo– *VAI* have one's fill, be full with food
miskwam– *VTA* find s.o. (e.g., coin) by mouth, find s.o. (e.g., coin) in one's food
mîcisowin– *NI* eating, meal; eating-habits; food, foodstuff; food supply
mîciwin– *NI* food
mîciwinis– *NI* some food, a little food
mosc-âsam– *VTA* simply provide food to s.o., supply food to s.o. without recompense
nawacî– *VAI* roast (it), roast (it) over an open fire; roast one's food
nôhtêhkatê– *VAI* be hungry, suffer want of food
paswêskôyo– *VAI* get sick from eating excessively fatty food
sakâwi-mîciwin– *NI* food from the bush

FOOL
kakêpâhkamikisi– *VAI* fool around, get in the way
mêtawâkê– *VAI* play with (it), use (it) to play; play around with (it), fool around with (it)

FOOLISH
môhcowi– *VAI* be foolish, be stupid, be silly; be mad, be crazy
môhcw-âyâ– *VAI* be foolish, be stupid, be silly; be mad, be crazy
môhcwahkamikisi– *VAI* behave foolishly, do crazy things

FOOT
–sicis– *NDI* foot
–sit– *NDI* foot
mostohtê– *VAI* simply walk, move along without instrument, be on foot
mostohtêyâciho– *VAI* travel on foot
pâkisitêpayi– *VAI* have one's foot swell up, have a swollen foot
pêyak-misit *IPC* one foot, for one foot; measuring one foot

FORCE
wîhkô– *VAI* strain oneself, use all one's force

FORCEFULLY
sôhkêhtatâ– *VAI* throw (it) vigorously, throw (it) forcefully
sôhkêwêpin– *VTI* throw s.t. vigorously, throw s.t. forcefully

FORECAST
kiskiwêhikê– *VAI* utter prophesies; make predictions, forecast things

kiskiwêhikêmakan– *VII* provide prophesies; make predictions, forecast things
kiskiwêhikêwin– *NI* prophesy; prediction, forecast
FORELEGS
nânapwahpiso– *VAI* have one's forelegs tied together (e.g., horse), be hobbled
FOREST-FIRES
âstawêhikê– *VAI* be a fire-fighter; fight forest-fires
FOREVER
kâkikê *IPC* always, at all times, forever; for a very long time, forever (metaphorically)
FORGET
wanêyiht– *VTI* forget s.t., be unsure of s.t.; have one's mind blurred, be confused
wanikiskisi– *VAI* forget (it/him); be forgetful
FORGIVE
kâsînamaw– *VTA* wipe (it) off for s.o.; *(fig.)* forgive s.o.
kâsînamâso– *VAI* wipe (it) off for oneself; *(fig.)* have one's sins forgiven, obtain forgivenness
kâsînamâto– *VAI* wipe (it) off for one another; *(fig.)* forgive one another
nânitaw itêyim– *VTA* hold (it) against s.o.; *(especially in negative constructions:)* not bear a grudge against s.o., forgive s.o.
pônêyihtamaw– *VTA* forgive s.o. for (it); forgive s.o.
pônêyihtamâto– *VAI* forgive one another
FORGOTTEN
kanihk *IPC* oh yes, I just remembered, I had forgotten
FORK
cîstâsêpon– *NI* fork
FORM
âtayôhkât– *VTA* tell about s.o. in the form of a sacred story, tell a sacred story of s.o.
âtayôhkât– *VTI* tell about s.t. in the form of a sacred story, tell a sacred story of s.t.
isi-mawimoscikêwin– *NI* worshipping thus, such a form of worship; rite of such a type
itâtayôhkât– *VTI* tell thus about s.t. in the form of a sacred story, tell such a sacred story of s.t.

itâtayôhkâtê– *VII* be told thus in the form of a sacred story, be told as such a sacred story
kwêskîmo– *VAI* change one's form
mawimoscikêwin– *NI* crying out in prayer, wailing; form of worship, rite
nîswayak isi *IPC* in both directions; in both forms of ritual (e.g., with both incense and sweetgrass)
FORMAL
aspitonâmo– *VAI* rely on the spoken word; rely on (it) as a formal confirmation of the spoken word
kîsîhcikê– *VAI* complete doing things; bring a ritual to its conclusion; conclude the formal signing of a treaty
FORMALLY
kihci *IPV* greatly; formally
kihci-wîki– *VAI* live formally; *(fig.)* live in residence
kihci-wîkihto– *VAI* be formally married, be married in church
kihci-wîkihtowin– *NI* formal marriage, Holy Matrimony
kihci-wîkim– *VTA* marry s.o. formally, marry s.o. in church
FORMERLY
kayâhtê *IPC* before, previously, formerly; before the appropriate time, prematurely
FORT CARLTON
pêhonânihk *INM* *(place-name:)* Fort Carlton (Saskatchewan)
FORTNIGHTLY
tahto-nîsw-âyamihêwi-kîsikâw *IPC* every second week, fortnightly
FORTY
nêmitanaw *IPC* forty
FORWARD
piyasêyimo– *VAI* look forward eagerly, wait in anticipation
yahkitisahw– *VTA* drive s.o. forward
FOUL
mâyâpaso– *VAI* smell foul, give off a bad smell, stink
mâyi-kîsikâ– *VII* be stormy weather, be foul weather, be a severe storm
wîhcêkimahkasikê– *VAI* give off a bad smell, produce a foul odour
FOUND
miskikâtê– *VII* be found
FOUR
nâh-nêwi– *VAI* be four each
nâh-nêwo *IPC* four each
nêw-âskiy *IPC* four years, for four years

nêwâw IPC four times
nêwi– VAI be four in number
nêwo IPC four
nêwo-kîsikâ– VII be four days, be the fourth day; be Thursday
nêwo-kîsikâw IPC four days, for four days
nêwo-tipiskâ– VII be four nights, be the fourth night
FOURTEEN
nêwosâp IPC fourteen
FRAGMENT
nanânistipit– VTA tear s.o. into bits and pieces; fragment s.o. (e.g., group of people), divide s.o. (e.g., community) against one another
FREE
kêcikopit– VTI pull s.t. free, pull s.t. out; take s.t. off by pulling; pull out of s.t.
manipit– VTA pull s.o. free (e.g., thorn, porcupine quills), pull s.o. in (e.g., net), pull s.o. out, obtain s.o. by pulling
manipit– VTI pull s.t. free, pull s.t. out (e.g., flower), obtain s.t. by pulling
pihkoh– VTA free s.o., release s.o.
pihkoho– VAI free oneself, escape; be released; *(fig.)* free oneself (e.g., to meet an obligation or duty); be saved
FREEZE
âhkwaci– VAI be cold, freeze, be frozen (e.g., fish)
âhkwatihtâ– VAI let (it) freeze, freeze (it)
âhkwatim– VTA let s.o. freeze (e.g., fish), freeze s.o.
FREEZE-UP
âhkwatin– VII be frozen, be frozen solid; be freeze-up
FREEZER
âhkwacihcikanis– NI small refrigerator, small freezer
âhkwatihcikan– NI refrigerator, freezer
FRENCH
wêmistikôsîmototaw– VTA speak French to s.o., address s.o. in French
FRENCHMAN
mistikôsiw– NA Frenchman, Hudson's Bay Company manager
wêmistikôsiw– NA Frenchman; non-Indian, White person
FRESH
miyân– VTI leave behind fresh tracks, have recently passed by

ENGLISH INDEX   281

oskaskosîwinâkwan– VII look green, have the appearance of fresh shoots
oski IPN young, fresh, new
oski-kinosêw– NA fresh fish
oski-napatâkw– NI new potato, fresh potato
FRET
nânitaw itêyiht– VTI worry about s.t., fret about s.t.; assign blame for s.t.; *(especially in negative constructions:)* not bear a grudge, be forgiving
FRIDAY
niyânano-kîsikâ– VII be the fifth day; be Friday
FRIED
sâsâpiskitê– VII be fried, be pan-fried
sâsâpiskitikâtê– VII be fried, be pan-fried
FRIEND
–ciwâm– NDA male parallel cousin (man speaking); *(fig.)* brother, friend, male of the same generation (man speaking); brother, brethren
–ciwâmis– NDA male parallel cousin (man speaking); *(fig.)* brother, friend, male of the same generation (man speaking); brother, brethren
–tôtêm– NDA kinsman; friend
otôtêmi– VAI have a kinsman or friend; have (her/him) as one's kinsman or friend
oyotôtêmi– VAI have a kinsman or friend; have (her/him) as one's kinsman or friend; be friendly
FRIENDLY
oyotôtêmi– VAI have a kinsman or friend; have (her/him) as one's kinsman or friend; be friendly
FRIGHTEN
astâh– VTA frighten s.o.; *(especially in inverse constructions:)* cause s.o. to be wary, worry s.o.
sêkih– VTA frighten s.o.
sêkim– VTA frighten s.o. by speech
FROG
ayîkis– NA frog
FRONT
nîkân IPC first, at the head, in front, in the lead; as a first step; in future
FROSTBITE
pasisêwaci– VAI suffer frostbite
FROZEN
âhkwaci– VAI be cold, freeze, be frozen (e.g., fish)
âhkwatihcikâtê– VII be frozen (e.g., in a freezer)

âhkwatin– *VII* be frozen, be frozen solid; be freeze-up
FRY
pahkwêsikanihkê– *VAI* fry bannock, bake bread
FRYING-PAN
napwênis– *NA* small frying-pan
FULFILLED
tâpwêmakan– *VII* come true; *(fig.)* be fulfilled (e.g., prophecy)
FULL
âkwâtaskinê– *VAI* be quite full (e.g., pail), be more than half full
kipwaskinê– *VII* be filled to the lid, be full to the brim
kisêwâtisi– *VAI* be kind, be of compassionate disposition; *(fig.)* be full of grace
kîspo– *VAI* have one's fill, be full with food
kîspôh– *VTA* feed s.o. until full, get s.o. (e.g., horse) fully fed
matwê– *IPV* audibly, visibly; perceptibly; in full view, in plain sight
sâkaskinahtâ– *VAI* make (it) full, fill (it) (e.g., audio-tape)
têpinêhamaw– *VTA* make full payment for (it/him) to s.o.
têpipayi– *VAI* have the full amount, put away enough; have enough, have a sufficiency; have enough of (it)
wâsakâ– *IPC* around a circle, in a full circle
wâsakâm– *IPC* around a circle, in a full circle
wâsakâyâskon– *VTA* point s.o. (e.g., pipe) around a full circle
FULLY
iyawis– *IPC* fully, entirely; the whole lot, the entire household; *(in negative constructions:)* only partially, not exclusively
kîsâpiskiso– *VAI* be completely heated as rock (e.g., in sweat-lodge), be fully heated as rock
mahkipakâ– *VII* be big leaves, be the time of fully grown leaves
mitoni– *IPC* intensively, fully, really
sâpo– *IPV* fully, exhaustively, through and through
têpâpam– *VTA* see plenty of s.o., see s.o. fully
têpi– *IPV* fully, sufficiently, enough
FUMES
âhkwâpahtê– *VII* give off a sharp odour, produce pungent fumes, emit acidic or caustic fumes

FUN
miyawât– *VTI* enjoy s.t., rejoice over s.t.; rejoice, be joyful, have fun
miyawâtamowin– *NI* enjoyment; fun, joyfulness
môcikan– *VII* be fun
môcikihcâsi– *VAI* have some fun with (it); have a little fun
môcikihtâ– *VAI* have fun with (it); have fun, have a good time
môcikipê– *VAI* have fun with alcohol, make merry with alcoholic drink
FUNCTION
itakiso– *VAI* be counted thus, be valued thus; be held in such esteem; be worth so much; have such a function
pimipayi– *VII* move along; run, run along; be on, work, function (e.g., motor, electricity); exist currently, take place
pimipayin– *VII* run, run along; go on, work, function
pimohtêmakisi– *VAI* go, go on, be in use, function
FUNERAL
akot– *VTA* hang s.o. up; place s.o. on a funeral scaffold
nahin– *VTA* bury s.o., hold a funeral for s.o.
FUNGUS
posâkan– *NA* touchwood, tinder fungus
FUNNY
wawiyas– *IPC* funny, amusing
wawiyasinâkosi– *VAI* look funny, look amusing
wawiyasipayin– *VII* be funny, be amusing
wawiyatâcimowinis– *NI* funny little story
wawiyatêyiht– *VTI* find s.t. funny, consider s.t. amusing; be funny about s.t., behave oddly
wawiyatêyim– *VTA* find s.o. funny, consider s.o. amusing; feel joy about s.o.
FUR
–pîway– *NDI* body-hair of animal, fur
ahtay– *NA* pelt, fur
FURNITURE
âpacihcikan– *NI* tool, appliance, machine; equipment, furnishings, furniture
FURTHER
awasitê– *IPC* further over there

kiyâm *IPC* oh well, never mind, so much for this; anyway, rather; let it be, let there be no further delay; please
konita *IPC* in vain, without reason, without purpose, for nothing; without further ado; anywhere, at random, in a random place
mosci-nôhâwaso– *VAI* simply breastfeed one's child, breastfeed one's child without further ado (e.g., sterilisation of bottles)
sôskwâc *IPC* simply, immediately, without further ado; without regard to the consequences; *(in negative constructions:)* not at all

FUTURE
–nîkânîm– *NDI* one's future
ati nîkân *IPC* in the future
niyâk *IPC* in the future
nîkân *IPC* first, at the head, in front, in the lead; as a first step; in future
nîkâniwi– *VII* be ahead, be the future; lie in the future

GALL
–îsopiy– *NDI* gall bladder; gall, bile

GALLON
pêyak-tipahôpân *IPC* one gallon of alcoholic drink (e.g., wine)

GAMBLE
mêtawê– *VAI* play; gamble

GAME
asawâpi– *VAI* be on the lookout; look out for game
minaho– *VAI* kill game, make a kill
môs-ôkimâw– *NA* game warden
nâciwanihikanê– *VAI* fetch game from traps, check one's traps

GARDEN
kiscikânis– *NI* garden
kiscikêsi– *VAI* plant seeds; have a small garden
kistikân– *NI* garden, field, farm, arable land
pîwi-kiscikânis– *NA* garden seed
pîwi-kiscikânis– *NI* vegetable garden
takahkikihtâ– *VAI* make (it) grow nicely, make (it) a nice garden; have a nice garden

GARMENT
kinwâpêkan– *VII* be a long garment, be a long piece of paper; be a long saw-blade, be a long saw
osîhtamowinihkê– *VAI* have a garment made, have clothes made

GARTERS
sîskêpison– *NI* garters

GATHER
mawiso– *VAI* pick berries, gather berries
mâwacih– *VTA* collect s.o. (e.g., pounded meat), gather s.o. up; save s.o.
mâwacihtâ– *VAI* collect (it), gather (it) up
mâwacisôniyâwê– *VAI* gather up money, pile up money
mâwacîhito– *VAI* collect one another, gather
mâwasakon– *VTA* gather s.o. up, collect s.o. (e.g., spruce-gum)
môsahkin– *VTA* gather s.o. up
môsahkin– *VTI* gather s.t. up

GATHERING
mâmawôpayi– *VAI* get together as a group, have a gathering

GENERATION
kâsispô– *VAI* reach beyond, exceed; survive into another generation
kâsispôhtêmakan– *VII* go on, reach beyond, exceed; survive into another generation

GENEROUS
sawêyim– *VTA* be generous towards s.o.; bless s.o.

GENTLY
pêyâhtik *IPC* quietly, gently, softly, slowly

GHOST-DANCE
wâsakâmêsimo– *VAI* dance the ghost-dance, participate in the ghost-dance
wâsakâmêsimowikamikw– *NI* ghost-dance lodge; ghost-dance
wâsakâmêsimowin– *NI* ghost-dance

GIFT
aspatot– *VTA* accompany one's request of s.o. with a gift
moscitôn *IPC* gratuitously by speech, without adding a gift or offering

GIRDLE
sîhtwahpisoso– *VAI* be braced, wear a girdle

GIRL
–oskinîkiskwêm– *NDA* young woman; hired girl
iskwêsis– *NI* girl, little girl, female infant
iskwêsisiwi– *VAI* be a little girl
iskwêwisîh– *VTA* dress s.o. as a girl, dress s.o. as a female
oskinîkiskwêsisiwi– *VAI* be a young girl (about 10-12 years old)
oskinîkiskwêwisi– *VAI* be a young girl (about 10-12 years old)

GIVE

âpacihtamôh– *VTA* make s.o. use (it/him), give (it/him) to s.o. to use; use (it/him) for s.o., use (it/him) on s.o.

mêki– *VAI* give (it/him) out as present; give (it/him) away, release (it/him); give (her) in marriage

mêkiskwêwê– *VAI* give a woman in marriage; give (her) in marriage

minah– *VTA* give s.o. to drink (e.g., tea, soup); give s.o. tea to drink; give s.o. an alcoholic drink, induce s.o. to drink an alcoholic drink

miy– *VTA* give (it/him) to s.o.

miyikowisi– *VAI* be given (it/him) by the powers

miyito– *VAI* give (it/him) to one another

mîcisôh– *VTA* give s.o. to eat, make s.o. eat

mosci-mêki– *VAI* simply give (her) in marriage

mosci-miy– *VTA* merely give (it/him) to s.o.

nîmihitowinihkê– *VAI* hold a dance, hold a dance ceremony; give a dance, organise a (secular) dance

pahkwênamaw– *VTA* pay a part of (it/him) to s.o., make partial payment to s.o.; parcel (it/him) out to s.o., give s.o. a share

pakicî– *VAI* let go, give up; release (it/him), let go of (it/him)

pakitin– *VTA* set s.o. down, allow s.o., permit s.o.; permit (it) to s.o., give permission to s.o.; let s.o. go, release s.o. (e.g., fish-spawn into lake), stock a lake with s.o. (e.g., fish); drop s.o. off (e.g., as an airplane)

pakitin– *VTI* let s.t. go, allow s.t., permit s.t.; release s.t.; give s.t. up, abandon s.t. (e.g., teaching, tradition); put s.t. down on earth; put s.t. in (e.g., seed potatoes)

pasakwâpisimowinihkê– *VAI* give a shut-eye dance, hold a shut-eye dance

GIVE UP

pômê– *VAI* be discouraged, be disappointed; give up

pômêh– *VTA* discourage s.o., disappoint s.o.; cause s.o. to give up

GIVE-AWAY

pakitinâso– *VAI* hold a give-away ceremony

pakitinâsowin– *NI* give-away ceremony

GLAD

miywêyiht– *VTI* consider s.t. good, like s.t.; be glad, be pleased

takahkêyiht– *VTI* think well of s.t., be glad about s.t., like s.t.; be glad, be pleased

GLANCE

âpasâpi– *VAI* look back, glance back

GLAND

–iyihkos– *NDA* gland

GLASSES

–skîsikos– *NDI* spectacles, glasses

oskîsikohkâ– *VAI* wear glasses

GLITTER

wâsihkopayi– *VAI* glitter (e.g., wedding-ring)

GLOVE

astis– *NA* mitten, glove

GLUE

pasakwahw– *VTA* glue s.o. down (e.g., figure cut out in paper)

GO

itohtê– *VAI* go there or thus

nitawi *IPV* go to, go and

niyâ *IPC* go!

pimohtê– *VAI* go along, walk along

GOAL

taskamohtê– *VAI* cut across, walk straight towards one's goal

GOD

kisê-manitow– *NA* God the kind, the compassionate God; *(name:)* Merciful God

kisê-manitowi-pîkiskwêwin– *NI* God's word

manitow– *NA* spirit; *(name:)* God

manitowi-masinahikan– *NI* God's book, bible

GOLD

osâwi-sôniyâwâpiskw– *NA* gold, yellow gold

sôniyâw– *NA* gold, silver; money; wages

sôniyâwâpiskw– *NA* gold; copper

GONE

awînipan *IPC* all gone, no longer present

mêscipayi– *VAI* be exhausted (e.g., snow), be gone entirely (e.g., snow)

GOOD

kakêhtawêyiht– *VTI* have good ideas about s.t.; be intelligent beyond one's years; be sensible

kanawêyihtamâso– *VAI* guard (it/him) closely for oneself, take good care of (it/him) oneself

miyo *IPV* good, well, beautiful, valuable

miyo-kakêskihkêmowin– *NI* good counselling, good preaching

miyo-kîkway *PR* something good, good things

miyo-kîsikâ– *VII* be good weather, be mild weather

miyo-nôcihtâ– *VAI* pursue good things; *(in negative constructions:)* pursue evil things, engage in bad medicine

miyo-pimâciho– *VAI* make a good life for oneself, live well; lead a proper life

miyo-pimâtisi– *VAI* llive a good life, live well; lead a proper life

miyo-pîkiskwêwin– *NI* good speech; *(fig.)* the good news of the bible

miyo-sôniyâhkê– *VAI* make good money; earn good wages

miyo-tôt– *VTI* do s.t. good; do a good thing

miyo-tôtamowin– *NI* good deed, good works

miyo-tôtaw– *VTA* do s.o. good, affect s.o. beneficially, do s.o. a good turn

miyokihtâ– *VAI* be good at growing (it)

miyomahciho– *VAI* fare well, be in good health or spirit; feel well, feel healthy; feel pleased

miyonâkohcikê– *VAI* be seen to be good at things, make things look nice, make things look prosperous

miyonâkwan– *VII* look good, have a nice appearance, look prosperous

miyosi– *VAI* be good, be beautiful

miyosîhtâ– *VAI* make (it) good, make (it) beautiful

miyoskaw– *VTA* *(especially in inverse constructions:)* go through s.o. to good effect, have a salutary effect on s.o., make s.o. well

miyô– *VAI* be good at (it)

miyw-âyâ– *VAI* be well, be in good health; have a good life

miywakihtê– *VII* be considered good; *(in negative constructions:)* be considered bad, be considered evil

miywakiso– *VAI* be considered good, be well esteemed; fetch a good price (e.g., tree)

miywâpacih– *VTA* use s.o. well, make good use of s.o., find s.o. useful

miywâpacihtâ– *VAI* use (it) well, make good use of (it)

miywâpatisi– *VAI* be of good use, be useful

miywâsin– *VII* be good, be valuable; *(in negative constructions:)* be bad, be evil

miywêyiht– *VTI* consider s.t. good, like s.t.; be glad, be pleased

miywêyim– *VTA* consider s.o. good, like s.o.; be pleased with s.o.

môcikihtâ– *VAI* have fun with (it); have fun, have a good time

nahî– *VAI* be adept at (it), be good at (it); be competent, be an expert

nitaka *IPC* it is a good thing, by a narrow escape

takahkatimw– *NA* good horse, beautiful horse

takahki *IPV* nice, good, beautiful

takahkipah– *VTA* make s.o. feel good, cause s.o. to be light-headed with an alcoholic drink, get s.o. inebriated

takahkipê– *VAI* feel good with drink, be light-headed with alcoholic drink, be inebriated

wîhkasin– *VAI* taste good

wîhkasin– *VII* taste good

wîhkimâkwan– *VII* smell good, give off a pleasant odour; have an aromatic odour

wîhkitisi– *VAI* taste good (e.g., beaver, fish, bannock)

GOOD AT

nihtâ *IPV* good at, doing much of, competent, practised, experienced

nihtâwâcimo– *VAI* be a good storyteller, tell stories expertly

nihtâwêyiht– *VTI* be good at thinking of s.t.; be knowledgeable; be innovative

nihtâwikwâso– *VAI* be good at sewing, sew expertly, be an experienced seamstress; do fancy sewing

nihtâwikwât– *VTI* be good at sewing s.t., sew s.t. expertly

nihtâwiminakinikê– *VAI* be good at sewing on beads

nihtâwisimo– *VAI* be good at dancing, be an expert dancer

nihtâwisîhcikê– *VAI* be good at doing things, make beautiful things

nihtâwitêpo– *VAI* be good at cooking, be an expert cook

nihtâwîhcikê– *VAI* be good at doing things, make beautiful things

GOOD-NATURED
miyohtwâ– *VAI* be good-natured, be of pleasant character

GOOSE
nisk– *NA* goose

GOPHER
anikwacâs– *NA* squirrel; gopher
miscanikwacâs– *NA* gopher
wâpiskatayêw– *NA* gopher

GOSSIP
âyimôhto– *VAI* discuss one another; gossip about one another
âyimôhtowin– *NI* discussing one another; gossiping about one another, gossip
âyimôm– *VTA* discuss s.o.; gossip about s.o.
âyimômiso– *VAI* discuss oneself; speak unguardedly about oneself, gossip about oneself
âyimôt– *VTI* speak of s.t., discuss s.t.; gossip about s.t.

GOVERN
tipêyihcikâtê– *VII* be owned, be controlled, be governed
tipêyimiso– *VAI* control oneself, govern oneself; be on one's own, be one's own boss

GOVERNMENT
kihc-ôkimâw– *NA* king; *(fig.)* government; royalty

GRAB
otihtin– *VTA* grab s.o., seize s.o.
otihtin– *VTI* grab s.t., seize s.t.

GRACE
kakwê *IPV* try to, attempt to; circumstances permitting, by divine grace
kisêwâtisi– *VAI* be kind, be of compassionate disposition; *(fig.)* be full of grace
kisêwâtisiwin– *NI* kindness, compassion; *(fig.)* grace

GRADUALLY
ati *IPC* gradually, progressively
âstê-ayâ– *VAI* recover from illness, have one's condition improve, be gradually restored
nisihkâc *IPC* slowly, gradually

GRAIN
cimacikê– *VAI* stook sheaves of grain, do one's stooking
kiscikânis– *NA* grain, seed
kistikân– *NA* grain, seed; sheaf of grain; oats

GRAINS
pîwên– *VTA* scatter s.o. (e.g., sugar), sprinkle s.o. (e.g., sugar) in small grains

GRANARY
kistikânikamikw– *NI* granary
okistikânikamiko– *VAI* have a granary

GRANDCHILD
–osk-âyim– *NDA* young people, children, grandchildren, the young
–ôsisim– *NDA* grandchild; *(fig.)* young person
oyôsisimi– *VAI* have a grandchild; have (her/him) as one's grandchild
oyôsisimimâw– *NA* a grandchild

GRANDFATHER
–mosôm– *NDA* grandfather, grandfather's brother; *(fig.)* old man, respected elder

GRANDMOTHER
–ôhkom– *NDA* grandmother, grandmother's sister, "great-aunt"; *(fig.)* old woman; Our Grandmother
oyôhkomi– *VAI* have a grandmother, have a grandmother living; have (her) as one's grandmother

GRANDPARENT
–kêhtê-ayim– *NDA* old person, parent, grandparent; elder

GRANT
kiskêyihtamôhikowisi– *VAI* be granted knowledge by the powers
manitowih– *VTA* grant s.o. supernatural power
nahêyihtamih– *VTA* cause s.o. to be satisfied with (it/him); grant s.o. peace of mind

GRASS
maskosiy– *NI* grass, hay; *(plural:)* reeds; pieces of sod
maskosîs– *NI* grass, hay; blade of grass

GRATEFUL
atamih– *VTA* make s.o. grateful, make s.o. indebted, please s.o.
atamim– *VTA* make s.o. grateful by speech, please s.o. by speech
nanâskom– *VTA* be grateful to s.o., give thanks to s.o.
nanâskomo– *VAI* be grateful, give thanks
nanâskot– *VTI* be grateful for s.t., give thanks for s.t.

GRATUITOUSLY
moscitôn *IPC* gratuitously by speech, without adding a gift or offering

GREASE
âhkwaci-pimiy– NI hard grease, solid grease
iyinico-pimîs– NI ordinary grease
iyinito-pimiy– NI ordinary grease
pimîwi– VII be grease, be greasy
tômâ– VII be greased, be greasy

GREAT
kihci IPV greatly; formally
mistahi IPN great

GREAT-AUNT
–ôhkom– NDA grandmother, grandmother's sister, "great-aunt"; *(fig.)* old woman; Our Grandmother

GREAT-GRANDCHILD
–âniskocâpânis– NDA great-grandchild
–âniskotâpân– NDA great-grandchild
–câpân– NDA great-grandchild

GREATLY
kakwâhyaki IPV greatly, extremely, tremendously, to an extraordinary extent
kakwâhyakih– VTA do a terrible thing to s.o., mistreat s.o. greatly
kihci IPV greatly; formally
miscahîs IPC quite greatly, quite a bit
misi IPV big, greatly
mistahi IPC greatly, very much so, very many
nipahi IPV deadly, terribly, greatly
sôhkahât IPV greatly, vigorously, powerfully

GREAVES
sîkosâkan– NA cracklings, greaves

GREEN
oskaskosîwinâkwan– VII look green, have the appearance of fresh shoots

GREEN LAKE
kwâkopîwi-sâkahikanihk INM *(place-name:)* Green Lake (Saskatchewan)

GREEN-FEED
asamastimwân– NA green-feed, oats

GREET
atamiskaw– VTA greet s.o., shake hands with s.o.

GRIEVE
mihtât– VTA deplore the loss of s.o., sorely miss s.o., grieve for s.o.
pîkiskât– VTA long for s.o., grieve for s.o.
pîkiskâtisi– VAI be lonesome, grieve

GRIND
pîkinatah– VTI grind s.t. to powder
tâsah– VTI grind s.t. (e.g., bone needle) to a point by tool
tâsahikâkê– VAI grind things with (it), use (it) to grind things

GROUND
ay-atâmaskamik IPC inside the earth, beneath the ground
ayâwahkahw– VTA bury s.o. in the ground
cahcakwahcâsin– VII be a small piece of level ground
kanâtahcâ– VII be clean ground, be clean land
kotâwiciwan– VII sink into the ground, run into the ground (e.g., water)
kotâwipayi– VAI rapidly sink into the ground (e.g., into bog or quicksand)
mohcihk IPC on the bare floor, on the bare ground
sâkawanêhtâ– VAI push (it) to emerge from the ground, make (it) come forth
sâkikin– VII grow forth, emerge from the ground

GROUP
asikâpawi– VAI stand about as a loose group
mâmaw-âyamihâ– VAI pray as a group, participate in a religious rite as a group, celebrate mass as a group; go on a pilgrimage as a group
mâmawatoskê– VAI work together as a group, work as a team
mâmawêyati– VAI be together as a group, be together in numbers
mâmawihkwâmi– VAI sleep together as a group, share a mattress
mâmawôhk– VTI work together at s.t. as a group; engage in a joint effort
mâmawôhkamâto– VAI work together at (it/him) as a group; do things together, help one another, cooperate
mâmawôpayi– VAI get together as a group, have a gathering
mâmawôpi– VAI sit as a group, get together; hold a meeting
takwâwahito– VAI bring one another to arrive, arrive as a group
wîcihiwê– VAI join in, be along, participate, be part of a group

GROW
kiyipikin– VII grow quickly
kîs-ôhpiki– VAI complete one's growing up, reach adulthood, be grown up

mahkipakâ– *VII* be big leaves, be the time of fully grown leaves
miyoki– *VAI* grow well
miyokihtâ– *VAI* be good at growing (it)
môniyâw-ôhpiki– *VAI* grow up like a White person
nayawaciki– *VAI* grow up to reach various ages, be variously grown up
nihtâwikin– *VII* grow forth (e.g., plant), come forth
ohpiki– *VAI* grow up, grow
ohpikih– *VTA* make s.o. grow up, raise s.o.
ohpikihâwaso– *VAI* make one's children grow up, raise one's children
ohpikihito– *VAI* make one another grow up, raise one another
ohpikihtamaw– *VTA* make (it/him) grow for s.o., raise (it/him) for s.o.
ohpikihtamâso– *VAI* make (it/him) grow for oneself, raise (it/him) for oneself
ohpikihtâ– *VAI* make (it) grow
ohpikin– *VII* grow up, grow
ohpikinâwaso– *VAI* make one's children grow up, raise one's children
sâkikin– *VII* grow forth, emerge from the ground
takahkikihtâ– *VAI* make (it) grow nicely, make (it) a nice garden; have a nice garden
wîc-ôhpikîm– *VTA* grow up together with s.o., be raised together with s.o.
wîpâcikin– *VII* grow out of place, grow wild, grow as weeds
GRUDGE
nânitaw itêyiht– *VTI* worry about s.t., fret about s.t.; assign blame for s.t.; *(especially in negative constructions:)* not bear a grudge, be forgiving
GUARD
kanawêyiht– *VTI* keep s.t., look after s.t., take care of s.t.; store s.t., preserve s.t.; guard s.t. closely
kanawêyihtamâso– *VAI* guard (it/him) closely for oneself, take good care of (it/him) oneself
kanawêyihtamôh– *VTA* make s.o. guard (it/him) closely; ask s.o. to look after (it/him), leave (it/him) to be looked after by s.o., get s.o. to babysit (her/him)
kanawêyihtâkwan– *VII* be kept, be looked after, the taken care of; be stored, be preserved; be closely guarded

kanawêyim– *VTA* keep s.o., look after s.o., take care of s.o.; guard s.o. closely
kanawêyimiwê– *VAI* look after people; guard people (e.g., girls) closely
GUARDIAN
âtayôhkan– *NA* spirit being, dream guardian
âtayôhkanakiso– *VAI* be held to be a spirit being, be recognised as a dream guardian
GUESS
êtokwê *IPC* presumably, I guess
GUIDE
mitimê– *VAI* track along a trail, follow a trail; *(fig.)* follow a path, be guided in one's life
miyohtah– *VTA* guide s.o. well
nâtakâsin– *VTI* guide s.t. (e.g., boat) to shore
pamih– *VTA* tend to s.o., look after s.o.; attend s.o. in childbirth, serve as midwife to s.o.; guide s.o. (e.g., sleigh), drive s.o. (e.g., sleigh)
pimohtah– *VTA* take s.o. along, go along with s.o., guide s.o. along; carry s.o. along, sustain s.o.
sîhkim– *VTA* urge s.o. by speech, encourage s.o. by speech; guide s.o. by speech
GUM
pasakoskiw– *NA* tree-gum, gum
pikiw– *NA* spruce-gum, gum
GUN
matwêwê– *VII* be heard as a gunshot, be the report of a gun
matwêwêhtâ– *VAI* detonate (it); shoot off one's gun
nîmâskwê– *VAI* carry a weapon; carry a gun
pâskisikan– *NI* gun
GUTS
–itâmiyaw *NDI* innards, guts
–takisiy– *NDI* intestines, guts, entrails
HABITUALLY
âhkosiski– *VAI* be habitually sick, be sickly
itwêski– *VAI* say thus habitually, always say thus
kiyâskiski– *VAI* habitually tell lies, be a liar
kîskwêpêski– *VAI* be habitually crazy with alcoholic drink, be habitually drunk
mâna *IPC* usually, habitually
minihkwêski– *VAI* habitually abuse alcohol, be an alcoholic

papâmitisahikêski– *VAI* habitually follow people about
HAIL
miskwamiy– *NA* ice, hail
HAILSTONES
miskwamîwâpoy– *NI* melted ice, melting hailstones
HAIR
–êscakâs– *NDI* hair
–êstakay– *NDI* hair
–stikwân– *NDI* head; head of hair; mind
itawêhikê– *VAI* wear one's hair thus
kisîpêkistikwânâkê– *VAI* wash one's head with (it), use (it) to wash one's hair
kisîpêkistikwânê– *VAI* wash one's head, wash one's hair
mihkostikwânê– *VAI* have red hair, be red-haired
sêkaho– *VAI* comb one's hair
sêkipatwâ– *VAI* braid one's hair, have braided hair, wear braids
wâpistikwânê– *VAI* have white hair; have light hair, be blond
HALF
âkwâtaskinê– *VAI* be quite full (e.g., pail), be more than half full
âpihtaw *IPC* half, in half, halfway
âpihtaw-tipahikan *IPC* half-hour, for half an hour
HALF-AND-HALF
ay-âpihtaw *IPC* half-and-half
HALF-HEARTEDLY
iyisâc *IPC* half-heartedly, resistingly
HALFBREED
âpihcaw-âyis– *NA* halfbreed, Métis
âpihtawikosisân– *NA* halfbreed, Métis
âpihtawikosisânaskiy– *NI* halfbreed settlement, Métis settlement
âpihtawikosisânôcênâs– *NI* little halfbreed town, Métis settlement
HALFWAY
âkwâc *IPC* well on its way, a long ways, more than halfway
âpihtaw *IPC* half, in half, halfway
âpihtawanohk *IPC* at the halfway point
âpistaw-âyihk *IPC* at the halfway point
HAMMER
pakamâkanis– *NI* hammer
wiyatah– *VTI* pound s.t., hammer s.t. together

HAND
–cihciy– *NDI* hand; paw (e.g., bear)
atamiskaw– *VTA* greet s.o., shake hands with s.o.
âh-âyin– *VTI* touch s.t. repeatedly, rub across s.t. by hand
âsônamaw– *VTA* pass (it/him) across to s.o., pass (it/him) on to s.o.; hand (it/him) down to s.o., bequeathe (it/him) to s.o.
itisinamaw– *VTA* thus hold (it/him) for s.o., thus hand (it/him) over to s.o.
îwâsên– *VTI* turn s.t. down by hand (e.g., by turning a knob), dim the light, turn s.t. too low
kihciniskihk *IPC* on the right hand, to the right
kisîwên– *VTI* turn s.t. (e.g., radio) loud by hand
kîkawin– *VTA* mix s.o. (e.g., tobacco) together by hand
kîskicihcêpit– *VTA* tear s.o.'s hand off
kwêskinisk *IPC* the other hand, changing one's hand
mâkon– *VTA* press upon s.o. by hand, press s.o.'s hand; push s.o. down (e.g., button on radio)
mâkon– *VTI* press upon s.t. by hand
miyoniskêhkât– *VTI* accomplish s.t. by the work of one's hands
mosci-kisîpêkinikê– *VAI* simply wash things, do one's laundry by hand
mosci-masinah– *VTI* simply write s.t., write s.t. down by hand
moscicihcên– *VTI* scoop s.t. up with bare hands
moscikwâso– *VAI* sew by hand
moscikwât– *VTI* sew s.t. by hand
namahtinihk *IPC* on the left hand, to the left
nîsôhkiniskê– *VAI* use two hands, use both hands
tâwin– *VTI* encounter s.t. by hand, come upon s.t., bump into s.t.
wâstinikê– *VAI* signal by hand, wave
wâwâstinamaw– *VTA* wave at s.o., signal to s.o. by hand
HAND-SAW
mosci-kîskipotâ– *VAI* simply cut (it) with a saw, cut (it) with a hand-saw
HANDIWORK
osîhcikêwin– *NI* what is made, handiwork, product

HANDLE
miyawâkâtinikê– *VAI* take particular care with things, handle ritual objects with particular care

HANDSOME
takahkâpêwi– *VAI* be a handsome man

HANG
akocikan– *NI* rack for hanging up fish or meat, storage-rack; cupboard, shelf
akocikê– *VAI* hang things up, hang up one's laundry
akocin– *VAI* hang, be suspended; hang in a swing, hang in a snare
akociwêpin– *VTA* throw s.o. to hang, throw s.o. to be suspended; throw s.o. over top (e.g., onto willow bushes)
akohcin– *VAI* hang in the water, be suspended in water
akot– *VTA* hang s.o. up; place s.o. on a funeral scaffold
akotâ– *VAI* hang (it) up; hang up one's snare, set one's snare
akotê– *VII* hang, be suspended
akwâwê– *VAI* hang sheets of meat on drying rack
âsipayin– *VII* move down, hang down, be dragged down
ispâhkêkocin– *VII* rise high up, hang high aloft, be suspended high in the air
itakocin– *VAI* hang thus or there, be suspended thus or there; fly thus or there
itakotâ– *VAI* hang (it) thus or there, suspend (it) thus or there
itakotê– *VII* hang thus or there, be suspended thus or there
nîpitêkotâ– *VAI* hang (it) up in a row, hang (it) up in a line
sâkakocin– *VAI* hang so as to project, hang out of the sky (e.g., snake)
waskitakotâ– *VAI* hang (it) on top, hang (it) over

HANGER-ON
pakosih– *VTA* beg from s.o.; be a hanger-on to s.o., go with s.o., be part of s.o.

HAPPEN
ihkin– *VII* happen thus; occur, take place
ispayih– *VTA* affect s.o. thus, happen thus to s.o.
kâkêswân *IPC* as it happens, by coincidence

HAPPY
môcikêyiht– *VTI* be happy about s.t., be excited about s.t.; be excited

HARASS
kwatakatot– *VTA* meanly order s.o. around, harass s.o.
pisiskêyim– *VTA* pay attention to s.o., take notice of s.o., tend to s.o.; bother s.o., harass s.o.

HARD
âhkwaci-pimiy– *NI* hard grease, solid grease
âyimî– *VAI* have a difficult time, have a difficult task; have a hard life
kakâyawâciho– *VAI* live an active life; work hard in one's life, lead an industrious life
kakâyawâtisi– *VAI* be active; be hard-working, be of industrious disposition
kakâyawi *IPV* actively; by working hard, industriously
kakâyawisî– *VAI* be active; be hard-working, be industrious
kakwâtakatoskê– *VAI* work dreadfully hard, do punishing work
manâhkwatatahw– *VTA* peel s.o. hardened off (e.g., spruce-gum)
maskawâ– *VII* be hard (e.g., fat); be strong, be sturdy
mistikwâhkatotê– *VII* be as hard as wood, be as solid as wood
sôhkatoskê– *VAI* work vigorously, work hard
sôhkêsimo– *VAI* dance hard, dance vigorously

HARDLY
mwâsi *IPC (in negative constructions:)* hardly ever, hardly any

HARM
mâyi-tôtaw– *VTA* do evil to s.o., harm s.o., make s.o. sick, put a curse on s.o.
mâyinikê– *VAI* act badly, do harmful things; experience bad things, come to harm
mâyinikêhkâto– *VAI* act badly towards one another, harm one another
opawâkanêyâspinat– *VTA* harm s.o. by means of dream spirits

HARMONY
miyo-wîcêhto– *VAI* get along well with one another, live in harmony with one another
wîcêhtowin– *NI* living with one another; getting along with one another, living in harmony with one another

HARNESS
atimotâpânêyâpiy– *NI* dog harness

nîswahpiso– *VAI* be harnessed as two, be a team of two, be yoked together
pêyakwahpit– *VTA* harness s.o. singly
wiyahpicikê– *VAI* harness one's horse; harness up
wiyahpit– *VTA* harness s.o. (e.g., horse)

HARPOON
cîstahikan– *NI* spear, harpoon

HARROW
sikwahcisikê– *VAI* cultivate, harrow

HAT
amiskwayânêscocinis– *NI* beaver-pelt hat
ascocinis– *NI* little hat, little cap; infant's bonnet
astotin– *NI* hat, cap
kêtastotinê– *VAI* take one's hat off

HATCH
wîtapiht– *VTI* sit by s.t.; hatch one's eggs (e.g., bird)

HATCHET
cîkahikanis– *NI* small axe, hatchet

HATE
pakwât– *VTA* hate s.o., dislike s.o., disapprove of s.o.
pakwât– *VTI* hate s.t., dislike s.t., disapprove of s.t.
pakwâtamaw– *VTA* hate (it/him) for s.o., dislike (it/him) for s.o., disapprove of (it/him) for s.o.

HAUL
âwacikê– *VAI* haul things, do one's hauling
âwacimihtê– *VAI* haul firewood
âwacipit– *VTI* haul s.t. by pulling
âwacitâpê– *VAI* haul (it/him) by dragging
âwatamâso– *VAI* haul (it/him) for oneself
âwatâ– *VAI* haul (it)
âwatôpê– *VAI* haul water, haul one's drinking water
kwâpikê– *VAI* dip out water, draw water, haul water, obtain one's drinking water
nâtâwatâ– *VAI* fetch (it) by hauling
pêtâwatâ– *VAI* haul (it) hither
pîhtikwê-âwacimihtêwin– *NI* hauling firewood indoors

HAVE
ayâ– *VAI* have (it)
ayâw– *VTA* have s.o.

HAY
maskosiy– *NI* grass, hay; *(plural:)* reeds; pieces of sod
maskosîhkê– *VAI* make hay
maskosîs– *NI* grass, hay; blade of grass
nâtaskosiwê– *VAI* fetch hay
wîscihkânis– *NI* hay-pile
wîscihkêsi– *VAI* pile hay into small heaps
wîstihkê– *VAI* pile hay into heaps

HAY-WAGON
âwataskosiwâkan– *NA* hay-wagon

HAZY
kaskâpahtê– *VII* be smoked; be smoky, be hazy

HE
wiya *PR* he, she
wîsta *PR* he, too; she, too; he by contrast, she by contrast; he himself, she herself

HEAD
–scikwân– *NDI* head
–scikwânis– *NDI* head
–stikwân– *NDI* head; head of hair; mind
âkwaskiskaw– *VTA* head s.o. off, get in s.o.'s way
kisîpêkistikwânâkê– *VAI* wash one's head with (it), use (it) to wash one's hair
kisîpêkistikwânê– *VAI* wash one's head, wash one's hair
kwêtatêyitiskwêyi– *VAI* be at a loss as to where to turn one's head; be at a loss for a response
nawakiskwêsimo– *VAI* dance with one's head down
nânâmiskwêyi– *VAI* nod one's head
nîkân *IPC* first, at the head, in front, in the lead; as a first step; in future
nîkânapi– *VAI* be at the head, be in the lead, be in charge; hold the office of director
nîkâni– *VAI* be at the head, be in the lead, take precedence (e.g., tobacco); be the prime element
nîkânîh– *VTA* place s.o. (e.g., tobacco) at the head, place s.o. in the lead
nîkânîst– *VTI* be at the head of s.t., lead s.t.
nîkânîstamaw– *VTA* be in the lead of s.o., be at the head of s.o., be a leader amongst s.o.
pîmiskwêyi– *VAI* turn one's head sideways, twist one's neck (e.g., owl)

sâkiskwêpayiho– VAI suddenly stick one's head out
tapâtiskwêyi– VAI hold one's head low, lower one's head
têyistikwânê– VAI have one's head hurt, have a headache
wîhkwêskaw– VTA go around s.o., head s.o. off

HEAD-SCARF
wêwêkiscikwânêhpisonis– NA head-scarf

HEADACHE
têyistikwânê– VAI have one's head hurt, have a headache

HEADLONG
pimakocin– VII make a rush in linear fashion, charge headlong

HEAL
iyinîhkah– VTA heal s.o.
nanâtawih– VTA treat s.o., doctor s.o.; heal s.o., cure s.o.
nanâtawihiwê– VAI treat people, doctor people; heal people, cure people
nanâtawihwâkê– VAI doctor oneself with (it), use (it) to heal oneself, use (it) medicinally

HEALING
nanâtawihitowin– NI doctoring one another; healing one another, curing one another

HEALTH
is-âyâ– VAI be thus in health; be unwell, be in poor health; be out of sorts, have something being the matter
itamahciho– VAI feel thus, be in such health
mâyamahciho– VAI feel poorly, be in ill health
miyomahciho– VAI fare well, be in good health or spirit; feel well, feel healthy; feel pleased
miyw-âyâ– VAI be well, be in good health; have a good life

HEAR
itiht– VTI hear s.t. thus
itihtaw– VTA hear s.o. thus
nahiht– VTI hear s.t. sharply; have acute hearing
pakahkihtaw– VTA hear s.o. clearly
pêht– VTI hear s.t.
pêhtaw– VTA hear s.o.
saskacihtaw– VTA be tired of hearing s.o., be fed up with hearing s.o.

HEARD
itihtâkosihkâso– VAI pretend to be heard making such a noise, act as if to make such a noise
itihtâkwan– VII be thus heard, sound thus
matwêwê– VII be heard as a gunshot, be the report of a gun
nitohtâkowisi– VAI be heard by the powers, be listened to by the powers
pêhtamowin– NI what one has heard
pêhtâkosi– VAI be heard, make oneself heard, make noise
pêhtâkwan– VII be heard

HEART
–cêhis– NDI heart
–têh– NDI heart; (fig.) heart, soul
wîsakitêhê– VAI (fig.) experience heart-ache, have a heavy heart

HEART-ACHE
wîsakitêhê– VAI (fig.) experience heart-ache, have a heavy heart

HEARTH-FIRE
iskotêw– NI fire, hearth-fire

HEAT
kâspihkas– VTI heat s.t. until crisp, heat s.t. until brittle; dry s.t. by heat until crisp
kâspis– VTI heat s.t. until crisp, heat s.t. until brittle
kisâkamis– VTI heat s.t. as liquid
kisâkamisikê– VAI heat a liquid; boil water for tea, make tea
kisâpiskisw– VTA heat s.o. as rock (e.g., in sweat-lodge)
kisis– VTI warm s.t. up, heat s.t. up
kisitê– VII be warmed up, be heated up, be hot; be a hot compress
kîsâpiskiso– VAI be completely heated as rock (e.g., in sweat-lodge), be fully heated as rock
nêstwâso– VAI be tired by the sun's heat, be exhausted by hot weather
ocipôhkahtê– VII shrink from heat
pâs– VTI dry s.t. by heat (e.g., meat, berries, moss)
pâsikâtê– VII be dried by heat
pâsw– VTA dry s.o. (e.g., rabbit) by heat
titipawêhkas– VTI curl s.t. (e.g., head) by heat; have a perm

HEATER
awasowi-kotawânâpiskw– NI warming-stove, heater
awaswâkan– NI heater

ENGLISH INDEX 293

HEAVE
pimwasinât– *VTA* throw (it/him) at s.o., heave (it/him) at s.o.
pimwasinê– *VAI* throw (it), heave (it)
HEAVEN
kihci-kîsikw– *NI* heaven
kîsikohk *IPC* in the sky; *(fig.)* in heaven
HEAVY
kosikwan– *VII* be heavy
wîsakitêhê– *VAI (fig.)* experience heart-ache, have a heavy heart
HEEL
–ahkwan– *NDI* heel
mistikwaskisin– *NI* heeled shoe, oxford
HEIGHT
iskosi– *VAI* extend so far, be so long, be so tall, be of such height
HELP
mâmawôhkamâto– *VAI* work together at (it/him) as a group; do things together, help one another, cooperate
nâtâmost– *VTI* flee to s.t., turn to s.t. for help, seek refuge in s.t.
nâtâmotot– *VTI* flee to s.t., turn to s.t. for help, seek refuge in s.t.
nâtâmototaw– *VTA* flee to s.o., turn to s.o. for help, seek refuge with s.o.
wîcih– *VTA* help s.o.
wîcihikowisi– *VAI* be helped by the powers
wîcihiso– *VAI* help oneself; apply oneself, study for oneself; rely on oneself in childbirth
wîcihito– *VAI* help one another, cooperate with one another
wîcihtâso– *VAI* help with things
wîcôhkamaw– *VTA* help s.o. by doing (it)
HELPING
mâmawi-wîcihitowin– *NI* all helping together, general cooperation
HERB
macipakw– *NI* herb; leaves, lettuce
maskihkiy– *NI* herb, plant; seneca-root; medicinal root; medicine; chemicals
HERBAL
maskihkîwâpôhkatiso– *VAI* prepare an herbal infusion for oneself; make a medicinal drink for oneself
maskihkîwâpôhkê– *VAI* prepare an herbal infusion; make tea

HERE
âstam *IPC* come here!
nanânis *IPC* variously, in bits and pieces, here and there
ôta *IPC* here
ôtê *IPC* over here, hither
papâ *IPV* around, about, here and there
papâmatoskê– *VAI* go about working, work here and there
papâmi *IPV* around, about, here and there
papâmipici– *VAI* move about, travel around, camp here and there, move around with one's camp
papâmohtah– *VTA* take s.o. about, take s.o. here and there, go about with s.o.
papâmohtatâ– *VAI* take (it) about, take (it) here and there, go about with (it)
papâmohtê– *VAI* walk about, go about, go here and there; run around, be promiscuous
pâh-pahki *IPC* here and there
HESITATE
mamihtisihkâso– *VAI* act proudly, hold back, hesitate with one's response
HIDDEN
âkaw-âyihk *IPC* hidden, out of view, behind an obstacle to vision
HIDE
kâcikê– *VAI* hide things
kâciwêpin– *VTI* throw s.t. so as to hide it
kâso– *VAI* hide, hide oneself
kât– *VTA* hide s.o.
mihkit– *VTI* scrape s.t. (meat) off the hide
misipocikê– *VAI* run hide over a sharp edge
pahkêkino-mîkiwâhp– *NI* skin-lodge, lodge made from hides
pahkêkinohkê– *VAI* prepare one's skins, dress one's hides; make dressed hides, make leather
pahkêkinos– *NI* small dressed hide, small piece of leather
pahkêkinw– *NI* dressed hide, tanned hide, finished hide, leather; tent-cover
pahkêkinw– *NA* raw hide
pahkêkinwêskisin– *NI* hide moccasin
pahkêkinwêtâs– *NA* hide leggings, hide trousers, hide pants
wayân– *NA* hide, skin

HIDE-SCRAPINGS
otamiskay– *NI* hide-scrapings (meat scraped from hide)

HIGH
ispastâ– *VAI* place (it) so high, pile (it) so high
ispâhkêkocin– *VII* rise high up, hang high aloft, be suspended high in the air
ispâhkêpayi– *VAI* reach a high level, be elevated (e.g., blood-sugar)
ispâhkêpit– *VTA* pull s.o. high up, pull s.o. high into the sky (e.g., snake)
ispâhkwanêyâ– *VII* be high-heeled (e.g., shoe)
ispimihk *IPC* high up, up above; upstairs
ispisîh– *VTA* make s.o. (e.g., cracklings being boiled) come up so high
kîhcêkosî– *VAI* climb high up, climb to a high place
kîhcêkosîw-ôhpî– *VAI* jump to a high place
kîhcêkosîwi *IPV* high up, towards a high place
kihkâtêyihtâkwan– *VII* be held in high esteem, be prominent
kihkâtêyim– *VTA* hold s.o. in high esteem
mis-âyamihâ– *VAI* hold mass, celebrate high mass
nîhtakocin– *VAI* descend from high up, fall down (e.g., star)
ohpatinâ– *VII* be a high hill
ohpohtât– *VTI* proceed high across s.t. (e.g., sky), rise up upon s.t. (e.g., sun upon sky)
ohpohtê– *VAI* rise up, proceed high in the sky
yôtinw– *NI* wind, high wind, tornado

HIGHLY
ayiwâkêyiht– *VTI* think more of s.t., regard s.t. more highly
ayiwâkêyim– *VTA* think more of s.o., regard s.o. more highly
ispîhtêyimiso– *VAI* think so highly of oneself
kihcêyiht– *VTI* think highly of s.t., hold s.t. in high regard, respect s.t.; hold s.t. sacred
kihcêyihcikâtê– *VII* be highly thought of, be respected; be held sacred
kihcêyihtamaw– *VTA* think highly of (it/him) for s.o.

kihcêyihtâkwan– *VII* be highly thought of, be respected; be held sacred
kihcêyim– *VTA* think highly of s.o., hold s.o. in high regard, respect s.o.; hold s.o. sacred

HILL
ayah– *VTI* cover s.t. with earth; hill s.t. (e.g., potatoes)
ayahikê– *VAI* cover things with earth, hill things (e.g., potatoes)
âmaciwê– *VAI* go uphill, ascend a hill
ispacinâs– *NI* small hill
ispacinâsin– *VII* be a small hill
ispatinâ– *VII* be a hill
ispatinâw– *NI* hill
nîhc-âyihk *IPC* down, downward; below; down the hill
ohpatinâ– *VII* be a high hill

HILLER
ayahikâkan– *NI* hiller, tool for covering potatoes with earth

HILLSIDE
osêhcâ– *VII* be a rise in the land, be a slope, be a gentle hillside
osêhcâw– *NI* rise in the land, slope, gentle hillside

HIND
otânihk *IPC* on one's hind part

HIRE
atoskah– *VTA* make s.o. work, employ s.o., hire s.o.
atoskêmo– *VAI* get people to do things, employ people, hire people
masinahikêh– *VTA* hire s.o., employ s.o.

HIRED
–oskinîkiskwêm– *NDA* young woman; hired girl
–oskinîkîmis– *NDA* young man; hired man
atoskahâkan– *NA* employee, hired man

HIT
pakamah– *VTI* strike s.t., hit s.t.; pound s.t. (e.g., meat); type s.t., type s.t. out
pakamahw– *VTA* hit s.o., strike s.o.; pound s.o. (e.g., earring)
pistah– *VTI* knock s.t. down inadvertently, hit s.t. accidentally
pistahw– *VTA* knock s.o. down inadvertently, hit s.o. accidentally
tâwin– *VTA* encounter s.o., come upon s.o., bump into s.o., hit s.o.

HITTING
nakâwâskwêsin– *VAI* be brought to a stop by hitting a tree

HOBBEMA
maskwacîsihk *INM (place-name:)* Hobbema (Alberta)
opîma *INM (place-name:)* Hobbema (Alberta)

HOBBLED
nânapwahpiso– *VAI* have one's forelegs tied together (e.g., horse), be hobbled

HOLD
asiskîhkê– *VAI* mud a log-house, do the mudding, hold a mudding bee
ayamihâ– *VAI* pray, say prayers; hold a church service, celebrate mass; participate in a religious rite, go to church; follow a religion
âyîtin– *VTI* hold fast onto s.t., hold on tightly to s.t.
cahkon– *VTA* carry s.o. small, hold s.o. small
isistâ– *VAI* hold such a rite, perform a rite thus
itakiht– *VTI* count s.t. thus, value s.t. thus, hold s.t. in such esteem; charge so much for s.t.
itakim– *VTA* count s.o. thus, value s.o. thus, hold s.o. in such esteem
itâskonikê– *VAI* thus point the pipe or pipestem; thus hold a pipe ceremony
itikwamikohkê– *VAI* hold such a lodge, hold such a rite
itin– *VTI* hold s.t. thus
itisinamaw– *VTA* thus hold (it/him) for s.o., thus hand (it/him) over to s.o.
kihcêyiht– *VTI* think highly of s.t., hold s.t. in high regard, respect s.t.; hold s.t. sacred
kihcêyim– *VTA* think highly of s.o., hold s.o. in high regard, respect s.o.; hold s.o. sacred
kihcikanisi– *VAI* hold a rite; spend Christmas
kisât– *VTI* stay with s.t., hold fast to s.t.; stay, stay back
kitin– *VTA* hold s.o. back
kîhkâtêyim– *VTA* hold s.o. in high esteem
kosâpaht– *VTI* hold a shaking-lodge, hold the shaking-lodge ceremony
matotisah– *VTA* make s.o. hold a sweat-lodge
matotisi– *VAI* hold a sweat-lodge
mâmawôpi– *VAI* sit as a group, get together; hold a meeting

mâmawôpîtot– *VTI* meet about s.t., hold a meeting about s.t.
micimâskwahw– *VTA* hold s.o. in place as or by wood
micimin– *VTA* hold on to s.o.; hold s.o. in place
micimin– *VTI* hold on to s.t.; hold s.t. in place
miciminamaw– *VTA* hold on to (it/him) for s.o.
miciminamôh– *VTA* make s.o. hold on to (it/him)
micimoskowahtâ– *VAI* make (it) hold together with mud, mud (it) with clay
mis-âyamihâ– *VAI* hold mass, celebrate high mass
nahin– *VTA* bury s.o., hold a funeral for s.o.
nânitaw itêyim– *VTA* hold (it) against s.o.; *(especially in negative constructions:)* not bear a grudge against s.o., forgive s.o.
nipâkwêsimowinihkê– *VAI* hold a sundance
nîkânakim– *VTA* count s.o. in first position, hold s.o. (e.g., tobacco) to be the prime element
nîkânapi– *VAI* be at the head, be in the lead, be in charge; hold the office of director
nîmihitowinihkê– *VAI* hold a dance, hold a dance ceremony; give a dance, organise a (secular) dance
nîmin– *VTI* hold s.t. aloft, offer s.t. up
nîminamaw– *VTA* hold (it/him) aloft for s.o., offer (it/him) up for s.o.
nîminikê– *VAI* hold things aloft, offer things up
nîpêpi– *VAI* sit up late at night with (her/him) (e.g., someone near death); hold a wake, take part in a wake
nîpêpîstaw– *VTA* sit up late at night with s.o.; sit at s.o.'s bedside, sit with s.o. near death; sit at a wake for s.o., hold a wake for s.o.
ohcih– *VTA* fight s.o. over (it/him); hold s.o. off
ohpâskwah– *VTI* raise s.t. (e.g., cloth) on a wooden pole, hold s.t. aloft on a wooden pole
otin– *VTA* take s.o., take s.o. in (e.g., orphan); choose s.o.; steal s.o.; *(especially in inverse constructions:)* take hold of s.o., possess s.o.
pakitinâso– *VAI* hold a give-away ceremony

pasakwâpisimowinihkê– *VAI* give a shut-eye dance, hold a shut-eye dance
pîhtwâ– *VAI* smoke, use the pipe; smoke (him) (e.g., pipe); hold a pipe ceremony; be a nicotine addict
sâkihtamaw– *VTA* hold on to (it/him) for s.o.; hold (it/him) back from s.o.
tahkon– *VTA* carry s.o., hold s.o.
tahkon– *VTI* carry s.t., hold s.t.
tahkonamôh– *VTA* make s.o. carry (it/him), make s.o. hold (it/him)
tahkonâwaso– *VAI* hold one's child, cuddle one's child
tahkwam– *VTA* hold s.o. fast by mouth, hold s.o. in one's mouth
tapâtiskwêyi– *VAI* hold one's head low, lower one's head
tâpwêwakêyiht– *VTI* hold s.t. to be true, believe in s.t.; regard s.t. positively
wiyasiwât– *VTA* decide about s.o.; sit in judgment on s.o., hold court over s.o.
wîhkohkât– *VTI* hold a feast for s.t. (e.g., medicinal herbs)
wîhkohkê– *VAI* hold a feast
wîhkohkêh– *VTA* hold a feast for s.o., hold a feast in s.o.'s honour

HOLE
mônâtihkê– *VAI* dig around, dig a hole
pakwanêh– *VTI* make a hole in s.t.; drill a hole
payipis– *VTI* cut s.t. out, cut a hole in s.t.
pôhtâskwah– *VTI* stick s.t. wooden into a hole; clean out one's ear, poke one's ear
pôskwahikâso– *VAI* have a hole punched, have oneself pierced
pôskwahw– *VTA* punch a hole in s.o. (e.g., in the reaches under a wagon)
pôskwatahw– *VTA* punch a hole in s.o. (e.g., earring), punch a hole in s.o.
wâtihkân– *NI* hole, cellar
wâtihkât– *VTI* make a hole for s.t., dig a hole for s.t.
wâtihkê– *VAI* make a hole, dig a hole
yahkâtihkât– *VTI* dig out more of a hole or cellar, push out the size of an existing hole or cellar

HOLLER
têpwê– *VAI* call out, shout, holler, yell

HOLY
ayamihêwi-saskamon– *NA* the host; Holy Communion

kihci-wîkihtowin– *NI* formal marriage, Holy Matrimony
kihcihtwâwi *IPN* of exalted character; venerable, holy

HOME
–îk– *NDI* house, dwelling, home
api– *VAI* sit, sit down; be situated, be present, stay; be at home, be available
kîwê *IPV* back, towards home
kîwê– *VAI* go home, return home
kîwêhtah– *VTA* take s.o. home, carry s.o. home, go home with s.o.
kîwêhtatamâkê– *VAI* take (it/him) home for people
kîwêhtatâ– *VAI* take (it) home, carry (it) home, go home with (it)
kîwêmakan– *VII* return home, come back
kîwêpayi– *VAI* drive home, drive back, ride home, ride back
kîwêtâpê– *VAI* drag (it) home
kîwêtisahw– *VTA* drive s.o. back, drive s.o. home
kîwêtot– *VTI* return home to s.t.
kîwêtotaw– *VTA* return home to s.o.
owîki– *VAI* live there, dwell there, have one's home there
pêtôpê– *VAI* bring an alcoholic drink hither, bring an alcoholic drink home or into the house
pîhcikwah– *VTA* take s.o. small indoors, go indoors with s.o. small; bring s.o. small (e.g., infant) home
tako-kîskwêpê– *VAI* arrive intoxicated with alcoholic drink, arrive inebriated, come home drunk
wîki– *VAI* live there, dwell there, have one's home there
wîkiwin– *NI* household; *(fig.)* home

HOME-MADE
mosc-ôsîh– *VTA* prepare s.o. (e.g., soap) without instrument; make s.o. (e.g., soap) at home
mosc-ôsîhcikâtê– *VII* be made by hand, be home-made
mosc-ôsîhtâ– *VAI* prepare (it) without instrument; make (it) at home

HOMESTEAD
otinaskê– *VAI* take land, settle the land, homestead

HOMEWORK
kiskinohamâkosiwin– *NI* being a student, going to school; schoolwork, homework

HONOUR
 wîhkohkêh– *VTA* hold a feast for s.o., hold a feast in s.o.'s honour
HOOFPRINT
 tahkoskê– *VAI* step, take a step, step upon, make a hoofprint
HOOT
 kâh-kito– *VAI* hoot (e.g., owl); be thunder
 kito– *VAI* utter a sound, call, sing (e.g., bird); make noises (e.g., animal), hoot; be a thunderclap
HORSE
 –têm– *NDA* dog; horse
 asamastimwê– *VAI* feed one's horses
 atimw– *NA* dog; horse
 ayiwêpihastimwê– *VAI* give one's horses a rest, rest one's horses
 âyimisîwatimw– *NA* wild horse, difficult horse
 mihcêtwastimwê– *VAI* have many horses
 misatimw– *NA* horse
 misatimwâyow– *NI* horse-tail; tail-hair of a horse
 mistatimw– *NA* horse
 nitawastimwê– *VAI* look for one's horses, search for one's horses
 otêhtapîwatimomi– *VAI* have a horse; have (him) for one's horse
 pamihastimwê– *VAI* drive one's horses
 pêyakw-âya *IPC* one team of horses, a single team of horses
 sipwêtâpâso– *VAI* leave with a team of horses, drive off by wagon
 takahkatimw– *NA* good horse, beautiful horse
 takahkipicikê– *VAI* drive a nice team, drive beautiful horses
 wâpastimw– *NA* white horse
 wiyahpicikê– *VAI* harness one's horse; harness up
HORSE-BARN
 misatimokamikw– *NI* horse-barn
 mistatimokamikw– *NI* horse-barn
HORSE-DUNG
 mistatimo-mêy– *NI* horse-dung
HORSE-HIDE
 misatimwayân– *NA* horse-hide
HORSE-TAIL
 misatimwâyow– *NI* horse-tail; tail-hair of a horse

HORSEBACK
 takopayi– *VAI* arrive on horseback, arrive driving, arrive by vehicle
 têhtapi– *VAI* be mounted, ride on horseback
HOSPITAL
 âhkosîwikamikw– *NI* hospital
 wayawî– *VAI* go outside, go outdoors; go to relieve oneself; leave school, leave hospital
HOST
 ayamihêwi-saskamon– *NA* the host; Holy Communion
 saskamonahiso– *VAI* give oneself communion, place the host into one's mouth
 saskamowin– *NI* host (e.g., in communion)
HOT
 kisâkamitêhkwe– *VAI* drink a hot liquid, have a hot drink
 kisâkamitêwâpoy– *NI* hot water
 kisâstê– *VII* be hot weather
 kisiso– *VAI* be warm, be hot; run a fever, be febrile
 kisitê– *VII* be warmed up, be heated up, be hot; be a hot compress
 nêstwâso– *VAI* be tired by the sun's heat, be exhausted by hot weather
HOTEL
 kapêsîwikamikw– *NI* inn, hotel
HOUR
 âpihtaw-tipahikan *IPC* half-hour, for half an hour
 nîso-tipahikan *IPC* two hours, for two hours
 pêyak-tipahikan *IPC* one hour
 tânitahto-tipahikan *IPC* what hour, what time; so many hours, that time; several hours
HOUSE
 –îk– *NDI* house, dwelling, home
 asahkêwikamikw– *NI* ration house
 asahtowikamikw– *NI* ration house
 kanawâpokê– *VAI* look after a household, keep house
 kanâtapi– *VAI* live in a clean house
 kayâsi-wâskahikan– *NI* old house, traditional house
 napakikamikos– *NI* little house made of lumber or boards
 napakikamikw– *NI* house made of lumber or boards; flat-top shack
 pêtôpê– *VAI* bring an alcoholic drink hither, bring an alcoholic drink home or into the house

pêyakwapi– VAI stay alone, be alone in the house
wâskahikan– NI house
wâskahikanihkê– VAI build a house
wâskahikanis– NI little house; shack, temporary building, trailer; play-house
wîhkwêhtakâw– NI corner made by wooden walls, corner of the floor, corner of the house

HOUSEHOLD
ispici– VAI move thus or there with one's camp, move one's household there
iyawis IPC fully, entirely; the whole lot, the entire household; *(in negative constructions:)* only partially, not exclusively
kanawâpokê– VAI look after a household, keep house
môniyâw-âpacihcikan– NI White apparatus, White household appliance
paskê– VAI branch off, go off to the side; set up a separate household
piskihci-wîki– VAI live separately, dwell separately, have a separate household
tipiyawêho– VAI live in one's own dwelling, have one's own household
wîkiwin– NI household; *(fig.)* home

HOUSEMATE
–wîkimâkan– NDA spouse, housemate
wîtokwêm– VTA share a dwelling with s.o., live with s.o., have s.o. as one's housemate

HOW
anis îsi IPC in that way; that is how it is
êkos îsi IPC thus, just so, in that way; that is how it is
ômis îsi IPC in this way; this is how it is
pikoyikohk IPC to any extent, no matter how much
tânimatahto IPC how many; so many, several
tânimatahtw-âskîwinê– VAI be how many years old; be so many years old
tânimayikohkêskamik IPC to which extent, for how long
tânisi IPC how, in what way
tânitahto IPC how many; so many
tânitahto-kîsikâw IPC how many days; so many days; several days
tânitahto-nîpin IPC how many summers; so many summers, a few summers
tânitahto-pîsim IPC how many months; so many months
tânitahtw-âskiy IPC how many years; so many years
tânitahtw-âya IPC how many kinds; so many kinds
tânitahtwayak IPC in how many places; in so many places
tânitahtwâw IPC how many times; so many times

HOWL
mawimohkê– VAI howl (e.g., dog)
oyoyo– VAI howl (e.g., dog, wolf)

HUDDLED
nawakapi– VAI sit bent down, sit huddled over
pitikwapi– VAI sit huddled together

HUDSON'S BAY COMPANY
Hudson's-Bay-ayiwinis– NI Hudson's Bay Company clothes, store-bought clothing
kihc-âtâwêwikamikowiyiniw– NA store manager, post manager, Hudson's Bay Company factor
kihc-âtâwêwikamikw– NI Hudson's Bay Company store
mistikôsiw– NA Frenchman, Hudson's Bay Company manager

HUG
âkwaskitin– VTA embrace s.o., hug s.o.
âkwaskitinito– VAI embrace one another, hug one another

HUMAN
–îcayisiyiniw– NDA fellow person, fellow human
ayisiyiniw– NA person, human being, people
ayisiyinîwi– VAI be a person, be a human being
ayisiyinîwin– NI being human, human existence
nâpêwinâkosi– VAI look like a man; be of human appearance

HUMBLE
pîwêyimo– VAI think little of oneself, have low self-esteem; *(fig.)* be humble

HUNDRED
mitâtahtomitanaw IPC one hundred
mitâtahtomitanaw-maskimot IPC a hundred bags, one hundred bags

HUNGRY
nipahâhkatoso– VAI starve to death, die from starvation; *(fig.)* be terribly hungry

nôhtêhkatê– VAI be hungry, suffer want of food
HUNT
mâcî– VAI hunt, go hunting
mâcîtotaw– VTA hunt for s.o.
mâcîwâkê– VAI hunt with (it/him), use (it/him) to hunt
mâcîwihkomân– NI hunting knife
mâcîwin– NI hunting, the hunt
nôcih– VTA pursue s.o., hunt for s.o. (e.g., animal); go after s.o., oppress s.o., beat s.o. up, fight with s.o.
nôcihcikê– VAI trap things, do one's trapping; do one's hunting
nôcihtâ– VAI pursue (it), work at (it); do one's hunting, hunt
nôcisipê– VAI hunt ducks, be engaged in duck-hunting
HUNTER
omâcîw– NA hunter
ominahowiyiniw– NA hunter; provisioner
HUNTING-KNIFE
mistihkomân– NI hunting-knife
HURRY
kakwêyâho– VAI hurry, hurry up
papâsi IPV fast, in a hurry
papâsim– VTA hurry s.o. by speech
papâtinikê– VAI hurry hither and thither, chase about
HURT
kitimahiso– VAI be mean to oneself, treat oneself cruelly; hurt oneself
manâcih– VTA be protective about s.o., be careful about s.o., spare s.o.; avoid hurting s.o.; treat s.o. with respect
manâcihito– VAI be protective about one another, be careful about one another; avoid hurting one another
moskâcih– VTA bother s.o., trouble s.o., hurt s.o.
nipahâhkwan– VII be terribly strong, be terribly powerful, hurt terribly
têyistikwânê– VAI have one's head hurt, have a headache
wîsakisin– VAI get hurt in a fall
HUSBAND
–kisêyinîm– NDA old man, husband
–nâpêm– NDA husband
–sis– NDA mother's brother, father's sister's husband; father-in-law, father-in-law's brother, "uncle"
–tawêmâw– NDA male parallel cousin (woman speaking); female cross-cousin's husband (woman speaking)

onâpêmi– VAI have a husband, be married (woman), have a husband living; get married (woman); have (him) as one's husband
HYMNS
ayamihêwi-nikamo– VAI sing hymns
nêhiyawi-nakamo– VAI sing hymns in Cree
I
niya PR I
nîsta PR I, too; I by contrast; I myself
ICE
miskwamiy– NA ice, hail
miskwamîs– NA a little ice (e.g., crushed ice, ice-cubes)
miskwamîwâpoy– NI melted ice, melting hailstones
IDEA
kakêhtawêyiht– VTI have good ideas about s.t.; be intelligent beyond one's years; be sensible
wiyêyiht– VTI have an idea, think of what to do
IDENTITY
kayâsi-nêhiyâwin– NI traditional Creeness, traditional Cree identity
nêhiyâwiwin– NI being Cree, Cree identity, Creeness
IF
ahpô piko IPC even if; and yet
itihtâkosihkâso– VAI pretend to be heard making such a noise, act as if to make such a noise
kanakê IPC at least, even if only
kîspin IPC if
kîspin êkâ ohci IPC if it were not for
tâpiskôc IPC as if; seemingly, apparently
yâhk îtâp IPC as if, pretendingly
IGNORE
patahôhkât– VTA overlook s.o., fail to notice s.o., ignore s.o.
ILL
âhkosi– VAI be sick, be ill; have contractions, be in labour
itâspinê– VAI be ill thus, suffer from such a disease
mâtahpinê– VAI begin to be ill, fall ill
mâyamahciho– VAI feel poorly, be in ill health
mâyipayi– VAI fare badly, suffer ill; suffer a death, be bereaved, have a death in the family; be bereaved of (her/him)
mâyiskaw– VTA go through s.o. to bad effect, affect s.o. negatively, fail to

agree with s.o.; *(especially in inverse constructions:)* have an adverse effect on s.o., make s.o. ill
ohcinê– *VAI* be ill on account of (it), suffer for (it); suffer in retribution
oskaninê– *VAI* be ill with arthritis, suffer from arthritis
sôkâwâspinê– *VAI* be ill with diabetes, suffer from diabetes, be a diabetic
taspinê– *VAI* be ill for such a time, be ill for the duration

ILLEGITIMATE
kimotôsê– *VAI* bear an illegitimate child

ILLNESS
âhkosiwin– *NI* illness
âstê-ayâ– *VAI* recover from illness, have one's condition improve, be gradually restored
iskwânê– *VAI* be left behind after a widespread illness, survive an epidemic
nihtâ-âhkosi– *VAI* fall sick easily, be prone to illness

IMITATOR
okiskinowâpiw– *NA* one who learns merely by watching, mere imitator

IMMEDIATE
cîkâhtaw *IPC* close, nearby, in the area, in the immediate vicinity

IMMEDIATELY
nama mayaw *IPC* not immediately, later; too late
sêmâk *IPC* right away, immediately, instantly
sôskwâc *IPC* simply, immediately, without further ado; without regard to the consequences; *(in negative constructions:)* not at all
tâpwê piko *IPC* straight away, immediately

IMMERSE
akohcim– *VTA* immerse s.o. in water (e.g., baby)
kohtân– *VTA* immerse s.o. (e.g., a piece of ice) in liquid, dunk s.o. into liquid
pakâhcikê– *VAI* immerse things in water; boil things in water
pakâhtâ– *VAI* immerse (it) in water; boil (it) in water
pakâhtê– *VII* be immersed in water; be boiled in water
pakâsim– *VTA* immerse s.o. in water; boil s.o. (e.g., rabbit) in water
pakâsimo– *VAI* be immersed, swim, have a bath
pakâsimonah– *VTA* immerse s.o., bathe s.o.
pakâsimonahâwaso– *VAI* immerse one's child, bathe one's child
pakâso– *VAI* be immersed in water; be boiled in water

IMPATIENT
ihkêyiht– *VTI* be tired of s.t.; be impatient

IMPLORE
mawimostaw– *VTA* cry out in prayer to s.o., wail before s.o., implore s.o.; worship s.o.

IMPORTANT
kihci-kîkway *PR* something important, big things
kihci-masinahikan– *NI (fig.)* important book; bible
sôhkan– *VII* be strong, be sturdy; be important; *(fig.)* be powerful, have supernatural power

IMPOSE
itasiwât– *VTA* decide thus with respect to s.o.; give s.o. such a command; impose such laws on s.o.
itasiwê– *VAI* decide thus for people, make such a plan for people; give such a command, impose such laws
kaskih– *VTA* prevail upon s.o., succeed in imposing one's will on s.o.; be able to deal with s.o.; earn s.o. (e.g., money)
mâyi-tôt– *VTI* do s.t. evil; do a bad thing, impose a curse

IMPRESSION
itiskwêhkê– *VAI* act thus as a woman; give the impression of being such a woman
kakâmwâtiskwêhkê– *VAI* act quietly as a woman; give the impression of being a quiet woman

IMPROVE
âstê-ayâ– *VAI* recover from illness, have one's condition improve, be gradually restored

IN LIEU
ciyêkwac *IPC* instead, in lieu

IN VAIN
konita *IPC* in vain, without reason, without purpose, for nothing; without further ado; anywhere, at random, in a random place

INADVERTENTLY
kitiskin– *VTA* inadvertently drop s.o., let s.o. fall by awkwardness
pistah– *VTI* knock s.t. down inadvertently, hit s.t. accidentally

ENGLISH INDEX 301

pistahw– *VTA* knock s.o. down inadvertently, hit s.o. accidentally
pistiskaw– *VTA* knock s.o. down inadvertently (by foot or body movement)
INAUGURATE
osîhtâ– *VAI* prepare (it), make (it); put (it) in service (e.g., hospital), inaugurate (it)
INCENSE
miyâhkasikâkê– *VAI* cense with (it), use (it) to cense with, use (it) as incense
INCLINED
wêpêyim– *VTA* be inclined to throw s.o. (e.g., money) away
INCOME
sôniyâhkêwin– *NI* earning money; wages; income
INCOMPLETELY
nôhtaw *IPC* less; minus; previously; prematurely, incompletely, short of attainment
INCOMPREHENSIBLE
mâmaskât– *VTA* find s.o. strange, find s.o. incomprehensible, marvel at s.o.
mâmaskât– *VTI* find s.t. strange, find s.t. incomprehensible, marvel at s.t.
INCREASINGLY
tahk âyiwâk *IPC* increasingly, more and more
INDEBTED
atamih– *VTA* make s.o. grateful, make s.o. indebted, please s.o.
pîkwasinahikê– *VAI* be loaded down with debt, be indebted in several places
INDEED
ahâw *IPC* now indeed! ready! let's go!
ani *IPC* then, indeed, surely
êcik âni *IPC* as it turns out, apparently, evidently, indeed
êkos âni *IPC* thus indeed
kosa *IPC* indeed
ohcitaw *IPC* expressly, specifically, purposely, necessarily; it is requisite, it is meet indeed
tâpwê *IPC* truly, indeed
INDIAN
iskonikan– *NI* reservation, Indian reserve
nêhiyaw– *NA* Cree; Indian
nêhiyaw-mihkw– *NI* Cree blood; Indian blood
nêhiyawaskamikâ– *VII* be Cree land, be Cree terrain; be Indian land, be Indian terrain

nêhiyawaskîwin– *VII* be Cree land, be Cree territory; be Indian land, be Indian territory
nêhiyawayisiyiniw– *NA* Cree person; Indian person
nêhiyawi *IPN* Cree; Indian
nêhiyawi *IPV* Cree; Indian
nêhiyawi-maskihkiy– *NI* Cree medicine; Indian medicine
nêhiyawi-maskihkîwiskwêw– *NA* Cree midwife; Indian midwife
nêhiyawi-mêskanaw– *NI* Cree path, Cree road; Indian path, Indian road
nêhiyawi-sîwîhtâkan– *NI* Cree salt; Indian salt
nêhiyawi-wîhowin– *NI* Cree name; Indian name
nêhiyawihtwâwin– *NI* the Cree way, Cree culture; Indian culture
nêhiyawisîhcikêwin– *NI* the Cree way, Cree culture; Indian culture
nêhiyawiskwêw– *NA* Cree woman; Indian woman
nêhiyawîhcikêwin– *NI* the Cree way, Cree culture; Indian culture
nêhiyâsis– *NA* young Cree; young Indian
nêhiyâwi– *VAI* be Cree; be an Indian
otasahkêw– *NA* dispenser of rations; Indian agent
sôniyâwikimâw– *NA* Indian agent
INDICATED
kiskinawâcihcikâcêsi– *VII* be marked, be indicated; be decorated (e.g., brooch, barrette)
kiskinowâcihcikâtê– *VII* be marked, be indicated; be decorated
INDISTINCTLY
wani *IPV* indistinctly, blurred
wanisîho– *VAI* be indistinctly dressed, be confusingly dressed, be wrongly dressed
INDIVIDUAL
ministikoskwâ– *VII* be an individual cloud
ministikwaskwâsin– *VII* be an individual small cloud, be an isolated small cloud
INDIVIDUALLY
pâh-pêyak *IPC* singly, one at a time; each one, each individually, each; one each
INDOORS
pîhcikwah– *VTA* take s.o. small indoors, go indoors with s.o. small; bring s.o. small (e.g., infant) home

pîhtikwê-âwacimihtêwin– *NI* hauling firewood indoors

pîhtikwêmakan– *VII* enter, go indoors

pîhtikwêpahtâ– *VAI* run indoors

pîhtikwêwêpin– *VTA* throw s.o. indoors

pîhtikwêyâmo– *VAI* flee indoors

pîhtikwêyâpâwê– *VII* be washed indoors as water, run indoors

pîhtokwah– *VTA* enter with s.o., take s.o. indoors

pîhtokwamik *IPC* indoors

pîhtokwatamâkê– *VAI* take (it/him) indoors for people

pîhtokwatâ– *VAI* take (it) indoors, enter with (it)

pîhtokwê *IPV* indoors

pîhtokwê– *VAI* enter, go indoors

INDUSTRIOUS
kakâyawâciho– *VAI* live an active life; work hard in one's life, lead an industrious life

kakâyawâtisi– *VAI* be active; be hard-working, be of industrious disposition

kakâyawi *IPV* actively; by working hard, industriously

kakâyawisî– *VAI* be active; be hard-working, be industrious

INEBRIATED
takahkipah– *VTA* make s.o. feel good, cause s.o. to be light-headed with an alcoholic drink, get s.o. inebriated

takahkipê– *VAI* feel good with drink, be light-headed with alcoholic drink, be inebriated

tako-kîskwêpê– *VAI* arrive intoxicated with alcoholic drink, arrive inebriated, come home drunk

INEXPENSIVE
wêhtakihtê– *VII* be cheap, be inexpensive

INFANT
–pêpîm *NDA* baby, infant; youngest child

iskwêsis– *NI* girl, little girl, female infant

nâpêsis– *NA* boy, little boy, male infant

opêpîmi– *VAI* have an infant, have a baby; have (her/him) as one's infant; be the mother of an infant; give birth, be delivered

oskawâsis– *NA* young child, infant

pêpîsis– *NA* baby, infant

pêpîwi– *VAI* be a baby, be an infant

INFECT
âsôskamaw– *VTA* infect s.o. with (it)

INFUSION
maskihkîwâpôhkatiso– *VAI* prepare an herbal infusion for oneself; make a medicinal drink for oneself

maskihkîwâpôhkê– *VAI* prepare an herbal infusion; make tea

INGEST
pisc-ôtin– *VTI* accidentally take s.t., accidentally ingest s.t. (e.g., pill)

INHERE
kikiskaw– *VTA* (especially in inverse constructions:) affect s.o., befall s.o.; inhere in s.o., engross s.o.

maci-kikiskaw– *VTA* (especially in inverse constructions:) inhere in s.o. as a bad thing, engross s.o. as an evil

INITIALLY
mâci *IPV* begin to; initially

nistam *IPC* first, at first, for the first time, initially, originally

INJURE ONESELF
cîkahoso– *VAI* chop oneself, injure oneself with an axe

osikôho– *VAI* injure oneself, be injured

INN
kapêsîwikamikw– *NI* inn, hotel

INNARDS
–itâmiyaw– *NDI* innards, guts

INNOVATIVE
nihtâwêyiht– *VTI* be good at thinking of s.t.; be knowledgeable; be innovative

INSECT
manicôs– *NA* insect, bug

sakimêwayânêkin– *NI* mosquito screen, insect screen

INSIDE
asiwacikê– *VAI* put things inside, enclose things, put things into boxes; have things inside; be pregnant

asiwacipayin– *VII* get placed inside, get enclosed; rapidly fill an enclosed space (e.g., water flowing into hoofprint)

asiwah– *VTA* place s.o. (e.g., sugar, fish) inside, enclose s.o.

asiwaso– *VAI* be inside, be enclosed; live inside, dwell inside

asiwatan– *VII* be inside, be enclosed

asiwatâ– *VAI* place (it) inside, enclose (it), put (it) into a bag or container

asiwatê– *VII* be placed inside, be enclosed

atâmihk *IPC* beneath, underneath, inside (e.g., clothing)

ay-atâmaskamik *IPC* inside the earth, beneath the ground
âpotah– *VTI* turn s.t. upside down, turn s.t. inside out
itâmihk *IPC* beneath, underneath, inside (e.g., clothing); inside (e.g., mouth)
pîhc-âyihk *IPC* inside (e.g., fish, house, hat)
pîhci *IPV* in between, inside
pîhciwêpin– *VTI* throw s.t. inside, throw s.t. into a wagon-box
pîhtêyask *IPC* at the central circle of poles inside the dance-lodge

INSISTENTLY
katâc *IPC* insistently; *(in negative constructions:)* not necessarily
kâkatâc *IPC* insistently; *(in negative constructions:)* not necessarily

INSTANCE
mâcika *IPC* for instance

INSTANTLY
sêmâk *IPC* right away, immediately, instantly

INSTEAD
ciyêkwac *IPC* instead, in lieu
ispîhci wiya *IPC* instead of
mêskoc *IPC* instead, in return, in exchange
mêskocikâpawi– *VAI* stand up instead

INSTRUMENT
kitohcikê– *VAI* play a musical instrument; play one's stereo-player
mosc-ôsîh– *VTA* prepare s.o. (e.g., soap) without instrument; make s.o. (e.g., soap) at home
mosc-ôsîhtâ– *VAI* prepare (it) without instrument; make (it) at home
mosci *IPV* simply, directly, without mediation; merely, without instrument; without recompense
mostohtê– *VAI* simply walk, move along without instrument, be on foot

INSUFFERABLY
kakwâtaki *IPV* dreadfully, insufferably

INSUFFLATION
nipiskât– *VTA* doctor s.o. by insufflation or aspiration

INTELLIGENT
kakêhtawêyiht– *VTI* have good ideas about s.t.; be intelligent beyond one's years; be sensible

INTEND
wî *IPV* intend to, be about to

INTENSIVELY
mitoni *IPC* intensively, fully, really

INTENT
mani *IPV* with the intent of, with the purpose of

INTENTLY
iyâyaw *IPC* eagerly, intently; by preference, rather

INTERPRET
itwêstamaw– *VTA* say thus for s.o.; speak for s.o.; interpret for s.o.; transmit s.o.'s message, relay s.o.'s message (e.g., by radio)

INTERPRETER
otitwêstamâkêw– *NA* interpreter; advocate

INTERVALS
tâh-têpi *IPC* at regular intervals
wâh-wîhkâc *IPC* at rare intervals, rarely now and again

INTERVIEW
pîkiskwêh– *VTA* make s.o. speak, get s.o. to speak; interview s.o.

INTESTINES
–takisiy– *NDI* intestines, guts, entrails

INTIMATE
kikisk– *VTI* wear s.t. (e.g., shoe), have s.t. as an intimate possession, carry s.t. in oneself (e.g., blood)
kikiskaw– *VTA* wear s.o. (e.g., ring), have s.o. as an intimate possession (e.g., stocking)

INTOXICATED
tako-kîskwêpê– *VAI* arrive intoxicated with alcoholic drink, arrive inebriated, come home drunk

INTRODUCE
nakiskamohtatamaw– *VTA* take (it/him) to meet s.o., meet s.o. with (it/him); introduce (it/him) to s.o.

INVIGORATING
maskawîskaw– *VTA* *(especially in inverse constructions:)* make s.o. strong in body, have an invigorating effect on s.o.

INVITE
nitom– *VTA* call s.o., beckon to s.o., invite s.o.
wîhkohkêmo– *VAI* invite people to a feast
wîhkohto– *VAI* invite one another to a feast
wîhkom– *VTA* invite s.o. to a feast

ITCHY
kiyakasê– *VAI* have itchy skin, suffer from eczema

JACKET
kispakiwêsâkay– *NI* thick coat, thick jacket

mîkisasâkay– NI beaded coat, beaded jacket
pahkêkinwêsâkay– NI leather coat, leather jacket

JACKFISH LAKE
kinosêwi-sâkahikanihk INM *(place-name:)* Jackfish Lake (Saskatchewan)

JAIL
kipahotowikamikw– NI jail, prison

JEALOUS
kâhkwêyim– VTA be jealous of s.o.
ohtêyim– VTA be jealous of s.o.

JIG
nîsosimo– VAI dance as two; dance a White dance, dance a jig

JOB
atoskêwin– NI work; job; contract (e.g., to complete an assignment)

JOIN
âniskê IPV successively, one joining the other, surviving
takwaskî– VAI arrive on the land, move onto the land, join those already on the land
wîc-âyamihâm– VTA pray together with s.o., join s.o. in prayer
wîcêhto– VAI live with one another, join with one another; get along with one another; breed with one another
wîcêw– VTA accompany s.o., get along with s.o., join s.o., live with s.o.
wîcihiwê– VAI join in, be along, participate, be part of a group
wîkihtah– VTA take s.o. to be married, arrange for s.o. to be married; join s.o. (e.g., a couple) in marriage

JOINTLY
mâmawi IPV collectively, jointly, all together
mâmawôhk– VTI work together at s.t. as a group; engage in a joint effort

JOKE
naniwêyatwê– VAI joke, tell a joke
pâhpih– VTA laugh at s.o., deride s.o.; joke with s.o.

JOSTLE
mâsihito– VAI wrestle with one another, wrestle, jostle one another

JOY
miywêyihtâkwan– VII be joy, be rejoicing
môsko-miywêyiht– VTI cry with joy about s.t.; be moved to tears of joy
wawiyatêyim– VTA find s.o. funny, consider s.o. amusing; feel joy about s.o.

JOYFUL
miyawât– VTI enjoy s.t., rejoice over s.t.; rejoice, be joyful, have fun

JOYFULNESS
miyawâtamowin– NI enjoyment; fun, joyfulness

JUDGMENT
wiyasiwât– VTA decide about s.o.; sit in judgment on s.o., hold court over s.o.

JUMP
kîhcêkosîw-ôhpî– VAI jump to a high place
kwâskwêkotê– VII jump up
nîhcipayiho– VAI jump down, jump off (e.g., vehicle)
pasikô-kwâskohti– VAI jump up from sitting or crouching
pôsi-kwâskohti– VAI jump aboard (e.g., boat or vehicle)
têhcipayiho– VAI jump on (e.g., on a horse)
waniskâpahtâ– VAI jump up (from lying)

JUST
êkos îsi IPC thus, just so, in that way; that is how it is
iyinitohk IPC simply; just as
kanihk IPC oh yes, I just remembered, I had forgotten
katisk IPC just now, a moment ago; recently, a while ago; exactly, just at that moment, at the very moment; *(in negative constructions:)* not merely
kêtisk IPC just barely, to exact measure
kêyiwêhk IPC just in case, nevertheless; despite shortcomings
konit-âcimowinis– NI mere story, simple story, just a little story
mwêsiskaw– VTA have chosen exactly the wrong time or place for s.o., just miss s.o.
nahiyikohk IPC to the proper degree, to the proper extent, just enough, just right, evenly, fittingly, appropriately
wawiyatisi– VAI be deservedly ridiculed, receive one's just deserts

KEEP
canawî– VAI keep busy in various ways
kanawâpokê– VAI look after a household, keep house
kanawêyiht– VTI keep s.t., look after s.t., take care of s.t.; store s.t., preserve s.t.; guard s.t. closely

kanawêyim– VTA keep s.o., look after s.o., take care of s.o.; guard s.o. closely
kanâciho– VAI clean oneself, keep oneself clean
kîsôn– VTA keep s.o. warm, warm s.o. by hand
nâkatawêyim– VTA watch s.o., keep one's mind trained on s.o.
nâkatôhkâtito– VAI take notice of one another, watch over one another, keep a careful eye on one another
os– VTI boil s.t. (e.g., water), keep s.t. at the boil
osw– VTA boil s.o. (e.g., porcupine quills), bring s.o. to the boil, keep s.o. (e.g., cracklings) at the boil
otamih– VTA keep s.o. busy, keep s.o. preoccupied; delay s.o.; *(especially in inverse constructions:)* get in s.o.'s way, be s.o.'s undoing
otamiyo– VAI busy oneself, keep busy, be preoccupied
pimahkamikisi– VAI work along, keep busy
pimipayihtâ– VAI run (it), operate (it) (e.g., machine); keep (it) up, exercise (it)
pônwêwit– VTI cease making noise; keep quiet
waskawîhtâ– VAI keep at (it), keep at one's work

KEPT
kanawêyihcikâtê– VII be kept, be preserved
kanawêyihtâkwan– VII be kept, be looked after, the taken care of; be stored, be preserved; be closely guarded

KETTLE
askihkw– NA kettle, pail; pot
mistaskihkw– NA big kettle, communal cooking pot
pêyakwêskihk IPC one kettle (measure)

KICK
kapatâsiwêpiskaw– VTA kick s.o. ashore, kick s.o. out of the water
tahkiskaw– VTA kick s.o.

KILL
iskwâhito– VAI kill one another off
mêscih– VTA kill s.o. off, annihilate s.o.
minaho– VAI kill game, make a kill
minahôstamaw– VTA kill an animal for s.o., make a kill for s.o.
minahôstamâso– VAI kill an animal for oneself, succeed in a kill

nipah– VTA kill s.o.
nipahcikê– VAI kill things (e.g., game), make a kill
nipahiso– VAI kill oneself, commit suicide
nipahtamaw– VTA kill (it/him) for s.o., make a kill for s.o.
nipahtamâso– VAI kill (it/him) for oneself, make a kill for oneself
nipahtâ– VAI kill (it) (e.g., game), make a kill
nipahtâkê– VAI kill people

KILLED
nipahisin– VAI get killed in a car accident

KIN-TERM
itâhkôm– VTA be thus related to s.o., have s.o. as such a relative, use such a kin-term for s.o.
wâhkôhto– VAI be related to one another, have one another as relatives; use kin-terms for one another
wâhkôm– VTA be related to s.o., have s.o. as one's relative; use a kin-term for s.o.

KIND
êkotowahk IPC of that kind
itowahk IPC this kind
kisê-manitow– NA God the kind, the compassionate God; *(name:)* Merciful God
kisêwâtisi– VAI be kind, be of compassionate disposition; *(fig.)* be full of grace
kitimâkêyihto– VAI feel pity towards one another, think of one another with compassion; take pity upon one another, be kind to one another, love one another
kitimâkêyihtowin– NI feeling pity towards one another, thinking of one another with compassion; taking pity upon one another, being kind to one another, loving one
kitimâkêyim– VTA feel pity towards s.o., think of s.o. with compassion; take pity upon s.o., be kind to s.o., love s.o.
kîkw-ây– NA which one; what kind
kîkwâpoy IPC what kind of liquid
nanâtohk IPC variously, of various kinds
nanâtohkôskân IPC various kinds, all kinds of things
nawac piko IPC sort of, kind of, approximately; more or less; even a little

nêmatowahk *IPC* of that kind yonder
ômatowahk *IPC* of this kind
pikw îtowahk *IPC* of any kind, no matter what kind; of all kinds
tânimatowâhtik *IPC* what kind of tree
tânitahtw-âya *IPC* how many kinds; so many kinds
tânitowahk *IPC* what kind

KINDNESS
kisêwâtisiwin– *NI* kindness, compassion; *(fig.)* grace

KING
kihc-ôkimâw– *NA* king; *(fig.)* government; royalty

KINSMAN
–tôtêm– *NDA* kinsman; friend
otôtêmi– *VAI* have a kinsman or friend; have (her/him) as one's kinsman or friend
oyotôtêmi– *VAI* have a kinsman or friend; have (her/him) as one's kinsman or friend; be friendly

KISS
ocêm– *VTA* kiss s.o.

KITCHEN
piminawasowikamikw– *NI* cookhouse, kitchen

KNEE
–hcikwan– *NDI* knee

KNEEL
ocihcihkwanapi– *VAI* kneel
ocihcihkwanapih– *VTA* make s.o. kneel
ocihkwanapi– *VAI* kneel

KNIFE
mâcîwihkomân– *NI* hunting knife
môhkomân– *NI* knife
môhkomânis– *NI* knife

KNIT
apihkât– *VTA* braid s.o., knit s.o. (e.g., stocking)
apihkât– *VTI* braid s.t., knit s.t.
apihkê– *VAI* braid, knit
apihkêpicikan– *NI* knitting machine
itapihkât– *VTI* braid s.t. thus, knit s.t. thus
itapihkê– *VAI* braid thus, knit thus
kîsapihkât– *VTI* braid s.t. to completion, complete the knitting of s.t.

KNOB
ocipâson– *NA* knob, button (e.g., on radio)

KNOCK
matwêhikâtê– *VII* be a knock; be a drum-beat
pahkwaciwêpah– *VTI* break s.t. off, pry s.t. off (e.g., hide-scrapings), knock s.t. off
pahkwatah– *VTI* break s.t. off, pry s.t. off (e.g., hide-scrapings), knock s.t. off
pistah– *VTI* knock s.t. down inadvertently, hit s.t. accidentally
pistahw– *VTA* knock s.o. down inadvertently, hit s.o. accidentally
pistiskaw– *VTA* knock s.o. down inadvertently (by foot or body movement)

KNOW
kiskêyiht– *VTI* know s.t.; have knowledge
kiskêyihtâkwan– *VII* be known
kiskêyim– *VTA* know s.o.
nisitawêyiht– *VTI* recognise s.t., know s.t.
nisitawêyim– *VTA* recognise s.o., know s.o.
pakwanawahtâ– *VAI* go on with (it) at random, know nothing about (it), be clueless about (it)

KNOWLEDGE
kiskêyiht– *VTI* know s.t.; have knowledge
kiskêyihtamâ– *VAI* have spiritual knowledge
kiskêyihtamôhikowisi– *VAI* be granted knowledge by the powers
môniyâw-kiskêyihtamowin– *NI* White knowledge

KNOWLEDGEABLE
nihtâwêyiht– *VTI* be good at thinking of s.t.; be knowledgeable; be innovative

LABOUR
âhkosi– *VAI* be sick, be ill; have contractions, be in labour

LABOURING
apwêsiwin– *NI* sweating, labouring

LABRADOR TEA
maskêko-*litea* *INM* labrador tea
maskêkwâpoy– *NI* labrador tea

LACE
tâpisah– *VTI* lace s.t. (e.g., mossbag)
wâspit– *VTA* wrap s.o. up in a mossbag, lace s.o. up in a mossbag, swaddle s.o.

LACK
kwîtâpacihtâ– *VAI* be short of (it) to use, lack tools

manêsi– *VAI* run short, be in want; have run out of (it), lack (it)

LADY
–nôtokwêm– *NDA* old lady, wife
kêhtêskwêw– *NA* old woman, old lady
kihc-îskwêwinâkosi– *VAI* look like a great lady

LAKE
akâmihk *IPC* across water, across the lake
sâkahikan– *NI* lake
sâkahikanisis– *NI* small lake
sîwihtâkani-sâkahikan– *NI* salty lake, salt lake
wâwiyêkamâ– *VII* be a round lake

LAMENT
mawîhkât– *VTA* cry out over s.o., lament s.o.
mawîhkât– *VTI* cry out over s.t., lament s.t.

LAMP
wâsaskocêpayîs– *NI* lamp, electric light
wâsaskotawêpi– *VAI* sit with a lamp, have light from a lamp
wâsaskotênikan– *NI* light, lamp, lantern
wâsaskotênikâkê– *VAI* light things with (it), use (it) to have light, use (it) as a lamp

LAND
askiy– *NI* land, region, area; earth, world; settlement, colony, country; Métis settlement; *(plural:)* fields under cultivation, pieces of farmland, the lands
ispisi-wîhkwêhcâhk *IPC* in such a sweep of the land, to the extent of the sweep of this valley
ispîhcâ– *VII* extend thus, reach so far as land, be of such size as country
ispîhtaskamikâ– *VII* extend so far as land
kanâtahcâ– *VII* be clean ground, be clean land
kistikân– *NI* garden, field, farm, arable land
kistikê– *VAI* seed things, plant things, do one's seeding, do one's planting; farm the land
kwêskahcâhk *IPC* on the opposite side of a rise in the land
misiwêskamik *IPC* all over the land, all over the world

nêhiyawaskamikâ– *VII* be Cree land, be Cree terrain; be Indian land, be Indian terrain
nêhiyawaskîwin– *VII* be Cree land, be Cree territory; be Indian land, be Indian territory
nêyâ– *VII* be a point of land
osêhcâ– *VII* be a rise in the land, be a slope, be a gentle hillside
osêhcâw– *NI* rise in the land, slope, gentle hillside
otaskî– *VAI* have land; have (it) as one's land, have (it) as one's territory
otinaskê– *VAI* take land, settle the land, homestead
takwaskî– *VAI* arrive on the land, move onto the land, join those already on the land
twêho– *VAI* alight, land (e.g., bird, airplane)
twêhômakan– *VII* alight, land (e.g., airplane)
wîhkwêhcâ– *VII* go around as land, be curved as land, be the sweep of the valley

LANGUAGE
âkayâsîmowin– *NI* speaking English, the English language
isi-pîkiskwêwin– *NI* speaking thus; such a language
itwêwin– *NI* what is being said, speech; word; language
nahkawêwin– *NI* speaking Saulteaux, the Saulteaux language
nêhiyawêwin– *NI* speaking Cree, the Cree language
pîkiskwêwin– *NI* word, phrase, expression, voice; what is being said; speech, language

LANTERN
wâsaskotê– *VII* be light, be lit; be a lantern
wâsaskotênikan– *NI* light, lamp, lantern

LARD
wâpiski-pimiy– *NI* lard, rendered lard

LARGE
misi-minahikw– *NA* large spruce-tree
mistiyâkan– *NI* big dish, platter, large bowl

LASSO
tâpakwêwêpin– *VTA* lasso s.o.

LAST
aspin *IPC* off, away, from a distance, in departing; since then, the last I knew; back then, so long ago; presumably, evidently

awasi-nîpinohk IPC the summer before last
iskwêyâc IPC to the end, to the last; the last time
nânapêc IPC late, at the last moment, barely in time (e.g., when it should have been done previously); *(in negative constructions:)* too late
piyisk IPC finally, at last
takwâkohk IPC last fall
tipiskohk IPC last night

LATE
âkwâ-tipiskâ– VII be late in the evening
nama mayaw IPC not immediately, later; too late
nânapêc IPC late, at the last moment, barely in time (e.g., when it should have been done previously); *(in negative constructions:)* too late
nîpâhtâ– VAI stay out until late in the night
nîpêpi– VAI sit up late at night with (her/him) (e.g., someone near death); hold a wake, take part in a wake
nîpêpîstaw– VTA sit up late at night with s.o.; sit at s.o.'s bedside, sit with s.o. near death; sit at a wake for s.o., hold a wake for s.o.

LATER
âstamita IPC later, more recently
ici IPC later, subsequently
itâp IPC then, later
kici IPC for then, for later
mwêstas IPC later, subsequently
nama mayaw IPC not immediately, later; too late
pâtimâ IPC no earlier, only later
pâtos IPC only later

LAUGH
kakwâtakâhpi– VAI laugh dreadfully
mosci-pâhpih– VTA merely laugh at s.o., merely deride s.o.
pâhpi– VAI laugh, smile
pâhpih– VTA laugh at s.o., deride s.o.; joke with s.o.
pâhpihtâ– VAI laugh at (it), deride (it)
pâhpîmakan– VII *(fig.)* laugh (e.g., one's heart)

LAUNDROMAT
kisîpêkinikêwikamikw– NI coin laundry, laundromat

LAUNDRY
akocikê– VAI hang things up, hang up one's laundry
ayiwinisis– NI clothes, clothing, laundry
kisêpêkinikê– VAI wash things, do the laundry
kisêpêkinikêwin– NI laundry, doing the laundry
kisîpêkinikêwikamikw– NI coin laundry, laundromat
mosci-kisîpêkinikê– VAI simply wash things, do one's laundry by hand

LAW
itasiwât– VTA decide thus with respect to s.o.; give s.o. such a command; impose such laws on s.o.
itasiwê– VAI decide thus for people, make such a plan for people; give such a command, impose such laws
kîsasiwât– VTI reach a decision about s.t.; complete making a law about s.t.
wiyasiwât– VTI decide s.t.; make a rule or law about s.t.
wiyasiwêwin– NI decision; rule, law; council, band council

LAY
âsosim– VTA lay s.o. to lean against something, lean s.o. against something
owâwi– VAI lay eggs
pimisim– VTA lay s.o. down, put s.o. to bed
sîhkitisahw– VTA urge s.o. along (e.g., horse); lay charges against s.o.

LAYER
âhkwêhtawêskaw– VTA wear s.o. (e.g., socks) over top of one another, wear several layers of s.o. (e.g., socks)
pîhton– VTA take the covering layer off s.o. (e.g., tree), peel s.o.
pîhton– VTI take s.t. (e.g., bark) off as the covering layer, peel s.t. off
pîhtopit– VTA pull the covering layer off s.o. (e.g., tree), peel the bark off s.o.
pîhtopit– VTI pull s.t. (e.g., bark) off as the covering layer, peel s.t. off
pîhtosw– VTA cut the covering layer off s.o. (e.g., tree), cut the bark off s.o.

LAZY
kihtimi– VAI be lazy; be self-indulgent
kihtimikanê– VAI be lazy, be a lazy-bones
nipahikanê– VAI be terribly lazy, be bone-lazy

LEAD
itâpêkin– VTA align s.o. (e.g., porcupine quills) thus (e.g., end-to-end); lead s.o. (e.g., horse) thus or there

itohtah– *VTA* take s.o. (e.g., pelt) there or thus; go there with s.o., lead s.o. there
nîkân *IPC* first, at the head, in front, in the lead; as a first step; in future
nîkânapi– *VAI* be at the head, be in the lead, be in charge; hold the office of director
nîkâni– *VAI* be at the head, be in the lead, take precedence (e.g., tobacco); be the prime element
nîkânîh– *VTA* place s.o. (e.g., tobacco) at the head, place s.o. in the lead
nîkânîmakan– *VII* be in the lead, take precedence
nîkânîst– *VTI* be at the head of s.t., lead s.t.
nîkânîstamaw– *VTA* be in the lead of s.o., be at the head of s.o., be a leader amongst s.o.
nîkânohk *IPC* in the lead position
nîkânohtatâ– *VAI* be in the lead with (it), carry (it) in the lead
nîkânohtê– *VAI* walk ahead, walk in the lead
nîkânohtêmakan– *VII* be in the lead, proceed in the lead position
pêtâwah– *VTA* lead s.o. hither as a crowd, pull s.o. hither
pimâwah– *VTA* lead s.o. along as a crowd, pull s.o. along
sakâpêkin– *VTA* lead s.o. (e.g., horse) by a rope
sakâpêkipah– *VTA* lead s.o. (e.g., horse) along by a rope
takohtah– *VTA* take s.o. to arrive, lead s.o. to one's destination, arrive with s.o.
wanâh– *VTA* lead s.o. astray, distract s.o.; disrupt s.o.'s life
wanisim– *VTA* cause s.o. to get lost, lead s.o. astray
wanisimôhâwaso– *VAI* lead one's children astray
wanisinohtah– *VTA* lead s.o. to lose (it/him)

LEAD-DOG
kihc-ônîkânohtêw– *NA* lead-dog

LEADER
nîkâni– *VAI* be a leader
nîkânîstamaw– *VTA* be in the lead of s.o., be at the head of s.o., be a leader amongst s.o.
okimâw– *NA* chief, leader, boss; *(fig.)* band council
onîkânîw– *NA* leader
onîkânohtêw– *NA* leader

LEAF
acikâsipakw– *NI* bearberry leaf
macipakw– *NI* herb; leaves, lettuce
mahkipakâ– *VII* be big leaves, be the time of fully grown leaves
nîpiy– *NI* leaf; leafy branch

LEAK
ohcikawan– *VII* leak out, drip out, trickle out; spring a leak (e.g., vessel)
ohcikawi– *VAI* leak out, drip out, trickle out (e.g., sap from tree)

LEAN
aspatisin– *VII* lie leaning upon (it), lie back upon (it), lie propped up
âsosim– *VTA* lay s.o. to lean against something, lean s.o. against something
âsôhtatâ– *VAI* lean (it) across something
âswastâ– *VAI* place (it) to lean against something, lean (it) against something
pâwani– *VAI* be lean, be skinny, be scrawny (e.g., rabbit, human)

LEARN
kiskinawâpi– *VAI* learn by observation, learn by example; learn merely by watching
kiskinowâpaht– *VTI* learn by watching s.t., learn by the example of s.t.; learn merely by watching s.t.
kiskinowâpam– *VTA* learn by watching s.o., learn by s.o.'s example
kiskinowâpiwin– *NI* learning by observation, learning by example; learning merely by watching
kiskinowâsoht– *VTI* learn merely by listening to s.t.
okiskinowâpiw– *NA* one who learns merely by watching, mere imitator

LEASK
pimicaskêkâs– *NI* *(place-name:)* Leask (Saskatchewan)

LEAST
kanakê *IPC* at least, even if only

LEATHER
pahkêkinohkê– *VAI* prepare one's skins, dress one's hides; make dressed hides, make leather
pahkêkinos– *NI* small dressed hide, small piece of leather
pahkêkinw– *NI* dressed hide, tanned hide, finished hide, leather; tent-cover
pahkêkinwêsâkay– *NI* leather coat, leather jacket

LEAVE

iskosâwât– VTA leave meat over in filleting s.o. (e.g., fish), leave some flesh on the bones in filleting s.o.

iskwaht– VTI leave so much of s.t. (e.g., food) over; have s.t. (e.g., food) left over

itiskaw– VTA *(especially in inverse constructions:)* have such an effect on s.o., leave s.o. thus affected

kanawêyihtamôh– VTA make s.o. guard (it/him) closely; ask s.o. to look after (it/him), leave (it/him) to be looked after by s.o., get s.o. to babysit (her/him)

kînwâhkwêh– VTA *(especially in inverse constructions:)* leave s.o. baffled, confound s.o.

kîskwêskaw– VTA *(especially in inverse constructions:)* make s.o. crazy, leave s.o. disoriented

miyân– VTI leave behind fresh tracks, have recently passed by

nakasiwê– VAI leave people behind, die

nakat– VTA leave s.o. behind; leave s.o. alone (e.g., helpless); abandon s.o. (e.g., child); leave s.o. behind in death, die leaving s.o. behind

nakat– VTI leave s.t. behind

nakatahw– VTA leave s.o. behind in departing by boat or airplane

nakatamaw– VTA leave (it/him) behind for s.o., bequeathe (it/him) to s.o.

nakataskê– VAI leave the earth behind, depart the world, die

ohtaskat– VTA leave s.o. behind thereby or from there, walk out on s.o.

ohtaskat– VTI leave s.t. behind thereby or from there

paskêwih– VTA part from s.o., leave s.o.; separate from s.o., divorce s.o.

paskêwihito– VAI part from one another, leave one another; separate from one another, divorce

pônihk– VTI cease of s.t., leave s.t. alone

sipwê IPV departing, leaving, starting off

sipwêcimê– VAI leave by boat, depart by boat

sipwêhotêwi– VAI leave by boat, depart by boat, go out by boat

sipwêhtah– VTA take s.o. away, leave with s.o., depart with s.o.

sipwêhtatâ– VAI leave taking (it), depart with (it)

sipwêhtê– VAI leave, depart

sipwêmon– VII leave as path, trail, road; begin as path, trail, road

sipwêpici– VAI leave with one's camp, depart with one's camp

sipwêtâpâso– VAI leave with a team of horses, drive off by wagon

sipwêwihw– VTA make s.o. leave by boat, depart with s.o. by boat

wanwêhkaw– VTA leave s.o. baffled by speech or in speech, confuse s.o.

wayawî– VAI go outside, go outdoors; go to relieve oneself; leave school, leave hospital

wâpanastâ– VAI place (it) until dawn, leave (it) until dawn

wêpin– VTA throw s.o. away; empty s.o. (e.g., pail); throw s.o. down or in (e.g., money in a card-game); leave s.o. (e.g., spouse); abandon s.o. (e.g., child)

wêpinamaw– VTA throw (it/him) on s.o., dump (it/him) on s.o., leave (it/him) with s.o., abandon (it/him) to s.o.

wêpinito– VAI leave one another, separate from one another, get divorced

wêpinitowin– NI leaving one another, separating from one another, divorce

LECTURE

kakêskihkêmo– VAI counsel people, lecture people, preach at people

kakêskim– VTA counsel s.o., lecture s.o., preach at s.o.

kakêskimâwaso– VAI counsel one's children, lecture one's children

kitot– VTA address s.o., speak to s.o.; lecture s.o.

LEFT

iskon– VTI have so much of s.t. left over

iskonikowisi– VAI be left over (e.g., to survive) by the powers

iskwaht– VTI leave so much of s.t. (e.g., food) over; have s.t. (e.g., food) left over

iskwahtâ– VAI have so much of (it) left over; have (it) left over, have a plentiful supply of (it)

iskwânê– VAI be left behind after a widespread illness, survive an epidemic

namahtinihk IPC on the left hand, to the left

pêyako– *VAI* be alone, be the only one; be left alone; go alone (e.g., as a woman, improperly)

LEG
  –skât– *NDI* leg
  –spiconis– *NDI* front and hind legs (e.g., of a rabbit)
  nîsokâtê– *VAI* have two legs, be two-legged

LEGGINGS
  –câsis– *NDA* loin-cloth; leggings; trousers, pants
  –tâs– *NDA* loin-cloth; leggings; trousers, pants
  pahkêkinwêtâs– *NA* hide leggings, hide trousers, hide pants

LEND
  awih– *VTA* lend (it/him) to s.o.; rent (it/him) out to s.o.
  awihiwê– *VAI* lend (it/him) to people; rent (it/him) out to people

LESS
  âstamipayi– *VAI* become less, run low (e.g., money)
  nawac piko *IPC* sort of, kind of, approximately; more or less; even a little
  nôhtaw *IPC* less; minus; previously; prematurely, incompletely, short of attainment

LET GO
  pakiciwêpin– *VTI* let go of s.t., abandon s.t.
  pakicî– *VAI* let go, give up; release (it/him), let go of (it/him)
  pakitin– *VTA* set s.o. down, allow s.o., permit s.o.; permit (it) to s.o., give permission to s.o.; let s.o. go, release s.o.; release s.o. (e.g., fish-spawn into lake), stock a lake with s.o. (e.g., fish); drop s.o. off (e.g., as an airplane)
  pakitin– *VTI* let s.t. go, allow s.t., permit s.t.; release s.t.; give s.t. up, abandon s.t. (e.g., teaching, tradition); put s.t. down on earth; put s.t. in (e.g., seed potatoes)

LET UP
  âstê-kimiwan– *VII* cease being rain, let up as rain
  âstê-kîsikâ– *VII* cease being stormy weather, let up as severe weather, be better weather

LET'S
  ahâw *IPC* now indeed! ready! let's go!
  kiyâm *IPC* oh well, never mind, so much for this; anyway, rather; let it be, let there be no further delay; please
  mahti *IPC* let's see, please

LETTER
  masinahikan– *NI* letter, mail; book; written document, will; *(fig.)* bible
  masinahikêwin– *NI* writing; letter, character

LETTUCE
  macipakw– *NI* herb; leaves, lettuce

LEVEL
  cahcakwahcâsin– *VII* be a small piece of level ground
  ispâhkêpayi– *VAI* reach a high level, be elevated (e.g., blood-sugar)
  tipiskôc *IPC* even, at the same level, parallel; directly overhead

LEVEL-HEADED
  âpahkawin– *VII* be level-headed, be sensible, be conscious

LIAR
  kiyâskiski– *VAI* habitually tell lies, be a liar

LICE
  nitihkomât– *VTA* pick lice off s.o., louse s.o.
  otihkomi– *VAI* have lice

LICK
  nôhkwât– *VTI* lick s.t.
  sisopât– *VTI* spread (it) on s.t.; lick s.t. off (e.g., sap)

LID
  akwanâpowêhikâso– *VAI* be covered as vessel containing liquid, have a cover, have a lid (e.g., pot)
  akwanâpowêhikâsosi– *VAI* be covered as a small vessel containing liquid, have a cover, have a lid (e.g., mussel)
  kipwaskinê– *VII* be filled to the lid, be full to the brim
  tasôh– *VTA* entrap s.o. (e.g., bird) by putting feed under a movable lid, trap s.o. underneath

LIE
  asawâpam– *VTA* watch for s.o., look out for s.o., lie in wait for s.o.
  aspatisin– *VII* lie leaning upon (it), lie back upon (it), lie propped up
  aspisimo– *VAI* lie upon (it), use (it) as one's mattress
  aspisin– *VAI* lie on (it), lie against (it)
  aswahikê– *VAI* watch with a weapon for people, be on the lookout with a weapon, lie in wait with a weapon
  itisin– *VAI* lie thus or there
  kakiyâskiwin– *NI* lie, tall tale
  kawisimo– *VAI* lie down, go to bed

kawisin– *VAI* fall down, lie fallen down
kiyâskiski– *VAI* habitually tell lies, be a liar
nôhtêsin– *VAI* be played out, lie exhausted
otihtapinahisin– *VAI* move to lie face-down
pimisin– *VAI* lie extended, lie down; lie confined, lie in childbed
sâsakitisin– *VAI* lie on one's back
wêwêkisin– *VAI* lie wrapped up

LIFE
–kîsikâm– *NDI* day, day of one's life; *(fig.)* [Our Father's] day, Christmas Day
–tipiskâm– *NDI* night, night of one's life
ahcâhko-pimâtisiwin– *NI* spiritual life
âpisisim– *VTA* revive s.o., bring s.o. back to life
âpisisimito– *VAI* revive one another, bring one another back to life
âpisisin– *VAI* revive, come back to life
âyimî– *VAI* have a difficult time, have a difficult task; have a hard life
itâciho– *VAI* travel thither or thus; lead one's life thus
itâcihowin– *NI* travelling thither or thus; leading one's life thus
kakâyawâciho– *VAI* live an active life; work hard in one's life, lead an industrious life
kayâsi-pimâcihowin– *NI* old life, traditional way of life
kistikêwi-pimâcihowin– *NI* agricultural way of life, farm economy
mitimê– *VAI* track along a trail, follow a trail; *(fig.)* follow a path, be guided in one's life
miyo-pimâciho– *VAI* make a good life for oneself, live well; lead a proper life
miyo-pimâtisi– *VAI* llive a good life, live well; lead a proper life
miyw-âyâ– *VAI* be well, be in good health; have a good life
pimâcih– *VTA* make s.o. live, give life to s.o., sustain s.o.'s life; revive s.o., save s.o.'s life; make a living for s.o.
pimâcihâwaso– *VAI* give life to one's children, make a living for one's children
pimâcihiwêwin– *NI* way of life; way of making a living
pimâciho– *VAI* make a life for oneself; make one's living; live
pimâcihowin– *NI* way of life, livelihood
pimâcisiwin– *NI* life
pimâtisiwin– *NI* life
pimâtisiwinê– *VAI* have life, seek life
pimâtisiwinowi– *VII* have life, provide life
pimâtisîtot– *VTI* live one's life; live one's life by s.t.
pimohtêho– *VAI* travel through life, live one's life
pimohtêhon– *NI* passage through life, travel through life
pîkon– *VTA* break s.o.; break up one's relation with s.o., disrupt s.o.'s life, spoil s.o.'s plans
sakâwi-pimâcihowin– *NI* life in the bush
wanâh– *VTA* lead s.o. astray, distract s.o.; disrupt s.o.'s life
wawânaskêhtamaw– *VTA* create a peaceful life for s.o.
wawânaskêhtâ– *VAI* live a peaceful life
wêhci-pimâtisi– *VAI* live in ease, have an easy life

LIFT
ohpaho– *VAI* fly up (e.g., bird); fly off, lift off by airplane
ohpin– *VTA* raise s.o. (e.g., pipe), lift s.o. up
ohpwêtot– *VTI* lift oneself upon s.t., rise up upon s.t. (e.g., moon upon night sky)
sâkôhtâ– *VAI* overcome (it), accomplish (it), lift (it) up

LIGHT
âhkasîho– *VAI* dress lightly
âstawêpayi– *VAI* have one's light go out (e.g., star), have one's fire extinguished (e.g., star)
îwâsên– *VTI* turn s.t. down by hand (e.g., by turning a knob), dim the light, turn s.t. too low
saskah– *VTI* light s.t. (e.g., lamp)
saskahamaw– *VTA* light (it/him) for s.o.; light the pipe for s.o.
saskahamâso– *VAI* light (it/him) for oneself (e.g., fire, pipe)
saskahw– *VTA* light s.o. (e.g., tobacco)
wâpistikwânê– *VAI* have white hair; have light hair, be blond
wâsaskocêpayîs– *NI* lamp, electric light
wâsaskotawêpi– *VAI* sit with a lamp, have light from a lamp

wâsaskotê– *VII* be light, be lit; be a lantern
wâsaskotênamaw– *VTA* light (it) for s.o., provide light to s.o.
wâsaskotênikan– *NI* light, lamp, lantern
wâsaskotênikâkê– *VAI* light things with (it), use (it) to have light, use (it) as a lamp
wâsaskotênikê– *VAI* light things, have light
yâhkasin– *VII* be light in weight

LIGHT-COLOURED
wâpâstê– *VII* be light-coloured, be faded in colour

LIGHT-HEADED
takahkipah– *VTA* make s.o. feel good, cause s.o. to be light-headed with an alcoholic drink, get s.o. inebriated
takahkipê– *VAI* feel good with drink, be light-headed with alcoholic drink, be inebriated

LIGHTNING
wâh-wâsaskotêpayi– *VII* be lightning
wâsaskotêpayi– *VII* be a bolt of lightning, be a lightning-strike

LIKE
cîhkêyiht– *VTI* like s.t., approve of s.t.; eagerly participate in s.t.
kisâstaw *IPC* roughly like, resembling
miyoht– *VTI* like the sound of s.t., consider s.t. to sound nice
miyonaw– *VTA* like the look of s.o., consider s.o. good-looking
miywâpisin– *VAI* like the look of (it)
miywêyihcikâtê– *VII* be liked, be enjoyed
miywêyiht– *VTI* consider s.t. good, like s.t.; be glad, be pleased
miywêyim– *VTA* consider s.o. good, like s.o.; be pleased with s.o.
mwêhci *IPC* exactly; like
takahkêyiht– *VTI* think well of s.t., be glad about s.t., like s.t.; be glad, be pleased
takahkêyim– *VTA* think well of s.o., consider s.o. nice, like s.o.
takahkêyimiso– *VAI* think well of oneself, like oneself
takahkinaw– *VTA* like the look of s.o., consider s.o. good-looking
wîhkipw– *VTA* like the taste of s.o. (e.g., duck, beaver), have a preference for the taste of s.o.
wîhkist– *VTI* like the taste of s.t.

LIMBS
sêsâwin– *VTA* stretch s.o. by hand, exercise s.o.'s limbs (in therapy)

LINE
nîpitêh– *VTA* place s.o. in a row, place s.o. abreast, place s.o. in a line
nîpitêkotâ– *VAI* hang (it) up in a row, hang (it) up in a line
pîhtawêkin– *VTI* line s.t., put a lining into s.t.

LINEAR
pimakocin– *VII* make a rush in linear fashion, charge headlong
pimastê– *VII* be placed in linear fashion, run along
pimi *IPV* along, in linear progression; while moving in linear progression

LINOLEUM
anâskânihtakw– *NI* floor-covering, linoleum

LIPSTICK
mihkotonê– *VAI* have a red mouth, wear lipstick
mihkotonêho– *VAI* paint one's mouth red, wear lipstick
mihkotonêhon– *NI* lipstick
mihkotonêhw– *VTA* paint s.o.'s mouth red, put lipstick on s.o.

LIQUID
akohtin– *VII* float on liquid (e.g., grease on soup)
akwanâpowêhikâso– *VAI* be covered as vessel containing liquid, have a cover, have a lid (e.g., pot)
akwanâpowêhikâsosi– *VAI* be covered as a small vessel containing liquid, have a cover, have a lid (e.g., mussel)
âsiciwan– *VII* run down as liquid
itâkami– *VII* be a liquid of such a colour
kakwâtakâpâkwaho– *VAI* suffer mortification by denying oneself liquid, make oneself suffer thirst
kisâkamis– *VTI* heat s.t. as liquid
kisâkamisikê– *VAI* heat a liquid; boil water for tea, make tea
kisâkamitêhkwê– *VAI* drink a hot liquid, have a hot drink
kîkwâpoy *IPC* what kind of liquid
kohtân– *VTA* immerse s.o. (e.g., a piece of ice) in liquid, dunk s.o. into liquid
mihkwâkami– *VII* be a red liquid
pîhtâpâwah– *VTA* pour liquid into s.o., give s.o. an enema

LIQUOR
iskotêwâpoy– NI alcoholic drink, liquor, whisky

LISTEN
kiskinowâsoht– VTI learn merely by listening to s.t.
kitimâkihtaw– VTA listen to s.o. with pity, listen to s.o. with compassion
mâmaskâsihtaw– VTA be amazed upon listening to s.o.
nanahiht– VTI listen well to s.t.; obey s.t.
nanahihtaw– VTA listen well to s.o.; obey s.o.
nitoht– VTI listen to s.t.
nitohtaw– VTA listen to s.o.
nitohtâkowisi– VAI be heard by the powers, be listened to by the powers
sasîpiht– VTI fail to listen to s.t., disobey s.t.
sasîpihtaw– VTA fail to listen to s.o., disobey s.o.

LITERATE
masinahikê– VAI write things; write, be literate; go into debt, have debts

LITTLE
apisîs IPC a little

LIVE
apîst– VTI sit by s.t., live by s.t., live near s.t.
asiwaso– VAI be inside, be enclosed; live inside, dwell inside
askîwisk– VTI subject the earth to oneself, populate the earth, make the earth live
ayâ– VAI be there, live there; exist
kakâyawâciho– VAI live an active life; work hard in one's life, lead an industrious life
kakwâtakâciho– VAI suffer dreadfully, live through a dreadful time
kanâtapi– VAI live in a clean house
kihci-wîki– VAI live formally; *(fig.)* live in residence
kîsikanisi– VAI spend one's day, live through the day
mâyi-wîcêhto– VAI live in discord with one another
miyo-pimâciho– VAI make a good life for oneself, live well; lead a proper life
miyo-pimâtisi– VAI llive a good life, live well; lead a proper life
miyo-wîcêhto– VAI get along well with one another, live in harmony with one another

miyo-wîki– VAI live comfortably, have a nice dwelling
ocihci IPV having lived long enough for something
otisâpaht– VTI have lived long enough to see s.t.
owîki– VAI live there, dwell there, have one's home there
papâmâciho– VAI travel about; live in various places; run about, be promiscuous
pêyakwâciho– VAI live alone, travel alone
pimâcih– VTA make s.o. live, give life to s.o., sustain s.o.'s life; revive s.o., save s.o.'s life; make a living for s.o.
pimâcihiso– VAI make oneself live; make a living for oneself
pimâciho– VAI make a life for oneself; make one's living; live
pimâtisi– VAI live, be alive, survive
pimâtisîtot– VTI live one's life; live one's life by s.t.
pimohtât– VTI travel to s.t. (e.g., work-site); live s.t. (e.g., day), live through s.t.; go through s.t. (e.g., as sun through the sky)
pimohtêho– VAI travel through life, live one's life
piskihci-wîki– VAI live separately, dwell separately, have a separate household
pôni-pimâtisi– VAI cease to live, die; be no longer alive, be dead
tipiskisi– VAI spend one's night, live through the night
tipiyawêho– VAI live in one's own dwelling, have one's own household
wawânaskêhtâ– VAI live a peaceful life
wêhci-pimâtisi– VAI live in ease, have an easy life
wîc-âyâhto– VAI live together; be married to one another
wîc-âyâm– VTA be together with s.o., live together with s.o.; be married to s.o.
wîcêhto– VAI live with one another, join with one another; get along with one another; breed with one another
wîcêw– VTA accompany s.o., get along with s.o., join s.o., live with s.o.
wîki– VAI live there, dwell there, have one's home there
wîkihto– VAI live together; marry one another, be married to one another

wîkim– VTA live with s.o.; be married to s.o.
wîtaskîwêm– VTA live together with s.o., have s.o. as one's compatriot; live in the same country with s.o., live in peace with s.o.
wîtokwêm– VTA share a dwelling with s.o., live with s.o., have s.o. as one's housemate

LIVELIHOOD
pimâcihowin– NI way of life, livelihood

LIVING
apîwikamikw– NI sitting room, living room
ohtâciho– VAI make one's living thereby or from there
pimâcih– VTA make s.o. live, give life to s.o., sustain s.o.'s life; revive s.o., save s.o.'s life; make a living for s.o.
pimâcihâwaso– VAI give life to one's children, make a living for one's children
pimâcihiso– VAI make oneself live; make a living for oneself
pimâcihiwêwin– NI way of life; way of making a living
pimâciho– VAI make a life for oneself; make one's living; live
pimâcihwâkê– VAI make one's living with (it), use (it) to make one's living
wîcêhtowin– NI living with one another; getting along with one another, living in harmony with one another
wîkihtowin– NI living together; marriage, matrimony; getting married, wedding

LOAD
nayôhcikê– VAI carry things on one's back, carry a load; carry a backpack
nîsotâpânâsk IPC two sleighs, two loads
pîkwasinahikê– VAI be loaded down with debt, be indebted in several places
pôsihtâ– VAI put (it) aboard (e.g., boat or vehicle), load (it) on
pôsihtâso– VAI load up, load one's boat or vehicle

LODGE
itikwamikohkê– VAI hold such a lodge, hold such a rite
mânokê– VAI build a lodge, set up a tent
mitêwiwin– NI mitewin lodge, medicine society
mîkiwâhp– NI lodge, tipi

mîkiwâhpis– NI little lodge
nipâkwêsimowikamikw– NI sundance lodge, sundance ceremony
nîmihitowikamikw– NI dance lodge, dance ceremony
pahkêkino-mîkiwâhp– NI skin-lodge, lodge made from hides
pîhtwâwikamikw– NI pipe lodge, pipe ceremony
wâsakâmêsimowikamikw– NI ghost-dance lodge; ghost-dance

LODGE-POLE
apasoy– NI lodge-pole

LOG
mistikw– NI stick, pole, post, log, wooden rail

LOG-HOUSE
asiskîhkê– VAI mud a log-house, do the mudding, hold a mudding bee
mistikokamikw– NI log-house
sisowaskinikê– VAI put on mud or plaster; mud one's log-house

LOIN-CLOTH
–câsis– NDA loin-cloth; leggings; trousers, pants
–tâs– NDA loin-cloth; leggings; trousers, pants
âsiyân– NA loin-cloth, diaper, menstrual napkin

LONESOME
kaskêyiht– VTI be sad over s.t.; be sad, be lonesome, have a longing
pîkiskâtisi– VAI be lonesome, grieve

LONG
âkwâc IPC well on its way, a long ways, more than halfway
iskosi– VAI extend so far, be so long, be so tall, be of such height
kakwêtawêyiht– VTI long for s.t., miss s.t.
kayâs IPC long ago, in earlier days; previously
kâkikê IPC always, at all times, forever; for a very long time, forever (metaphorically)
kinosi– VAI be long (e.g., sock), be tall
kinwâ– VII be long, be tall
kinwâpêkan– VII be a long garment, be a long piece of paper; be a long saw-blade, be a long saw
kinwâpêkasâkê– VAI wear a long skirt; wear a long robe (e.g., as a Roman Catholic priest)
kinwâpêkisi– VAI be long as string, be long as fishing-net

kinwêsêskamik *IPC* for a very long time
kinwêsîs *IPC* for quite a long time
kinwêsk *IPC* for a long time
kîskipocikan– *NI* saw, long saw (e.g., with two handles)
nayawâs *IPC* after a long wait
ocihci *IPV* having lived long enough for something
otisâpaht– *VTI* have lived long enough to see s.t.
pîkiskât– *VTA* long for s.o., grieve for s.o.
tânimayikohkêskamik *IPC* to which extent, for how long
têpihkwâmi– *VAI* sleep long enough, have enough sleep
têpiyâhk *IPC* merely; barely, the most (if any); the only thing; so long as; *(in negative constructions:)* all but

LONG-LODGE
sâpohtawân– *NI* long-lodge, through-lodge

LOOK
asawâpam– *VTA* watch for s.o., look out for s.o., lie in wait for s.o.
asawâpi– *VAI* be on the lookout; look out for game
awêska *IPC* behold! look at that!
âpasâpi– *VAI* look back, glance back
isinaw– *VTA* look thus to s.o., present such an appearance to s.o.
isinâkosi– *VAI* look thus, give such an appearance
isinâkwan– *VII* look thus, give such an appearance
itâpaminâkwan– *VII* give such an appearance to look at
itâpi– *VAI* look thus or there; take aim thus or there
îh *IPC* lo! look! behold!
kanawâpam– *VTA* look at s.o., watch s.o., observe s.o.; look after s.o.
kanawâpokê– *VAI* look after a household, keep house
kanawêyiht– *VTI* keep s.t., look after s.t., take care of s.t.; store s.t., preserve s.t.; guard s.t. closely
kanawêyihtamaw– *VTA* look after (it/him) for s.o., take care of (it/him) for s.o.
kanawêyihtamôh– *VTA* make s.o. guard (it/him) closely; ask s.o. to look after (it/him), leave (it/him) to be looked after by s.o., get s.o. to babysit (her/him)

kanawêyim– *VTA* keep s.o., look after s.o., take care of s.o.; guard s.o. closely
kanawêyimiwê– *VAI* look after people; guard people (e.g., girls) closely
kanâcinâkosi– *VAI* look clean, give a clean appearance
kihc-îskwêwinâkosi– *VAI* look like a great lady
kitâpaht– *VTI* look at s.t.
kitâpam– *VTA* look at s.o. (e.g., sun), watch s.o.; look at s.o. with respect, regard s.o. with respect; *(fig.)* watch over s.o.
kitâpamikowisi– *VAI* be looked upon by the powers
kitêyiht– *VTI* look after s.t., be responsible for s.t.
kitêyihtamaw– *VTA* look after (it/him) for s.o., be responsible (for it/him) to s.o.
kitimâkinaw– *VTA* look with pity upon s.o., look with compassion upon s.o., feel sorry for s.o.; take pity upon s.o., lovingly tend s.o.; regard s.o. with respect
kitimâkinâkosi– *VAI* look pitiable, look miserable; look poor
kîmôtâpi– *VAI* look stealthily, look secretly
kwayâci-niton– *VTI* look for s.t. to hold in readiness
kwêskinâkwan– *VII* look changed around, look turned around to the opposite side
miyonaw– *VTA* like the look of s.o., consider s.o. good-looking
miyonâkohcikê– *VAI* be seen to be good at things, make things look nice, make things look prosperous
miyonâkwan– *VII* look good, have a nice appearance, look prosperous
miywâpisin– *VAI* like the look of (it)
nanâtawâpi– *VAI* look around
nâkatawâpam– *VTA* pay attention in looking at s.o., observe s.o.
nâkatêyiht– *VTI* pay attention to s.o., attend to s.o., look after s.o.
nâkatowâpaht– *VTI* pay attention in looking at s.t., observe s.t.
nâpêwinâkosi– *VAI* look like a man; be of human appearance
nitawastimwê– *VAI* look for one's horses, search for one's horses
nitawâwê– *VAI* go looking for eggs, go to collect eggs
nitâmiso– *VAI* look for berries, go berry-picking

niton– *VTI* look for s.t., seek s.t., search for s.t.
nitonaw– *VTA* look for s.o., seek s.o. (e.g., tree), search for s.o.
nitonikâtê– *VII* be looked for, be searched for
nitonikê– *VAI* take a look, search for things, make a search
nitot– *VTI* look for s.t.; order s.t. (e.g., in a restaurant)
osâpaht– *VTI* look at s.t. from there
osâpam– *VTA* look at s.o. from there
oskaskosîwinâkwan– *VII* look green, have the appearance of fresh shoots
pamih– *VTA* tend to s.o., look after s.o.; attend s.o. in childbirth, serve as midwife to s.o.; guide s.o. (e.g., sleigh), drive s.o. (e.g., sleigh)
pamihikowin– *NI* being looked after, welfare
pamihiso– *VAI* tend to oneself, look after oneself; attend oneself in childbirth, serve as one's own midwife
pamiho– *VAI* look after oneself; be well off
pamihtamaw– *VTA* tend to (it/him) for s.o., look after (it/him) for s.o.
pamihtamâso– *VAI* tend to (it/him) for or by oneself, look after (it/him) for or by oneself
pamihtâ– *VAI* look after (it)
pamin– *VTA* tend to s.o., look after s.o.; attend s.o. in childbirth, serve as midwife to s.o.
pamin– *VTI* tend to s.t., look after s.t.
paminiso– *VAI* tend to oneself, look after oneself
paminiwê– *VAI* tend to people, look after people
paspâpam– *VTA* look out (e.g., through a window or crack) at s.o.
paspâpi– *VAI* look out (e.g., through a hole or crack), peep out
piyasêyimo– *VAI* look forward eagerly, wait in anticipation
pîtosinâkwan– *VII* look different; look strange
saskaci-wâpaht– *VTI* be tired of looking at s.t.
takahkinaw– *VTA* like the look of s.o., consider s.o. good-looking
takahkinâkohtâ– *VAI* make (it) look nice, make (it) look beautiful
wawiyasinâkosi– *VAI* look funny, look amusing

yêyâpisin– *VAI* look on with favour; be tempted by looking at (it)

LOOKOUT
asawâpi– *VAI* be on the lookout; look out for game
aswahikê– *VAI* watch with a weapon for people, be on the lookout with a weapon, lie in wait with a weapon
aswahw– *VTA* watch with a weapon for s.o., be on the lookout with a weapon for s.o.

LOON
mâkw– *NA* loon

LOOSE
asikâpawi– *VAI* stand about as a loose group
pimw– *VTA* shoot at s.o., loose an arrow at s.o.

LOOSEN
âpah– *VTI* loosen s.t., untie s.t.
âpahw– *VTA* loosen s.o., uncover s.o., unbundle s.o. (e.g., child)
tahtinikâtê– *VII* be loosened, be taken off

LORD
tipêyihcikê– *VAI* be master over things, be in charge; *(fig.)* be the Lord
tipêyim– *VTA* own s.o., control s.o., rule s.o.; *(fig.)* be the Lord over s.o.; have s.o. in one's clutches (e.g., devil)

LOSE
wanahâht– *VTA* lose s.o.'s tracks
wanih– *VTA* lose s.o.; lose s.o. (e.g., to death)
wanihtâ– *VAI* lose (it); get relief from (it)
wanisinohtah– *VTA* lead s.o. to lose (it/him)

LOSS
kôtatê *IPC* at a loss; due to limitations beyond one's control; it cannot be helped
kôtawêyiht– *VTI* be at a loss for s.t., miss s.t.
kôtawêyim– *VTA* be aware of s.o.'s absence, feel the loss of s.o., miss s.o.
kwêtatêyitiskwêyi– *VAI* be at a loss as to where to turn one's head; be at a loss for a response
mihtât– *VTA* deplore the loss of s.o., sorely miss s.o., grieve for s.o.
mihtât– *VTI* deplore the loss of s.t., be sorry about s.t.
wawânêyiht– *VTI* be at a loss for s.t.; worry about s.t.; be worried
wawânêyihtamih– *VTA* cause s.o. to be at a loss; cause s.o. to worry about

(it/him); *(especially in inverse constructions:)* place s.o. in a bind

LOST
waniho– VAI be lost, get lost
wanisim– VTA cause s.o. to get lost, lead s.o. astray
wanisin– VAI get lost, be lost
wêpinikâtê– VII be thrown away, be abandoned, be discarded; be lost (e.g., blood)

LOT
iyawis IPC fully, entirely; the whole lot, the entire household; *(in negative constructions:)* only partially, not exclusively
misahcinêh– VTI buy s.t. in great numbers, buy a lot of s.t.
misi-mîci– VAI eat much of (it), eat a lot of (it)
mistakihtê– VII be counted for much, be worth a lot, be valuable, be expensive
namôy âpisis IPC not a little, quite a lot

LOUD
kisîwê– VAI speak angrily; speak loudly
kisîwê– VII be loud, speak loudly (e.g., audio-recorder)
kisîwêhkahtaw– VTA speak angrily to s.o.; speak loudly to s.o., scold s.o. loudly
kisîwên– VTI turn s.t. (e.g., radio) loud by hand
kisîwi IPV loudly, angrily, in anger

LOUSE
nitihkomât– VTA pick lice off s.o., louse s.o.

LOVE
kitimâkêyihto– VAI feel pity towards one another, think of one another with compassion; take pity upon one another, be kind to one another, love one another
kitimâkêyim– VTA feel pity towards s.o., think of s.o. with compassion; take pity upon s.o., be kind to s.o., love s.o.
sâkih– VTA love s.o., be attached to s.o.
sâkihâwaso– VAI love one's children
sâkihito– VAI love one another
sâkihito-maskihkiy– NI love medicine
sâkihitowaskw– NI love medicine
sâkihitowin– NI mutual love; charity

sâkihtâ– VAI love (it), be attached to (it)

LOW
âstamipayi– VAI become less, run low (e.g., money)
capahcâsin– VII be quite low
capasis IPC down, down low
îwâsên– VTI turn s.t. down by hand (e.g., by turning a knob), dim the light, turn s.t. too low
pîwêyiht– VTI think little of s.t., have a low opinion of s.t.
pîwêyim– VTA think little of s.o., have a low opinion of s.o.; be disrespectful of s.o.
pîwêyimo– VAI think little of oneself, have low self-esteem; *(fig.)* be humble
tapahcipayiho– VAI swoop down, swoop low
tapâtiskwêyi– VAI hold one's head low, lower one's head

LUCK
miyopayi– VAI fare well, be in luck

LUMBER
napakihtakw– NI flat lumber, board, floor-board
napakikamikos– NI little house made of lumber or boards
napakikamikw– NI house made of lumber or boards; flat-top shack

LUNCH
âpihtâ-kîsikani-mîciso– VAI eat one's mid-day meal, eat one's lunch
nîmâ– VAI take provisions; take a packed lunch
nîmâh– VTA make s.o. take provisions; add (it) to s.o.'s packed lunch
nîmâsi– VAI take some provisions; take some packed lunch
nîmâwin– NI provisions; packed lunch
nîmâwinihkê– VAI arrange provisions; prepare a packed lunch

LUNCH-BOX
nîmâwiwat– NI box for provisions; lunch-box

LUST
akâwât– VTA desire s.o., lust for s.o.; want s.o. (e.g., rabbit for food)

LYE
pihkwâpoy– NI lye

LYNX
pisiw– NA lynx

MACHINE
apihkêpicikan– NI knitting machine

âpacihcikan– NI tool, appliance, machine; equipment, furnishings, furniture
kaskikwâsopayihcikanis– NI sewing machine
kaskikwâswâkan– NI sewing machine

MACHINE-SEW
kaskikwâsopayihcikâkê– VAI machine-sew with (it), use (it) to machine-sew

MAD
kîskwê– VAI be mentally disturbed, be mad, be crazy
môhcowi– VAI be foolish, be stupid, be silly; be mad, be crazy
môhcw-âyâ– VAI be foolish, be stupid, be silly; be mad, be crazy

MAIL
masinahikan– NI letter, mail; book; written document, will; *(fig.)* bible

MAIL-ORDER
nâtitisahikêwasinahikan– NI mail-order catalogue

MAINLY
osâm piko IPC mainly, mostly

MAJOR
kihci-wayawî– VAI go to relieve oneself in a major way, go to defecate
mistah-âtoskêwin– NI big task, major task

MAKE-BELIEVE
yâhki IPC pretend, make-believe

MALE
–ciwâm– NDA male parallel cousin (man speaking); *(fig.)* brother, friend, male of the same generation (man speaking); brother, brethren
–ciwâmis– NDA male parallel cousin (man speaking); *(fig.)* brother, friend, male of the same generation (man speaking); brother, brethren
–îscâs– NDA male cross-cousin (man speaking); brother-in-law (man speaking)
–îstâw– NDA male cross-cousin (man speaking); brother-in-law (man speaking)
–stês– NDA older brother, older male parallel cousin
–tawêmâw– NDA male parallel cousin (woman speaking); female cross-cousin's husband (woman speaking)
nâpêsis– NA boy, little boy, male infant
nâpêw– NA man, male, adult male
nâpêwi– VAI be a man, be male

nâpêwisîh– VTA dress s.o. as a boy, dress s.o. as a male
nâpêwisîho– VAI be dressed as a man, dress as a male

MAN
–îci-kisêyin– NDA fellow old man, co-elder
–îci-kisêyiniw– NDA fellow old man, co-elder
–kisêyinîm– NDA old man, husband
–kosis– NDA son, parallel nephew; *(fig.)* younger man
–mosôm– NDA grandfather, grandfather's brother; *(fig.)* old man, respected elder
–oskinîkîm– NDA young man, follower; *(fig.)* servant
–oskinîkîmis– NDA young man; hired man
atoskahâkan– NA employee, hired man
kisêyiniw– NA old man
kisêyinîsis– NA little old man, wizened old man
kisêyinîw-âcimowin– NI old man's story, report of the old men
kisêyinîw-ôhpikihâkan– NA old man's pupil, ward of the old men
kisêyinîwi IPN of an old man, befitting an old man
kisêyinîwi– VAI be an old man
kisêyinîwi-pîkiskwêwin– NI old man's word, word of the old men
nâpêw– NA man, male, adult male
nâpêw-âya IPC men's things, men's stuff, men's clothing
nâpêwasikan– NA men's socks
nâpêwatoskê– VAI work like a man, do man's work
nâpêwi– VAI be a man, be male
nâpêwinâkosi– VAI look like a man; be of human appearance
nâpêwisîho– VAI be dressed as a man, dress as a male
oskinîki– VAI be a young man
oskinîkiw– NA young man
oskinîkiwiyinîs– NI youth, young man (about 12-13 years old)
oskinîkiwiyinîsiwi– VAI be a youth, be a young man (about 12-13 years old)
oskinîkîwiyinîsiwi– VAI be a youth, be a young man (about 12-13 years old)
takahkâpêwi– VAI be a handsome man

MANAGE
kaskihtâ– *VAI* be able to do (it), be competent at (it), manage (it)
MANAGER
kihc-âtâwêwikamikowiyiniw– *NA* store manager, post manager, Hudson's Bay Company factor
mistikôsiw– *NA* Frenchman, Hudson's Bay Company manager
MANITO LAKE
manitowi-sâkahikanihk *INM (place-name:)* Manito Lake (Saskatchewan)
MANNER
katawâhk *IPC* properly, in seemly manner
MANNIKIN
ayisiyinîhkân– *NA* doll, mannikin; cartoon figure
MANY
icahcopiponêsi– *VAI* be so many years old (e.g., infant)
ihtahtopiponwêwin– *NI* having so many years, the number of one's years, one's age
ihtasi– *VAI* be so many, be as many
itahtin– *VII* be so many
itahtopiponê– *VAI* be so many years old
itahtw-âskîwinê– *VAI* be so many years old
itahtwapi– *VAI* sit as so many, be present as so many
itahtwâkin– *VTI* bend so many of s.t. (e.g., willows), bend s.t. (e.g., willows) in such numbers
itêyati– *VAI* be such in number, be so many
mihcêt *IPC* many, much
mihcêtôsê– *VAI* have many children, have numerous offspring
mihcêtwastimwê– *VAI* have many horses
mihcêtwâw *IPC* many times
misahkamik *IPC* a great many, in great number
mistahi *IPC* greatly, very much so, very many
mistahi-kîkway *PR* many things, a great deal of something
môy kakêtihk *IPC* a great many
namôya kakêtihk *IPC* a great many
osâmêyatin– *VII* be too many, be plentiful
tahto *IPC* so many, as many

tahto-aya *IPC* so many
tahto-kîkway *PR* so many things, as many things, everything
tahtw-âskiy *IPC* so many years, as many years
tahtwayak *IPC* in so many places, in so many ways
tahtwâpisk *IPC* so many dollars
tahtwâw *IPC* so many times, each time
tânimatahto *IPC* how many; so many, several
tânimatahtw-âskîwinê– *VAI* be how many years old; be so many years old
tânitahto *IPC* how many; so many
tânitahto-kîsikâw *IPC* how many days; so many days; several days
tânitahto-nîpin *IPC* how many summers; so many summers, a few summers
tânitahto-pîsim *IPC* how many months; so many months
tânitahto-tipahikan *IPC* what hour, what time; so many hours, that time; several hours
tânitahtw-âskiy *IPC* how many years; so many years
tânitahtw-âya *IPC* how many kinds; so many kinds
tânitahtwayak *IPC* in how many places; in so many places
tânitahtwâw *IPC* how many times; so many times
tâniyikohk *IPC* to what extent; to such an extent; so many, plenty
MANYPLIES
omâw– *NA* "bible", manyplies, omasum
MARK
itasinah– *VTI* mark s.t. thus, draw s.t. thus; write s.t. thus; thus write s.t. down
masinah– *VTI* mark s.t., draw s.t.; write s.t.; write s.t. down, record s.t. in writing; sign s.t. (e.g., treaty)
MARKED
kiskinawâcihcikâcêsi– *VII* be marked, be indicated; be decorated (e.g., brooch, barrette)
kiskinowâcihcikâtê– *VII* be marked, be indicated; be decorated
masinâso– *VAI* be marked, be striped
MARKINGS
kaskicêwasinâsosi– *VAI* have black markings (e.g., dog)

MARKS
masinahikâtê– *VII* be pictured, be depicted; have marks, have writing; be written

MARRIAGE
kihci-wîkihtowin– *NI* formal marriage, Holy Matrimony
mêki– *VAI* give (it/him) out as present; give (it/him) away, release (it/him); give (her) in marriage
mêkiskwêwê– *VAI* give a woman in marriage; give (her) in marriage
mosci-mêki– *VAI* simply give (her) in marriage
têpwât– *VTA* call out to s.o., yell at s.o.; publish the marriage banns for s.o.
wîkihtah– *VTA* take s.o. to be married, arrange for s.o. to be married; join s.o. (e.g., a couple) in marriage
wîkihtowin– *NI* living together; marriage, matrimony; getting married, wedding

MARRIED
kihci-wîkihto– *VAI* be formally married, be married in church
onâpêmi– *VAI* have a husband, be married (woman), have a husband living; get married (woman); have (him) as one's husband
wîc-âyâhto– *VAI* live together; be married to one another
wîc-âyâm– *VTA* be together with s.o., live together with s.o.; be married to s.o.
wîkihtah– *VTA* take s.o. to be married, arrange for s.o. to be married; join s.o. (e.g., a couple) in marriage
wîkihto– *VAI* live together; marry one another, be married to one another
wîkihtowin– *NI* living together; marriage, matrimony; getting married, wedding
wîkim– *VTA* live with s.o.; be married to s.o.
wîwi– *VAI* have a wife, be married (man); have (her) as one's wife; take a wife

MARRY
kihci-wîkim– *VTA* marry s.o. formally, marry s.o. in church
otinito– *VAI* take one another; marry each other
wîkihto– *VAI* live together; marry one another, be married to one another

MARSH
îhkatawâw– *NI* slough, marsh
îhkatawâwipêyâw– *NI* wet slough, marsh

MARVEL
koskwêyiht– *VTI* be surprised about s.t., marvel at s.t.; be surprised
mâmaskât– *VTA* find s.o. strange, find s.o. incomprehensible, marvel at s.o.
mâmaskât– *VTI* find s.t. strange, find s.t. incomprehensible, marvel at s.t.

MARVELLOUSLY
mâmaskâc *IPC* strangely, marvellously, amazingly; *(in negative constructions:)* not surprisingly, no wonder

MASS
ayamihâ– *VAI* pray, say prayers; hold a church service, celebrate mass; participate in a religious rite, go to church; follow a religion
ayamihâhtah– *VTA* make s.o. go to church, take s.o. to mass, go to church with s.o.
mâmaw-âyamihâ– *VAI* pray as a group, participate in a religious rite as a group, celebrate mass as a group; go on a pilgrimage as a group
mis-âyamihâ– *VAI* hold mass, celebrate high mass
nîpâ-ayamihâ– *VAI* celebrate midnight mass (e.g., at Christmas)

MASTER
tipêyihcikê– *VAI* be master over things, be in charge; *(fig.)* be the Lord
tipêyiht– *VTI* own s.t., control s.t., rule s.t., be master over s.t.; have a voice in the affairs of s.t. (e.g., reserve)

MAT
anâskânis– *NI* covering, mat, rug
anâskât– *VTA* spread matting for s.o.; provide s.o. with bedsheets
anâskê– *VAI* have a mat, spread a blanket; use (it) as matting or floor-covering

MATCH
kocawâkanis– *NI* match, match-stick

MATTER
is-âyâ– *VAI* be thus in health; be unwell, be in poor health; be out of sorts, have something being the matter
sapiko *IPC* actually, as a matter of fact
tâspwâw *IPC* in fact, as a matter of fact

MATTRESS
aspisimo– *VAI* lie upon (it), use (it) as one's mattress
aspisimowin– *NI* mattress

mâmawihkwâmi– *VAI* sleep together as a group, share a mattress

MEADOW LAKE
paskwâwi-sâkahikanihk *INM (place-name:)* Meadow Lake (Saskatchewan)

MEAL
âpihtâ-kîsikani-mîciso– *VAI* eat one's mid-day meal, eat one's lunch
mîciso– *VAI* eat, have a meal; feed (e.g., bird); chew the cud (e.g., ruminant)
mîcisosi– *VAI* eat a little, have a small meal
mîcisowin– *NI* eating, meal; eating-habits; food, foodstuff, food supply
wîci-mîcisôm– *VTA* eat together with s.o., share one's meal with s.o.

MEAN
âyimisi– *VAI* have a difficult time; be of difficult disposition, be wild, be mean
kakwâtakih– *VTA* make s.o. suffer; be mean to s.o., be abusive to s.o.; *(especially in inverse constructions:)* affect s.o. terribly (e.g., as disease), ravage s.o.
kicimah– *VTA* be mean to s.o., treat s.o. cruelly
kitimah– *VTA* be mean to s.o., treat s.o. cruelly; bring misery upon s.o.
kitimahiso– *VAI* be mean to oneself, treat oneself cruelly; hurt oneself
kitimaho– *VAI* be mean to oneself, treat oneself cruelly; bring misery upon oneself
kwatakatot– *VTA* meanly order s.o. around, harass s.o.
kwatakim– *VTA* speak meanly to s.o., nag s.o.

MEANING
itwê– *VAI* say thus, call (it) thus; have such a meaning
itwêmakan– *VII* say thus, have such a meaning
itwêmakisi– *VAI* say thus, have such a meaning

MEANTIME
ispîhci *IPC* for now, in the meantime; *(in comparative constructions:)* by comparison; than
mêkwâc *IPC* while, during, in the course of; in the meantime

MEANWHILE
mêkwâ *IPV* while, during, in the course of; meanwhile; in the midst of

MEASURE
katiskaw *IPC* to exact measure, no more than, barely

kêtisk *IPC* just barely, to exact measure
tako-tipah– *VTI* measure s.t. in addition; pay s.t. extra, pay for s.t. in addition; pay (it) in addition for s.t.
tipah– *VTI* measure s.t.; pay s.t., pay for s.t.; pay (it) for s.t.
tipahâkê– *VAI* measure things with (it/him), measure things against (it/him), use (it/him) as a benchmark; measure things; rely on things

MEASURING
pêyak-misit *IPC* one foot, for one foot; measuring one foot

MEAT
akocikan– *NI* rack for hanging up fish or meat, storage-rack; cupboard, shelf
akwâwân– *NI* rack for drying meat
akwâwê– *VAI* hang sheets of meat on drying rack
cîhcîkos– *VTI* cut meat off s.t. (e.g., bone)
iskosâwât– *VTA* leave meat over in filleting s.o. (e.g., fish), leave some flesh on the bones in filleting s.o.
îwahikan– *NA* pounded meat
kâhkêwakw– *NI* dried meat, sheet of dried meat
pânisâwê– *VAI* cut meat into sheets; cut fish into fillets
wiyâs– *NI* meat
wiyâsowi– *VAI* be meaty, have meat still attached (e.g., cracklings)
wiyinw– *NI* fat, fat meat, piece of fat
yîwahikan– *NA* pounded meat

MEATBALL
pitikonikanâpoy– *NI* meatball soup

MECHANICAL
pîkonikê– *VAI* break things; have things break, experience a mechanical breakdown

MEDICATION
misiwêpayihcikan– *NI* pill, medication
misiwêpayihcikanis– *NI* little pill, medication

MEDICINAL
maskihkiy– *NI* herb, plant; seneca-root; medicinal root; medicine; chemicals
maskihkîwâpôhkatiso– *VAI* prepare an herbal infusion for oneself; make a medicinal drink for oneself
maskihkîwin– *NI* medicinal preparation, medicine

nanâtawâpôhkân– NI medicinal draught
nanâtawihwâkê– VAI doctor oneself with (it), use (it) to heal oneself, use (it) medicinally

MEDICINE
akopiso– VAI put on medicine, tie on a bandage
maci-maskihkiy– NI evil medicine
maci-nôcihtâ– VAI pursue evil things, engage in bad medicine
maskihkiy– NI herb, plant; senecaroot; medicinal root; medicine; chemicals
maskihkîwin– NI medicinal preparation, medicine
maskihkîwiwacis– NI medicine chest
miskîsik-maskihkiy– NI eye medicine
mitêwiwin– NI mitewin lodge, medicine society
miyo-nôcihtâ– VAI pursue good things; *(in negative constructions:)* pursue evil things, engage in bad medicine
nâcinêhamaw– VTA obtain (it/him) from s.o. by payment, seek to buy medicine from s.o.
nâcinêhikê– VAI obtain things by payment, seek to buy medicine
nêhiyawi-maskihkiy– NI Cree medicine; Indian medicine
sâkihito-maskihkiy– NI love medicine
sâkihitowaskw– NI love medicine

MEET
mâmawôpîtot– VTI meet about s.t., hold a meeting about s.t.
nakiskamohtatamaw– VTA take (it/him) to meet s.o., meet s.o. with (it/him); introduce (it/him) to s.o.
nakiskaw– VTA encounter s.o., meet s.o.
ohcitaw IPC expressly, specifically, purposely, necessarily; it is requisite, it is meet indeed

MEETING
mâmawopiwin– NI meeting, assembly
mâmawôpi– VAI sit as a group, get together; hold a meeting
mâmawôpîtot– VTI meet about s.t., hold a meeting about s.t.

MELT
kîsohpihkê– VAI melt snow into water
miskwamîwâpoy– NI melted ice, melting hailstones

tihkis– VTI melt s.t. down
tihkiso– VAI melt, thaw out (e.g., snow, ice, tree, hibernating animal)
tihkisw– VTA melt s.o.; render s.o. (e.g., cracklings)

MEMBER
akiso– VAI be counted; be counted in, be a band member

MEND
mîsah– VTI mend s.t.
nânapâcih– VTA fix s.o. up, mend s.o. (e.g., pants)
nânapâcihtâ– VAI fix (it) up, mend (it)

MENSTRUAL
âsiyân– NA loin-cloth, diaper, menstrual napkin
tahto-pîsim IPC every month, each month, monthly, menstrual

MENTAL
itâpatakêyimo– VAI use one's mind thus, make such use of one's mental faculties
pîkwêyihtamih– VTA worry s.o., cause s.o. mental anguish
pîkwêyihtamowin– NI mental anguish

MENTION
wîh– VTA name s.o., mention s.o. by name
wîht– VTI name s.t., mention s.t. by name; tell about s.t., report s.t.; decree s.t.

MERCIFUL
kisê-manitow– NA God the kind, the compassionate God; *(name:)* Merciful God

MERE
konit-âcimowinis– NI mere story, simple story, just a little story
mosti-tôhtôsâpoy– NI mere milk, mere cow's milk

MERELY
katisk IPC just now, a moment ago; recently, a while ago; exactly, just at that moment, at the very moment; *(in negative constructions:)* not merely
kiskinawâpi– VAI learn by observation, learn by example; learn merely by watching
kiskinowâpaht– VTI learn by watching s.t., learn by the example of s.t.; learn merely by watching s.t.
kiskinowâpiwin– NI learning by observation, learning by example; learning merely by watching

kiskinowâsoht– *VTI* learn merely by listening to s.t.
mosci *IPC* simply, directly, without mediation; merely, without instrument; without recompense
mosci-miy– *VTA* merely give (it/him) to s.o.
mosci-pâhpih– *VTA* merely laugh at s.o., merely deride s.o.
mosci-wêwêkin– *VTA* merely wrap s.o. up (e.g., an infant without moss)
okiskinowâpiw– *NA* one who learns merely by watching, mere imitator
têpiyâhk *IPC* merely; barely, the most (if any); the only thing; so long as; *(in negative constructions:)* all but

MERRY
môcikipê– *VAI* have fun with alcohol, make merry with alcoholic drink

MESSAGE
ayamiwin– *NI* speech, message
itwêstamaw– *VTA* say thus for s.o.; speak for s.o.; interpret for s.o.; transmit s.o.'s message, relay s.o.'s message (e.g., by radio)

METAL
pîwâpiskw– *NI* metal, metal object; steel blade; screen of wire-mesh
pîwâpiskwâ– *VII* be metal
sôniyâwi– *VII* be precious metal; be money
wanihikan– *NI* trap, metal trap

MÉTIS
askiy– *NI* land, region, area; earth, world; settlement, colony, country; Métis settlement; *(plural:)* fields under cultivation, pieces of farmland, the lands
âpihcaw-âyis– *NA* halfbreed, Métis
âpihtawikosisân– *NA* halfbreed, Métis
âpihtawikosisânaskiy– *NI* halfbreed settlement, Métis settlement
âpihtawikosisânôcênâs– *NI* little halfbreed town, Métis settlement

MID-AIR
nayêwac *IPC* in mid-air

MID-DAY
âpihtâ-kîsikani-mîciso– *VAI* eat one's mid-day meal, eat one's lunch
âpihtâ-kîsikâ– *VII* be mid-day, be noon, be lunchtime

MIDDLE
nîpâ-tipisk *IPC* in the dark of the night, in the middle of the night
tastawayas *IPC* in between, in the middle

tâsawisâwât– *VTI* cut into the middle of s.t., slice s.t. open (e.g., veal belly cordon-bleu)
tâwic *IPC* in the middle (e.g., lake)

MIDNIGHT
âpihtâ-tipiskâ– *VII* be midnight
nîpâ-ayamihâ– *VAI* celebrate midnight mass (e.g., at Christmas)

MIDST
mêkwâ *IPV* while, during, in the course of; meanwhile; in the midst of
mêkwâskaw– *VTA* encounter s.o. in the midst of (it), catch s.o. in the act

MIDWIFE
nêhiyawi-maskihkîwiskwêw– *NA* Cree midwife; Indian midwife
pamih– *VTA* tend to s.o., look after s.o.; attend s.o. in childbirth, serve as midwife to s.o.; guide s.o. (e.g., sleigh), drive s.o. (e.g., sleigh)
pamihiso– *VAI* tend to oneself, look after oneself; attend oneself in childbirth, serve as one's own midwife
pamin– *VTA* tend to s.o., look after s.o.; attend s.o. in childbirth, serve as midwife to s.o.

MIGRATE
pimipayiho– *VAI* move along, migrate (e.g., fish)

MILD
miyo-kîsikâ– *VII* be good weather, be mild weather

MILK
îkin– *VTA* milk s.o. (e.g., cow)
îkinamaw– *VTA* milk (it/him) for s.o.
îkinikêsi– *VAI* milk, do one's milking
mosti-tôhtôsâpoy– *NI* mere milk, mere cow's milk
sîkopit– *VTA* press s.o. out by pulling; drain the milk from s.o. (e.g., cow)
tôhtôsâpoy– *NI* milk; milk come in (e.g., seen to have come down into the cow's udder at calving time)
yîkinikê– *VAI* milk, do the milking
yîkinikêstamâso– *VAI* do the milking for oneself

MILK-COW
yîkinikan– *NA* milk-cow

MINCED
sikwatahikanâpoy– *NI* minced-meat soup
sikwatahikâtê– *VII* be pounded, be minced (e.g., meat)

MIND
–stikwân– *NDI* head; head of hair; mind

awâska-mâmitonêyihcikan– NI stable mind, steady mind, balanced mind

itâpatakêyimo– VAI use one's mind thus, make such use of one's mental faculties

itêyimo– VAI think thus of (it/him) for oneself, have (it/him) in mind for oneself

kiskisoh– VTA make s.o. remember, remind s.o., put s.o. in mind

kiskisopayi– VAI suddenly remember, remember in a flash; suddenly think of (it), have (it) come to mind

kîsêyiht– VTI make up one's mind about s.t., decide on s.t., complete one's plan for s.t.; be decisive

kotêyiht– VTI try s.t. in one's mind, think strenuously about s.t., test s.t.; challenge s.t.

kotêyim– VTA try s.o., test s.o., put s.o.'s mind to the test; challenge s.o.

mâmitonêyihcikan– NI mind; troubled mind; thought, worry

mâmitonêyim– VTA think about s.o., have s.o. on one's mind; worry about s.o.

miskwêyihtamipayi– VAI suddenly have (it/him) come to mind

mitonêyihcikan– NI mind

nahêyiht– VTI be satisfied with s.t.; have peace of mind

nahêyihtamih– VTA cause s.o. to be satisfied with (it/him); grant s.o. peace of mind

nâkatawêyim– VTA watch s.o., keep one's mind trained on s.o.

wanêyiht– VTI forget s.t., be unsure of s.t.; have one's mind blurred, be confused

MINISTER
ayamihêwiyiniw– NA priest; minister; missionary

MINUS
nôhtaw IPC less; minus; previously; prematurely, incompletely, short of attainment

MIRROR
wâpamon– NI mirror

MISERABLE
kicimâkisi– VAI be pitiable, be miserable; be poor

kitimâkan– VII be pitiable, be miserable

kitimâkêyimo– VAI feel pitiable, feel miserable; feel poor

kitimâkinâkosi– VAI look pitiable, look miserable; look poor

kitimâkisi– VAI be pitiable, be miserable; be poor

MISERY
kitimah– VTA be mean to s.o., treat s.o. cruelly; bring misery upon s.o.

kitimaho– VAI be mean to oneself, treat oneself cruelly; bring misery upon oneself

kitimâkisiwin– NI misery; poverty

MISFORTUNE
nanayêhtâwipayiwin– NI misfortune, breakdown

MISPLACE
wanastâ– VAI misplace (it), mislay (it)

MISS
kakwêtawêyiht– VTI long for s.t., miss s.t.

kôtawêyiht– VTI be at a loss for s.t., miss s.t.

kôtawêyim– VTA be aware of s.o.'s absence, feel the loss of s.o., miss s.o.

kwîtawêyihcikâtê– VII be missed, be in short supply

mihtât– VTA deplore the loss of s.o., sorely miss s.o., grieve for s.o.

mwêsiskaw– VTA have chosen exactly the wrong time or place for s.o., just miss s.o.

patakwât– VTA miss s.o. with one's snare, fail to snare s.o.

patisk– VTI miss s.t. (by foot or body movement)

MISSIONARY
ayamihêwiyiniw– NA priest; minister; missionary

MISSOURI RIVER
pîkanowi-sîpiy– NI (place-name:) Missouri River

MISSPEAK
patowât– VTI misspeak s.t.; commit an error in one's prayers

MISTAKE
patinikê– VAI make a mistake, take a wrong step, transgress; (fig.) sin

pistin– VTI take s.t. accidentally, take s.t. by mistake

wanitonâmo– VAI make a mistake in speaking, commit a slip of the tongue

wanohtê– VAI err, make a mistake, take the wrong road

MISTREAT
kakwâhyakih– VTA do a terrible thing to s.o., mistreat s.o. greatly

MITTEN
astis– NA mitten, glove
MIX
kikin– VTA add s.o. (e.g., tobacco) in, mix s.o. in
kîkawên– VTI mix s.t. in, sprinkle s.t. over
kîkawin– VTA mix s.o. (e.g., tobacco) together by hand
takon– VTA add (it) to s.o. (e.g., flour), mix (it) into s.o. (e.g., dough); add s.o. to (it), enrich (it) with s.o.
takwastâ– VAI add something to (it), mix something in with (it)
MOAN
mamâhpinêmakan– VII moan, emit a moaning sound
MOCCASIN
asêsinw– NI beaded top of moccasin, vamp of moccasin
maskisin– NI moccasin, shoe
maskisinihkê– VAI make moccasins
maskisinihkêhkâso– VAI pretend to make moccasins
napakaskisin– NI flat moccasin
ocîhkwêhikan– NI pleated moccasin
pahkêkinwêskisin– NI hide moccasin
MOM
–mâmâ– NDA mom, mother
omâmâ– VAI have a mom or mother, have ones' mom living; have (her) as one's mom
MOMENT
katisk IPC just now, a moment ago; recently, a while ago; exactly, just at that moment, at the very moment; *(in negative constructions:)* not merely
nânapêc IPC late, at the last moment, barely in time (e.g., when it should have been done previously); *(in negative constructions:)* too late
MONDAY
pôn-âyamihêwi-kîsikâ– VII be Monday
MONEY
kaskihtamâso– VAI earn (it) for oneself, deserve (it); make money for oneself
mâwacisôniyâwê– VAI gather up money, pile up money
mêstinikê– VAI use things up, exhaust things, spend all of (it); spend all of one's money on things
miyo-sôniyâhkê– VAI make good money; earn good wages
osôniyâmi– VAI have money, carry money on oneself
sôniyâhkâkê– VAI make money with (it), use (it) to earn wages
sôniyâhkât– VTI make money at s.t., earn wages at s.t.
sôniyâhkê– VAI make money; earn wages; earn (it) as wages
sôniyâhkêsi– VAI make some money, earn a little money; earn some wages
sôniyâhkêwin– NI earning money; wages; income
sôniyâs– NA coin; 25-cents coin, quarter; a little money, some money
sôniyâw– NA gold, silver; money; wages
sôniyâwi IPV with respect to money, in financial matters
sôniyâwi– VII be precious metal; be money
tipahamâtowi-sôniyâw– NA Treaty money, Treaty payment
MONSTER
maci-pisiskiw– NA evil animal, monster
wîhtikow– NA cannibal monster; *(name:)* Wihtikow, Windigo
MONTH
ayîki-pîsimw– NA the month of April
kisipakim– VTA count s.o. (e.g., sun) as the end of the month
ohpahowi-pîsimw– NA the month of August
pêyak-pîsim IPC one month, for one month
pîsimw– NA sun; moon; month
tahto-pîsim IPC every month, each month, monthly, menstrual
tânitahto-pîsim IPC how many months; so many months
MOON
pîsimw– NA sun; moon; month
tipiskâwi-pîsimw– NA moon
MOOSE
apisi-môsw– NA small moose
môsw– NA moose
MOOSE-HAIR
môsopîway– NI moose-hair
MOOSE-HIDE
môso-pahkêkin– NI finished moose-hide
môswêkinw– NI moose-hide
MOOSE-MEAT
môso-wiyâs– NI moose-meat

MORE
  ayiwâk IPC more; *(in numeral phrases:)* plus
  ayiwâk ihkin IPC ever more so! this cannot be! would anyone believe this!
  ayiwâkêyiht– VTI think more of s.t., regard s.t. more highly
  ayiwâkêyim– VTA think more of s.o., regard s.o. more highly
  ayiwâkipayi– VAI have more than enough, have a surplus, have plenty; run to more, be a surplus, (e.g., money)
  âhkwakihtê– VII cost dearly, cost more, be worth a top-up amount
  âkwâc IPC well on its way, a long ways, more than halfway
  âkwâtaskinê– VAI be quite full (e.g., pail), be more than half full
  âstamispîhk IPC at a time closer to the present; more recently
  âstamita IPC later, more recently
  kanakêkâ IPC more especially
  katiskaw IPC to exact measure, no more than, barely
  kîhtwâm IPC again, once more, the next
  mis-âyiwâk IPC much more
  nawac IPC by comparison; more, better, rather
  nawac piko IPC sort of, kind of, approximately; more or less; even a little
  nowâhc IPC more properly
  tahk âyiwâk IPC increasingly, more and more
  wâwâc IPC especially, even, even more
  wâwîs cî IPC especially, all the more so
  yahkâtihkât– VTI dig out more of a hole or cellar, push out the size of an existing hole or cellar
  yâyâhk IPC really, for sure, to be sure; especially, all the more so
MORNING
  kîkisêpâ IPC early in the morning
  kîkisêpâyâ– VII be early in the morning
  tahto-kîkisêpâ IPC every morning, early each morning
  wâpan– VII be dawn, be early morning; be the next day
MORNING-STAR
  wâpanatâhkw– NA morning-star, Venus
MORTIFICATION
  kakwâtakâpâkwaho– VAI suffer mortification by denying oneself liquid, make oneself suffer thirst
MOSQUITO
  sakimêskâw– NI abundance of mosquitoes
  sakimêwayânêkin– NI mosquito screen, insect screen
MOSS
  askiy– NI moss
MOSSBAG
  wâspison– NI mossbag
  wâspisonis– NI mossbag
  wâspit– VTA wrap s.o. up in a mossbag, lace s.o. up in a mossbag, swaddle s.o.
MOST
  mâmawaci IPC *(in superlative constructions:)* most, the very most
  mâmâwacêyas IPC *(in superlative constructions:)* most, the very most
  mâwacêyas IPC *(in superlative constructions:)* most, the very most
  mâwaci IPV *(in superlative constructions:)* the most
  mistahi-pîtos IPC very strangely, most strangely, very differently
  têpiyâhk IPC merely; barely, the most (if any); the only thing; so long as; *(in negative constructions:)* all but
MOSTLY
  osâm piko IPC mainly, mostly
MOTHER
  –kâwiy– NDA mother, mother's sister; [*fig.*] Our Mother
  –kâwîs– NDA mother's sister, parallel aunt; step-mother
  –mâmâ– NDA mom, mother
  –sikos– NDA father's sister, mother's brother's wife; mother-in-law, father-in-law's brother's wife, "aunt"
  –sis– NDA mother's brother, father's sister's husband; father-in-law, father-in-law's brother, "uncle"
  kihc-ôkâwîmâw– NA *(name:)* Great Mother, Mother Earth
  ocawâsimisi– VAI have a child; have offspring, have a calf (as cow); have (her/him) as one's child; be the mother of a child; give birth, be delivered; calve (as cow)
  okâwîmâw– NA a mother
  okâwîmâwaskiy– NI *(name:)* Mother Earth

omâmâ– VAI have a mom or mother, have ones' mom living; have (her) as one's mom

opêpîmi– VAI have an infant, have a baby; have (her/him) as one's infant; be the mother of an infant; give birth, be delivered

osisi– VAI have a mother's brother or father-in-law; have (him) as one's mother's brother or father-in-law

MOTHER-IN-LAW

–sikos– NDA father's sister, mother's brother's wife; mother-in-law, father-in-law's brother's wife, "aunt"

osikosi– VAI have a father's sister or mother-in-law; have (her) as one's father's sister or mother-in-law

MOTIF

nêhiyaw-masinîwin– NI Cree design, Cree motif

MOTION

nîmihito– VAI dance with one another, dance; dance a (secular) dance; dance as prairie-chicken; move about in a dancing motion, dance (e.g., northern lights)

MOULD

wiyatahw– VTA pound s.o. (e.g., earring), mould s.o., shape s.o.

MOUNTED

itamon– VII run thus or there as a path; be thus attached, be mounted thus

têhtapi– VAI be mounted, ride on horseback

MOUSE

âpakosîs– NA mouse

MOUTH

–cônis– NDI mouth

–tôn– NDI mouth

kêcikonêwên– VTA take (it/him) out of s.o.'s mouth

mêscitonêsin– VAI have exhausted one's mouth, wear one's mouth out

mihkotonê– VAI have a red mouth, wear lipstick

mihkotonêho– VAI paint one's mouth red, wear lipstick

mihkotonêhw– VTA paint s.o.'s mouth red, put lipstick on s.o.

miskwam– VTA find s.o. (e.g., coin) by mouth, find s.o. (e.g., coin) in one's food

pîkokonêwêpayi– VAI have cracks erupt in one's mouth, have one's mouth break out in sores (e.g., with thrush)

saskamonahiso– VAI give oneself communion, place the host into one's mouth

sôpaht– VTI put s.t. in one's mouth

tahkwam– VTA hold s.o. fast by mouth, hold s.o. in one's mouth

tâwati– VAI have one's mouth open

tâwatipayi– VAI suddenly open one's mouth

MOUTHPIECE

otônihkâ– VAI use (it/him) as one's mouthpiece, make (it/him) one's advocate

MOVE

atimipayi– VAI move the other way, speed away

âhc-âyâ– VAI move one's abode, move from one place to another

âhtahpit– VTI move and tie s.t., tie s.t. differently; change the bandage on s.t.

âhtin– VTI move s.t. over, push s.t. aside

âhtohtê– VAI move to a different place, go elsewhere

âhtokê– VAI move camp, move one's camp elsewhere

âsipayin– VII move down, hang down, be dragged down

asîmakan– VII go down, move down

âsowakâmêpici– VAI move one's camp across a body of water

âsô-nakî– VAI stop in moving across (e.g., the prairies), stop in one's transit

cacâstapipayin– VII move rapidly

isiniskêyi– VAI move one's arm thus or there, point in that direction with one's arm

isiwêpin– VTA move s.o. (e.g., wing) thus

ispayi– VAI move thus, drive there

ispayiho– VAI throw oneself thus or there, move thus or there

ispici– VAI move thus or there with one's camp, move one's household there

itâpihkêpayi– VAI move thus or there as a rope or snake, swing thus as a rope or snake

kisîkotê– VII move fast through the sky (e.g., cloud)

kospî– VAI move away from the water, move off into the bush

masinipayi– VAI be depicted as moving (e.g., on film)

matâwisi– VAI move into the open, come out onto the open prairie

mitâsipici– *VAI* move camp into the open, move one's camp out onto the open prairie
mostohtê– *VAI* simply walk, move along without instrument, be on foot
môsko-miywêyiht– *VTI* cry with joy about s.t.; be moved to tears of joy
naskwên– *VTA* collect s.o. while moving, pick s.o. up on one's way
natahipayiho– *VAI* move upriver, spawn (e.g., fish)
nîhcipayi– *VAI* come down, move down, fall down
nîmihito– *VAI* dance with one another, dance; dance a (secular) dance; dance as prairie-chicken; move about in a dancing motion, dance (e.g., northern lights)
ocipicikâtê– *VII* be pulled off, be moved (e.g., house, granary)
ocipit– *VTI* pull s.t. out (e.g., from the ground), pull s.t. off; extract s.t. (e.g., grease from soup); move s.t. (e.g., house)
otihtapinahisin– *VAI* move to lie face-down
papâmipici– *VAI* move about, travel around, camp here and there, move around with one's camp
paskêpayi– *VAI* branch off, move off to the side; stop off there
paskêtâpaso– *VAI* branch off with one's wagon, move off to the side with one's vehicle; pull over with a vehicle
pâpici– *VAI* move one's camp hither
pici– *VAI* move camp, move with one's camp
pimakocin– *VAI* move along, go by; work, be in working order (e.g., clock, car)
pimi *IPV* along, in linear progression; while moving in linear progression
pimipayi– *VII* move along; run, run along; be on, work, function (e.g., motor, electricity); exist currently, take place
pimipayiho– *VAI* move along, migrate (e.g., fish)
pimipici– *VAI* move camp, move along with one's camp
pimiskâ– *VAI* swim by, swim along; go by in a boat, move along by one's own power
pimitâpaso– *VAI* move along in a vehicle
pimohtêmakan– *VII* go along, move along; go on, be in effect (e.g., treaty)

sâkohtê– *VAI* walk into view, move into view
takwaskî– *VAI* arrive on the land, move onto the land, join those already on the land
waskawipit– *VTI* move s.t. by pulling, shake s.t. by pulling
waskawî– *VAI* move, move about, be energetic
waskawîmakan– *VII* move, move about, be shaken by an earthquake
yîkatêpayin– *VII* move off to the side, move sideways (e.g., braided strips of rabbitskin)

MUCH
ahpihc *IPC* very much
âkwâskam *IPC* really, rather; *(in negative constructions:)* not really, not as much
êkoyikohk *IPC* that much, up to that point, to that degree, to that extent
iskon– *VTI* have so much of s.t. left over
iskwaht– *VTI* leave so much of s.t. (e.g., food) over; have s.t. (e.g., food) left over
iskwahtâ– *VAI* have so much of (it) left over; have (it) left over, have a plentiful supply of (it)
ispîhtêyihtâkwan– *VII* be considered worth so much
itakiht– *VTI* count s.t. thus, value s.t. thus, hold s.t. in such esteem; charge so much for s.t.
itakihtê– *VII* be counted thus, be valued thus, be held in such esteem; be worth so much, cost so much
itakiso– *VAI* be counted thus, be valued thus; be held in such esteem; be worth so much; have such a function
iyikohk *IPC* so much, to such a degree, to such an extent
mihcêt *IPC* many, much
mis-âyiwâk *IPC* much more
misi-mîci– *VAI* eat much of (it), eat a lot of (it)
mistahi *IPC* greatly, very much so, very many
mistakihtê– *VII* be counted for much, be worth a lot, be valuable, be expensive
nihtâ *IPV* good at, doing much of, competent, practised, experienced
osâm *IPC* too much, excessively
ômayikohk *IPC* this much, to this degree, to this extent

pikoyikohk *IPC* to any extent, no matter how much

MUD
asiskiy– *NI* earth, soil, mud; clay; sod
asiskîhkât– *VTI* mud s.t., plaster s.t.
asiskîhkê– *VAI* mud a log-house, do the mudding, hold a mudding bee
asiskîwi-kocawânâpiskos– *NA* mud stove
asiskîwikamikos– *NI* mud shack
micimoskowahtâ– *VAI* make (it) hold together with mud, mud (it) with clay
micimoskowahtê– *VII* be held together with mud, be mudded with clay
micimoskowê– *VAI* be stuck in mud or bog
sisoskiwakin– *VTI* mud s.t. (e.g., log-house), plaster s.t.
sisoskiwakinamâso– *VAI* do the mudding for oneself
sisoskiwakinikâtê– *VII* be mudded
sisoskiwakinikê– *VAI* do the mudding
sisowaskinikê– *VAI* put on mud or plaster; mud one's log-house

MUD-PIE
asiskîwi-pahkwêsikan– *NA* mud-pie

MUSIC
kitohcikêmakan– *VII* blare out music (e.g., as stereo-player)

MUSICAL
kitohcikê– *VAI* play a musical instrument; play one's stereo-player

MUSKEG
maskêkw– *NI* swamp, bog, muskeg

MUSKEG LAKE
maskêko-sâkahikanihk *INM* (place-name:) Muskeg Lake (Saskatchewan); *opitihkwahâkêw*'s Reserve
maskêkowiyiniw– *NA* Muskeg Lake person, member of *opitihkwahâkêw*'s band

MUSKRAT
wacaskw– *NA* muskrat

MUST
piko *IPC* must, have to

MUTUAL
asotamâtowin– *NI* mutual promise, promises made to one another
sâkihitowin– *NI* mutual love; charity

NAG
kwatakim– *VTA* speak meanly to s.o., nag s.o.

NAIL
kiposakahikâtê– *VII* be nailed shut
pimâskwamon– *VII* run fastened along as wood, be nailed along (e.g., at regular intervals)
sakah– *VTI* nail s.t. on, attach s.t. by nails
sakahikan– *NI* nail
sâposci-sakah– *VTI* nail s.t. through, nail through s.t.

NAME
isiyîhkâso– *VAI* be called thus, have such a name
isiyîhkât– *VTA* call s.o. thus, use such a name for s.o.
isiyîhkât– *VTI* call s.t. thus, use such a name for s.t.
isiyîhkâtê– *VII* be called thus, have such a name
itâspinêm– *VTA* call s.o. thus in anger, angrily call s.o. such a name, thus scold s.o. in anger
môniyâwi-wîhowin– *NI* White name, English name
nêhiyaw-îsiyîhkâtê– *VII* have a Cree name
nêhiyawi-wîh– *VTA* use s.o.'s Cree name, call s.o. by a Cree name
nêhiyawi-wîhowin– *NI* Cree name; Indian name
nêhiyawi-wîht– *VTI* use the Cree name of s.t., call s.t. by a Cree name
nêhiyawiyîhkâso– *VAI* have a Cree name
nêhiyawiyîhkât– *VTA* give s.o. a Cree name
nêhiyawiyîhkât– *VTI* give s.t. a Cree name
nêhiyawiyîhkâtê– *VII* be a Cree name
owîhowini– *VAI* have a name; have (it) as one's name
wîh– *VTA* name s.o., mention s.o. by name
wîhowin– *NI* name
wîht– *VTI* name s.t., mention s.t. by name; tell about s.t., report s.t.; decree s.t.

NAMESAKE
okwêmêsi– *VAI* have a namesake; have (her/him) as one's namesake, be named after (her/him)

NAP
nipâsi– *VAI* sleep a little, take a nap

NAPKIN
âsiyân– *NA* loin-cloth, diaper, menstrual napkin

NATURAL ORDER
pâstâho– *VAI* breach the natural order, transgress; *(fig.)* sin, be a sinner
pâstâhowi-mihkw– *NI* blood tainted by a breach of the natural order; *(fig.)* blood tainted by deicide, sinful blood
pâstâhowin– *NI* transgression, breach of the natural order; *(fig.)* sin

NEAR
apîst– *VTI* sit by s.t., live by s.t., live near s.t.
cîki *IPC* close, close by, nearby, near to
itakâm *IPC* on the hither side of a body of water, on the near side of a body of water
nêsowisi– *VAI* be weak, be exhausted, be near death
nîpêpîstaw– *VTA* sit up late at night with s.o.; sit at s.o.'s bedside, sit with s.o. near death; sit at a wake for s.o., hold a wake for s.o.

NEARBY
câh-cîkâhtaw *IPC* quite close, quite nearby
cîkâhtaw *IPC* close, nearby, in the area, in the immediate vicinity
cîki *IPC* close, close by, nearby, near to
kisâcî– *VAI* stay behind, stay around, stay nearby
kisiwâk *IPC* nearby

NECESSARILY
katâc *IPC* insistently; *(in negative constructions:)* not necessarily
kâkatâc *IPC* insistently; *(in negative constructions:)* not necessarily
môy êkâ êtokwê *IPC* without any doubt, of necessity
ohcitaw *IPC* expressly, specifically, purposely, necessarily; it is requisite, it is meet indeed

NECK
–kwayaw– *NDI* neck
pîmiskwêyi– *VAI* turn one's head sideways, twist one's neck (e.g., owl)
sâkiskwêhpit– *VTA* wrap s.o. up to the neck, swaddle s.o. up to the neck
tâpisk– *VTI* wear s.t. fitted, wear s.t. around the neck
wîpakwêpayi– *VAI* have one's neck snapped (e.g., in a snare)

NEGATIVELY
mâyiskaw– *VTA* go through s.o. to bad effect, affect s.o. negatively, fail to agree with s.o.; *(especially in inverse constructions:)* have an adverse effect on s.o., make s.o. ill

NEGLECTED
wêpinikan– *NA* abandoned child, neglected child

NEGOTIATIONS
isîhcikê– *VAI* do things thus, proceed thus, arrange things thus; perform such a rite, perform a rite thus; conduct negotiations thus
wiyîhcikê– *VAI* conduct negotiations, conclude negotiations

NEGRO
kaskitêwiyâs– *NA* Negro, Black person

NEPHEW
–kosis– *NDA* son, parallel nephew; *(fig.)* younger man

NEST
wacistwan– *NI* nest

NET
ayapiy– *NA* net, fishing-net
nâtahapê– *VAI* check one's nets
pakitahwâ– *VAI* fish by net, set nets

NEVER
nama wîhkâc *IPC* never
wîhkâc *IPC* ever; *(in negative constructions:)* never

NEVER MIND
kiyâm *IPC* oh well, never mind, so much for this; anyway, rather; let it be, let there be no further delay; please

NEVERTHELESS
âhci *IPC* still, nevertheless, despite everything
âhci piko *IPC* still, nevertheless, despite everything
kêyiwêhk *IPC* just in case, nevertheless; despite shortcomings
kîhkîhk *IPC* nevertheless

NEW
oski *IPN* young, fresh, new
oski-napatâkw– *NI* new potato, fresh potato
oskiskwêwê– *VAI* have a new wife

NEW YEAR'S
ocêhtowi-kîsikâ– *VII* be New Year's Day

NEWLY
mastaw *IPC* newly, recently

NEXT
iyaskohc *IPC* next in sequence
kîhtwâm *IPC* again, once more, the next
wâpan– *VII* be dawn, be early morning; be the next day

NICE
cakahki-nôcikwêsîwi– *VAI* be a nice old woman, be a wonderful old woman
miyo-wîki– *VAI* live comfortably, have a nice dwelling
miyoht– *VTI* like the sound of s.t., consider s.t. to sound nice
miyonâkohcikê– *VAI* be seen to be good at things, make things look nice, make things look prosperous
miyonâkwan– *VII* look good, have a nice appearance, look prosperous
takahkâciwasw– *VTA* boil s.o. (e.g., rabbit) nicely, boil s.o. well
takahkâpâwê– *VII* be nicely washed with water
takahkêyim– *VTA* think well of s.o., consider s.o. nice, like s.o.
takahki *IPN* nice, good, beautiful
takahki *IPV* nice, good, beautiful
takahkihtaw– *VTA* like the sound of s.o., consider s.o. to sound nice
takahkihtâkosi– *VAI* sound nice, sound beautiful
takahkihtâkwan– *VII* sound nice, sound beautiful
takahkikihtâ– *VAI* make (it) grow nicely, make (it) a nice garden; have a nice garden
takahkinâkohtâ– *VAI* make (it) look nice, make (it) look beautiful
takahkipahtâ– *VAI* run nicely (e.g., horse), run beautifully
takahkipicikê– *VAI* drive a nice team, drive beautiful horses
takahkisîhtâ– *VAI* make (it) nice, make (it) beautiful
takahkwêwêhtitâ– *VAI* make (it) sound nice by drumming or tapping; make a nice drumming or tapping sound
takahkwêwêsin– *VAI* fall with nice sounds, make nice sounds with one's shoes

NICOTINE
pîhtwâ– *VAI* smoke, use the pipe; smoke (him) (e.g., pipe); hold a pipe ceremony; be a nicotine addict

NIECE
–cânis– *NDA* daughter, parallel niece
–tânis– *NDA* daughter, parallel niece
–tôsimiskwêm– *NDA* sister's daughter (woman speaking), parallel niece (woman speaking)

NIGHT
–tipiskâm– *NDI* night, night of one's life
kapê-tipisk *IPC* all night long, throughout the night
kaski-tipiskâ– *VII* be the dark of the night
katikoni– *VAI* sleep over, spend the night
kîsi-tipiskâ– *VII* be completely night
nêwo-tipiskâ– *VII* be four nights, be the fourth night
nîpâ *IPV* in the dark of the night
nîpâ-tipisk *IPC* in the dark of the night, in the middle of the night
nîpâhtâ– *VAI* stay out until late in the night
nîpêpi– *VAI* sit up late at night with (her/him) (e.g., someone near death); hold a wake, take part in a wake
nîpêpîstaw– *VTA* sit up late at night with s.o.; sit at s.o.'s bedside, sit with s.o. near death; sit at a wake for s.o., hold a wake for s.o.
nîso-tipiskâ– *VII* be two nights, be the second night
nîso-tipiskâw *IPC* two nights, for two nights
pêyak-tipiskâw *IPC* one night, for one night
tipiskâ– *VII* be night
tipiskâw– *NI* night, night sky
tipiskisi– *VAI* spend one's night, live through the night
tipiskohk *IPC* last night
wani-tipiskâ– *VII* be dark night
wani-tipiskin– *VTI* perceive s.t. as darkness; merely see night, perceive merely darkness
wâpanwêwit– *VTI* make noise until dawn, bark through the night (e.g., dog)

NINETY
kêkâ-mitâtahtomitanaw *IPC* ninety

NO
mwâc *IPC* no, not
namôya *IPC* not; no
namwâc *IPC* not; no

NOBILITY
okimâsis– *NA* little chief, boss; *(fig.)* nobility

NOD
nânâmiskwêyi– *VAI* nod one's head

NOISE
itihtâkosihkâso– *VAI* pretend to be heard making such a noise, act as if to make such a noise
itwêwit– *VTI* make such a noise

ENGLISH INDEX   333

kito– VAI utter a sound, call, sing (e.g., bird); make noises (e.g., animal), hoot; be a thunderclap
kitowêyêkinikê– VAI make a noise with paper, rustle one's paper
mwêstâtwêwit– VTI make troublesome noise, make a nuisance of oneself by being noisy
pêhtâkosi– VAI be heard, make oneself heard, make noise
pitihkwê– VII thud, make a thudding noise (e.g., the rushing of water, the fall of hooves, the rapid wing movements of a dancing prairie-chicken)
pônwêwit– VTI cease making noise; keep quiet
tasin– VTI pull the trigger on s.t. (e.g., gun), shoot s.t. off (e.g., gun); emit a sharp noise, make a shot-like noise; sound a thunderclap (e.g., as Thunderbird)
wâpanwêwit– VTI make noise until dawn, bark through the night (e.g., dog)

NON-CATHOLIC
môniyâw-âyamihâwin– NI White religion; non-Catholic denomination

NON-EXISTENT
namatakon– VII be non-existent, be absent; have disappeared, be no longer in existence
namatê– VAI be non-existent, be absent; have disappeared, be no longer in existence

NON-INDIAN
môniyâs– NA non-Indian, White person
môniyâw– NA non-Indian, White person
wâpiski-wiyâs– NA non-Indian, White person
wêmistikôsiw– NA Frenchman; non-Indian, White person

NONE
nama kîkway PR nothing; not at all; there is none

NOON
âpihtâ-kîsikâ– VII be mid-day, be noon, be lunchtime

NORTH
kîwêtinohk IPC north, in the north
nâtakâm IPC in the north, to the north

NOSE
–skiwan– NDI nose

NOT
ahpônâni IPC of course not, not any
âkwâskam IPC really, rather; *(in negative constructions:)* not really, not as much
êkamâ IPC it is not the case
êkâ IPC not to
êkâya IPC not to; do not!
êkwayâc IPC only then, not until then; only now, for the first time
iyawis IPC fully, entirely; the whole lot, the entire household; *(in negative constructions:)* only partially, not exclusively
katisk IPC just now, a moment ago; recently, a while ago; exactly, just at that moment, at the very moment; *(in negative constructions:)* not merely
kîspin êkâ ohci IPC if it were not for
manâ IPC in avoiding, in sparing, being careful not to
manâ-koskon– VTA avoid waking s.o. up, be careful not to wake s.o. up
mâmaskâc IPC strangely, marvellously, amazingly; *(in negative constructions:)* not surprisingly, no wonder
mosciwâk IPC *(in negative constructions:)* not at all, not under any circumstances
môy misikiti– VAI be not big, be small
môya IPC not
nam êskwa IPC not yet
nama IPC not
nama cî IPC is it not the case
nama kîkway PR nothing; not at all; there is none
nama mayaw IPC not immediately, later; too late
namôy âhpô IPC not even
namôy âpisis IPC not a little, quite a lot
namôya IPC not; no
namôya cî IPC is it not the case
namwâc IPC not; no

NOTHING
konita IPC in vain, without reason, without purpose, for nothing; without further ado; anywhere, at random, in a random place
môy nânitaw IPC it is alright, there is nothing wrong with that
nama kîkway PR nothing; not at all; there is none

pakwanawahtâ– VAI go on with (it) at random, know nothing about (it), be clueless about (it)

NOTICE

nâkatâpam– VTA notice s.o. by sight

nâkatôhkâtito– VAI take notice of one another, watch over one another, keep a careful eye on one another

nâkatôhkê– VAI take notice, pay attention, be observant; attend to people, watch over people

patahôhkât– VTA overlook s.o., fail to notice s.o., ignore s.o.

pisiskâpam– VTA notice s.o.

pisiskêyiht– VTI pay attention to s.t., take notice of s.t.; bother with s.t.

pisiskêyim– VTA pay attention to s.o., take notice of s.o., tend to s.o.; bother s.o., harass s.o.

NOW

ahâw IPC now indeed! ready! let's go!

anohc IPC now, today

êkwa IPC then, now; and

êkwayâc IPC only then, not until then; only now, for the first time

hâm IPC now then

hâw IPC now, now then

ispîhci IPC for now, in the meantime; *(in comparative constructions:)* by comparison; than

iyaw IPC well now; ho!

katisk IPC just now, a moment ago; recently, a while ago; exactly, just at that moment, at the very moment; *(in negative constructions:)* not merely

kâh-kipîhci IPC stopping now and then

wâh-wîhkâc IPC at rare intervals, rarely now and again

NUISANCE

mwêstâcîhkaw– VTA bother s.o., annoy s.o., make a nuisance of oneself to s.o., be troublesome for s.o.

mwêstâtwêwêm– VTA speak about s.o. as troublesome, complain about s.o. being a nuisance

mwêstâtwêwit– VTI make troublesome noise, make a nuisance of oneself by being noisy

NUMBER

ihtahtopiponwêwin– NI having so many years, the number of one's years, one's age

itêyati– VAI be such in number, be so many

misahkamik IPC a great many, in great number

NUMEROUS

kakwâhyakêyati– VAI be in great numbers, be plentiful, be very numerous

mihcêti– VAI be numerous, be plentiful

mihcêtin– VII be numerous, be plentiful

mihcêtôsê– VAI have many children, have numerous offspring

NUN

ayamihêwiskwêw– NA nun

NURSE

maskihkîwiskwêw– NA nurse

nôh– VTA suckle s.o., nurse s.o., breastfeed s.o.

nôhâwaso– VAI nurse one's child, breastfeed one's child; suckle the young one (of the species), suckle one's calf (as cow)

nôni– VAI suck at the breast, nurse at the breast; suck at the teats (e.g., calf)

pôni-nôhâwaso– VAI stop nursing one's child, wean one's child

NWMP

mihkwasâkay– NA red-coat, officer of the NWMP

OATS

asamastimwân– NA green-feed, oats

kistikân– NA grain, seed; sheaf of grain; oats

OBEY

nanahiht– VTI listen well to s.t.; obey s.t.

nanahihtaw– VTA listen well to s.o.; obey s.o.

OBSCENE

wiyâhkwêwi-âcimo– VAI swear in telling stories; tell obscene stories, tell risqué stories

OBSCENITIES

wiyâhkwât– VTA swear at s.o., speak to s.o. in obscenities

OBSERVATION

kiskinawâpi– VAI learn by observation, learn by example; learn merely by watching

kiskinowâpiwin– NI learning by observation, learning by example; learning merely by watching

OBSERVE

kanawâpahkê– VAI watch things, watch people, observe people

kanawâpam– VTA look at s.o., watch s.o., observe s.o.; look after s.o.

kitâpahkê– VAI watch things, observe people

nâkatawâpam– *VTA* pay attention in looking at s.o., observe s.o.

nâkatowâpaht– *VTI* pay attention in looking at s.t., observe s.t.

nâkatôhkê– *VAI* take notice, pay attention, be observant; attend to people, watch over people

nitawâpahkê– *VAI* watch things, observe people

nitawâpaht– *VTI* go to see s.t., observe s.t., check s.t. out

wâpahkê– *VAI* watch things, observe people

OBSTACLE

âkaw-âyihk *IPC* hidden, out of view, behind an obstacle to vision

âkwaskikâpawi– *VAI* stand in the way, stand as an obstacle

OBTAIN

kâhcitin– *VTA* catch s.o., seize s.o., get s.o. (e.g., a spouse); obtain s.o. (e.g., money)

kâhcitin– *VTI* catch s.t., seize s.t., obtain s.t.; get s.t. back

kâsînamâso– *VAI* wipe (it) off for oneself; *(fig.)* have one's sins forgiven, obtain forgiveness

kwâpikê– *VAI* dip out water, draw water, haul water, obtain one's drinking water

manipit– *VTA* pull s.o. free (e.g., thorn, porcupine quills), pull s.o. in (e.g., net), pull s.o. out, obtain s.o. by pulling

manipit– *VTI* pull s.t. free, pull s.t. out (e.g., flower), obtain s.t. by pulling

nâcinêhamaw– *VTA* obtain (it/him) from s.o. by payment, seek to buy medicine from s.o.

nâcinêhikê– *VAI* obtain things by payment, seek to buy medicine

nâtamawât– *VTI* seek to obtain s.t. for (it/him); take s.t. up for (it/him)

ohtahipê– *VAI* obtain water from there, draw one's drinking water from there

ohtin– *VTI* take s.t. from there, obtain s.t. thereby or from there

ohtinikê– *VAI* take things from there, obtain things thereby or from there

ohtisi– *VAI* earn (it) thereby or from there, earn (it) for that; obtain payment thereby or from there

otinikâtê– *VII* be taken, be obtained; be chosen

OBVIOUSLY

cikêmâ *IPC* of course, obviously, as might be expected

OCCUR

ihkin– *VII* happen thus; occur, take place

ispayin– *VII* take place thus, occur thus; run thus (in a cycle), be there (in a cycle), come around (in a cycle), be that time again; come by, go by, have passed (e.g., days, years)

ODD

pîtotêyihtâkosi– *VAI* be thought strange, be considered odd

wawiyatêyiht– *VTI* find s.t. funny, consider s.t. amusing; be funny about s.t., behave oddly

ODOUR

âhkwâpahtê– *VII* give off a sharp odour, produce pungent fumes, emit acidic or caustic fumes

wîhcêkimahkasikê– *VAI* give off a bad smell, produce a foul odour

wîhkimâkwan– *VII* smell good, give off a pleasant odour; have an aromatic odour

OF COURSE

ahpônâni *IPC* of course not, not any

cikêmâ *IPC* of course, obviously, as might be expected

pîhtaw *IPC* in the event, of course

wiy âta wiya *IPC* but of course

OFFER

nîmin– *VTI* hold s.t. aloft, offer s.t. up

nîminamaw– *VTA* hold (it/him) aloft for s.o., offer (it/him) up for s.o.

nîminikê– *VAI* hold things aloft, offer things up

pîsâkwan– *VII* contain plenty, offer lots of room; be plentiful, be rich

OFFERING

kîskisamaw– *VTA* cut (it/him) off for s.o.; cut tobacco as an offering to s.o., present tobacco to s.o.

moscitôn *IPC* gratuitously by speech, without adding a gift or offering

wêpinâson– *NI* draped cloth, flag, cloth offering

OFFICE

nîkânapi– *VAI* be at the head, be in the lead, be in charge; hold the office of director

tâpapîstamaw– *VTA* sit in s.o.'s place, succeed s.o. in office

OFFSPRING

mihcêtôsê– *VAI* have many children, have numerous offspring

ocawâsimisi– VAI have a child; have offspring, have a calf (as cow); have (her/him) as one's child; be the mother of a child; give birth, be delivered; calve (as cow)

OFTEN
wâh-wîpac IPC quite often, again and again, repeatedly

OIL
askîwi-pimiy– NI coal oil, petroleum
pimiy– NI fat, oil; crude petroleum

OLD
–îci-kisêyin– NDA fellow old man, co-elder
–îci-kisêyiniw– NDA fellow old man, co-elder
–îci-kîhkâw– NDA aged spouse, fellow old person, fellow oldster, companion of one's old age
–kêhtê-ayim– NDA old person, parent, grandparent; elder
–kisêyinîm– NDA old man, husband
–mosôm– NDA grandfather, grandfather's brother; *(fig.)* old man, respected elder
–nôtokwêm– NDA old lady, wife
–ôhkom– NDA grandmother, grandmother's sister, "great-aunt"; *(fig.)* old woman; Our Grandmother
cakahki-nôcikwêsîwi– VAI be a nice old woman, be a wonderful old woman
icahcopiponêsi– VAI be so many years old (e.g., infant)
itahtopiponê– VAI be so many years old
itahtw-âskîwinê– VAI be so many years old
kayâs-ây– NI old stuff
kayâs-isîhcikêwin– NI the old way of doing things, traditional culture
kayâsi-pimâcihowin– NI old life, traditional way of life
kayâsi-wâskahikan– NI old house, traditional house
kêhcê-ayiwi– VAI be old
kêhtê-ay– NA old person, the old; elder
kêhtê-ayisiyiniw– NDA old person
kêhtê-ayiwi– VAI be an old person, get old; be an elder
kêhtêskwêw– NA old woman, old lady
kêhtêyâtisi– VAI be old, be advanced in age
kisêyiniw– NA old man
kisêyinîsis– NA little old man, wizened old man
kisêyinîw-âcimowin– NI old man's story, report of the old men
kisêyinîw-ôhpikihâkan– NA old man's pupil, ward of the old men
kisêyinîwi IPN of an old man, befitting an old man
kisêyinîwi– VAI be an old man
kisêyinîwi-pîkiskwêwin– NI old man's word, word of the old men
nistopiponwê– VAI be three years old
nôtokwêsiw– NA old woman
nôtokwêw– NA old woman
nôtokwêwi– VAI be an old woman
tânimatahtw-âskîwinê– VAI be how many years old; be so many years old

OLD-AGE
kêhtêwasinahikan– NI pension cheque, old-age pension

OLDER
–mis– NDA older sister, older female parallel cousin
–stês– NDA older brother, older male parallel cousin
omisi– VAI have an older sister; have (her) as one's older sister

OLDEST
omisimâs– NI the oldest sister
omisimâw– NA the oldest sister
ostêsimâw– NA the oldest brother
ostêsimâwi– VAI be the oldest brother

OMASUM
omâw– NA "bible", manyplies, omasum

ONCE
âskaw IPC sometimes; once in a while
kîhtwâm IPC again, once more, the next
kîtahtawê IPC at times, sometimes; at one time, all at once, suddenly
nîsowê– VAI speak as two at once
pêyakwâw IPC once

ONE
aya PR the one
êwako PR that one
kîkw-ây– NA which one; what kind
kîtahtawê IPC at times, sometimes; at one time, all at once, suddenly
napatê IPC on one side
nâha PR that one yonder
nikotwâw IPC either one, anyone
nistamêmâkan– NA the first one, the original one

ôyâ PR that one no longer here
pâh-pêyak IPC singly, one at a time; each one, each individually, each; one each
pêh-pêyak IPC one after another, one by one
pêyak IPC one, alone, a single one; the only one; a certain one
pêyak-askiy IPC one year, for one year
pêyak-ispayiw IPC one week, for one week
pêyak-kîsikâw IPC one day, for one day, in one day; per day
pêyak-misit IPC one foot, for one foot; measuring one foot
pêyak-pîsim IPC one month, for one month
pêyak-tipahikan IPC one hour
pêyak-tipahôpân IPC one gallon of alcoholic drink (e.g., wine)
pêyak-tipiskâw IPC one night, for one night
pêyako- VAI be alone, be the only one; be left alone; go alone (e.g., as a woman, improperly)
pêyako-kosikwan IPC one pound; per pound
pêyakoh- VTA have s.o. as the only one, be faithful to s.o. (e.g., spouse)
pêyakoyâkan IPC one dish (measure)
pêyakw-ây- NA a single one (e.g., stocking); one pair
pêyakw-âya IPC one team of horses, a single team of horses
pêyakwahpitêw IPC one team (of two horses)
pêyakwanohk IPC in one place, in a single place; in the same place
pêyakwayak IPC in one place, in a certain place; in the same place
pêyakwâpisk IPC one dollar
pêyakwêskihk IPC one kettle (measure)
tâna PR which one

ONION
wîhcêkaskosiy- NI onion, wild onion

ONION LAKE
wîhcêkaskosîwi-sâkahikanihk INM (place-name:) Onion Lake (Saskatchewan)

ONLY
êkwayâc IPC only then, not until then; only now, for the first time
iyawis IPC fully, entirely; the whole lot, the entire household; (in negative constructions:) only partially, not exclusively
kanakê IPC at least, even if only
kîkwây piko IPC the only thing is
nayêstaw IPC only, exclusively; it is only that
pâtimâ IPC no earlier, only later
pâtos IPC only later
pêyak IPC one, alone, a single one; the only one; a certain one
pêyako- VAI be alone, be the only one; be left alone; go alone (e.g., as a woman, improperly)
pêyakoh- VTA have s.o. as the only one, be faithful to s.o. (e.g., spouse)
piko IPC only
têpiyâhk IPC merely; barely, the most (if any); the only thing; so long as; (in negative constructions:) all but

OPEN
côhkâpisi- VAI open one's eyes a little, have one's eyes open a little
kotawân- NI campfire, open fire
matâwisi- VAI move into the open, come out onto the open prairie
matâwisipit- VTI pull s.t. into the open, pull s.t. out onto the open prairie
mitâsipici- VAI move camp into the open, move one's camp out onto the open prairie
nawacî- VAI roast (it), roast (it) over an open fire; roast one's food
pasahkâpi- VAI blink, shut and open one's eyes
pâskihtên- VTI open s.t. (e.g., window)
pâskin- VTI open s.t. up, take the cover off s.t.; fold s.t. (e.g., book) open
pâskiwêpin- VTI throw s.t. open (e.g., lodge-cover)
sâpotawâ- VII be open through and through
taswêkin- VTI unfold s.t. as cloth; open s.t. (e.g., book) up flat
tawâ- VII be open, have room
tawâtamaw- VTA open (it) up for s.o.; clear the way for s.o.
tawin- VTI open s.t. (e.g., house, bottle); turn s.t. on (e.g., stereo, TV)
tawinamaw- VTA open (it/him) for s.o.; (fig.) open the door to s.o. (e.g., devil)
tâsawisâwât- VTI cut into the middle of s.t., slice s.t. open (e.g., veal belly cordon-bleu)

tâwati– VAI have one's mouth open
tâwatipayi– VAI suddenly open one's mouth
tôhkâpi– VAI open one's eyes, have one's eyes open
yôhtên– VTI open s.t.; turn s.t. (e.g., television set) on
yôhtênamaw– VTA open (it/him) for s.o.; turn (it/him) (e.g., television set) on for s.o.
yôhtêwêpin– VTI throw s.t. open (e.g., lodge-cover)

OPENING
cawâsin– VII be a little opening

OPERATE
pimipayihtâ– VAI run (it), operate (it) (e.g., machine); keep (it) up, exercise (it)

OPINION
pîwêyiht– VTI think little of s.t., have a low opinion of s.t.
pîwêyim– VTA think little of s.o., have a low opinion of s.o.; be disrespectful of s.o.

OPPOSITE
kwêsk-âyâ– VAI turn around to the opposite side, be turned around (e.g., a pivot)
kwêsk-âyihk IPC on the opposite side
kwêskahcâhk IPC on the opposite side of a rise in the land
kwêskâskon– VTA turn s.o. (e.g., pipe) to the opposite side
kwêski IPV turned around, turned to the opposite side
kwêskin– VTA change s.o. around, turn s.o. around to the opposite side; *(fig.)* convert s.o. to Christianity
kwêskinâkwan– VII look changed around, look turned around to the opposite side

OPPRESS
mâkoh– VTA press upon s.o., bear down upon s.o., oppress s.o.; worry s.o., trouble s.o., throw s.o. into crisis
nôcih– VTA pursue s.o., hunt for s.o. (e.g., animal); go after s.o., oppress s.o., beat s.o. up, fight with s.o.

OR
ahpô cî IPC or else
awêkâ IPC or else

ORANGES
k-ôsâwisicik INM oranges

ORDER
kîsakim– VTA finish counting s.o.; finish giving orders to s.o., complete one's charge to s.o.
kwatakatot– VTA meanly order s.o. around, harass s.o.
nâtitisahikê– VAI send for things, place an order from a catalogue
nâtitisahw– VTA go to fetch s.o. (e.g., horses); send for s.o., order s.o. (e.g., chickens) by catalogue
nitot– VTI look for s.t.; order s.t. (e.g., in a restaurant)
pimakocin– VAI move along, go by; work, be in working order (e.g., clock, car)
pimakotê– VII be in working order, run (e.g., tape-recorder)
wiyakim– VTA set a price on s.o. (e.g., bread); arrange (it) for s.o.; decide on s.o.; give orders to s.o.

ORDINARY
iyinico-pimîs– NI ordinary grease
iyinito IPN plain, ordinary
iyinito-pimiy– NI ordinary grease

ORGANISE
nîmihitowinihkê– VAI hold a dance, hold a dance ceremony; give a dance, organise a (secular) dance

ORIGINAL
nistam IPC first, at first, for the first time, initially, originally
nistamêmâkan– NA the first one, the original one

ORPHAN
kitimâk-ôhpikih– VTA raise s.o. in poverty; raise s.o. as an orphan
kîwâc-âwâsis– NA orphan
kîwâtisi– VAI be orphaned, be an orphan

OTHER
kotak PR other, another

OUTDOORS
wayawî IPV outside, outdoors
wayawî– VAI go outside, go outdoors; go to relieve oneself; leave school, leave hospital
wayawîhtatâ– VAI have (it) go outdoors; take (it) out, get (it) back (e.g., from photographer)
wayawîkâpawi– VAI stand outside, go outdoors
wayawîpahtâ– VAI run outside, run outdoors
wayawîpakitin– VTA put s.o. (e.g., diaper) down outdoors
wayawîsimo– VAI dance outdoors, dance towards the outside
wayawîstamâso– VAI go outdoors for oneself, go to relieve oneself

wayawîtimihk *IPC* outside, outdoors
wayawîtisahw– *VTA* send s.o. outdoors; send s.o. off the reserve, banish s.o. from the reserve
wayawîwin– *NI* going outside, being outdoors; going to relieve oneself, going to the toilet
wayawîyâmohkê– *VAI* arrange for s.o. to flee outdoors

OUTHOUSE
mîsîwikamikw– *NI* outhouse, toilet
wayawîwikamikw– *NI* outhouse, toilet

OVEN
sêkwâpiskin– *VTA* place s.o. beneath the coals, place s.o. (e.g., beaver) in the oven
sêkwâpiskin– *VTI* place s.t. beneath the coals, place s.t. in the oven

OVERCAST
titipikwanah– *VTI* sew s.t. in overcast stitch (e.g., the spiral loops around the vamp of a moccasin)

OVERCOAT
waskitasâkay– *NI* overcoat

OVERCOME
pônêyiht– *VTI* cease thinking of s.t.; overcome a worrying preoccupation
sâkôcih– *VTA* overcome s.o., defeat s.o.
sâkôcim– *VTA* overcome s.o. by speech; convince s.o. by speech, win s.o. over
sâkôh– *VTA* overcome s.o., overpower s.o., overwhelm s.o.
sâkôhtâ– *VAI* overcome (it), accomplish (it), lift (it) up

OVERHEAD
tipiskôc *IPC* even, at the same level, parallel; directly overhead

OVERLOOK
patahôhkât– *VTA* overlook s.o., fail to notice s.o., ignore s.o.

OVERNIGHT
kapêsi– *VAI* stay overnight
kapêsimostaw– *VTA* stay overnight with s.o., stay overnight at s.o.'s place

OVERSEAS
akâmaskîhk *IPC* across the water, overseas

OVERSHOE
waskicaskisinis– *NI* overshoe, rubber
waskipicikan– *NI* pull-on, overshoe, rubber
waskitaskisin– *NI* overshoe, rubber

OWL
ôhow– *NA* owl

OWN
tipêyihcikâtê– *VII* be owned, be controlled, be governed
tipêyiht– *VTI* own s.t., control s.t., rule s.t., be master over s.t.; have a voice in the affairs of s.t. (e.g., reserve)
tipêyim– *VTA* own s.o., control s.o., rule s.o.; *(fig.)* be the Lord over s.o.; have s.o. in one's clutches (e.g., devil)
tipêyimiso– *VAI* control oneself, govern oneself; be on one's own, be one's own boss

OX
ayêhkwêw– *NA* castrated bull; ox

OXFORD
miscikwaskisinis– *NI* firm shoe, sturdy shoe, oxford
mistikwaskisin– *NI* heeled shoe, oxford

PADDLE
papâmiskâ– *VAI* paddle about, go about in a boat

PAIL
askihkos– *NA* little pail, little pot
askihkw– *NA* kettle, pail; pot
mitâtaht-kosikwan– *NA* ten-pound pail

PAIN
kâkîtisi– *VAI* ache, experience pain
wîsakêyiht– *VTI* have pain in s.t. (e.g., neck)

PAINFULLY
wîsaki *IPV* sharply, painfully; sorely

PAINT
câhcahkipêkahw– *VTA* paint dots on s.o.
mihkotonêho– *VAI* paint one's mouth red, wear lipstick
mihkotonêhw– *VTA* paint s.o.'s mouth red, put lipstick on s.o.
sisopêkah– *VTI* rub (it) flat on s.t. by tool; paint s.t.
sisopêkahw– *VTA* rub (it/him) flat on s.o. by tool; paint s.o.
wâpiskipêkahw– *VTA* paint s.o. white

PAIR
nîsonito– *VAI* dance two-and-two with one another, dance in pairs
nîsw-âya *IPC* two pairs, two sets
pêyakw-ây– *NA* a single one (e.g., stocking); one pair

PALPABLE
sawôhkât– *VTA* bestow a palpable blessing upon s.o.

PAN-FRIED
sâsâpiskitê– *VII* be fried, be pan-fried
sâsâpiskitikâtê– *VII* be fried, be pan-fried
PANTRY
wiyâkanikamikw– *NI* pantry, scullery; walk-in closet
PANTS
–câsis– *NDA* loin-cloth; leggings; trousers, pants
–tâs– *NDA* loin-cloth; leggings; trousers, pants
pahkêkinwêtâs– *NA* hide leggings, hide trousers, hide pants
PAPER
kinwâpêkan– *VII* be a long garment, be a long piece of paper; be a long saw-blade, be a long saw
kitowêyêkinikê– *VAI* make a noise with paper, rustle one's paper
masinahikanêkinowatis– *NI* paper bag
masinahikanêkinw– *NI* paper; wallpaper
pâskêkin– *VTA* break s.o. made of paper, break the paper of s.o. (e.g., cigarette)
PARCEL
pahkwênamaw– *VTA* pay a part of (it/him) to s.o., make partial payment to s.o.; parcel (it/him) out to s.o., give s.o. a share
PARENTS
–kêhtê-ayim– *NDA* old person, parent, grandparent; elder
–nîkihikw– *NDA* parent
onîkihiko– *VAI* have parents; have (them) as one's parents
onîkihikomâw– *NA* parents
PART
paskêwih– *VTA* part from s.o., leave s.o.; separate from s.o., divorce s.o.
paskêwihito– *VAI* part from one another, leave one another; separate from one another, divorce
PARTIAL
iyawis *IPC* fully, entirely; the whole lot, the entire household; *(in negative constructions:)* only partially, not exclusively
pahkwênamaw– *VTA* pay a part of (it/him) to s.o., make partial payment to s.o.; parcel (it/him) out to s.o., give s.o. a share
PARTICIPATE
ayamihâ– *VAI* pray, say prayers; hold a church service, celebrate mass; participate in a religious rite, go to church; follow a religion
cîhkêyiht– *VTI* like s.t., approve of s.t.; eagerly participate in s.t.
mâmaw-âyamihâ– *VAI* pray as a group, participate in a religious rite as a group, celebrate mass as a group; go on a pilgrimage as a group
nipâkwêsimo– *VAI* attend a sundance, participate in a sundance, dance the sundance
wâsakâmêsimo– *VAI* dance the ghost-dance, participate in the ghost-dance
wîci-tôtamôm– *VTA* do (it) together with s.o., participate with s.o. in doing (it)
wîcihiwê– *VAI* join in, be along, participate, be part of a group
PARTICULAR
âsônê *IPC* especially, in particular
mêmohci *IPC* in particular, above all; exactly, precisely
miyawâkâc *IPV* with particular care
miyawâkâtinikê– *VAI* take particular care with things, handle ritual objects with particular care
PARTICULARLY
wâwîs *IPC* especially, particularly
PARTNER
–wîcêwâkan– *NDA* companion, partner; spouse
wîcêwâkani– *VAI* have a companion or partner, have (her/him) as one's companion or partner
wîcêwâkanihto– *VAI* find one another as partner or spouse
wîcêwâkanim– *VTA* have s.o. as partner, be in partnership with s.o.
wîci-piponisîm– *VTA* winter together with s.o., have s.o. as one's wintering partner
PARTRIDGE
paspaskiw– *NI* partridge, bush-partridge
PASS
âsawi *IPV* in passing something on, in continuation
âsawinamaw– *VTA* pass (it/him) on to s.o.
âsô *IPV* in passing something on, in continuation
âsônamaw– *VTA* pass (it/him) across to s.o., pass (it/him) on to s.o.; hand (it/him) down to s.o., bequeathe (it/him) to s.o.
miyân– *VTI* leave behind fresh tracks, have recently passed by

miyâsk– *VTI* pass around s.t., bypass s.t.
miyopayi– *VII* work well, run well; work out, come to pass
ocihcipayi– *VII* come to pass, take place
ocihciskâmakan– *VII* come to pass, take place (by foot or body movement)
sîkwanisi– *VAI* be there in spring, pass the spring, spend the spring
wîmâskaw– *VTA* pass around s.o., pass s.o. by

PASSAGE
pimohtêhon– *NI* passage through life, travel through life

PAST
kî *IPV* to completion, completely; in the past
nâway *IPC* behind, at the rear; in the past
ohci *IPC* thence, from there; with, by means of; for that reason; *(in negative constructions: perfective)* in the past
ohci *IPV* thence, from there; with, by means of; for that reason; *(in negative constructions: perfective)* in the past
otâhk *IPC* behind, at the rear, in the past
otâskanâhk *IPC* behind, at the rear; in the past
ôh *IPV* thence, from there; with, by means of; for that reason; *(in negative constructions: perfective)* in the past
pêc-âskiy *IPC* in a past year, in past years
pêci-nâway *IPC* back then, far in the past; from the earliest times

PATCHWORK
nanâcohkokwacês– *NI* patchwork quilt
nanâtohkokwâso– *VAI* sew various things; sew a patchwork blanket

PATH
itamon– *VII* run thus or there as a path; be thus attached, be mounted thus
mêskanaw– *NI* path, trail, road
mêskanâs– *NI* path, trail
mitimê– *VAI* track along a trail, follow a trail; *(fig.)* follow a path, be guided in one's life
môniyâwi-mêskanaw– *NI* White path, White road
nâsipêskanaw– *NI* path towards the water
nêhiyawi-mêskanaw– *NI* Cree path, Cree road; Indian path, Indian road

patitisahamaw– *VTA* drive (it/him) off the path for s.o., send (it/him) awry for s.o., spoil (it/him) for s.o.
pimohtêskanaw– *NI* walking path
sipwêmon– *VII* leave as path, trail, road; begin as path, trail, road

PATTERN
apiscâpakwanîs– *NI* small flower, flower pattern (e.g., printed on fabric)
masinihtatâ– *VAI* trace (it), use (it) as pattern
wiyis– *VTI* cut s.t. out, cut s.t. to a pattern
wiyisamaw– *VTA* cut a pattern for s.o.
wiyisamâso– *VAI* cut a pattern for oneself, cut one's own pattern

PATTIES
pitikon– *VTI* make small patties of s.t. (e.g., crushed chokecherries)
pitikonikâtê– *VII* be made into small patties (e.g., crushed chokecherries)

PAUNCH
wînâstakay– *NI* "tripe", paunch

PAW
–cihciy– *NDI* hand; paw (e.g., bear)

PAY
pahkwênamaw– *VTA* pay a part of (it/him) to s.o., make partial payment to s.o.; parcel (it/him) out to s.o., give s.o. a share
tako-tipah– *VTI* measure s.t. in addition; pay s.t. extra, pay for s.t. in addition; pay (it) in addition for s.t.
têpinêh– *VTI* have enough to pay for s.t.
tipah– *VTI* measure s.t.; pay s.t., pay for s.t.; pay (it) for s.t.
tipahamaw– *VTA* pay s.o. for (it/him), repay a debt to s.o.; pay s.o. a pension
tipahikê– *VAI* pay for things, make a payment
tipahw– *VTA* pay (it) for s.o. (e.g., stove)

PAYMENT
nâcinêhamaw– *VTA* obtain (it/him) from s.o. by payment, seek to buy medicine from s.o.
nâcinêhikê– *VAI* obtain things by payment, seek to buy medicine
ohtisi– *VAI* earn (it) thereby or from there, earn (it) for that; obtain payment thereby or from there
pahkwênamaw– *VTA* pay a part of (it/him) to s.o., make partial payment to s.o.; parcel (it/him) out to s.o., give s.o. a share

têpinêhamaw– VTA make full payment for (it/him) to s.o.
tipahamâto– VAI receive one's Treaty payment, be paid Treaty
tipahamâtowi-sôniyâw– NA Treaty money, Treaty payment
tipahikê– VAI pay for things, make a payment

PEACE
nahêyiht– VTI be satisfied with s.t.; have peace of mind
nahêyihtamih– VTA cause s.o. to be satisfied with (it/him); grant s.o. peace of mind
wânaskêwin– NI being at peace with oneself
wîtaskîwêm– VTA live together with s.o., have s.o. as one's compatriot; live in the same country with s.o., live in peace with s.o.

PEACEFUL
wawânaskêhtamaw– VTA create a peaceful life for s.o.
wawânaskêhtâ– VAI live a peaceful life

PEARS
kâ-cîposicik INM pears

PEAS
âyîcimin– NA peas

PEEL
manâhkwatatahw– VTA peel s.o. hardened off (e.g., spruce-gum)
pîhton– VTA take the covering layer off s.o. (e.g., tree), peel s.o.
pîhton– VTI take s.t. (e.g., bark) off as the covering layer, peel s.t. off
pîhtopit– VTA pull the covering layer off s.o. (e.g., tree), peel the bark off s.o.
pîhtopit– VTI pull s.t. (e.g., bark) off as the covering layer, peel s.t. off

PEEP
paspâpi– VAI look out (e.g., through a hole or crack), peep out

PELT
ahtay– NA pelt, fur
mânahtê– VAI get one's pelts

PEMMICAN
pimîhkân– NI pemmican

PENSION
kêhtêwasinahikan– NI pension cheque, old-age pension
tipahamaw– VTA pay s.o. for (it/him), repay a debt to s.o.; pay s.o. a pension

PEOPLE
–ayisiyinîm– NDA people, follower
–iyinîm– NDA people, followers

PEPPER
papêskomin– NI peppercorn, pepper

PERCEIVE
âmatisôst– VTI perceive the spirit of s.t. (e.g., spirit-bundle)
môsih– VTA sense s.o., feel s.o. approaching, perceive s.o.'s presence
môsihtâ– VAI sense (it), feel (it) approaching, perceive (it)
tahkêyiht– VTI consider s.t. cold; perceive the cold
wani-tipiskin– VTI perceive s.t. as darkness; merely see night, perceive merely darkness

PERCEPTIBLY
matwê IPV audibly, visibly; perceptibly; in full view, in plain sight

PERCH
akosî– VAI perch aloft, be perched (e.g., on a tree)

PERFORM
isistâ– VAI hold such a rite, perform a rite thus
isîhcikê– VAI do things thus, proceed thus, arrange things thus; perform such a rite, perform a rite thus; conduct negotiations thus
isîhtwâwin– NI performing a rite thus; such a rite; way of worship, way of doing things
manisw– VTA cut s.o.; perform surgery on s.o.

PERHAPS
mâskôc IPC perhaps, I suppose, undoubtedly
pakahkam IPC I think; perhaps

PERISH
misiwanâtan– VII be ruined, perish; be spoiled, spoil (e.g., meat)
misiwanâtisi– VAI be ruined, perish

PERM
titipawêhkas– VTI curl s.t. (e.g., head) by heat; have a perm

PERMIT
pakitin– VTA set s.o. down, allow s.o., permit s.o.; permit (it) to s.o., give permission to s.o.; let s.o. go, release s.o.; release s.o. (e.g., fish-spawn into lake), tock a lake with s.o. (e.g., fish); drop s.o. off (e.g., as an airplane)
pakitin– VTI let s.t. go, allow s.t., permit s.t.; release s.t.; give s.t. up, abandon s.t. (e.g., teaching, tradition); put s.t. down on earth; put s.t. in (e.g., seed potatoes)
pakitinikâso– VAI be allowed, have permission; be released

pakitinikâtê– *VII* be permitted
pakitinikowisi– *VAI* be permitted by the powers; be put down on earth by the powers

PERSEVERE
âhkamêyimo– *VAI* persist in one's will, persevere
âhkamêyimotot– *VTI* persist in s.t., persevere in s.t.
sîpihkêyiht– *VTI* endure s.t.; persevere in s.t.; persevere

PERSIST
sâpohtêmakan– *VII* go through; persist

PERSISTENTLY
âhkami *IPV* persistently, unceasingly, unwaveringly
mâninakisk *IPC* continually, on and on, persistently

PERSON
ayisiyiniw– *NA* person, human being, people
ayisiyinîwi– *VAI* be a person, be a human being

PERSONALITY
wiyâhtikosi– *VAI* be ebullient, have a bubbly personality

PERSONALLY
tipiyawê *IPC* personally, in person; really

PERSPIRE
apwêsi– *VAI* sweat, perspire; work up a sweat

PETROLEUM
askîwi-pimiy– *NI* coal oil, petroleum
pimiy– *NI* fat, oil; crude petroleum

PHOTOGRAPH
masinipayiwin– *NI* picture, photograph

PHRASE
pîkiskwêwin– *NI* word, phrase, expression, voice; what is being said; speech, language

PHYSICIAN
maskihkîwiyiniw– *NA* doctor, physician

PICK
mawiso– *VAI* pick berries, gather berries
naskwên– *VTA* collect s.o. while moving, pick s.o. up on one's way
nâtahw– *VTA* fetch s.o. by boat or airplane; pick s.o. up (e.g., as an airplane)
nitihkomât– *VTA* pick lice off s.o., louse s.o.

otin– *VTI* take s.t.; pick s.t., choose s.t., select s.t. (e.g., moss); steal s.t.; take s.t. over; extract s.t. (e.g., grease from soup), remove s.t. (e.g., glands in butchering beaver), extract s.t.; accept s.t. (e.g., contract); capture s.t., record s.t. on audio-tape

PICTURE
masinahikâso– *VAI* be drawn, be pictured, be depicted; be written on
masinahikâtê– *VII* be pictured, be depicted; have marks, have writing; be written
masinipayiwin– *NI* picture, photograph

PIECE
mâmawokwât– *VTI* sew s.t. together into one, piece s.t. together in sewing
miht– *NI* firewood, piece of firewood
nîpisîhtakw– *NI* willow piece, willow trunk
sakâs– *NI* piece of bush, bluff of woodland
wiyinw– *NI* fat, fat meat, piece of fat

PIERCED
pôskwahikâso– *VAI* have a hole punched, have oneself pierced

PIG
kôhkôs– *NA* pig, domestic pig

PILE
asastê– *VII* be piled up
astê– *VII* be placed, be in place; be piled up; be out (e.g., leaves)
âhkwêhtawastê– *VII* be piled one over top of the other
ispastâ– *VAI* place (it) so high, pile (it) so high
mâwacisôniyâwê– *VAI* gather up money, pile up money
wîscihkêsi– *VAI* pile hay into small heaps
wîstihkê– *VAI* pile hay into heaps

PILGRIMAGE
mâmaw-âyamihâ– *VAI* pray as a group, participate in a religious rite as a group, celebrate mass as a group; go on a pilgrimage as a group
nitaw-âyamihâ– *VAI* *(fig.)* go on a pilgrimage

PILL
misiwêpayihcikan– *NI* pill, medication
misiwêpayihcikanis– *NI* little pill, medication

PILLOW
aspiskwêsimon– *NI* pillow

otaspiskwêsimoni– *VAI* have a pillow; use (it) as one's pillow

PIPE

itâskonamaw– *VTA* thus point the pipe for s.o., thus point the pipe at s.o.

itâskonamawât– *VTI* thus point the pipe at s.t.

itâskonikâkê– *VAI* point the pipe or pipestem with (it), use (it) to point the pipe or pipestem

itâskonikê– *VAI* thus point the pipe or pipestem; thus hold a pipe ceremony

itâskonikêwin– *NI* thus pointing the pipe or pipestem; such a pipe ceremony

mâtâskonikê– *VAI* begin to point the pipe or pipestem

ospwâkan– *NA* pipe

pîhtwâ– *VAI* smoke, use the pipe; smoke (him) (e.g., pipe); hold a pipe ceremony; be a nicotine addict

pîhtwâkê– *VAI* smoke with (it/him), use (it/him) in the pipe

pîhtwâwikamikw– *NI* pipe lodge, pipe ceremony

saskahamaw– *VTA* light (it/him) for s.o.; light the pipe for s.o.

PIPESTEM

itâskonikâkê– *VAI* point the pipe or pipestem with (it), use (it) to point the pipe or pipestem

itâskonikê– *VAI* thus point the pipe or pipestem; thus hold a pipe ceremony

itâskonikêwin– *NI* thus pointing the pipe or pipestem; such a pipe ceremony

mâtâskonikê– *VAI* begin to point the pipe or pipestem

oskiciy– *NI* pipestem

oskicîwâhtikw– *NI* wood of pipestem

PITIABLE

kicimâkisi– *VAI* be pitiable, be miserable; be poor

kitimâkan– *VII* be pitiable, be miserable

kitimâkêyimo– *VAI* feel pitiable, feel miserable; feel poor

kitimâkinâkosi– *VAI* look pitiable, look miserable; look poor

kitimâkisi– *VAI* be pitiable, be miserable; be poor

PITY

kitimâkêyihto– *VAI* feel pity towards one another, think of one another with compassion; take pity upon one another, be kind to one another, love one another

kitimâkêyihtowin– *NI* feeling pity towards one another, thinking of one another with compassion; taking pity upon one another, being kind to one another, loving one

kitimâkêyim– *VTA* feel pity towards s.o., think of s.o. with compassion; take pity upon s.o., be kind to s.o., love s.o.

kitimâkihtaw– *VTA* listen to s.o. with pity, listen to s.o. with compassion

kitimâkinaw– *VTA* look with pity upon s.o., look with compassion upon s.o., feel sorry for s.o.; take pity upon s.o., lovingly tend s.o.; regard s.o. with respect

kitimâkinâso– *VAI* pity oneself, feel sorry for oneself

PLACE

ah– *VTA* place s.o. there, put s.o. there, set s.o. down

astâ– *VAI* place (it) there, put (it) there

êkotowihk *IPC* in that place

itastâ– *VAI* place (it) thus or there

itowihk *IPC* in this place

ômatowihk *IPC* in this place

pêyakwanohk *IPC* in one place, in a single place; in the same place

pêyakwayak *IPC* in one place, in a certain place; in the same place

pikw îta *IPC* in any place, no matter where; everywhere

pikw îtowihk *IPC* in any place, no matter where; in all places

tahtwayak *IPC* in so many places, in so many ways

tânitahtwayak *IPC* in how many places; in so many places

tânitowihk *IPC* in what place

PLACED

asiwacipayin– *VII* get placed inside, get enclosed; rapidly fill an enclosed space (e.g., water flowing into hoofprint)

asiwatê– *VII* be placed inside, be enclosed

astê– *VII* be placed, be in place; be piled up; be out (e.g., leaves)

itastê– *VII* be placed thus or there; be written thus

kikastê– *VII* be placed along with something

ohtastê– *VII* be placed thereby or from there

pimastê– *VII* be placed in linear fashion, run along

pimitastê– VII be placed crosswise; be the bunk of a wagon

PLAIN
iyinito IPN plain, ordinary
matwê IPV audibly, visibly; perceptibly; in full view, in plain sight

PLAINS CREE
paskwâwiyiniw– NA prairie person; Plains Cree

PLAN
itasiwê– VAI decide thus for people, make such a plan for people; give such a command, impose such laws
kîsêyiht– VTI make up one's mind about s.t., decide on s.t., complete one's plan for s.t.; be decisive
mâmitonêyihtêstamâso– VAI think about (it/him) for oneself; plan for oneself
pîkon– VTA break s.o.; break up one's relation with s.o., disrupt s.o.'s life, spoil s.o.'s plans
wiyasiwâtiso– VAI make a plan for oneself, make one's plan

PLANT
cimah– VTA place s.o. (e.g., tree) upright, plant s.o. upright
cimatâ– VAI place (it) upright, plant (it) upright
kiscikêsi– VAI plant seeds; have a small garden
kistikê– VAI seed things, plant things, do one's seeding, do one's planting; farm the land
maskihkiy– NI herb, plant; seneca-root; medicinal root; medicine; chemicals
miscikos– NI little stick (e.g., in collecting sap); little pole, rod, rail (e.g., on drying rack); branch of a small plant (e.g., labrador tea)
sâkikihtâ– VAI make (it) (e.g., earth) bring forth plants

PLASTER
asiskîhkât– VTI mud s.t., plaster s.t.
sisocêskiwakinikê– VAI plaster things, do the plastering
sisoskiwakin– VTI mud s.t. (e.g., log-house), plaster s.t.
sisowaskinikê– VAI put on mud or plaster; mud one's log-house

PLATTER
mistiyâkan– NI big dish, platter, large bowl

PLAY
kitohcikê– VAI play a musical instrument; play one's stereo-player
mêtawâkâniwi– VII be general playing around
mêtawâkê– VAI play with (it), use (it) to play; play around with (it), fool around with (it)
mêtawê– VAI play; gamble
pâkâhtowê– VAI play ball; play soccer
wîci-mêtawêm– VTA play together with s.o., have s.o. as one's playmate

PLAY-HOUSE
mêtawêwikamikw– NI play-house
wâskahikanis– NI little house; shack, temporary building, trailer; play-house

PLAYED OUT
nôhtêsin– VAI be played out, lie exhausted

PLAYING-CARD
pêyakopêhikan– NA card, playing-card

PLAYMATE
wîci-mêtawêm– VTA play together with s.o., have s.o. as one's playmate

PLEAD
kâkîsimo– VAI pray, plead, chant prayers

PLEASANT
miyohtwâ– VAI be good-natured, be of pleasant character
wîhkimâkwan– VII smell good, give off a pleasant odour; have an aromatic odour

PLEASE
atamih– VTA make s.o. grateful, make s.o. indebted, please s.o.
atamim– VTA make s.o. grateful by speech, please s.o. by speech
kiyâm IPC oh well, never mind, so much for this; anyway, rather; let it be, let there be no further delay; please
mahti IPC let's see, please
miyomahciho– VAI fare well, be in good health or spirit; feel well, feel healthy; feel pleased
miywêyiht– VTI consider s.t. good, like s.t.; be glad, be pleased
miywêyim– VTA consider s.o. good, like s.o.; be pleased with s.o.
miywêyimo– VAI think well of oneself; be pleased with oneself; think well for oneself, take a fancy
takahkêyiht– VTI think well of s.t., be glad about s.t., like s.t.; be glad, be pleased
takahkêyihtamih– VTA please s.o.
takahkêyimo– VAI be pleased with oneself

PLEATED
ocîhkwêhikan– NI pleated moccasin
PLENTIFUL
iskwahtâ– VAI have so much of (it) left over; have (it) left over, have a plentiful supply of (it)
kakwâhyakêyati– VAI be in great numbers, be plentiful, be very numerous
mihcêti– VAI be numerous, be plentiful
mihcêtin– VII be numerous, be plentiful
osâmêyatin– VII be too many, be plentiful
pîsâkwan– VII contain plenty, offer lots of room; be plentiful, be rich
PLENTY
ayiwâkipayi– VAI have more than enough, have a surplus, have plenty; run to more, be a surplus (e.g., money)
pîsâkwan– VII contain plenty, offer lots of room; be plentiful, be rich
tâniyikohk IPC to what extent; to such an extent; so many, plenty
têpâpam– VTA see plenty of s.o., see s.o. fully
PLOUGH
pîkopicikâtê– VII be ploughed soil, be cultivated
pîkopicikê– VAI plough, do one's ploughing; break soil
pîkopicikêh– VTA make s.o. plough, use s.o. (e.g., oxen) in ploughing
pîkopit– VTI break s.t. (e.g., soil), plough s.t. (e.g., field)
pîkopitamaw– VTA break (it) for s.o., plough (it) for s.o.
PLUCK
paskopit– VTA pluck s.o. (e.g., bird)
PLUMP
wiyino– VAI be fat (e.g., animal); be fat, be plump (e.g., little girl)
PLUS
ayiwâk IPC more; *(in numeral phrases:)* plus
POCKET
asiwacikan– NI pocket; container
asiwacikanis– NI little pocket
POINT
cîposi– VAI be pointed
isiniskêyi– VAI move one's arm thus or there, point in that direction with one's arm

itâskonamaw– VTA thus point the pipe for s.o., thus point the pipe at s.o.
itâskonamawât– VTI thus point the pipe at s.t.
itâskonikâkê– VAI point the pipe or pipestem with (it), use (it) to point the pipe or pipestem
itâskonikê– VAI thus point the pipe or pipestem; thus hold a pipe ceremony
itwahw– VTA point one's finger at s.o., point at s.o.
kâsisi– VAI be sharp, be scratchy (e.g., wool); be sharply pointed
kînikatahamaw– VTA chop (it/him) to a point for s.o.
kînikatahikê– VAI chop things to a point, sharpen posts
mâtâskonikê– VAI begin to point the pipe or pipestem
nêyâ– VII be a point of land
tâsah– VTI grind s.t. (e.g., bone needle) to a point by tool
wâsakâyâskon– VTA point s.o. (e.g., pipe) around a full circle
POINTING
itâskonikêwin– NI thus pointing the pipe or pipestem; such a pipe ceremony
POISON
pihcipo– VAI be poisoned
pihcipohtâ– VAI poison (it)
pihcipôh– VTA poison s.o.
piscipowin– NI poison
piscipôskaw– VTA poison s.o.
POKE
pôhtâskwah– VTI stick s.t. wooden into a hole; clean out one's ear, poke one's ear
POLE
ispâhtêhikan– NI pole supporting tent-flap (e.g., to permit air-flow)
miscikos– NI little stick (e.g., in collecting sap); little pole, rod, rail (e.g., on drying rack); branch of a small plant (e.g., labrador tea)
mistikw– NI stick, pole, post, log, wooden rail
ohpâskwah– VTI raise s.t. (e.g., cloth) on a wooden pole, hold s.t. aloft on a wooden pole
pîhtêyask IPC at the central circle of poles inside the dance-lodge
POLICE
simâkanis– NA policeman; *(plural:)* the police

POOR
   is-âyâ– *VAI* be thus in health; be unwell, be in poor health; be out of sorts, have something being the matter
   kicimâkisi– *VAI* be pitiable, be miserable; be poor
   kitimâkêyimo– *VAI* feel pitiable, feel miserable; feel poor
   kitimâkinâkosi– *VAI* look pitiable, look miserable; look poor
   kitimâkisi– *VAI* be pitiable, be miserable; be poor
   mamâyî– *VAI* be poor at (it), do (it) poorly
   mâyamahciho– *VAI* feel poorly, be in ill health

POPLAR
   mîtos– *NA* poplar; tree

POPULATE
   askîwisk– *VTI* subject the earth to oneself, populate the earth, make the earth live
   nihtâwikîst– *VTI* populate s.t. (e.g., the earth)

PORCUPINE
   kâkw– *NA* porcupine
   kâwiy– *NA* porcupine quill

PORTAGE
   onikahp– *NI* portage

POSITIVELY
   tâpwêwakêyiht– *VTI* hold s.t. to be true, believe in s.t.; regard s.t. positively

POSSESS
   otin– *VTA* take s.o., take s.o. in (e.g., orphan); choose s.o.; steal s.o.; *(especially in inverse constructions:)* take hold of s.o., possess s.o.

POSSESSION
   kikisk– *VTI* wear s.t. (e.g., shoe), have s.t. as an intimate possession, carry s.t. in oneself (e.g., blood)
   kikiskaw– *VTA* wear s.o. (e.g., ring), have s.o. as an intimate possession (e.g., stocking)
   wiyakihtâ– *VAI* treat (it) as worthless; *(especially in negative constructions:)* not waste (it); not destroy a valuable possession

POSSIBLY
   ahpô *IPC* even, possibly; or

POST
   cîkahikê– *VAI* chop things, chop wood, chop posts
   kihc-âtâwêwikamikowiyiniw– *NA* store manager, post manager, Hudson's Bay Company factor
   kînikatahikê– *VAI* chop things to a point, sharpen posts
   mistikw– *NA* tree, post [*sic*]
   mistikw– *NI* stick, pole, post, log, wooden rail

POST-SECONDARY
   kihci-kiskinahamâtowikamikw– *NI* university; post-secondary education
   kihci-kiskinahamâtowin– *NI* higher education, post-secondary education

POT
   askihkos– *NA* little pail, little pot
   askihkw– *NA* kettle, pail; pot
   mistaskihkw– *NA* big kettle, communal cooking pot
   pakâhcikanaskihkw– *NA* cooking pot
   wiyâkan– *NI* dish, bowl, vessel, pot

POTATO
   askipwâw– *NI* potato
   ayahikâkan– *NI* hiller, tool for covering potatoes with earth
   napatâkw– *NI* potato
   oski-napatâkw– *NI* new potato, fresh potato

POUND
   îwahikan– *NA* pounded meat
   kwayâci-sikwatahikâtê– *VII* be pounded in readiness, be pre-pounded
   mitâtaht-kosikwan *IPC* ten pounds
   pakamah– *VTI* strike s.t., hit s.t.; pound s.t. (e.g., meat); type s.t., type s.t. out
   pakamahw– *VTA* hit s.o., strike s.o.; pound s.o. (e.g., earring)
   pêyako-kosikwan *IPC* one pound; per pound
   sikwatah– *VTI* pound s.t. (by tool with handle) until small
   sikwatahikâtê– *VII* be pounded, be minced (e.g., meat)
   wiyatah– *VTI* pound s.t., hammer s.t. together
   wiyatahamâso– *VAI* pound (it/him) into shape for oneself
   wiyatahw– *VTA* pound s.o. (e.g., earring), mould s.o., shape s.o.
   yîwahikan– *NA* pounded meat

POUR
   pîhtâpawah– *VTA* pour liquid into s.o., give s.o. an enema
   sîkahasinê– *VAI* pour water on rocks (e.g., in sweat-lodge), sprinkle rocks with water
   sîkihtatamaw– *VTA* pour (it) for s.o.
   sîkin– *VTA* pour s.o. in (e.g., soap)

sîkin– *VTI* pour s.t.; pour s.t. in (e.g., lye); let it rain

sîkinamaw– *VTA* pour (it) for s.o. (e.g., tea)

sîkipêstâ– *VII* pour down as a rain shower

sîkipicikê– *VAI* pour things out; spill things

sîkiwêpin– *VTI* pour s.t. out

tahkâpâwat– *VTA* pour water to cool s.o. (e.g., rock), cool s.o. (e.g., rock) with water (e.g., in sweat-lodge)

POVERTY

kitimâk-ôhpikih– *VTA* raise s.o. in poverty; raise s.o. as an orphan

kitimâkisiwin– *NI* misery; poverty

POWDER

pîkinatah– *VTI* grind s.t. to powder

pîkinâ– *VII* be powder, be powdered

pîwêyâwahkwâ– *VII* be powdery

POWER

mamâhtâwisi– *VAI* have supernatural power

manitowakim– *VTA* endow s.o. (e.g., tobacco) with supernatural power; attribute spirit power to s.o.

manitowi– *VAI* be a spirit; have spirit power

manitowih– *VTA* grant s.o. supernatural power

pawâmiwin– *NI* spirit power; *(fig.)* witchcraft

sôhkan– *VII* be strong, be sturdy; be important; *(fig.)* be powerful, have supernatural power

sôhkisi– *VAI* be strong, be vigorous; be powerful, have supernatural power

sôhkisiwin– *NI* strength, vigour; power, supernatural power; authority

POWERFUL

nipahâhkwan– *VII* be terribly strong, be terribly powerful, hurt terribly

sôhkahât *IPV* greatly, vigorously, powerfully

sôhkan– *VII* be strong, be sturdy; be important; *(fig.)* be powerful, have supernatural power

sôhki *IPC* strongly, vigorously, powerfully

sôhkisi– *VAI* be strong, be vigorous; be powerful, have supernatural power

PRACTICABLE

osiskêpayi– *VII* fall into place, work itself out, be practicable

PRACTISED

nakacihtâ– *VAI* be familiar with doing (it), be practised at (it)

nihtâ *IPV* good at, doing much of, competent, practised, experienced

PRAIRIE

matâwisi– *VAI* move into the open, come out onto the open prairie

matâwisipit– *VTI* pull s.t. into the open, pull s.t. out onto the open prairie

mitâsipici– *VAI* move camp into the open, move one's camp out onto the open prairie

paskwâwiyiniw– *NA* prairie person; Plains Cree

PRAIRIE-CHICKEN

nîmihito– *VAI* dance with one another, dance; dance a (secular) dance; dance as prairie-chicken; move about in a dancing motion, dance (e.g., northern lights)

pihêsis– *NA* little prairie-chicken

pihêw– *NA* prairie-chicken

pihêwisimo– *VAI* dance the prairie-chicken dance

PRAY

ayamihâ– *VAI* pray, say prayers; hold a church service, celebrate mass; participate in a religious rite, go to church; follow a religion

kâkîsimo– *VAI* pray, plead, chant prayers

mâmaw-ayamihâ– *VAI* pray as a group, participate in a religious rite as a group, celebrate mass as a group; go on a pilgrimage as a group

nitotamâ– *VAI* ask for (it/him) (e.g., sugar), make a request for (it), pray for (it); make a request

nitotamâkêstamaw– *VTA* make a request for s.o., pray on s.o.'s behalf, ask for (it/him) on s.o.'s behalf

pîkiskwê– *VAI* use words, speak; speak a prayer, pray

wîc-âyamihâm– *VTA* pray together with s.o., join s.o. in prayer

PRAYER

ayamihâwin– *NI* prayer, praying, saying prayers; church service; religious rite; religion, religious denomination; the Roman Catholic church

ayamihêstamaw– *VTA* say Christian prayers for s.o.

kâkîsimo– *VAI* pray, plead, chant prayers

kâkîsimotot– *VTI* chant prayers for s.t.; chant prayers over s.t.

kâkîsimototaw– VTA chant prayers for s.o.; chant prayers over s.o.
kâkîsimowin– NI chanting prayers
kâkîsimwâkê– VAI chant prayers with (it), use (it) to chant prayers
kîsowât– VTI complete one's words, complete one's prayers
kîsowâtamaw– VTA complete one's words for s.o., complete one's prayers for s.o.
mawimo– VAI cry out; cry out in prayer, wail
mawimoscikê– VAI cry out in prayer, wail; worship with (it)
mawimoscikêwin– NI crying out in prayer, wailing; form of worship, rite
mawimost– VTI cry out in prayer to s.t., wail before s.t.
mawimostaw– VTA cry out in prayer to s.o., wail before s.o., implore s.o.; worship s.o.
mawîhkâtamaw– VTA cry out over (it/him) in prayer to s.o., wail over (it/him) before s.o.
naskom– VTA respond to s.o. with (it/him), answer s.o.'s prayer with (it/him)
patowât– VTI misspeak s.t.; commit an error in one's prayers
pîkiskwât– VTI speak about s.t., speak about s.t. with concern; speak a prayer over s.t.; address s.t., speak to s.t. (e.g., spirit-bundle)
pîkiskwê– VAI use words, speak; speak a prayer, pray
tâpowê– VAI speak correctly; recite one's prayer correctly
wîc-âyamihâm– VTA pray together with s.o., join s.o. in prayer

PREACH
kakêskihkêmo– VAI counsel people, lecture people, preach at people
kakêskim– VTA counsel s.o., lecture s.o., preach at s.o.

PRECEDENCE
nîkâni– VAI be at the head, be in the lead, take precedence (e.g., tobacco); be the prime element
nîkâninikâso– VAI take precedence, rank first; be the prime element
nîkânîmakan– VII be in the lead, take precedence

PRECIOUS
sôniyâwi– VII be precious metal; be money

PRECISELY
mêmohci IPC in particular, above all; exactly, precisely

PREDICTION
kiskiwêhikê– VAI utter prophesies; make predictions, forecast things
kiskiwêhikêmakan– VII provide prophesies; make predictions, forecast things
kiskiwêhikêwin– NI prophesy; prediction, forecast

PREFERENCE
iyâyaw IPC eagerly, intently; by preference, rather
wîhkipw– VTA like the taste of s.o. (e.g., duck, beaver), have a preference for the taste of s.o.

PREGNANT
asiwacikê– VAI put things inside, enclose things, put things into boxes; have things inside; be pregnant
kikiskawâwaso– VAI carry a child, be with child, be pregnant
misikiti– VAI be big (in height or girth); be pregnant

PREMATURELY
kayâhtê IPC before, previously, formerly; before the appropriate time, prematurely
kikask IPC too soon, prematurely
nôhtaw IPC less; minus; previously; prematurely, incompletely, short of attainment

PREOCCUPATION
pônêyiht– VTI cease thinking of s.t.; overcome a worrying preoccupation

PREOCCUPIED
otamih– VTA keep s.o. busy, keep s.o. preoccupied; delay s.o.; *(especially in inverse constructions:)* get in s.o.'s way, be s.o.'s undoing
otamiyo– VAI busy oneself, keep busy, be preoccupied

PREPARATION
kîsâc IPC beforehand, in advance, in preparation
maskihkîwin– NI medicinal preparation, medicine

PREPARATIONS
wawêyî– VAI get ready, make preparations

PREPARE
isîh– VTA make s.o. thus, prepare s.o. thus
isîhtâ– VAI prepare (it) thus, make (it) thus

kawisimonihkê– *VAI* prepare the bed, get ready for bed

kîsih– *VTA* complete s.o. (e.g., stocking), finish preparing s.o.

kwayâc *IPC* ready, prepared in advance

kwayâcihtâ– *VAI* get (it) ready, prepare (it) in advance

kwayâtah– *VTA* place s.o. (e.g., rock) in readiness, prepare s.o. (e.g., rock) in advance

maskihkîwâpôhkatiso– *VAI* prepare an herbal infusion for oneself; make a medicinal drink for oneself

maskihkîwâpôhkê– *VAI* prepare an herbal infusion; make tea

mosc-osîh– *VTA* prepare s.o. (e.g., soap) without instrument; make s.o. (e.g., soap) at home

mosc-ôsîhtâ– *VAI* prepare (it) without instrument; make (it) at home

nîmâwinihkê– *VAI* arrange provisions; prepare a packed lunch

osîh– *VTA* prepare s.o. (e.g., game animal, porcupine quills, rattle), make s.o. (e.g., bread)

osîhcikâkê– *VAI* prepare things with (it/him), use (it/him) to prepare things

osîhcikâtê– *VII* be made, be prepared; be built, be constructed

osîhikinosêwê– *VAI* prepare one's fish, process one's fish

osîhtamaw– *VTA* prepare (it/him) for s.o., make (it/him) for s.o.

osîhtâ– *VAI* prepare (it), make (it); put (it) in service (e.g., hospital), inaugurate (it)

pahkêkinohkê– *VAI* prepare one's skins, dress one's hides; make dressed hides, make leather

wawêyîst– *VTI* prepare s.t., be prepared

PRESENCE

miyâm– *VTA* smell s.o., smell s.o.'s presence

môsih– *VTA* sense s.o., feel s.o. approaching, perceive s.o.'s presence

PRESENT

api– *VAI* sit, sit down; be situated, be present, stay; be at home, be available

awînipan *IPC* all gone, no longer present

âstamispîhk *IPC* at a time closer to the present; more recently

itahtwapi– *VAI* sit as so many, be present as so many

itapi– *VAI* sit thus or there, be present thus or there

kîskisamaw– *VTA* cut (it/him) off for s.o.; cut tobacco as an offering to s.o., present tobacco to s.o.

mêki– *VAI* give (it/him) out as present; give (it/him) away, release (it/him); give (her) in marriage

wîtapim– *VTA* sit with s.o., sit beside s.o., be present with s.o.; work together with s.o.

PRESERVE

kanawêyiht– *VTI* keep s.t., look after s.t., take care of s.t.; store s.t., preserve s.t.; guard s.t. closely

kaskâpiskah– *VTI* can s.t., preserve s.t.

kaskâpiskahikan– *NI* can, preserve, canned goods

PRESERVED

kanawêyihcikâtê– *VII* be kept, be preserved

kanawêyihtâkwan– *VII* be kept, be looked after, the taken care of; be stored, be preserved; be closely guarded

kaskâpiskahikâtê– *VII* be canned, be preserved

PRESS

mâkoh– *VTA* press upon s.o., bear down upon s.o., oppress s.o.; worry s.o., trouble s.o., throw s.o. into crisis

mâkon– *VTA* press upon s.o. by hand, press s.o.'s hand; push s.o. down (e.g., button on radio)

mâkon– *VTI* press upon s.t. by hand

mâkoskaw– *VTA* press upon s.o. (by foot or body movement)

sîkopit– *VTA* press s.o. out by pulling; drain the milk from s.o. (e.g., cow)

PRESUMABLY

aspin *IPC* off, away, from a distance, in departing; since then, the last I knew; back then, so long ago; presumably, evidently

êtokwê *IPC* presumably, I guess

PRETEND

itihtâkosihkâso– *VAI* pretend to be heard making such a noise, act as if to make such a noise

maskisinihkêhkâso– *VAI* pretend to make moccasins

nâkasohtamohkâso– *VAI* pretend to pay attention

nisitohtamôhkâso– *VAI* pretend to understand (it/him)

yâhk îtâp *IPC* as if, pretendingly

yâhki *IPC* pretend, make-believe

PREVAIL
   kaskih– *VTA* prevail upon s.o., succeed in imposing one's will on s.o.; be able to deal with s.o.; earn s.o. (e.g., money)
   kaskim– *VTA* prevail upon s.o. by speech

PREVIOUS
   otâkosihk *IPC* the previous evening; yesterday

PRICE
   miywakiso– *VAI* be considered good, be well esteemed; fetch a good price (e.g., tree)
   wiyakiht– *VTI* set a price for s.t.
   wiyakihtamaw– *VTA* set a price on (it/him) for s.o., charge s.o. for (it/him)
   wiyakim– *VTA* set a price on s.o. (e.g., bread); arrange (it) for s.o.; decide on s.o.; give orders to s.o.

PRICK
   cîsw– *VTA* sting s.o., prick s.o.

PRIDE
   mamihcih– *VTA* *(especially in inverse constructions:)* make s.o. proud, fill s.o. with pride

PRIEST
   ayamihêwiyiniw– *NA* priest; minister; missionary
   pâhkw-âyamihêwiyiniw– *NA* Roman Catholic priest

PRIME
   nîkânakim– *VTA* count s.o. in first position, hold s.o. (e.g., tobacco) to be the prime element
   nîkâni– *VAI* be at the head, be in the lead, take precedence (e.g., tobacco); be the prime element
   nîkâninikâso– *VAI* take precedence, rank first; be the prime element

PRISON
   kipahotowikamikw– *NI* jail, prison

PRIVATE
   kîmôc *IPC* secretly, in secret, stealthily, privately, in private
   piskihcikamikos– *NI* separate room, private room

PROBLEMS
   nayêhtâw-âyâ– *VAI* be troubled, have problems (e.g., health problems)
   nayêhtâwipayin– *VII* there is trouble, there are problems

PROCEED
   ati *IPV* progressively, proceed to
   isîhcikât– *VTI* do things thus for s.t., proceed thus for s.t.
   isîhcikê– *VAI* do things thus, proceed thus, arrange things thus; perform such a rite, perform a rite thus; conduct negotiations thus
   nîkânohtêmakan– *VII* be in the lead, proceed in the lead position
   ohpohtât– *VTI* proceed high across s.t. (e.g., sky), rise up upon s.t. (e.g., sun upon sky)
   ohpohtê– *VAI* rise up, proceed high in the sky

PROCESS
   osîhikinosêwê– *VAI* prepare one's fish, process one's fish

PROCLAMATION
   sâkito– *VAI* make an announcement, make a proclamation

PROD
   cahkatayên– *VTA* prod s.o. at the belly, spur s.o.'s belly

PRODUCE
   âhkwâpahtê– *VII* give off a sharp odour, produce pungent fumes, emit acidic or caustic fumes
   wîhcêkimahkasikê– *VAI* give off a bad smell, produce a foul odour

PRODUCT
   osîhcikêwin– *NI* what is made, handiwork, product

PROGRESS
   pimi-nakî– *VAI* stop in one's progress, stop in one's travelling

PROGRESSION
   pimi *IPV* along, in linear progression; while moving in linear progression

PROGRESSIVELY
   ati *IPV* progressively, proceed to

PROJECT
   cîpatamo– *VAI* be attached so as to project out
   sâkakocin– *VAI* hang so as to project, hang out of the sky (e.g., snake)
   sâkamon– *VII* stick out, be attached so as to project
   sâkêkamon– *VII* stick out as cloth, project as cloth

PROMINENT
   kîhkâtêyihtâkwan– *VII* be held in high esteem, be prominent

PROMISCUOUS
   papâmâciho– *VAI* travel about; live in various places; run about, be promiscuous
   papâmipahtâ– *VAI* run about (e.g., as a child); run around, be promiscuous

papâmohtê– VAI walk about, go about, go here and there; run around, be promiscuous

PROMISE
asotamaw– VTA promise (it) to s.o.
asotamâkê– VAI make a promise
asotamâkêwin– NI promise, vow
asotamâkowin– NI promise, promise made
asotamâtowin– NI mutual promise, promises made to one another

PROMOTE
sôhkêpit– VTI stand firmly behind s.t., promote s.t.

PRONE
nihtâ-âhkosi– VAI fall sick easily, be prone to illness

PROPER
miyo-pimâciho– VAI make a good life for oneself, live well; lead a proper life
miyo-pimâtisi– VAI llive a good life, live well; lead a proper life
nahâwaso– VAI have one's child in the proper place, carry one's child with one
nahiyikohk IPC to the proper degree, to the proper extent, just enough, just right, evenly, fittingly, appropriately

PROPERLY
katawâhk IPC properly, in seemly manner
kwayask IPC properly, by rights
nahapi– VAI sit down in one's place, be properly seated
nowâhc IPC more properly

PROPHESY
kiskinawêhikê– VAI utter prophesies, prophesy
kiskiwêhikê– VAI utter prophesies; make predictions, forecast things
kiskiwêhikêmakan– VII provide prophesies; make predictions, forecast things
kiskiwêhikêwin– NI prophesy; prediction, forecast
kiskiwêh– VTI utter s.t. as a prophesy; utter prophesies
kiskiwêhw– VTA utter prophesies to s.o., utter prophesies about s.o.

PROPPED UP
aspatisin– VII lie leaning upon (it), lie back upon (it), lie propped up

PROSPEROUS
miyonâkohcikê– VAI be seen to be good at things, make things look nice, make things look prosperous
miyonâkwan– VII look good, have a nice appearance, look prosperous

PROSTRATED
kawikîhkâ– VAI be bent with age, be prostrated by age

PROTECTION
kanôsimon– NI protective talisman (usually worn around the neck, wrapped in leather)
kanôsimototaw– VTA have s.o. (e.g., rattle) as protection
manâcih– VTA be protective about s.o., be careful about s.o., spare s.o.; avoid hurting s.o.; treat s.o. with respect
manâcihito– VAI be protective about one another, be careful about one another; avoid hurting one another

PROUD
mamihcih– VTA *(especially in inverse constructions:)* make s.o. proud, fill s.o. with pride
mamihcisi– VAI be proud
mamihtisihkâso– VAI act proudly, hold back, hesitate with one's response
mamistêyimo– VAI be proud of oneself, be boastful

PROVISIONER
ominahowiyiniw– NA hunter; provisioner

PROVISIONS
nîmâ– VAI take provisions; take a packed lunch
nîmâh– VTA make s.o. take provisions; add (it) to s.o.'s packed lunch
nîmâsi– VAI take some provisions; take some packed lunch
nîmâwin– NI provisions; packed lunch
nîmâwinihkê– VAI arrange provisions; prepare a packed lunch
nîmâwiwat– NI box for provisions; lunch-box

PROVOKE
naniwacihito– VAI tease one another, provoke one another
paciyawêh– VTA wrong s.o. by one's utterance, provoke s.o.'s anger

PRY
pahkwaciwêpah– VTI break s.t. off, pry s.t. off (e.g., hide-scrapings), knock s.t. off
pahkwatah– VTI break s.t. off, pry s.t. off (e.g., hide-scrapings), knock s.t. off

pahkwatin– VTI break s.t. off by hand, pry s.t. off by hand (e.g., caked dirt from laundry)

pahkwêh– VTI break a part off s.t., pry a part off s.t.

PUBLISH

têpwât– VTA call out to s.o., yell at s.o.; publish the marriage banns for s.o.

PULL

âsipit– VTA pull s.o. down

âwacipit– VTI haul s.t. by pulling

iskon– VTI pull s.t. (e.g., dress) up so far

ispâhkêpit– VTA pull s.o. high up, pull s.o. high into the sky (e.g., snake)

ispit– VTI pull s.t. thither or thus; pull a trailer

kêcikopit– VTI pull s.t. free, pull s.t. out; take s.t. off by pulling; pull out of s.t.

kêcikwahw– VTA pull s.o. (e.g., thorns) out, remove s.o. by tool

kêcikwâpitêpit– VTA pull a tooth for s.o., pull s.o.'s tooth

kipwahpit– VTI pull s.t. closed, tie s.t. shut

manipit– VTA pull s.o. free (e.g., thorn, porcupine quills), pull s.o. in (e.g., net), pull s.o. out, obtain s.o. by pulling

manipit– VTI pull s.t. free, pull s.t. out (e.g., flower), obtain s.t. by pulling

matâwisipit– VTI pull s.t. into the open, pull s.t. out onto the open prairie

nâhnâskon– VTA pull s.o. in (on a rope)

nîhcipit– VTA pull s.o. down, drag s.o. down

ocipit– VTA pull s.o. along, pull s.o. in; pull s.o. out (e.g., rabbit from snare, fish out of water)

ocipit– VTI pull s.t. out (e.g., from the ground), pull s.t. off; extract s.t. (e.g., grease from soup); move s.t. (e.g., house)

ocipitamâso– VAI pull (it/him) in for oneself, secure (it/him) for oneself

ohpipit– VTA pull s.o. up

paskêtâpâso– VAI branch off with one's wagon, move off to the side with one's vehicle; pull over with a vehicle

pêtâwah– VTA lead s.o. hither as a crowd, pull s.o. hither

pimâwah– VTA lead s.o. along as a crowd, pull s.o. along

pîhtopit– VTA pull the covering layer off s.o. (e.g., tree), peel the bark off s.o.

pîhtopit– VTI pull s.t. (e.g., bark) off as the covering layer, peel s.t. off

tasin– VTI pull the trigger on s.t. (e.g., gun), shoot s.t. off (e.g., gun); emit a sharp noise, make a shot-like noise; sound a thunderclap (e.g., as Thunderbird)

waskicipit– VTI pull s.t. over top

wayawîpit– VTI pull s.t. (e.g., fence-post) out of the bush

PULL-ON

waskipicikan– NI pull-on, overshoe, rubber

PULLING

nâtwâpit– VTI split s.t. (e.g., branch) off by pulling, break s.t. off

patakopit– VTA squash s.o. in pulling, flatten s.o. down by pulling

pêcipit– VTI bring s.t. hither by pulling

sîkopit– VTA press s.o. out by pulling; drain the milk from s.o. (e.g., cow)

waskawipit– VTI move s.t. by pulling, shake s.t. by pulling

PUNCH

pôskwahikâso– VAI have a hole punched, have oneself pierced

pôskwahw– VTA punch a hole in s.o. (e.g., in the reaches under a wagon)

pôskwatahw– VTA punch a hole in s.o. (e.g., earring), punch a hole in s.o.

PUNCTURED

cahkâpicin– VAI have one's eye punctured (e.g., by branches or thorns)

PUNGENT

âhkwâpahtê– VII give off a sharp odour, produce pungent fumes, emit acidic or caustic fumes

PUNISHING

kakwâtakatoskê– VAI work dreadfully hard, do punishing work

PUPIL

kisêyinîw-ôhpikihâkan– NA old man's pupil, ward of the old men

PUPPY

acimosis– NA puppy, young dog, little dog

PURCHASE

nîhcipicikâtê– VII be taken down (e.g., from a shelf), be chosen for purchase (e.g., in self-service store)

otinikê– VAI take things; buy things, do one's shopping, make a purchase; take away winnings (e.g., in a card-game)

PURPOSE
konita *IPC* in vain, without reason, without purpose, for nothing; without further ado; anywhere, at random, in a random place
mani *IPV* with the intent of, with the purpose of

PURPOSELY
ohcitaw *IPC* expressly, specifically, purposely, necessarily; it is requisite, it is meet indeed

PURSUE
maci-nôcihtâ– *VAI* pursue evil things, engage in bad medicine
miyo-nôcihtâ– *VAI* pursue good things; *(in negative constructions:)* pursue evil things, engage in bad medicine
nawaswât– *VTA* pursue s.o., chase after s.o.
nawaswât– *VTI* pursue s.t., chase after s.t.
nawaswê– *VAI* give chase, be in pursuit
nôcih– *VTA* pursue s.o., hunt for s.o. (e.g., animal); go after s.o., oppress s.o., beat s.o. up, fight with s.o.
nôcihtâ– *VAI* pursue (it), work at (it); do one's hunting, hunt

PUSH
âhtin– *VTI* move s.t. over, push s.t. aside
mâkon– *VTA* press upon s.o. by hand, press s.o.'s hand; push s.o. down (e.g., button on radio)
sâkâwanêhtâ– *VAI* push (it) to emerge from the ground, make (it) come forth
wêpah– *VTI* sweep s.t. up; throw s.t. by tool, push s.t. by tool; cock s.t. (e.g., gun)
wîkatêwêpin– *VTA* push s.o. aside, push s.o. away
yahkâtihkât– *VTI* dig out more of a hole or cellar, push out the size of an existing hole or cellar

QUADRUPED
onîcâniw– *NA* female of large quadrupeds; cow, cow-moose, female elk

QUARREL
kîhkihto– *VAI* resist one another, quarrel

QUARTER
pêyak-sôniyâs *IPC* twenty-five cents, a quarter
sôniyâs– *NA* coin; 25-cents coin, quarter; a little money, some money

QUEEN
kihc-ôkimâskwêw– *NA* queen

QUICKLY
kisiskâ *IPV* quickly, fast
kiyipa *IPC* quickly, soon
kiyipi *IPV* quickly, fast
kiyipikin– *VII* grow quickly
mâmâsîs *IPC* sparingly, delicately; quickly, roughly, without care

QUICKSAND
tastôstôkan– *VII* be bog, be quicksand

QUIET
kakâmwâtisi– *VAI* be of quiet disposition
kakâmwâtiskwêhkê– *VAI* act quietly as a woman; give the impression of being a quiet woman
pêyâhtik *IPC* quietly, gently, softly, slowly
pônwêwit– *VTI* cease making noise; keep quiet
wâskamisî– *VAI* settle down; be of quiet disposition
wêtinahk *IPC* quietly

QUILL
kâwiy– *NA* porcupine quill

QUILT
nanâcohkokwâcês– *NI* patchwork quilt

QUIT
pôyo– *VAI* cease, quit

RABBIT
câpakwânis– *NI* snare, rabbit snare
câpakwêsi– *VAI* set small snares, set rabbit snares; do a little snaring
wâposo-câpakwêsi– *VAI* set small snares, set rabbit snares
wâposo-mîcimâpoy– *NI* rabbit broth, rabbit soup
wâposos– *NA* young rabbit, small rabbit
wâposw– *NA* rabbit

RABBITSKIN
wâposwayân– *NA* rabbitskin, raw rabbitskin
wâposwayân– *NI* rabbitskin, dressed rabbitskin
wâposwayânakohp– *NI* rabbitskin blanket

RACE
kotiskâwê– *VAI* race, be in a race

RACE-HORSE
kotiskâwêwatimw– *NA* race-horse

ENGLISH INDEX

RACK
akocikan– *NI* rack for hanging up fish or meat, storage-rack; cupboard, shelf
akwâwân– *NI* rack for drying meat
akwâwânâhcikos– *NI* rail of drying rack
akwâwê– *VAI* hang sheets of meat on drying rack
paskiciwêpin– *VTA* throw s.o. across; throw s.o. (e.g., rabbit) over drying rack

RADIO
orêtiyow– *NI* radio

RAGE
kisiwipayi– *VAI* get angry, fly into rage

RAGGED
mêscihtatâ– *VAI* get all of (it) torn, get all of (it) ragged
sikohtatâ– *VAI* get (it) torn; go ragged
yâyikâskocin– *VAI* have one's clothes ripped ragged on branches or thorns
yîwêpayi– *VAI* be ragged, be in rags
yîwêyâskocin– *VAI* have one's clothes torn ragged on branches or thorns

RAGS
ayiwinis– *NI* clothes, clothing; rags (e.g., as used in bitch-light)
yîwêpayi– *VAI* be ragged, be in rags

RAIL
akwâwânâhcikos– *NI* rail of drying rack
miscikos– *NI* little stick (e.g., in collecting sap); little pole, rod, rail (e.g., on drying rack); branch of a small plant (e.g., labrador tea)
mistikw– *NI* stick, pole, post, log, wooden rail
nîsopîwâpiskw– *NI* double rail, railway track
wâsakâmêyâpôyo– *VAI* go around a circle by railway, describe a circuit by rail

RAILWAY
nîsopîwâpiskw– *NI* double rail, railway track
pîwâpiskomêskanaw– *NI* railway
takwâpôyo– *VAI* arrive by railway, arrive by train
wâsakâmêyâpôyo– *VAI* go around a circle by railway, describe a circuit by rail

RAIN
âstê-kimiwan– *VII* cease being rain, let up as rain
kaskawanipêstâ– *VII* be drizzle, be rainy
kimiwan– *VII* rain, be rain
sâpohci-kimiwan– *VII* rain through, come raining through
sîkin– *VTI* pour s.t.; pour s.t. in (e.g., lye); let it rain
sîkipêstâ– *VII* pour down as a rain shower

RAISE
kitimâk-ôhpikih– *VTA* raise s.o. in poverty; raise s.o. as an orphan
ohpahpahtên– *VTI* raise up the smoke of s.t.
ohpahtên– *VTI* raise up the smoke of s.t.
ohpâskon– *VTA* raise s.o. (e.g., pipe)
ohpâskon– *VTI* raise s.t. (e.g., pipestem)
ohpâskwah– *VTI* raise s.t. (e.g., cloth) on a wooden pole, hold s.t. aloft on a wooden pole
ohpikih– *VTA* make s.o. grow up, raise s.o.
ohpikihâwaso– *VAI* make one's children grow up, raise one's children
ohpikihito– *VAI* make one another grow up, raise one another
ohpikihtamaw– *VTA* make (it/him) grow for s.o., raise (it/him) for s.o.
ohpikihtamâso– *VAI* make (it/him) grow for oneself, raise (it/him) for oneself
ohpikinâwaso– *VAI* make one's children grow up, raise one's children
ohpin– *VTA* raise s.o. (e.g., pipe), lift s.o. up
ohpin– *VTI* raise s.t., create s.t.
ohpwên– *VTI* make s.t. fly up, raise s.t. up (e.g., dust)
pasikôn– *VTA* raise s.o. (e.g., to a position of leadership)
pasikôn– *VTI* raise s.t. (e.g., lodge)
wîc-ôhpikîm– *VTA* grow up together with s.o., be raised together with s.o.

RAISIN
sôminis– *NA* raisin

RANDOM
konita *IPC* in vain, without reason, without purpose, for nothing; without further ado; anywhere, at random, in a random place
nânitaw isi *IPC* in some way, in any way; in various ways; in a random direction
pakwanaw *IPC* by chance, at random

pakwanawahtâ– *VAI* go on with (it) at random, know nothing about (it), be clueless about (it)

waniyaw *IPC* any, somebody; at random

RAPIDLY

asiwacipayin– *VII* get placed inside, get enclosed; rapidly fill an enclosed space (e.g., water flowing into hoofprint)

cacâstapipayin– *VII* move rapidly

kotâwipayi– *VAI* rapidly sink into the ground (e.g., into bog or quicksand)

sipwêtâcimopahtâ– *VAI* rapidly crawl away, depart crawling fast

RARE

wâh-wîhkâc *IPC* at rare intervals, rarely now and again

wiyâ wîpac cî wiya *IPC* it is a rare and welcome event that

RASH

môskipayi– *VAI* break out in a rash, erupt in sores (e.g., with thrush)

RASPBERRY

ayôskan– *NA* raspberry

RATHER

âkwâskam *IPC* really, rather; *(in negative constructions:)* not really, not as much

iyâyaw *IPC* eagerly, intently; by preference, rather

kiyâm *IPC* oh well, never mind, so much for this; anyway, rather; let it be, let there be no further delay; please

nawac *IPC* by comparison; more, better, rather

RATION

asahkêwikamikw– *NI* ration house

asahtowikamikw– *NI* ration house

asahtowin– *NI* feeding one another; rations

asam– *VTA* feed s.o., give s.o. to eat; hand out rations to s.o.

otasahkêw– *NA* dispenser of rations; Indian agent

RATROOT

wîhkês– *NI* ratroot

RATTLE

papâsiwih– *VTA* rattle s.o., cause s.o. to be unsettled

sîsîkwan– *NA* rattle

RAVAGE

kakwâtakih– *VTA* make s.o. suffer; be mean to s.o., be abusive to s.o.; *(especially in inverse constructions:)* affect s.o. terribly (e.g., as disease), ravage s.o.

RAW

âskiti– *VAI* be raw, be uncooked (e.g., flour)

pahkêkinw– *NA* raw hide

pâpakwâtahw– *VTA (especially in inverse constructions:)* rub s.o. raw, cause s.o. blisters

wâposwayân– *NA* rabbitskin, raw rabbitskin

RAWHIDE

mâhmâkwahcikanêyâpiy– *NI* rawhide rope

REACH

iskopitonê– *VAI* have one's arm reach so far, extend one's arm so far

iskwâpêkamon– *VII* reach so far as rope

ispâhkêpayi– *VAI* reach a high level, be elevated (e.g., blood-sugar)

ispîhcâ– *VII* extend thus, reach so far as land, be of such size as country

kâsispô– *VAI* reach beyond, exceed; survive into another generation

kâsispôhtêmakan– *VII* go on, reach beyond, exceed; survive into another generation

kisipipayin– *VII* come to an end, reach the end, run out

kisipîmakan– *VII* come to an end, reach the end; have an end

kîs-ôhpiki– *VAI* complete one's growing up, reach adulthood, be grown up

kîsasiwât– *VTI* reach a decision about s.t.; complete making a law about s.t.

nayawaciki– *VAI* grow up to reach various ages, be variously grown up

otiht– *VTA* reach s.o.

otiht– *VTI* reach s.t.

otihtamâso– *VAI* reach (it/him) for oneself

takopayi– *VII* arrive, have sufficient reach

REACHES

pasiposôs– *NA* reach (long beam running from front to back in the centre of the undercarriage of a wagon)

sâpostamon– *VII* run through; be the reaches (under a wagon)

READ

ayamihcikê– *VAI* read things, read; go to school

ayamihtâ– *VAI* read (it); read

READINESS

kwayâc-âstâ– *VAI* place (it) in readiness (e.g., drinking water)

ENGLISH INDEX 357

kwayâci-niton– *VTI* look for s.t. to hold in readiness
kwayâci-sikwatahikâtê– *VII* be pounded in readiness, be pre-pounded
kwayâtah– *VTA* place s.o. (e.g., rock) in readiness, prepare s.o. (e.g., rock) in advance
kwayâtastamaw– *VTA* put (it/him) aside in readiness for s.o.
kwayâtastamâso– *VAI* put (it/him) aside in readiness for oneself
kwayâtastâ– *VAI* place (it) in readiness, put (it) aside in advance
wawêyapi– *VAI* sit in readiness

READING
ayamihcikêwin– *NI* reading; *(fig.)* a reading, bible verse

READY
ahâw *IPC* now indeed! ready! let's go!
kawisimonihkê– *VAI* prepare the bed, get ready for bed
kwayâc *IPC* ready, prepared in advance
kwayâci *IPV* ready, prepared in advance
kwayâcihtâ– *VAI* get (it) ready, prepare (it) in advance
mamanê– *VAI* get ready, be busy
nêhpêmapi– *VAI* be at the ready, sit at the ready
wawêyî– *VAI* get ready, make preparations
wawêyîh– *VTA* get s.o. ready, get s.o. dressed

REALISE
môyêyiht– *VTI* sense s.t.; suspect s.t.; realise s.t.

REALLY
âkwâskam *IPC* really, rather; *(in negative constructions:)* not really, not as much
mitoni *IPC* intensively, fully, really
tipiyawê *IPC* personally, in person; really
yâyâhk *IPC* really, for sure, to be sure; especially, all the more so

REAR
nâway *IPC* behind, at the rear; in the past
otâhk *IPC* behind, at the rear, in the past
otâskanâhk *IPC* behind, at the rear; in the past
simacî– *VAI* stand upright; rear up (e.g., horse)

RECEIVE
tipahamâto– *VAI* receive one's Treaty payment, be paid Treaty
wawiyatisi– *VAI* be deservedly ridiculed, receive one's just deserts

RECENTLY
anohcihkê *IPC* recently
âstamispîhk *IPC* at a time closer to the present; more recently
âstamita *IPC* later, more recently
katisk *IPC* just now, a moment ago; recently, a while ago; exactly, just at that moment, at the very moment; *(in negative constructions:)* not merely
mastaw *IPC* newly, recently
miyân– *VTI* leave behind fresh tracks, have recently passed by

RECITE
tâpowê– *VAI* speak correctly; recite one's prayer correctly

RECOGNISE
âtayôhkanakiso– *VAI* be held to be a spirit being, be recognised as a dream guardian
nisitawêyihcikâtê– *VII* be recognised
nisitawêyiht– *VTI* recognise s.t., know s.t.
nisitawêyim– *VTA* recognise s.o., know s.o.
nisitawin– *VTI* recognise s.t.

RECOMPENSE
mosc-âsam– *VTA* simply provide food to s.o., supply food to s.o. without recompense
mosci *IPC* simply, directly, without mediation; merely, without instrument; without recompense

RECORD
masinah– *VTI* mark s.t., draw s.t.; write s.t.; write s.t. down, record s.t. in writing; sign s.t. (e.g., treaty)
otin– *VTI* take s.t.; pick s.t., choose s.t., select s.t. (e.g., moss); steal s.t.; take s.t. over; extract s.t. (e.g., grease from soup), remove s.t. (e.g., glands in butchering beaver), extract s.t.; accept s.t. (e.g., contract); capture s.t., record s.t. on audio-tape

RECOVER
âstê-ayâ– *VAI* recover from illness, have one's condition improve, be gradually restored

RED
mihkon– *VTI* make s.t. red, redden s.t.
mihkonikâtê– *VII* be made red, be reddened
mihkosi– *VAI* be red

mihkostikwânê– VAI have red hair, be red-haired

mihkotonê– VAI have a red mouth, wear lipstick

mihkotonêho– VAI paint one's mouth red, wear lipstick

mihkotonêhw– VTA paint s.o.'s mouth red, put lipstick on s.o.

mihkwawê– VAI have a red coat (e.g., animal)

mihkwâ– VII be red

mihkwâkami– VII be a red liquid

mihkwâpêmakos– NI young red willow, little red willow

mihkwâpêmakw– NI red willow, red willow scrapings

mihkwâpêmakw-âya IPC red willow stuff

RED-COAT

mihkwasâkay– NA red-coat, officer of the NWMP

RED-DEER

apisi-môsos– NA deer, red-deer

REDUCED

sikopayi– VII be crushed, be reduced to small pieces

REED

maskosiy– NI grass, hay; *(plural:)* reeds; pieces of sod

mwâskosiwân– NI bulrush, edible reed

pasân– NA cattail, edible reed

REFER

mâmiskôm– VTA talk about s.o., discuss s.o., refer to s.o.

mâmiskôt– VTI talk about s.t., discuss s.t., expound s.t., refer to s.t.

mâmiskôtamaw– VTA discuss (it/him) for s.o., expound (it/him) for s.o., refer to (it/him) for s.o.

miskôt– VTI discuss s.t., refer to s.t.

REFRIGERATOR

âhkwacihcikanis– NI small refrigerator, small freezer

âhkwatihcikan– NI refrigerator, freezer

REFUGE

itâmo– VAI flee thither or thus, seek such refuge

itâmôh– VTA make s.o. flee thus or there, direct s.o. to seek such refuge

nâtâmost– VTI flee to s.t., turn to s.t. for help, seek refuge in s.t.

nâtâmotot– VTI flee to s.t., turn to s.t. for help, seek refuge in s.t.

nâtâmototaw– VTA flee to s.o., turn to s.o. for help, seek refuge with s.o.

REGARD

ayiwâkêyiht– VTI think more of s.t., regard s.t. more highly

ayiwâkêyim– VTA think more of s.o., regard s.o. more highly

itêyiht– VTI think thus of s.t., regard s.t. thus

itêyim– VTA think thus of s.o., regard s.o. thus

itêyimikowisi– VAI be thus thought of by the powers, be thus regarded by the powers

itêyimiso– VAI think thus of oneself, regard oneself thus

kihcêyiht– VTI think highly of s.t., hold s.t. in high regard, respect s.t.; hold s.t. sacred

kihcêyim– VTA think highly of s.o., hold s.o. in high regard, respect s.o.; hold s.o. sacred

kitâpam– VTA look at s.o. (e.g., sun), watch s.o.; look at s.o. with respect, regard s.o. with respect; *(fig.)* watch over s.o.

kitimâkinaw– VTA look with pity upon s.o., look with compassion upon s.o., feel sorry for s.o.; take pity upon s.o., lovingly tend s.o.; regard s.o. with respect

sôskwâc IPC simply, immediately, without further ado; without regard to the consequences; *(in negative constructions:)* not at all

tâpwêwakêyiht– VTI hold s.t. to be true, believe in s.t.; regard s.t. positively

REGION

askiy– NI land, region, area; earth, world; settlement, colony, country; Métis settlement; *(plural:)* fields under cultivation, pieces of farmland, the lands

itêhkêskamik IPC thitherward, in thither region

REGRETTABLE

wiyakâc IPC it is regrettable

REGULARLY

kâhtap IPC differently; regularly

tâh-têpi IPC at regular intervals

REJECT

asên– VTA reject s.o., turn s.o. back

asên– VTI reject s.t., turn s.t. back, run away from s.t.

asênikâtê– VII be rejected, be turned back

âtawêyihcikê– *VAI* reject things; be dissatisfied with things
âtawêyiht– *VTI* reject s.t.; be dissatisfied with s.t.
âtawêyim– *VTA* reject s.o.; be dissatisfied with s.o.

REJOICE
miyawâcikâtê– *VII* be rejoiced over, be cause for rejoicing
miyawât– *VTI* enjoy s.t., rejoice over s.t.; rejoice, be joyful, have fun
miywêyihtâkwan– *VII* be joy, be rejoicing

RELATED
itâhkôm– *VTA* be thus related to s.o., have s.o. as such a relative, use such a kin-term for s.o.
wâhkôhto– *VAI* be related to one another, have one another as relatives; use kin-terms for one another
wâhkôm– *VTA* be related to s.o., have s.o. as one's relative; use a kin-term for s.o.

RELATIVE
–wâhkômâkan– *NDA* relative

RELAY
itwêstamaw– *VTA* say thus for s.o.; speak for s.o.; interpret for s.o.; transmit s.o.'s message, relay s.o.'s message (e.g., by radio)

RELEASE
mêki– *VAI* give (it/him) out as present; give (it/him) away, release (it/him); give (her) in marriage
pakicî– *VAI* let go, give up; release (it/him), let go of (it/him)
pakitin– *VTA* set s.o. down, allow s.o., permit s.o.; permit (it) to s.o., give permission to s.o.; let s.o. go, release s.o.; release s.o. (e.g., fish-spawn into lake), stock a lake with s.o. (e.g., fish); drop s.o. off (e.g., as an airplane)
pakitin– *VTI* let s.t. go, allow s.t., permit s.t.; release s.t.; give s.t. up, abandon s.t. (e.g., teaching, tradition); put s.t. down on earth; put s.t. in (e.g., seed potatoes)
pakitinamaw– *VTA* allow (it) for s.o., arrange (it) for s.o.; release (it/him) for s.o.
pakitinikâso– *VAI* be allowed, have permission; be released
pihkoh– *VTA* free s.o., release s.o.
pihkoho– *VAI* free oneself, escape; be released; *(fig.)* free oneself (e.g., to meet an obligation or duty); be saved

RELIEF
wanihtâ– *VAI* lose (it); get relief from (it)

RELIEVE ONESELF
kihci-wayawî– *VAI* go to relieve oneself in a major way, go to defecate
sêskisi– *VAI* go into the bush; go into the bush to relieve oneself
wayawî– *VAI* go outside, go outdoors; go to relieve oneself; leave school, leave hospital
wayawîstamâso– *VAI* go outdoors for oneself, go to relieve oneself
wayawîwin– *NI* going outside, being outdoors; going to relieve oneself, going to the toilet

RELIGION
ayamihâ– *VAI* pray, say prayers; hold a church service, celebrate mass; participate in a religious rite, go to church; follow a religion
ayamihâwin– *NI* prayer, praying, saying prayers; church service; religious rite; religion, religious denomination; the Roman Catholic church
ayamihêwâtisi– *VAI* be of religious disposition
mâmaw-ayamihâ– *VAI* pray as a group, participate in a religious rite as a group, celebrate mass as a group; go on a pilgrimage as a group
môniyâw-âyamihâwin– *NI* White religion; non-Catholic denomination
pâhkw-âyamihâwin– *NI* Roman Catholic religion; the Roman Catholic church
pimitisah– *VTI* follow s.t.; *(fig.)* adhere to a religion

RELY
aspahâkêmo– *VAI* rely upon (it/him) in speaking, rely upon (it/him) in telling a story; use (it/him) as an excuse
aspitonâmo– *VAI* rely on the spoken word; rely on (it) as a formal confirmation of the spoken word
mamisî– *VAI* rely on (it/him); place reliance
mamisîtot– *VTI* rely on s.t.
mamisîtotaw– *VTA* rely on s.o.
mamisîwât– *VTA* rely on s.o. for (it/him)
tipahâkê– *VAI* measure things with (it/him), measure things against (it/him), use (it/him) as a benchmark; measure things; rely on things

wîcihiso– *VAI* help oneself; apply oneself, study for oneself; rely on oneself in childbirth

REMEMBER
kanihk *IPC* oh yes, I just remembered, I had forgotten
kiskisi– *VAI* remember; remember (it/him)
kiskisoh– *VTA* make s.o. remember, remind s.o., put s.o. in mind
kiskisopayi– *VAI* suddenly remember, remember in a flash; suddenly think of (it), have (it) come to mind
kiskisototaw– *VTA* remember s.o.; remember (it) about s.o.
ocihcikiskisi– *VAI* remember (it) far back; have memories far back
sîpikiskisi– *VAI* remember far back

REMIND
kiskisoh– *VTA* make s.o. remember, remind s.o., put s.o. in mind
kiskisohto– *VAI* remind one another
kiskisom– *VTA* remind s.o.
kiskisomito– *VAI* remind one another

REMOVE
kêcikwahw– *VTA* pull s.o. (e.g., thorns) out, remove s.o. by tool
manin– *VTI* take s.t. down, remove s.t. (e.g., snare)
otin– *VTI* take s.t.; pick s.t., choose s.t., select s.t. (e.g., moss); steal s.t.; take s.t. over; extract s.t. (e.g., grease from soup), remove s.t. (e.g., glands in butchering beaver), extract s.t.; accept s.t. (e.g., contract); capture s.t., record s.t. on audio-tape

RENDER
tihkisw– *VTA* melt s.o.; render s.o. (e.g., cracklings)
wâpiski-pimiy– *NI* lard, rendered lard

RENT
awih– *VTA* lend (it/him) to s.o.; rent (it/him) out to s.o.
awihiwê– *VAI* lend (it/him) to people; rent (it/him) out to people

REPAY
tipahamaw– *VTA* pay s.o. for (it/him), repay a debt to s.o.; pay s.o. a pension

REPEATEDLY
âh-âyin– *VTI* touch s.t. repeatedly, rub across s.t. by hand
wâh-wîpac *IPC* quite often, again and again, repeatedly

REPLACE
âhci *IPV* by change, by replacement
mêskotin– *VTI* change s.t., replace s.t.

REPORT
âcimowin– *NI* story, account, report
kisêyinîw-âcimowin– *NI* old man's story, report of the old men
matwêwê– *VII* be heard as a gunshot, be the report of a gun
wîht– *VTI* name s.t., mention s.t. by name; tell about s.t., report s.t.; decree s.t.

REPORTEDLY
êsa *IPC* reportedly

REPREHENSIBLY
nânitaw itahkamikisi– *VAI* behave reprehensibly, be up to something

REPRESENT
masinisin– *VAI* be drawn, be represented, be shaped (e.g., star, sun)
pimohtêstamaw– *VTA* go along for s.o., represent s.o.

REQUEST
aspatot– *VTA* accompany one's request of s.o. with a gift
kakwêcim– *VTA* ask s.o.; make a request of s.o.; ask s.o. about (it/him)
nitotamâ– *VAI* ask for (it/him) (e.g., sugar), make a request for (it), pray for (it); make a request
nitotamâkêstamaw– *VTA* make a request for s.o., pray on s.o.'s behalf, ask for (it/him) on s.o.'s behalf
nitotamâwin– *NI* request
nitôsk– *VTI* seek s.t.; make a request for s.t. (e.g., medicine)
nitôskamaw– *VTA* seek (it/him) of s.o., make a request for (it/him) of s.o.

REQUISITE
ohcitaw *IPC* expressly, specifically, purposely, necessarily; it is requisite, it is meet indeed

RESEMBLING
kisâstaw *IPC* roughly like, resembling

RESERVE
askîhkân– *NI* reserve; band
iskonikan– *NI* reservation, Indian reserve
tipahaskân– *NI* reserve
wayawîtisahw– *VTA* send s.o. outdoors; send s.o. off the reserve, banish s.o. from the reserve

RESIDENCE
ihtâwin– *NI* abode, place of residence; community
kihci-wîki– *VAI* live formally; *(fig.)* live in residence
otihtâwini– *VAI* have a dwelling, have a place of residence; have (it) as one's

dwelling, have (it) as one's place of residence

RESIST
iyisâc *IPC* half-heartedly, resistingly
iyisâho– *VAI* resist, resist temptation, exercise restraint
kîhkihto– *VAI* resist one another, quarrel

RESISTANCE
iyisâhowin– *NI* resistance, resisting temptation, restraint

RESPECT
itasiwât– *VTA* decide thus with respect to s.o.; give s.o. such a command; impose such laws on s.o.
kanâtêyim– *VTA* have respect for s.o.
kêhtin– *VTA* treat s.o. with respect, show deference to s.o.
kihcêyiht– *VTI* think highly of s.t., hold s.t. in high regard, respect s.t.; hold s.t. sacred
kihcêyim– *VTA* think highly of s.o., hold s.o. in high regard, respect s.o.; hold s.o. sacred
kitâpam– *VTA* look at s.o. (e.g., sun), watch s.o.; look at s.o. with respect, regard s.o. with respect; *(fig.)* watch over s.o.
kitimâkinaw– *VTA* look with pity upon s.o., look with compassion upon s.o., feel sorry for s.o.; take pity upon s.o., lovingly tend s.o.; regard s.o. with respect
manâcih– *VTA* be protective about s.o., be careful about s.o., spare s.o.; avoid hurting s.o.; treat s.o. with respect
manâcihtâ– *VAI* treat (it) with respect
manâcim– *VTA* speak to s.o. with respect, speak of s.o. with respect

RESPECTED
–mosôm– *NDA* grandfather, grandfather's brother; *(fig.)* old man, respected elder
kihcêyihcikâtê– *VII* be highly thought of, be respected; be held sacred
kihcêyihtâkwan– *VII* be highly thought of, be respected; be held sacred

RESPOND
kwêtatêyitiskwêyi– *VAI* be at a loss as to where to turn one's head; be at a loss for a response
mamihtisihkâso– *VAI* act proudly, hold back, hesitate with one's response

naskom– *VTA* respond to s.o. with (it/him), answer s.o.'s prayer with (it/him)
naskomo– *VAI* respond, make a verbal response
naskot– *VTI* respond to s.t.; swear upon s.t. in response
naskwahamaw– *VTA* respond to s.o.; sing in response to s.o.
naskwahamâkê– *VAI* respond; sing in response, sing one's response
naskwêwasim– *VTA* speak to s.o. in response, respond to s.o. by speech; answer back to s.o., respond to s.o. (e.g., inappropriately)
naskwêwasimo– *VAI* speak in response, respond by speech

RESPONSIBLE
kitêyiht– *VTI* look after s.t., be responsible for s.t.
kitêyihtamaw– *VTA* look after (it/him) for s.o., be responsible (for it/him) to s.o.

REST
ayiwêpi– *VAI* rest, take a rest; retire, take retirement
ayiwêpihastimwê– *VAI* give one's horses a rest, rest one's horses

RESTAURANT
mîcisowikamikw– *NI* cafe, restaurant
môniyâwi-mîcisowikamikw– *NI* White restaurant

RESTORED
âstê-ayâ– *VAI* recover from illness, have one's condition improve, be gradually restored

RESTRAINT
iyisâho– *VAI* resist, resist temptation, exercise restraint
iyisâhowin– *NI* resistance, resisting temptation, restraint

RESULT
ohcipayin– *VII* come from there, result from that

RETIRE
ayiwêpi– *VAI* rest, take a rest; retire, take retirement

RETRIBUTION
ohcinê– *VAI* be ill on account of (it), suffer for (it); suffer in retribution

RETURN
kâwi *IPC* again; back, in return
kîwê– *VAI* go home, return home
kîwêmakan– *VII* return home, come back
kîwêtot– *VTI* return home to s.t.

kîwêtotaw– *VTA* return home to s.o.
mêskoc *IPC* instead, in return, in exchange
wâyonî– *VAI* turn back, return

REVIVE
âpisisim– *VTA* revive s.o., bring s.o. back to life
âpisisimito– *VAI* revive one another, bring one another back to life
âpisisin– *VAI* revive, come back to life
pimâcih– *VTA* make s.o. live, give life to s.o., sustain s.o.'s life; revive s.o., save s.o.'s life; make a living for s.o.

REWARD
kîspinat– *VTI* earn enough to buy s.t.; earn s.t. as reward; earn one's reward
kîspinatamaw– *VTA* earn one's reward in s.o., earn s.o. (e.g., grandchild) as one's reward

RIB
–spikêkan– *NDI* rib

RIBBON
sênipân– *NA* ribbon, satin ribbon

RICH
mis-ôtinikê– *VAI* come away with rich winnings (e.g., in a card-game)
pîsâkwan– *VII* contain plenty, offer lots of room; be plentiful, be rich
wêyôtisi– *VAI* be wealthy, be rich

RIDE
kiwêpayi– *VAI* drive home, drive back, ride home, ride back
nayahto– *VAI* carry one another on one's back; ride up on one another (e.g., beads)
papâmipayi– *VAI* ride about, drive about
papâmitâpâso– *VAI* ride about on a wagon; go on a wagon-ride
pâpayi– *VAI* come hither, ride hither
pôsi– *VAI* board, be aboard (e.g., boat or vehicle); ride the train
pôsih– *VTA* make s.o. board (e.g., boat or vehicle), give s.o. a ride; put s.o. on a sleigh, give s.o. a ride on a sleigh
têhtapi– *VAI* be mounted, ride on horseback
têhtapîwitâs– *NA* riding breeches

RIDICULED
wawiyatisi– *VAI* be deservedly ridiculed, receive one's just deserts

RIGHT
kihciniskihk *IPC* on the right hand, to the right
kwayask *IPC* properly, by rights
nahiyikohk *IPC* to the proper degree, to the proper extent, just enough, just right, evenly, fittingly, appropriately

RING
âhcanis– *NA* ring, wedding-ring
cowêskihtê– *VAI* have one's ears ring, have ringing in one's ears, suffer from tinnitus
kihci-wîkihtowin-âhcanis– *NA* wedding ring
kîhkâtah– *VTI* make the sound of (it/him) ring out clearly
kîhkâtahamaw– *VTA* make the sound of (it/him) ring out clearly to s.o.
sêwêpin– *VTA* make s.o. (e.g., rattle) ring out
sêwêpitamaw– *VTA* make (it) ring out for s.o.; call s.o. by telephone

RIPE
atihtê– *VII* be ripe, be of ripe colouring

RIPPED
yâyikâskocin– *VAI* have one's clothes ripped ragged on branches or thorns

RISE
ispâhkêkocin– *VII* rise high up, hang high aloft, be suspended high in the air
kwêskahcâhk *IPC* on the opposite side of a rise in the land
ohpohtât– *VTI* proceed high across s.t. (e.g., sky), rise up upon s.t. (e.g., sun upon sky)
ohpohtê– *VAI* rise up, proceed high in the sky
ohpwêtot– *VTI* lift oneself upon s.t., rise up upon s.t. (e.g., moon upon night sky)
osêhcâ– *VII* be a rise in the land, be a slope, be a gentle hillside
osêhcâw– *NI* rise in the land, slope, gentle hillside
sâkêwêtot– *VTI* come out upon s.t., rise (e.g., sun) upon s.t.

RISQUÉ
wiyâhkwêwi-âcimo– *VAI* swear in telling stories; tell obscene stories, tell risqué stories

RITE
ayamihâ– *VAI* pray, say prayers; hold a church service, celebrate mass; participate in a religious rite, go to church; follow a religion
ayamihâwin– *NI* prayer, praying, saying prayers; church service; religious rite; religion, religious denomination; the Roman Catholic church

isi-mawimoscikêwin– NI worshipping thus, such a form of worship; rite of such a type
isistâ– VAI hold such a rite, perform a rite thus
isîhcikê– VAI do things thus, proceed thus, arrange things thus; perform such a rite, perform a rite thus; conduct negotiations thus
isîhtwâwin– NI performing a rite thus; such a rite; way of worship, way of doing things
itikwamikohkê– VAI hold such a lodge, hold such a rite
kihcikanisi– VAI hold a rite; spend Christmas
mawimoscikêwin– NI crying out in prayer, wailing; form of worship, rite
mâmaw-âyamihâ– VAI pray as a group, participate in a religious rite as a group, celebrate mass as a group; go on a pilgrimage as a group

RITUAL
isîhcikêwin– NI what is done, activities; culture; ritual
kihc-ôskâpêwis– NA main ritual server
kîsitêpo– VAI cook; cook a feast, cook ritual food
kîsitêw– NI food, ritual food
kîsîhcikê– VAI complete doing things; bring a ritual to its conclusion; conclude the formal signing of a treaty
miyawâkâtinikê– VAI take particular care with things, handle ritual objects with particular care
môniyâw-îhtwâwin– NI White ritual, White custom
nikamo– VAI sing, sing a ritual song
nikamon– NI song, ritual song
nîswayak isi IPC in both directions; in both forms of ritual (e.g., with both incense and sweetgrass)
oskâpêwis– NA ritual server, servitor (e.g., in ritual)

RIVER
sîpiy– NI river
sîpîsis– NI small river, creek

ROAD
âsowohtê– VAI walk across, cross the road
mêskanaw– NI path, trail, road
môniyâwi-mêskanaw– NI White path, White road
nêhiyawi-mêskanaw– NI Cree path, Cree road; Indian path, Indian road

sipwêmon– VII leave as path, trail, road; begin as path, trail, road
wanohtê– VAI err, make a mistake, take the wrong road

ROAST
maskatêpo– VAI roast (it) on a spit
nawacî– VAI roast (it), roast (it) over an open fire; roast one's food

ROB
maskahto– VAI seize (it/him) from one another; rob one another
maskam– VTA seize (it/him) from s.o.; rob s.o.

ROBE
kinwâpêkasâkê– VAI wear a long skirt; wear a long robe (e.g., as a Roman Catholic priest)

ROBIN
pihpihcêw– NA robin

ROCK
asiniy– NA rock, stone
kisâpiskisw– VTA heat s.o. as rock (e.g., in sweat-lodge)
kîsâpiskiso– VAI be completely heated as rock (e.g., in sweat-lodge), be fully heated as rock
mistasiniy– NA big stone, big rock
sîkahasinê– VAI pour water on rocks (e.g., in sweat-lodge), sprinkle rocks with water

ROCKY MOUNTAINS
asinîwaciy– NI the Rocky Mountains

ROD
kwâskwêpicikê– VAI fish with a rod
miscikos– NI little stick (e.g., in collecting sap); little pole, rod, rail (e.g., on drying rack); branch of a small plant (e.g., labrador tea)

ROLL
pitikwêkin– VTI roll s.t. up as cloth
tihtipin– VTI twist s.t. (e.g., rope); roll s.t. up
titipahpit– VTA roll and tie (it) around s.o., bandage s.o. with (it)
titipahpit– VTI roll and tie (it) around s.t.
titipihtin– VII be rolled up, be twisted
titipin– VTI twine s.t., twist s.t.; roll s.t. up
titipisim– VTA roll s.o. (e.g., thread) up

ROMAN CATHOLIC
ayamihâwin– NI prayer, praying, saying prayers; church service; religious rite; religion, religious denomination; the Roman Catholic church

pâhkw-âyamihâwin– NI Roman Catholic religion; the Roman Catholic church
pâhkw-âyamihêwiyiniw– NA Roman Catholic priest

ROOF
apahkwân– NI roof
apahkwât– VTI make a roof over s.t.
apahkwâtê– VII have a roof, be roofed; be the roof
apahkwê– VAI roof (it); make a roof

ROOM
apîwikamikw– NI sitting room, living room
ascikêwikamikw– NI storage room, storage building
piskihcikamikos– NI separate room, private room
pîsâkwan– VII contain plenty, offer lots of room; be plentiful, be rich
tawâ– VII be open, have room

ROOT
maskihkiy– NI herb, plant; seneca-root; medicinal root; medicine; chemicals
mônah– VTI dig for s.t.; dig roots
ocêpihk– NI root
ocêpihkis– NI little root
ocêpihkos– NI little root
otêhiminâni-cêpihk– NI strawberry root

ROPE
iskwâpêkamon– VII reach so far as rope
itâpihkêpayi– VAI move thus or there as a rope or snake, swing thus as a rope or snake
mâhmâkwahcikanêyâpiy– NI rawhide rope
osâwâpêkan– VII be yellow (as rope); be yellow rope
pîminahkwân– NI rope
pîminahkwânis– NI string, rope
sakâpêkin– VTA lead s.o. (e.g., horse) by a rope
sakâpêkipah– VTA lead s.o. (e.g., horse) along by a rope

ROSARY
ayamihêmin– NA rosary-bead; rosary

ROSEHIP
okiniy– NA rosehip

ROTTEN
pîkwatowan– VII be rotten (e.g., tooth)

ROUGHLY
kisâstaw IPC roughly like, resembling
mâmâsîs IPC sparingly, delicately; quickly, roughly, without care
nânitaw IPC simply; *(with numbers:)* roughly, approximately; variously; something, at some undetermined place; *(in negative constructions:)* not anything; something bad, anything bad; somewhere

ROUND
wâwiyê IPV round, in a ball
wâwiyêkamâ– VII be a round lake
wâwiyêkwât– VTI sew s.t. round (e.g., rug)
wâwiyên– VTI bend s.t. round
wâwiyêyâ– VII be round

ROUNDED
wîhkwêtâpânâskw– NA rounded toboggan, curved sleigh

ROUTINELY
pisisik IPC always, every time, routinely

ROW
nîpitêh– VTA place s.o. in a row, place s.o. abreast, place s.o. in a line
nîpitêkotâ– VAI hang (it) up in a row, hang (it) up in a line
nîpitêpi– VAI sit in a row, sit abreast

ROYALTY
kihc-ôkimâw– NA king; *(fig.)* government; royalty

RUB
âh-âyin– VTI touch s.t. repeatedly, rub across s.t. by hand
pâpakwâtahw– VTA *(especially in inverse constructions:)* rub s.o. raw, cause s.o. blisters
sâmiskaw– VTA rub against s.o.
sinikon– VTA rub s.o. (e.g., soap)
sisopêkah– VTI rub (it) flat on s.t. by tool; paint s.t.
sisopêkahw– VTA rub (it/him) flat on s.o. by tool; paint s.o.
sisopêkin– VTA rub (it/him) flat on s.o. by hand

RUBBER
waskicaskisinis– NI overshoe, rubber
waskipicikan– NI pull-on, overshoe, rubber
waskitaskisin– NI overshoe, rubber

RUG
anâskânis– NI covering, mat, rug

RUIN
misiwanâcihcikêmakan– *VII* ruin things, destroy things
misiwanâcihiso– *VAI* ruin oneself, destroy oneself; *(fig.)* commit suicide
misiwanâcihtamaw– *VTA* ruin (it/him) for s.o., destroy (it/him) for s.o.
misiwanâcihtâ– *VAI* ruin (it), destroy (it)
misiwanâtan– *VII* be ruined, perish; be spoiled, spoil (e.g., meat)
misiwanâtisi– *VAI* be ruined, perish

RUINOUS
misiwanâcisîmakan– *VII* be ruinous, be destructive

RULE
tipêyiht– *VTI* own s.t., control s.t., rule s.t., be master over s.t.; have a voice in the affairs of s.t. (e.g., reserve)
tipêyim– *VTA* own s.o., control s.o., rule s.o.; *(fig.)* be the Lord over s.o.; have s.o. in one's clutches (e.g., devil)
wiyasiwât– *VTI* decide s.t.; make a rule or law about s.t.
wiyasiwêwin– *NI* decision; rule, law; council, band council

RUN
âsiciwan– *VII* run down as liquid
iskwâhtawîpahtâ– *VAI* climb up so far at a run; climb up (e.g., a tree) at a run
ispahtâ– *VAI* run there or thus
ispayin– *VII* take place thus, occur thus; run thus (in a cycle), be there (in a cycle), come around (in a cycle), be that time again; come by, go by, have passed (e.g., days, years)
itamon– *VII* run thus or there as a path; be thus attached, be mounted thus
kisipipayin– *VII* come to an end, reach the end, run out
kotâwiciwan– *VII* sink into the ground, run into the ground (e.g., water)
kwâsih– *VTA* steal s.o., run away with s.o. (e.g., of the opposite sex)
manâpâwê– *VII* be washed down as water, come running down
manêsi– *VAI* run short, be in want; have run out of (it), lack (it)
mâcipayin– *VII* begin to run (e.g., tape-recorder)
mâtopahtâ– *VAI* cry while running
mêscipayin– *VII* run out, be exhausted on the way
miyopayi– *VII* work well, run well; work out, come to pass
nakacipah– *VTA* run away from s.o.
nayêhtâwipayi– *VAI* run into difficulties, experience trouble
nâcipah– *VTA* run to fetch s.o., make a run for s.o.
nâcipahiwê– *VAI* run to fetch things, make a run for things
nâsipêpahtâ– *VAI* run towards the water
nipahipahtâ– *VAI* run to excess, collapse from running
nîhtâhtawîpahtâ– *VAI* climb down (e.g., a tree) at a run
ohcipahtâ– *VAI* run from there
papâmâciho– *VAI* travel about; live in various places; run about, be promiscuous
papâmipahtâ– *VAI* run about (e.g., as a child); run around, be promiscuous
papâmohtê– *VAI* walk about, go about, go here and there; run around, be promiscuous
pâpahtâ– *VAI* run hither, come running
pimakotê– *VII* be in working order, run (e.g., tape-recorder)
pimamon– *VII* run along (e.g., road, rail)
pimastê– *VII* be placed in linear fashion, run along
pimâskwamon– *VII* run fastened along as wood, be nailed along (e.g., at regular intervals)
pimihtin– *VII* go along (e.g., river, road); run along, flow by (e.g., creek)
pimipayi– *VII* move along; run, run along; be on, work, function (e.g., motor, electricity); exist currently, take place
pimipayihtâ– *VAI* run (it), operate (it) (e.g., machine); keep (it) up, exercise (it)
pîhtikwêpahtâ– *VAI* run indoors
pîhtikwêyâpâwê– *VII* be washed indoors as water, run indoors
sêkopayin– *VII* run beneath, go underneath, get caught underneath
sipwêpahtâ– *VAI* run off, drive off
sipwêpayin– *VII* start off to run (e.g., tape-recorder)
sôskwakotê– *VII* simply run down, run off (e.g., water)
takahkipahtâ– *VAI* run nicely (e.g., horse), run beautifully

takopahtâ– VAI arrive running
tapasî– VAI flee, run away
wayawîpahtâ– VAI run outside, run outdoors

RUNNER
pimipayîs– NA runner (e.g., on sleigh)

RUPTURED
pâskâpi– VAI have a ruptured eye; have only one eye

RUSH
pimakocin– VII make a rush in linear fashion, charge headlong

RUSTLE
kitowêyêkinikê– VAI make a noise with paper, rustle one's paper

SACK
maskimotêkinw– NI sack, sacking, sack-cloth; flour-bag, cloth from flour-bag

SACK-CLOTH
maskimotêkinw– NI sack, sacking, sack-cloth; flour-bag, cloth from flour-bag

SACRED
âtayôhkan– NI sacred story
âtayôhkaw– VTA tell s.o. a sacred story
âtayôhkât– VTA tell about s.o. in the form of a sacred story, tell a sacred story of s.o.
âtayôhkât– VTI tell about s.t. in the form of a sacred story, tell a sacred story of s.t.
âtayôhkê– VAI tell a sacred story
âtayôhkêwin– NI sacred story
itâtayôhkaw– VTA tell s.o. such a sacred story
itâtayôhkât– VTI tell thus about s.t. in the form of a sacred story, tell such a sacred story of s.t.
itâtayôhkâtê– VII be told thus in the form of a sacred story, be told as such a sacred story
kihcêyihcikâtê– VII be highly thought of, be respected; be held sacred
kihcêyiht– VTI think highly of s.t., hold s.t. in high regard, respect s.t.; hold s.t. sacred
kihcêyihtâkwan– VII be highly thought of, be respected; be held sacred
kihcêyim– VTA think highly of s.o., hold s.o. in high regard, respect s.o.; hold s.o. sacred
ma-môhcw-âtayôhkêwin– NI stupid sacred story, crazy sacred story
nayôhcikan– NI bundle, sacred bundle, spirit-bundle (e.g., in ghost-dance)
takahk-âtayôhkêwin– NI fine sacred story

SACRILEGE
pâstâhôtot– VTI commit a transgression in s.t., commit sacrilege in s.t.

SAD
kaskêyiht– VTI be sad over s.t.; be sad, be lonesome, have a longing

SADDLE
aspapiwin– NI saddle

SADDLE LAKE
onihcikiskwapiwinihk INM (place-name:) Saddle Lake (Alberta)

SAIL
yâhkâstimon– NI sail

SALT
nêhiyawi-sîwîhtâkan– NI Cree salt; Indian salt
sîwihtâkan– NI salt
sîwihtâkani-sâkahikan– NI salty lake, salt lake

SALUTARY
miyoskaw– VTA (especially in inverse constructions:) go through s.o. to good effect, have a salutary effect on s.o., make s.o. well

SAME
kisik IPC at the same time, simultaneously, coincidentally
pâh-pêyakwan IPC the same for each
pêskis IPC besides; at the same time, simultaneously
pêyakwan IPC the same
pêyakwan ispî IPC at the same time
pêyakwanohk IPC in one place, in a single place; in the same place
pêyakwayak IPC in one place, in a certain place; in the same place
tipiskôc IPC even, at the same level, parallel; directly overhead
wîc-îspîhcisîm– VTA be of the same age as s.o., have s.o. as one's age-mate
wîc-ôhcîm– VTA come from the same time or place as s.o., share the year of birth with s.o.
wîtaskîwêm– VTA live together with s.o., have s.o. as one's compatriot; live in the same country with s.o., live in peace with s.o.

SANDY LAKE
yêkawiskâwikamâhk INM (place-name:) Sandy Lake (Saskatchewan); *atâhk-akohp*'s Reserve

SAP
  mêstan– *NA* sap, tree-sap
SARCI
  sasîwiskwêw– *NA* Sarci woman
SASKATOON
  misâskwatômin– *NI* saskatoon berry
SATIN
  sênipân– *NA* ribbon, satin ribbon
  sênipânasâkay– *NI* satin dress
SATISFIED
  nahêyiht– *VTI* be satisfied with s.t.; have peace of mind
  nahêyihtamih– *VTA* cause s.o. to be satisfied with (it/him); grant s.o. peace of mind
SATURDAY
  nikotwâsiko-kîsikâ– *VII* be six days, be the sixth day; be Saturday
SAULTEAUX
  nahkawêwin– *NI* speaking Saulteaux, the Saulteaux language
  nahkawiyiniw– *NA* Saulteaux
SAUSAGE
  otakisîhkân– *NI* sausage
SAVE
  mâwacih– *VTA* collect s.o. (e.g., pounded meat), gather s.o. up; save s.o.
  pihkoho– *VAI* free oneself, escape; be released; *(fig.)* free oneself (e.g., to meet an obligation or duty); be saved
  pimâcih– *VTA* make s.o. live, give life to s.o., sustain s.o.'s life; revive s.o., save s.o.'s life; make a living for s.o.
SAW
  kinwâpêkan– *VII* be a long garment, be a long piece of paper; be a long saw-blade, be a long saw
  kîskipocikan– *NI* saw, long saw (e.g., with two handles)
  kîskipocikê– *VAI* cut things with a saw, cut cordwood
  kîskipotâ– *VAI* cut (it) with a saw (e.g., cordwood), saw (it) through
  mosci-kîskipotâ– *VAI* simply cut (it) with a saw, cut (it) with a hand-saw
SAY
  it– *VTA* say thus to s.o., say thus of s.o.
  it– *VTI* say thus of s.t., say thus about s.t.
  itito– *VAI* say thus to one another, say thus about one another
  itwê– *VAI* say thus, call (it) thus; have such a meaning
  itwêmakan– *VII* say thus, have such a meaning
  itwêmakisi– *VAI* say thus, have such a meaning
  itwêski– *VAI* say thus habitually, always say thus
  itwêstamaw– *VTA* say thus for s.o.; speak for s.o.; interpret for s.o.; transmit s.o.'s message, relay s.o.'s message (e.g., by radio)
  kîskwêtonâmo– *VAI* say all manner of things, chatter on
  môniyâwi-itwê– *VAI* say the White word, say the English word
SCAB
  –mikiy– *NDI* scab
  omikî– *VAI* have a scab, have a sore; have (it) as one's scab
SCAFFOLD
  akot– *VTA* hang s.o. up; place s.o. on a funeral scaffold
SCARCELY
  êtataw *IPC* barely, scarcely
SCATTER
  pîwên– *VTA* scatter s.o. (e.g., sugar), sprinkle s.o. (e.g., sugar) in small grains
  pîwêwêpin– *VTI* scatter s.t., sprinkle in a pinch of s.t.
SCHOOL
  ayamihcikê– *VAI* read things, read; go to school
  iskôl– *NI* school
  iskôliwi– *VAI* be in school, go to school
  kiskinohamâkosi– *VAI* be taught; be a student, attend school
  kiskinohamâkosiwin– *NI* being a student, going to school; schoolwork, homework
  kiskinohamâso– *VAI* teach oneself; be taught; be a student, attend school
  kiskinohamâtowikamikw– *NI* school-house; school
  kiskinohamâtowin– *NI* teaching, education; education system, school board
  wayawî– *VAI* go outside, go outdoors; go to relieve oneself; leave school, leave hospital
  wîci-kiskinohamâkosîm– *VTA* be in school together with s.o., have s.o. as a fellow student
SCHOOL-MATE
  –îci-kiskinohamawâkan– *NDA* fellow student, school-mate
SCHOOLING
  kiskinohamâsowin– *NI* schooling, education

SCOLD
itâspinêm– *VTA* call s.o. thus in anger, angrily call s.o. such a name, thus scold s.o. in anger
kisîwêhkahtaw– *VTA* speak angrily to s.o.; speak loudly to s.o., scold s.o. loudly
kîhkâm– *VTA* scold s.o.

SCOOP
moscicihcên– *VTI* scoop s.t. up with bare hands

SCOUT
onitawahtâw– *NA* scout, explorer, spy

SCRAPE
kâskah– *VTI* scrape s.t., scrape s.t. off
kâskâskihkot– *VTA* scrape s.o. (e.g., touchwood) off
mâtah– *VTI* scrape s.t. (e.g., hide)
mihkit– *VTI* scrape s.t. (meat) off the hide
yôskipotâ– *VAI* soften (it) by scraping (e.g., hide)

SCRAPINGS
mihkwâpêmakw– *NI* red willow, red willow scrapings

SCRATCH
cîhcîkin– *VTI* scratch s.t. (e.g., one's hip)
cîhcîkî– *VAI* scratch oneself, scratch

SCRATCHY
kâsisi– *VAI* be sharp, be scratchy (e.g., wool); be sharply pointed

SCRAWNY
pâwanî– *VAI* be lean, be skinny, be scrawny (e.g., rabbit, human)

SCREEN
pîwâpiskw– *NI* metal, metal object; steel blade; screen of wire-mesh
sakimêwayânêkin– *NI* mosquito screen, insect screen

SCRIBE
omasinahikêsîs– *NA* scribe, clerk

SCRUB
sinikohtakahikan– *NI* scrub-brush, floor brush, brush for wood
sinikohtakinikan– *NI* scrubber, brush; wash-board

SCULLERY
wiyâkanikamikw– *NI* pantry, scullery; walk-in closet

SEAMSTRESS
nihtâwikwâso– *VAI* be good at sewing, sew expertly, be an experienced seamstress; do fancy sewing

SEARCH
nitawastimwê– *VAI* look for one's horses, search for one's horses
niton– *VTI* look for s.t., seek s.t., search for s.t.
nitonaw– *VTA* look for s.o., seek s.o. (e.g., tree), search for s.o.
nitonikâtê– *VII* be looked for, be searched for
nitonikê– *VAI* take a look, search for things, make a search
nitopahtwâ– *VAI* search for (it/him)

SEAT
apiwinis– *NI* seat, chair

SEATED
ay-api– *VAI* sit, be seated
nahapi– *VAI* sit down in one's place, be properly seated

SECOND
nîso-tipiskâ– *VII* be two nights, be the second night
tahto-nîso-kîsikâw *IPC* every second day, every other day
tahto-nîsw-âyamihêwi-kîsikâw *IPC* every second week, fortnightly

SECRETLY
kîmôc *IPC* secretly, in secret, stealthily, privately, in private
kîmôtâpi– *VAI* look stealthily, look secretly

SECURE
ocipitamâso– *VAI* pull (it/him) in for oneself, secure (it/him) for oneself

SEE
mahti *IPC* let's see, please
mâcikôtitan *IPC* wait and see! lo!
miskwâpam– *VTA* see s.o., espy s.o. (e.g., star)
miyonâkohcikê– *VAI* be seen to be good at things, make things look nice, make things look prosperous
nitawâpaht– *VTI* go to see s.t., observe s.t., check s.t. out
nitawâpam– *VTA* go to see s.o., go to visit s.o.
otisâpaht– *VTI* have lived long enough to see s.t.
pêtisâpam– *VTA* see s.o. coming
têpâpam– *VTA* see plenty of s.o., see s.o. fully
wani-tipiskin– *VTI* perceive s.t. as darkness; merely see night, perceive merely darkness
wâpahcikâtê– *VII* be seen, be witnessed
wâpaht– *VTI* see s.t., witness s.t.

wâpahtih– *VTA* make s.o. see (it), show (it) to s.o.
wâpam– *VTA* see s.o., witness s.o.
wâpi– *VAI* see, be sighted, have vision; *(in negative constructions:)* be blind

SEED
kiscikânis– *NA* grain, seed
kiscikêsi– *VAI* plant seeds; have a small garden
kistikân– *NA* grain, seed; sheaf of grain; oats
kistikê– *VAI* seed things, plant things, do one's seeding, do one's planting; farm the land
pîwi-kiscikânis– *NA* garden seed

SEEK
itâmo– *VAI* flee thither or thus, seek such refuge
itâmôh– *VTA* make s.o. flee thus or there, direct s.o. to seek such refuge
nâcikâpawist– *VTI* seek to shift one's position to s.t.
nâcinêhamaw– *VTA* obtain (it/him) from s.o. by payment, seek to buy medicine from s.o.
nâcinêhikê– *VAI* obtain things by payment, seek to buy medicine
nâtamawât– *VTI* seek to obtain s.t. for (it/him); take s.t. up for (it/him)
nâtâmost– *VTI* flee to s.t., turn to s.t. for help, seek refuge in s.t.
nâtâmotot– *VTI* flee to s.t., turn to s.t. for help, seek refuge in s.t.
nâtâmototaw– *VTA* flee to s.o., turn to s.o. for help, seek refuge with s.o.
niton– *VTI* look for s.t., seek s.t., search for s.t.
nitonaw– *VTA* look for s.o., seek s.o. (e.g., tree), search for s.o.
nitôsk– *VTI* seek s.t.; make a request for s.t. (e.g., medicine)
nitôskamaw– *VTA* seek (it/him) of s.o., make a request for (it/him) of s.o.
pimâtisiwinê– *VAI* have life, seek life

SEEMINGLY
tâpiskôc *IPC* as if; seemingly, apparently

SEEMLY
katawâhk *IPC* properly, in seemly manner

SEIZE
kâhcitin– *VTA* catch s.o., seize s.o., get s.o. (e.g., a spouse); obtain s.o. (e.g., money)
kâhcitin– *VTI* catch s.t., seize s.t., obtain s.t.; get s.t. back

maskahcih– *VTA* seize (it/him) from s.o.
maskahto– *VAI* seize (it/him) from one another; rob one another
maskam– *VTA* seize (it/him) from s.o.; rob s.o.
otihtin– *VTA* grab s.o., seize s.o.
otihtin– *VTI* grab s.t., seize s.t.

SELECT
otin– *VTI* take s.t.; pick s.t., choose s.t., select s.t. (e.g., moss); steal s.t.; take s.t. over; extract s.t. (e.g., grease from soup), remove s.t. (e.g., glands in butchering beaver), extract s.t.; accept s.t. (e.g., contract); capture s.t., record s.t. on audio-tape

SELF-ESTEEM
pîwêyimo– *VAI* think little of oneself, have low self-esteem; *(fig.)* be humble

SELF-INDULGENT
kihtimi– *VAI* be lazy; be self-indulgent

SELL
atâwâkê– *VAI* sell (it/him), sell things
ohtatâwâkê– *VAI* sell (it) thus, sell (it) for that amount

SEND
itisahamaw– *VTA* send (it/him) to s.o. thus or there
itisahamâto– *VAI* send (it/him) to one another thus or there
itisahw– *VTA* send s.o. thus or there
nâtitisahikê– *VAI* send for things, place an order from a catalogue
nâtitisahw– *VTA* go to fetch s.o. (e.g., horses); send for s.o., order s.o. (e.g., chickens) by catalogue
patitisahamaw– *VTA* drive (it/him) off the path for s.o., send (it/him) awry for s.o., spoil (it/him) for s.o.
pêtitisahw– *VTA* drive s.o. hither, send s.o. hither
sipwêtisah– *VTI* send s.t. off
sipwêtisahw– *VTA* send s.o. off
wayawîtisahw– *VTA* send s.o. outdoors; send s.o. off the reserve, banish s.o. from the reserve

SENECA-ROOT
maskihkiy– *NI* herb, plant; seneca-root; medicinal root; medicine; chemicals
mînisîhkês– *NI* seneca-root
mônahaskwâkan– *NI* digger, tool used to dig seneca-root
mônahaskwân– *NI* digger, tool used to dig seneca-root
mônahaskwê– *VAI* dig seneca-root

SENSE
môsih– VTA sense s.o., feel s.o. approaching, perceive s.o.'s presence
môsihtâ– VAI sense (it), feel (it) approaching, perceive (it)
môyêyiht– VTI sense s.t.; suspect s.t.; realise s.t.
môyêyim– VTA sense s.o., suspect s.o.

SENSIBLE
âpahkawin– VII be level-headed, be sensible, be conscious
kakêhtawêyiht– VTI have good ideas about s.t.; be intelligent beyond one's years; be sensible

SEPARATE
paskê– VAI branch off, go off to the side; set up a separate household
paskêwih– VTA part from s.o., leave s.o.; separate from s.o., divorce s.o.
paskêwihito– VAI part from one another, leave one another; separate from one another, divorce
piskihci-wîki– VAI live separately, dwell separately, have a separate household
piskihcikamikos– NI separate room, private room
wêpinito– VAI leave one another, separate from one another, get divorced

SEPARATELY
pâh-piskihc IPC each separately
piskihci IPV separately
piskihci-wîki– VAI live separately, dwell separately, have a separate household

SEPARATING
wêpinitowin– NI leaving one another, separating from one another, divorce

SEQUENCE
askôskaw– VTA follow s.o. in birth sequence
iyaskohc IPC next in sequence

SERVANT
–oskinîkîm– NDA young man, follower; *(fig.)* servant

SERVE
okimâhkâniwi– VAI be chief, serve as elected chief
pamih– VTA tend to s.o., look after s.o.; attend s.o. in childbirth, serve as midwife to s.o.; guide s.o. (e.g., sleigh), drive s.o. (e.g., sleigh)
pamihiso– VAI tend to oneself, look after oneself; attend oneself in childbirth, serve as one's own midwife
pamin– VTA tend to s.o., look after s.o.; attend s.o. in childbirth, serve as midwife to s.o.

SERVER
kihc-ôskâpêwis– NA main ritual server
oskâpêwis– NA ritual server, servitor (e.g., in ritual)

SERVICE
ayamihâ– VAI pray, say prayers; hold a church service, celebrate mass; participate in a religious rite, go to church; follow a religion
ayamihâwin– NI prayer, praying, saying prayers; church service; religious rite; religion, religious denomination; the Roman Catholic church
âpacih– VTA *(especially in inverse constructions:)* be of use to s.o., be of service to s.o.
itâpacih– VTA *(especially in inverse constructions:)* be of such use to s.o., be thus of service to s.o.
osîhtâ– VAI prepare (it), make (it); put (it) in service (e.g., hospital), inaugurate (it)

SERVITOR
oskâpêwis– NA ritual server, servitor (e.g., in ritual)

SET
ah– VTA place s.o. there, put s.o. there, set s.o. down
akotâ– VAI hang (it) up; hang up one's snare, set one's snare
câpakwêsi– VAI set small snares, set rabbit snares; do a little snaring
kwâhkotênikê– VAI start a fire, set things aflame
mânokê– VAI build a lodge, set up a tent
ohpahamaw– VTA set a trap for s.o. (e.g., prairie-chicken)
pakitahwâ– VAI fish by net, set nets
pakitin– VTA set s.o. down, allow s.o., permit s.o.; permit (it) to s.o., give permission to s.o.; let s.o. go, release s.o. (e.g., fish-spawn into lake), stock a lake with s.o. (e.g., fish); drop s.o. off (e.g., as an airplane)
paskê– VAI branch off, go off to the side; set up a separate household
tâpakwê– VAI set snares
wanihikamaw– VTA set traps for s.o. (e.g., animal)
wanihikê– VAI trap, set traps
wâposo-câpakwêsi– VAI set small snares, set rabbit snares

wiyakiht– *VTI* set a price for s.t.
wiyakihtamaw– *VTA* set a price on (it/him) for s.o., charge s.o. for (it/him)
wiyakim– *VTA* set a price on s.o. (e.g., bread); arrange (it) for s.o.; decide on s.o.; give orders to s.o.
wiyastamaw– *VTA* set the table for s.o.
wîtapihtah– *VTA* set s.o. (e.g., chicken) to brood
yîkatên– *VTI* set s.t. aside

SETS
nisto-aya *IPC* three sets
nîsw-âya *IPC* two pairs, two sets

SETTLE
otinaskê– *VAI* take land, settle the land, homestead
wâskamisî– *VAI* settle down; be of quiet disposition

SETTLEMENT
akâmôtênaw *IPC* across the camp-circle; across the settlement, across town
askiy– *NI* land, region, area; earth, world; settlement, colony, country; Métis settlement; *(plural:)* fields under cultivation, pieces of farmland, the lands
âpihtawikosisânaskiy– *NI* halfbreed settlement, Métis settlement
âpihtawikosisânôcênâs– *NI* little halfbreed town, Métis settlement
ôtênaw– *NI* camp-circle; settlement, town

SEVEN
têpakohp *IPC* seven
têpakohp-askiy *IPC* seven years, for seven years

SEVENTEEN
têpakohposâp *IPC* seventeen

SEVENTY
têpakohpomitanaw *IPC* seventy

SEVERAL
âhkwêhtawêskaw– *VTA* wear s.o. (e.g., socks) over top of one another, wear several layers of s.o. (e.g., socks)
pîkwasinahikê– *VAI* be loaded down with debt, be indebted in several places
tânimatahto *IPC* how many; so many, several
tânitahto-kîsikâw *IPC* how many days; so many days; several days
tânitahto-tipahikan *IPC* what hour, what time; so many hours, that time; several hours

SEVERE
âhkwâtisi– *VAI* be stern, be sharp, be of severe disposition
âstê-kîsikâ– *VII* cease being stormy weather, let up as severe weather, be better weather
maci-kîsikâ– *VII* be a bad storm, be a severe storm
mâyahpinat– *VTA* treat s.o. badly, beat s.o. severely
mâyi-kîsikâ– *VII* be stormy weather, be foul weather, be a severe storm

SEW
âniskôkwât– *VTI* sew s.t. on as an extension
isikwât– *VTI* sew s.t. thus, sew s.t. to such a design
itistahikê– *VAI* sew things on thus
itistahw– *VTA* sew s.o. (e.g., porcupine quills) on thus
kaskikwâcikâkê– *VAI* sew things with (it), use (it) to sew things
kaskikwâso– *VAI* sew, do one's sewing; sew (it)
kaskikwâsopayihcikanis– *NI* sewing machine
kaskikwâsowin– *NI* doing one's sewing, the art of sewing; sewing needs, sewing-kit
kaskikwâswâkan– *NI* sewing machine
kaskikwâswâkê– *VAI* sew with (it), use (it) in sewing
kaskikwât– *VTA* sew s.o. (e.g., pants)
kaskikwât– *VTI* sew s.t.
kaskikwâtamaw– *VTA* sew (it/him) for s.o.
kaskikwâtamâso– *VAI* sew (it/him) for oneself
kaskikwâtê– *VII* be sewn
kaskikwâtiso– *VAI* sew for oneself
kipokwât– *VTI* sew s.t. closed, sew s.t. shut; close s.t. up by sewing
kipokwâtâ– *VAI* sew (it) closed, sew (it) shut, close (it) up by sewing
kispakikwât– *VTI* sew s.t. thickly
mâmawin– *VTI* put s.t. together, sew s.t. together (e.g., quilted squares)
mâmawokwât– *VTI* sew s.t. together into one, piece s.t. together in sewing
moscikwâso– *VAI* sew by hand
moscikwât– *VTI* sew s.t. by hand
nanâtohkokwâso– *VAI* sew various things; sew a patchwork blanket

nihtâwikwâso– *VAI* be good at sewing, sew expertly, be an experienced seamstress; do fancy sewing
nihtâwikwâsowin– *NI* fancy sewing
nihtâwikwât– *VTI* be good at sewing s.t., sew s.t. expertly
nihtâwiminakinikê– *VAI* be good at sewing on beads
piskihcikwât– *VTI* sew an extension on s.t.
pîhtawêkwât– *VTI* sew s.t. in between, sew covers on s.t.
sakâpât– *VTI* attach s.t. by sewing, sew s.t. on
titipikwanah– *VTI* sew s.t. in overcast stitch (e.g., the spiral loops around the vamp of a moccasin)
wâwiyêkwât– *VTI* sew s.t. round (e.g., rug)
wiyikwât– *VTI* sew s.t. together, sew s.t. up

SEWING-BOX
kaskikwâsowat– *NI* sewing-box

SEWING-KIT
kaskikwâsowin– *NI* doing one's sewing, the art of sewing; sewing needs, sewing-kit

SHACK
asiskîwikamikos– *NI* mud shack
napakikamikw– *NI* house made of lumber or boards; flat-top shack
wâskahikanis– *NI* little house; shack, temporary building, trailer; play-house

SHAKE
atamiskaw– *VTA* greet s.o., shake hands with s.o.
pahpawiwêpin– *VTI* shake s.t. out
pawahikê– *VAI* shake things out by tool; thresh, do one's threshing
pawin– *VTI* shake s.t. out
waskawipit– *VTI* move s.t. by pulling, shake s.t. by pulling
waskawîmakan– *VII* move, move about, be shaken by an earthquake

SHAKING-LODGE
kosâpaht– *VTI* hold a shaking-lodge, hold the shaking-lodge ceremony

SHAME
nêpêwih– *VTA* shame s.o., put s.o. to shame
onêpêwisiwini– *VAI* have shame

SHAPE
masinisin– *VAI* be drawn, be represented, be shaped (e.g., star, sun)
pihkin– *VTI* shape s.t., bend s.t., fold s.t.
wiyatahamâso– *VAI* pound (it/him) into shape for oneself
wiyatahw– *VTA* pound s.o. (e.g., earring), mould s.o., shape s.o.
wîhkwêstê– *VII* be placed around, stand in the shape of a curve

SHARE
mâmawihkwâmi– *VAI* sleep together as a group, share a mattress
pahkwênamaw– *VTA* pay a part of (it/him) to s.o., make partial payment to s.o.; parcel (it/him) out to s.o., give s.o. a share
wîc-ôhcîm– *VTA* come from the same time or place as s.o., share the year of birth with s.o.
wîci-mîcisôm– *VTA* eat together with s.o., share one's meal with s.o.
wîtokwêm– *VTA* share a dwelling with s.o., live with s.o., have s.o. as one's housemate

SHARP
âhkohtêwiso– *VAI* be sharp, be caustic (e.g., soap)
âhkwâpahtê– *VII* give off a sharp odour, produce pungent fumes, emit acidic or caustic fumes
âhkwâtisi– *VAI* be stern, be sharp, be of severe disposition
kâsisi– *VAI* be sharp, be scratchy (e.g., wool); be sharply pointed
kâsisin– *VII* be sharp (e.g., knife)
kînikâ– *VII* be sharp; be well-defined (e.g., hoofprint)
misipocikê– *VAI* run hide over a sharp edge
misipotâ– *VAI* run (it) (e.g., hide) over a sharp edge
tasin– *VTI* pull the trigger on s.t. (e.g., gun), shoot s.t. off (e.g., gun); emit a sharp noise, make a shot-like noise; sound a thunderclap (e.g., as Thunderbird)

SHARPEN
kînikatahikê– *VAI* chop things to a point, sharpen posts
papakipotâ– *VAI* sharpen (it) to a thin edge

SHARPLY
nahiht– *VTI* hear s.t. sharply; have acute hearing
wîsaki *IPV* sharply, painfully; sorely

SHATTER
nanânistiwêpahw– *VTA* shoot s.o. (e.g., rock) into bits and pieces, shatter s.o. (e.g., rock) into pieces

SHAWL
akwanân– NA shawl
SHE
wiya PR he, she
wîsta PR he, too; she, too; he by contrast, she by contrast; he himself, she herself
SHEAF
cimacikê– VAI stook sheaves of grain, do one's stooking
kistikân– NA grain, seed; sheaf of grain; oats
SHEEP
mâyatihkopîway– NI sheep's fleece; wool
SHEET
akwâwê– VAI hang sheets of meat on drying rack
kâhkêwakw– NI dried meat, sheet of dried meat
pânis– VTI cut s.t. (e.g., meat) into sheets
pânisâwê– VAI cut meat into sheets; cut fish into fillets
pânisw– VTA cut s.o. (e.g., animal) into sheets
taswêkisâwât– VTI cut s.t. (e.g., leg of rabbit) into thin sheets
SHELF
akocikan– NI rack for hanging up fish or meat, storage-rack; cupboard, shelf
akocikanis– NI little shelf
SHELL
êsis– NA little shell (mollusc)
môsosiniy– NI shell, bullet
SHIELDED
âkô IPV covered, shielded
SHIFT
nâcikâpawist– VTI seek to shift one's position to s.t.
SHIRT
papakiwayân– NI shirt
SHIVER
nanamaci– VAI shiver with cold
SHOCKED
sisikotêyiht– VTI find s.t. surprising, find s.t. shocking; be surprised, be shocked
SHOE
itwêwêsin– VAI fall with such a sound, make such a sound with one's shoes
kikaskisinê– VAI wear shoes
maskisin– NI moccasin, shoe
maskisinis– NI shoe, little shoe

miscikwaskisinis– NI firm shoe, sturdy shoe, oxford
mistikwaskisin– NI heeled shoe, oxford
sâpopatâ– VAI get (it) wet throughout; get one's shoes wet
takahkwêwêsin– VAI fall with nice sounds, make nice sounds with one's shoes
SHOE-LEATHER
maskisinêkinw– NI shoe-leather
SHOOT
matwêwêhtâ– VAI detonate (it); shoot off one's gun
nanânistiwêpahw– VTA shoot s.o. (e.g., rock) into bits and pieces, shatter s.o. (e.g., rock) into pieces
nawatahikê– VAI shoot (it/him) in flight, shoot ducks as they fly
nawatahw– VTA shoot s.o. in flight
oskaskosîwinâkwan– VII look green, have the appearance of fresh shoots
pâskis– VTI shoot at s.t.
pâskisikê– VAI shoot at things, shoot, take a shot
pâskisw– VTA shoot at s.o.
pimocikê– VAI shoot arrows
pimot– VTA shoot an arrow at s.o.
pimw– VTA shoot at s.o., loose an arrow at s.o.
tasin– VTI pull the trigger on s.t. (e.g., gun), shoot s.t. off (e.g., gun); emit a sharp noise, make a shot-like noise; sound a thunderclap (e.g., as Thunderbird)
tâskiwêpahw– VTA split s.o. (e.g., rock) by arrow, shoot s.o. (e.g., rock) apart
SHOPPING
otinikê– VAI take things; buy things, do one's shopping, make a purchase; take away winnings (e.g., in a card-game)
SHORE
nâtakâsin– VTI guide s.t. (e.g., boat) to shore
SHORT
aciyaw IPC for a short while
cimâsin– VII be short
kanak IPC for a short while
kwîtawêyihcikâtê– VII be missed, be in short supply
kwîtâpacihtâ– VAI be short of (it) to use, lack tools
manêsi– VAI run short, be in want; have run out of (it), lack (it)

nôhtaw IPC less; minus; previously; prematurely, incompletely, short of attainment
nôhtêpayi– VAI run short, be in want; run short of supplies; run short of (it), have (it) in short supply

SHORT-SLEEVED
kiskanakwêwayân– NI waistcoat, short-sleeved vest

SHOUT
têpwê– VAI call out, shout, holler, yell

SHOW
kiskinohtah– VTA show (it/him) to s.o.; show s.o. the way, direct s.o.
mamacikastâkê– VAI show off with (it), use (it) to show off
mamacikastê– VAI show off
nôkohtâ– VAI let (it) appear, show (it)
ohtiskawapi– VAI sit facing, sit so as to show one's face
wâpahtih– VTA make s.o. see (it), show (it) to s.o.

SHOWER
sîkipêstâ– VII pour down as a rain shower

SHRINK
ocipôhkahtê– VII shrink from heat
ocipwâpâwê– VII be shrunk from washing in water

SHUT
kipah– VTI close s.t., shut s.t.
kipokwât– VTI sew s.t. closed, sew s.t. shut; close s.t. up by sewing
kipokwâtâ– VAI sew (it) closed, sew (it) shut, close (it) up by sewing
kiposakahikâtê– VII be nailed shut
kipwahpit– VTI pull s.t. closed, tie s.t. shut
pasahkâpi– VAI blink, shut and open one's eyes
pasakwâpi– VAI close one's eyes, have one's eyes shut
tahkopit– VTI tie s.t. fast, tie s.t. shut (e.g., swim-bladder), tie s.t. in, tie s.t. up

SHUT-EYE
pasakwâpisimowin– NI shut-eye dance
pasakwâpisimowinihkê– VAI give a shut-eye dance, hold a shut-eye dance

SHY
nêpêwisi– VAI be bashful, be shy; be ashamed, be ashamed of oneself
nêpêwisîstaw– VTA be bashful before s.o., be shy towards s.o.

SIBLING
–îc-âyis– NDA fellow youngster; sibling, parallel cousin
–îtisân– NDA sibling
–sîm– NDA younger sibling, younger parallel cousin
–sîmis– NDA younger sibling, younger parallel cousin
osîmihto– VAI be siblings to one another
osîmimâs– NA the youngest sibling
osîmimâw– NA the youngest sibling
osîmimâwi– VAI be the youngest sibling
osîmisi– VAI have a younger sibling; have (him/her) as one's younger sibling
osîmisimâw– NA the youngest sibling
owîcisânihto– VAI have one another as siblings
owîtisâni– VAI have a sibling, have (her/him) as one's sibling

SICK
âhkosi– VAI be sick, be ill; have contractions, be in labour
âhkosiski– VAI be habitually sick, be sickly
mâyi-tôtaw– VTA do evil to s.o., harm s.o., make s.o. sick, put a curse on s.o.
nihtâ-âhkosi– VAI fall sick easily, be prone to illness
otâhkosiw– NA sick person
paswêskôyo– VAI get sick from eating excessively fatty food

SIDE
awas-âyihk IPC on the other side, on the far side
âh-âyîtaw IPC on both sides
itakâm IPC on the hither side of a body of water, on the near side of a body of water
îkatê IPV to the side, aside
kwêsk-âyihk IPC on the opposite side
kwêskahcâhk IPC on the opposite side of a rise in the land
kwêskâskon– VTA turn s.o. (e.g., pipe) to the opposite side
kwêski IPV turned around, turned to the opposite side
kwêskin– VTA change s.o. around, turn s.o. around to the opposite side; (fig.) convert s.o. to Christianity
kwêskinâkwan– VII look changed around, look turned around to the opposite side
napatê IPC on one side

ohpimê *IPC* off, away, to the side; elsewhere, anywhere

ohpimês *IPC* a little off, a little away, a little to the side

paskê– *VAI* branch off, go off to the side; set up a separate household

paskêpayi– *VAI* branch off, move off to the side; stop off there

paskêtâpâso– *VAI* branch off with one's wagon, move off to the side with one's vehicle; pull over with a vehicle

wîkatêtâpê– *VAI* drag (it) off to the side, drag (it) away

yîkatêhtê– *VAI* walk off to the side; *(fig.)* walk away

yîkatêpayin– *VII* move off to the side, move sideways (e.g., braided strips of rabbitskin)

yîkatêstaw– *VTA* go off to the side from s.o., go away from s.o.

SIDEWAYS
pimic-âyihk *IPC* across, athwart, crosswise, sideways

pimicikâpawi– *VAI* stand sideways, stand across

pîmiskwêyi– *VAI* turn one's head sideways, twist one's neck (e.g., owl)

yîkatêpayin– *VII* move off to the side, move sideways (e.g., braided strips of rabbitskin)

SIGHT
matwê *IPV* audibly, visibly; perceptibly; in full view, in plain sight

nâkatâpam– *VTA* notice s.o. by sight

SIGHTED
wâpi– *VAI* see, be sighted, have vision; *(in negative constructions:)* be blind

SIGN
masinah– *VTI* mark s.t., draw s.t.; write s.t.; write s.t. down, record s.t. in writing; sign s.t. (e.g., treaty)

SIGNAL
wâstinikê– *VAI* signal by hand, wave

wâwâstinamaw– *VTA* wave at s.o., signal to s.o. by hand

SILLY
môhcowi– *VAI* be foolish, be stupid, be silly; be mad, be crazy

môhcw-âyâ– *VAI* be foolish, be stupid, be silly; be mad, be crazy

SILVER
sôniyâw– *NA* gold, silver; money; wages

SIMPLE
konit-âcimowinis– *NI* mere story, simple story, just a little story

SIMPLY
iyinitohk *IPC* simply; just as

mosc-âsam– *VTA* simply provide food to s.o., supply food to s.o. without recompense

mosci *IPC* simply, directly, without mediation; merely, without instrument; without recompense

mosci-kisîpêkinikê– *VAI* simply wash things, do one's laundry by hand

mosci-kîskipotâ– *VAI* simply cut (it) with a saw, cut (it) with a hand-saw

mosci-masinah– *VTI* simply write s.t., write s.t. down by hand

mosci-mêki– *VAI* simply give (her) in marriage

mosci-nôhâwaso– *VAI* simply breastfeed one's child, breastfeed one's child without further ado (e.g., sterilisation of bottles)

mostohtê– *VAI* simply walk, move along without instrument, be on foot

nânitaw *IPC* simply; *(with numbers:)* roughly, approximately; variously; something, at some undetermined place; *(in negative constructions:)* not anything; something bad, anything bad; somewhere

sôskwakotê– *VII* simply run down, run off (e.g., water)

sôskwâc *IPC* simply, immediately, without further ado; without regard to the consequences; *(in negative constructions:)* not at all

SIMULTANEOUSLY
kisik *IPC* at the same time, simultaneously, coincidentally

pêskis *IPC* besides; at the same time, simultaneously

SIN
kâsînamâso– *VAI* wipe (it) off for oneself; *(fig.)* have one's sins forgiven, obtain forgiveness

patinikê– *VAI* make a mistake, take a wrong step, transgress; *(fig.)* sin

pâstâho– *VAI* breach the natural order, transgress; *(fig.)* sin, be a sinner

pâstâhowin– *NI* transgression, breach of the natural order; *(fig.)* sin

SINCE
aspin *IPC* off, away, from a distance, in departing; since then, the last I knew; back then, so long ago; presumably, evidently

SINEW
astinwân– *NI* sinew

SING
ayamihêwi-nikamo– VAI sing hymns
kito– VAI utter a sound, call, sing (e.g., bird); make noises (e.g., animal), hoot; be a thunderclap
naskwahamaw– VTA respond to s.o.; sing in response to s.o.
naskwahamâkê– VAI respond; sing in response, sing one's response
nêhiyawi-nakamo– VAI sing hymns in Cree
nikamo– VAI sing, sing a ritual song
nikamosi– VAI sing a little song
takahkatâmo– VAI sing out beautifully
wîhtaskât– VTA sing about s.o. with words, sing a texted song about s.o.
wîhtaskât– VTI sing about s.t. with words, sing a texted song
yahkatâmo– VAI sing out vigorously

SINGLE
môsâpêwi– VAI be a bachelor, be unmarried, be single
môsiskwêw– NA single woman, widow
môsiskwêwi– VAI be a single woman, be a widow
pêyak IPC one, alone, a single one; the only one; a certain one
pêyakw-ây– NA a single one (e.g., stocking); one pair
pêyakw-âya IPC one team of horses, a single team of horses
pêyakwanohk IPC in one place, in a single place; in the same place

SINGLY
pâh-pêyak IPC singly, one at a time; each one, each individually, each; one each
pêyakwahpit– VTA harness s.o. singly

SINK
kotâwiciwan– VII sink into the ground, run into the ground (e.g., water)
kotâwipayi– VAI rapidly sink into the ground (e.g., into bog or quicksand)

SIOUX
pwât– NA Sioux

SISTER
–kâwiy– NDA mother, mother's sister; *(fig.)* Our Mother
–kâwîs– NDA mother's sister, parallel aunt; step-mother
–mis– NDA older sister, older female parallel cousin

–ôhkom– NDA grandmother, grandmother's sister, "great-aunt"; *(fig.)* old woman; Our Grandmother
–sikos– NDA father's sister, mother's brother's wife; mother-in-law, father-in-law's brother's wife, "aunt"
–sis– NDA mother's brother, father's sister's husband; father-in-law, father-in-law's brother, "uncle"
–tôsimiskwêm– NDA sister's daughter (woman speaking), parallel niece (woman speaking)
omisi– VAI have an older sister; have (her) as one's older sister
omisimâs– NI the oldest sister
omisimâw– NA the oldest sister
osikosâhkôm– VTA have s.o. as one's father's sister, call s.o. one's father's sister
osikosi– VAI have a father's sister or mother-in-law; have (her) as one's father's sister or mother-in-law

SISTER-IN-LAW
–câhkos– NDA female cross-cousin (woman speaking); sister-in-law (woman speaking)
ocâhkosi– VAI have a female cross-cousin or sister-in-law (woman speaking), have (her) as one's female cross-cousin or sister-in-law (woman speaking)

SIT
api– VAI sit, sit down; be situated, be present, stay; be at home, be available
apîst– VTI sit by s.t., live by s.t., live near s.t.
aspapi– VAI sit against (it), sit on (it) (e.g., blanket)
ay-api– VAI sit, be seated
cîpatapi– VAI sit up, sit upright, sit erect
itahtwapi– VAI sit as so many, be present as so many
itapi– VAI sit thus or there, be present thus or there
kikapi– VAI sit along with something
mâmawôpi– VAI sit as a group, get together; hold a meeting
nahapi– VAI sit down in one's place, be properly seated
nawakapi– VAI sit bent down, sit huddled over
nêhpêmapi– VAI be at the ready, sit at the ready
nîpêpi– VAI sit up late at night with (her/him) (e.g., someone near death); hold a wake, take part in a wake

nîpêpîstaw– *VTA* sit up late at night with s.o.; sit at s.o.'s bedside, sit with s.o. near death; sit at a wake for s.o., hold a wake for s.o.
nîpitêpi– *VAI* sit in a row, sit abreast
ohtiskawapi– *VAI* sit facing, sit so as to show one's face
ohtiskawapîstaw– *VTA* sit facing s.o., sit with one's face towards s.o.
pimitapi– *VAI* sit crosswise, sit across (e.g., path)
pitikwapi– *VAI* sit huddled together
pôsapi– *VAI* be aboard (e.g., boat or vehicle), sit aboard, get aboard
tâpapîstamaw– *VTA* sit in s.o.'s place, succeed s.o. in office
wanâtapi– *VAI* sit so as to expose oneself
wawêyapi– *VAI* sit in readiness
wâsakâpi– *VAI* sit in a circle
wâsaskotawêpi– *VAI* sit with a lamp, have light from a lamp
wêwêkapi– *VAI* sit wrapped up, sit bundled up
wiyasiwât– *VTA* decide about s.o.; sit in judgment on s.o., hold court over s.o.
wîtapiht– *VTI* sit by s.t.; hatch one's eggs (e.g., bird)
wîtapim– *VTA* sit with s.o., sit beside s.o., be present with s.o.; work together with s.o.

SITTING
apîwikamikw– *NI* sitting room, living room
pasikô-kwâskohti– *VAI* jump up from sitting or crouching

SITUATED
api– *VAI* sit, sit down; be situated, be present, stay; be at home, be available
nîswapi– *VAI* be situated as two, come together as two

SITUATION
mâyahkamikan– *VII* be a bad deed; be a bad situation

SIX
nikotwâsik *IPC* six
nikotwâsik-askiy *IPC* six years, for six years
nikotwâsik-tipahamâtowin– *NI* Treaty Number Six, Treaty Six
nikotwâsiko-kîsikâ– *VII* be six days, be the sixth day; be Saturday

SIXTEEN
nikotwâsosâp *IPC* sixteen

SIXTY
nikotwâsikomitanaw *IPC* sixty
nikotwâsomitanaw *IPC* sixty
nikotwâsomitanaw-askiy *IPC* sixty years, for sixty years

SKIM
manah– *VTI* skim s.t. off (e.g., grease, cream)

SKIN
kiyakasê– *VAI* have itchy skin, suffer from eczema
pahkon– *VTA* skin s.o. (e.g., animal)
pahkonikê– *VAI* skin things (e.g., animals), do one's skinning
wayân– *NA* hide, skin

SKIN-LODGE
pahkêkino-mîkiwâhp– *NI* skin-lodge, lodge made from hides

SKINNY
pâwanî– *VAI* be lean, be skinny, be scrawny (e.g., rabbit, human)

SKIRT
kinwâpêkasâkê– *VAI* wear a long skirt; wear a long robe (e.g., as a Roman Catholic priest)
kîskasâkay– *NI* skirt
kîskasâkê– *VAI* wear a skirt

SKUNK
sikâkw– *NA* skunk

SKY
ispâhkêpit– *VTA* pull s.o. high up, pull s.o. high into the sky (e.g., snake)
kisîkotê– *VII* move fast through the sky (e.g., cloud)
kîsikâw– *NI* day, daylight, day sky
kîsikohk *IPC* in the sky; *(fig.)* in heaven
kîsikw– *NI* sky
ohpohtê– *VAI* rise up, proceed high in the sky
sâkakocin– *VAI* hang so as to project, hang out of the sky (e.g., snake)
takwakotê– *VII* arrive across the sky (e.g., cloud)
tipiskâw– *NI* night, night sky

SLEEP
itihkwâmi– *VAI* sleep thus
katikoni– *VAI* sleep over, spend the night
mâmawihkwâmi– *VAI* sleep together as a group, share a mattress
nipâ– *VAI* sleep, be asleep
nipâsi– *VAI* sleep a little, take a nap
nipâwin– *NI* sleeping, sleep

têpihkwâmi– VAI sleep long enough, have enough sleep

SLEEPY
nôhtêhkwasîwipayi– VAI suddenly become sleepy

SLEIGH
nîsotâpânâsk IPC two sleighs, two loads
ocâpânâskos– NA cart; small wagon, small sleigh
pôsih– VTA make s.o. board (e.g., boat or vehicle), give s.o. a ride; put s.o. on a sleigh, give s.o. a ride on a sleigh
pôsiwêpin– VTI throw s.t. on board (e.g., boat or vehicle), throw s.t. on a sleigh
wîhkwêtâpânâskw– NA rounded toboggan, curved sleigh

SLICE
tâsawisâwât– VTI cut into the middle of s.t., slice s.t. open (e.g., veal belly cordon-bleu)

SLIP
pîhcawêsâkânis– NI slip, undershirt
pîhtawêsâkân– NI slip, undergarment
wanitonâmo– VAI make a mistake in speaking, commit a slip of the tongue

SLOPE
osêhcâ– VII be a rise in the land, be a slope, be a gentle hillside
osêhcâw– NI rise in the land, slope, gentle hillside

SLOUGH
îhkatawâw– NI slough, marsh
îhkatawâwipêyâw– NI wet slough, marsh

SLOWLY
nisihkâc IPC slowly, gradually
pêyâhtik IPC quietly, gently, softly, slowly

SMALL
apisâsin– VII be small
apisîsi– VAI be small
apisîsisi– VAI be quite small, be very small
ispîhcisi– VAI be so small, be so young
môy misikiti– VAI be not big, be small

SMART
iyinîsi– VAI be clever, be smart

SMELL
mâyâpaso– VAI smell foul, give off a bad smell, stink
miyâhcikê– VAI smell things, sniff about
miyâhkaso– VAI give off a burning smell
miyâht– VTI smell s.t., sniff s.t.
miyâm– VTA smell s.o., smell s.o.'s presence
nitawâpaso– VAI smell around, sniff about
paso– VAI smell (it)
wîhcêkimahkasikê– VAI give off a bad smell, produce a foul odour
wîhkimahkaso– VAI smell sweet in burning
wîhkimâkwan– VII smell good, give off a pleasant odour; have an aromatic odour

SMILE
pâhpi– VAI laugh, smile

SMOKE
kakwâhyakâpasikê– VAI make a great deal of smoke
kaskâpahtê– VII be smoked; be smoky, be hazy
kaskâpas– VTI smoke s.t.
kaskâpaso– VAI be smoked (e.g., rabbit)
kaskâpasw– VTA smoke s.o. (e.g., fish, rabbit)
kaskitêwâpahtê– VII give off black smoke
namêstikw– NA smoked fish
ohpahpahtên– VTI raise up the smoke of s.t.
ohpahtên– VTI raise up the smoke of s.t.
osikwânâs– VTI smoke-dry s.t.
osikwânâstê– VII be smoke-dried
pîhtwâ– VAI smoke, use the pipe; smoke (him) (e.g., pipe); hold a pipe ceremony; be a nicotine addict
pîhtwâh– VTA make s.o. smoke, give s.o. to smoke
pîhtwâkê– VAI smoke with (it/him), use (it/him) in the pipe
pîhtwât– VTI smoke s.t., use s.t. to smoke
wîci-pîhtwâm– VTA smoke together with s.o., have s.o. as one's fellow smoker
wîskwas– VTI smoke s.t. (e.g., fish, hide)
wîskwasw– VTA smoke s.o. (e.g., fish)

SMOKING
pîhtwâwin– NI smoking; *(fig.)* cannabis abuse

ENGLISH INDEX 379

SMUDGE
miyâhkas– *VTI* cense s.t., smudge s.t. with sweetgrass
miyâhkasamaw– *VTA* cense (it/him) for s.o., smudge (it/him) with sweetgrass for s.o.
miyâhkasikê– *VAI* cense things, smudge things with sweetgrass
miyâhkasw– *VTA* cense s.o. (e.g., pipe), smudge s.o. (e.g., pipe) with sweetgrass
tasamân– *NI* smudge (smoky fire, often of sage-brush, made to protect cattle against insects)
tasamânihkê– *VAI* make a smudge (smoky fire, often of sage-brush, made to protect cattle against insects)

SNAKE
itâpihkêpayi– *VAI* move thus or there as a rope or snake, swing thus as a rope or snake
kinêpikw– *NA* snake

SNAKE PLAIN
kinêpiko-maskotêhk *INM (place-name:)* Snake Plain (Saskatchewan); *mistawâsis*'s Reserve

SNAPPED
wîpakwêpayi– *VAI* have one's neck snapped (e.g., in a snare)

SNARE
akocin– *VAI* hang, be suspended; hang in a swing, hang in a snare
akotâ– *VAI* hang (it) up; hang up one's snare, set one's snare
câpakwânis– *NI* snare, rabbit snare
câpakwêsi– *VAI* set small snares, set rabbit snares; do a little snaring
kîh– *VTA* get away from s.o., escape from s.o.'s snare
nakwâso– *VAI* be snared, be stopped by a snare
nakwât– *VTA* snare s.o.
nâcakwêsi– *VAI* check one's small snares (e.g., for rabbits)
nâtakwê– *VAI* check one's snares
paskakwaw– *VTA* break a snare on s.o., break through s.o.'s snare
patakwât– *VTA* miss s.o. with one's snare, fail to snare s.o.
tâpakwamahw– *VTA* snare s.o., trap s.o.
tâpakwân– *NI* snare
tâpakwânihkê– *VAI* make a snare
tâpakwâso– *VAI* get oneself snared, be caught in a snare
tâpakwât– *VTA* snare s.o.

tâpakwê– *VAI* set snares
wâposo-câpakwêsi– *VAI* set small snares, set rabbit snares

SNARE-WIRE
apiscâpêkasin– *VII* be thin string, be thin snare-wire
tâpakwânêyâpiy– *NI* snare-wire

SNEAK UP
nâciyôscikê– *VAI* sneak up to people

SNIFF
miyâhcikê– *VAI* smell things, sniff about
miyâht– *VTI* smell s.t., sniff s.t.
nitawâpaso– *VAI* smell around, sniff about

SNOW
kîsohpihkê– *VAI* melt snow into water
kôn– *NA* snow
kôniwâpoy– *NI* snow water
mispon– *VII* be falling snow, be a snow-fall
timikoni– *VII* be deep snow

SNOWSHOE
asâm– *NA* snowshoe

SOAP
kisêpêkinikan– *NI* soap
kisîpêkinikan– *NA* soap
sâponikan– *NI* soap

SOCCER
pâkâhtowê– *VAI* play ball; play soccer

SOCK
asikan– *NA* sock, stocking
nâpêwasikan– *NA* men's socks

SOD
asiskiy– *NI* earth, soil, mud; clay; sod
maskosiy– *NI* grass, hay; *(plural:)* reeds; pieces of sod

SODDEN
sâpopê– *VAI* get wet, be drenched, be wet throughout, be sodden
sâpopê– *VII* get wet, be drenched, be wet throughout, be sodden

SOFT
yôskâ– *VII* be soft
yôskisi– *VAI* be soft

SOFTEN
yôskipotâ– *VAI* soften (it) by scraping (e.g., hide)

SOFTLY
pêyâhtik *IPC* quietly, gently, softly, slowly

SOIL
asiskiy– *NI* earth, soil, mud; clay; sod

asiskîwihkwê– *VAI* have soil on one's face, have dirt on one's face
îpâcihtâ– *VAI* make (it) dirty, soil (it)
pîkopicikâtê– *VII* be ploughed soil, be cultivated
pîkopicikê– *VAI* plough, do one's ploughing; break soil

SOILED
mêyiwiciskê– *VAI* have feces stuck to one's anus, have one's anus soiled with feces
wiyîpâ– *VII* be soiled, be dirty
wîpayiwinis– *NI* dirty clothes, soiled clothing
wîpâtayiwinis– *NI* dirty clothes, soiled clothing

SOLDIER
simâkanisihkâniwi– *VAI* be a soldier; take part in war (e.g., World War II)

SOLELY
pêyakwêyimiso– *VAI* think solely of oneself

SOLID
âhkwaci-pimiy– *NI* hard grease, solid grease
âhkwatin– *VII* be frozen, be frozen solid; be freeze-up
mistikwâhkatotê– *VII* be as hard as wood, be as solid as wood

SOME
âtiht *IPC* some
kayâsês *IPC* quite some time ago; a while ago
nânitaw *IPC* simply; *(with numbers:)* roughly, approximately; variously; something, at some undetermined place; *(in negative constructions:)* not anything; something bad, anything bad; somewhere
nânitaw isi *IPC* in some way, in any way; in various ways; in a random direction

SOMEBODY
awiyak *PR* someone, somebody; *(in negative constructions:)* not anyone, not anybody
waniyaw *IPC* any, somebody; at random

SOMEONE
awiyak *PR* someone, somebody; *(in negative constructions:)* not anyone, not anybody

SOMETHING
kîkway *PR* something, thing; things; *(in negative constructions:)* not anything, nothing, not any
kîkwâs *PR* something, thing; things; *(in negative constructions:)* not anything, nothing, not any
konita-kîkway *PR* something or other, random things
piko kîkway *PR* something or other; anything at all
piko kîkwâs *PR* something or other; anything at all

SOMETIMES
âskaw *IPC* sometimes; once in a while
kîtahtawê *IPC* at times, sometimes; at one time, all at once, suddenly

SOMEWHERE
nânitaw *IPC* simply; *(with numbers:)* roughly, approximately; variously; something, at some undetermined place; *(in negative constructions:)* not anything; something bad, anything bad; somewhere

SON
–kosis– *NDA* son, parallel nephew; *(fig.)* younger man

SON-IN-LAW
–tihkwatim– *NDA* cross-nephew; son-in-law

SONG
nikamo– *VAI* sing, sing a ritual song
nikamon– *NI* song, ritual song
nikamosi– *VAI* sing a little song
wîhtaskât– *VTA* sing about s.o. with words, sing a texted song about s.o.
wîhtaskât– *VTI* sing about s.t. with words, sing a texted song

SOON
cêskwa *IPC* wait! soon; *(in negative constructions:)* not yet
kikask *IPC* too soon, prematurely
kiyipa *IPC* quickly, soon
mayaw *IPC* as soon as
wîpac *IPC* soon, early

SORE
môskipayi– *VAI* break out in a rash, erupt in sores (e.g., with thrush)
omikî– *VAI* have a scab, have a sore; have (it) as one's scab
pîkokonêwêpayi– *VAI* have cracks erupt in one's mouth, have one's mouth break out in sores (e.g., with thrush)

SORELY
mihtât– *VTA* deplore the loss of s.o., sorely miss s.o., grieve for s.o.
wîsaki *IPV* sharply, painfully; sorely

SORRY
kitimâkinaw– *VTA* look with pity upon s.o., look with compassion upon s.o., feel sorry for s.o.; take pity upon s.o., lovingly tend s.o.; regard s.o. with respect

kitimâkinâso– *VAI* pity oneself, feel sorry for oneself

mihtât– *VTI* deplore the loss of s.t., be sorry about s.t.

SOUL
–têh– *NDI* heart; *(fig.)* heart, soul

ahcâhkw– *NA* soul

SOUND
itihtâkwan– *VII* be thus heard, sound thus

itwêwêsin– *VAI* fall with such a sound, make such a sound with one's shoes

kito– *VAI* utter a sound, call, sing (e.g., bird); make noises (e.g., animal), hoot; be a thunderclap

kîhkâtah– *VTI* make the sound of (it/him) ring out clearly

kîhkâtahamaw– *VTA* make the sound of (it/him) ring out clearly to s.o.

kîskosîmakan– *VII* whistle, emit a whistling sound

mamâhpinêmakan– *VII* moan, emit a moaning sound

matwêhw– *VTA* sound a beat upon s.o. (e.g., drum), drum on s.o.

miyoht– *VTI* like the sound of s.t., consider s.t. to sound nice

takahkihtaw– *VTA* like the sound of s.o., consider s.o. to sound nice

takahkihtâkosi– *VAI* sound nice, sound beautiful

takahkihtâkwan– *VII* sound nice, sound beautiful

takahkwêwêhtitâ– *VAI* make (it) sound nice by drumming or tapping; make a nice drumming or tapping sound

takahkwêwêsin– *VAI* fall with nice sounds, make nice sounds with one's shoes

tasin– *VTI* pull the trigger on s.t. (e.g., gun), shoot s.t. off (e.g., gun); emit a sharp noise, make a shot-like noise; sound a thunderclap (e.g., as Thunderbird)

SOUP
kikâpôhkê– *VAI* add (it) to soup, enhance one's soup with (it)

mîcimâpoy– *NI* broth, soup

mîcimâpôhkâkê– *VAI* make soup with (it), use (it) to make soup

mîcimâpôs– *NI* broth, soup

pitikonikanâpoy– *NI* meatball soup

sikwatahikanâpoy– *NI* minced-meat soup

sîsîpi-mîcimâpoy– *NI* duck broth, duck soup

wâposo-mîcimâpoy– *NI* rabbit broth, rabbit soup

SOURCE
mônahipân– *NI* source, well

SOUTH
âpihtâ-kîsikâhk *IPC* in the south, to the south

SPARE
kayâcic *IPC* the spare, the surplus

manâ *IPC* in avoiding, in sparing, being careful not to

manâ *IPV* in avoiding, in sparing, being careful not to

manâcih– *VTA* be protective about s.o., be careful about s.o., spare s.o.; avoid hurting s.o.; treat s.o. with respect

manâtâstim– *VTA* be careful in making s.o. wave, avoid making s.o. weave about; spare s.o. in driving a wagon, be considerate of s.o.

SPARINGLY
mâmâsîs *IPC* sparingly, delicately; quickly, roughly, without care

SPATTERED
sisopâcikâtê– *VII* be spattered, be sprayed

SPAWN
natahipayiho– *VAI* move upriver, spawn (e.g., fish)

SPEAK
ayami– *VAI* speak

ayamih– *VTA* speak to s.o.

ayamihâ– *VAI* speak, talk; speak about (it), talk about (it)

ayamihito– *VAI* speak to one another

âkayâsîmo– *VAI* speak English

âkayâsîmosi– *VAI* speak a little English

âyimômiso– *VAI* discuss oneself; speak unguardedly about oneself, gossip about oneself

âyimôt– *VTI* speak of s.t., discuss s.t.; gossip about s.t.

itwêstamaw– *VTA* say thus for s.o.; speak for s.o.; interpret for s.o.; transmit s.o.'s message, relay s.o.'s message (e.g., by radio)

kisîkitot– *VTA* speak to s.o. in anger
kisîwê– *VAI* speak angrily; speak loudly
kisîwê– *VII* be loud, speak loudly (e.g., audio-recorder)
kisîwêhkahtaw– *VTA* speak angrily to s.o.; speak loudly to s.o., scold s.o. loudly
kitot– *VTA* address s.o., speak to s.o.; lecture s.o.
kitot– *VTI* address s.t., speak to s.t. (e.g., spirit-bundle)
kwatakim– *VTA* speak meanly to s.o., nag s.o.
manâcim– *VTA* speak to s.o. with respect, speak of s.o. with respect
miyiskwê– *VAI* have a dry throat; speak with a weak voice
mwêstâtwêwêm– *VTA* speak about s.o. as troublesome, complain about s.o. being a nuisance
naskwêwasim– *VTA* speak to s.o. in response, respond to s.o. by speech; answer back to s.o., respond to s.o. (e.g., inappropriately)
naskwêwasimo– *VAI* speak in response, respond by speech
nêhiyawê– *VAI* speak Cree
nêhiyawêmototaw– *VTA* speak Cree to s.o.
nêhiyawi-pîkiskwê– *VAI* speak Cree, use Cree words
nîsowê– *VAI* speak as two at once
ohtowâtamaw– *VTA* speak for s.o. therefore or from there
pîkiskwât– *VTA* speak to s.o., address s.o.
pîkiskwât– *VTI* speak about s.t., speak about s.t. with concern; speak a prayer over s.t.; address s.t., speak to s.t. (e.g., spirit-bundle)
pîkiskwê– *VAI* use words, speak; speak a prayer, pray
pîkiskwêh– *VTA* make s.o. speak, get s.o. to speak; interview s.o.
pîkiskwêmakan– *VII* speak (e.g., spirit-bundle)
pîkiskwêmohtâ– *VAI* cause (it) to speak; make an audio-recording
pîkiskwêmôh– *VTA* cause s.o. to speak with concern
pîkiskwêpayi– *VAI* speak suddenly, burst into speech
pîkiskwêstamaw– *VTA* speak for s.o., speak on s.o.'s behalf
pîkiskwêstamâso– *VAI* speak for oneself, do one's own speaking
tâpowê– *VAI* speak correctly; recite one's prayer correctly
tâpwê– *VAI* speak true, speak the truth
wêmistikôsîmototaw– *VTA* speak French to s.o., address s.o. in French
wiyâhkwât– *VTA* swear at s.o., speak to s.o. in obscenities
wîci-pîkiskwêm– *VTA* speak together with s.o., have s.o. as one's fellow speaker

SPEAR
cîstahikan– *NI* spear, harpoon
cîstahw– *VTA* spear s.o.

SPECIFICALLY
ohcitaw *IPC* expressly, specifically, purposely, necessarily; it is requisite, it is meet indeed

SPECTACLES
–skîsikos– *NDI* spectacles, glasses

SPEECH
atamim– *VTA* make s.o. grateful by speech, please s.o. by speech
atâmim– *VTA* blame s.o. by speech
ayamiwin– *NI* speech, message
âyimim– *VTA* make things difficult for s.o. by speech
itwêwin– *NI* what is being said, speech; word; language
kaskim– *VTA* prevail upon s.o. by speech
kisîhto– *VAI* anger one another by speech
kisîm– *VTA* anger s.o. by speech
koskom– *VTA* awaken s.o. by speech; surprise s.o. by speech
mâmitonêyihtamim– *VTA* worry s.o. by speech
miyo-pîkiskwêwin– *NI* good speech; *(fig.)* the good news of the bible
moscitôn *IPC* gratuitously by speech, without adding a gift or offering
môskom– *VTA* make s.o. cry by tears or speech
mwêstâcim– *VTA* bother s.o. by speech, wear s.o. out by speech
naskwêwasim– *VTA* speak to s.o. in response, respond to s.o. by speech; answer back to s.o., respond to s.o. (e.g., inappropriately)
naskwêwasimo– *VAI* speak in response, respond by speech
papâsim– *VTA* hurry s.o. by speech
pîkiskwêpayi– *VAI* speak suddenly, burst into speech

pîkiskwêwin– NI word, phrase, expression, voice; what is being said; speech, language
sâkôcim– VTA overcome s.o. by speech; convince s.o. by speech, win s.o. over
sêkim– VTA frighten s.o. by speech
sîhkim– VTA urge s.o. by speech, encourage s.o. by speech; guide s.o. by speech
tâpwêwin– NI true speech, truth
wanâm– VTA distract s.o. by speech
wanwêhkaw– VTA leave s.o. baffled by speech or in speech, confuse s.o.
wayêsim– VTA trick s.o. by speech
wîhtamâkowin– NI speech, what is said to s.o.

SPEED
atimipayi– VAI move the other way, speed away
kakwâyakinikê– VAI act with great speed, act abruptly; buck violently (e.g., horse)
sôhkêkocin– VAI travel vigorously, travel at great speed

SPEND
katikoni– VAI sleep over, spend the night
kihcikanisi– VAI hold a rite; spend Christmas
kîsikanisi– VAI spend one's day, live through the day
mêstinikê– VAI use things up, exhaust things, spend all of (it); spend all of one's money on things
sîkwanisi– VAI be there in spring, pass the spring, spend the spring
tipiskisi– VAI spend one's night, live through the night

SPILL
sîkipicikê– VAI pour things out; spill things

SPINE
–âwikan– NDI backbone, spine (e.g., fish)

SPINNING
cicipahwânis– NI top, spinning top

SPIRIT
–pawâkan– NDA dream spirit
âmatisôst– VTI perceive the spirit of s.t. (e.g., spirit-bundle)
âtayôhkan– NA spirit being, dream guardian
âtayôhkanakiso– VAI be held to be a spirit being, be recognised as a dream guardian

maci-pawâmi– VAI have an evil dream spirit
manitow– NA spirit; *(name:)* God
manitowakim– VTA endow s.o. (e.g., tobacco) with supernatural power; attribute spirit power to s.o.
manitowi– VAI be a spirit; have spirit power
miyomahciho– VAI fare well, be in good health or spirit; feel well, feel healthy; feel pleased
opawâkanêyâspinat– VTA harm s.o. by means of dream spirits
opawâmi– VAI have a dream spirit
pawâmi– VAI have a dream spirit
pawâmiwin– NI spirit power; *(fig.)* witchcraft

SPIRIT-BUNDLE
nayôhcikan– NI bundle, sacred bundle, spirit-bundle (e.g., in ghost-dance)

SPIRITUAL
ahcâhko-pimâtisiwin– NI spiritual life
kiskêyihtamâ– VAI have spiritual knowledge

SPIT
maskatêpo– VAI roast (it) on a spit
sihko– VAI spit, spit out
sîkatêhtamaw– VTA spit (it/him) out for s.o.

SPLIT
mihcis– NI split wood, small firewood, sticks
nâtwâh– VTI split s.t., chop s.t. apart
nâtwân– VTI split s.t. apart, break s.t. off
nâtwâpayi– VII split off (e.g., branch), break off
nâtwâpit– VTI split s.t. (e.g., branch) off by pulling, break s.t. off
nâtwâwêpah– VTI split s.t. (e.g., branch) off and throw it down, break s.t. off and throw it down
tâskatah– VTI split s.t. (e.g., cordwood) by tool
tâskatahimihtê– VAI split firewood
tâskipayi– VAI split apart (e.g., reaches under a wagon)
tâskipit– VTI split s.t. apart
tâskiwêpahw– VTA split s.o. (e.g., rock) by arrow, shoot s.o. (e.g., rock) apart

SPOIL
misiwanâtan– VII be ruined, perish; be spoiled, spoil (e.g., meat)

patitisahamaw– VTA drive (it/him) off the path for s.o., send (it/him) awry for s.o., spoil (it/him) for s.o.
pîkon– VTA break s.o.; break up one's relation with s.o., disrupt s.o.'s life, spoil s.o.'s plans

SPOKEN
aspitonâmo– VAI rely on the spoken word; rely on (it) as a formal confirmation of the spoken word

SPOON
êmihkwânis– NA spoon

SPOUSE
–îci-kîhkâw– NDA aged spouse, fellow old person, fellow oldster, companion of one's old age
–wîcêwâkan– NDA companion, partner; spouse
–wîkimâkan– NDA spouse, housemate
miskamâso– VAI find (it/him) for oneself; find oneself a spouse
wîcêwâkanihto– VAI find one another as partner or spouse

SPRAY
sîkahâht– VTI spray s.t. (e.g., the land)

SPREAD
anâskât– VTA spread matting for s.o.; provide s.o. with bedsheets
anâskê– VAI have a mat, spread a blanket; use (it) as matting or floor-covering
sisopât– VTA spread (it) on s.o., apply (it) to s.o.'s chest
sisopât– VTI spread (it) on s.t.; lick s.t. off (e.g., sap)
taswêkiwêpin– VTA spread s.o. (e.g., wing) flat

SPRING
miyoskamin– VII be early spring
môhkiciwanipêyâ– VII be a spring, be a well
ohcikawan– VII leak out, drip out, trickle out; spring a leak (e.g., vessel)
ohpipayi– VAI spring up, be catapulted up (e.g., in a snare)
sîkwanisi– VAI be there in spring, pass the spring, spend the spring
sîkwâ– VII be spring

SPRINKLE
kîkawên– VTI mix s.t. in, sprinkle s.t. over
pîwên– VTA scatter s.o. (e.g., sugar), sprinkle s.o. (e.g., sugar) in small grains
pîwêwêpin– VTI scatter s.t., sprinkle in a pinch of s.t.
siswêwêpin– VTI sprinkle s.t. about (e.g., ashes in cleaning)
sîkahasinê– VAI pour water on rocks (e.g., in sweat-lodge), sprinkle rocks with water
sîkahâhtaw– VTA sprinkle s.o. with water; (fig.) baptise s.o., accept s.o. into the Catholic church

SPRUCE
minahikosis– NA small spruce, young spruce-tree
minahikoskâ– VII be a spruce thicket, be an abundance of spruce
minahikw– NA spruce, spruce-tree; spruce-bough

SPRUCE-GUM
pikiw– NA spruce-gum, gum

SPUR
cahkatayên– VTA prod s.o. at the belly, spur s.o.'s belly

SPY
onitawahtâw– NA scout, explorer, spy

SQUASH
patakopit– VTA squash s.o. in pulling, flatten s.o. down by pulling

SQUIRREL
anikwacâs– NA squirrel; gopher

STAB
tahkam– VTA stab s.o.

STABLE
awâska-mâmitonêyihcikan– NI stable mind, steady mind, balanced mind

STAND
asikâpawi– VAI stand about as a loose group
âkwaskikâpawi– VAI stand in the way, stand as an obstacle
cimaso– VAI stand upright, stand erect (e.g., tree)
cimatê– VII stand upright, stand erect
itaskitê– VII stand thus (e.g., lodge)
mêskocikâpawi– VAI stand up instead
nîpawi– VAI stand, stand up, stand upright, stand fast
nîpawipayiho– VAI stand up suddenly
nîpawistamaw– VTA stand up for s.o., be a witness (e.g., at wedding) for s.o.
nîpisîhkopâw– NI stand of willows, willow patch
pimicikâpawi– VAI stand sideways, stand across
sâkaskinêkâpawi– VAI stand crowded in, stand to fill a place

simacî– *VAI* stand upright; rear up (e.g., horse)
sôhkêpit– *VTI* stand firmly behind s.t., promote s.t.
wayawîkâpawi– *VAI* stand outside, go outdoors
wîhkwêstê– *VII* be placed around, stand in the shape of a curve

STAR
acâhkos– *NA* star, little star

START
kwâhkotênikê– *VAI* start a fire, set things aflame
sipwêpayin– *VII* start off to run (e.g., tape-recorder)

STARTLE
koskoh– *VTA* startle s.o., surprise s.o.
koskon– *VTA* awaken s.o. by hand, wake s.o. up; startle s.o.

STARVE
nipahâhkatoso– *VAI* starve to death, die from starvation; *(fig.)* be terribly hungry

STAY
api– *VAI* sit, sit down; be situated, be present, stay; be at home, be available
kapêsi– *VAI* stay overnight
kapêsimostaw– *VTA* stay overnight with s.o., stay overnight at s.o.'s place
kisâcî– *VAI* stay behind, stay around, stay nearby
kisât– *VTI* stay with s.t., hold fast to s.t.; stay, stay back
kisîstaw– *VTA* be angry with s.o., stay angry with s.o.
kîsôsi– *VAI* keep warm, stay warm; be warm (e.g., pants)
nîpâhtâ– *VAI* stay out until late in the night
pêyakwapi– *VAI* stay alone, be alone in the house

STEADY
awâska-mâmitonêyihcikan– *NI* stable mind, steady mind, balanced mind

STEAL
kimotamaw– *VTA* steal (it/him) from s.o.
kimoti– *VAI* steal (him/it); be a thief
kwâsih– *VTA* steal s.o., run away with s.o. (e.g., of the opposite sex)
otin– *VTA* take s.o., take s.o. in (e.g., orphan); choose s.o.; steal s.o.; *(especially in inverse constructions:)* take hold of s.o., possess s.o.
otin– *VTI* take s.t.; pick s.t., choose s.t., select s.t. (e.g., moss); steal s.t.; take s.t. over; extract s.t. (e.g., grease from soup), remove s.t. (e.g., glands in butchering beaver), extract s.t.; accept s.t. (e.g., contract); capture s.t., record s.t. on audio-tape
otinamâso– *VAI* take (it/him) for oneself, get (it/him) for oneself; steal (it/him)

STEALTHILY
kîmôci *IPV* secretly, in secret, stealthily, privately, in private
kîmôtâpi– *VAI* look stealthily, look secretly

STEEL
pîwâpiskw– *NI* metal, metal object; steel blade; screen of wire-mesh

STEER
ayêhkwêsis– *NA* young castrated bull; steer

STEP
patinikê– *VAI* make a mistake, take a wrong step, transgress; *(fig.)* sin
pêtwêwên– *VTI* come hither audibly, come with audible steps
tahkoskê– *VAI* step, take a step, step upon, make a hoofprint

STEP-CROSS-NIECE
–stimihkâwin– *NDA* step-cross-niece, step-daughter-in-law; daughter-in-law-in-common-law

STEP-DAUGHTER-IN-LAW
–stimihkâwin– *NDA* step-cross-niece, step-daughter-in-law; daughter-in-law-in-common-law

STEP-FATHER
–ôhcâwîs– *NDA* father's brother, parallel uncle; step-father
–ôhtâwîhkâwin– *NDA* step-father

STEP-MOTHER
–kâwîs– *NDA* mother's sister, parallel aunt; step-mother

STEREO-PLAYER
kitohcikê– *VAI* play a musical instrument; play one's stereo-player

STERN
âhkwâtisi– *VAI* be stern, be sharp, be of severe disposition

STICK
mihcis– *NI* split wood, small firewood, sticks
miscikos– *NI* little stick (e.g., in collecting sap); little pole, rod, rail (e.g., on drying rack); branch of a small plant (e.g., labrador tea)
mistikw– *NI* stick, pole, post, log, wooden rail

pôhtâskwah– *VTI* stick s.t. wooden into a hole; clean out one's ear, poke one's ear
sâkamon– *VII* stick out, be attached so as to project
sâkêkamon– *VII* stick out as cloth, project as cloth
sâkiskwêpayiho– *VAI* suddenly stick one's head out

STICKY
pasakoskiw-âya *IPC* sticky stuff

STIFF
sîtawâ– *VII* be stiff

STILL
âhci *IPC* still, nevertheless, despite everything
âhci piko *IPC* still, nevertheless, despite everything
kêyâpic *IPC* still, in continuity; yet

STING
cîsw– *VTA* sting s.o., prick s.o.

STINK
mâyâpaso– *VAI* smell foul, give off a bad smell, stink

STIR
itêh– *VTI* stir s.t., stir s.t. in
itêhw– *VTA* stir s.o., stir s.o. in; stir s.o. (flour) in as thickening

STITCH
mîkisihkaht– *VTI* bead s.t., stitch beads on s.t.
mîkisistah– *VTI* bead s.t., stitch beads on s.t.
titipikwanah– *VTI* sew s.t. in overcast stitch (e.g., the spiral loops around the vamp of a moccasin)

STOCK
pakitin– *VTA* set s.o. down, allow s.o., permit s.o.; permit (it) to s.o., give permission to s.o.; let s.o. go, release s.o.; release s.o. (e.g., fish-spawn into lake), stock a lake with s.o. (e.g., fish); drop s.o. off (e.g., as an airplane)

STOCKING
asikan– *NA* sock, stocking

STONE
asiniy– *NA* rock, stone
asinîs– *NA* stone
mistasiniy– *NA* big stone, big rock

STOOK
cimacikê– *VAI* stook sheaves of grain, do one's stooking

STOP
âsô-nakî– *VAI* stop in moving across (e.g., the prairies), stop in one's transit

kâh-kipîhci *IPC* stopping now and then
nakân– *VTA* stop s.o.
nakâwâskwêsin– *VAI* be brought to a stop by hitting a tree
nakin– *VTA* stop s.o., make s.o. stop; turn s.o. off (e.g., kitchen-stove)
nakipicikê– *VAI* stop one's team
nakî– *VAI* stop, come to a stop
nakwâso– *VAI* be snared, be stopped by a snare
paskêpayi– *VAI* branch off, move off to the side; stop off there
pimi-nakî– *VAI* stop in one's progress, stop in one's travelling
pôni-nôhâwaso– *VAI* stop nursing one's child, wean one's child
pônipayi– *VII* cease, stop, come to an end

STORAGE
ascikêwikamikw– *NI* storage room, storage building

STORAGE-RACK
akocikan– *NI* rack for hanging up fish or meat, storage-rack; cupboard, shelf

STORE
ascikê– *VAI* put things away, store things
atâwêwikamikw– *NI* store, trading-post
kanawêyiht– *VTI* keep s.t., look after s.t., take care of s.t.; store s.t., preserve s.t.; guard s.t. closely
kanawêyihtâkwan– *VII* be kept, be looked after, the taken care of; be stored, be preserved; be closely guarded
kihc-âtâwêwikamikowiyiniw– *NA* store manager, post manager, Hudson's Bay Company factor
kihc-âtâwêwikamikw– *NI* Hudson's Bay Company store
nahah– *VTA* put s.o. away, store s.o. (e.g., duck)
nahascikê– *VAI* put things away, store things
nahastâ– *VAI* put (it) in its place, put (it) away; store (it)

STORE-BOUGHT
***Hudson's-Bay*-ayiwinis–** *NI* Hudson's Bay Company clothes, store-bought clothing

STORE-KEEPER
otatâwêw– *NA* store-keeper, store-manager
otatâwêwi– *VAI* be the store-keeper, be the store-manager

STORM
âstê-kîsikâ– VII cease being stormy weather, let up as severe weather, be better weather
maci-kîsikâ– VII be a bad storm, be a severe storm
mâyi-kîsikâ– VII be stormy weather, be foul weather, be a severe storm

STORY
aspahâkêmo– VAI rely upon (it/him) in speaking, rely upon (it/him) in telling a story; use (it/him) as an excuse
âcimiso– VAI tell things about oneself, tell a story about oneself; *(fig.)* confess oneself, go to confession
âcimo– VAI tell things, tell a story, give an account
âcimostaw– VTA tell s.o. about (it/him), tell s.o. a story, give s.o. an account
âcimostâto– VAI tell one another about (it/him), tell stories to one another
âcimowin– NI story, account, report
âcimowinis– NI little story
âcimôh– VTA make s.o. tell about (it/him), make s.o. tell a story
âtayôhkan– NI sacred story
âtayôhkaw– VTA tell s.o. a sacred story
âtayôhkât– VTA tell about s.o. in the form of a sacred story, tell a sacred story of s.o.
âtayôhkât– VTI tell about s.t. in the form of a sacred story, tell a sacred story of s.t.
âtayôhkê– VAI tell a sacred story
âtayôhkêwin– NI sacred story
itâcimo– VAI tell thus, tell a story thus, tell such a story, give such an account
itâcimostaw– VTA tell s.o. thus about (it/him), tell s.o. such a story, give s.o. such an account
itâcimowinihkât– VTI tell thus about s.t., make such a story of s.t., give such an account of s.t.
itâcimômakan– VII tell thus about (it/him), tell such a story, give such an account
itâtayôhkaw– VTA tell s.o. such a sacred story
itâtayôhkât– VTI tell thus about s.t. in the form of a sacred story, tell such a sacred story of s.t.
itâtayôhkâtê– VII be told thus in the form of a sacred story, be told as such a sacred story
kisêyiniw-âcimowin– NI old man's story, report of the old men
konit-âcimowinis– NI mere story, simple story, just a little story
ma-môhcw-âtayôhkêwin– NI stupid sacred story, crazy sacred story
mâtâcimo– VAI begin to tell a story
nihtâwâcimo– VAI be a good storyteller, tell stories expertly
takahk-âcim– VTA tell a beautiful story about s.o.
takahk-âtayôhkêwin– NI fine sacred story
wawiyatâcimowinis– NI funny little story
wiyâhkwêwi-âcimo– VAI swear in telling stories; tell obscene stories, tell risqué stories

STORYTELLER
nihtâwâcimo– VAI be a good storyteller, tell stories expertly

STOVE
asiskîwi-kocawânâpiskos– NA mud stove
kotawânâpiskw– NA stove, cook-stove
kotawânâpiskw– NI stove, cook-stove

STRAIGHT
taskamohtê– VAI cut across, walk straight towards one's goal
tâpwê piko IPC straight away, immediately

STRAIGHTEN
mînom– VTA straighten s.o. out, correct s.o. verbally
mînwâskonamaw– VTA straighten (it/him) as wood for s.o.

STRAIN
sîhcihtâ– VAI strain (it) (e.g., one's eyes)
sîhcî– VAI strain, be strained
wîhkô– VAI strain oneself, use all one's force

STRANGE
mamâhtâwêyihtâkwan– VII be thought strange, be thought supernatural
mâmaskâc IPC strangely, marvellously, amazingly; *(in negative constructions:)* not surprisingly, no wonder
mâmaskât– VTA find s.o. strange, find s.o. incomprehensible, marvel at s.o.

mâmaskât– VTI find s.t. strange, find s.t. incomprehensible, marvel at s.t.
misi-pîtos IPC very different; very strange
mistahi-pîtos IPC very strangely, most strangely, very differently
pîtos IPC strangely, differently
pîtos-kîkway PR something strange, strange things
pîtosinâkwan– VII look different; look strange
pîtotêyihtâkosi– VAI be thought strange, be considered odd

STRAWBERRY
otêhiminâni-cêpihk– NI strawberry root

STRENGTH
maskawisîwin– NI strength
sôhkisiwin– NI strength, vigour; power, supernatural power; authority

STRENUOUSLY
kotêyiht– VTI try s.t. in one's mind, think strenuously about s.t., test s.t.; challenge s.t.

STRETCH
âsowahpitê– VII be stretched across, be strung across
sêsâwin– VTA stretch s.o. by hand, exercise s.o.'s limbs (in therapy)
sêsâwipayi– VAI stretch, become stretched
sîpah– VTI stretch s.t.
sîpahw– VTA stretch s.o. (e.g., an animal in processing skins)
sîpêkaht– VTI stretch s.t. with one's teeth
sîpi IPV stretching far back

STRIKE
pakamah– VTI strike s.t., hit s.t.; pound s.t. (e.g., meat); type s.t., type s.t. out
pakamahw– VTA hit s.o., strike s.o.; pound s.o. (e.g., earring)

STRING
apiscâpêkasin– VII be thin string, be thin snare-wire
kinwâpêkisi– VAI be long as string, be long as fishing-net
pîminahkwânis– NI string, rope

STRIPED
masinâso– VAI be marked, be striped

STRONG
maskawâ– VII be hard (e.g., fat); be strong, be sturdy
maskawâtisi– VAI be strong, be of sturdy disposition

maskawisî– VAI be strong, be vigorous
maskawîskaw– VTA *(especially in inverse constructions:)* make s.o. strong in body, have an invigorating effect on s.o.
nipahâhkwan– VII be terribly strong, be terribly powerful, hurt terribly
sôhkan– VII be strong, be sturdy; be important; *(fig.)* be powerful, have supernatural power
sôhkâtisi– VAI be strong in body, be fit, have a vigorous disposition
sôhkêpayin– VII be strong, work effectively (e.g., medicine)
sôhkisi– VAI be strong, be vigorous; be powerful, have supernatural power

STRONGEST
mâwaci-sôhkan– VII be strongest, be sturdiest

STRONGLY
sôhki IPC strongly, vigorously, powerfully

STRUCTURED
wiyastê– VII be arranged, be structured

STRUNG
âsowahpitê– VII be stretched across, be strung across

STUBBLE
kîsisikê– VAI burn things; burn stubble, burn the fields
pasisâwê– VAI burn stubble, burn the fields

STUCK
mêyiwiciskê– VAI have feces stuck to one's anus, have one's anus soiled with feces
miciminikâtê– VII be held onto, be stuck
micimoskowê– VAI be stuck in mud or bog
micimôh– VTA *(especially in inverse constructions:)* cause s.o. to get stuck
micimôho– VAI be held fast, be stuck

STUDENT
–îci-kiskinohamawâkan– NDA fellow student, school-mate
kiskinohamawâkan– NA student
kiskinohamâkosi– VAI be taught; be a student, attend school
kiskinohamâkosiwin– NI being a student, going to school; schoolwork, homework
kiskinohamâso– VAI teach oneself; be taught; be a student, attend school
takahki-kiskinahamawâkanis– NA excellent student

ENGLISH INDEX 389

wîci-kiskinohamâkosîm– VTA be in school together with s.o., have s.o. as a fellow student

STUDY
  wîcihiso– VAI help oneself; apply oneself, study for oneself; rely on oneself in childbirth

STUFF
  kayâs-ây– NI old stuff
  mihkwâpêmakw-âya IPC red willow stuff
  môniyâw-âya IPC White things, White stuff
  nâpêw-âya IPC men's things, men's stuff, men's clothing
  pasakoskiw-âya IPC sticky stuff
  sîpaskwât– VTI stuff s.t. (e.g., head of an animal)

STUPID
  ma-môhcw-âtayôhkêwin– NI stupid sacred story, crazy sacred story
  môhcowi– VAI be foolish, be stupid, be silly; be mad, be crazy
  môhcw-âyâ– VAI be foolish, be stupid, be silly; be mad, be crazy
  môhcwêyim– VTA consider s.o. stupid

STURDY
  maskawâ– VII be hard (e.g., fat); be strong, be sturdy
  maskawâtisi– VAI be strong, be of sturdy disposition
  miscikwaskisinis– NI firm shoe, sturdy shoe, oxford
  sôhkan– VII be strong, be sturdy; be important; *(fig.)* be powerful, have supernatural power

SUBJECT
  askîwisk– VTI subject the earth to oneself, populate the earth, make the earth live

SUBSEQUENTLY
  ici IPC later, subsequently
  mwêstas IPC later, subsequently

SUCCEED
  kaskih– VTA prevail upon s.o., succeed in imposing one's will on s.o.; be able to deal with s.o.; earn s.o. (e.g., money)
  minahôstamâso– VAI kill an animal for oneself, succeed in a kill
  tâpapîstamaw– VTA sit in s.o.'s place, succeed s.o. in office

SUCCESSIVELY
  âniskê IPV successively, one joining the other, surviving
  âsowi IPV in turn, in succession

SUCK
  nôni– VAI suck at the breast, nurse at the breast; suck at the teats (e.g., calf)

SUCKLE
  nôh– VTA suckle s.o., nurse s.o., breastfeed s.o.
  nôhâwaso– VAI nurse one's child, breastfeed one's child; suckle the young one (of the species), suckle one's calf (as cow)

SUDDENLY
  kîtahtawê IPC at times, sometimes; at one time, all at once, suddenly
  sisikoc IPC suddenly

SUFFER
  cowêskihtê– VAI have one's ears ring, have ringing in one's ears, suffer from tinnitus
  itâspinê– VAI be ill thus, suffer from such a disease
  kakwâtakâciho– VAI suffer dreadfully, live through a dreadful time
  kakwâtakâpâkwaho– VAI suffer mortification by denying oneself liquid, make oneself suffer thirst
  kakwâtakih– VTA make s.o. suffer; be mean to s.o., be abusive to s.o.; *(especially in inverse constructions:)* affect s.o. terribly (e.g., as disease), ravage s.o.
  kakwâtakihiso– VAI make oneself suffer; torture oneself, deny oneself food and drink
  kakwâtakiho– VAI make oneself suffer; torture oneself, experience suffering; deny oneself food and drink
  kakwâtakihowin– NI making oneself suffer; denying oneself food and drink
  kakwâtakihtâ– VAI suffer (it), suffer because of (it), have difficulties because of (it); suffer; experience a crisis (e.g., in the course of an illness)
  kakwâtakî– VAI suffer, experience difficulty, experience torment
  kawaci– VAI be cold, experience cold; suffer chills
  kiyakasê– VAI have itchy skin, suffer from eczema
  kwatakiho– VAI suffer
  mâyipayi– VAI fare badly, suffer ill; suffer a death, be bereaved, have a death in the family; be bereaved of (her/him)
  nôhtêhkatê– VAI be hungry, suffer want of food
  nôhtêyâpâkwê– VAI be thirsty, suffer want of water

ohcinê– *VAI* be ill on account of (it), suffer for (it); suffer in retribution
oskaninê– *VAI* be ill with arthritis, suffer from arthritis
pasisêwaci– *VAI* suffer frostbite
sôkâwâspinê– *VAI* be ill with diabetes, suffer from diabetes, be a diabetic

SUFFERING
kakwâtakêyihtamih– *VTA* bring torment upon s.o., bring suffering upon s.o.
kakwâtakiho– *VAI* make oneself suffer; torture oneself, experience suffering; deny oneself food and drink

SUFFICIENTLY
têpi *IPV* fully, sufficiently, enough

SUGAR
sîwinikan– *NA* sugar
sôkâs– *NA* sugar; candy
sôkâw– *NA* sugar

SUICIDE
misiwanâcihiso– *VAI* ruin oneself, destroy oneself; *(fig.)* commit suicide
nipahiso– *VAI* kill oneself, commit suicide

SUMMER
awasi-nîpinohk *IPC* the summer before last
kapê-nîpin *IPC* all summer long, throughout the summer
nîpin– *VII* be summer
tahto-nîpin *IPC* every summer, each summer
tânitahto-nîpin *IPC* how many summers; so many summers, a few summers

SUN
kîsikâwi-pîsimw– *NA* sun
nêstwâso– *VAI* be tired by the sun's heat, be exhausted by hot weather
pîsimw– *NA* sun; moon; month

SUNDANCE
nipâkwêsimo– *VAI* attend a sundance, participate in a sundance, dance the sundance
nipâkwêsimowikamikw– *NI* sundance lodge, sundance ceremony
nipâkwêsimowin– *NI* sundance
nipâkwêsimowinihkê– *VAI* hold a sundance

SUNDAY
ayamihêwi-kîsikâ– *VII* be Sunday
ayamihêwi-kîsikâw– *NI* Sunday
tahtw-âyamihêwi-kîsikâw *IPC* every Sunday

SUNRISE
naspâpan *IPC* at daybreak, before sunrise

SUNSET
pahkisimon– *VII* be sunset, be west

SUPER-WOMAN
kakwâhyaki-iskwêw– *NA* extraordinary woman, super-woman

SUPERB
kihci *IPC* great, superb; the best

SUPERNATURAL
mamâhtâwêyihtâkwan– *VII* be thought strange, be thought supernatural
mamâhtâwisi– *VAI* have supernatural power
manitowakim– *VTA* endow s.o. (e.g., tobacco) with supernatural power; attribute spirit power to s.o.
manitowih– *VTA* grant s.o. supernatural power
sôhkan– *VII* be strong, be sturdy; be important; *(fig.)* be powerful, have supernatural power
sôhkisi– *VAI* be strong, be vigorous; be powerful, have supernatural power
sôhkisiwin– *NI* strength, vigour; power, supernatural power; authority

SUPPLICATION
nêhiyaw-nitotamâwin– *NI* Cree supplication, the Cree way of supplication

SUPPLY
iskwahtâ– *VAI* have so much of (it) left over; have (it) left over, have a plentiful supply of (it)
kitâpayihtamaw– *VTA* eat all of (it/him) on s.o., eat s.o.'s entire supply
kwîtawêyihcikâtê– *VII* be missed, be in short supply
mêstasahkê– *VAI* feed people until the supply is exhausted, exhaust one's supply by feeding people
mîcisowin– *NI* eating, meal; eating-habits; food, foodstuff, food supply
mosc-âsam– *VTA* simply provide food to s.o., supply food to s.o. without recompense
nôhtêpayi– *VAI* run short, be in want; run short of supplies; run short of (it), have (it) in short supply

SUPPORT
wîcêht– *VTI* go along with s.t., support s.t., cooperate with s.t.

SUPPOSE
mâskôc *IPC* perhaps, I suppose, undoubtedly

SURELY
ani *IPC* then, indeed, surely
kêhcinâ *IPC* surely, for certain
yâyâhk *IPC* really, for sure, to be sure; especially, all the more so
SURFACE
waskic *IPC* on top, on the surface
SURGERY
manisw– *VTA* cut s.o.; perform surgery on s.o.
SURNAME
aspiyîhkâso– *VAI* have a surname; have (it) as one's surname
SURPLUS
ayiwâkipayi– *VAI* have more than enough, have a surplus, have plenty; run to more, be a surplus (e.g., money)
kayâcic *IPC* the spare, the surplus
SURPRISE
koskoh– *VTA* startle s.o., surprise s.o.
koskom– *VTA* awaken s.o. by speech; surprise s.o. by speech
koskwêyiht– *VTI* be surprised about s.t., marvel at s.t.; be surprised
koskwêyihtâkwan– *VII* be surprising, be amazing
koskwêyim– *VTA* be surprised about s.o.; find s.o. surprising
sisikotêyiht– *VTI* find s.t. surprising, find s.t. shocking; be surprised, be shocked
SURPRISINGLY
mâmaskâc *IPC* strangely, marvellously, amazingly; *(in negative constructions:)* not surprisingly, no wonder
SURVIVE
âniskê *IPV* successively, one joining the other, surviving
iskwânê– *VAI* be left behind after a widespread illness, survive an epidemic
kâsispô– *VAI* reach beyond, exceed; survive into another generation
kâsispôhtêmakan– *VII* go on, reach beyond, exceed; survive into another generation
pimâtisi– *VAI* live, be alive, survive
SUSPECT
mac-îtêyiht– *VTI* suspect s.t. bad; suspect evil
môyêyiht– *VTI* sense s.t.; suspect s.t.; realise s.t.
môyêyim– *VTA* sense s.o., suspect s.o.
SUSPEND
itakotâ– *VAI* hang (it) thus or there, suspend (it) thus or there

SUSPENDED
akocin– *VAI* hang, be suspended; hang in a swing, hang in a snare
akociwêpin– *VTA* throw s.o. to hang, throw s.o. to be suspended; throw s.o. over top (e.g., onto willow bushes)
akohcin– *VAI* hang in the water, be suspended in water
akotê– *VII* hang, be suspended
ispâhkêkocin– *VII* rise high up, hang high aloft, be suspended high in the air
itakocin– *VAI* hang thus or there, be suspended thus or there; fly thus or there
itakotê– *VII* hang thus or there, be suspended thus or there
SUSTAIN
asamâwaso– *VAI* feed one's children, sustain one's children
pimâcih– *VTA* make s.o. live, give life to s.o., sustain s.o.'s life; revive s.o., save s.o.'s life; make a living for s.o.
pimohtah– *VTA* take s.o. along, go along with s.o., guide s.o. along; carry s.o. along, sustain s.o.
SWADDLE
kîsowâspiso– *VAI* be warmly swaddled
sâkiskwêhpit– *VTA* wrap s.o. up to the neck, swaddle s.o. up to the neck
tahkopitâwaso– *VAI* swaddle one's child; *(fig.)* be delivered of a child
wâspit– *VTA* wrap s.o. up in a mossbag, lace s.o. up in a mossbag, swaddle s.o.
SWALLOW
kohcipayihtâ– *VAI* swallow (it)
SWAMP
maskêkw– *NI* swamp, bog, muskeg
SWAYED
wâhkêyêyiht– *VTI* be easily swayed; *(fig.)* be too weak
SWEAR
naskot– *VTI* respond to s.t.; swear upon s.t. in response
wiyâhkwât– *VTA* swear at s.o., speak to s.o. in obscenities
wiyâhkwêwi-âcimo– *VAI* swear in telling stories; tell obscene stories, tell risqué stories
SWEAT
apwêsi– *VAI* sweat, perspire; work up a sweat
SWEAT-LODGE
matotisah– *VTA* make s.o. hold a sweat-lodge
matotisahtâ– *VAI* take (it) into the sweat-lodge

matotisân– *NI* sweat-lodge
matotisi– *VAI* hold a sweat-lodge
SWEATER
sîpêkiskâwasâkâs– *NI* sweater
SWEATING
apwêsiwin– *NI* sweating, labouring
SWEEP
ispisi-wîhkwêhcâhk *IPC* in such a sweep of the land, to the extent of the sweep of this valley
mâwasakowêpah– *VTI* sweep s.t. together
wêpah– *VTI* sweep s.t. up; throw s.t. by tool, push s.t. by tool; cock s.t. (e.g., gun)
wêpahikâkê– *VAI* sweep things with (it), use (it) to sweep, use (it) as a broom
wêpahikê– *VAI* sweep things, do the sweeping
wîhkwêhcâ– *VII* go around as land, be curved as land, be the sweep of the valley
SWEET
wîhkimahkaso– *VAI* smell sweet in burning
SWEETEN
sîwinikê– *VAI* sweeten things; sweeten one's tea
SWEETGRASS
miyâhkas– *VTI* cense s.t., smudge s.t. with sweetgrass
miyâhkasamaw– *VTA* cense (it/him) for s.o., smudge (it/him) with sweetgrass for s.o.
miyâhkasikê– *VAI* cense things, smudge things with sweetgrass
miyâhkasw– *VTA* cense s.o. (e.g., pipe), smudge s.o. (e.g., pipe) with sweetgrass
wîhkaskw– *NI* sweetgrass
SWEETS
sîwahcikê– *VAI* eat sweets
SWELL
pâkisitêpayi– *VAI* have one's foot swell up, have a swollen foot
SWIM
pakâsimo– *VAI* be immersed, swim, have a bath
pimiskâ– *VAI* swim by, swim along; go by in a boat, move along by one's own power
SWIM-BLADDER
wîhkway– *NI* craw (e.g., bird); swim-bladder (e.g., fish)

SWING
akocin– *VAI* hang, be suspended; hang in a swing, hang in a snare
itâpihkêpayi– *VAI* move thus or there as a rope or snake, swing thus as a rope or snake
wêwêpison– *NI* swing
wêwêpisonihkê– *VAI* make a swing, arrange a swing
SWITCH
nîpisîs– *NI* willow branch, willow switch; little willow
SWOLLEN
pâkisitêpayi– *VAI* have one's foot swell up, have a swollen foot
SWOOP
tapahcipayiho– *VAI* swoop down, swoop low
SYLLABICS
nêhiyawastê– *VII* be written in Cree; be written in syllabics
SYRUP
lamilâs– *NI* syrup
TABLE
mîcisowinâhtikw– *NI* dining table, table
wiyastamaw– *VTA* set the table for s.o.
TACKLE
mâyêyiht– *VTI* consider s.t. a challenge; be willing to tackle a difficult task, venture out
mâyêyim– *VTA* consider s.o. a challenge; be willing to tackle s.o.
TAG ALONG
pimitisahikê– *VAI* follow people, tag along, be a follower
TAIL
–soy– *NDI* tail
TAIL-HAIR
misatimwâyow– *NI* horse-tail; tail-hair of a horse
TAINTED
pâstâhowi-mihkw– *NI* blood tainted by a breach of the natural order; *(fig.)* blood tainted by deicide, sinful blood
TAKE
itohtatamaw– *VTA* take (it/him) to s.o.
itohtatâ– *VAI* take (it) there or thus, go there with (it)
kêcikon– *VTI* take s.t. off (e.g., glasses, clothing)
miy-ôtin– *VTA* take s.o. in, accept s.o.
ohtin– *VTI* take s.t. from there, obtain s.t. thereby or from there

ohtinikê– *VAI* take things from there, obtain things thereby or from there

otin– *VTA* take s.o., take s.o. in (e.g., orphan); choose s.o.; steal s.o.; *(especially in inverse constructions:)* take hold of s.o., possess s.o.

otin– *VTI* take s.t.; pick s.t., choose s.t., select s.t. (e.g., moss); steal s.t.; take s.t. over; extract s.t. (e.g., grease from soup), remove s.t. (e.g., glands in butchering beaver), extract s.t.; accept s.t. (e.g., contract); capture s.t., record s.t. on audio-tape

otinamâso– *VAI* take (it/him) for oneself, get (it/him) for oneself; steal (it/him)

otinikê– *VAI* take things; buy things, do one's shopping, make a purchase; take away winnings (e.g., in a card-game)

otinikêmakan– *VII* take things away; take the fever away

sipwêhtatâ– *VAI* leave taking (it), depart with (it)

TAKE CARE

kanawêyiht– *VTI* keep s.t., look after s.t., take care of s.t.; store s.t., preserve s.t.; guard s.t. closely

kanawêyihtamaw– *VTA* look after (it/him) for s.o., take care of (it/him) for s.o.

kanawêyihtamâso– *VAI* guard (it/him) closely for oneself, take good care of (it/him) oneself

kanawêyim– *VTA* keep s.o., look after s.o., take care of s.o.; guard s.o. closely

miyawâkâtinikê– *VAI* take particular care with things, handle ritual objects with particular care

TAKE PLACE

ispayin– *VII* take place thus, occur thus; run thus (in a cycle), be there (in a cycle), come around (in a cycle), be that time again; come by, go by, have passed (e.g., days, years)

nânitaw ispayi– *VII* take place as an unwelcome event

ocihcipayi– *VII* come to pass, take place

ocihciskâmakan– *VII* come to pass, take place (by foot or body movement)

pimipayi– *VII* move along; run, run along; be on, work, function (e.g., motor, electricity); exist currently, take place

TAKEN

nîhcipicikâtê– *VII* be taken down (e.g., from a shelf), be chosen for purchase (e.g., in self-service store)

otinikâtê– *VII* be taken, be obtained; be chosen

otinikowisi– *VAI* be taken by the powers

tahtinikâtê– *VII* be loosened, be taken off

TALISMAN

kanôsimon– *NI* protective talisman (usually worn around the neck, wrapped in leather)

TALK

ayamihâ– *VAI* speak, talk; speak about (it), talk about (it)

mâmiskôm– *VTA* talk about s.o., discuss s.o., refer to s.o.

mâmiskôt– *VTI* talk about s.t., discuss s.t., expound s.t., refer to s.t.

môskomo– *VAI* talk oneself into crying, cry while talking

tasîhcikâtê– *VII* be talked about, be discussed

tasîht– *VTI* talk about s.t., discuss s.t.

TALL

iskosi– *VAI* extend so far, be so long, be so tall, be of such height

kakiyâskiwin– *NI* lie, tall tale

kinosi– *VAI* be long (e.g., sock), be tall

kinwâ– *VII* be long, be tall

TAME

nakayâh– *VTA* get s.o. accustomed to something, break s.o. (e.g., horse), tame s.o., train s.o.

TAMPER

mikoskâcihtâ– *VAI* trifle with (it), tamper with (it)

TANNED

pahkêkinw– *NI* dressed hide, tanned hide, finished hide, leather; tent-cover

TAPE

têpiwi– *VAI* tape (it), make an audio-recording of (it)

TAPPING

takahkwêwêhtitâ– *VAI* make (it) sound nice by drumming or tapping; make a nice drumming or tapping sound

TASK

âyimî– *VAI* have a difficult time, have a difficult task; have a hard life

mâyêyiht– *VTI* consider s.t. a challenge; be willing to tackle a difficult task, venture out

mistah-âtoskêwin– *NI* big task, major task

TASTE
ispakwan– *VII* taste thus
kotist– *VTI* taste s.t., try the taste of s.t.
sâmaht– *VTI* taste s.t.
wîhkasin– *VAI* taste good
wîhkasin– *VII* taste good
wîhkipw– *VTA* like the taste of s.o. (e.g., duck, beaver), have a preference for the taste of s.o.
wîhkist– *VTA* like the taste of s.o. (e.g., bread, duck)
wîhkist– *VTI* like the taste of s.t.
wîhkitisi– *VAI* taste good (e.g., beaver, fish, bannock)

TAUGHT
kiskinohamâkosi– *VAI* be taught; be a student, attend school
kiskinohamâso– *VAI* teach oneself; be taught; be a student, attend school

TEA
kisâkamisikê– *VAI* heat a liquid; boil water for tea, make tea
maskêko-*litea* *INM* labrador tea
maskêkwâpoy– *NI* labrador tea
maskihkîwâpoy– *NI* tea
maskihkîwâpôhkê– *VAI* prepare an herbal infusion; make tea
minah– *VTA* give s.o. to drink (e.g., tea, soup); give s.o. tea to drink; give s.o. an alcoholic drink, induce s.o. to drink an alcoholic drink
nihtiy– *NI* tea
sîwinikê– *VAI* sweeten things; sweeten one's tea

TEACH
kiskinahamâwaso– *VAI* teach one's children
kiskinohamaw– *VTA* teach (it) to s.o.; teach s.o.
kiskinohamâkê– *VAI* teach (it) to people; teach things; teach, be a teacher
kiskinohamâso– *VAI* teach oneself; be taught; be a student, attend school
kiskinohamâto– *VAI* teach one another
kiskinowâpahtih– *VTA* teach s.o. by example
kiskinowâpahtihiwê– *VAI* teach people by example

TEACHER
kiskinohamâkê– *VAI* teach (it) to people; teach things; teach, be a teacher
okiskinohamâkêw– *NA* teacher
okiskinohamâkêwiskwêw– *NA* female teacher; teacher's wife

TEACHING
kiskinahamâkêwin– *NI* teaching, education
kiskinohamâtowin– *NI* teaching, education; education system, school board
nêhiyawi-wîhtamawâkan– *NI* Cree etymology; Cree teaching

TEAM
mâmawatoskê– *VAI* work together as a group, work as a team
nakipicikê– *VAI* stop one's team
nîswahpiso– *VAI* be harnessed as two, be a team of two, be yoked together
pamihcikê– *VAI* drive one's team
pêyakw-âya *IPC* one team of horses, a single team of horses
pêyakwahpitêw *IPC* one team (of two horses)
sipwêtâpâso– *VAI* leave with a team of horses, drive off by wagon
takahkipicikê– *VAI* drive a nice team, drive beautiful horses

TEAR
kîskicihcêpit– *VTA* tear s.o.'s hand off
nanânistipit– *VTA* tear s.o. into bits and pieces; fragment s.o. (e.g., group of people), divide s.o. (e.g., community) against one another
tâtopit– *VTI* tear s.t. up into small pieces

TEARS
môsko-miywêyiht– *VTI* cry with joy about s.t.; be moved to tears of joy
môskom– *VTA* make s.o. cry by tears or speech

TEASE
naniwacihito– *VAI* tease one another, provoke one another

TEAT
–tôhtôsim– *NDA* female breast; teat (e.g., cow)
nôni– *VAI* suck at the breast, nurse at the breast; suck at the teats (e.g., calf)

TEETH
–îpitihkân– *NDI* false teeth, dentures
kîskaht– *VTI* cut s.t. with one's teeth, bite s.t. off

ENGLISH INDEX 395

sîpêkaht– *VTI* stretch s.t. with one's teeth

TELEPHONE
sêwêpitamaw– *VTA* make (it) ring out for s.o.; call s.o. by telephone

TELL
aspahâkêmo– *VAI* rely upon (it/him) in speaking, rely upon (it/him) in telling a story; use (it/him) as an excuse
âcim– *VTA* tell s.o., tell things to s.o., tell about s.o.
âcimiso– *VAI* tell things about oneself, tell a story about oneself; *(fig.)* confess oneself, go to confession
âcimo– *VAI* tell things, tell a story, give an account
âcimostaw– *VTA* tell s.o. about (it/him), tell s.o. a story, give s.o. an account
âcimostâto– *VAI* tell one another about (it/him), tell stories to one another
âcimôh– *VTA* make s.o. tell about (it/him), make s.o. tell a story
âcimômakan– *VII* tell things, provide an account
âtayôhkaw– *VTA* tell s.o. a sacred story
âtayôhkât– *VTA* tell about s.o. in the form of a sacred story, tell a sacred story of s.o.
âtayôhkât– *VTI* tell about s.t. in the form of a sacred story, tell a sacred story of s.t.
âtayôhkê– *VAI* tell a sacred story
âtot– *VTI* tell about s.t., give an account of s.t.
itâcim– *VTA* tell s.o. thus, tell s.o. such things, tell thus about s.o.
itâcimo– *VAI* tell thus, tell a story thus, tell such a story, give such an account
itâcimostaw– *VTA* tell s.o. thus about (it/him), tell s.o. such a story, give s.o. such an account
itâcimowinihkât– *VTI* tell thus about s.t., make such a story of s.t., give such an account of s.t.
itâcimômakan– *VII* tell thus about (it/him), tell such a story, give such an account
itâtayôhkaw– *VTA* tell s.o. such a sacred story
itâtayôhkât– *VTI* tell thus about s.t. in the form of a sacred story, tell such a sacred story of s.t.

itâtot– *VTI* tell thus about s.t., give such an account of s.t.
kiyâskiski– *VAI* habitually tell lies, be a liar
mâtâcimo– *VAI* begin to tell a story
naniwêyatwê– *VAI* joke, tell a joke
nihtâwâcimo– *VAI* be a good storyteller, tell stories expertly
takahk-âcim– *VTA* tell a beautiful story about s.o.
tâpâtot– *VTI* tell s.t. fittingly, tell s.t. correctly, tell s.t. faithfully
wiyâhkwêwi-âcimo– *VAI* swear in telling stories; tell obscene stories, tell risqué stories
wîht– *VTI* name s.t., mention s.t. by name; tell about s.t., report s.t.; decree s.t.
wîhtamaw– *VTA* tell s.o. about (it/him)
wîhtamâto– *VAI* tell one another about (it/him)
wîhtamâwaso– *VAI* tell (it/him) to one's children

TEMPT
yêyâpisin– *VAI* look on with favour; be tempted by looking at (it)
yêyih– *VTA* get s.o. excited by one's action, tempt s.o. by one's action

TEMPTATION
iyisâho– *VAI* resist, resist temptation, exercise restraint
iyisâhowin– *NI* resistance, resisting temptation, restraint

TEN
mitâtaht *IPC* ten
mitâtaht-kosikwan *IPC* ten pounds
mitâtaht-kosikwan– *NA* ten-pound pail
mitâtaht-tipahikan *IPC* at ten o'clock
mitâtahto-pîwâpiskos *IPC* ten cents
mitâtahtwâpisk *IPC* ten dollars

TEND
kitimâkinaw– *VTA* look with pity upon s.o., look with compassion upon s.o., feel sorry for s.o.; take pity upon s.o., lovingly tend s.o.; regard s.o. with respect
pamih– *VTA* tend to s.o., look after s.o.; attend s.o. in childbirth, serve as midwife to s.o.; guide s.o. (e.g., sleigh), drive s.o. (e.g., sleigh)
pamihiso– *VAI* tend to oneself, look after oneself; attend oneself in childbirth, serve as one's own midwife

pamihtamaw– *VTA* tend to (it/him) for s.o., look after (it/him) for s.o.

pamihtamâso– *VAI* tend to (it/him) for or by oneself, look after (it/him) for or by oneself

pamin– *VTA* tend to s.o., look after s.o.; attend s.o. in childbirth, serve as midwife to s.o.

pamin– *VTI* tend to s.t., look after s.t.

paminiso– *VAI* tend to oneself, look after oneself

paminiwê– *VAI* tend to people, look after people

pisiskêyim– *VTA* pay attention to s.o., take notice of s.o., tend to s.o.; bother s.o., harass s.o.

TENDER

kaskâciwahtê– *VII* be boiled until tender

kaskâciwas– *VTI* boil s.t. until tender

kaskihkasw– *VTA* cook s.o. (e.g., skunk) until tender

TENT

mânokê– *VAI* build a lodge, set up a tent

papakiwayânikamikw– *NI* tent

papakwânikamikos– *NI* small tent

TENT-COVER

pahkêkinw– *NI* dressed hide, tanned hide, finished hide, leather; tent-cover

TENT-FLAP

ispâhtêhikan– *NI* pole supporting tent-flap (e.g., to permit air-flow)

TERRAIN

nêhiyawaskamikâ– *VII* be Cree land, be Cree terrain; be Indian land, be Indian terrain

TERRIBLY

kakwâhyakicin– *VAI* be terribly torn (e.g., by porcupine quills)

kakwâhyakih– *VTA* do a terrible thing to s.o., mistreat s.o. greatly

kakwâtakih– *VTA* make s.o. suffer; be mean to s.o., be abusive to s.o.; *(especially in inverse constructions:)* affect s.o. terribly (e.g., as disease), ravage s.o.

kakwâyakiyawêh– *VTA* make s.o. terribly angry

nipahâhkatoso– *VAI* starve to death, die from starvation; *(fig.)* be terribly hungry

nipahâhkwan– *VII* be terribly strong, be terribly powerful, hurt terribly

nipahâpâkwê– *VAI* die of thirst; *(fig.)* be terribly thirsty

nipahi *IPV* deadly, terribly, greatly

nipahikanê– *VAI* be terribly lazy, be bone-lazy

TERRITORY

nêhiyawaskîwin– *VII* be Cree land, be Cree territory; be Indian land, be Indian territory

nôcihcikêwaskiy– *NI* trapping territory, trapline

otaskî– *VAI* have land; have (it) as one's land, have (it) as one's territory

TEST

kotêyiht– *VTI* try s.t. in one's mind, think strenuously about s.t., test s.t.; challenge s.t.

kotêyihto– *VAI* test one another, try one another's determination, challenge one another

kotêyim– *VTA* try s.o., test s.o., put s.o.'s mind to the test; challenge s.o.

TEXTED

wîhtaskât– *VTA* sing about s.o. with words, sing a texted song about s.o.

wîhtaskât– *VTI* sing about s.t. with words, sing a texted song

THAN

ayiwâkipayi– *VAI* have more than enough, have a surplus, have plenty; run to more, be a surplus (e.g., money)

âkwâc *IPC* well on its way, a long ways, more than halfway

âkwâtaskinê– *VAI* be quite full (e.g., pail), be more than half full

ispîhci *IPC* for now, in the meantime; *(in comparative constructions:)* by comparison; than

katiskaw *IPC* to exact measure, no more than, barely

THANKS

nanâskom– *VTA* be grateful to s.o., give thanks to s.o.

nanâskomo– *VAI* be grateful, give thanks

nanâskot– *VTI* be grateful for s.t., give thanks for s.t.

THAT

ana *PR* that

êwako *PR* that one

THAW

tihkiso– *VAI* melt, thaw out (e.g., snow, ice, tree, hibernating animal)

THEN

ani *IPC* then, indeed, surely

aspin *IPC* off, away, from a distance, in departing; since then, the last I knew; back then, so long ago; presumably, evidently

êkos êsa *IPC* thus then

êkospîhk *IPC* then, at that time
êkw âni *IPC* it is then
êkwa *IPC* then, now; and
êkwayâc *IPC* only then, not until then; only now, for the first time
ispî *IPC* at such a time, then; when
itâp *IPC* then, later
kici *IPC* for then, for later
ôma *IPC* then; when; it is this; the fact that
pêci-nâway *IPC* back then, far in the past; from the earliest times

THENCE
ohci *IPC* thence, from there; with, by means of; for that reason; *(in negative constructions: perfective)* in the past
ohci *IPV* thence, from there; with, by means of; for that reason; *(in negative constructions: perfective)* in the past
ôh *IPV* thence, from there; with, by means of; for that reason; *(in negative constructions: perfective)* in the past
pê *IPV* thence, from there on down, hither
pêci *IPC* thence, from there on down, hither

THERE
êkota *IPC* there, right there, at that place
êkotê *IPC* over there
isi *IPC* thus, this way; there, in the direction of
isi *IPV* thus, this way; there
ita *IPC* there
itê *IPC* there, over there; thither
nêta *IPC* over there, over yonder
nêtê *IPC* over there, over yonder; in that direction

THEY
wiyawâw *PR* they
wîstawâw *PR* they, too; they, by contrast; they themselves

THICK
ispîhtâskosi– *VAI* be so thick (as tree-trunk, braid of tobacco or snake)
ispîhtâskwapihkê– *VAI* have braids of such thickness
kispaki *IPV* thickly
kispakikwât– *VTI* sew s.t. thickly
kispakiwêsâkay– *NI* thick coat, thick jacket

THICKENING
itêhw– *VTA* stir s.o., stir s.o. in; stir s.o. (flour) in as thickening

THICKET
minahikoskâ– *VII* be a spruce thicket, be an abundance of spruce

THIEF
kimoti– *VAI* steal (him/it); be a thief

THIN
apiscâpêkasin– *VII* be thin string, be thin snare-wire
papakipotâ– *VAI* sharpen (it) to a thin edge
papakiwânêkinw– *NI* thin cloth, cotton; canvas
taswêkisâwât– *VTI* cut s.t. (e.g., leg of rabbit) into thin sheets

THING
kihci-kîkway *PR* something important, big things
kîkway *PR* something, thing; things; *(in negative constructions:)* not anything, nothing, not any
kîkwâs *PR* something, thing; things; *(in negative constructions:)* not anything, nothing, not any
kîkwây piko *IPC* the only thing is
pîtos-kîkway *PR* something strange, strange things
têpiyâhk *IPC* merely; barely, the most (if any); the only thing; so long as; *(in negative constructions:)* all but

THINK
ayiwâkêyiht– *VTI* think more of s.t., regard s.t. more highly
ayiwâkêyim– *VTA* think more of s.o., regard s.o. more highly
ispîhtêyimiso– *VAI* think so highly of oneself
itêyiht– *VTI* think thus of s.t., regard s.t. thus
itêyihtamopayi– *VAI* suddenly think thus of (it/him)
itêyim– *VTA* think thus of s.o., regard s.o. thus
itêyimiso– *VAI* think thus of oneself, regard oneself thus
itêyimo– *VAI* think thus of (it/him) for oneself, have (it/him) in mind for oneself
kihcêyiht– *VTI* think highly of s.t., hold s.t. in high regard, respect s.t.; hold s.t. sacred
kihcêyihtamaw– *VTA* think highly of (it/him) for s.o.
kihcêyim– *VTA* think highly of s.o., hold s.o. in high regard, respect s.o.; hold s.o. sacred

kiskisopayi– *VAI* suddenly remember, remember in a flash; suddenly think of (it), have (it) come to mind
kitimâkêyihtamâso– *VAI* think of (it/him) with compassion for one's own sake
kitimâkêyihto– *VAI* feel pity towards one another, think of one another with compassion; take pity upon one another, be kind to one another, love one another
kitimâkêyim– *VTA* feel pity towards s.o., think of s.o. with compassion; take pity upon s.o., be kind to s.o., love s.o.
kotêyiht– *VTI* try s.t. in one's mind, think strenuously about s.t., test s.t.; challenge s.t.
mâmitonêyiht– *VTI* think about s.t.; worry about s.t.
mâmitonêyihtamih– *VTA* cause s.o. to think about (it/him), cause s.o. to worry about (it/him); worry s.o.
mâmitonêyihtêstamâso– *VAI* think about (it/him) for oneself; plan for oneself
mâmitonêyim– *VTA* think about s.o., have s.o. on one's mind; worry about s.o.
miskwêyiht– *VTI* find s.t., think of s.t., come to think of s.t.
miywêyimo– *VAI* think well of oneself; be pleased with oneself; think well for oneself, take a fancy
nihtâwêyiht– *VTI* be good at thinking of s.t.; be knowledgeable; be innovative
pakahkam *IPC* I think; perhaps
pêyakwêyimiso– *VAI* think solely of oneself
piwêyiht– *VTI* think little of s.t., have a low opinion of s.t.
piwêyim– *VTA* think little of s.o., have a low opinion of s.o.; be disrespectful of s.o.
piwêyimo– *VAI* think little of oneself, have low self-esteem; *(fig.)* be humble
pônêyiht– *VTI* cease thinking of s.t.; overcome a worrying preoccupation
takahkêyiht– *VTI* think well of s.t., be glad about s.t., like s.t.; be glad, be pleased
takahkêyim– *VTA* think well of s.o., consider s.o. nice, like s.o.
takahkêyimiso– *VAI* think well of oneself, like oneself
wiyêyiht– *VTI* have an idea, think of what to do

THINKING
itêyihcikan– *NI* thinking thus; such thought
kitimâkêyihtowin– *NI* feeling pity towards one another, thinking of one another with compassion; taking pity upon one another, being kind to one another, loving one

THIRST
kakwâtakâpâkwaho– *VAI* suffer mortification by denying oneself liquid, make oneself suffer thirst
nipahâpâkwê– *VAI* die of thirst; *(fig.)* be terribly thirsty
nôhtêyâpâkwê– *VAI* be thirsty, suffer want of water

THIRTEEN
nistosâp *IPC* thirteen

THIRTY
nistomitanaw *IPC* thirty

THIS
awa *PR* this
ôma *IPC* then; when; it is this; the fact that

THITHER
itê isi *IPC* thither, in that direction
itêhkê isi *IPC* thither, in that direction
itêhkêskamik *IPC* thitherward, in thither region

THORN
akwâminakasiy– *NA* thorn, thornbush

THOUGHT
atâmêyim– *VTA* blame s.o. in one's thoughts, accuse s.o. in one's thoughts
itêyihcikan– *NI* thinking thus; such thought
itêyihtâkwan– *VII* be thus thought of
itêyimikowisi– *VAI* be thus thought of by the powers, be thus regarded by the powers
kihcêyihcikâtê– *VII* be highly thought of, be respected; be held sacred
kihcêyihtâkwan– *VII* be highly thought of, be respected; be held sacred
mamâhtâwêyihtâkwan– *VII* be thought strange, be thought supernatural
mâmitonêyihcikan– *NI* mind; troubled mind; thought, worry
misawâc *IPC* in any case, whatever might be thought
pîtotêyihtâkosi– *VAI* be thought strange, be considered odd

THREAD
asapâp– NA thread
sêstakw– NA yarn, thread

THREAD-SPOOL
asapâpâhtikw– NA thread-spool

THREAT
astâhtâso– VAI be watched, be considered a threat; evoke fear, be fearsome, be awe-inspiring, be awesome

THREE
nisti– VAI be three in number
nistin– VII be three in number
nisto IPC three
nisto-aya IPC three sets
nisto-kîsikâw IPC three days, for three days
nistopiponwê– VAI be three years old
nistôskwêwê– VAI have three wives
nistw-âskiy IPC three years, for three years
nistwapihkât– VTI braid s.t. in three
nistwâw IPC three times

THRESH
pawahikê– VAI shake things out by tool; thresh, do one's threshing

THROAT
–kohtaskway– NDI throat
miyiskwê– VAI have a dry throat; speak with a weak voice

THROUGH
kîskatah– VTI chop s.t. through
kîskatahikâso– VAI be chopped through by tool (e.g., tree)
kîskatahikâtê– VII be chopped through by tool (e.g., branch)
kîskipayi– VAI break off, be cut through, break apart
kîskipotâ– VAI cut (it) with a saw (e.g., cordwood), saw (it) through
kîskis– VTI cut s.t. through
mâyiskaw– VTA go through s.o. to bad effect, affect s.o. negatively, fail to agree with s.o.; *(especially in inverse constructions:)* have an adverse effect on s.o., make s.o. ill
miyoskaw– VTA *(especially in inverse constructions:)* go through s.o. to good effect, have a salutary effect on s.o., make s.o. well
paskaht– VTI bite through s.t.
sâpo IPV fully, exhaustively, through and through
sâpohci IPV through, all the way through
sâpohci-kimiwan– VII rain through, come raining through
sâpohtê– VAI walk through (e.g., through a snare)
sâpohtêmakan– VII go through; persist
sâposci-sakah– VTI nail s.t. through, nail through s.t.
sâpostamon– VII run through; be the reaches (under a wagon)
sâpotawâ– VII be open through and through
sâpoyowê– VII be blown through by wind
tipiskisi– VAI spend one's night, live through the night
wâpanwêwit– VTI make noise until dawn, bark through the night (e.g., dog)

THROUGH-LODGE
sâpohtawân– NI long-lodge, through-lodge

THROUGHOUT
âpihci IPV completely, throughout
kapê-ayi IPC all along, all the time, for the entire period, throughout
kapê-kîsik IPC all day long, throughout the day
kapê-nîpin IPC all summer long, throughout the summer
kapê-tipisk IPC all night long, throughout the night
misakâmê IPC all along, all the way, in continuity, throughout
sâpopatâ– VAI get (it) wet throughout; get one's shoes wet
sâpopê– VAI get wet, be drenched, be wet throughout, be sodden
sâpopê– VII get wet, be drenched, be wet throughout, be sodden

THROW
akociwêpin– VTA throw s.o. to hang, throw s.o. to be suspended; throw s.o. over top (e.g., onto willow bushes)
ispayiho– VAI throw oneself thus or there, move thus or there
kawipayiho– VAI throw oneself down
kawiwêpin– VTA throw s.o. down
kâciwêpin– VTI throw s.t. so as to hide it
kwatapiwêpin– VTA throw s.o. over, flip s.o. upside down
macostêh– VTI throw s.t. into the fire
mâkoh– VTA press upon s.o., bear down upon s.o., oppress s.o.; worry s.o., trouble s.o., throw s.o. into crisis

mêsciwêpah– *VTI* throw away all of s.t.
nawakipayiho– *VAI* throw oneself down, duck down
nâtwâwêpah– *VTI* split s.t. (e.g., branch) off and throw it down, break s.t. off and throw it down
nîhciwêpin– *VTI* throw s.t. down
nîhtin– *VTI* take s.t. down, throw s.t. down, unload s.t.
pakamisim– *VTA* throw s.o. down
paskiciwêpin– *VTA* throw s.o. across; throw s.o. (e.g., rabbit) over drying rack
pâskiwêpin– *VTI* throw s.t. open (e.g., lodge-cover)
pimwasinât– *VTA* throw (it/him) at s.o., heave (it/him) at s.o.
pimwasinê– *VAI* throw (it), heave (it)
pîhciwêpin– *VTI* throw s.t. inside, throw s.t. into a wagon-box
pîhtikwêwêpin– *VTA* throw s.o. indoors
pôsiwêpin– *VTI* throw s.t. on board (e.g., boat or vehicle), throw s.t. on a sleigh
sôhkêhtatâ– *VAI* throw (it) vigorously, throw (it) forcefully
sôhkêwêpin– *VTI* throw s.t. vigorously, throw s.t. forcefully
wêpah– *VTI* sweep s.t. up; throw s.t. by tool, push s.t. by tool; cock s.t. (e.g., gun)
wêpêyim– *VTA* be inclined to throw s.o. (e.g., money) away
wêpin– *VTA* throw s.o. away; empty s.o. (e.g., pail); throw s.o. down or in (e.g., money in a card-game); leave s.o. (e.g., spouse); abandon s.o. (e.g., child)
wêpin– *VTI* throw s.t. away; abandon s.t.
wêpinamaw– *VTA* throw (it/him) on s.o., dump (it/him) on s.o., leave (it/him) with s.o., abandon (it/him) to s.o.
wêpinikâtê– *VII* be thrown away, be abandoned, be discarded; be lost (e.g., blood)
wêpinikê– *VAI* throw things about; throw people about, dance a European dance
yôhtêwêpin– *VTI* throw s.t. open (e.g., lodge-cover)

THUD
pitihkwê– *VII* thud, make a thudding noise (e.g., the rushing of water, the fall of hooves, the rapid wing movements of a dancing prairie-chicken)

THUNDER
kâh-kito– *VAI* hoot (e.g., owl); be thunder

THUNDERCLAP
kito– *VAI* utter a sound, call, sing (e.g., bird); make noises (e.g., animal), hoot; be a thunderclap
tasin– *VTI* pull the trigger on s.t. (e.g., gun), shoot s.t. off (e.g., gun); emit a sharp noise, make a shot-like noise; sound a thunderclap (e.g., as Thunderbird)

THURSDAY
nêwo-kîsikâ– *VII* be four days, be the fourth day; be Thursday

THUS
êkos îsi *IPC* thus, just so, in that way; that is how it is
êkosi *IPC* thus, in that way; that is all
ômisi *IPC* thus, in this way

THWARTED
pwâtawihtâ– *VAI* be thwarted at (it), fail of (it)

TIE
akopiso– *VAI* put on medicine, tie on a bandage
âhtahpit– *VTI* move and tie s.t., tie s.t. differently; change the bandage on s.t.
kaskipitê– *VII* be tied up, be wrapped up
kipwahpit– *VTI* pull s.t. closed, tie s.t. shut
kîsahpit– *VTI* complete tying s.t. up, complete tying s.t. in
mâwasakwahpit– *VTI* tie s.t. together in a bunch
nânapwahpiso– *VAI* have one's forelegs tied together (e.g., horse), be hobbled
nîswahpit– *VTI* tie s.t. together as two (e.g., bones)
pitikwahpit– *VTI* tie s.t. into a bundle
sakahpit– *VTA* tie s.o. up (e.g., horses)
tahkopiso– *VAI* be tied fast
tahkopit– *VTA* tie s.o. fast (e.g., horse), tie s.o. on (e.g., to a sleigh)
tahkopit– *VTI* tie s.t. fast, tie s.t. shut (e.g., swim-bladder), tie s.t. in, tie s.t. up
titipahpit– *VTA* roll and tie (it) around s.o., bandage s.o. with (it)
titipahpit– *VTI* roll and tie (it) around s.t.

ENGLISH INDEX   401

wêwêkahpit– VTA wrap and tie (it) around s.o., bandage s.o. with (it)
wêwêkahpit– VTI wrap and tie (it) around s.t.
wiyahpit– VTI tie s.t. together, tie s.t. into a bundle

TIGHTLY
âyîtin– VTI hold fast onto s.t., hold on tightly to s.t.

TIME
ay-âskawi IPC from time to time, a few at a time
âstamispîhk IPC at a time closer to the present; more recently
êkospîhk IPC then, at that time
êkwayâc IPC only then, not until then; only now, for the first time
iskwêyâc IPC to the end, to the last; the last time
ispayin– VII take place thus, occur thus; run thus (in a cycle), be there (in a cycle), come around (in a cycle), be that time again; come by, go by, have passed (e.g., days, years)
ispî IPC at such a time, then; when
kapê-ayi IPC all along, all the time, for the entire period, throughout
kayâhtê IPC before, previously, formerly; before the appropriate time, prematurely
kayâsês IPC quite some time ago; a while ago
kâh-kapê-ayi IPC all the time
kâkikê IPC always, at all times, forever; for a very long time, forever (metaphorically)
kinwêsêskamik IPC for a very long time
kinwêsîs IPC for quite a long time
kinwêsk IPC for a long time
kisik IPC at the same time, simultaneously, coincidentally
kîtahtawê IPC at times, sometimes; at one time, all at once, suddenly
mâmawaci-kayâs IPC at the very earliest time
mâmawo-kayâs IPC at the very earliest time
mâtayak IPC ahead of time, beforehand, in advance
mihcêtwâw IPC many times
mwêsiskaw– VTA have chosen exactly the wrong time or place for s.o., just miss s.o.
nânapêc IPC late, at the last moment, barely in time (e.g., when it should have been done previously); *(in negative constructions:)* too late
nêwâw IPC four times
nistam IPC first, at first, for the first time, initially, originally
nistwâw IPC three times
pâh-pêyak IPC singly, one at a time; each one, each individually, each; one each
pêskis IPC besides; at the same time, simultaneously
pêyakwan ispî IPC at the same time
pisisik IPC always, every time, routinely
tahki IPC always, all the time
tahtwâw IPC so many times, each time
tasi IPC along in time, at the same time; for suck a time, for the duration
taspinê– VAI be ill for such a time, be ill for the duration
tânispî IPC when, at what time
tânitahto-tipahikan IPC what hour, what time; so many hours, that time; several hours
tânitahtwâw IPC how many times; so many times
tâpitawi IPC all the time, at all times
wîc-ôhcîm– VTA come from the same time or place as s.o., share the year of birth with s.o.

TINDER
posâkan– NA touchwood, tinder fungus

TINNITUS
cowêskihtê– VAI have one's ears ring, have ringing in one's ears, suffer from tinnitus

TIP
kwatapisim– VTA tip s.o. over, turn s.o. over (e.g., car in an accident)
wanaskoc IPC at the end, at the tip, at the top

TIPI
mîkiwâhp– NI lodge, tipi

TIRE
ayêskotisahw– VTA tire s.o. out
ihkêyiht– VTI be tired of s.t.; be impatient
kihtimêyiht– VTI be tired of s.t.
mwêstât– VTA be tired of s.o., be fed up with s.o.
nêstosi– VAI be tired
nêstosiwin– NI being tired

nêstwâso– VAI be tired by the sun's heat, be exhausted by hot weather
saskaci-wâpaht– VTI be tired of looking at s.t.
saskacihtaw– VTA be tired of hearing s.o., be fed up with hearing s.o.
saskatam– VTA be tired of eating s.o. (e.g., fish, duck)

TITIVATED
wawêsî– VAI dress up, get titivated
wawêsîh– VTA dress s.o. up, get s.o. titivated

TOBACCO
cistêmâw– NA tobacco
kîskisamaw– VTA cut (it/him) off for s.o.; cut tobacco as an offering to s.o., present tobacco to s.o.
manipîhtwâh– VTA provide tobacco for s.o.
môniyâwi-cistêmâw– NA White tobacco, trade tobacco
ocistêmâ– VAI have tobacco; have (it/him) as tobacco

TOBOGGAN
wîhkwêtâpânâskw– NA rounded toboggan, curved sleigh

TODAY
anohc IPC now, today
anohc-kaskâpiskahikan– NI today's canned goods

TOE
–misisitân– NDI big toe

TOGETHER
asici IPC also, in addition, along with, together with
mâmawatoskê– VAI work together as a group, work as a team
mâmawêyati– VAI be together as a group, be together in numbers
mâmawi IPV collectively, jointly, all together
mâmawi-wîcihitowin– NI all helping together, general cooperation
mâmawihkwâmi– VAI sleep together as a group, share a mattress
mâmawin– VTI put s.t. together, sew s.t. together (e.g., quilted squares)
mâmawokwât– VTI sew s.t. together into one, piece s.t. together in sewing
mâmawôhk– VTI work together at s.t. as a group; engage in a joint effort
mâmawôhkamâto– VAI work together at (it/him) as a group; do things together, help one another, cooperate
mâmawôpayi– VAI get together as a group, have a gathering
mâmawôpi– VAI sit as a group, get together; hold a meeting
mâwasakowêpah– VTI sweep s.t. together
mâwasakwahpit– VTI tie s.t. together in a bunch
micimoskowahtâ– VAI make (it) hold together with mud, mud (it) with clay
micimoskowahtê– VII be held together with mud, be mudded with clay
nânapwahpiso– VAI have one's forelegs tied together (e.g., horse), be hobbled
nîsi– VAI be two in number, be two together
nîso IPV two, as two, two together
nîsôhkamâto– VAI work together at (it/him) as two
nîswahpiso– VAI be harnessed as two, be a team of two, be yoked together
nîswahpit– VTI tie s.t. together as two (e.g., bones)
nîswapi– VAI be situated as two, come together as two
wiyikwât– VTI sew s.t. together, sew s.t. up
wîc-âyâhto– VAI live together; be married to one another
wîc-âyâm– VTA be together with s.o., live together with s.o.; be married to s.o.

TOILET
mîsîwikamikw– NI outhouse, toilet
wayawîwikamikw– NI outhouse, toilet
wayawîwin– NI going outside, being outdoors; going to relieve oneself, going to the toilet

TOLD
âtotâkosi– VAI be told about, be told of
âtotâkwan– VII be told, be told about, be told of
iskw-âcimikosi– VAI be told about up to such a point
itâtayôhkâtê– VII be told thus in the form of a sacred story, be told as such a sacred story
wîhtamâkowisi– VAI be told about (it/him) by the powers

TOMORROW
wâpahki IPC tomorrow

ENGLISH INDEX 403

TONGUE
wanitonâmo– *VAI* make a mistake in speaking, commit a slip of the tongue

TOO
kikask *IPC* too soon, prematurely
nama mayaw *IPC* not immediately, later; too late
nânapêc *IPC* late, at the last moment, barely in time (e.g., when it should have been done previously); *(in negative constructions:)* too late
osâm *IPC* too much, excessively
osâmêyatin– *VII* be too many, be plentiful

TOOL
ayahikâkan– *NI* hiller, tool for covering potatoes with earth
âpacihcikan– *NI* tool, appliance, machine; equipment, furnishings, furniture
âpacihcikanis– *NI* small tool, small appliance
kwîtâpacihtâ– *VAI* be short of (it) to use, lack tools
mônahaskwâkan– *NI* digger, tool used to dig seneca-root
mônahaskwân– *NI* digger, tool used to dig seneca-root
pawahikê– *VAI* shake things out by tool; thresh, do one's threshing

TOOTH
–îpit– *NDI* tooth
kêcikwâpitêpit– *VTA* pull a tooth for s.o., pull s.o.'s tooth

TOP
akociwêpin– *VTA* throw s.o. to hang, throw s.o. to be suspended; throw s.o. over top (e.g., onto willow bushes)
asêsinw– *NI* beaded top of moccasin, vamp of moccasin
âhkwêhtawastê– *VII* be piled one over top of the other
âhkwêhtawêskaw– *VTA* wear s.o. (e.g., socks) over top of one another, wear several layers of s.o. (e.g., socks)
cicipahwânis– *NI* top, spinning top
pâskac *IPC* on top of that, to top it all off, to cap it all, as the final touch; coincidentally
tahkohc *IPC* on top
tahkohcipahkisin– *VAI* fall on top
tahkohcipicikê– *VAI* drive on top of things, drive over things
tahkohtastâ– *VAI* place (it) on top
têhtastâ– *VAI* place (it) on top

wanaskoc *IPC* at the end, at the tip, at the top
waskic *IPC* on top, on the surface
waskicipit– *VTI* pull s.t. over top
waskitakotâ– *VAI* hang (it) on top, hang (it) over

TOP-UP
âhkwakihtê– *VII* cost dearly, cost more, be worth a top-up amount

TORMENT
kakwâtakêyiht– *VTI* be tormented, be tormented about s.t.
kakwâtakêyihtamih– *VTA* bring torment upon s.o., bring suffering upon s.o.
kakwâtakî– *VAI* suffer, experience difficulty, experience torment

TORN
kakwâhyakicin– *VAI* be terribly torn (e.g., by porcupine quills)
kîskicin– *VAI* be cut (e.g., by branches or thorns), be torn
manâskocihtâ– *VAI* be left in want by having (it) torn by branches or thorns
mêscihtatâ– *VAI* get all of (it) torn, get all of (it) ragged
mêstâskocihtâ– *VAI* get all of (it) torn by branches or thorns
pîkocin– *VAI* be torn (e.g., by branches or thorns)
pîkonikâtê– *VII* be torn; be broken down (e.g., institution)
pîkopayi– *VAI* break down, be broken; be torn (e.g., trousers); *(fig.)* go broke, go bankrupt
sikohtatâ– *VAI* get (it) torn; go ragged
sikwâskocin– *VAI* be cut by branches or thorns, have one's clothes torn
yîwêyâskocin– *VAI* have one's clothes torn ragged on branches or thorns

TORNADO
yôtinw– *NI* wind, high wind, tornado

TORTURE
kakwâtakihiso– *VAI* make oneself suffer; torture oneself, deny oneself food and drink
kakwâtakiho– *VAI* make oneself suffer; torture oneself, experience suffering; deny oneself food and drink

TOUCH
âh-âyin– *VTI* touch s.t. repeatedly, rub across s.t. by hand
câhkin– *VTA* touch s.o. small, touch s.o. a little
misaskê– *VAI* touch the earth (e.g., as a falling star)

TOUCHWOOD
posâkan– *NA* touchwood, tinder fungus

TOWARDS
kîhcêkosîwi *IPV* high up, towards a high place
nâsipê– *VAI* go towards the water
nâsipêpahtâ– *VAI* run towards the water
nâsipêskanaw– *NI* path towards the water
nâsipêtimihk *IPC* towards the water, by the water's edge
ohtiskawapîstaw– *VTA* sit facing s.o., sit with one's face towards s.o.
taskamohtê– *VAI* cut across, walk straight towards one's goal

TOWEL
pâhkohkwêhon– *NI* towel
pâhkohkwêhonis– *NI* small towel
pâhkwahikâkanis– *NI* small towel, dish-towel

TOWN
akâmôtênaw *IPC* across the camp-circle; across the settlement, across town
âpihtawikosisânôcênâs– *NI* little halfbreed town, Métis settlement
ôcênâs– *NI* small town
ôtênaw– *NI* camp-circle; settlement, town

TRACE
masinihtatâ– *VAI* trace (it), use (it) as pattern

TRACK
mitiht– *VTA* track s.o., follow s.o.'s tracks
mitiht– *VTI* track s.t., follow the tracks of s.t.
mitimê– *VAI* track along a trail, follow a trail; *(fig.)* follow a path, be guided in one's life
miyân– *VTI* leave behind fresh tracks, have recently passed by
wanahâht– *VTA* lose s.o.'s tracks

TRADE
minihkwât– *VTA* trade s.o. for a drink
mîskotônikê– *VAI* exchange things, trade things (e.g., horse, wagon)
môniyâwi-cistêmâw– *NA* White tobacco, trade tobacco

TRADE-DYE
atisikan– *NI* dye, trade-dye

TRADING-POST
atâwêwikamikw– *NI* store, trading-post

TRADITIONAL
kayâs-isîhcikêwin– *NI* the old way of doing things, traditional culture
kayâsi-nêhiyâwin– *NI* traditional Creeness, traditional Cree identity
kayâsi-pimâcihowin– *NI* old life, traditional way of life
kayâsi-wâskahikan– *NI* old house, traditional house

TRAIL
mêskanaw– *NI* path, trail, road
mêskanâs– *NI* path, trail
mitimê– *VAI* track along a trail, follow a trail; *(fig.)* follow a path, be guided in one's life
sipwêmon– *VII* leave as path, trail, road; begin as path, trail, road

TRAILER
ispit– *VTI* pull s.t. thither or thus; pull a trailer
wâskahikanis– *NI* little house; shack, temporary building, trailer; play-house

TRAIN
nakayâh– *VTA* get s.o. accustomed to something, break s.o. (e.g., horse), tame s.o., train s.o.
pôsi– *VAI* board, be aboard (e.g., boat or vehicle); ride the train
pôsiwin– *NA* train
takwâpôyo– *VAI* arrive by railway, arrive by train

TRANSGRESS
patinikê– *VAI* make a mistake, take a wrong step, transgress; *(fig.)* sin
pâstâho– *VAI* breach the natural order, transgress; *(fig.)* sin, be a sinner

TRANSGRESSION
pâstâhowin– *NI* transgression, breach of the natural order; *(fig.)* sin
pâstâhôtot– *VTI* commit a transgression in s.t., commit sacrilege in s.t.

TRANSIT
âsô-nakî– *VAI* stop in moving across (e.g., the prairies), stop in one's transit

TRANSMIT
itwêstamaw– *VTA* say thus for s.o.; speak for s.o.; interpret for s.o.; transmit s.o.'s message, relay s.o.'s message (e.g., by radio)

TRAP
mistiko-wanihikan– *NI* trap, wooden trap
nâciwanihikanê– *VAI* fetch game from traps, check one's traps
nôcihcikâkê– *VAI* trap with (it/him) (e.g., dog), use (it/him) to trap

nôcihcikê– *VAI* trap things, do one's trapping; do one's hunting
ohpahamaw– *VTA* set a trap for s.o. (e.g., prairie-chicken)
tasôh– *VTA* entrap s.o. (e.g., bird) by putting feed under a movable lid, trap s.o. underneath
tâpakwamahw– *VTA* snare s.o., trap s.o.
wanihikamaw– *VTA* set traps for s.o. (e.g., animal)
wanihikan– *NI* trap, metal trap
wanihikê– *VAI* trap, set traps

TRAPLINE
nôcihcikêwaskiy– *NI* trapping territory, trapline
nôcihcikêwin– *NI* trapping, one's trapping; trapline
wanihikêskanaw– *NI* trapline

TRAPPER
onôcihcikêw– *NA* trapper
owanihikêw– *NA* trapper

TRAVEL
itâciho– *VAI* travel thither or thus; lead one's life thus
itâcihowin– *NI* travelling thither or thus; leading one's life thus
kiyôtê– *VAI* visit afar, travel to visit
mostohtêyâciho– *VAI* travel on foot
papâmâciho– *VAI* travel about; live in various places; run about, be promiscuous
papâmipici– *VAI* move about, travel around, camp here and there, move around with one's camp
pêyakwâciho– *VAI* live alone, travel alone
pimi-nakî– *VAI* stop in one's progress, stop in one's travelling
pimohtatâ– *VAI* take (it) along, carry (it) along, travel with (it)
pimohtât– *VTI* travel to s.t. (e.g., work-site); live s.t. (e.g., day), live through s.t.; go through s.t. (e.g., as sun through the sky)
pimohtêho– *VAI* travel through life, live one's life
pimohtêhon– *NI* passage through life, travel through life
pimohtêwin– *NI* travel
sipwêyâciho– *VAI* travel away, depart in travel; depart as a camp
sôhkêkocin– *VAI* travel vigorously, travel at great speed

TRAVOIS
îkihtawitâpân– *NA* travois

TREAT
itôtaw– *VTA* do (it) thus to s.o., treat s.o. thus
kêhtin– *VTA* treat s.o. with respect, show deference to s.o.
kicimah– *VTA* be mean to s.o., treat s.o. cruelly
kitimah– *VTA* be mean to s.o., treat s.o. cruelly; bring misery upon s.o.
kitimahiso– *VAI* be mean to oneself, treat oneself cruelly; hurt oneself
kitimaho– *VAI* be mean to oneself, treat oneself cruelly; bring misery upon oneself
manâcih– *VTA* be protective about s.o., be careful about s.o., spare s.o.; avoid hurting s.o.; treat s.o. with respect
manâcihtâ– *VAI* treat (it) with respect
mâyahpinat– *VTA* treat s.o. badly, beat s.o. severely
nanâtawih– *VTA* treat s.o., doctor s.o.; heal s.o., cure s.o.
nanâtawihiwê– *VAI* treat people, doctor people; heal people, cure people
tôtaw– *VTA* do (it) thus to s.o., treat s.o. thus
wiyakihtâ– *VAI* treat (it) as worthless; *(especially in negative constructions:)* not waste (it); not destroy a valuable possession

TREATY
kâ-tipahamâtohk *INM* at Treaty time, during Treaty Days
kîsîhcikê– *VAI* complete doing things; bring a ritual to its conclusion; conclude the formal signing of a treaty
nikotwâsik-tipahamâtowin– *NI* Treaty Number Six, Treaty Six
tipahamâto– *VAI* receive one's Treaty payment, be paid Treaty
tipahamâtowi-sôniyâw– *NA* Treaty money, Treaty payment
tipahamâtowin– *NI* Treaty

TREE
mistikw– *NA* tree, post [sic]
mîtos– *NA* poplar; tree
nakâwâskwêsin– *VAI* be brought to a stop by hitting a tree
tânimatowâhtik *IPC* what kind of tree

TREE-GUM
pasakoskiw– *NA* tree-gum, gum

TREE-SAP
mêstan– *NA* sap, tree-sap

TREE-STUMP
iskwatahikan– NA tree-stump

TREMENDOUSLY
kakwâhyaki IPV greatly, extremely, tremendously, to an extraordinary extent

TRICK
wayêsih– VTA trick s.o., deceive s.o.; take advantage of s.o.

wayêsim– VTA trick s.o. by speech

TRICKLE
ohcikawan– VII leak out, drip out, trickle out; spring a leak (e.g., vessel)

ohcikawi– VAI leak out, drip out, trickle out (e.g., sap from tree)

TRIFLE
mikoskâcihtâ– VAI trifle with (it), tamper with (it)

tasîhk– VTI bother with s.t., trifle with s.t.; be engaged in s.t.

TRIGGER
tasin– VTI pull the trigger on s.t. (e.g., gun), shoot s.t. off (e.g., gun); emit a sharp noise, make a shot-like noise; sound a thunderclap (e.g., as Thunderbird)

TRIM
kaskitêwasinâstê– VII be black trim, be black edging

TRIPE
wînâstakay– NI "tripe", paunch

TROPHY
manâho– VAI collect (it); take (it) as trophy; take a trophy

TROUBLE
mâkoh– VTA press upon s.o., bear down upon s.o., oppress s.o.; worry s.o., trouble s.o., throw s.o. into crisis

moskâcih– VTA bother s.o., trouble s.o., hurt s.o.

nayêhtâwipayi– VAI run into difficulties, experience trouble

nayêhtâwipayin– VII there is trouble, there are problems

tasîhkaw– VTA be busy with s.o., work on s.o. (e.g., fish), trouble oneself with s.o. (e.g., fish)

TROUBLED
mâkwêyimo– VAI be worried, be troubled

mâmitonêyihcikan– NI mind; troubled mind; thought, worry

nayêhtâw-âyâ– VAI be troubled, have problems (e.g., health problems)

nayêhtâwiki– VAI have experienced a troubled birth, be born with a birth defect

TROUBLESOME
mwêstâcîhkaw– VTA bother s.o., annoy s.o., make a nuisance of oneself to s.o., be troublesome for s.o.

mwêstâtahkamikisi– VAI be troublesome, behave annoyingly

mwêstâtwêwêm– VTA speak about s.o. as troublesome, complain about s.o. being a nuisance

mwêstâtwêwit– VTI make troublesome noise, make a nuisance of oneself by being noisy

nayêhtâwan– VII be difficult, be troublesome

nayêhtâwêyim– VTA find s.o. difficult, find s.o. troublesome

TROUSERS
–câsis– NDA loin-cloth; leggings; trousers, pants

–tâs– NDA loin-cloth; leggings; trousers, pants

pahkêkinwêtâs– NA hide leggings, hide trousers, hide pants

TROUT
namêkosis– NA little trout

TRUE
tâpwê IPC truly, indeed

tâpwê– VAI speak true, speak the truth

tâpwêmakan– VII come true; (fig.) be fulfilled (e.g., prophecy)

tâpwêwakêyiht– VTI hold s.t. to be true, believe in s.t.; regard s.t. positively

tâpwêwin– NI true speech, truth

TRUNK
mistikowat– NI wooden box, trunk; wood-box, box for wood; wagon-box

nîpisîhtakw– NI willow piece, willow trunk

TRUTH
tâh-tâpwê IPC in fact, in truth

tâpwê– VAI speak true, speak the truth

tâpwêwin– NI true speech, truth

TRY
kakwê IPV try to, attempt to; circumstances permitting, by divine grace

kocihtâ– VAI try (it), try to do (it)

kocî– VAI try (it); try, have a try

kotêyiht– VTI try s.t. in one's mind, think strenuously about s.t., test s.t.; challenge s.t.

kotêyihto– VAI test one another, try one another's determination, challenge one another

ENGLISH INDEX 407

kotêyim– VTA try s.o., test s.o., put s.o.'s mind to the test; challenge s.o.
kotist– VTI taste s.t., try the taste of s.t.

TUB
mahkahkw– NI barrel, tub

TUCK
kîsôsim– VTA place s.o. to lie warmly, tuck s.o. into bed

TURN
asên– VTA reject s.o., turn s.o. back
asên– VTI reject s.t., turn s.t. back, run away from s.t.
asênikâtê– VII be rejected, be turned back
âpocikwânipayin– VII turn upside down
âpocikwânipit– VTA turn s.o. (e.g., sleigh) upside down
âpocikwânîmakan– VII turn upside down, be turned upside down
âpotah– VTI turn s.t. upside down, turn s.t. inside out
âsowi IPV in turn, in succession
îwâsên– VTI turn s.t. down by hand (e.g., by turning a knob), dim the light, turn s.t. too low
kisîwên– VTI turn s.t. (e.g., radio) loud by hand
kwatapisim– VTA tip s.o. over, turn s.o. over (e.g., car in an accident)
kwêsk-âyâ– VAI turn around to the opposite side, be turned around (e.g., a pivot)
kwêskâskon– VTA turn s.o. (e.g., pipe) to the opposite side
kwêski IPV turned around, turned to the opposite side
kwêskin– VTA change s.o. around, turn s.o. around to the opposite side; *(fig.)* convert s.o. to Christianity
kwêskinâkwan– VII look changed around, look turned around to the opposite side
kwêskî– VAI turn around
kwêtatêyitiskwêyi– VAI be at a loss as to where to turn one's head; be at a loss for a response
mâh-mêskoc IPC each in turn
miyo-tôtaw– VTA do s.o. good, affect s.o. beneficially, do s.o. a good turn
nakin– VTA stop s.o., make s.o. stop; turn s.o. off (e.g., kitchen-stove)
nâtâmost– VTI flee to s.t., turn to s.t. for help, seek refuge in s.t.
nâtâmotot– VTI flee to s.t., turn to s.t. for help, seek refuge in s.t.
nâtâmototaw– VTA flee to s.o., turn to s.o. for help, seek refuge with s.o.
pîmin– VTI twist s.t.; turn s.t. on (e.g., equipment); turn s.t. down (e.g., electric appliance)
pîmiskwêyi– VAI turn one's head sideways, twist one's neck (e.g., owl)
tawin– VTI open s.t. (e.g., house, bottle); turn s.t. on (e.g., stereo, TV)
wâpiskâpâwê– VAI be white from water (e.g., skin), turn white with washing (e.g., pants); turn white under a compress (e.g., skin)
wâsakân– VTI turn s.t. around a circle; make s.t. go around, turn s.t. (e.g. treadle), crank s.t.
wâskân– VTI turn s.t. around a circle; make s.t. go around, turn s.t. (e.g., treadle), crank s.t.
wâyonî– VAI turn back, return
yôhtên– VTI open s.t.; turn s.t. on (e.g., television set) on
yôhtênamaw– VTA open (it/him) for s.o.; turn (it/him) (e.g., television set) on for s.o.

TURNIP
otisîhkân– NI turnip

TWELVE
nîsosâp IPC twelve

TWENTY
nîstanaw IPC twenty
nîstanaw-askiy IPC twenty years, for twenty years
nîstanaw-tahtwâpisk IPC twenty dollars

TWENTY-FIVE
pêyak-sôniyâs IPC twenty-five cents, a quarter

TWICE
nîswâw IPC twice

TWIN
nîsôcêsis– NA twin

TWINE
titipin– VTI twine s.t., twist s.t.; roll s.t. up

TWIST
pîmah– VTI twist s.t. (e.g., rags for bitch-light)
pîmin– VTI twist s.t.; turn s.t. on (e.g., equipment); turn s.t. down (e.g., electric appliance)
pîmiskwêyi– VAI turn one's head sideways, twist one's neck (e.g., owl)

tihtipin– VTI twist s.t. (e.g., rope); roll s.t. up
tihtipiwêpin– VTA twist s.o.
titipihtin– VII be rolled up, be twisted
titipin– VTI twine s.t., twist s.t.; roll s.t. up

TWIST-TOBACCO
pîminikan– NA twist-tobacco

TWO
nîsi– VAI be two in number, be two together
nîso IPV two, as two, two together
nîso-kîkway PR two things
nîso-kîsikâw IPC two days, for two days
nîso-tipahikan IPC two hours, for two hours
nîso-tipiskâ– VII be two nights, be the second night
nîso-tipiskâw IPC two nights, for two nights
nîsokâtê– VAI have two legs, be two-legged
nîsonito– VAI dance two-and-two with one another, dance in pairs
nîsosimo– VAI dance as two; dance a White dance, dance a jig
nîsotâpânâsk IPC two sleighs, two loads
nîsowê– VAI speak as two at once
nîsôhkamâto– VAI work together at (it/him) as two
nîsôhkiniskê– VAI use two hands, use both hands
nîsôskwêwê– VAI have two wives
nîsw-âskiy IPC two years, for two years
nîsw-âya IPC two pairs, two sets
nîsw-âyamihêwi-kîsikâw IPC two weeks, for two weeks
nîswahpiso– VAI be harnessed as two, be a team of two, be yoked together
nîswahpit– VTI tie s.t. together as two (e.g., bones)
nîswapi– VAI be situated as two, come together as two
nîswâpisk IPC two dollars

TWO-LEGGED
nîsokâtê– VAI have two legs, be two-legged

TYPE
pakamah– VTI strike s.t., hit s.t.; pound s.t. (e.g., meat); type s.t., type s.t. out

UGLY
mâyâtan– VII be ugly, be bad

UKRAINIAN
opîtatowêw– NA Ukrainian

UNBUNDLE
âpahw– VTA loosen s.o., uncover s.o., unbundle s.o. (e.g., child)

UNCEASINGLY
âhkami IPV persistently, unceasingly, unwaveringly

UNCLE
–ôhcâwîs– NDA father's brother, parallel uncle; step-father
–pâpâsis– NDA dad's brother, father's brother, parallel uncle
–sis– NDA mother's brother, father's sister's husband; father-in-law, father-in-law's brother, "uncle"

UNCOOKED
âskiti– VAI be raw, be uncooked (e.g., flour)

UNCOVER
âpahw– VTA loosen s.o., uncover s.o., unbundle s.o. (e.g., child)

UNDERCLOTHES
pîhtawêwayiwinis– NI underclothes, underwear
wiyâht– VTI wear s.t., wear s.t. as underclothing

UNDERGARMENT
pîhtawêsâkân– NI slip, undergarment

UNDERNEATH
atâmihk IPC beneath, underneath, inside (e.g., clothing)
itâmihk IPC beneath, underneath, inside (e.g., clothing); inside (e.g., mouth)
sêkon– VTI place s.t. underneath; place s.t. beneath the coals
sêkopayin– VII run beneath, go underneath, get caught underneath
sêkw-âyihk IPC underneath
sêkwamon– VII be underneath, be attached underneath
sêkwâ IPC underneath
sêkwâhtawî– VAI crawl underneath (e.g., a tree)
sîpâ IPC beneath, underneath
sîpâhtawî– VAI crawl underneath (e.g., a tree)
tasôh– VTA entrap s.o. (e.g., bird) by putting feed under a movable lid, trap s.o. underneath

UNDERSHIRT
pîhcawêsâkânis– NI slip, undershirt

UNDERSTAND
nisitoht– *VTI* understand s.t.
nisitohtamohtâ– *VAI* cause (it) to be understood, make (it) understood
nisitohtamôh– *VTA* make s.o. understand (it/him)
nisitohtamôhkâso– *VAI* pretend to understand (it/him)
nisitohtaw– *VTA* understand s.o.
nisitohtâto– *VAI* understand one another

UNDERWEAR
pîhtawêwayiwinis– *NI* underclothes, underwear

UNDETERMINED
nânitaw *IPC* simply; *(with numbers:)* roughly, approximately; variously; something, at some undetermined place; *(in negative constructions:)* not anything; something bad, anything bad; somewhere

UNDO
tahcipit– *VTI* undo s.t.

UNDOING
otamih– *VTA* keep s.o. busy, keep s.o. preoccupied; delay s.o.; *(especially in inverse constructions:)* get in s.o.'s way, be s.o.'s undoing

UNDOUBTEDLY
mâskôc *IPC* perhaps, I suppose, undoubtedly

UNFAITHFUL
kîmôcih– *VTA* be stealthily unfaithful to s.o. (e.g., spouse), cheat on s.o. (e.g., spouse)

UNFOLD
taswêkin– *VTI* unfold s.t. as cloth; open s.t. (e.g., book) up flat

UNGUARDEDLY
âyimômiso– *VAI* discuss oneself; speak unguardedly about oneself, gossip about oneself

UNITED STATES
akâmi-tipahaskân *IPC* across the border; across the forty-ninth parallel, in the United States
kihci-môhkomânaskiy– *NI* America, the USA

UNIVERSITY
kihci-kiskinahamâtowikamikw– *NI* university; post-secondary education

UNLOAD
nîhtin– *VTI* take s.t. down, throw s.t. down, unload s.t.

UNMARRIED
môsâpêwi– *VAI* be a bachelor, be unmarried, be single

UNSETTLED
papâsiwih– *VTA* rattle s.o., cause s.o. to be unsettled

UNSMOKED
wâpiskâ– *VII* be white, be unsmoked (e.g., leather)

UNSURE
wanêyiht– *VTI* forget s.t., be unsure of s.t.; have one's mind blurred, be confused

UNTIE
âpah– *VTI* loosen s.t., untie s.t.
âpihkon– *VTI* untie s.t.

UNTIL
êkwayâc *IPC* only then, not until then; only now, for the first time
wâpanastâ– *VAI* place (it) until dawn, leave (it) until dawn
wâpani *IPV* until dawn
wâpanisimo– *VAI* dance until dawn
wâpanwêwit– *VTI* make noise until dawn, bark through the night (e.g., dog)

UNWAVERINGLY
âhkami *IPV* persistently, unceasingly, unwaveringly

UNWELCOME
nânitaw ispayi– *VII* take place as an unwelcome event

UNWELL
is-âyâ– *VAI* be thus in health; be unwell, be in poor health; be out of sorts, have something being the matter
nânitaw itamahciho– *VAI* feel unwell

UPHILL
âmaciwê– *VAI* go uphill, ascend a hill

UPLIFTED
pasikô– *VAI* arise (from sitting or crouching); be uplifted

UPRIGHT
cimah– *VTA* place s.o. (e.g., tree) upright, plant s.o. upright
cimaso– *VAI* stand upright, stand erect (e.g., tree)
cimatâ– *VAI* place (it) upright, plant (it) upright
cimatê– *VII* stand upright, stand erect
cîpatapi– *VAI* sit up, sit upright, sit erect
nîpawi– *VAI* stand, stand up, stand upright, stand fast
simacî– *VAI* stand upright; rear up (e.g., horse)

UPRIVER
natahipayiho– *VAI* move upriver, spawn (e.g., fish)

UPSIDE DOWN
âpocikwânipayin– *VII* turn upside down
âpocikwânipit– *VTA* turn s.o. (e.g., sleigh) upside down
âpocikwânîmakan– *VII* turn upside down, be turned upside down
âpotah– *VTI* turn s.t. upside down, turn s.t. inside out
kwatapiwêpin– *VTA* throw s.o. over, flip s.o. upside down

UPSTAIRS
ispimihk *IPC* high up, up above; upstairs

UPWARD
kwâskwê *IPV* upward

URGE
sîhkim– *VTA* urge s.o. by speech, encourage s.o. by speech; guide s.o. by speech
sîhkiskaw– *VTA* urge s.o. (by foot or body movement)
sîhkitisahw– *VTA* urge s.o. along (e.g., horse); lay charges against s.o.

USE
âpacih– *VTA* use s.o., make use of s.o., find s.o. useful
âpacihtâ– *VAI* use (it), make use of (it)
mêstin– *VTA* use all of s.o. (e.g., thread)

USEFUL
âpacih– *VTA* use s.o., make use of s.o., find s.o. useful
âpatan– *VII* be used, be useful
âpatisi– *VAI* be used, be useful
itâpacih– *VTA* use s.o. thus, make such use of s.o., thus find s.o. useful
itâpatan– *VII* be thus used, be of such use
miywâpacih– *VTA* use s.o. well, make good use of s.o., find s.o. useful
miywâpatisi– *VAI* be of good use, be useful

USUAL
âsay mîna *IPC* as usual
mâka mîna *IPC* also, on the other hand; as usual
mâna *IPC* usually, habitually

UTTER
kiskinawêhikê– *VAI* utter prophesies, prophesy
kiskiwêh– *VTI* utter s.t. as a prophesy; utter prophesies
kiskiwêhikê– *VAI* utter prophesies; make predictions, forecast things
kiskiwêhw– *VTA* utter prophesies to s.o., utter prophesies about s.o.
kito– *VAI* utter a sound, call, sing (e.g., bird); make noises (e.g., animal), hoot; be a thunderclap

UTTERANCE
paciyawêh– *VTA* wrong s.o. by one's utterance, provoke s.o.'s anger

VALUABLE
mistakihtê– *VII* be counted for much, be worth a lot, be valuable, be expensive
miyo *IPV* good, well, beautiful, valuable
miywâsin– *VII* be good, be valuable; *(in negative constructions:)* be bad, be evil
wiyakihtâ– *VAI* treat (it) as worthless; *(especially in negative constructions:)* not waste (it); not destroy a valuable possession

VALUE
itakiht– *VTI* count s.t. thus, value s.t. thus, hold s.t. in such esteem; charge so much for s.t.
itakihtê– *VII* be counted thus, be valued thus, be held in such esteem; be worth so much, cost so much
itakim– *VTA* count s.o. thus, value s.o. thus, hold s.o. in such esteem
itakiso– *VAI* be counted thus, be valued thus; be held in such esteem; be worth so much; have such a function

VAMP
asêsinw– *NI* beaded top of moccasin, vamp of moccasin

VARIOUS
nanânis *IPC* variously, in bits and pieces, here and there
nanâtohk *IPC* variously, of various kinds
nanâtohk isi *IPC* in various ways, in various directions
nanâtohkokwâso– *VAI* sew various things; sew a patchwork blanket
nanâtohkôskân *IPC* various kinds, all kinds of things
nayawaciki– *VAI* grow up to reach various ages, be variously grown up
nânitaw *IPC* simply; *(with numbers:)* roughly, approximately; variously; something, at some undetermined place; *(in negative constructions:)* not anything; something bad, anything bad; somewhere
nânitaw isi *IPC* in some way, in any way; in various ways; in a random direction

VEGETABLE
pîsi-kiscikânis– *NI* vegetable
pîwi-kiscikânis– *NI* vegetable garden
VEHICLE
otâpân– *NA* wagon, vehicle
otâpânâskw– *NA* wagon, vehicle; automobile
otâpâso– *VAI* drive a vehicle
paskêtâpâso– *VAI* branch off with one's wagon, move off to the side with one's vehicle; pull over with a vehicle
pimitâpâso– *VAI* move along in a vehicle
pôsihtâso– *VAI* load up, load one's boat or vehicle
sipwêkocin– *VII* depart in water or air, or by vehicle; fly off, depart flying
takopayi– *VAI* arrive on horseback, arrive driving, arrive by vehicle
VENERABLE
kihcihtwâwi *IPN* of exalted character; venerable, holy
VENTURE
mâyêyiht– *VTI* consider s.t. a challenge; be willing to tackle a difficult task, venture out
VENUS
wâpanatâhkw– *NA* morning-star, Venus
VERBAL
mînom– *VTA* straighten s.o. out, correct s.o. verbally
naskomo– *VAI* respond, make a verbal response
VERSE
ayamihcikêwin– *NI* reading; *(fig.)* a reading, bible verse
VERY
ahpihc *IPC* very much
katisk *IPC* just now, a moment ago; recently, a while ago; exactly, just at that moment, at the very moment; *(in negative constructions:)* not merely
mâmawaci *IPC (in superlative constructions:)* most, the very most
misi-pîtos *IPC* very different; very strange
mistahi *IPC* greatly, very much so, very many
VESSEL
akwanâpowêhikâso– *VAI* be covered as vessel containing liquid, have a cover, have a lid (e.g., pot)
akwanâpowêhikâsosi– *VAI* be covered as a small vessel containing liquid, have a cover, have a lid (e.g., mussel)

wiyâkan– *NI* dish, bowl, vessel, pot
VEST
kîskanakwêwayân– *NI* waistcoat, short-sleeved vest
VIEW
awaswêwê– *VAI* disappear from view (e.g., sun)
âkaw-âyihk *IPC* hidden, out of view, behind an obstacle to vision
matwê *IPV* audibly, visibly; perceptibly; in full view, in plain sight
sâkêwê– *VAI* appear, come into view
sâkêwêtâpâso– *VAI* come into view with one's wagon, drive into view
sâkohtê– *VAI* walk into view, move into view
VIGOROUS
maskawisî– *VAI* be strong, be vigorous
sôhkahât *IPV* greatly, vigorously, powerfully
sôhkatoskê– *VAI* work vigorously, work hard
sôhkâtisi– *VAI* be strong in body, be fit, have a vigorous disposition
sôhkêhtatâ– *VAI* throw (it) vigorously, throw (it) forcefully
sôhkêkocin– *VAI* travel vigorously, travel at great speed
sôhkêsimo– *VAI* dance hard, dance vigorously
sôhkêwêpin– *VTI* throw s.t. vigorously, throw s.t. forcefully
sôhki *IPC* strongly, vigorously, powerfully
sôhkisi– *VAI* be strong, be vigorous; be powerful, have supernatural power
yahkatâmo– *VAI* sing out vigorously
VIGOUR
sôhkisiwin– *NI* strength, vigour; power, supernatural power; authority
VIOLENTLY
kakwâyakinikê– *VAI* act with great speed, act abruptly; buck violently (e.g., horse)
VISIBLE
kîhkânâkwan– *VII* be clearly visible
nôkosi– *VAI* be visible, become visible; be born
nôkwan– *VII* be visible, become visible
VISION
âkaw-âyihk *IPC* hidden, out of view, behind an obstacle to vision
nahâpi– *VAI* have one's eyes focussed, have acute vision

wâpi– *VAI* see, be sighted, have vision; *(in negative constructions:)* be blind

VISIT
kiyokaw– *VTA* visit s.o.
kiyokâto– *VAI* visit one another
kiyokê– *VAI* visit people, pay a visit, go visiting
kiyôtê– *VAI* visit afar, travel to visit
nitawâpam– *VTA* go to see s.o., go to visit s.o.

VOICE
miyiskwê– *VAI* have a dry throat; speak with a weak voice
pîkiskwêwin– *NI* word, phrase, expression, voice; what is being said; speech, language

VOW
asotamâkêwin– *NI* promise, vow

WAGES
miyo-sôniyâhkê– *VAI* make good money; earn good wages
sôniyâhkâkê– *VAI* make money with (it), use (it) to earn wages
sôniyâhkât– *VTI* make money at s.t., earn wages at s.t.
sôniyâhkê– *VAI* make money; earn wages; earn (it) as wages
sôniyâhkêsi– *VAI* make some money, earn a little money; earn some wages
sôniyâhkêwin– *NI* earning money; wages; income
sôniyâw– *NA* gold, silver; money; wages

WAGON
manâtâstim– *VTA* be careful in making s.o. wave, avoid making s.o. weave about; spare s.o. in driving a wagon, be considerate of s.o.
ocâpânâskos– *NA* cart; small wagon, small sleigh
otâpân– *NA* wagon, vehicle
otâpânâskw– *NA* wagon, vehicle; automobile
papâmitâpâso– *VAI* ride about on a wagon; go on a wagon-ride
paskêtâpâso– *VAI* branch off with one's wagon, move off to the side with one's vehicle; pull over with a vehicle
pimitastê– *VII* be placed crosswise; be the bunk of a wagon
sâkêwêtâpâso– *VAI* come into view with one's wagon, drive into view
sipwêtâpâso– *VAI* leave with a team of horses, drive off by wagon

WAGON-BOX
mistikowat– *NI* wooden box, trunk; wood-box, box for wood; wagon-box
pîhciwêpin– *VTI* throw s.t. inside, throw s.t. into a wagon-box

WAGON-RIDE
papâmitâpâso– *VAI* ride about on a wagon; go on a wagon-ride

WAIL
mawimo– *VAI* cry out; cry out in prayer, wail
mawimoscikê– *VAI* cry out in prayer, wail; worship with (it)
mawimost– *VTI* cry out in prayer to s.t., wail before s.t.
mawimostaw– *VTA* cry out in prayer to s.o., wail before s.o., implore s.o.; worship s.o.
mawîhkâtamaw– *VTA* cry out over (it/him) in prayer to s.o., wail over (it/him) before s.o.
mâto– *VAI* cry, wail

WAILING
mawimoscikêwin– *NI* crying out in prayer, wailing; form of worship, rite
mâtowin– *NI* crying, wailing

WAISTCOAT
kîskanakwêwayân– *NI* waistcoat, short-sleeved vest

WAIT
asawâpam– *VTA* watch for s.o., look out for s.o., lie in wait for s.o.
aswahikê– *VAI* watch with a weapon for people, be on the lookout with a weapon, lie in wait with a weapon
cêskwa *IPC* wait! soon; *(in negative constructions:)* not yet
mâcikôtitan *IPC* wait and see! lo!
nayawâs *IPC* after a long wait
pêh– *VTA* wait for s.o.
pêho– *VAI* wait
piyasêyimo– *VAI* look forward eagerly, wait in anticipation

WAKE
koskon– *VTA* awaken s.o. by hand, wake s.o. up; startle s.o.
koskopayi– *VAI* wake up
manâ-koskon– *VTA* avoid waking s.o. up, be careful not to wake s.o. up
nîpêpi– *VAI* sit up late at night with (her/him) (e.g., someone near death); hold a wake, take part in a wake
nîpêpîstaw– *VTA* sit up late at night with s.o.; sit at s.o.'s bedside, sit with s.o. near death; sit at a wake for s.o., hold a wake for s.o.

ENGLISH INDEX 413

pêkopayi– *VAI* awake, wake up
WALK
âsowohtê– *VAI* walk across, cross the road
îkatêhtê– *VAI* walk off to the side
mostohtê– *VAI* simply walk, move along without instrument, be on foot
nîkânohtê– *VAI* walk ahead, walk in the lead
ohtaskat– *VTA* leave s.o. behind thereby or from there, walk out on s.o.
ohtohtê– *VAI* come from there, come walking from there
pahkopê– *VAI* walk into the water
papâmohtê– *VAI* walk about, go about, go here and there; run around, be promiscuous
pêtâstamohtê– *VAI* walk hither, come walking
pimohtê– *VAI* go along, walk along
pimohtêskanaw– *NI* walking path
sâkohtê– *VAI* walk into view, move into view
sâpohtê– *VAI* walk through (e.g., through a snare)
takohtê– *VAI* arrive, arrive walking
taskamohtê– *VAI* cut across, walk straight towards one's goal
wâsakâhtê– *VAI* walk around a circle, walk a circuit
wâskâhtê– *VAI* walk around a circle, walk a circuit
yîkatêhtê– *VAI* walk off to the side; *(fig.)* walk away
WALL
–askatay– *NDI* abdominal wall of animal
wîhkwêhtakâw– *NI* corner made by wooden walls, corner of the floor, corner of the house
WALLPAPER
masinahikanêkinw– *NI* paper; wallpaper
WANT
akâwât– *VTA* desire s.o., lust for s.o.; want s.o. (e.g., rabbit for food)
manâskocihtâ– *VAI* be left in want by having (it) torn by branches or thorns
manêsi– *VAI* run short, be in want; have run out of (it), lack (it)
nitawêyihcikâtê– *VII* be wanted, be wished for
nitawêyiht– *VTI* want s.t.
nitawêyihtamaw– *VTA* want (it/him) for s.o., want (it/him) from s.o.

nitawêyim– *VTA* want s.o., want (it/him) of s.o.
nôhtê *IPV* want to, desire to
nôhtêhkatê– *VAI* be hungry, suffer want of food
nôhtêpayi– *VAI* run short, be in want; run short of supplies; run short of (it), have (it) in short supply
nôhtêyâpâkwê– *VAI* be thirsty, suffer want of water
WAR
nôtinikê– *VAI* fight people, put up a fight; take part in war (e.g., World War II)
simâkanisihkâniwi– *VAI* be a soldier; take part in war (e.g., World War II)
WARD
kisêyinîw-ôhpikihâkan– *NA* old man's pupil, ward of the old men
mîtâkwêwi– *VAI* ward (it/him) off
WARDEN
môs-ôkimâw– *NA* game warden
WARM
kisâkamicêwâpôs– *NI* warm water
kisis– *VTI* warm s.t. up, heat s.t. up
kisiso– *VAI* be warm, be hot; run a fever, be febrile
kisitê– *VII* be warmed up, be heated up, be hot; be a hot compress
kîsapwê– *VII* be warm weather
kîsopwê– *VII* be warm weather
kîsowaho– *VAI* dress warmly, be warmly dressed
kîsowâ– *VII* be warm, provide warmth
kîsowâspiso– *VAI* be warmly swaddled
kîsowihkaso– *VAI* warm oneself by a burning fire
kîsôn– *VTA* keep s.o. warm, warm s.o. by hand
kîsôsi– *VAI* keep warm, stay warm; be warm (e.g., pants)
kîsôsim– *VTA* place s.o. to lie warmly, tuck s.o. into bed
WARMING-STOVE
awasowi-kotawânâpiskw– *NI* warming-stove, heater
WARN
kitahamaw– *VTA* advise s.o. against (it/him), warn s.o. about (it/him)
kitâsôm– *VTA* warn s.o. about (it/him)
WARY
astâh– *VTA* frighten s.o.; *(especially in inverse constructions:)* cause s.o. to be wary, worry s.o.

WASH

kanâtâpâwahiso– *VAI* wash oneself clean with water

kanâtâpâwatâ– *VAI* wash (it) clean with water

kanâtâpâwê– *VII* be washed clean with water

kâsîhkwâkê– *VAI* wash one's face with (it), use (it) to wash one's face

kâsîhkwê– *VAI* wash one's face

kâsîyâkanê– *VAI* wash dishes, do the dishes

kisêpêkihtakinikê– *VAI* wash a wooden floor, wash floor-boards

kisêpêkin– *VTA* wash s.o.

kisêpêkinikê– *VAI* wash things, do the laundry

kisêpêkiniso– *VAI* wash oneself

kisîpêkin– *VTI* wash s.t.

kisîpêkinihtakwâkê– *VAI* wash one's floor-boards with (it), use (it) to wash one's floor-boards

kisîpêkinihtakwê– *VAI* wash one's floor-boards

kisîpêkinikâtê– *VII* be washed

kisîpêkistikwânâkê– *VAI* wash one's head with (it), use (it) to wash one's hair

kisîpêkistikwânê– *VAI* wash one's head, wash one's hair

manâpâwê– *VII* be washed down as water, come running down

mosci-kisîpêkinikê– *VAI* simply wash things, do one's laundry by hand

ocipwâpâwê– *VII* be shrunk from washing in water

pîhtikwêyâpâwê– *VII* be washed indoors as water, run indoors

takahkâpâwê– *VII* be nicely washed with water

wâpiskâpâwê– *VAI* be white from water (e.g., skin), turn white with washing (e.g., pants); turn white under a compress (e.g., skin)

WASH-BASIN

kâsîhkwêwiyâkan– *NI* wash-basin

WASH-BOARD

sinikohtakinikan– *NI* scrubber, brush; wash-board

WASTE

wiyakihtâ– *VAI* treat (it) as worthless; *(especially in negative constructions:)* not waste (it); not destroy a valuable possession

WATCH

asawâpam– *VTA* watch for s.o., look out for s.o., lie in wait for s.o.

aswahikê– *VAI* watch with a weapon for people, be on the lookout with a weapon, lie in wait with a weapon

aswahw– *VTA* watch with a weapon for s.o., be on the lookout with a weapon for s.o.

kanawâpahkê– *VAI* watch things, watch people, observe people

kanawâpam– *VTA* look at s.o., watch s.o., observe s.o.; look after s.o.

kitâpahkê– *VAI* watch things, observe people

kitâpam– *VTA* look at s.o. (e.g., sun), watch s.o.; look at s.o. with respect, regard s.o. with respect; *(fig.)* watch over s.o.

nâkatawêyim– *VTA* watch s.o., keep one's mind trained on s.o.

nâkatôhkâtito– *VAI* take notice of one another, watch over one another, keep a careful eye on one another

nâkatôhkê– *VAI* take notice, pay attention, be observant; attend to people, watch over people

nitawâpahkê– *VAI* watch things, observe people

pîsimôhkân– *NI* clock, watch

wâpahkê– *VAI* watch things, observe people

WATCHED

astâhtaso– *VAI* be watched, be considered a threat; evoke fear, be fearsome, be awe-inspiring, be awesome

WATCHING

kiskinawâpam– *VTA* learn by watching s.o., learn by s.o.'s example

kiskinawâpi– *VAI* learn by observation, learn by example; learn merely by watching

kiskinowâpaht– *VTI* learn by watching s.t., learn by the example of s.t.; learn merely by watching s.t.

kiskinowâpam– *VTA* learn by watching s.o., learn by s.o.'s example

kiskinowâpiwin– *NI* learning by observation, learning by example; learning merely by watching

okiskinowâpiw– *NA* one who learns merely by watching, mere imitator

WATER

akâmaskîhk *IPC* across the water, overseas

akâmihk *IPC* across water, across the lake
akohcim– *VTA* immerse s.o. in water (e.g., baby)
akohcin– *VAI* hang in the water, be suspended in water
akohtitâ– *VAI* put (it) in water, add (it) to water (e.g., boric acid)
âsowakâmêpici– *VAI* move one's camp across a body of water
âwatôpê– *VAI* haul water, haul one's drinking water
itakâm *IPC* on the hither side of a body of water, on the near side of a body of water
kanâtâpâwahiso– *VAI* wash oneself clean with water
kanâtâpâwatâ– *VAI* wash (it) clean with water
kanâtâpâwê– *VII* be washed clean with water
kapatâsiwêpiskaw– *VTA* kick s.o. ashore, kick s.o. out of the water
kapatên– *VTA* take s.o. ashore, take s.o. out of the water
kapâ– *VAI* come ashore, come out of the water
kisâkamicêwâpôs– *NI* warm water
kisâkamisikê– *VAI* heat a liquid; boil water for tea, make tea
kisâkamitêwâpoy– *NI* hot water
kîsohpihkê– *VAI* melt snow into water
kospî– *VAI* move away from the water, move off into the bush
kôniwâpoy– *NI* snow water
kwâpikê– *VAI* dip out water, draw water, haul water, obtain one's drinking water
manâpâwê– *VII* be washed down as water, come running down
nâsipê– *VAI* go towards the water
nâsipêpahtâ– *VAI* run towards the water
nâsipêskanaw– *NI* path towards the water
nâsipêtimihk *IPC* towards the water, by the water's edge
nâtôpê– *VAI* go to fetch water; go for a drink; go for alcoholic drink
nipiy– *NI* water
nipîs– *NI* a little water, a small amount of water
nôhcimihk *IPC* in the bush, away from the water

nôhtêyâpâkwê– *VAI* be thirsty, suffer want of water
ocipwâpâwê– *VII* be shrunk from washing in water
ohtahipê– *VAI* obtain water from there, draw one's drinking water from there
pahkopê– *VAI* walk into the water
pahkopêtisahw– *VTA* drive s.o. into the water
pakastawê *IPV* into the water
pakastawêh– *VTI* place s.t. in water
pakastawêhw– *VTA* place s.o. in water
pakâhcikê– *VAI* immerse things in water; boil things in water
pakâhtâ– *VAI* immerse (it) in water; boil (it) in water
pakâhtê– *VII* be immersed in water; be boiled in water
pakâsim– *VTA* immerse s.o. in water; boil s.o. (e.g., rabbit) in water
pakâso– *VAI* be immersed in water; be boiled in water
pîhtikwêyâpâwê– *VII* be washed indoors as water, run indoors
sipwêkocin– *VII* depart in water or air, or by vehicle; fly off, depart flying
sîkahasinânâpoy– *NI* rock-sprinkling water (e.g., in sweat-lodge)
sîkahasinê– *VAI* pour water on rocks (e.g., in sweat-lodge), sprinkle rocks with water
sîkahâhtaw– *VTA* sprinkle s.o. with water; *(fig.)* baptise s.o., accept s.o. into the Catholic church
tahkâpâwat– *VTA* pour water to cool s.o. (e.g., rock), cool s.o. (e.g., rock) with water (e.g., in sweat-lodge)
tahkikamâpoy– *NI* cold water
takahkâpâwê– *VII* be nicely washed with water
wâpiskâpâwê– *VAI* be white from water (e.g., skin), turn white with washing (e.g., pants); turn white under a compress (e.g., skin)

WAVE

manâtâstim– *VTA* be careful in making s.o. wave, avoid making s.o. weave about; spare s.o. in driving a wagon, be considerate of s.o.
wâstinikê– *VAI* signal by hand, wave
wâwâstinamaw– *VTA* wave at s.o., signal to s.o. by hand

WAY

anis îsi *IPC* in that way; that is how it is

atimipayi– *VAI* move the other way, speed away

âkwaskikâpawi– *VAI* stand in the way, stand as an obstacle

âkwaskiskaw– *VTA* head s.o. off, get in s.o.'s way

âkwâc *IPC* well on its way, a long ways, more than halfway

êkos îsi *IPC* thus, just so, in that way; that is how it is

êkosi *IPC* thus, in that way; that is all

isi *IPC* thus, this way; there, in the direction of

misakâmê *IPC* all along, all the way, in continuity, throughout

nanâtohk isi *IPC* in various ways, in various directions

nânitaw isi *IPC* in some way, in any way; in various ways; in a random direction

otamih– *VTA* keep s.o. busy, keep s.o. preoccupied; delay s.o.; *(especially in inverse constructions:)* get in s.o.'s way, be s.o.'s undoing

ômis îsi *IPC* in this way; this is how it is

ômisi *IPC* thus, in this way

tahtwayak *IPC* in so many places, in so many ways

tawâtamaw– *VTA* open (it) up for s.o.; clear the way for s.o.

tânisi *IPC* how, in what way

WE

kiyânaw *PR* you-and-I (incl.), you-and-we (incl.), we (incl.)

kîstanaw *PR* you-and-I (incl.), too; you-and-we (incl.) by contrast; we ourselves

niyanân *PR* we (excl.)

nîstanân *PR* we (excl.), too; we (excl.) by contrast; we (excl.) ourselves

WEAK

êtatawisi– *VAI* be barely alive, be weak unto death, be about to die

miyiskwê– *VAI* have a dry throat; speak with a weak voice

nêsowan– *VII* be weak (e.g., eyes)

nêsowâtisi– *VAI* be weak, have a weak constitution

nêsowisi– *VAI* be weak, be exhausted, be near death

wâhkêyêyiht– *VTI* be easily swayed; *(fig.)* be too weak

WEALTHY

wêyôtisi– *VAI* be wealthy, be rich

WEAN

pôni-nôhâwaso– *VAI* stop nursing one's child, wean one's child

WEAPON

aswahikê– *VAI* watch with a weapon for people, be on the lookout with a weapon, lie in wait with a weapon

aswahw– *VTA* watch with a weapon for s.o., be on the lookout with a weapon for s.o.

nîmâskwê– *VAI* carry a weapon; carry a gun

WEAR

âhkwêhtawêskaw– *VTA* wear s.o. (e.g., socks) over top of one another, wear several layers of s.o. (e.g., socks)

itawêhikê– *VAI* wear one's hair thus

kikaskisinê– *VAI* wear shoes

kikisk– *VTI* wear s.t. (e.g., shoe), have s.t. as an intimate possession, carry s.t. in oneself (e.g., blood)

kikiskaw– *VTA* wear s.o. (e.g., ring), have s.o. as an intimate possession (e.g., stocking)

kinwâpêkasâkê– *VAI* wear a long skirt; wear a long robe (e.g., as a Roman Catholic priest)

kîskasâkê– *VAI* wear a skirt

mâtitâpihtêpiso– *VAI* begin to wear earrings

mêscisk– *VTI* wear s.t. out

mêscitonêsin– *VAI* have exhausted one's mouth, wear one's mouth out

mihkotonê– *VAI* have a red mouth, wear lipstick

mihkotonêho– *VAI* paint one's mouth red, wear lipstick

mîstowê– *VAI* be bearded, wear a beard

mwêstâcim– *VTA* bother s.o. by speech, wear s.o. out by speech

oskîsikohkâ– *VAI* wear glasses

pohtisk– *VTI* put s.t. on (e.g., clothing), get dressed in s.t., wear s.t.; be enclosed by s.t. (e.g., mossbag)

postiskaw– *VTA* put s.o. on, wear s.o. (e.g., pants)

sêkipatwâ– *VAI* braid one's hair, have braided hair, wear braids

sîhtwahpisoso– *VAI* be braced, wear a girdle

tâpisk– *VTI* wear s.t. fitted, wear s.t. around the neck

wiyâht– *VTI* wear s.t., wear s.t. as underclothing

WEASEL
sihkos– *NA* weasel

WEATHER
âstê-kîsikâ– *VII* cease being stormy weather, let up as severe weather, be better weather
kisâstê– *VII* be hot weather
kisin– *VII* be cold weather, be very cold weather
kîsapwê– *VII* be warm weather
kîsopwê– *VII* be warm weather
mâyi-kîsikâ– *VII* be stormy weather, be foul weather, be a severe storm
miyo-kîsikâ– *VII* be good weather, be mild weather
nêstwâso– *VAI* be tired by the sun's heat, be exhausted by hot weather
tahkâyâ– *VII* be cold weather

WEAVE
manâtâstim– *VTA* be careful in making s.o. wave, avoid making s.o. weave about; spare s.o. in driving a wagon, be considerate of s.o.

WEDDING
âhcanis– *NA* ring, wedding-ring
kihci-wîkihtowin-âhcanis– *NA* wedding ring
wîkihtowin– *NI* living together; marriage, matrimony; getting married, wedding

WEED
macikwanâs– *NI* weed
wîpâcikin– *VII* grow out of place, grow wild, grow as weeds

WEEK
ayamihêwi-kîsikâw *IPC* a week, for a week
nîsw-âyamihêwi-kîsikâw *IPC* two weeks, for two weeks
pêyak-ispayiw *IPC* one week, for one week
tahto-nîsw-âyamihêwi-kîsikâw *IPC* every second week, fortnightly

WEIGHT
yâhkasin– *VII* be light in weight

WELCOME
wiyâ wîpac cî wiya *IPC* it is a rare and welcome event that

WELFARE
pamihikowin– *NI* being looked after, welfare

WELL
miyw-âyâ– *VAI* be well, be in good health; have a good life
môhkiciwanipêyâ– *VII* be a spring, be a well
mônahipân– *NI* source, well

WELL-DEFINED
kînikâ– *VII* be sharp; be well-defined (e.g., hoofprint)

WEST
pahkisimohk *IPC* in the west, to the west
pahkisimon– *VII* be sunset, be west

WET
îhkatawâwipêyâw– *NI* wet slough, marsh
sâpopatâ– *VAI* get (it) wet throughout; get one's shoes wet
sâpopê– *VAI* get wet, be drenched, be wet throughout, be sodden
sâpopê– *VII* get wet, be drenched, be wet throughout, be sodden

WHAT
kîkw-ây– *NA* which one; what kind
kîkwâpoy *IPC* what kind of liquid
kîkwây *PR* what
pôti *IPC* lo and behold! what is this!
pwêti *IPC* lo and behold! what is this!
tânimatowâhtik *IPC* what kind of tree
tânisi *IPC* how, in what way
tânispî *IPC* when, at what time
tânitahto-tipahikan *IPC* what hour, what time; so many hours, that time; several hours
tânitowahk *IPC* what kind
tânitowihk *IPC* in what place
tâniyikohk *IPC* to what extent; to such an extent; so many, plenty

WHEN
ispî *IPC* at such a time, then; when
ôma *IPC* then; when; it is this; the fact that
tânispî *IPC* when, at what time

WHERE
pikw îta *IPC* in any place, no matter where; everywhere
pikw îtowihk *IPC* in any place, no matter where; in all places
tânita *IPC* where
tânitê *IPC* where over there, whither

WHICH
kîkw-ây– *NA* which one; what kind
tâna *PR* which one
tânimayikohk *IPC* to which extent; to such an extent
tânimayikohkêskamik *IPC* to which extent, for how long

WHILE
aciyaw *IPC* for a short while
âskaw *IPC* sometimes; once in a while
kanak *IPC* for a short while
katisk *IPC* just now, a moment ago; recently, a while ago; exactly, just at that moment, at the very moment; *(in negative constructions:)* not merely
kayâsês *IPC* quite some time ago; a while ago
mêkwâ *IPV* while, during, in the course of; meanwhile; in the midst of
mêkwâc *IPC* while, during, in the course of; in the meantime
nômanak *IPC* a while
pita *IPC* first, first of all; for a while
pitamâ *IPC* first, first of all; for a while

WHIP
pasastêhw– *VTA* whip s.o.

WHISKEY-JACK
wîskipôs– *NA* whiskey-jack

WHISKY
iskotêwâpoy– *NI* alcoholic drink, liquor, whisky

WHISTLE
kîskosîmakan– *VII* whistle, emit a whistling sound

WHITE
môniyâhkâso– *VAI* be like a White person, act White
môniyâs– *NA* non-Indian, White person
môniyâskwêw– *NA* White female, White woman
môniyâw– *NA* non-Indian, White person
môniyâw-âpacihcikan– *NI* White apparatus, White household appliance
môniyâw-âya *IPC* White things, White stuff
môniyâw-âyamihâwin– *NI* White religion; non-Catholic denomination
môniyâw-âyisiyiniw– *NA* White person
môniyâw-îhtwâwin– *NI* White ritual, White custom
môniyâw-kiskêyihtamowin– *NI* White knowledge
môniyâw-kîkway *PR* something White, White things
môniyâw-ôhpiki– *VAI* grow up like a White person
môniyâwi-cistêmâw– *NA* White tobacco, trade tobacco
môniyâwi-itwê– *VAI* say the White word, say the English word
môniyâwi-mêskanaw– *NI* White path, White road
môniyâwi-mîcisowikamikw– *NI* White restaurant
môniyâwi-wîhowin– *NI* White name, English name
nîsosimo– *VAI* dance as two; dance a White dance, dance a jig
wâpastimw– *NA* white horse
wâpatonisk– *NA* white clay
wâpisk-ânâskât– *VTA* provide s.o. with white bedsheets
wâpiskayiwinis– *NI* white cloth
wâpiskâ– *VII* be white, be unsmoked (e.g., leather)
wâpiskâpâwê– *VAI* be white from water (e.g., skin), turn white with washing (e.g., pants); turn white under a compress (e.g., skin)
wâpiski-wiyâs– *NA* non-Indian, White person
wâpiskihtakâ– *VII* be white boards, be white floor
wâpiskinikêmakisi– *VAI* make things white, whiten things (e.g., as soap)
wâpiskipêkahw– *VTA* paint s.o. white
wâpiskisi– *VAI* be white
wâpistikwânê– *VAI* have white hair; have light hair, be blond
wêmistikôsiw– *NA* Frenchman; non-Indian, White person

WHITEFISH
atihkamêkw– *NA* whitefish

WHITEWASH
wâpiskah– *VTI* whitewash s.t.
wâpiskahikê– *VAI* do the whitewashing

WHITHER
pikw îtê *IPC* to any place, no matter whither; everywhere
tânitê *IPC* where over there, whither

WHO
awîna *PR* who

WHOLE
iyawis *IPC* fully, entirely; the whole lot, the entire household; *(in negative constructions:)* only partially, not exclusively

WHY
tânêhki *IPC* why

WIDOW
môsiskwêw– *NA* single woman, widow
môsiskwêwi– *VAI* be a single woman, be a widow

ENGLISH INDEX 419

WIFE
-îw- NDA wife
-nôtokwêm- NDA old lady, wife
-okimâskwêm- NDA female boss, boss's wife
-sikos- NDA father's sister, mother's brother's wife; mother-in-law, father-in-law's brother's wife, "aunt"
nistôskwêwê- VAI have three wives
nîsôskwêwê- VAI have two wives
nôtiniskwêwê- VAI beat one's wife
okiskinohamâkêwiskwêw- NA female teacher; teacher's wife
oskiskwêwê- VAI have a new wife
wîcêwiskwêwê- VAI have one's wife along
wîwi- VAI have a wife, be married (man); have (her) as one's wife; take a wife

WILD
âyimisi- VAI have a difficult time; be of difficult disposition, be wild, be mean
âyimisîwatimw- NA wild horse, difficult horse
sakâwi-pisiskiw- NA bush animal, wild animal
wîhcêkaskosiy- NI onion, wild onion
wîpâcikin- VII grow out of place, grow wild, grow as weeds

WILL
âhkamêyimo- VAI persist in one's will, persevere
kaskih- VTA prevail upon s.o., succeed in imposing one's will on s.o.; be able to deal with s.o.; earn s.o. (e.g., money)
masinahikan- NI letter, mail; book; written document, will; *(fig.)* bible

WILLING
mâyêyiht- VTI consider s.t. a challenge; be willing to tackle a difficult task, venture out
mâyêyim- VTA consider s.o. a challenge; be willing to tackle s.o.
têpêyimo- VAI be content, be willing

WILLOW
mihkwâpêmakos- NI young red willow, little red willow
mihkwâpêmakw- NI red willow, red willow scrapings
mihkwâpêmakw-âya IPC red willow stuff
nîpisiy- NI willow, willow bush; willow branch
nîpisîhkopâw- NI stand of willows, willow patch
nîpisîhtakw- NI willow piece, willow trunk
nîpisîs- NI willow branch, willow switch; little willow

WIN
ohciyaw- VTA win from s.o. with (it), win over s.o. with (it)
ohciyâkê- VAI win from people with (it), use (it) to win from people
otahw- VTA beat s.o. in competition, win over s.o., win from s.o.
sâkôcim- VTA overcome s.o. by speech; convince s.o. by speech, win s.o. over

WIND
kêcikwâstan- VII be blown down by wind
pimâsi- VAI be blown along by wind
sâpoyowê- VII be blown through by wind
yôtin- VII be wind, be a windstorm
yôtinw- NI wind, high wind, tornado

WINDIGO
wîhtikow- NA cannibal monster; *(name:)* Wihtikow, Windigo

WINDOW
wâsênamân- NI window
wâsênamâwin- NI window

WINDSTORM
misi-yôtin- VII be a big windstorm
yôtin- VII be wind, be a windstorm

WING
-tahtahkwan- NDA wing

WINNINGS
mis-ôtinikê- VAI come away with rich winnings (e.g., in a card-game)
otinikê- VAI take things; buy things, do one's shopping, make a purchase; take away winnings (e.g., in a card-game)

WINTER
pipon- VII be winter
wîci-piponisîm- VTA winter together with s.o., have s.o. as one's wintering partner

WIPE
kâsînamaw- VTA wipe (it) off for s.o.; *(fig.)* forgive s.o.
kâsînamâso- VAI wipe (it) off for oneself; *(fig.)* have one's sins forgiven, obtain forgiveness
kâsînamâto- VAI wipe (it) off for one another; *(fig.)* forgive one another

kimisâhowin– NI wiping oneself, wiping one's anus
WIRE-MESH
pîwâpiskw– NI metal, metal object; steel blade; screen of wire-mesh
WISAHKETCHAHK
wîsahkêcâhkw– NA *(name:)* Wisahketchahk
WISH
akâwât– VTI desire s.t., wish for s.t.
nitawêyihcikâtê– VII be wanted, be wished for
pakosêyim– VTA wish for (it/him) of s.o., expect (it/him) of s.o.
pakosêyimo– VAI wish for (it); have an expectation
pitanê IPC wish that
WITCHCRAFT
pawâmiwin– NI spirit power; *(fig.)* witchcraft
WITHOUT
âstawê– VII be without fire; be extinct (e.g., fire)
konita IPC in vain, without reason, without purpose, for nothing; without further ado; anywhere, at random, in a random place
mâmâsîs IPC sparingly, delicately; quickly, roughly, without care
mosc-âsam– VTA simply provide food to s.o., supply food to s.o. without recompense
mosc-ôsîh– VTA prepare s.o. (e.g., soap) without instrument; make s.o. (e.g., soap) at home
mosc-ôsîhtâ– VAI prepare (it) without instrument; make (it) at home
mosci IPV simply, directly, without mediation; merely, without instrument; without recompense
mosci-nôhâwaso– VAI simply breastfeed one's child, breastfeed one's child without further ado (e.g., sterilisation of bottles)
moscitôn IPC gratuitously by speech, without adding a gift or offering
mostohtê– VAI simply walk, move along without instrument, be on foot
môy êkâ êtokwê IPC without any doubt, of necessity
sôskwâc IPC simply, immediately, without further ado; without regard to the consequences; *(in negative constructions:)* not at all
WITNESS
nîpawistamaw– VTA stand up for s.o., be a witness (e.g., at wedding) for s.o.

wâpahcikâtê– VII be seen, be witnessed
wâpaht– VTI see s.t., witness s.t.
wâpam– VTA see s.o., witness s.o.
WOLF-HOLE
mahîhkani-wât– NI wolf-hole
WOMAN
–oskinîkiskwêm– NDA young woman; hired girl
–ôhkom– NDA grandmother, grandmother's sister, "great-aunt"; *(fig.)* old woman; Our Grandmother
cakahki-nôcikwêsîwi– VAI be a nice old woman, be a wonderful old woman
iskwêw– NA woman, female, female adult
iskwêwi– VAI be a woman, be female
itiskwêhkê– VAI act thus as a woman; give the impression of being such a woman
kakâmwâtiskwêhkê– VAI act quietly as a woman; give the impression of being a quiet woman
kakwâhyaki-iskwêw– NA extraordinary woman, super-woman
kêhtêskwêw– NA old woman, old lady
mêkiskwêwê– VAI give a woman in marriage; give (her) in marriage
môniyâskwêw– NA White female, White woman
môsiskwêw– NA single woman, widow
môsiskwêwi– VAI be a single woman, be a widow
nêhiyawiskwêw– NA Cree woman; Indian woman
nôtokwêsiw– NA old woman
nôtokwêw– NA old woman
nôtokwêwi– VAI be an old woman
osk-îskwêw– NA young woman
oskinîkiskwêmakisi– VAI be a young woman
oskinîkiskwêw– NA young woman
oskinîkiskwêwi– VAI be a young woman
sasîwiskwêw– NA Sarci woman
WONDER
matwân cî IPC I wonder
mâmaskâc IPC strangely, marvellously, amazingly; *(in negative constructions:)* not surprisingly, no wonder
WOOD
cîkahikê– VAI chop things, chop wood, chop posts

micimâskwahw– VTA hold s.o. in place as or by wood
mihcis– NI split wood, small firewood, sticks
mistikowat– NI wooden box, trunk; wood-box, box for wood; wagon-box
mistikwâhkatotê– VII be as hard as wood, be as solid as wood
mînwâskonamaw– VTA straighten (it/him) as wood for s.o.
oskicîwâhtikw– NI wood of pipestem
pimâskwamon– VII run fastened along as wood, be nailed along (e.g., at regular intervals)
pônasi– VAI add a little wood to one's fire
sinikohtakahikan– NI scrub-brush, floor brush, brush for wood

WOOD-BOX
mistikowat– NI wooden box, trunk; wood-box, box for wood; wagon-box

WOOD-CHIPS
pîwihtakahikan– NI wood-chips

WOOD-COCK
sakâwi-pihêw– NA wood-cock, wood-partridge, wood-chicken

WOODEN
kisêpêkihtakinikê– VAI wash a wooden floor, wash floor-boards
mistiko-nipêwin– NI wooden bed, bedstead
mistiko-wanihikan– NI trap, wooden trap
mistikowat– NI wooden box, trunk; wood-box, box for wood; wagon-box
mistikw– NI stick, pole, post, log, wooden rail
ohpâskwah– VTI raise s.t. (e.g., cloth) on a wooden pole, hold s.t. aloft on a wooden pole
pôhtâskwah– VTI stick s.t. wooden into a hole; clean out one's ear, poke one's ear
sînâskwah– VTI wring s.t. out with a wooden tool
wîhkwêhtakâw– NI corner made by wooden walls, corner of the floor, corner of the house

WOODLAND
sakâ– VII be bush, be woodland
sakâs– NI piece of bush, bluff of woodland
sakâw– NI bush, woodland

WOOL
mâyatihkopîway– NI sheep's fleece; wool

WORD
aspitonâmo– VAI rely on the spoken word; rely on (it) as a formal confirmation of the spoken word
itwêwin– NI what is being said, speech; word; language
kisê-manitowi-pîkiskwêwin– NI God's word
kisêyinîwi-pîkiskwêwin– NI old man's word, word of the old men
kîsowât– VTI complete one's words, complete one's prayers
kîsowâtamaw– VTA complete one's words for s.o., complete one's prayers for s.o.
môniyâwi-itwê– VAI say the White word, say the English word
nêhiyawi-pîkiskwê– VAI speak Cree, use Cree words
pîkiskwê– VAI use words, speak; speak a prayer, pray
pîkiskwêwin– NI word, phrase, expression, voice; what is being said; speech, language
wîhtaskât– VTA sing about s.o. with words, sing a texted song about s.o.
wîhtaskât– VTI sing about s.t. with words, sing a texted song

WORK
acoskâcasi– VAI do some work on (it)
apwêsi– VAI sweat, perspire; work up a sweat
atoskah– VTA make s.o. work, employ s.o., hire s.o.
atoskaw– VTA work for s.o.
atoskât– VTI work at s.t.
atoskê– VAI work
atoskêstamaw– VTA work for s.o.
atoskêwin– NI work; job; contract (e.g., to complete an assignment)
itahkamikan– VII go on thus, work thus
itahkamikisi– VAI do things thus, behave thus; work thus or there, busy oneself thus or there
itatoskê– VAI work thus or there
kakâyawâciho– VAI live an active life; work hard in one's life, lead an industrious life
kakâyawi IPV actively; by working hard, industriously
kakwâtakatoskê– VAI work dreadfully hard, do punishing work
kisiwiyo– VAI complain, be angry at one's work

mâmawatoskê– VAI work together as a group, work as a team

mâmawôhk– VTI work together at s.t. as a group; engage in a joint effort

mâmawôhkamâto– VAI work together at (it/him) as a group; do things together, help one another, cooperate

mâtatoskaw– VTA begin to work for s.o.

mâtatoskê– VAI begin to work, begin one's work

mistiko-nâpêwi– VAI work as a carpenter, do carpentry

miyoniskêhkât– VTI accomplish s.t. by the work of one's hands

miyopayi– VII work well, run well; work out, come to pass

nâpêwatoskê– VAI work like a man, do man's work

nîsôhkamâto– VAI work together at (it/him) as two

nôcihtâ– VAI pursue (it), work at (it); do one's hunting, hunt

osiskêpayi– VII fall into place, work itself out, be practicable

papâmatoskê– VAI go about working, work here and there

pimahkamikisi– VAI work along, keep busy

pimakocin– VAI move along, go by; work, be in working order (e.g., clock, car)

pimipayi– VII move along; run, run along; be on, work, function (e.g., motor, electricity); exist currently, take place

pônatoskê– VAI cease working

sôhkatoskê– VAI work vigorously, work hard

sôhkêpayin– VII be strong, work effectively (e.g., medicine)

tasîhkaw– VTA be busy with s.o., work on s.o. (e.g., fish), trouble oneself with s.o. (e.g., fish)

waskawîhtâ– VAI keep at (it), keep at one's work

waskawîstamâso– VAI work for oneself, be enterprising

wîtapim– VTA sit with s.o., sit beside s.o., be present with s.o.; work together with s.o.

wîtatoskêm– VTA work together with s.o., have s.o. as one's fellow worker

WORKER

–wîtatoskêmâkan– NDA fellow worker, co-worker

wîtatoskêm– VTA work together with s.o., have s.o. as one's fellow worker

WORLD

askiy– NI land, region, area; earth, world; settlement, colony, country; Métis settlement; *(plural:)* fields under cultivation, pieces of farmland, the lands

askîwi– VII be the earth, exist as world; be a year

misiwêskamik IPC all over the land, all over the world

nakataskê– VAI leave the earth behind, depart the world, die

WORRY

astâh– VTA frighten s.o.; *(especially in inverse constructions:)* cause s.o. to be wary, worry s.o.

mâkoh– VTA press upon s.o., bear down upon s.o., oppress s.o.; worry s.o., trouble s.o., throw s.o. into crisis

mâkwêyimo– VAI be worried, be troubled

mâmitonêyihcikan– NI troubled mind; thought, worry

mâmitonêyiht– VTI think about s.t.; worry about s.t.

mâmitonêyihtamih– VTA cause s.o. to think about (it/him), cause s.o. to worry about (it/him); worry s.o.

mâmitonêyihtamim– VTA worry s.o. by speech

mâmitonêyim– VTA think about s.o., have s.o. on one's mind; worry about s.o.

nânitaw itêyiht– VTI worry about s.t., fret about s.t.; assign blame for s.t.; *(especially in negative constructions:)* not bear a grudge, be forgiving

pîkwêyiht– VTI be worried about s.t.

pîkwêyihtamih– VTA worry s.o., cause s.o. mental anguish

pônêyiht– VTI cease thinking of s.t.; overcome a worrying preoccupation

wawânêyiht– VTI be at a loss for s.t.; worry about s.t.; be worried

wawânêyihtamih– VTA cause s.o. to be at a loss; cause s.o. to worry about (it/him); *(especially in inverse constructions:)* place s.o. in a bind

WORSHIP

isi-mawimoscikêwin– NI worshipping thus, such a form of worship; rite of such a type

isîhtwâwin– NI performing a rite thus; such a rite; way of worship, way of doing things

mawimoscikê– *VAI* cry out in prayer, wail; worship with (it)
mawimoscikêwin– *NI* crying out in prayer, wailing; form of worship, rite
mawimostaw– *VTA* cry out in prayer to s.o., wail before s.o., implore s.o.; worship s.o.

WORTH
âhkwakihtê– *VII* cost dearly, cost more, be worth a top-up amount
ispîhtêyihtâkwan– *VII* be considered worth so much
itakihtê– *VII* be counted thus, be valued thus, be held in such esteem; be worth so much, cost so much
itakiso– *VAI* be counted thus, be valued thus; be held in such esteem; be worth so much; have such a function
mistakihtê– *VII* be counted for much, be worth a lot, be valuable, be expensive

WORTHLESS
wiyakihtâ– *VAI* treat (it) as worthless; *(especially in negative constructions:)* not waste (it); not destroy a valuable possession

WRAP
kaskipitê– *VII* be tied up, be wrapped up
mosci-wêwêkin– *VTA* merely wrap s.o. up (e.g., an infant without moss)
sâkiskwêhpit– *VTA* wrap s.o. up to the neck, swaddle s.o. up to the neck
wâspit– *VTA* wrap s.o. up in a mossbag, lace s.o. up in a mossbag, swaddle s.o.
wêwêkahpit– *VTA* wrap and tie (it) around s.o., bandage s.o. with (it)
wêwêkahpit– *VTI* wrap and tie (it) around s.t.
wêwêkapi– *VAI* sit wrapped up, sit bundled up
wêwêkin– *VTA* wrap (it) around s.o., wrap s.o. up
wêwêkin– *VTI* wrap (it) around s.t.; wrap s.t. around
wêwêkisin– *VAI* lie wrapped up

WRESTLE
mâsihito– *VAI* wrestle with one another, wrestle, jostle one another

WRING
sîn– *VTI* wring s.t. out
sînâskwah– *VTI* wring s.t. out with a wooden tool

WRITE
itasinah– *VTI* mark s.t. thus, draw s.t. thus; write s.t. thus; thus write s.t. down
masinah– *VTI* mark s.t., draw s.t.; write s.t.; write s.t. down, record s.t. in writing; sign s.t. (e.g., treaty)
masinahamâso– *VAI* draw (it) for oneself, write (it) for oneself; write oneself
masinahikê– *VAI* write things; write, be literate; go into debt, have debts
masinahikêstamaw– *VTA* write things for s.o., write things down for s.o.
masinahikêwin– *NI* writing; letter, character
mosci-masinah– *VTI* simply write s.t., write s.t. down by hand

WRITTEN
itastê– *VII* be placed thus or there; be written thus
masinahikan– *NI* letter, mail; book; written document, will; *(fig.)* bible
masinahikâso– *VAI* be drawn, be pictured, be depicted; be written on
masinahikâtê– *VII* be pictured, be depicted; have marks, have writing; be written
nêhiyawastê– *VII* be written in Cree; be written in syllabics

WRONG
môy nânitaw *IPC* it is alright, there is nothing wrong with that
mwêsiskaw– *VTA* have chosen exactly the wrong time or place for s.o., just miss s.o.
paci *IPV* wrongly, in error
paci-tôtaw– *VTA* wrong s.o.
paciyawêh– *VTA* wrong s.o. by one's utterance, provoke s.o.'s anger
patinikê– *VAI* make a mistake, take a wrong step, transgress; *(fig.)* sin
wanisîho– *VAI* be indistinctly dressed, be confusingly dressed, be wrongly dressed
wanohtê– *VAI* err, make a mistake, take the wrong road

WRONG-DOING
mâyinikêwin– *NI* wrong-doing; evil deed

YARN
sêstakw– *NA* yarn, thread

YEAR
askîwi– *VII* be the earth, exist as world; be a year

icahcopiponêsi– VAI be so many years old (e.g., infant)
ihtahtopiponwêwin– NI having so many years, the number of one's years, one's age
itahtopiponwê– VAI be so many years old
itahtw-âskîwinê– VAI be so many years old
kakêhtawêyiht– VTI have good ideas about s.t.; be intelligent beyond one's years; be sensible
nêw-âskiy IPC four years, for four years
nikotwâsik-askiy IPC six years, for six years
nikotwâsomitanaw-askiy IPC sixty years, for sixty years
nistopiponwê– VAI be three years old
nistw-âskiy IPC three years, for three years
nîso-askiy IPC two years, for two years
nîstanaw-askiy IPC twenty years, for twenty years
nîsw-âskiy IPC two years, for two years
ocêhtowi-kîsikâ– VII be New Year's Day
pêc-âskiy IPC in a past year, in past years
pêyak-askiy IPC one year, for one year
tahtw-âskiy IPC so many years, as many years
tânimatahtw-âskîwinê– VAI be how many years old; be so many years old
tânitahtw-âskiy IPC how many years; so many years
têpakohp-askiy IPC seven years, for seven years
wîc-ôhcîm– VTA come from the same time or place as s.o., share the year of birth with s.o.

YELL
têpwât– VTA call out to s.o., yell at s.o.; publish the marriage banns for s.o.
têpwê– VAI call out, shout, holler, yell

YELLOW
osâwâpêkan– VII be yellow (as rope); be yellow rope
osâwi-sôniyâwâpiskw– NA gold, yellow gold
osâwisi– VAI be yellow, be brown

YES
êha IPC yes

YESTERDAY
awasitâkosihk IPC the day before yesterday
otâkosihk IPC the previous evening; yesterday

YET
ahpô piko IPC even if; and yet
cêskwa IPC wait! soon; *(in negative constructions:)* not yet
kêyâpic IPC still, in continuity; yet
nam êskwa IPC not yet

YOKED
nîswahpiso– VAI be harnessed as two, be a team of two, be yoked together

YONDER
nâha PR that one yonder
nêmatowahk IPC of that kind yonder
nêta IPC over there, over yonder
nêtê IPC over there, over yonder; in that direction

YOU
kiya PR you (sg.)
kiyawâw PR you (pl.)
kîsta PR you (sg.), too; you (sg.), by contrast; you yourself
kîstawâw PR you (pl.), too; you (pl.) by contrast; you yourselves

YOU-AND-I, YOU-AND-WE
kiyânaw PR you-and-I (incl.), you-and-we (incl.), we (incl.)
kîstanaw PR you-and-I (incl.), too; you-and-we (incl.) by contrast; we ourselves

YOUNG
–osk-âyim– NDA young people, children, grandchildren, the young
–oskinîkiskwêm– NDA young woman; hired girl
–oskinîkîm– NDA young man, follower; *(fig.)* servant
–oskinîkîmis– NDA young man; hired man
–ôsisim– NDA grandchild; *(fig.)* young person
acimosis– NA puppy, young dog, little dog
ayêhkwêsis– NA young castrated bull; steer
ayisiyinîsis– NA young person
ispîhcisi– VAI be so small, be so young
kakêskimâwasowin– NI counselling the young
mihkwâpêmakos– NI young red willow, little red willow

ENGLISH INDEX   425

minahikosis– *NA* small spruce, young spruce-tree
nêhiyâsis– *NA* young Cree; young Indian
nihtâwikihâwaso– *VAI* give birth to one's child, bring forth a child, bring forth a young one (of the species)
nihtâwikinâwaso– *VAI* give birth to one's child, bring forth a child, bring forth a young one (of the species)
nôhâwaso– *VAI* nurse one's child, breastfeed one's child; suckle the young one (of the species), suckle one's calf (as cow)
osk-ây– *NA* young one (of the species); young person, the young
osk-âyiwi– *VAI* be young; be a young person
osk-îskwêw– *NA* young woman
oskawâsis– *NA* young child, infant
oskayisiyiniw– *NA* young person
oski *IPN* young, fresh, new
oskinîki– *VAI* be a young man
oskinîkiskwêmakisi– *VAI* be a young woman
oskinîkiskwêsisiwi– *VAI* be a young girl (about 10-12 years old)
oskinîkiskwêw– *NA* young woman
oskinîkiskwêwi– *VAI* be a young woman
oskinîkiskwêwisi– *VAI* be a young girl (about 10-12 years old)
oskinîkiw– *NA* young man
oskinîkiwiyinîs– *NI* youth, young man (about 12-13 years old)
oskinîkîs– *NA* young boy, youth
oskinîkîwiyinîsiwi– *VAI* be a youth, be a young man (about 12-13 years old)
pâhpahâhkwânisis– *NA* young chicken, chick
pisiskisîs– *NA* animal; young animal; small animal (e.g., bird, gopher)
wâposos– *NA* young rabbit, small rabbit

YOUNGER
–kosis– *NDA* son, parallel nephew; *(fig.)* younger man
–sîm– *NDA* younger sibling, younger parallel cousin
–sîmis– *NDA* younger sibling, younger parallel cousin
osîmisi– *VAI* have a younger sibling; have (him/her) as one's younger sibling

YOUNGEST
–pêpîm– *NDA* baby, infant; youngest child
osîmimâs– *NA* the youngest sibling
osîmimâw– *NA* the youngest sibling
osîmimâwi– *VAI* be the youngest sibling
osîmisimâw– *NA* the youngest sibling

YOUNGSTER
–îc-âyis– *NDA* fellow youngster; sibling, parallel cousin